ANGAZA AFRIKA

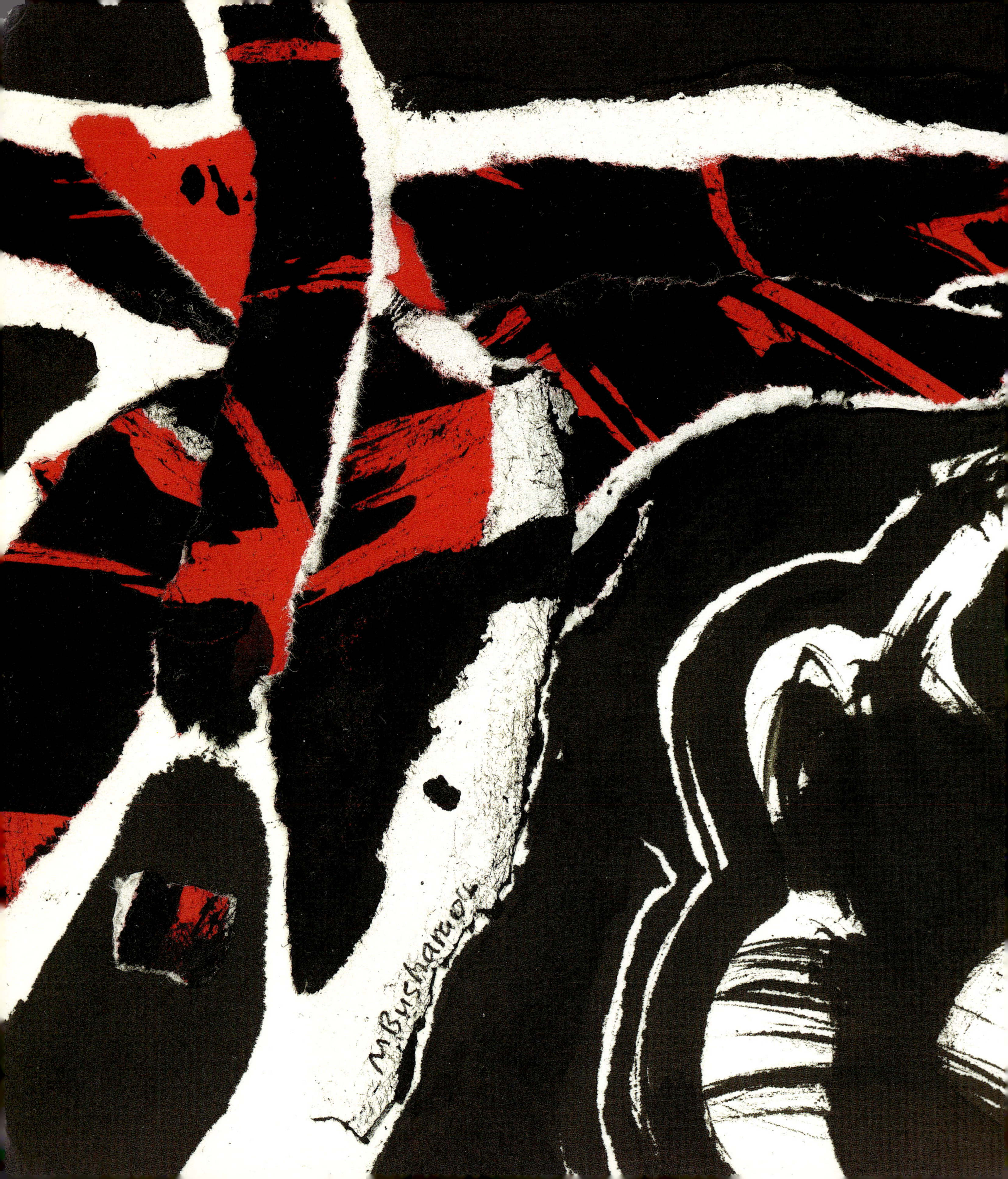

ANGAZA AFRIKA

AFRICAN ART NOW

CHRIS SPRING

LAURENCE KING PUBLISHING

LAURENCE KING

Published in 2008 by
Laurence King Publishing Ltd
361–373 City Road
London EC1V 1LR

tel: +44 20 7841 6900
fax: +44 20 7841 6910
email: enquiries@laurenceking.co.uk
www.laurenceking.co.uk

A catalogue record of this book is available from the British Library.

ISBN: 978 1 85669 548 0

Design: Studio8 Design
Picture Research: Annalaura Palma

Printed and bound in China.

ANGAZA AFRIKA
AFRICAN ART NOW

PREFACE

'To hell with African art'; 'I don't give a toss about Africa!'; 'I'm an artist who paints for humankind and who just happens to come from Africa.' These remarks by Hassan Musa, Yinka Shonibare, MBE and Owusu-Ankomah, working in France, the UK and Germany respectively, though obviously taken out of context, nonetheless reflect a growing impatience among 'African' artists with the labels imposed on them, largely by Western aesthetics. However, many artists do acknowledge that such labels may still be necessary in order to give their works sufficient 'visibility' to question the validity of these very labels.

Artists working within Africa are generally not so concerned by such issues. As Kwame Anthony Appiah observed in the introduction to the catalogue of the exhibition 'Africa: The Art of a Continent' in 1995: 'Only recently has the idea of Africa come to figure importantly in the thinking of many Africans; and those who took up this idea got it, by and large, from European culture.'

'I think we've gone past the stage of African group highlights, whether continental or regional', observed the artist and curator Olu Oguibe at the 2007 Venice Biennale. 'People must begin to show confidence in the ability of individual African artists to stand shoulder-to-shoulder with their peers on the global stage.' Yet the very fact that African artists featured so strongly at the 2007 Biennale, despite controversy over the call for proposals, is highly significant when one considers that the entire continent of Africa was not represented at the Biennale until 1990, and then by only five artists. Add to that the fact that most of the well-known curators of African art are now African, and the picture becomes even more positive. The sophistication and vigour of the recent art historical discourse engendered by three major exhibitions of contemporary African art and their accompanying catalogues is drawn together in a review article by Elizabeth Harney (*Art Journal*, summer 2007). Despite the feuding among curators it (painfully at times) lays bare, it reveals an enormous groundswell of creativity. As Simon Njami, curator of the touring exhibition 'Africa Remix', refreshingly observes: 'It is through the works, and the works alone, that the answers will transpire, or at least the routes towards renewed reflection.'

The idea of what 'African art' is, or ought to be, has been increasingly challenged over the past decade, though for the vast majority the definition that immediately comes to mind is still that of the masks, woodcarvings, ceramics and metalwork that are the staples of the 'ethnographical' display. In academic circles, archaeologists, anthropologists and art historians still tend to be polarized in their views about the African artistic heritage, though more and more the commonalities between art from today and from the distant past are tending to squeeze the rather artificial category of 'ethnography' sits uneasily between them. The Sainsbury African Galleries at the British Museum are a physical manifestation of these changing views. Yet, despite the success of celebrations of African art and culture such as Africa '95 and Africa '05 and a growing global appreciation of contemporary African art, there is still a sense in which the art remains remote from a far wider potential audience. One reason for this may be that writers and curators have tended to use works of art as illustrative of the complexities of Africa's post-colonial heritage (political, social, sexual, racial and religious) rather than trying to elucidate and make accessible the works of art themselves. Furthermore, in at least three of the major publications of the last decade dealing with contemporary African art, the writer/curator has arbitrarily decided that North Africa – and in one case 'the Indian Ocean' – should be excluded from the discussion. This approach simply reinforces popular notions of the African continent as a sub-Saharan entity, somehow imploded into a single country, frozen in time and hermetically sealed from the rest of the world. 'This kind of revisionism', as Simon Njami observes, '... is pathological, for it seeks to negate the multiple influences fuelled by exchanges between the large Sahelian cities and their North African neighbours since the Middle Ages... In short, it seeks to negate the common history that united the destinies of nations colonized by the same powers and their ensuing struggles for liberation.'

The title of this book, *Angaza Afrika*, is from the Swahili, and translates roughly as 'Shed Light on Africa' or 'Look Around Africa'. And it is in such a spirit that this group of artists and artworks have been brought together. I acknowledge that my choice of artists is, inevitably and to a large extent, personal. As an artist myself, and as a result of the approach we have taken in curating the new African galleries at the British Museum, I have grown to know and deeply respect many of these creators and their works over the past decade. While I accept that others could choose equally valid alternative lists, I believe that those I have selected will help to emphasize the sheer diversity of Africa, embracing not only the whole continent and its diaspora, but also its inclusion in the cultural complexes that make up the Mediterranean, Atlantic and Indian Ocean worlds. Africa is as much a global phenomenon as a continent. As Appiah put it back in 1995, there is 'not one Africa, but many' in the world today.

Chris Spring, October 2007

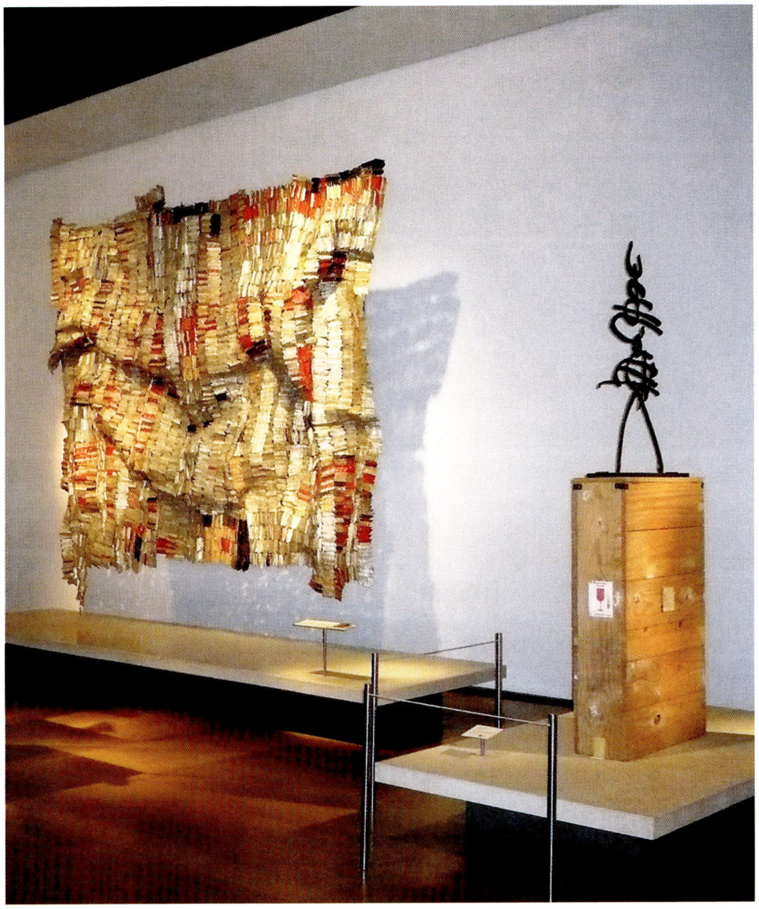

Above Installation view of works by El Anatsui and Rachid Koraïchi in the Sainsbury African Galleries at the British Museum, London.

ACKNOWLEDGEMENTS

My heartfelt thanks go to the artists who generously contributed their remarkable works to this book; to my wife Yvonne and my children, Willoughby and Madeleine, for their love and support; to my friends, Elsbeth Court and Gus Casely-Hayford, who, in their different ways, fed my growing appreciation of contemporary African art (and Elsbeth also provided detailed comments on the text); to Robert Loder, who did something similar, as well as generously lending images from his collection; to Elisabeth Lalouschek, Chili Hawes and Gerard Houghton at the October Gallery, for all their help and enthusiasm; to Laurence King, for conceiving the book, to Kara Hattersley Smith, for realizing it, and especially to my editor Donald Dinwiddie, for his wisdom and calm good humour; to Matt Willey and Zoë Bather of Studio8 Design, who did such a fantastic job designing the book; to Annalaura Palma, who sorted out all the images to go into this book; to Simon Walsh who saw the book through all the stages of production and printing; to Anna Lethbridge, who copy-edited my prose into shape; to Judy Joseph, for her invaluable research, grapes and bananas; to Margaret Solomon, Joe and Peaw, who lowered my stress levels and kept me in one piece; to Rachel, for keeping a song in my heart; to my friends and colleagues Julie Hudson, Heidi Cutts and Ryszard Lewandowski; and finally to Jonathan King, Claude Ardouin and Neil MacGregor, for supporting the project from the start.

For my Dad, Mike Spring

INTRODUCTION
ART IS ALL AROUND

Right Appliqué canvas-backed patterned hangings strung between lamp posts and rolled up on transverse poles spanning a street in Cairo, Egypt. In the evening they were unfurled to form a marquee to accommodate the mourners at a funeral.

A recent visitor from South Africa to the Sainsbury African Galleries at the British Museum in London when asked if she was surprised that the public should be introduced to Africa's artistic heritage through the works of contemporary artists replied, 'Why should I be surprised? Art is all around in Africa – everywhere you look there is art. What could be more natural than to begin with the work of modern, living artists?'

What did the visitor mean when she said that 'art is all around' in Africa? Walking down the street in a large town anywhere on the continent of Africa you would not necessarily see the works of any of the artists in this book, though commissioned works by a number of them do grace many public spaces and buildings. However, you would be likely to see art forms – many of which are represented in the British Museum's African galleries – that, in many cases, have inspired, informed or otherwise affected their work.

In 2002, the Ghanaian artist Atta Kwami showed his work alongside that of 11 sign-painters based in Kumasi, Ghana ('Kumasi Junction', Oriel Mostyn Gallery, Llandudno, UK). The aim of the exhibition was not to suggest a comparative discussion over Kwami's and the sign-painters' respective artistic practice but, amongst other things, to subvert some of our Western categories of artist and artisan, art and craft, and so on. As Kwami himself states: 'My work is part of the commonality of Kumasi painting; it is similar in regard to the materials used: paint, canvas, wood, paper. In its techniques, themes and concepts, however, it offers a contrast.'

The complex and dynamic artistic practices that I have (all too briefly) summarized are particular case studies, but they are representative of far broader artistic traditions and movements that may involve literally thousands of artists. They are as 'contemporary' as the work of the other artists represented in this book – they simply 'offer a contrast.'

THE TENT-MAKERS OF CAIRO

The art of the *khiyamiya* (from the Arabic *khayma*, 'tent'), the tent-makers of Cairo, goes back to the very origins of the Egyptian capital. Even to this day, the tent-makers' intricate and brilliantly coloured appliqué designs regularly transform the city's streets, creating a suitable backdrop to numerous important events and festivals.

The tent-makers are situated among the many tiny shops located in and around the covered *suq* or market in old Cairo that leads to the imposing city gate of Bab Zuwayla. Working in the great lofts above the *suq*, the tent-makers have, for many generations, created the arabesque hanging panels that adorn large marquees, called *suadiq* or *siwan*. The products of the *khiyamiya* probably developed from the embellishments of great tents that were once erected to welcome desert caravans at the end of their long and exhausting journeys, or to provide cool shelter from the rays of the sun for the guests of princes and noblemen while travelling or on hunting expeditions. Their modern-day usage is not totally dissimilar, in that they decorate the marquees that are set up to accommodate people at weddings, funerals, religious festivals and other important events. On such occasions the hangings are often strung between lamp posts and also from transverse poles spanning the narrow streets, thus creating the sides and roof of the tent.

Today, flimsy, factory-printed cloth, imitating the designs produced by the *khiyamiya*, may be seen throughout Egypt. However, the fact that the poorest stallholder may now have a piece of *khiyamiya*-inspired cloth on the front of his barrow does not mean that he is a customer lost to the tent-makers themselves. The cost of the genuine article would always have been beyond the pocket of such citizens. In fact, almost any manufacturing industry will attest that a proliferation of imitations increases rather than reduces the demand for 'the real thing'. The art of the *khiyamiya* is part of a dynamic living tradition that ensures the continued flourishing of old techniques and styles while readily adapting itself to changing tastes and to new designs, materials and markets.

FANTASY COFFINS OF TESHIE

One of the most remarkable traditions anywhere in Africa is centred on the town of Teshie, near Accra in Ghana. There, artists of the Ga people create an extraordinary array of 'fantasy' coffins, the designs of which are intended to echo their occupants' professions in life. It is an art that has grown out of an older tradition of creating palanquins for the prestige funerals of well-to-do members of the community. Today, it is much more available to all, especially the new and burgeoning middle class. The products of the coffin-makers of Teshie are in big demand, not only from local clients but also from the international community. Skilled carpenters create large guns for hunters and soldiers, rainbow-coloured fish for fishermen, Coca-Cola bottles for market traders, saloon cars for chauffeurs and even eagles for pilots. It is by no means an exclusively African idea – a British WWII fighter pilot was recently buried in a coffin in the form of his Hurricane – but nowhere else in the world has the custom-made coffin been developed into such a remarkable art form.

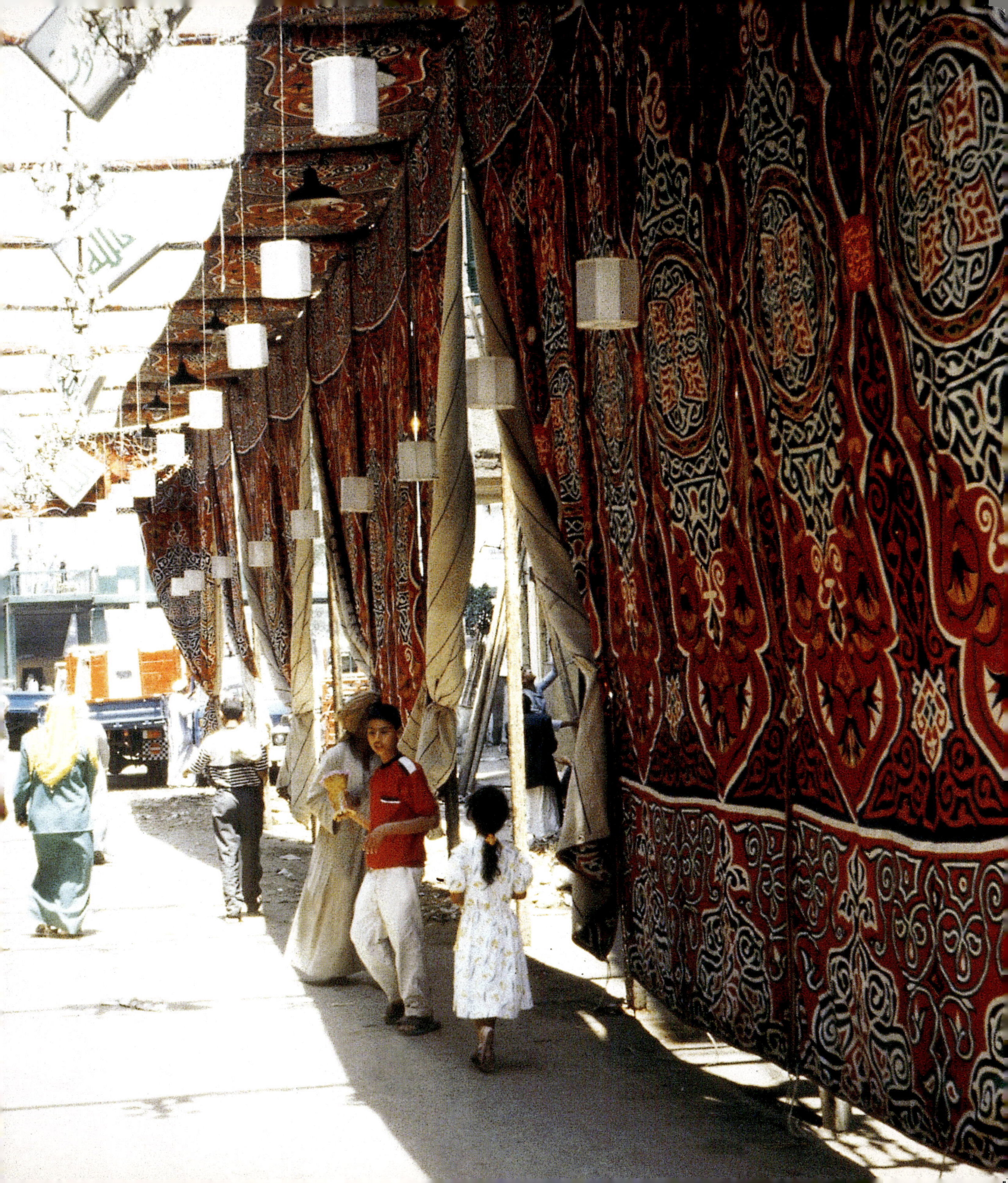

Christian sects around Accra in southern Ghana have debated the acceptability of such an array of coffin designs entering the church. In most cases a compromise was reached whereby the deceased was permitted to enter the church in a Bible-shaped coffin for the duration of the funeral service, and was transferred to a coffin of his or her choosing for the interment in the graveyard outside.

THE TINGATINGA COOPERATIVE SOCIETY

The Tingatinga Cooperative Society art collective in Oyster Bay, Dar Es Salaam, is composed of the latter-day disciples of a single artist, Edward Saidi (later known as Tingatinga), who died in 1972 – only four years after he began to paint. Today, Tingatinga artists across Tanzania paint pictures on subjects ranging from flora and fauna to the battle against HIV/AIDS.

The Tingatinga collective has much in common with organizations in other parts of Africa where there are masters, assistants and apprentices, and where a collective style and creativity are fostered above and beyond individual talent. Though clearly some artists are more gifted than others and attempt more difficult and challenging subjects – judged from a Western standpoint at least – their contributions are seen as simply a part of the collective talent of the group. Stylistically, much of the work is quite closely related to Ethiopian popular painting, which itself derived from an ancient tradition of religious art; there are also possible influences from the modern sculpture of the Makonde people of southern Tanzania and northern Mozambique. However, there are continuous innovations in style and subject matter that ensure the dynamism of the tradition. Genre themes abound, painted again and again by different artists in slightly different styles. The subject matter can broadly be divided between the worlds of men and nature. The content may vary from strictly representational to highly allegorical/symbolic pieces, which shed interesting light on the social, political and religious life of Tanzania, particularly the all-pervading presence of and response to *ukimwi* (HIV/AIDS), which saw many Tanzanians turning away from Western biomedicine to seek the help of the *mganga* (spirit healer) or of Indian and Chinese traditional medicine.

SIGN-PAINTERS

There are numerous collectives of artists across Africa that specialize in sign-painting, their works advertising an enormous range of products and professions, from cinema films to the latest hairstyles. Although machine-printed posters and neon illuminations

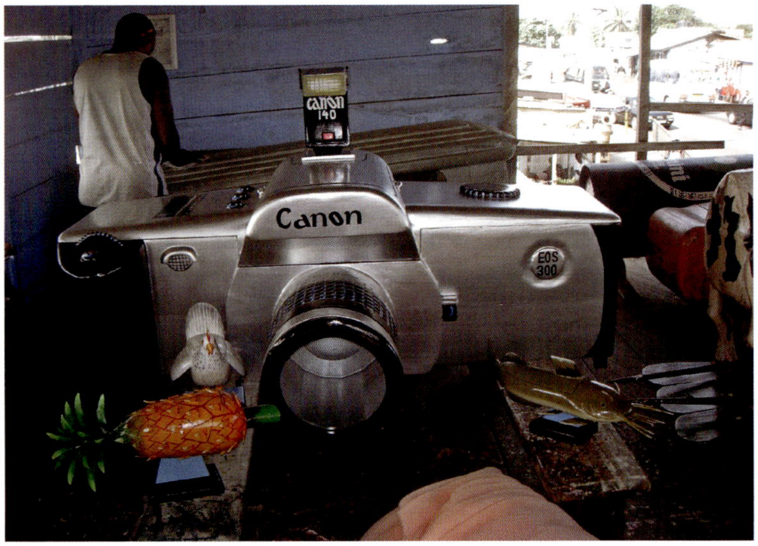

Below Coffin of wood in the form of a Canon camera designed by Daniel Oblie; in the foreground are miniature 'sample' coffins (catfish, pineapple, chicken) to show to potential customers. Hello Design Coffins, Teshie, Ghana, 2006.

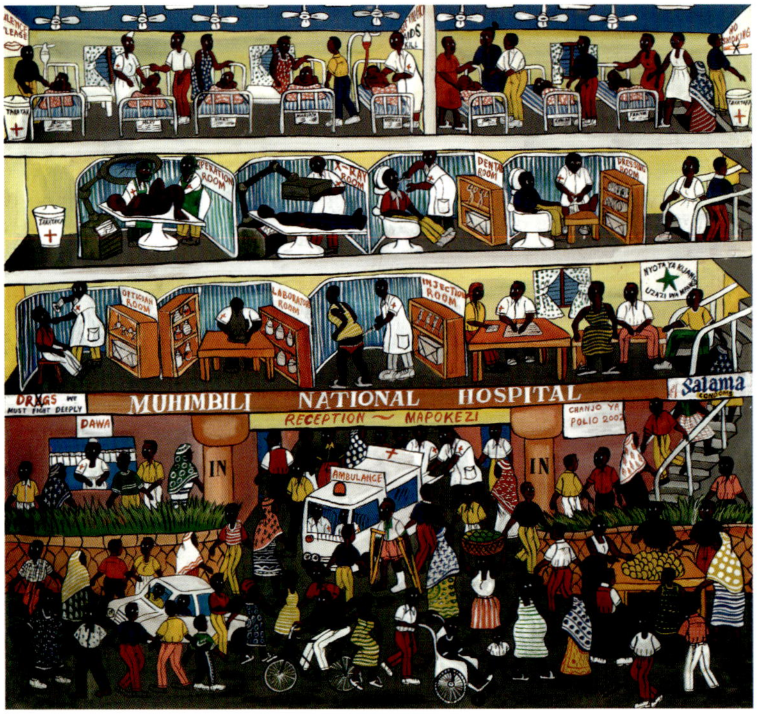

Bottom *Muhimbili Hospital* by Hassan Mocha of Zanzibar, 2002. The big general hospital in Dar Es Salaam is one of the subjects painted regularly by artists of the Tingatinga Cooperative Society. The immunization and birth control clinics and the HIV/AIDS ward are always featured.

Below top Isa Saidi Mitole with his painting *DAR ES SALAAM USIKU* ('Dar Es Salaam by Night'), 2002. Mitole is a member of the Tingatinga Cooperative Society, based in Oyster Bay, Dar Es Salaam, Tanzania. The painting depicts the lurid night life of Dar Es Salaam, though its subtext is the fight against HIV/AIDS.

Below middle RossArt Best sign studios, Kumasi, Ghana, 2006.

Bottom Three women wearing *kangas* in a style known as *ushungu* on the beach in Bagamoyo, Tanzania.

advertising major companies and their wares are to be found no less in African cities than in any other urban environment around the world, small businesses in Africa still promote themselves largely by means of hand-painted signs, despite an increasing threat from new digital technology.

Hand-painted hairdressers' signs are ubiquitous in Africa and have blossomed since the mid-twentieth century as they reflect the multitude of styles dictated by fashion, popular music, television, sport and movies worldwide. Studios such as MIKE ARTS in Nairobi, Kenya, specialize in depicting upbeat and daring styles for the city's barber shops. Many of the haircuts for both men and women relate to individual celebrities; others refer to wider categories such as Europeans, or to certain professions such as 'police cut'; still others are the invention of individual hairdressers, 'house-styles' which, it is hoped, will catch on and entice customers away from rival businesses.

In Kumasi, Ghana, dozens of separate studios have sprung up, the most famous of which is the Almighty God Art Works, headed by master artist Almighty God, aka Kwame Akoto. Since establishing his business in the mid-1970s, he has trained at least 15 master artists, each of whom runs his own studio. Today, these businesses have expanded far beyond their local clientele, selling pictures to foreigners and showing their works in exhibitions worldwide – such as the earlier mentioned 'Kumasi Junction' of 2002–3, which featured the work of 11 sign-painters from Kumasi.

The sign-painter's art in Africa is also highly visible on various means of transport, particularly long-distance buses and the smaller mini-van taxis, or *daladalas* as they are known in Tanzania. The rear panels of buses going up-country from Dar Es Salaam are particularly popular with the sign-painters, allowing drivers behind the buses time to contemplate the full range of the artist's skills and the messages he may wish to convey.

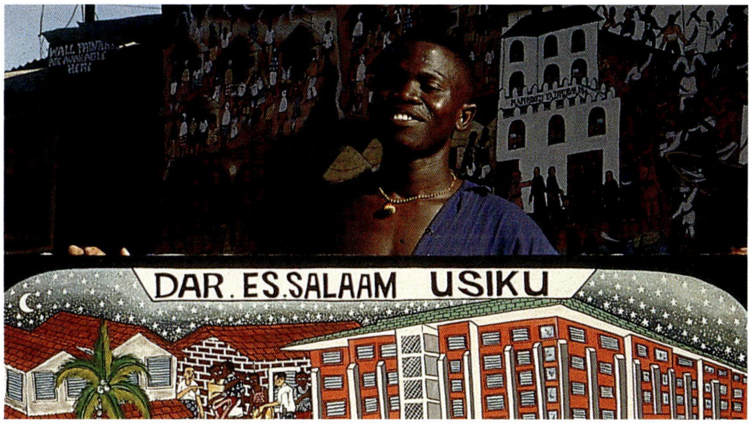

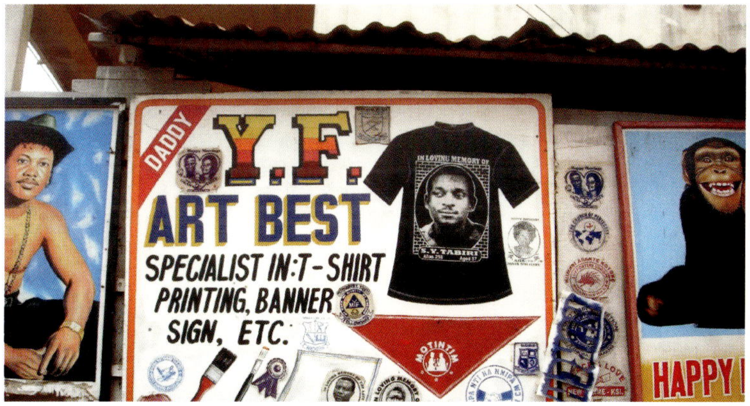

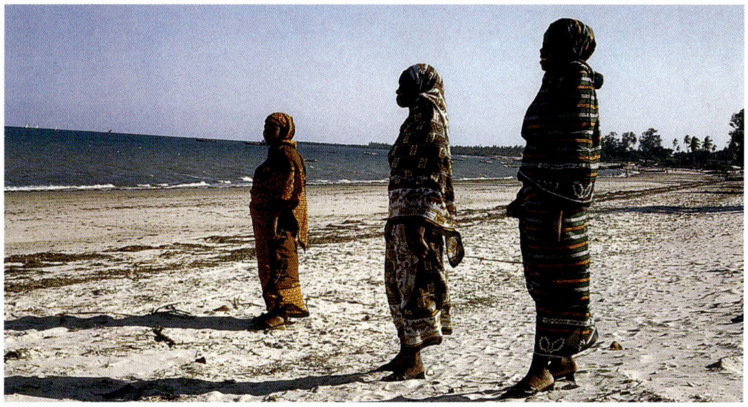

KANGAS

The printed cloths known as *kangas* are worn by millions of women in eastern Africa, from southern Somalia to northern Mozambique. They are sold and worn in pairs, one as a wraparound skirt, the other as a shawl or headscarf. Their complex designs, often including enigmatic inscriptions, make them emblematic of multifaceted Swahili society. The tradition has grown up in and around the great trading ports on the Indian Ocean coast of eastern Africa: Mombasa, Dar Es Salaam and Zanzibar. Legend has it that the first *kanga* sprang from a single textile created in the late nineteenth century, shortly

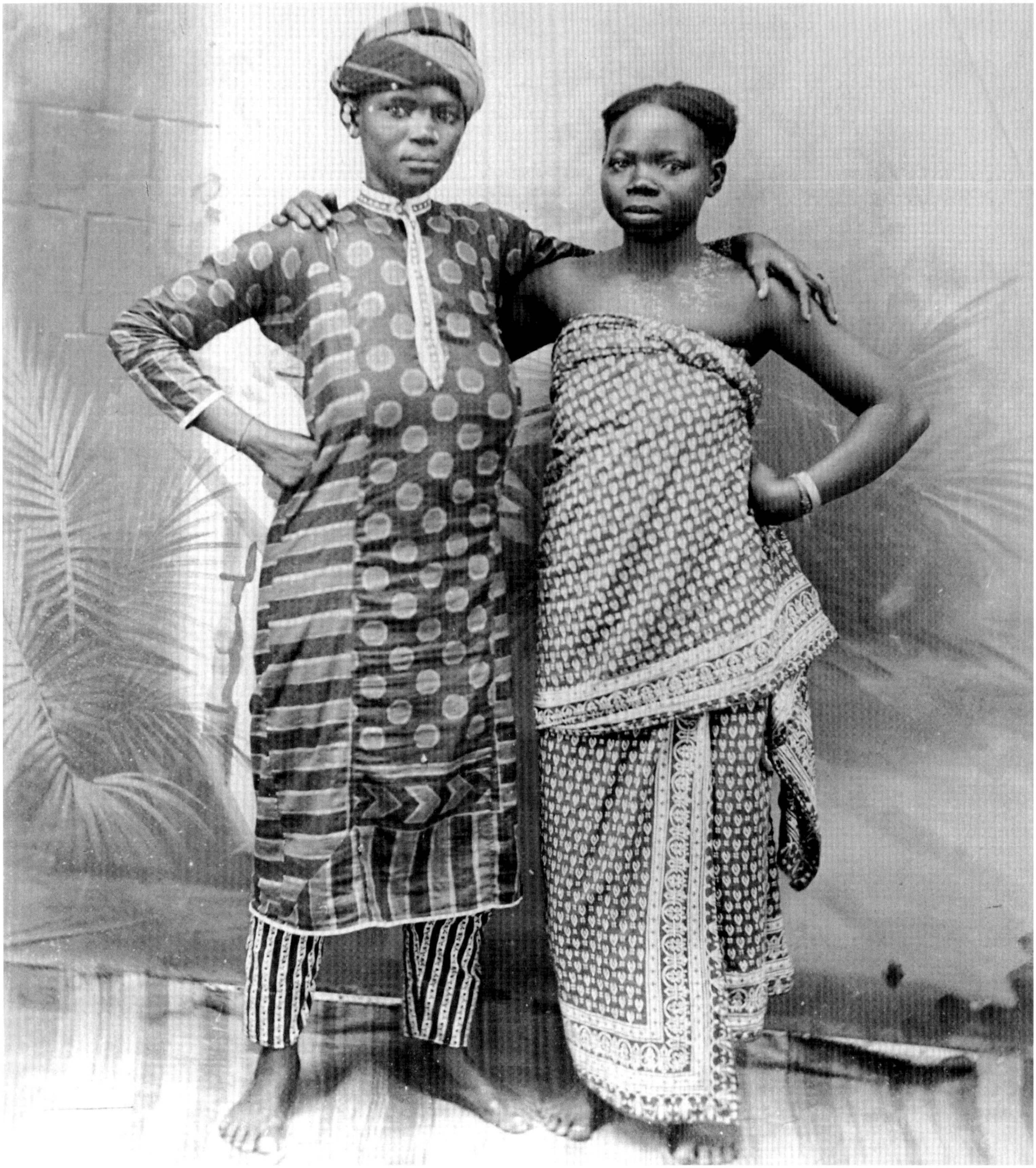

Left Two women of Zanzibar, late nineteenth century.

Below Woman and child, Mozambique, photograph by Rui Assubuji.

after the abolition of slavery in that part of Africa, an act that created a whole new market for colourful cloth amongst women who formerly would not have been permitted to wear garments of such material. This new textile was created by sewing together six of the printed handkerchiefs, known as *leso*, which the Portuguese had first traded to eastern Africa in the sixteenth century, but which by the late nineteenth century were being printed in England, the Netherlands and Switzerland.

Soon the prototype *kanga* was being locally printed, using wood blocks, on a single piece of cloth, and it wasn't long before the textile mills of Europe were mass-producing *kangas*. Today, *kangas* are still imported from overseas – mainly from India – but large quantities are also printed in Kenya and in Tanzania at the integrated textile mills of URAFIKI and KARIBU in Dar Es Salaam.

In the 1900s the familiar size, shape and pattern of today's *kanga* began to predominate, with a patterned border enclosing a central design, and an inscription in KiSwahili centrally placed just above the lower border. The first inscriptions were printed in Arabic script, though since the 1960s most of the inscriptions have been printed in the Roman script. Manufacturers have always consulted their customers about the most appropriate or topical design and inscription for the *kangas* they produce, knowing that if they do not, eastern African women will quickly advise them of their mistake, or simply refuse to buy or wear their products. *Kangas* may carry a political or social message, may urge people to prevent soil erosion or extol the virtues of cleanliness in the home – or they may reflect the ongoing horror of the HIV/AIDS pandemic in inscriptions such as, 'Don't be boastful – have you been checked?', or 'Whatever begins must come to an end'. *Kangas* reflect changing times, fashions and tastes; inscriptions will also vary according to the age of the wearer and the context in which the *kanga* is worn. Certain themes, by contrast, have changed relatively little over the years, especially those governing intimate social and sexual relationships and marriage. 'Your problem is that you can't stop backbiting' is a popular inscription worn by the bride and her female entourage at her wedding as a means of heading off any malicious rumours.

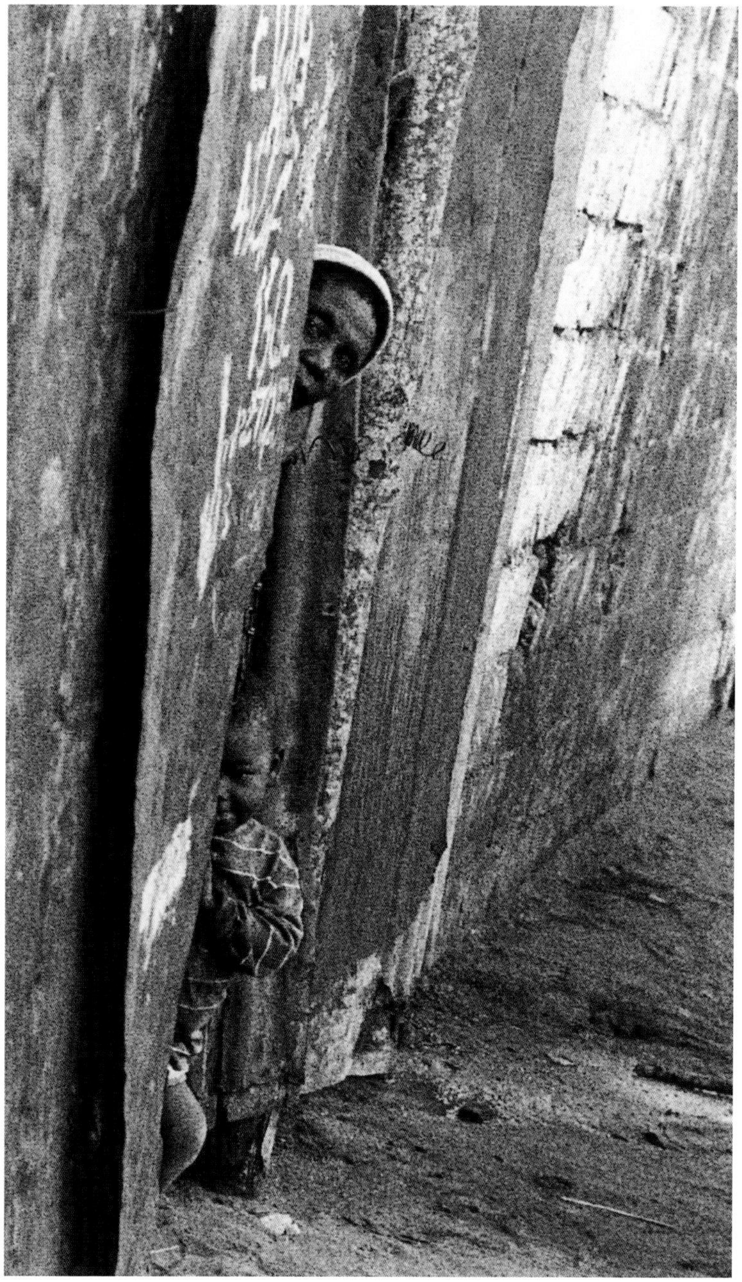

PORTRAIT AND STUDIO PHOTOGRAPHY

Studio photography has flourished in many parts of Africa for more than a century and has been a source of inspiration for many of Africa's contemporary artist/photographers, such as Rui Assubuji of Mozambique. The first studios were set up in Cairo and South

Below Pots (including a collection of *garra* beneath the palm trees) drying in the sun. Qasr, Dakhla Oasis, Egypt.

Bottom The potter Nkubwa Kondo shaping a traditional Zanzibari cooking vessel (*chungu chenye kifuniko*).

Right The master weaver Muhammed Tobji with the prestigious marriage shawl (*biskri*). Djerba Island, Tunisia.

Africa, followed quickly by Sierra Leone and Ghana in West Africa, and by the great Indian Ocean ports, such as Zanzibar and Mombasa. In West Africa some of the studios were owned by Africans from the beginning, though there is often no documentation to determine the identity of many early photographers and their customers. Some studios catered mainly for foreigners and were part of the colonial establishment, their customers probably being colonial officials wanting portraits of local people and dress to take home as souvenirs. However, African photographers attracted clients who could express their identities through dress and hairstyle and who felt uneasy in front of foreign photographers. The popularity of local photographic studios grew enormously after WWII, particularly after the introduction of electricity in many towns, which greatly increased the range of effects available to the photographer through studio lighting. Photography was an important element in the creation of African modernity – the Malian photographer Seydou Keïta (1921–2001) was the first to build an international reputation, followed by Malick Sidibé (Mali), Philip Kwame Apagya (Ghana) and Samuel Fosso (Central African Republic).

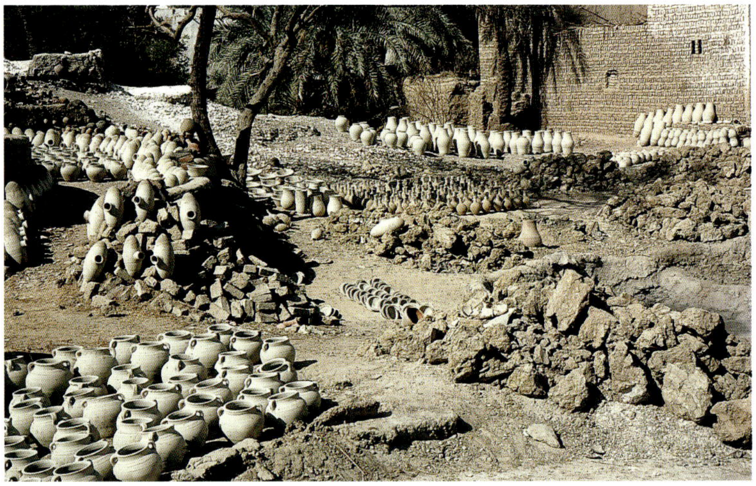

POTTERS OF DAKHLA AND ZANZIBAR

Despite the introduction of factory-made vessels of plastic and metal, the art of pottery, in its innumerable forms and methods of production, is still flourishing in Africa and has been a constant source of inspiration for the studio potters featured in this book. In order to give some idea of the diversity of practice throughout Africa I will give a brief overview of the very different working methods and products of the group of male potters at Dakhla Oasis in the Western Desert of Egypt, and of the female potter Nkubwa Kondo, who works on her own in Zanzibar. Although there are increasing exceptions to the rule, most domestic pottery in urban areas of North Africa is produced by male potters using a wheel and is often glazed and fired in a kiln, whereas in most of sub-Saharan Africa women create unglazed pots shaped by hand and fired in the open at relatively low temperatures.

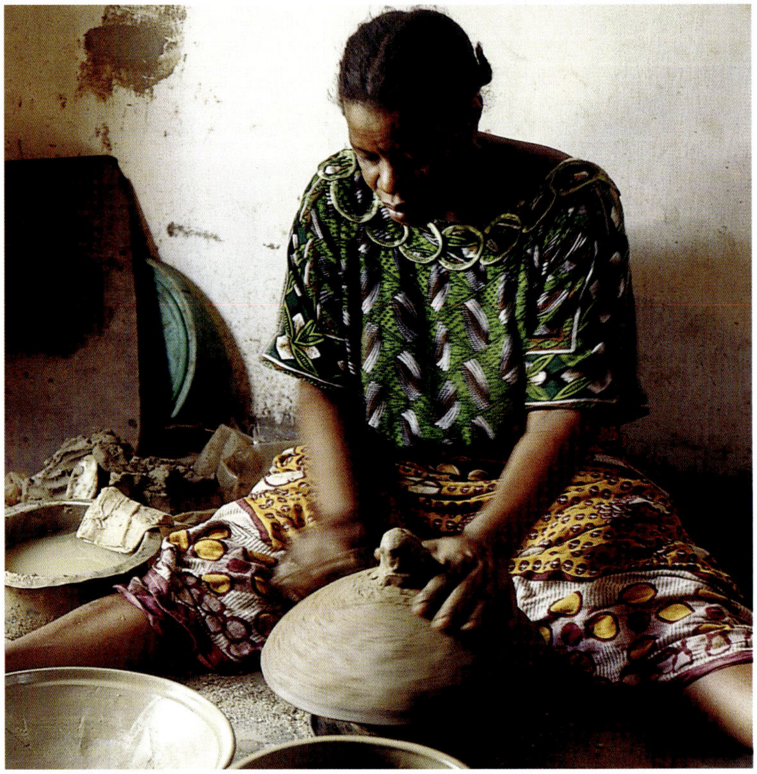

Dakhla

Dakhla is one of a string of Egyptian oases, each with its own very distinctive character and culture, which stretch out into the Sahara to the west of the Nile. Around the village of Qasr there are large deposits of clay that are used by a group of male potters to create vessels for much of the Western Desert. Working in a long, dark hut, the potters use foot-powered wheels to create at least a dozen types of vessel, one of which, the *garra*, is peculiar to Dakhla and is of great antiquity, its use being recorded in hieroglyphic inscriptions dating to the reign of Thutmose III (1504–1450 BC). A cigar-shaped vessel with a central spout, the *garra* is designed so that a number may be carried at the same time. Women can often be seen with two tucked under their arms and another balanced on the head. The principal function of the *garra* is to store and carry water, but it has other uses, such as the separation of curds and whey in cheese-making, by rhythmically tilting the vessel from side to side.

Another of the Dakhla potters' products, though dating from the much more recent Islamic period, is the *zir*, a large water vessel. Because of its great size, the potter deftly wraps a rope around the vessel as soon as he removes it from the wheel in order to prevent the wet clay from sagging; the rope is removed when the vessel is almost dry and ready to be fired in a large kiln. As in much of North Africa and the Middle East, water is cooled by evaporation and purified in the porous *zir*, which can often be seen at the roadside.

Zanzibar

The potter Nkubwa Kondo lives and works in her house in the small village of Kiembe Samaki ('the mango tree beneath which fish are sold') on Zanzibar Island. She uses two types of clay, red and white, to make her pots, which she sells in the market to her local clientele and to the wider Zanzibari community. As a first step she kneads a small amount of white clay into a loaf-sized slab of red; she shapes each slab into a cone, spreads a little sand on the concrete floor of her studio, then puts down a small round disc about the size of a vacuum cleaner filter on which the pot will revolve and take shape. She then begins to create the vessel, using a damp cloth to shape it and a seashell as a rib. Once the basic shape of, for example, the base of the lidded Zanzibari cooking pot has been achieved, it is allowed to dry for a day before being further shaped with a knife and a smooth stone. The lid of the pot is initially made using a similar procedure to the base; additional clay is then worked around the rim to create a wall, into which Nkubwa puts a decorative wave using the edge of her finger so that it begins to look a bit like a traditional pastry pie-crust. She then adds a triangular handle to the top of the lid.

The pots are then left to dry for four days before being taken for firing on a piece of waste ground near Nkubwa's house. She only fires about a dozen pots at a time, laying them on a small blaze of palm leaves and coconut husks. She then covers them with more leaves and husks, as well as old, cracked pots, to block out any direct gusts

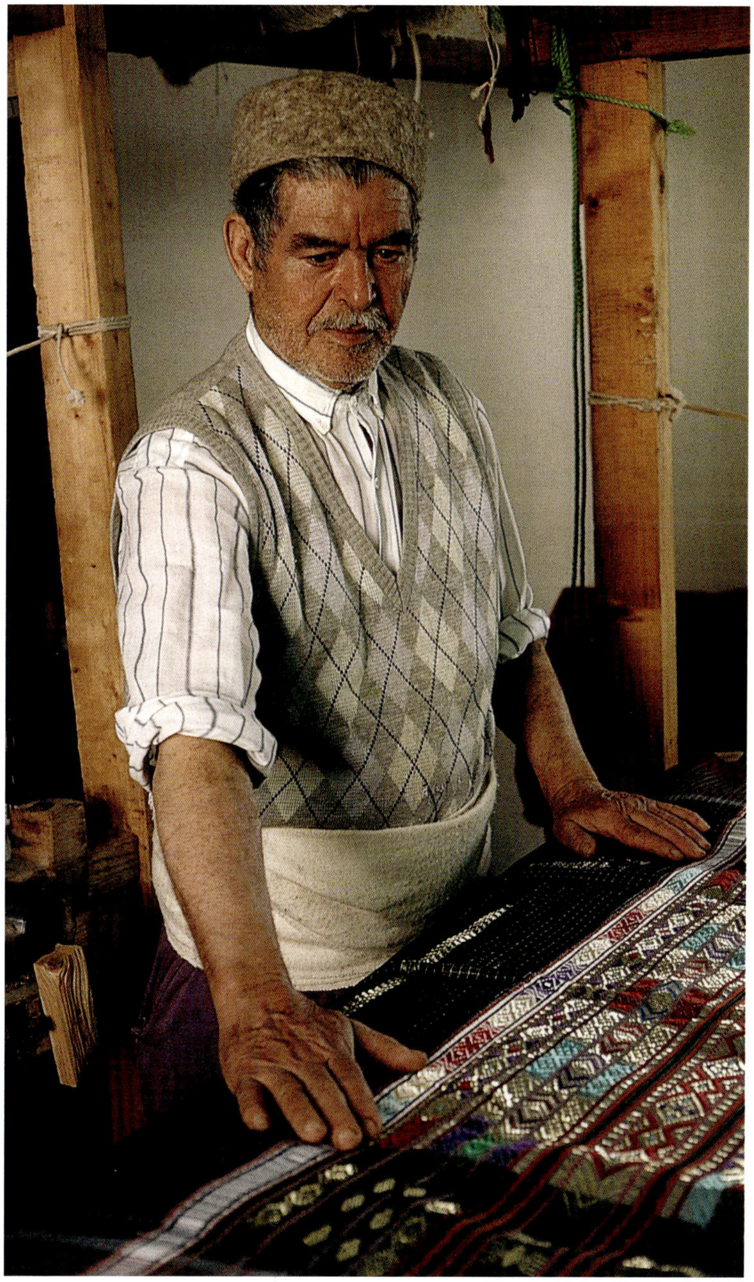

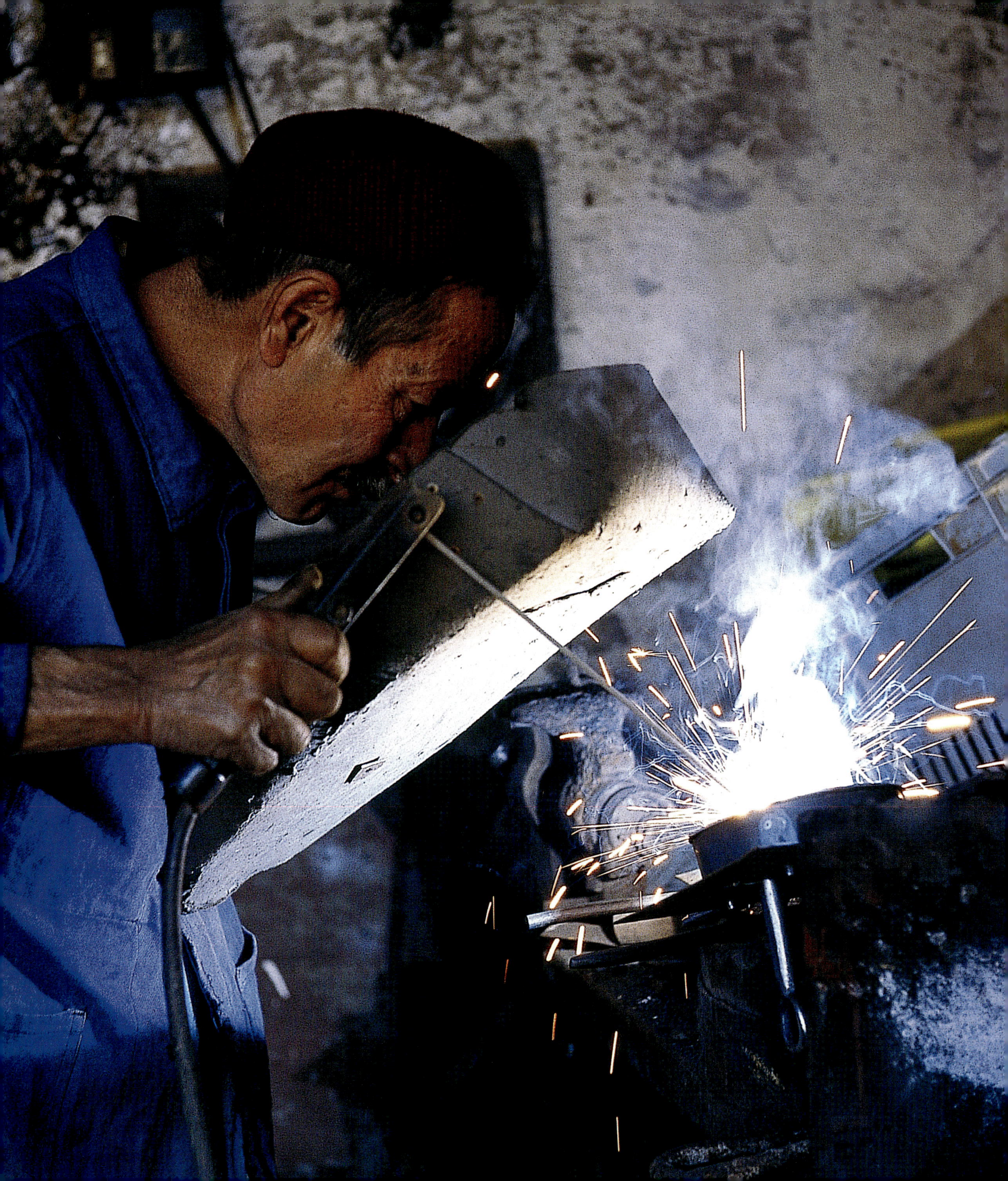

Left Blacksmith Fathi El Abassi working in the old caravanserai of Sfax, Tunisia.

of wind. Once the pile of pots has been completely covered, she leaves them for no more than an hour before carefully removing each fired pot with a long metal rod.

URBAN TEXTILES OF TUNISIA

In contrast to the rural weaving traditions in Tunisia, in which women use woollen yarn on upright, single-heddle looms, urban traditions are predominantly the preserve of male weavers, using treadle looms and a range of luxury yarns such as silk and metallic thread. Similar divisions exist throughout North Africa. Bearing witness to many centuries of cross-cultural and ideological exchange, these urban textiles nonetheless represent an internal dynamic through which the living history and the distinctive nature of Tunisia's culture may be read and understood. Contemporary artists throughout Africa, including El Anatsui of Ghana and Abdoulaye Konaté of Mali, have been inspired by indigenous textile traditions. In Tunisia Nja Mahdaoui, Rachid Koraïchi and even the ceramicist Khaled Ben Slimane all reference local textile traditions in their work.

Muhammed Tobji is a master weaver on Djerba Island, producing a range of cloth for local women, the most prestigious of which are known as *biskri* and may take several weeks to weave. It is a cotton cloth four metres (13 feet) long, embellished at one end with numerous named pattern bands of complex design in silk and cotton thread. The cloth is worn initially as part of a woman's wedding dress, and the names of the pattern bands – 'beans', 'rice', 'heart', 'eyes', 'chair', and so on – reflect a concern for fertility and domestic harmony, as well as protection from the Evil Eye. Older *biskri* incorporate the Star of David in their pattern bands because, it is said, most of the Djerban weavers who originally wove such cloth were of Jewish ancestry.

The Star of David still appears on the *rida' ahmar* (literally 'red outer-garment') woven in the coastal town of Mahdia to the north of Djerba. In the old medina of Mahdia the *rida' ahmar* is woven in many of the small ateliers owned by Karim el-Arousse, the latest in a long line of master weavers in his family. This cloth isn't actually red – its base cloth is black – but the word 'red' has a wider significance in the function and social context of marriage, where it represents wealth and fertility. All the design bands at each end of the cloth are named, the central band including a stylized representation of a mosque in the form of a star with a gold lozenge representing the *imam* at its centre.

Karim also researches the old patterns once used by weavers in Mahdia and has woven samples with colour combinations quite unlike anything else his workshops produce. This may be a way to expand his business into a new market and to satisfy his own creativity, while at the same time remaining true to what he sees as his responsibilities in maintaining living weaving traditions in Mahdia.

BLACKSMITHS AND METALWORKERS

Blacksmiths throughout Africa have always held a special position in society. Sometimes revered, sometimes despised, their magical transformation of one substance into another through the medium of fire has always set them apart. Today, some of the old taboos and beliefs surrounding the smiths are gradually disappearing, and they no longer make all the metal artefacts, from weapons to ploughs, that a society would need to survive. Today, very little ore is taken from the ground for smelting, as the smiths acquire their raw material from many more easily available sources, including large numbers of junked automobiles. The spot-welder and the blowtorch have made the process of moulding and joining metal a different art, but the metalworkers of Africa, in common with weavers, potters and sign-painters, have adapted to new markets and means of production. Blacksmiths create a vast range of artefacts, from the most delicate jewellery to large sheet metal ovens and carts.

Metalworkers may form into collectives that help to attract a large clientele through the sheer range of artefacts produced. In Nairobi, Kenya, a group of metalworkers called Jua Kali ('Fierce Heat'/ 'Sun') has taken over a two-acre site on which the members produce an extraordinary range of items, many made with great skill, including milk churns, pots and pans, furniture and ornamental lamps. As always in a collective, there are master craftsmen who pass on their skills to others. Francis Kuaya Kiare is one such among the Jua Kali, producing highly imaginative work that has been exhibited in Kenyan galleries and internationally.

Art is all around in Africa.

ARTISTS

AKINBODE AKINBIYI
NIGERIA/GERMANY

Below *Lagos: All Roads.* Victoria Island, 2006. B&W photograph.
'I love to wander, to go out for hours in the great wide open and simply wander. In cities and also in the countryside.'

Right *Lagos: All Roads.* Surulere, 2006. B&W photograph.
'*Lagos: All Roads* is a still ongoing work on the city that has the largest sub-Saharan population, roughly 15 million inhabitants. Its vitality and energy are hard to capture visually, a constant onward drive to manage the daily upheavals and downturns.'

Akinbode Akinbiyi may be seen as one of the greatest observers of city life through the lens of his camera. Born in Oxford, UK, in 1946, he studied literature at the universities of Ibadan (Nigeria), Lancaster (UK) and Heidelberg (Germany), but did not take up photography until 1974. Since then he has shown his work in numerous solo and group exhibitions, particularly in Germany, including the large touring exhibition 'Africa Remix' (2005–7). He has been a mentor to Depth of Field, a collective of young artist/photographers (including Toyin Sokefun) working in Lagos.

> *I love to wander. I photograph in as relaxed a mode as possible, wandering quietly along the highways and byways, dancing in and out of crowds and ever-swirling traffic... The resulting photographs are a constantly ongoing attempt at understanding, at coming to a more perceptive inner image.*

Akinbiyi is currently involved in *Lagos: All Roads*, taking as his subject the vast, sprawling Nigerian city and its 15 million inhabitants. He is fascinated by the 'mega-cities' of Africa – Lagos, Cairo, Johannesburg and Kinshasa; how they compare with smaller cities such as Bamako, but also with the older cities of Europe – London, Paris, Barcelona and Berlin. He brings his calm, deeply humane eye to bear on the realities of these urban landscapes, each photograph taking him a little further on his journey.

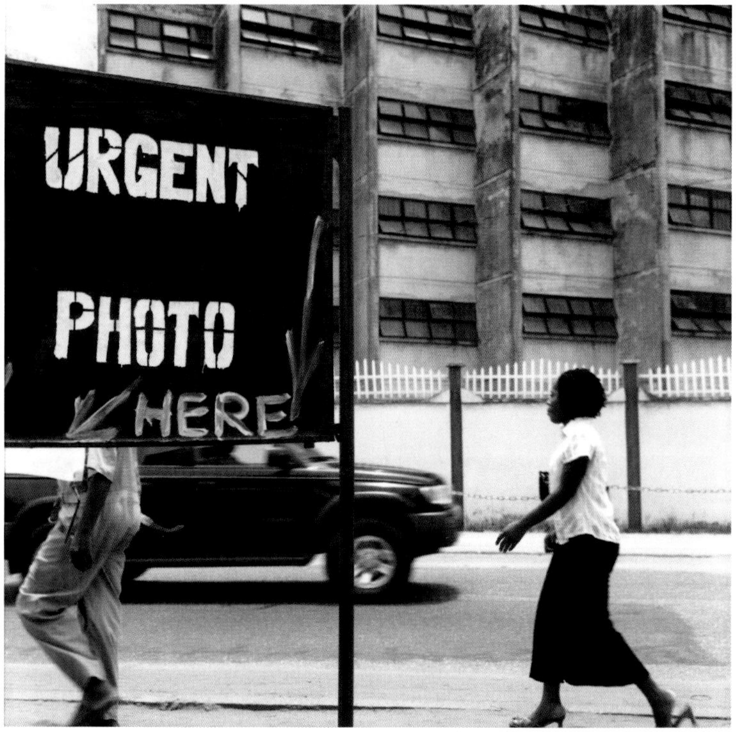

'It is very much a case of taking in the immediate surroundings and gradually trying to come to a deeper understanding of the relationships between things. The road, the pathway, the street assume a primary importance in this scheme, the mapping out of the lines of involvement and engagement.'
Akinbode Akinbiyi

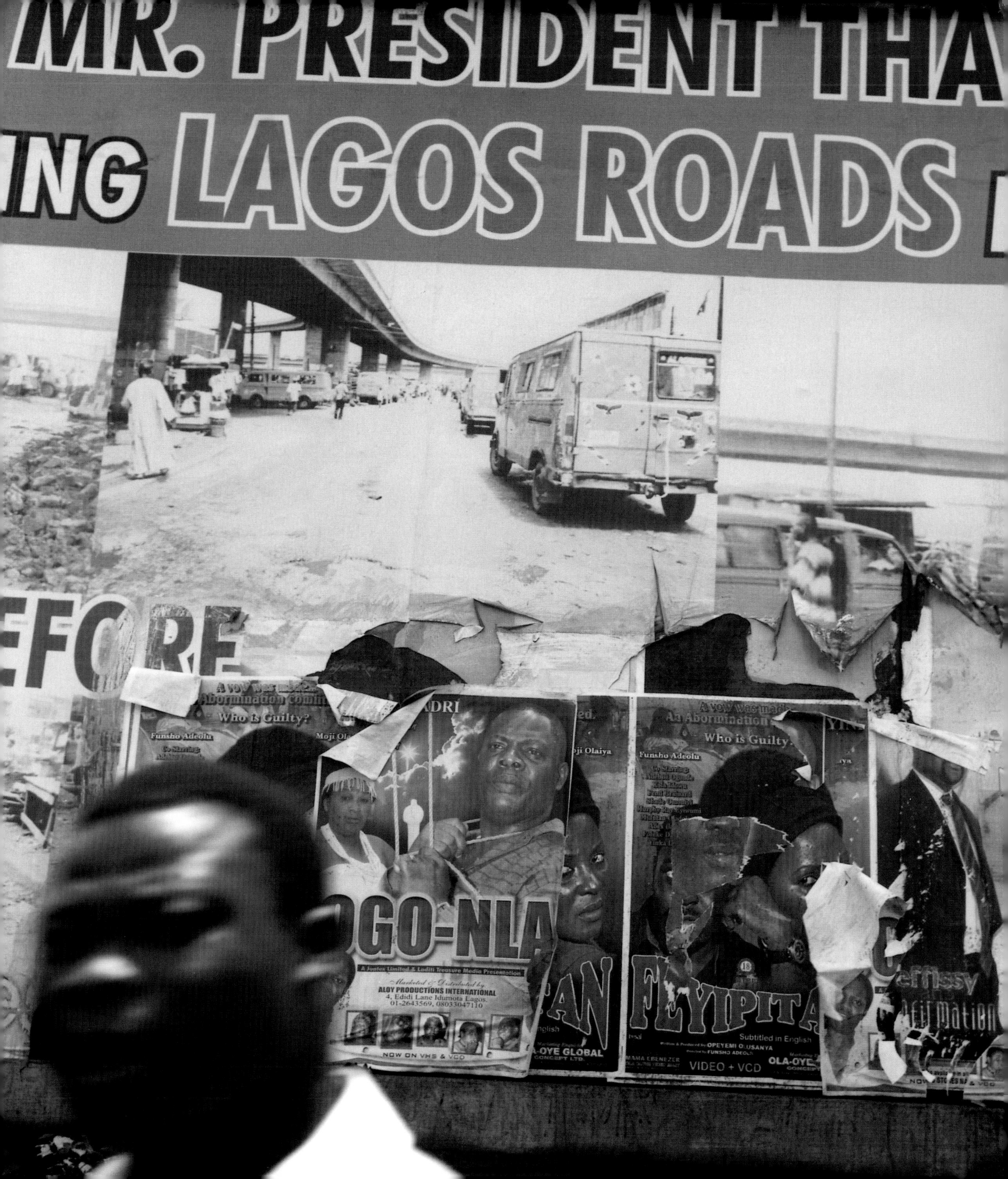
MR. PRESIDENT THA
ING LAGOS ROADS
EFORE
Who is Guilty?
Funsho Adeolu
Moji Olaiya
OGO-NLA
A Jontex Limited & Loditi Treasure Media Presentation
ALOY PRODUCTIONS INTERNATIONAL
4, Edidi Lane Idumota Lagos.
01-2643569, 08033047110
NOW ON VHS & VCD
Who is Guilty?
Funsho Adeolu
EYIPITA
Subtitled in English
VIDEO + VCD
OLA-OYE GLOBAL
CONCEPT LTD.

Below *Lagos: All Roads.* Lagos Island, 2006. B&W photograph.
'The dust eats into your sight as the heat fades into the evening twilight, but even at night the city still pulses and vibrates.'

Right *Lagos: All Roads.* Bar Beach, Victoria Island, 2006. B&W photograph.
'My wanderings also include the greater picture, the landscape in which a city is embedded.'

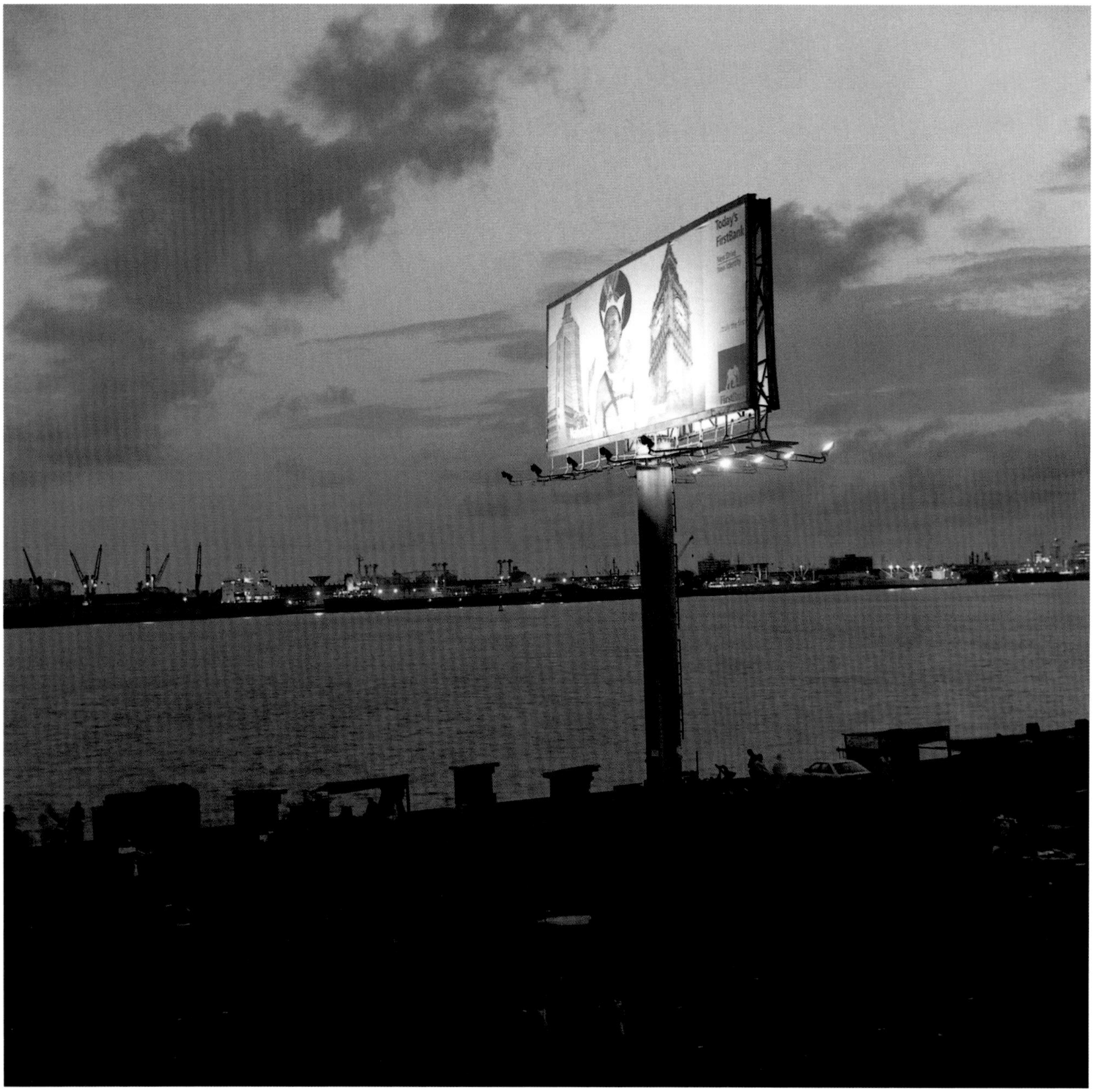

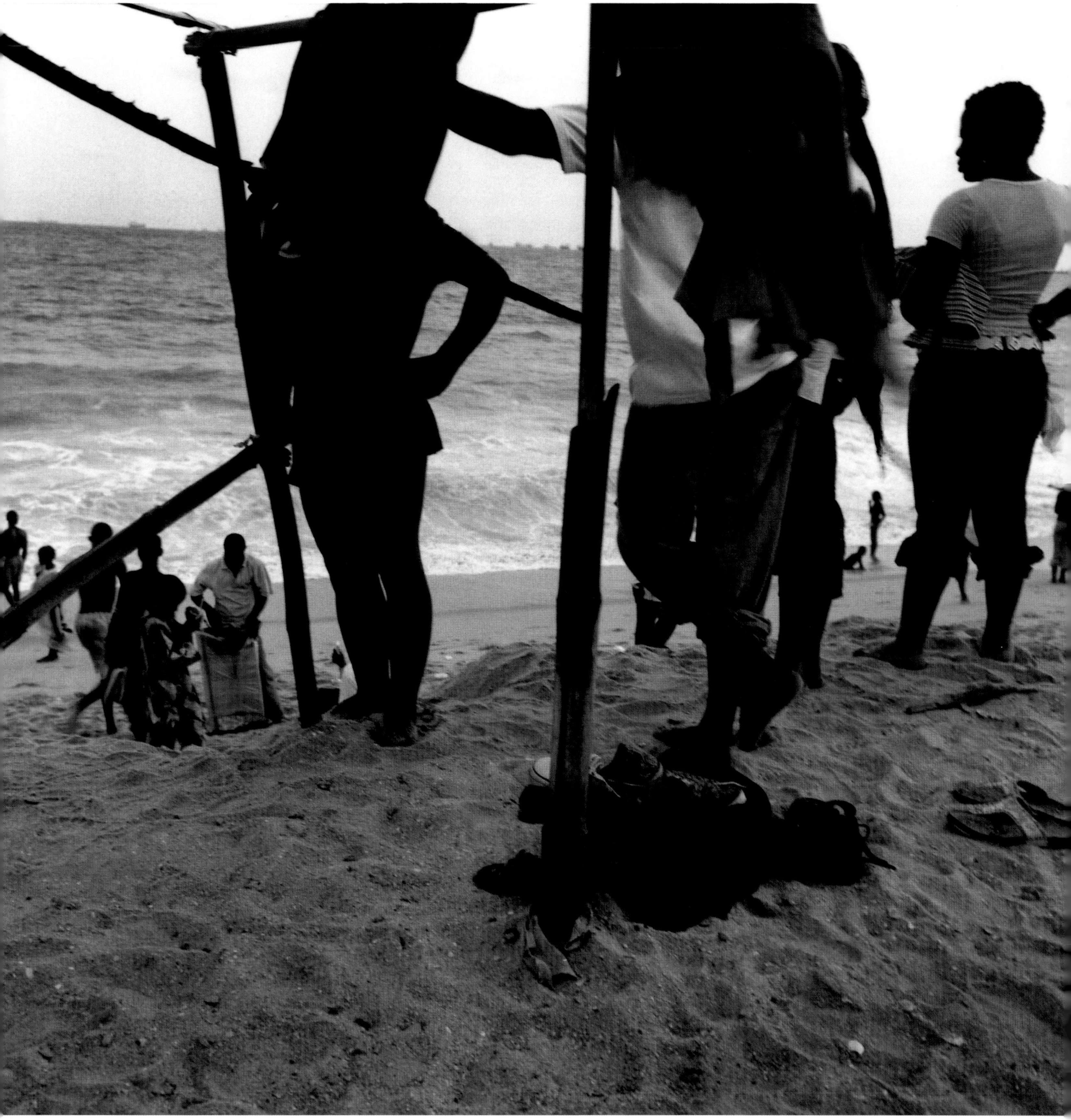

Below *Lagos: All Roads.*
Obalende, 2006.
B&W photograph.
'The resulting photographs are a constantly ongoing attempt at understanding...'

Right *Lagos: All Roads.*
Lagos Island, 2006.
B&W photograph.
'...at coming to a more perceptive inner image.'

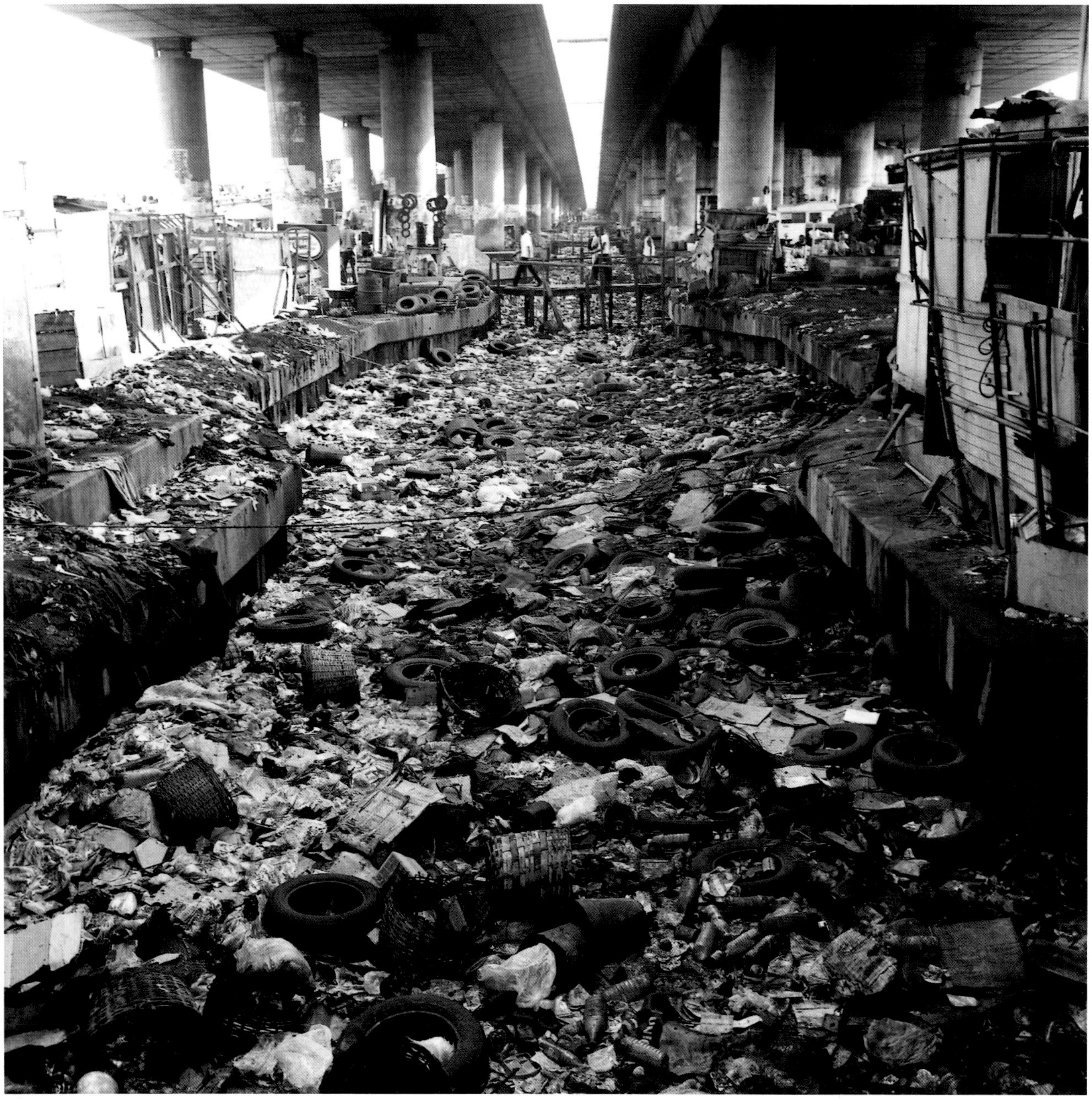

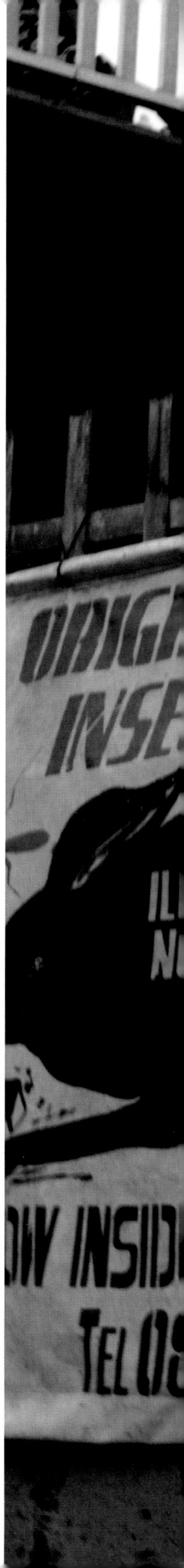

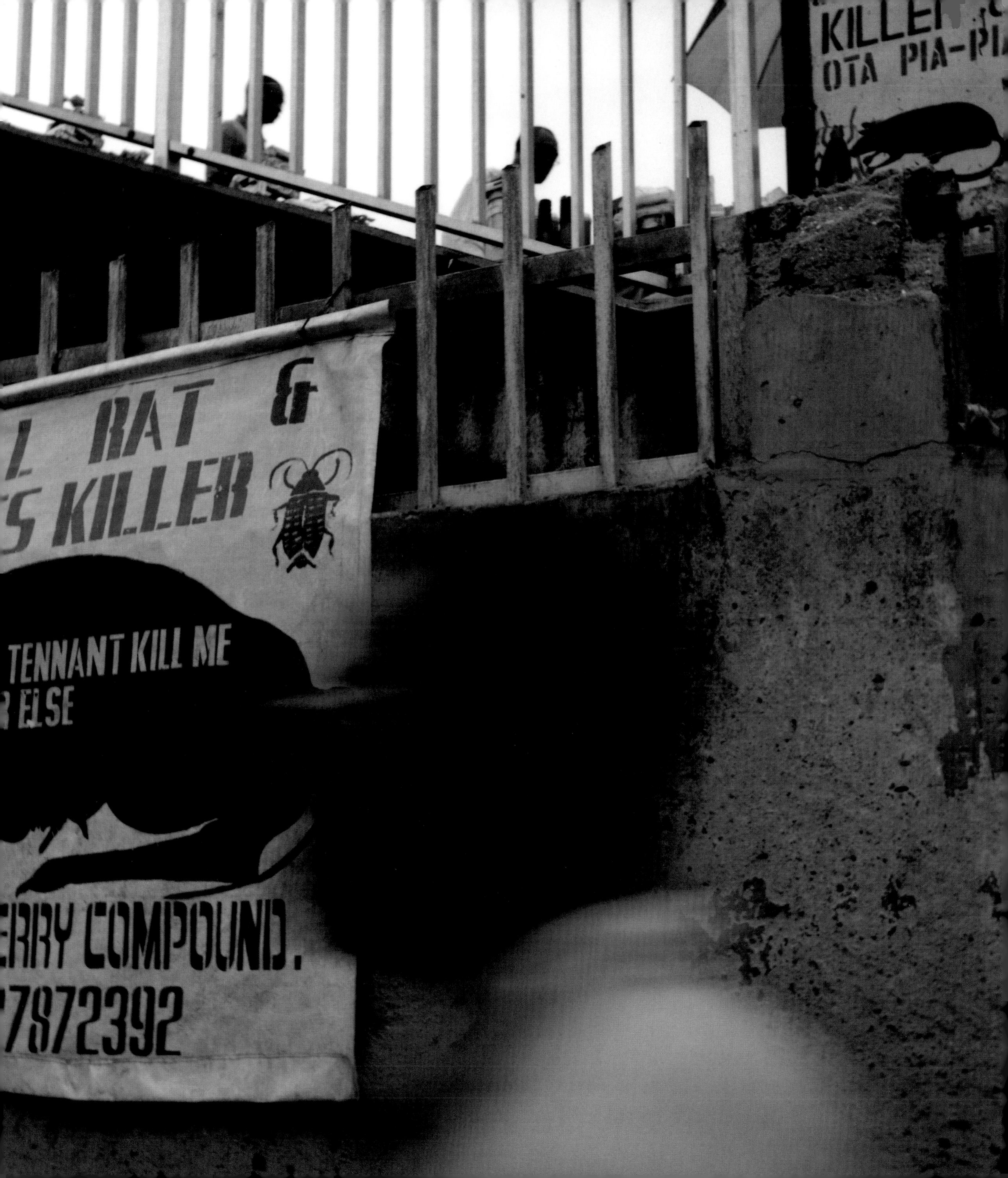
KILLE
OTA PIA-PI
L RAT &
S KILLER
TENNANT KILL ME
R ELSE
ERRY COMPOUND.
7872392

JANE ALEXANDER
SOUTH AFRICA

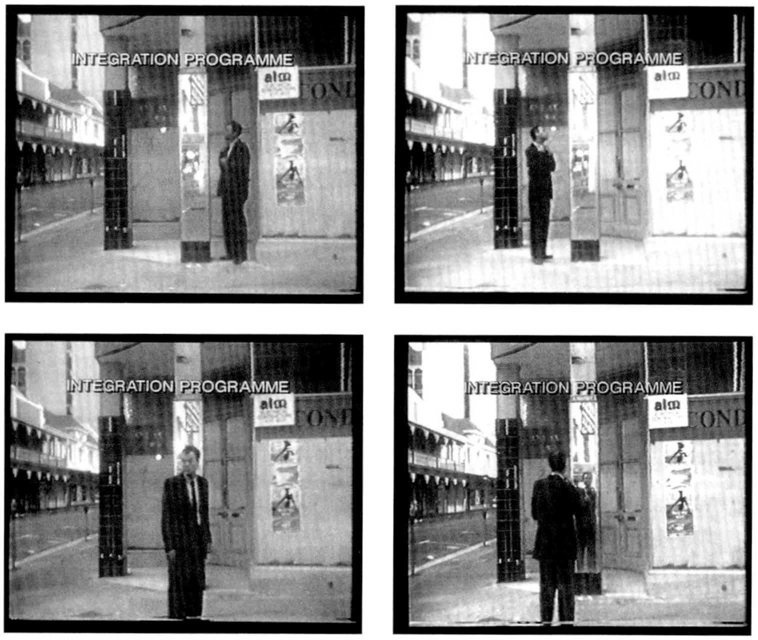

Below Stills from the video of *Integration Programme: man with TV.*

Right *Integration Programme: man with TV,* 1995. Plaster, oil paint, clothing, found objects and video recording, 138 x 100 x 220cm ($54\frac{1}{3}$ x $39\frac{2}{5}$ x $86\frac{3}{5}$ in). Collection of the South African National Gallery, Cape Town.

A man sits in his Sunday best, staring in amazement at a television. On the screen appears the image of another man, also dressed in a suit, who repeatedly adjusts his tie in a shopfront mirror, smoothes his hair, adjusts his tie again, perpetually grooming himself in anticipation of the arrival of someone he will never meet.

Jane Alexander is a South African artist whose father left Germany in 1936 due to anti-semitism. Although Alexander rarely speaks about herself or her work, her art seems to spring from first-hand experience of one repressive, dehumanizing regime (apartheid South Africa) and an imaginative recreation of another (Nazi Germany). Perhaps it is the very lack of comment or explanation that makes Alexander's work so powerful – in the society she portrays, appalling things happen without explanation or justification. An early work, *Butcher Boys* (1985–6) was created while she was still a student, yet remains the most popular work of contemporary art in the South African National Gallery. The meticulous modelling of the life-size, grotesque, yet disturbingly familiar *Butcher Boys* has remained her artistic signature throughout her career.

Alexander was born in 1959 in Johannesburg. She studied Fine Art at the University of Witwatersrand, gaining her Masters degree in 1988. She has taught art at university level for the past ten years, and is currently Professor at the Michaelis School of Fine Art of the University of Cape Town. She has won many awards and prizes and has exhibited widely, including at the Venice Biennale (1995) and in 'The Short Century' (2001–2) and 'Africa Remix' (2005–7).

Alexander's sculpted figures seem to be in a permanent state of mutation: from human to animal and back; from naked to clothed and back. Only occasionally do 'normal' figures appear, such as the man in *Integration Programme: Man with TV* (1995). The spurious notion of 'integration', and all the disintegration and segregation committed in its name, remains a central theme in Alexander's work. Her concern for children and the way in which they are abused and damaged in dysfunctional societies is another pervasive theme; they are often portrayed wearing masks, as if they have not completely mutated and still have the chance to remove the mask before it becomes a permanent feature. Alexander's poignant depictions of children reveal most clearly the deep humanity that pervades all her work.

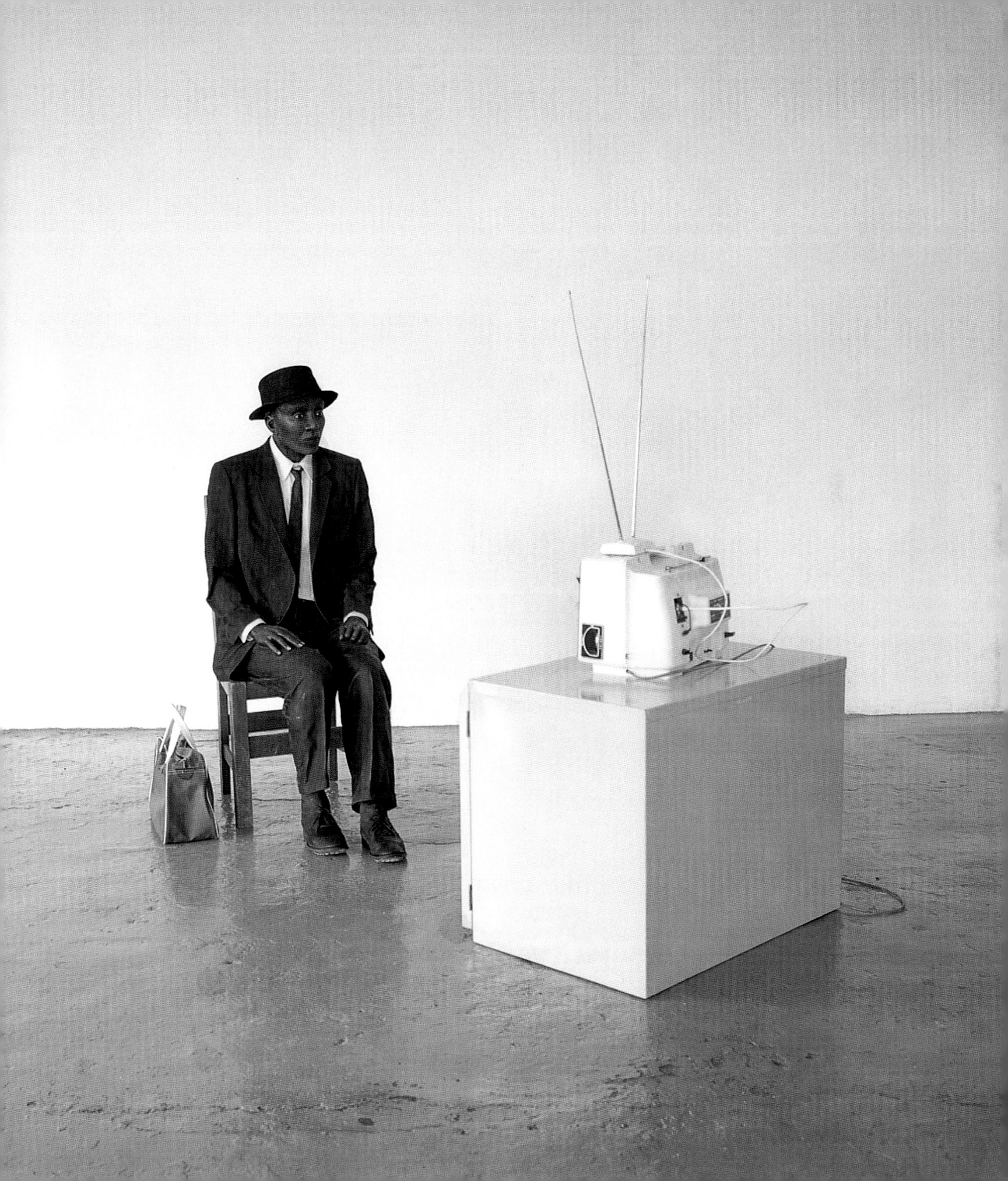

Below *African Adventure*, 1999–2002. Informal security guard, reinforced plaster, oil paint, fibreglass, acrylic paint, synthetic clay, ammunition boxes, clothing, Venetian gloves, gold, diamonds, jackal skin, machetes, sickles, toy tractors, child's car, child's pushchair, oil drum, wood, steel and Bushmanland earth, dimensions variable. Collection of the artist.

A man carries a machete in one hand and drags behind him dozens of similar implements as well as tractors and trailers, perhaps symbolizing not only the weight of his own labour, but also the restrictions placed on African agriculture by world trading tariffs. Meanwhile, mutants jealously stand guard on an oil drum and on boxes of explosives used in mining Africa's diamond and mineral wealth.

Right *Butcher Boys*, 1985/86. Plaster, oil paint, bone, horns and wood, 128.5 x 213.5 x 88.5 cm (50½ x 84 x 34⅘ in). Collection of the South African National Gallery, Cape Town.

They could be waiting for a bus, these three unconcernedly naked horned figures – one staring into space, the other two idly watching something across the road. Their sternums and spines are raw, as if they have recently been split open and had all their vital organs removed before being roughly sewn up. It is frightening to think what such creatures might be capable of.

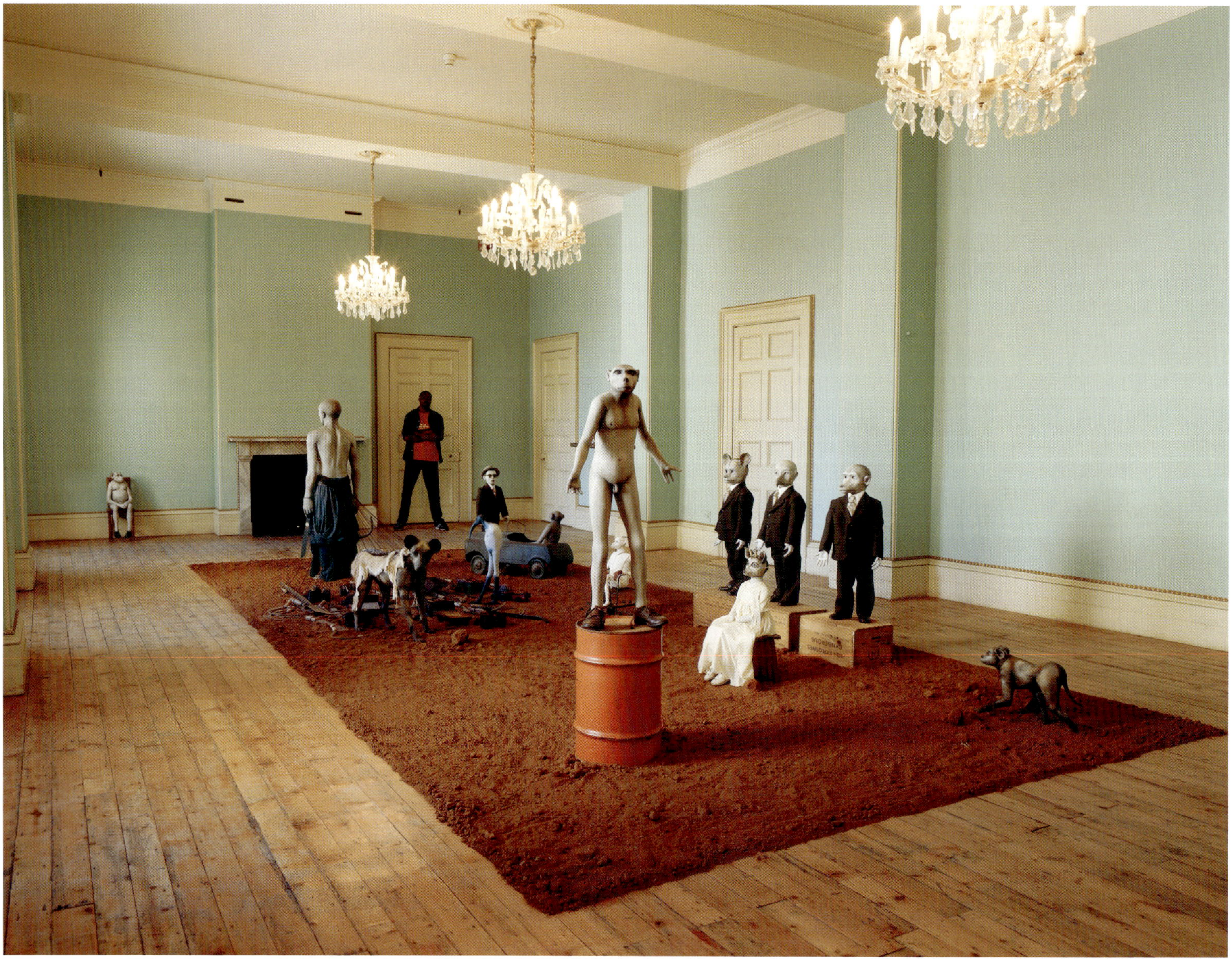

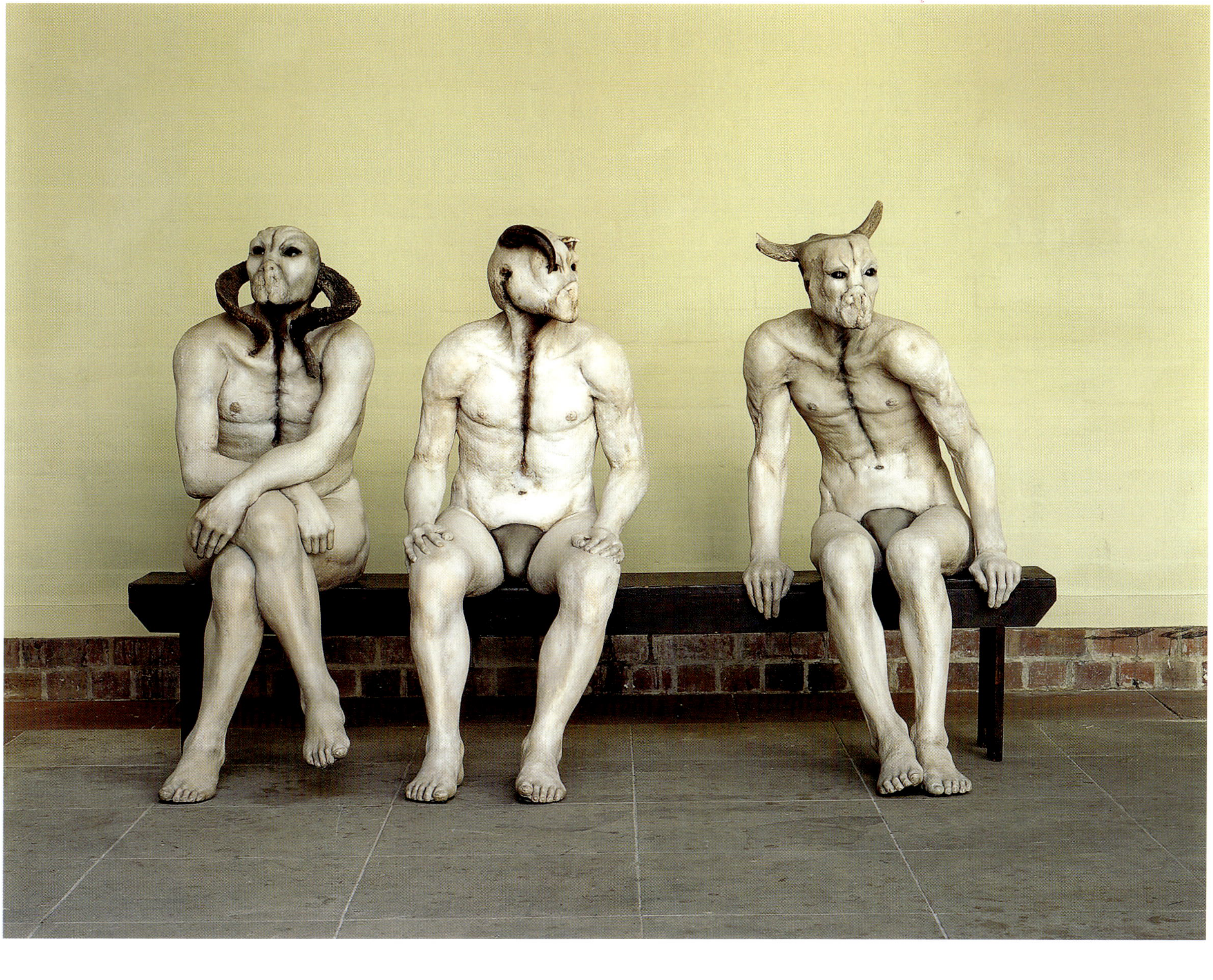

Right *Bom Boys,* 1998. Fibreglass, acrylic paint, found clothing and wood, 105 x 360 x 360cm (41⅓ x 141¾ x 141¾ in). Collection of the artist.

'A child understands fear, and the hurt and hate it brings.'
Nadine Gordimer

'The deformed and stunted relations between human beings that were created under colonialism and exacerbated under what is loosely called apartheid have their psychic representation in a deformed and stunted inner life.'
J.M. Coetzee

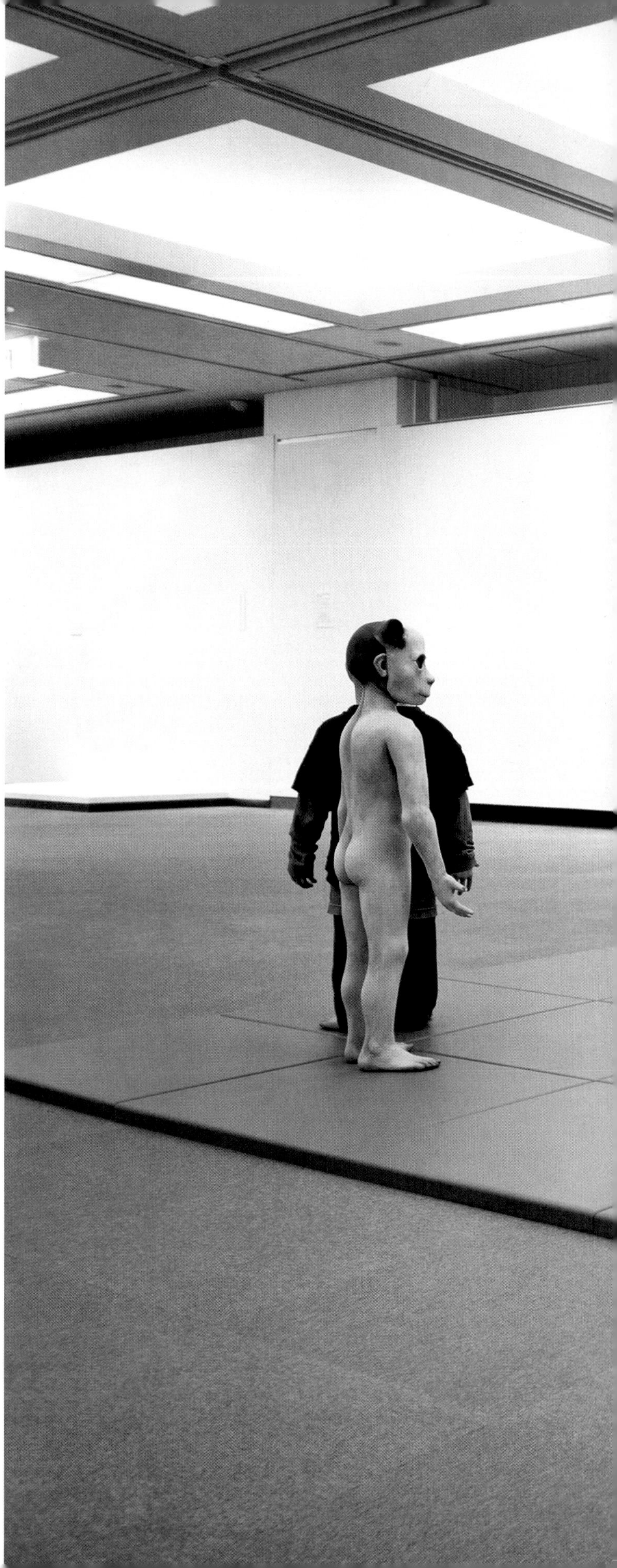

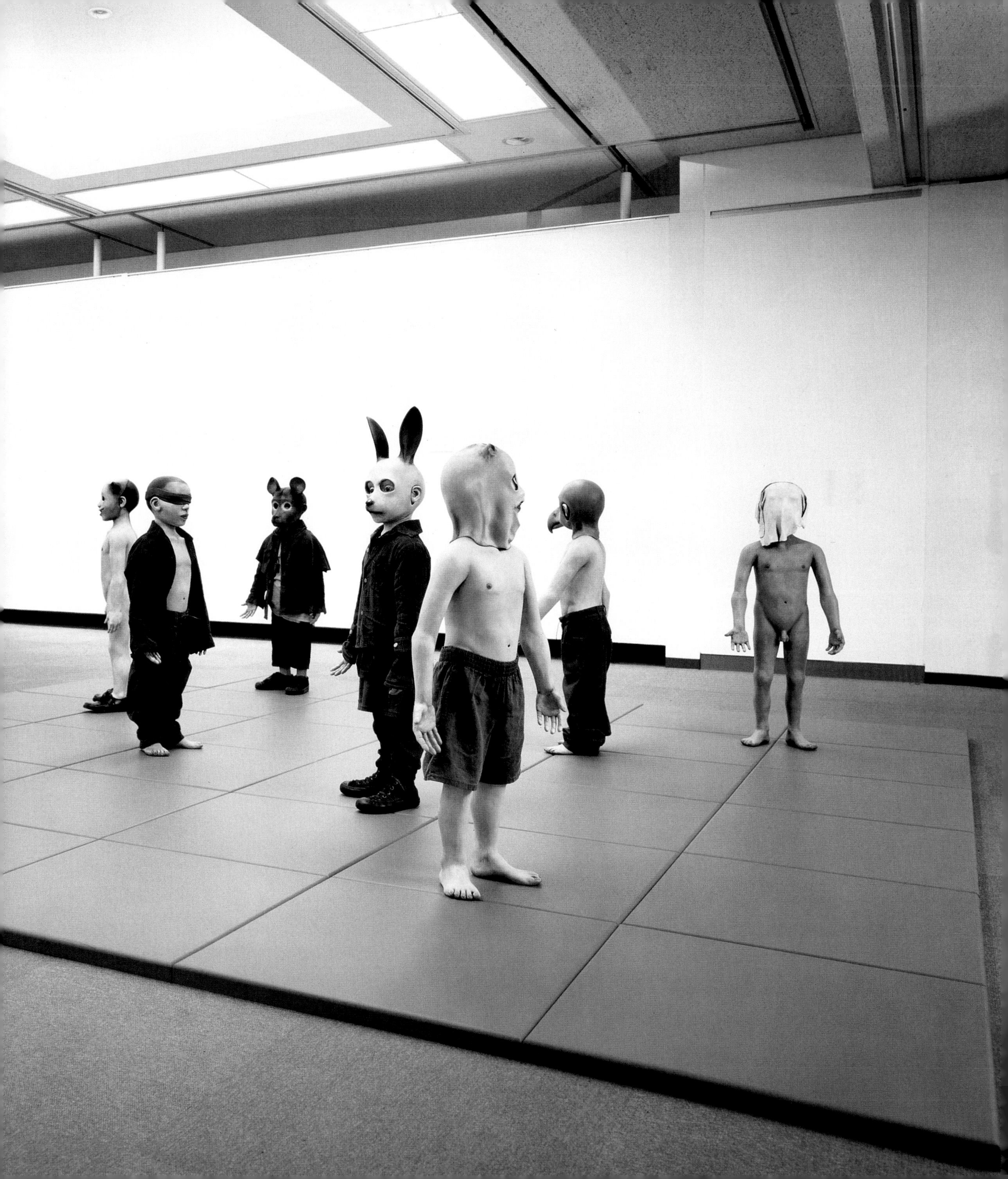

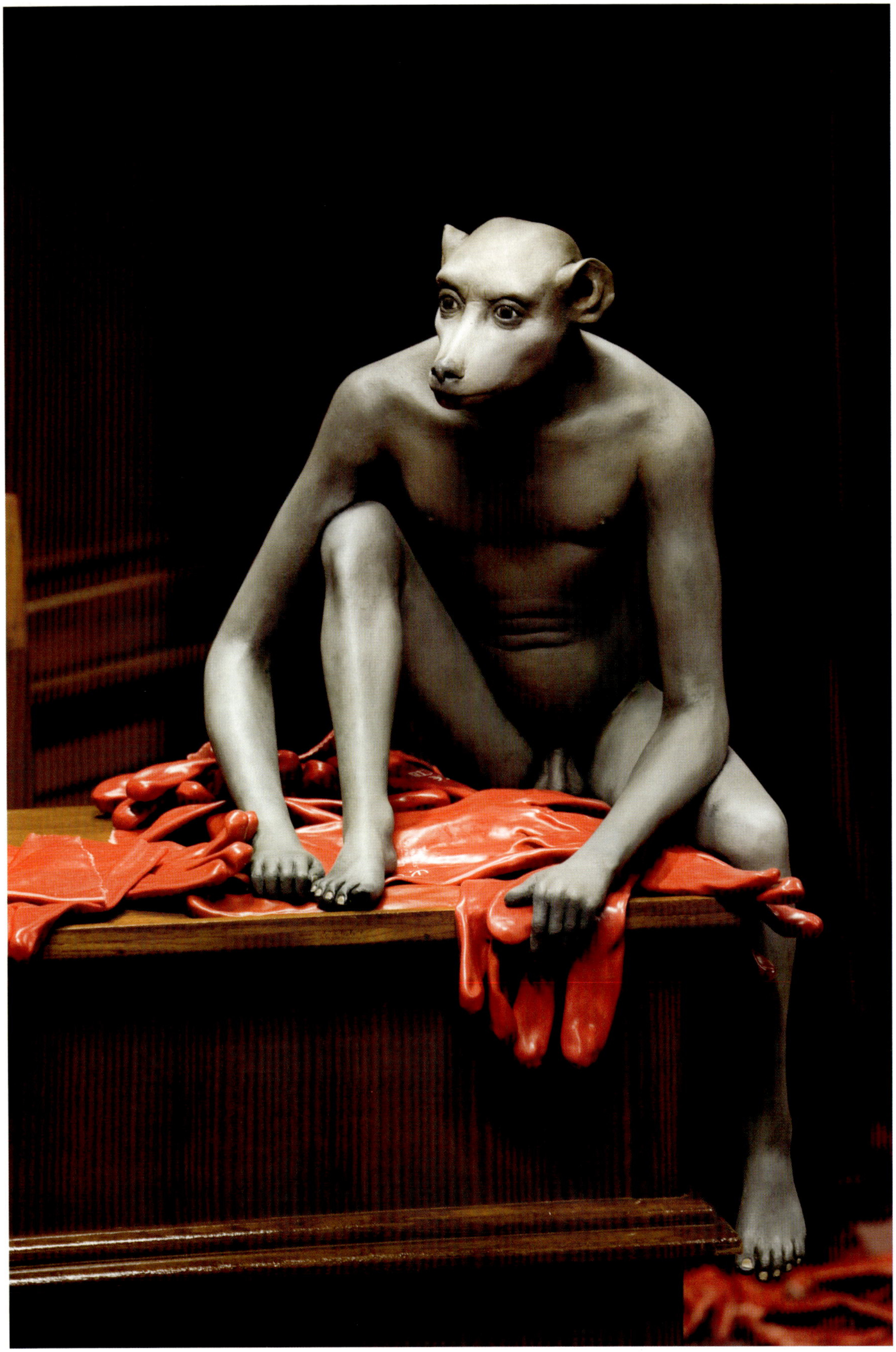

Left *Custodian*, detail of ~~*Courtroom 21 (in the absence of Judge Woo Bih Li)*~~ ~~*Courtroom 21*~~ ~~*Title withdrawn*~~ *Verity, Faith and Justice*, site-specific installation, Courtroom 21, City Hall, Singapore, for Belief: first Singapore Biennale 2006. 100 smooth black thread sewn gilt edge 100 gram 1000 page blank wood free books; 1000 new red industrial strength gloves; 1 Singaporean judicial ceremonial robe sewn by a judicial seamstress, Cape Town; 1 set of South African pre democracy prisoner's clothing issue; 1 set of shackles loaned from Pollsmoor Maximum Security Prison Cape Town; 2 VOC (Dutch East India Company) and 2 British East India Company flags; 10 sculptures: Harbinger in correctional uniform, Custodian, Monkey boy, Hobbled ruminant, Lamb with stolen boots, Beast, Offenders (3), Bird, dimensions variable. Collection of the artist.

'Censorship is never over for those who have experienced it. It is a brand on the imagination that affects the individual who has suffered it, forever.'
Nadine Gordimer

Right *Street cadets with harbinger: wish, walk/Loop Long*, 1997–8. Reinforced plaster, oil paint, wood, steel, clothing, sheep and rabbit skin, greatest height 112 cm (44 in). Private collection.
It is when Alexander is portraying children that her work is at its most powerful. At once highly amusing and achingly pathetic, the two masked 'Street Cadets', mounted on their handcarts, are being pushed and pulled by the 'harbinger', a foretaste of what is to become of them. As yet the children still wear clothes that fit and masks that can be removed; soon they will mutate irrevocably.

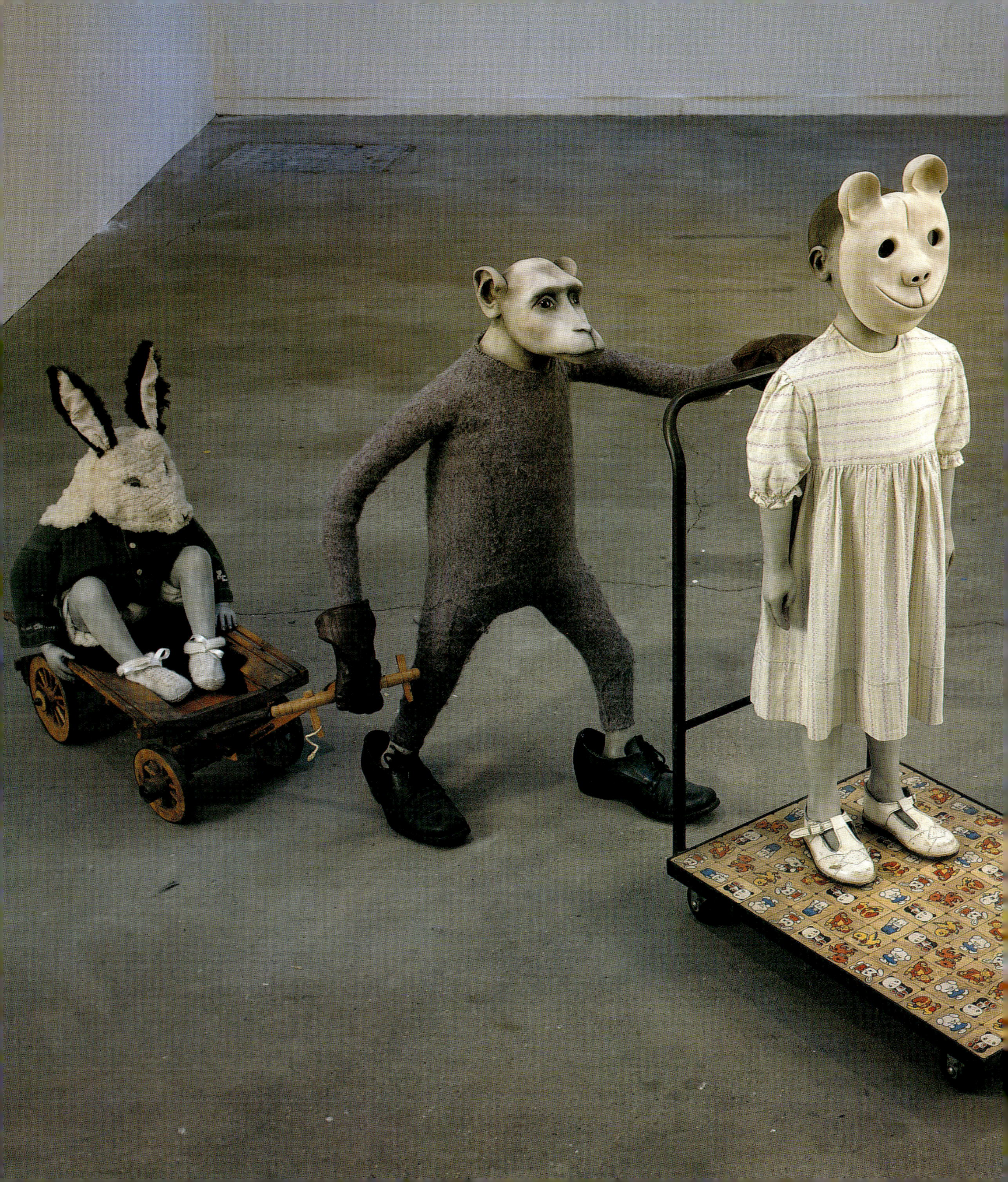

EL ANATSUI
GHANA/NIGERIA

Below *Takpekpe (Conference)*, 2006. Aluminium and copper wire, 240 x 340cm (94½ x 133⅞ in). Seattle Art Museum. Cloth in Africa is a way of memorializing something that in other parts of the world might require a statue or a plaque. A famous *kente* cloth in Ghana is called *Takpekpe le Anloga* meaning 'Conference at Anloga'.

Right *Duvor (Communal Cloth)*, 2007 (detail). Aluminium and copper wire, 400 x 500cm (157½ x 196⅞ in). Indianapolis Museum of Art. The bottle tops that El Anatsui uses to create his 'cloths' come from brands of liquor whose names are linked to events, people, historical or current issues. Traditional silk *kente* cloths are also named in this way.

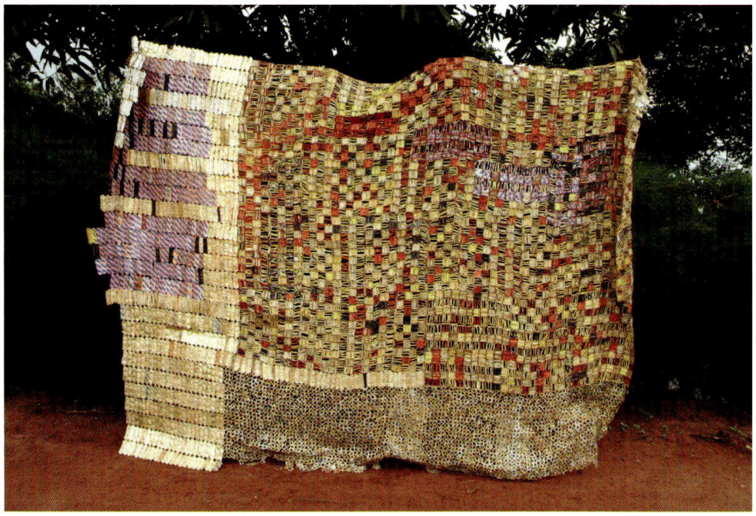

Born in 1944, El Anatsui studied in Kumasi, Ghana, during the late 1960s when an English art-school curriculum was taught. Anatsui recalls 'that there had to be something else!' In 1975, he became a lecturer at the University of Nigeria, Nsukka, together with Uche Okeke who, with Bruce Onobrakpeya and others, had formed the 'Zaria Rebels' at the Ahmadu Bello University in the late 1950s. They had a manifesto based on 'Natural Synthesis', which appealed strongly to Anatsui. This entailed interpreting indigenous cultural traditions through modern materials and techniques, though Anatsui rejected 'professional' artists' materials: 'Art grows out of each particular situation, and I believe that artists are better off working with whatever their environment throws up.'

In 1980, while in the USA, Anatsui began working with power tools, particularly the chainsaw, as a means of exploring African hardwoods – often old house posts or other found wooden objects – and the history locked within them. 'Each process has its own peculiarities or language. [The chainsaw's] language [is] of violence, of tearing, of clawing, of dividing'. El Anatsui uses the chainsaw as a metaphor for the long history of violence to Africa's cultural traditions, not only the atrocities such as the slave trade, but also the subtler damage to African history, either not told at all or misrepresented.

Recently, Anatsui, in his vast, tinfoil 'cloths', has pursued his theme of transformation, by 'subverting the stereotype of metal as a stiff, rigid medium and rather showing it as a soft, pliable, almost sensuous material... You know you can memorialize a lot of things in cloth instead of having a statue in bronze.'

Created by many hands, these metal cloths constantly change in shape and colour according to the different hands that install them. As such they represent the strength and beauty of African oral history:

> *Oral histories have the chance of being amended in the process of transfer through generations, without compromising their essential bases. It is easier to resolve varieties of the history and, in the process, history is edited by the owners of that history.*

El Anatsui's work – with Bruce Onobrakpeya's and others' – was shown at the 1990 Venice Biennale; since then he has held numerous solo exhibitions worldwide, including at the October Gallery, London in 1995, 1998, 2002 and 2005. In 2007, he showed a series of major metal 'cloths' at the Venice Biennale. His work is in many public collections, including the British Museum, London; the Smithsonian Institution, Washington DC; the Pompidou Centre, Paris, and the Museum Kunst Palast, Düsseldorf.

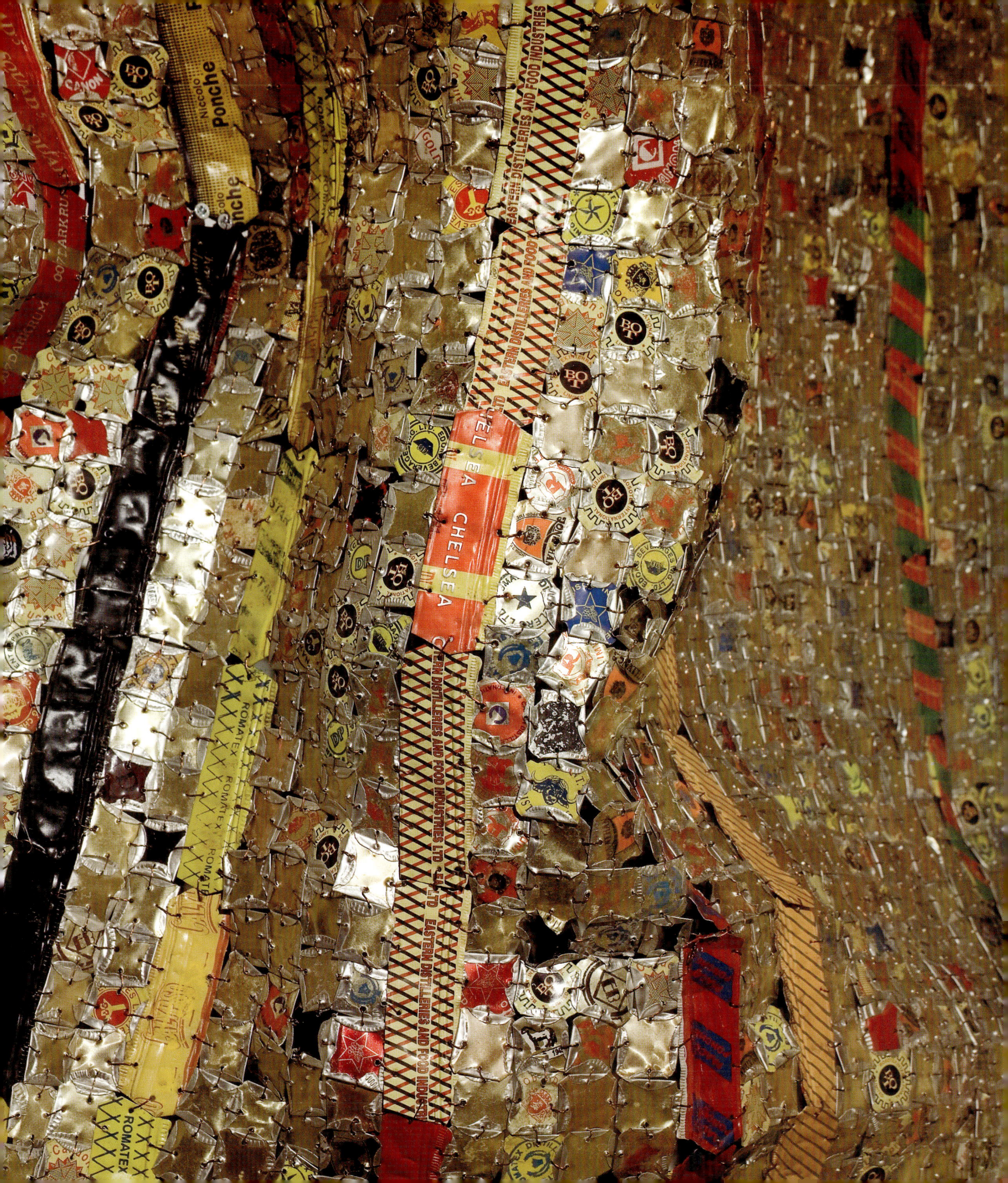
Niccolo
Ponche
CHELSEA
CHELSEA
EASTERN DISTILLERIES AND FOOD INDUSTRIES
ROMATEX

Below *Taago,* 2006. Aluminium and copper wire, approximately 240 x 340 cm (94½ x 133⅞ in). Collection of the artist.
'The nomadic aesthetic is about fluidity of ideas and impermanence of form, indeterminacy, as well as giving others the freedom, the authority to try their hands at forming what the artist has provided as a starting point.'

Right View of installation at Venice Biennale, 2007. Aluminium and copper wire, approximately 500 x 400 cm (94½ x 133⅞ in). Collection of the artist.
History in Africa may be read in cloth. Despite the beauty of this transformation of a Venetian façade, the grim realities of the European trade to Africa, in which liquor was one of the primary commodities exchanged for slaves, is never far away.

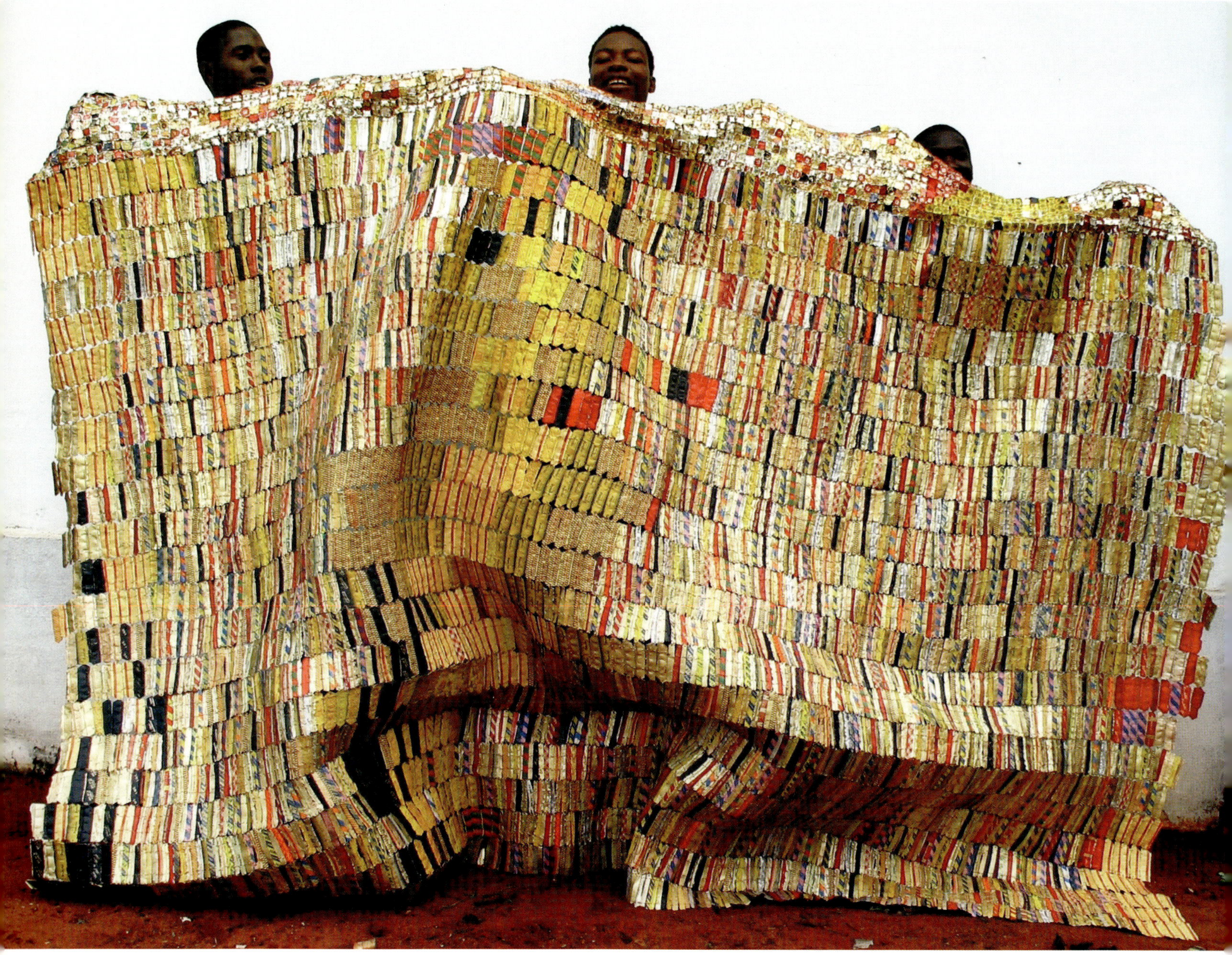

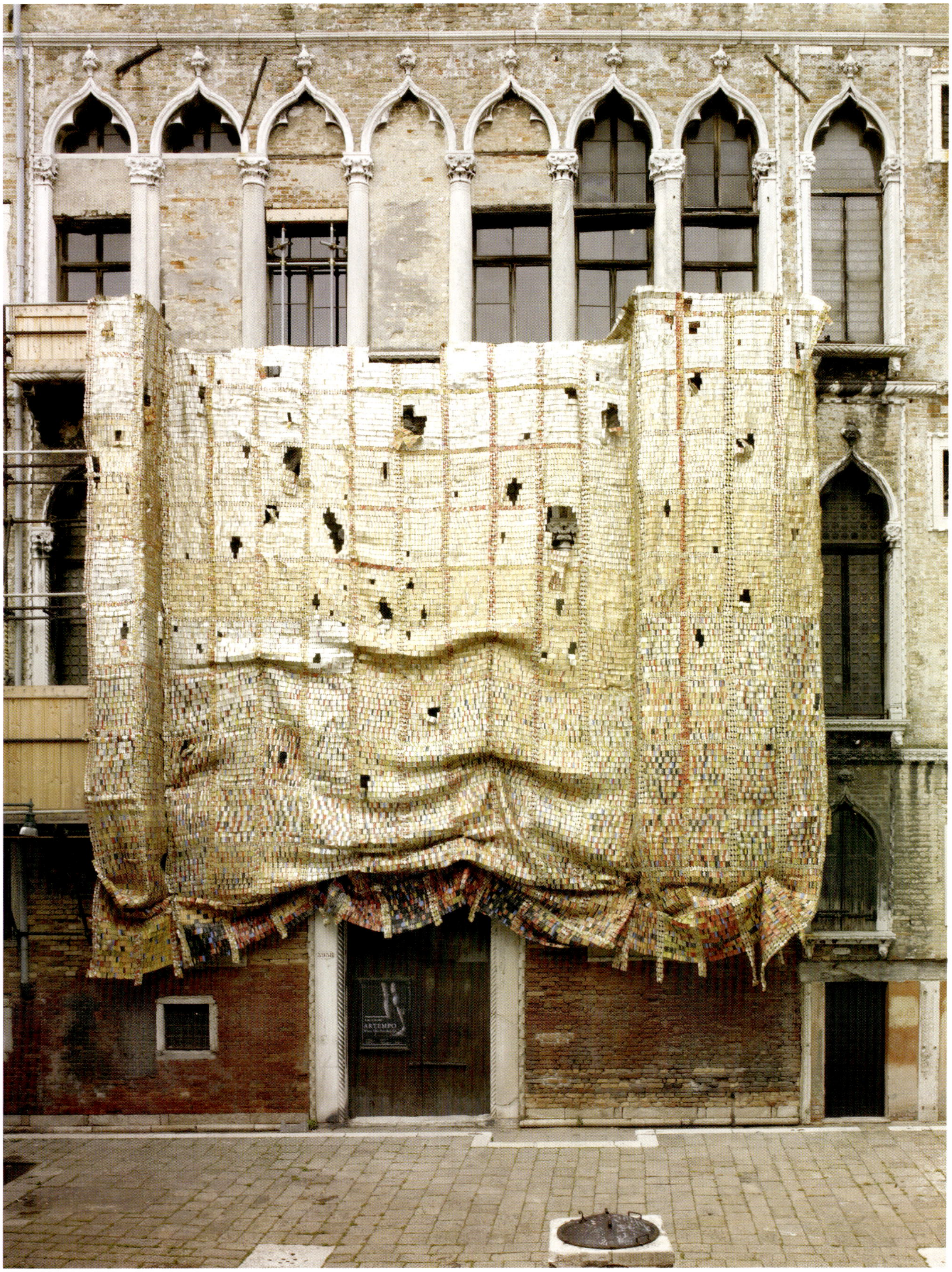
ARTEMPO

Below *Crumbling Wall*, 2003 (detail). Steel sheets, 400 x 500 x 70cm (157½ x 196⅞ x 27½ in). Collection of the artist.
This work is composed of dozens of cassava graters, sheets of galvanized metal punched with holes. Each sheet would have been made and used by different hands, and each has a different tone, from the darkest rusty brown to shiny silver. The sculpture crumbles and creases like cloth, so that it seems both ephemeral and monumental.

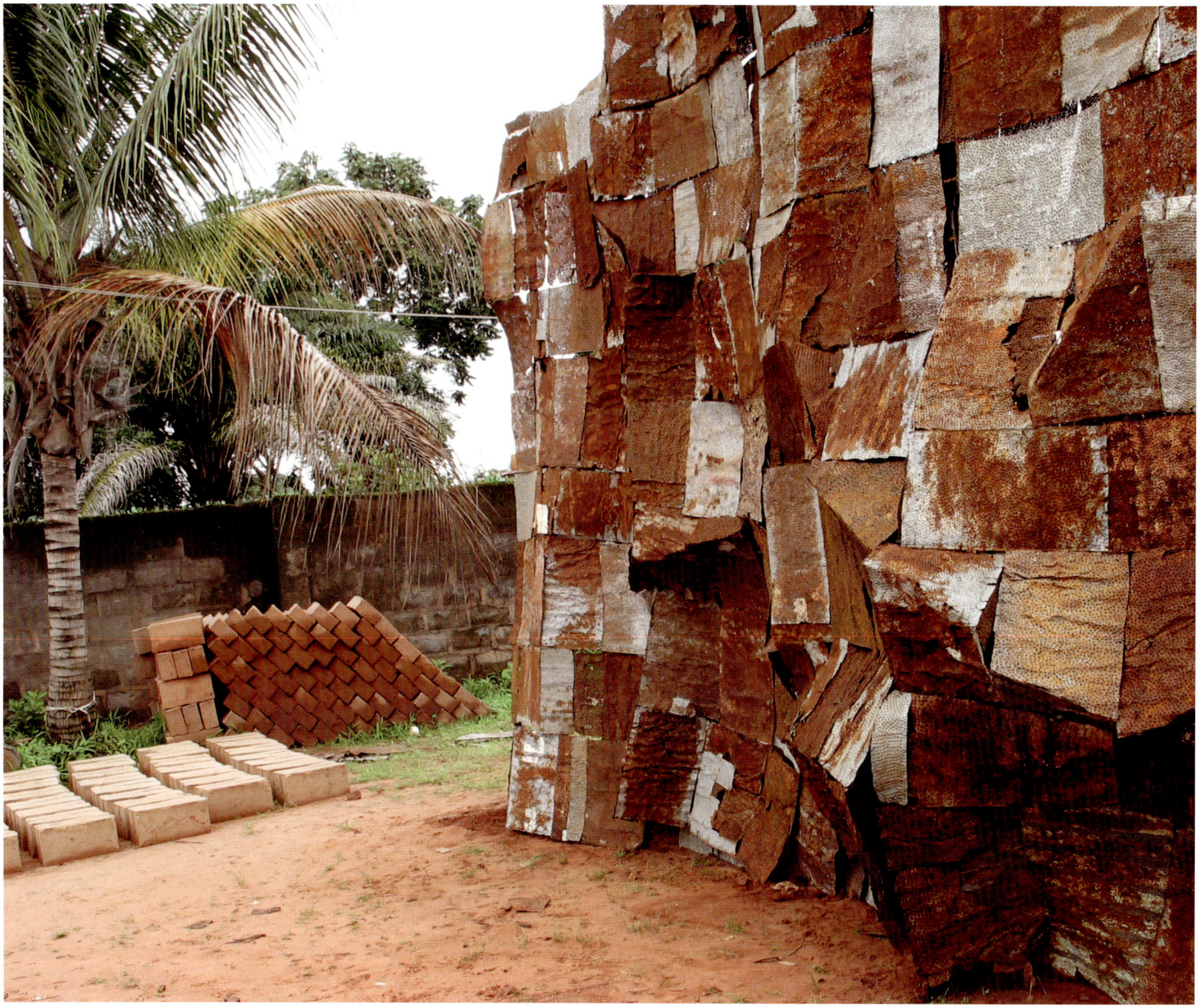

Below *Crumbling Wall*, 2000 (detail).
Much of El Anatsui's recent work uses consumption of food and drink, 'building in the stomach' in the Ghanaian vernacular, as a way of transforming objects and telling new stories. The cassava grater is used to create flour (*gari*), a staple food in much of West Africa.

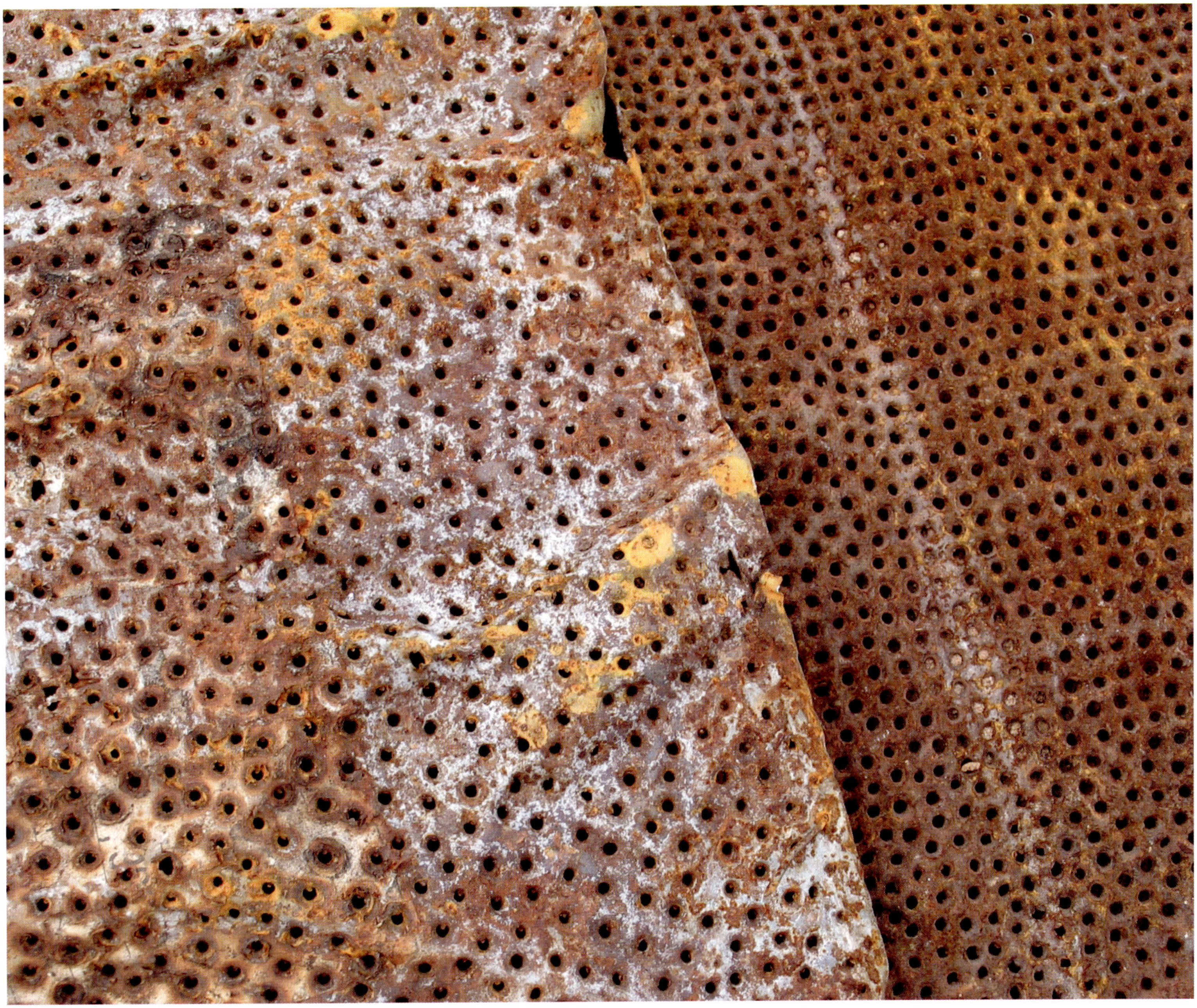

Right *Akua's Surviving Children*, 1996. Driftwood, greatest height 165 cm (65 in). Collection of the artist.

This work was created from driftwood during a residency in Denmark while researching the Danish slave trade. 'The wood having (like the slaves) been torn from its land source and exposed to the hostile elements of water and wind only required fire (a symbolic reversal) to complete the full cycle of its experience. The title... identifies the work with the Gold Coast, the land of the Akua-ba (Akua's child) fertility symbol, and fertile source (for slave traders) from which so many of Akua's "children" were unprotected.'

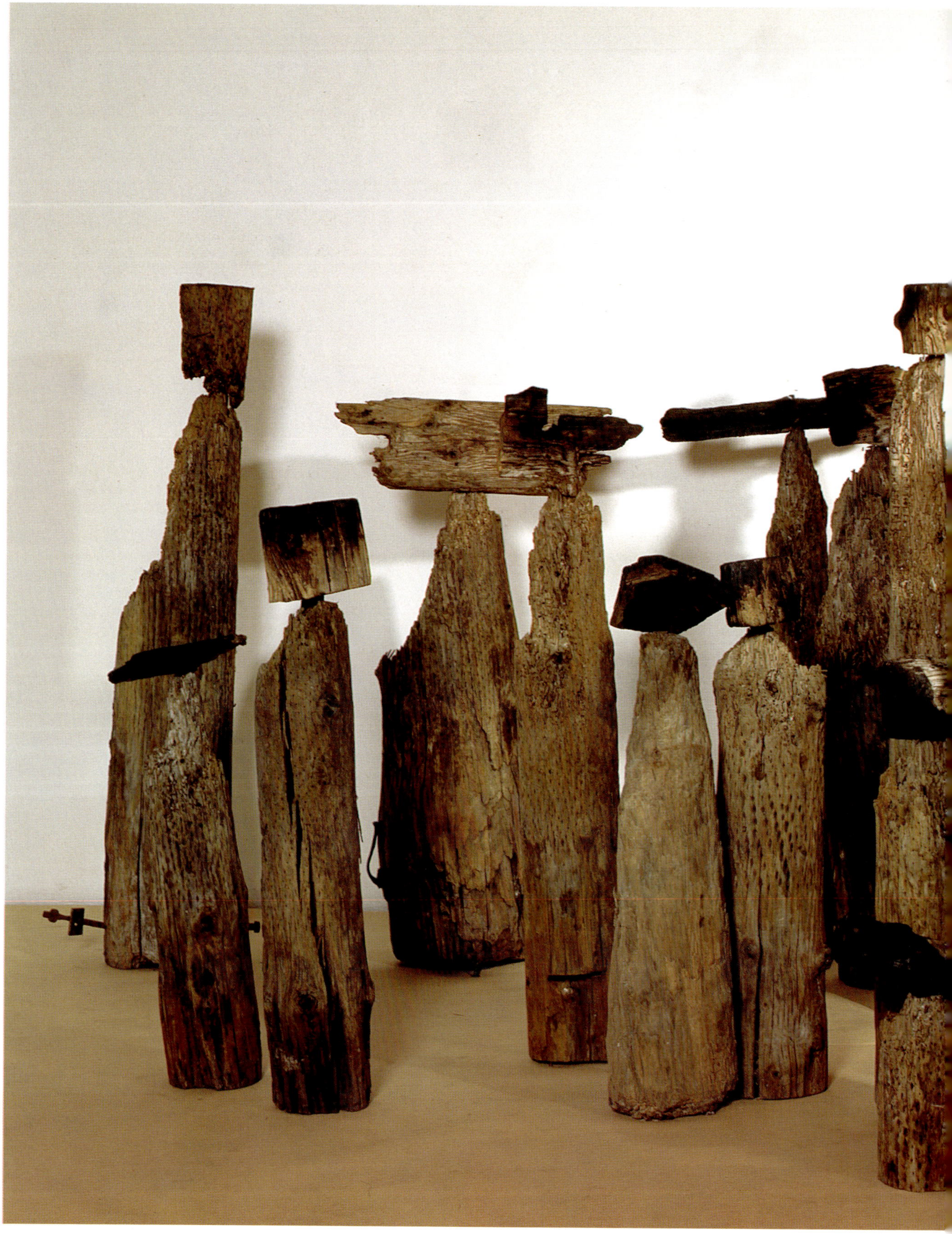

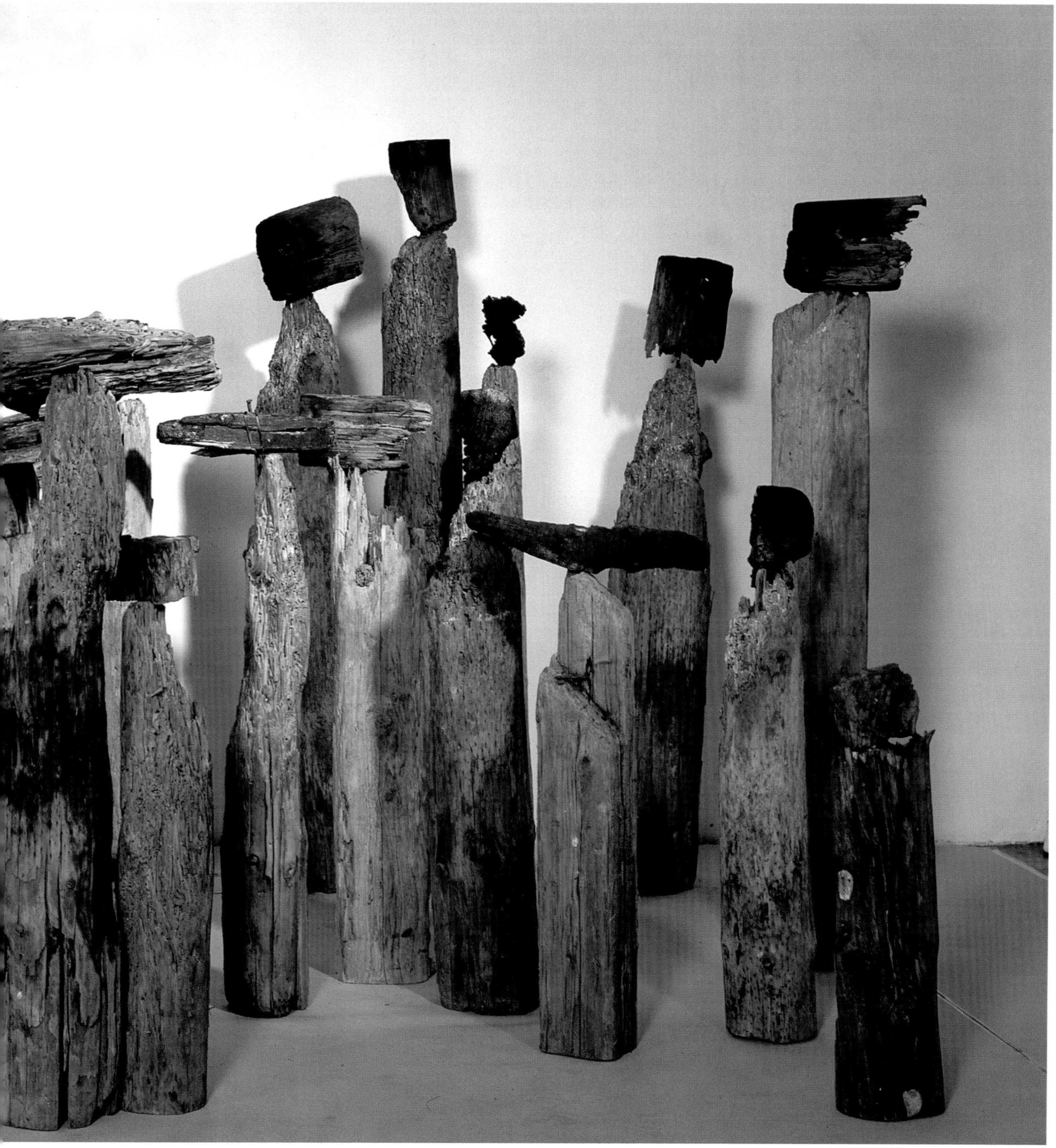

CHANT AVEDISSIAN
EGYPT

Below *Appliqué wall-hanging*, 1989–90. Dyed cotton, 264 x 310 cm (104 x 122 in). British Museum, London.
Avedissian drew inspiration from a number of sources in creating this cotton appliqué textile, including the art of the tent-makers (*khiyamiyya*) of Cairo and the coloured marble panels surrounding worshippers in Cairo's al-Ghouri mosque. 'The colours have been altered, but the essence of the composition – meditation – has been retained.'

Right *Bus Tickets*, 1993 (detail). Cardboard, gum Arabic, cotton, metal, 250 x 151 cm (98⅖ x 59 in). British Museum, London. Gift of Rose Issa in Memory of Philip Ravenhill.
Stencilled onto a roll of corrugated cardboard is a series of bus tickets upon which images that evoke the life of Cairo past and present are superimposed, including the artist's signature sunglasses, the notoriously busy al-'Ataba street and the famous thief, Mohammed Fahmy al-Darestawy.

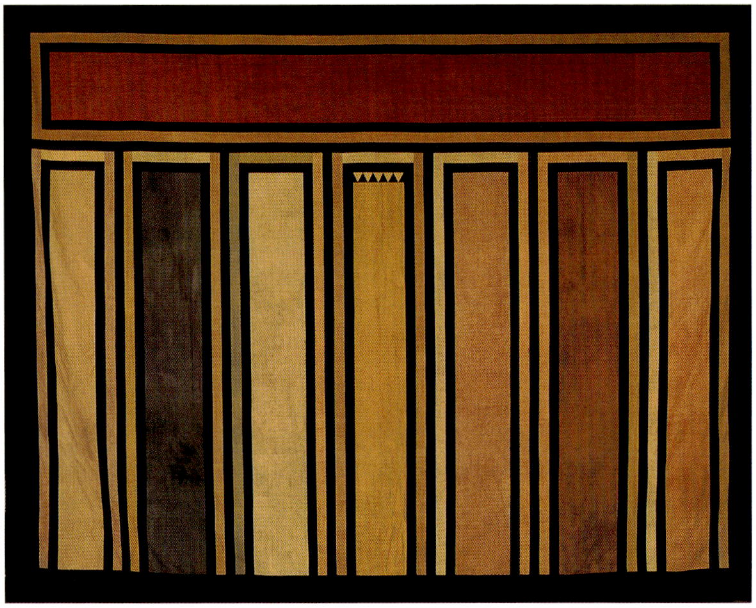

While the millions of tourists who visit Egypt and Cairo each year think only of the Pharaonic past, Avedissian's art celebrates a less well-known Egypt, in which the distant past and the present come together as elements in a patterned cloth of infinite variety.

Chant Avedissian was born in Cairo in 1951, the grandson of Armenian refugees who had fled the 1915–16 massacres in Turkey. He studied fine art in Montreal and applied arts in Paris, before returning to Egypt in 1980. Between 1983 and 1989 Avedissian worked for the revolutionary Egyptian architect Hassan Fathy, whose buildings reflect his profound appreciation of traditional indigenous architecture, which he combined with modern materials, skills and techniques.

Avedissian's own works constantly reference themes of architecture, both 'permanent' and transitory. Like the tents created by the *khiyamiya* or 'tent-makers' of Cairo, Avedissian's textile works and stencils created on corrugated cardboard are moveable, adaptable, transitory – yet in many ways that is their enduring strength.

The first Gulf war of 1991 acted as a catalyst for the creation of more than 150 works by Avedissian. Any war creates a terrible uncertainty; in Avedissian's case he was inspired to capture what he perceived to be the essence of life in Egypt – and in particular Cairo – in the face of elemental forces of change.

'In Cairo today temporary tents are still used for numerous occasions, including weddings, political meetings and funerals, three non-permanent events that ironically create so many permanent situations in human destiny.'
Chant Avedissian

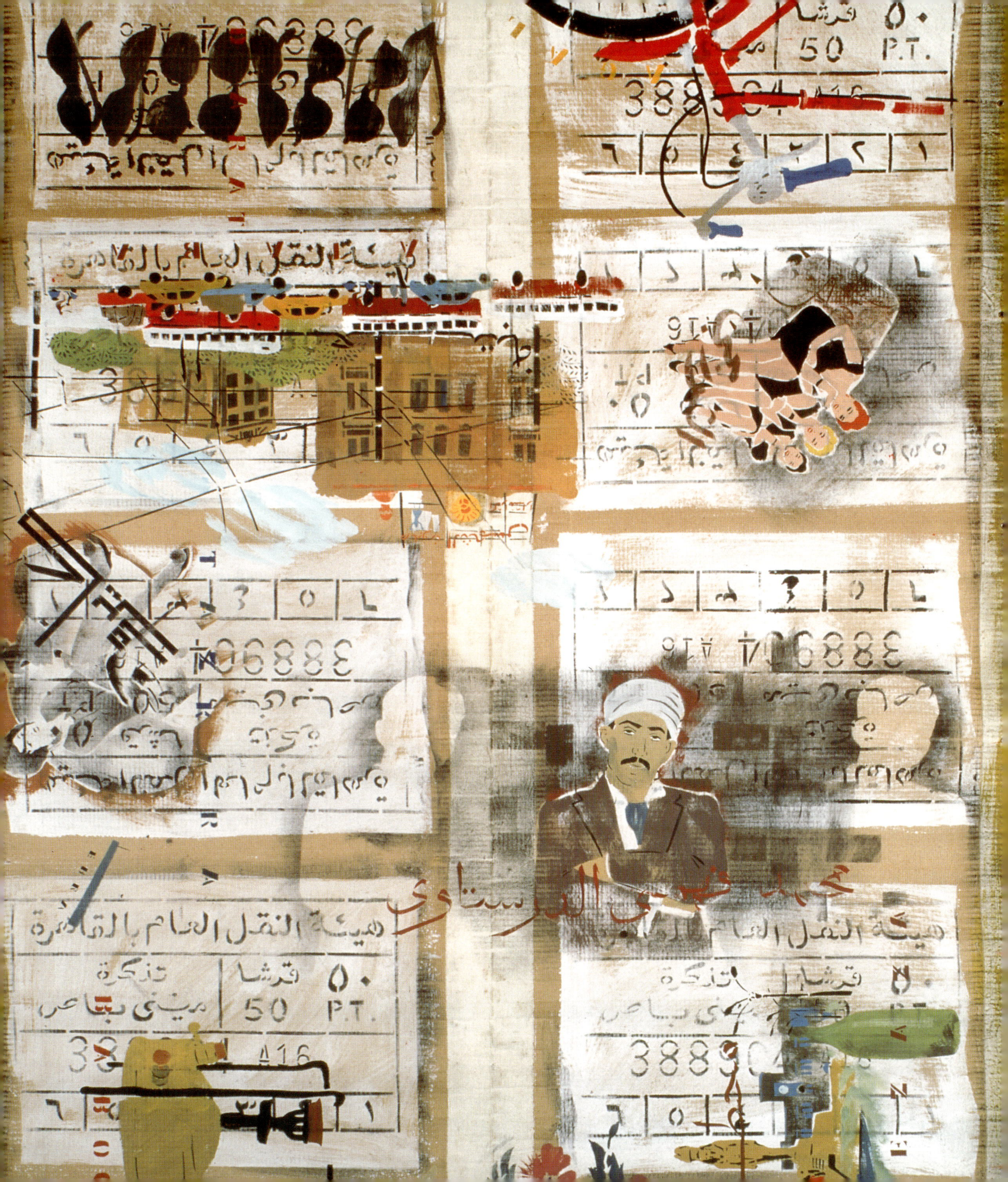

٥٠ قرشا
50 P.T.
هيئة النقل العام بالقاهرة
تذكرة
قرشا
٥٠
مينى باص
50
P.T.
A16

Below *The Best Lady of Them All*, 2002. Colour pigments on recycled cardboard, 50 x 70cm (19⅔ x 27½ in). Private collection, London.
The famous 'diva', Umm Kulthum (1904–75), rose to fame in the 1930s, appearing in numerous films and recording hundreds of songs. Throughout the 1940s, 1950s and 1960s she remained the most popular entertainer in North Africa and the Middle East; huge crowds attended her funeral in 1975.

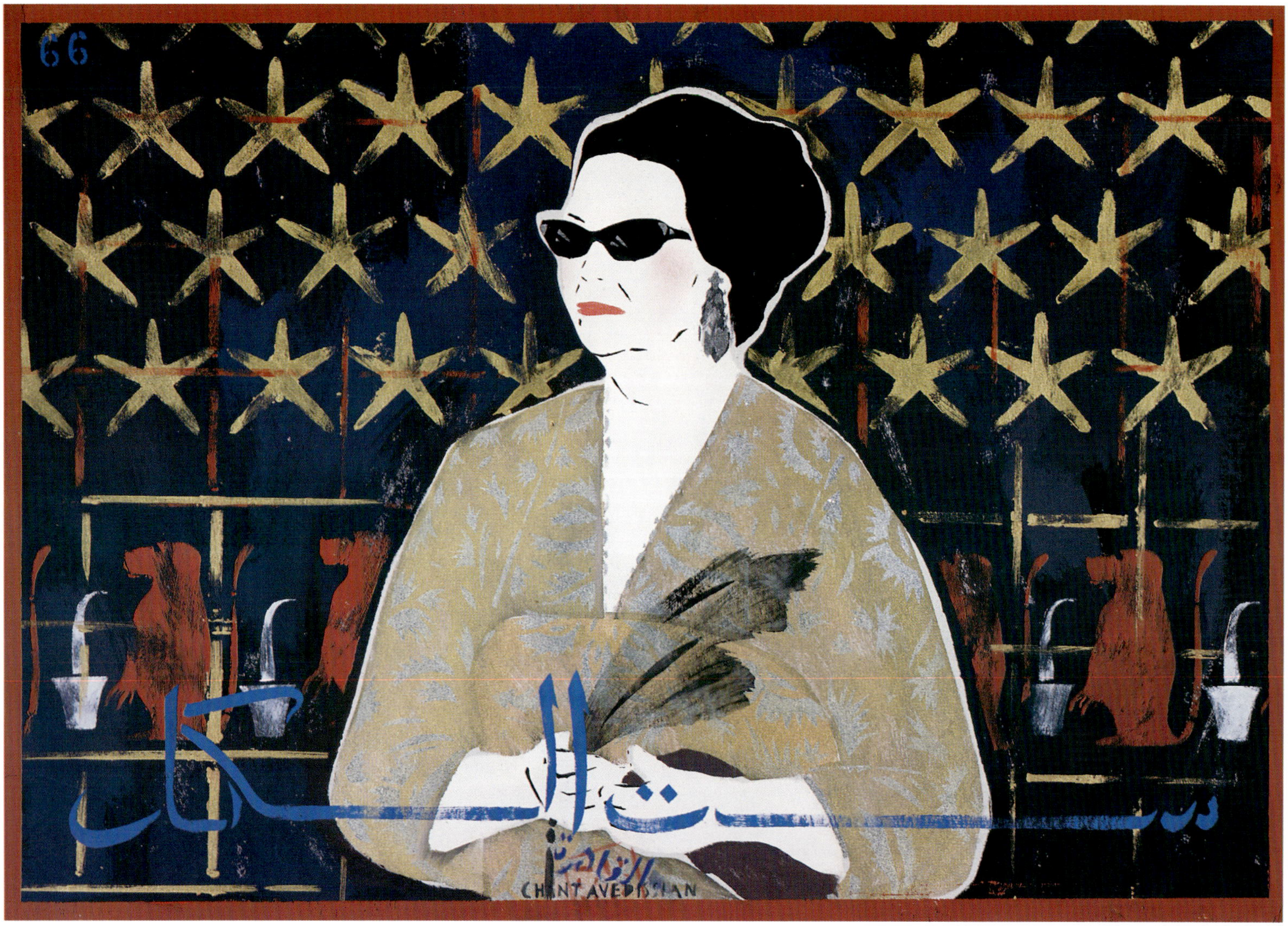

Below *Mohammad Ali Street,* 2003. Colour pigments on recycled cardboard, 50 x 70cm (19⅔ x 27½ in). Private collection, London.
The ghostly image of the moon rising over the domes and minarets of Old Cairo is imprisoned in a grid of street lamps and telegraph wires, while the dark, modern dwellings in the foreground seem oblivious to the past, the thunderous roar of traffic obliterating all other sounds.

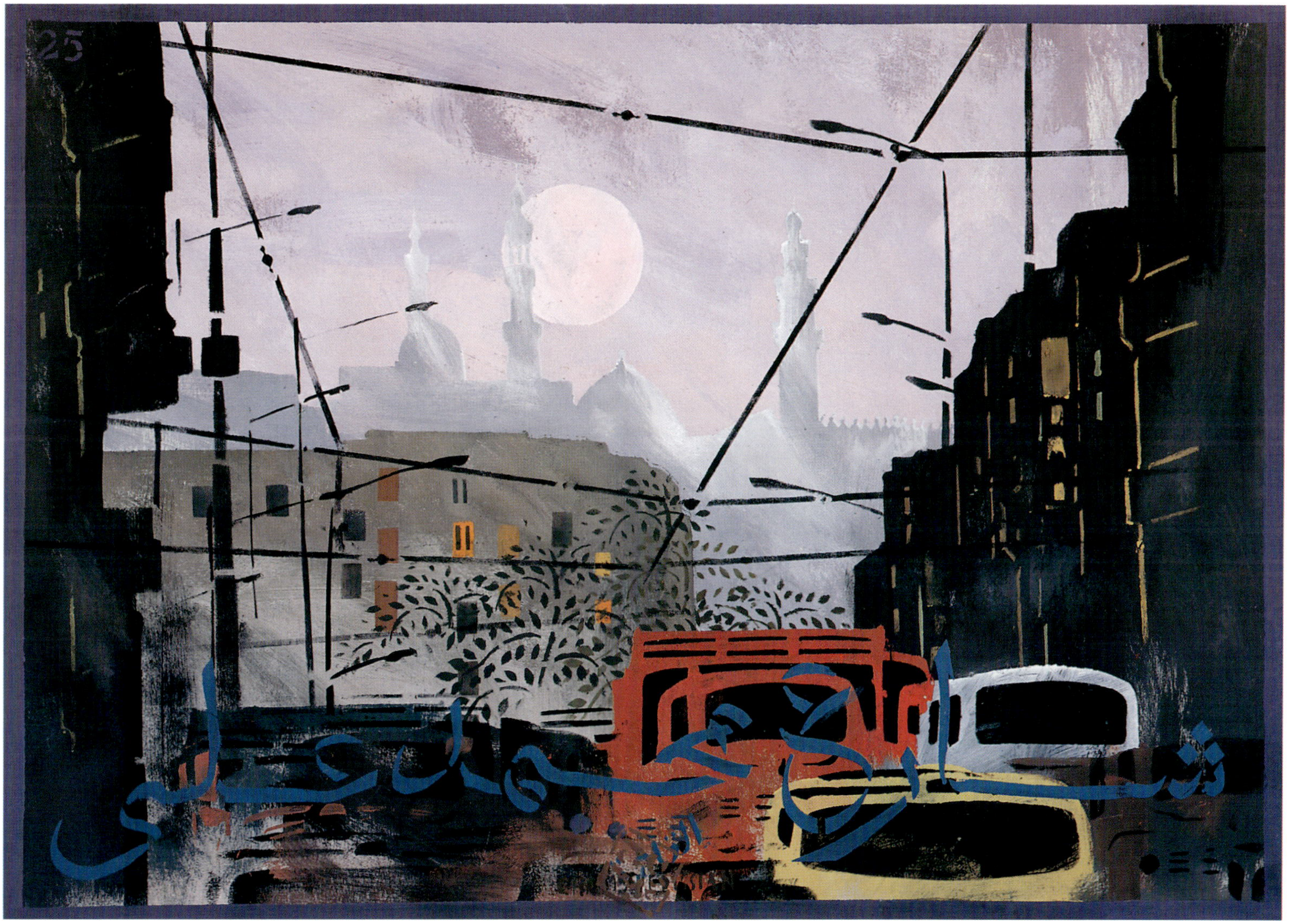

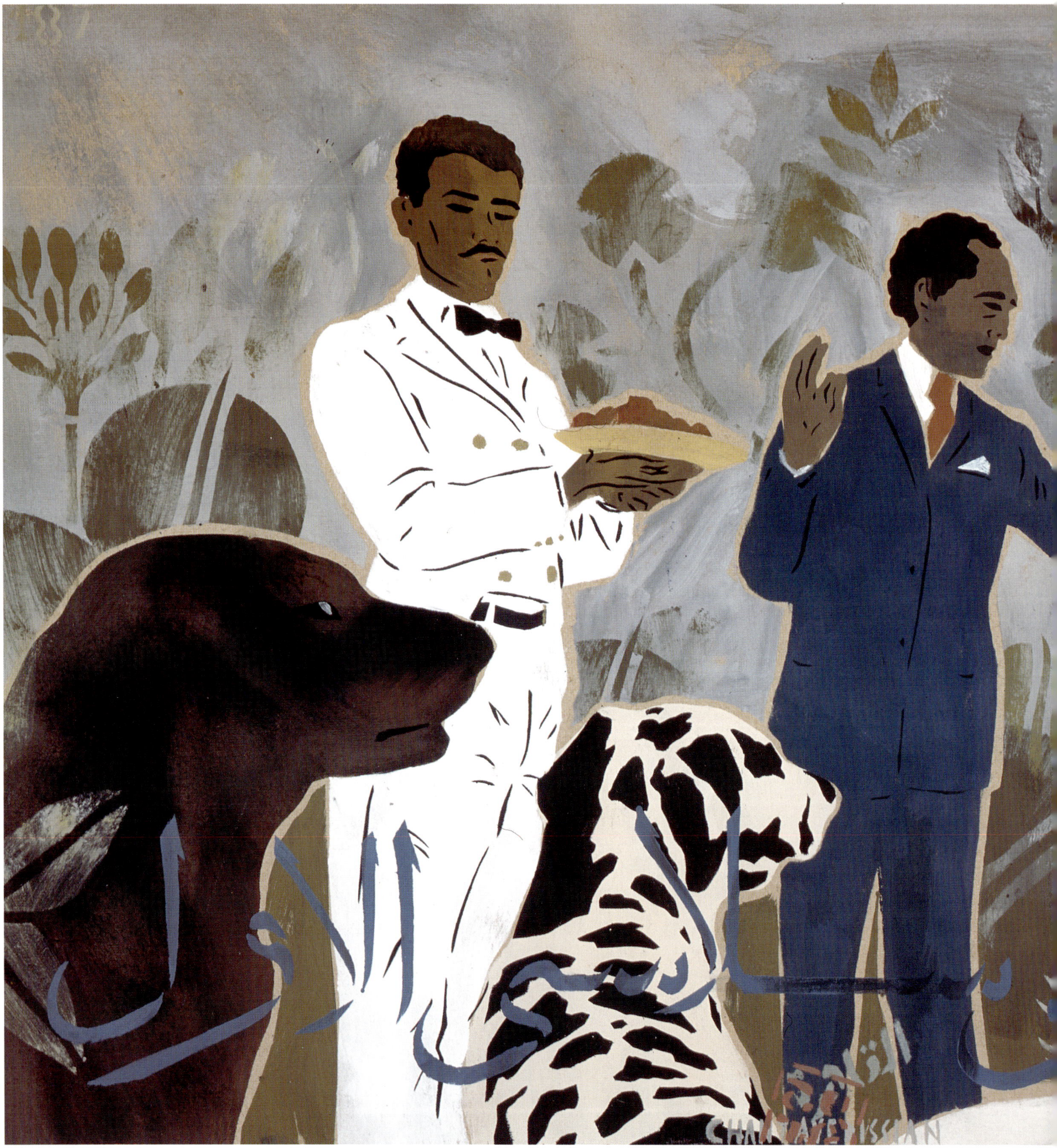

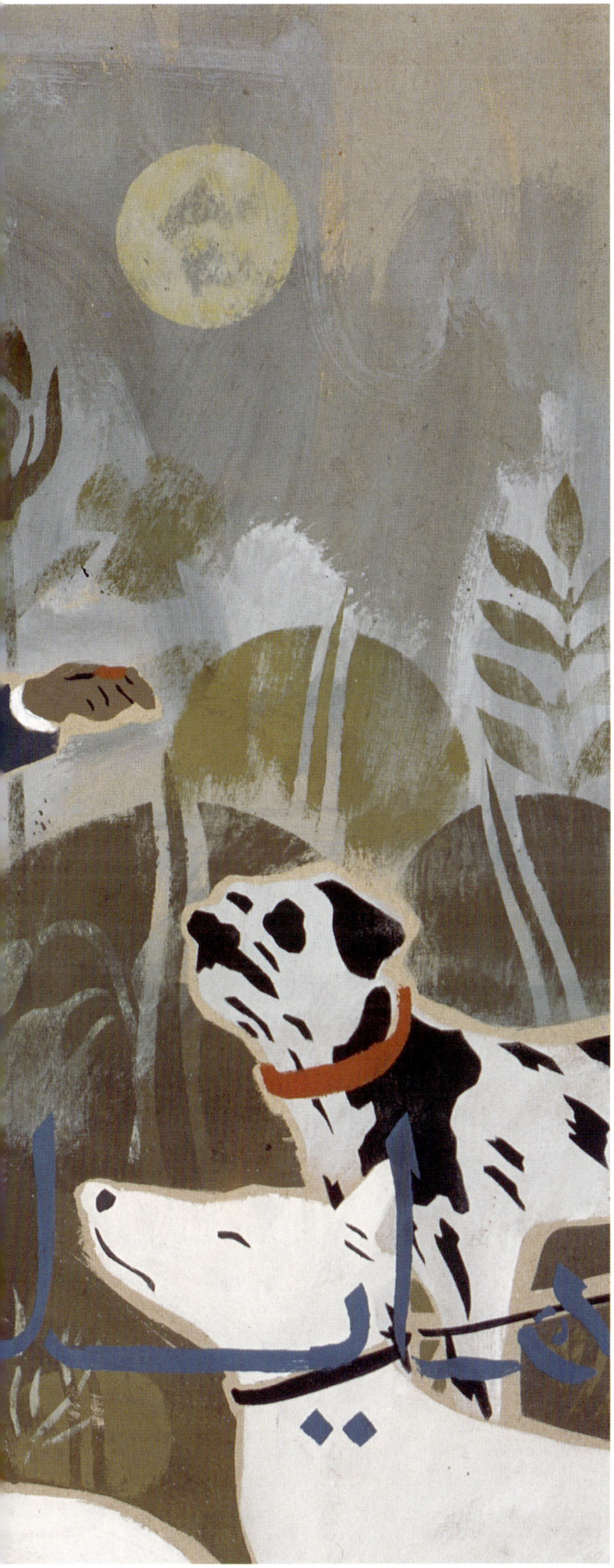

Left *Emperor Haile Selassie the First, of Ethiopia,* 2003. Colour pigments on recycled cardboard, 50 x 70 cm (19⅔ x 27½ in). Private collection, London.

Below *Soviet–African Cooperation*, 2003. Colour pigments on recycled cardboard, 50 x 70 cm (19⅔ x 27½ in). Private collection, London.
Many of Avedissian's stencils reference the revolutionary socialism of the 1950s and 1960s introduced by Egypt's charismatic leader Gamal Abdel Nasser. As in many parts of Africa, it was a time to collaborate, not with the colonial, imperial past but with what the Soviet Union seemed to offer for a bright, egalitarian future. The transitory nature of this vision is suggested by the contrast between the solidity of the African driver and his spectral adviser.

Bottom *The Mummy*, 2003. Colour pigments on recycled cardboard, 50 x 70 cm (19⅔ x 27½ in). Private collection, London.
This stencil takes its title from the film by Shadi Abdel Salam, which protested against the erosion of Egypt's cultural heritage, in particular the neglect of archaeological sites from the Pharaonic period.

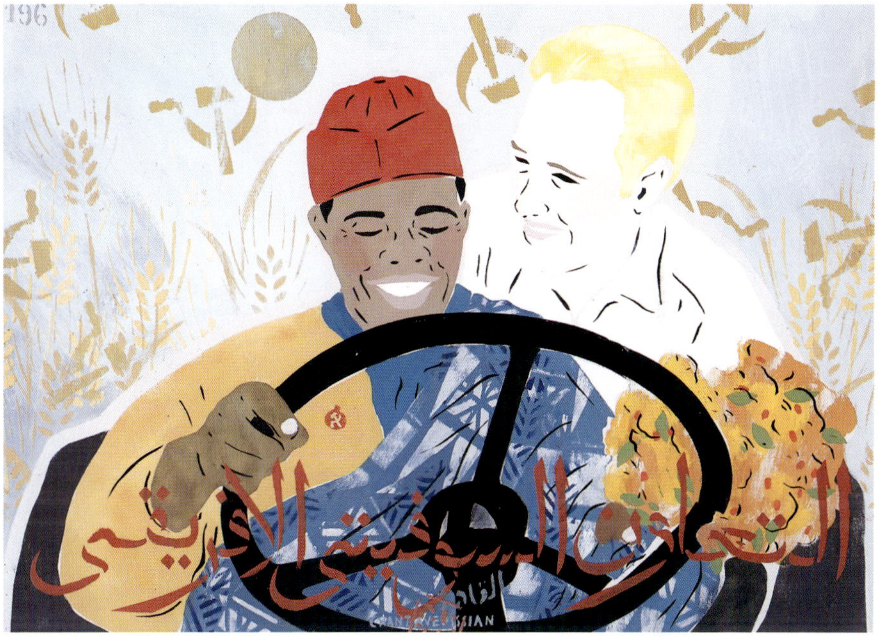

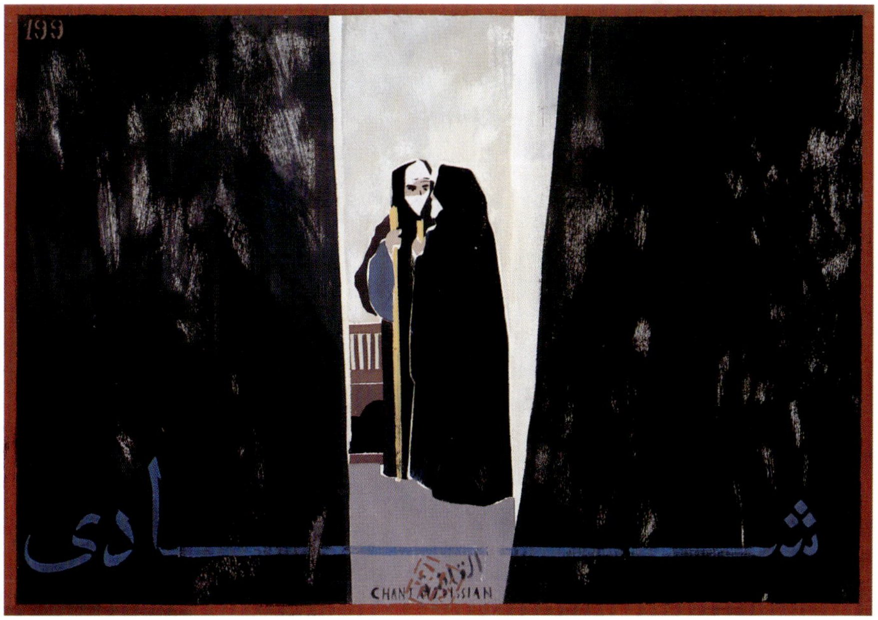

LARA BALADI
EGYPT

Below *Roba Vecchia (The Wheel of Fortune)*, 'Art projects', Gulf Art Fair, 2007. 1120 x 245 cm (441 x 96½ in).
The visitor enters what appears from the outside to be a triangular construction, but the senses are tricked into seeing it as a circular passageway at the end of which spins a never ending and constantly changing 'Wheel of Fortune'. The visitor's reflections immediately become the spokes in that wheel, parts of stories that endlessly repeat themselves, but are infinitely variable.

Right *Roba Vecchia (The Wheel of Fortune)*, 'Art projects', Gulf Art Fair, 2007 (detail).

Born in Beirut, Lebanon, in 1969, Lara Baladi moved regularly between the Middle East, North Africa and Europe as she grew up. She studied international business in London, and now lives and works in Cairo. Baladi's primary medium is photography, presented through installation, photomontage, video and collage in ways that are interactive and invite the viewer to participate in the process. Baladi's work has been exhibited in many shows worldwide over the past decade.

The title of one of her works, *Sandouk El Dounia* (*The World in a Box*) refers directly to the traditional children's street theatre of Cairo (a little like the British Punch and Judy) and also to the 'box' that rules the world – television. This is a world that on one level seems to be full of fun and entertainment, but on another is an oppressive box where people, often against their will, are crowded together and where individual and cultural beliefs, rights and liberties are ignored.

Baladi is fascinated by identity and personal or cultural perceptions of the world. The Egyptian artist Chant Avedissian noted that 'no matter what we do, we will always be exotic. Egypt is exotic, so is India. But the truth is that, seen by an Egyptian, the Italian *cinquecento* was folklore, and it was Paris that seemed a distant exotic land'. Baladi's imagery also explores a world of 'universal' signs and symbols, yet one in which the same image and the same words might be perceived by different people in very different ways. It is a world of genuine fun and good humour, yet one in which tragedy is never far away.

'It's important to me to treat photos other than in frames on a wall. A framed picture has no more substance, it is a simple image and no longer an object.'
Lara Baladi

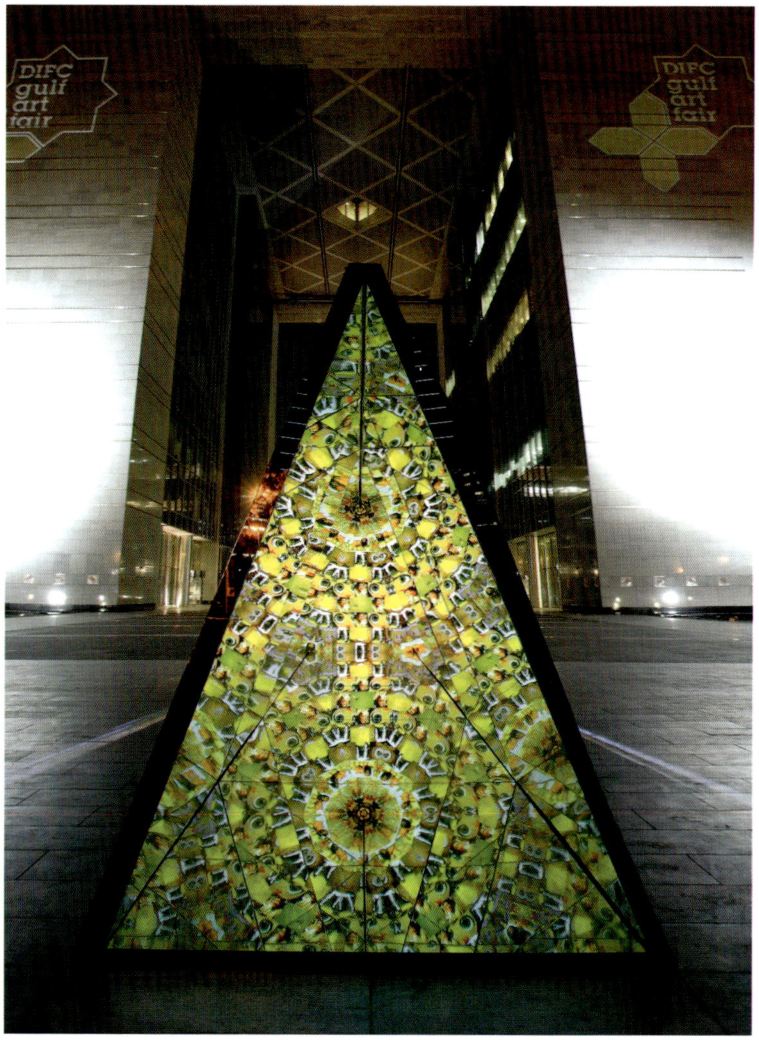

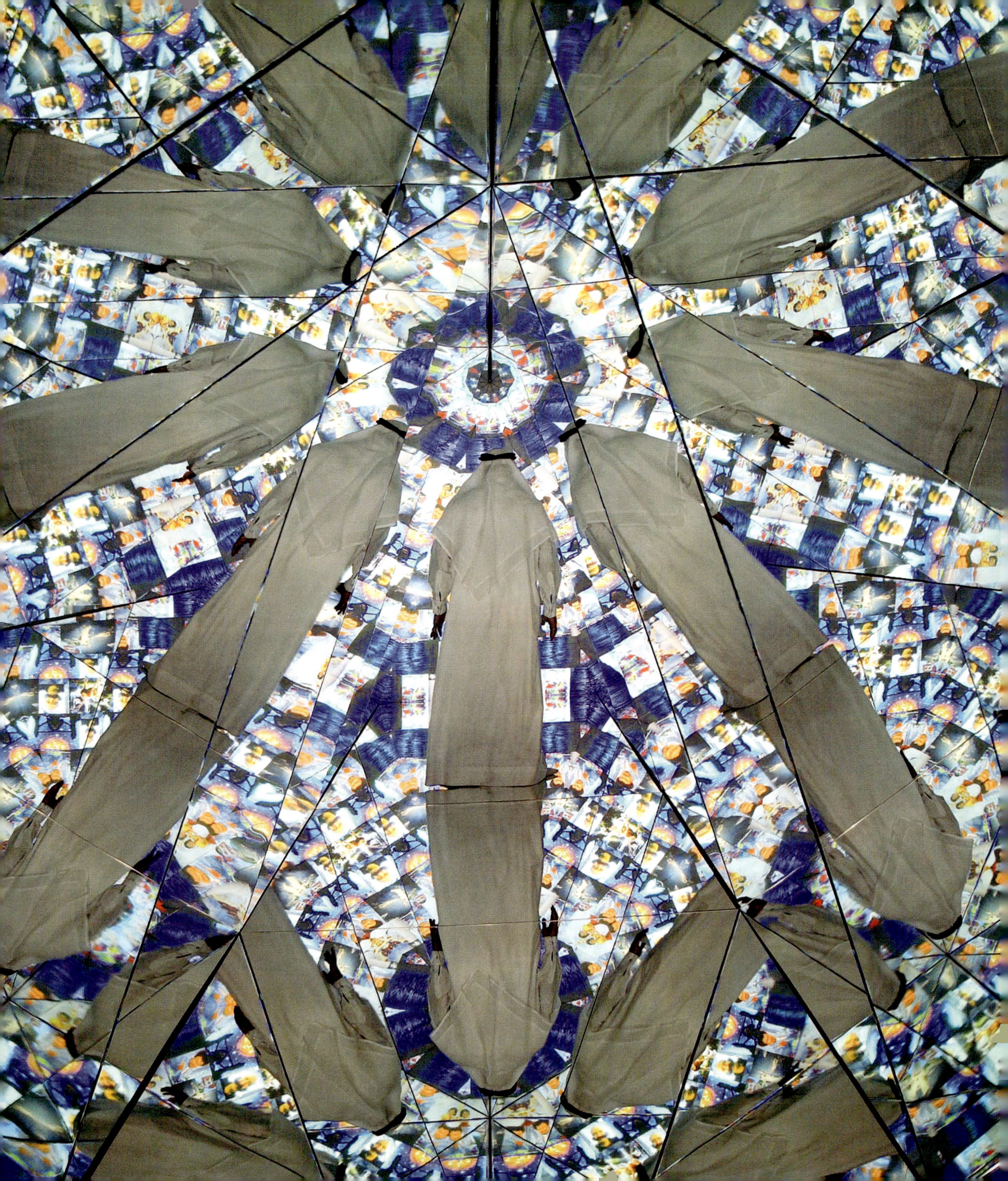

Right *Sandouk El Dounia (The World in a Box)*, 2001. 10 x 15 cm (7½ x 6 in) colour photographic prints, 250 x 315 cm (98½ x 124 in). Collection of the artist.

Next spread *Justice for the Mother*, 2007. Digital montage, printing material variable, produced by the Sharjah Biennial, 248 x 560 cm (97½ x 220½ in). Collection of the artist.

This is a playground for the natural and human worlds, full of male macho posturing, laughter, pain and sex, a wonderland, where Alice is just as likely to carry a gun as a hairband, where there is apparently no logic, save that men and women are bound – literally as well as figuratively – by their own fantasies. Into this world, a bit like the foot in the opening sequence of *Monty Python*, comes a hand clutching a photograph. Like the Python foot, it squashes the fun and the fantasy, bringing us back to the 'real' world. Yet look closely at the photograph and we see that it's just another male fantasy: the wife and two kids.

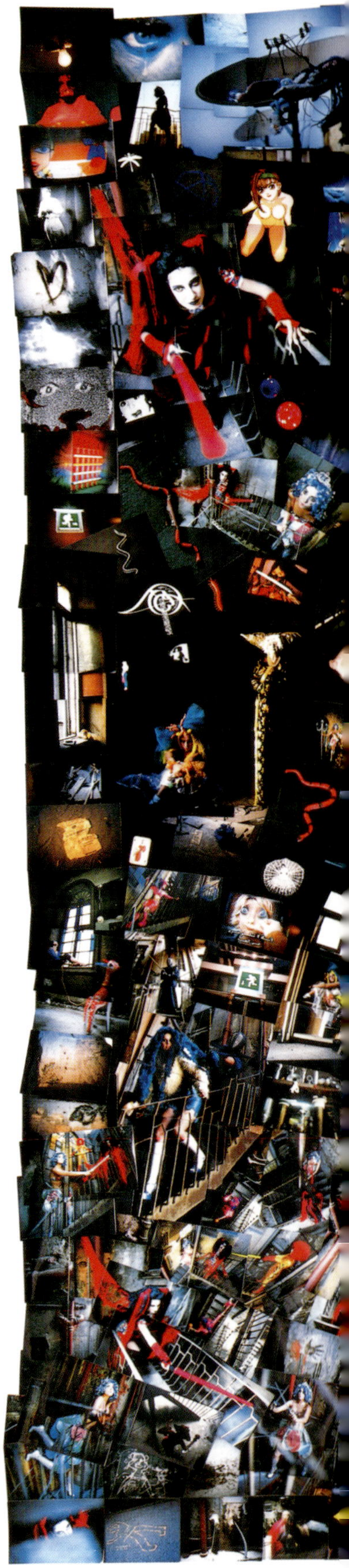

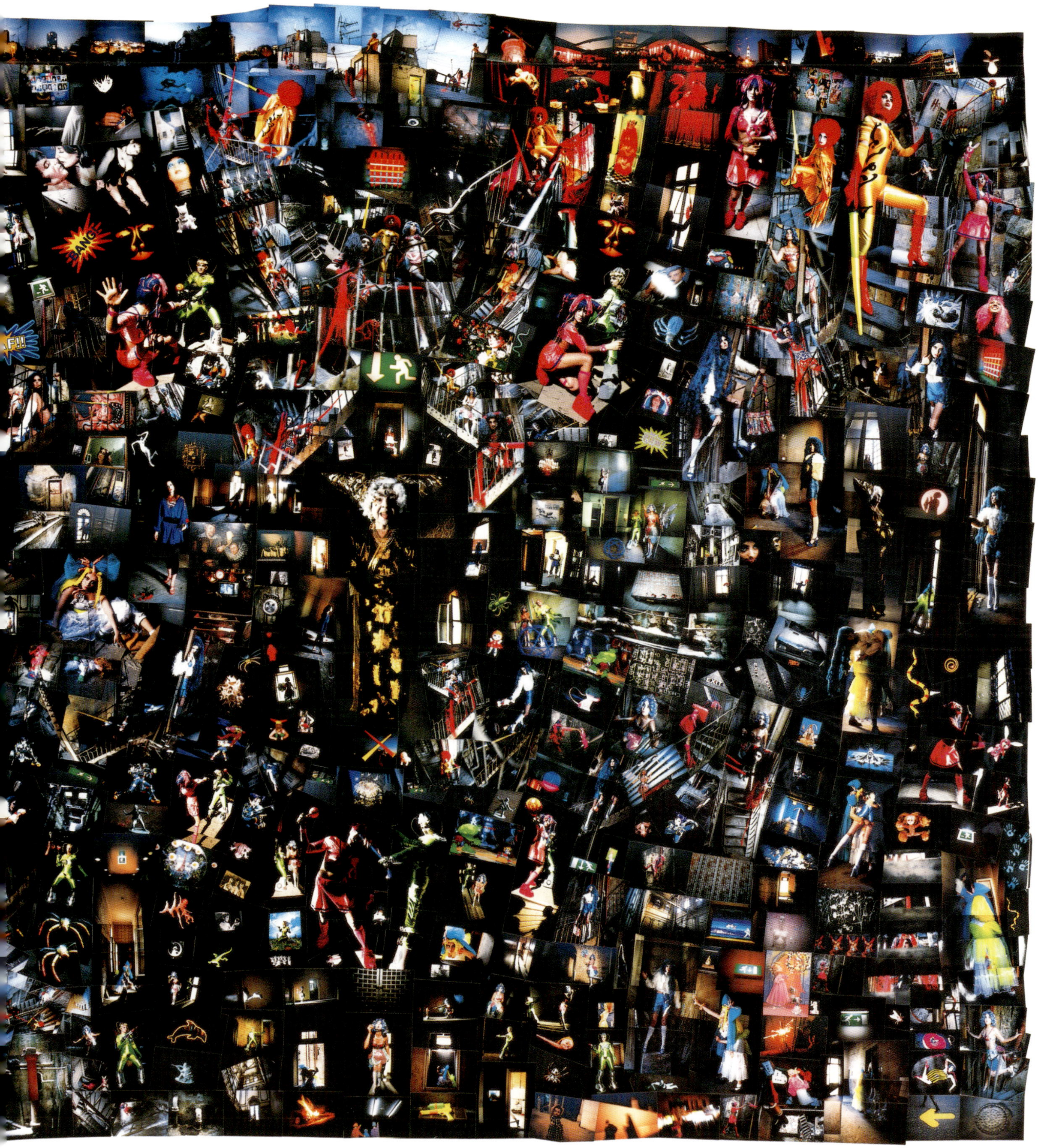
BANG

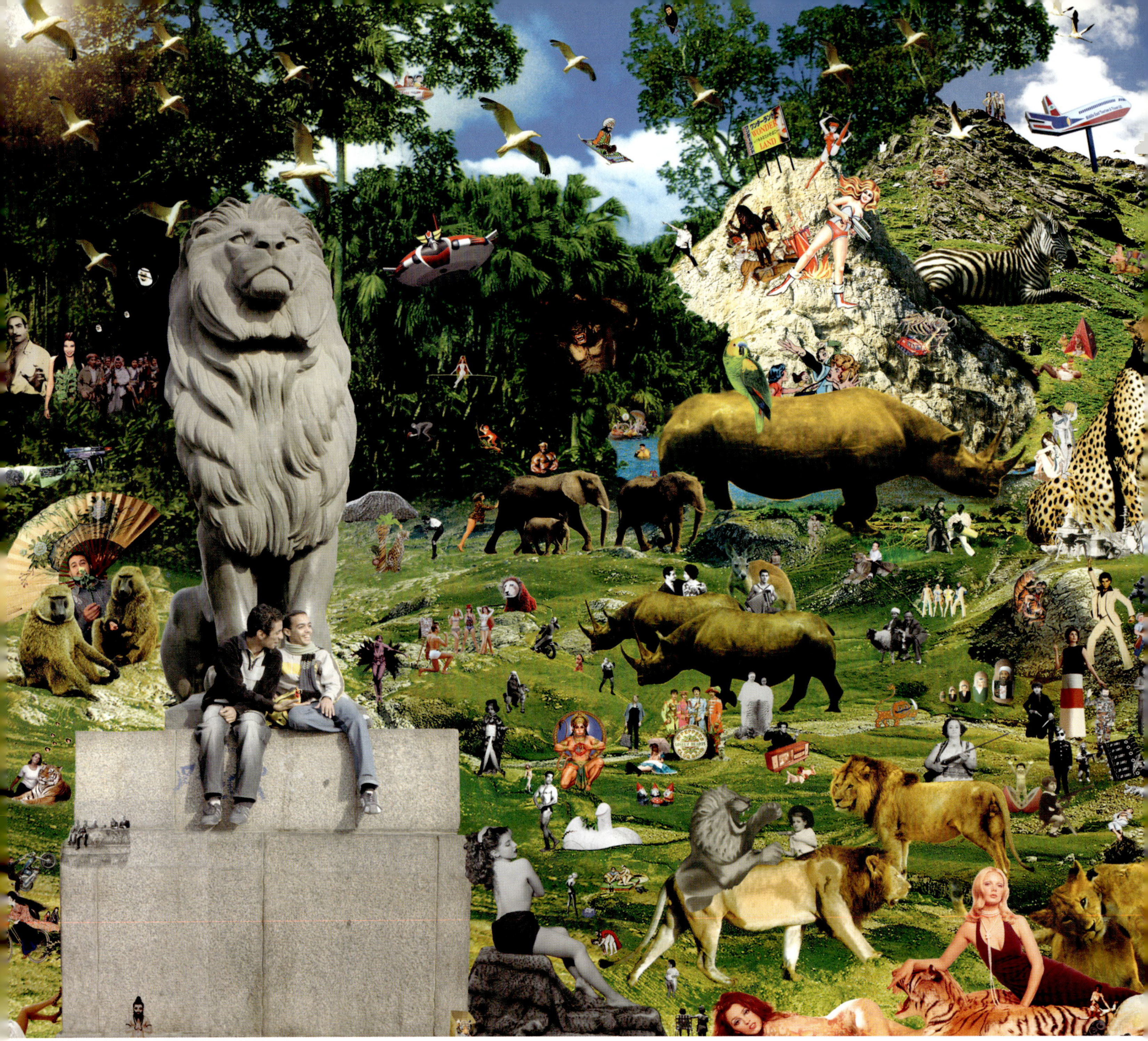
ワンダーランド
WONDER
LAND

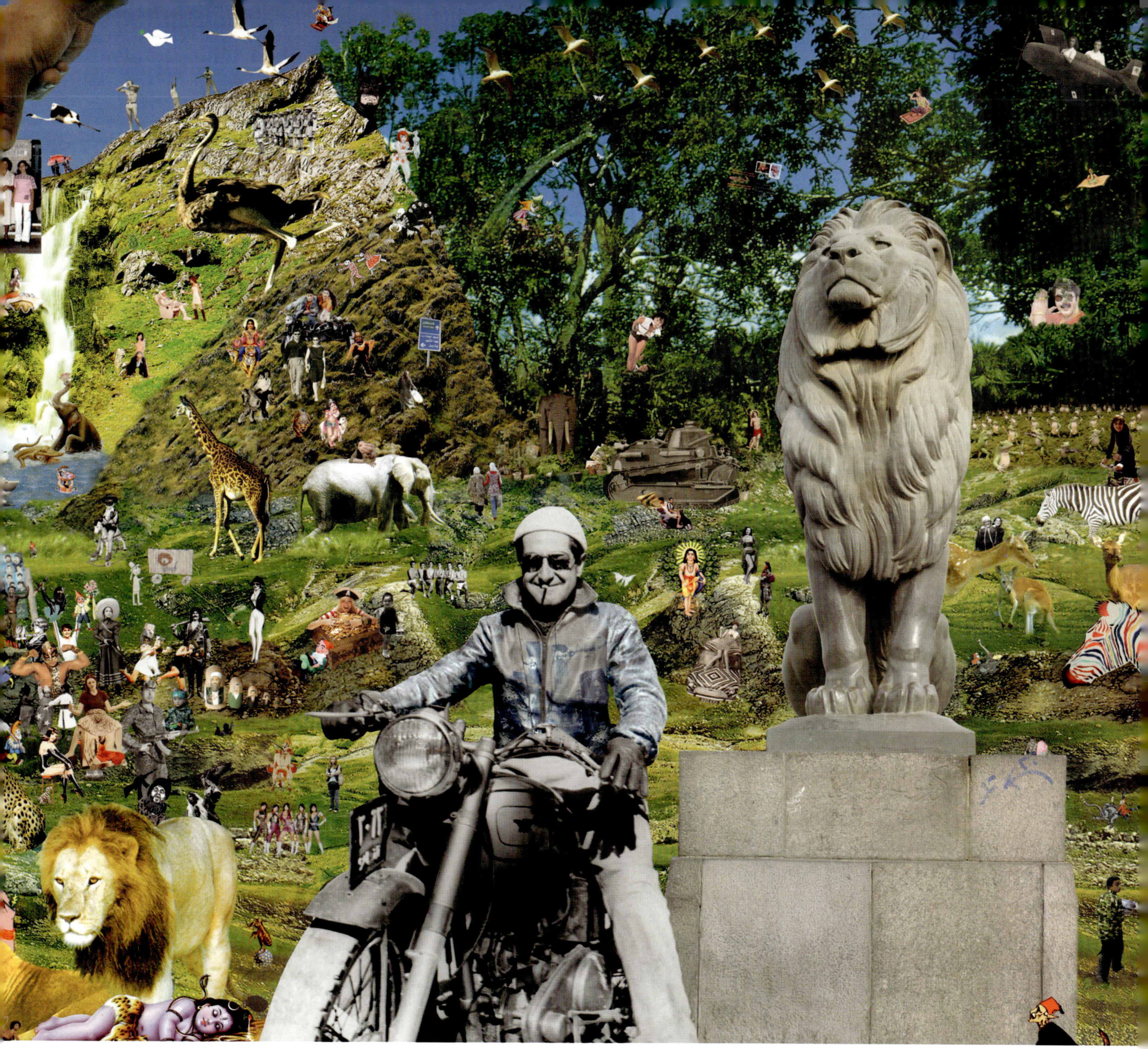

DOMINIC BENHURA
ZIMBABWE

Below *Butterfly*, 2006. Stone, acrylic on canvas and glass, 92 x 111 x 192 cm (36⅕ x 43⅔ x 75⅔ in). Collection of the artist.
The depiction of such a delicate, beautiful yet fragile and vulnerable creature through the medium of stone helps the viewer to think again about what is really strong and what is transitory in relationships between humans and the natural world – and between fellow human beings.

Right *Bull*, 2006. Stone, 143 x 314 x 84 cm (56⅓ x 123⅔ x 33 in). Collection of the artist.
'Bulls are symbols of power, force and energy. They suggest the ability to charge and conquer. For me this is a positive power. They inspire me not to feel vulnerable or sorry for myself.'

The contemporary stone sculpture tradition in Zimbabwe is a twentieth-century phenomenon, though the lack of connection with the remarkable stone carvings of Great Zimbabwe does not necessarily preclude a much more ancient tradition. The great 'first generation' Shona stone carvers were championed by Frank McEwen, founder and director of the National Gallery of Zimbabwe, in the 1950s and 60s. The sculptors created highly accomplished and imaginative work, drawing heavily on traditional beliefs and mythology. The tradition has had its apologists and its critics, but Dominic Benhura's works have taken it in a radically new direction in recent years.

Born in Murewa Town, Zimbabwe, in 1968, Dominic Benhura began assisting in the studio of his cousin, the artist Tapfuma Gutsa, at the age of ten. Gutsa often incorporates a number of different materials into his work, and this may have helped to inspire Benhura to use steel, wire and other materials in his own stone sculptures.

Benhura's work does not aspire to great psychological or metaphysical depths; instead it champions the concept of the artists' commune – he has stayed in Zimbabwe among his community of sculptors – and basic human rights and values – in particular stable and loving relationships between men and women in which children are both protected and respected. Benhura has shown his work in many parts of the world, though none gave him greater pleasure than when, in 2003, his work *Swing Me Mama* became part of the permanent collection of the Nelson Mandela Foundation in Johannesburg, South Africa.

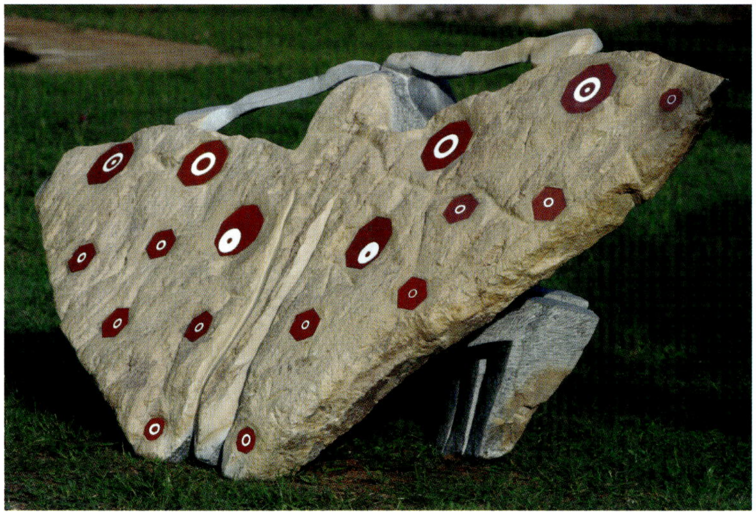

'Why should I make a sculpture of a baboon spirit when I do not believe that a baboon is inhabited by a spirit? The past is not my world, what I respond to. I respond to what is around me today. I see what is wrong and I try to redress it in sculptures in which I speak about what is right.'
Dominic Benhura

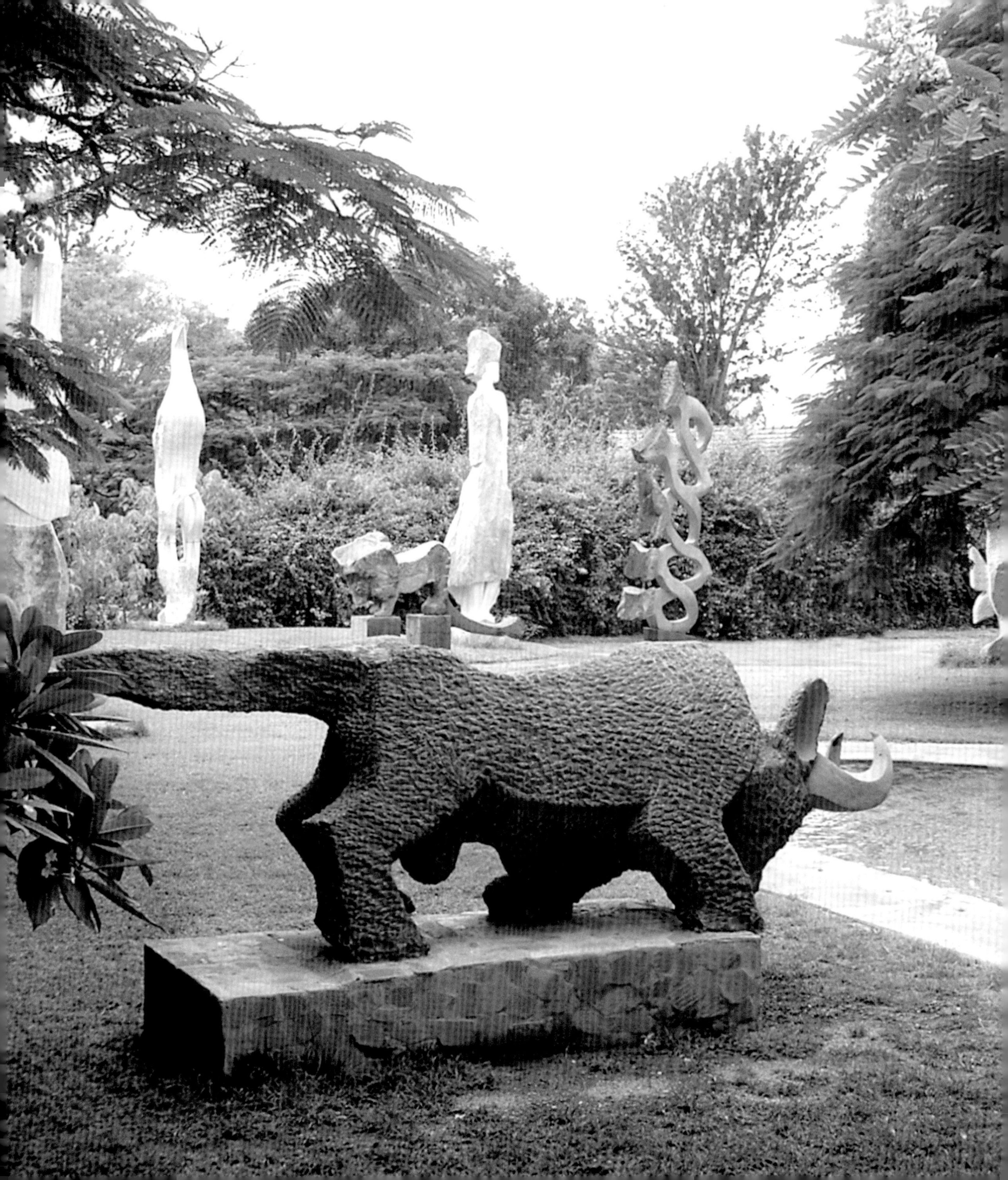

This spread *Chameleon Concept*, 2006. Glass, canvas and acrylics on stone, 300 x 600 x 300cm (118⅛ x 236¼ x 118⅛ in). Private collection.
A girl dances between three stone walls on which Benhura has painted falling leaves of many colours, leaves that are reflected in the glass panels on the girl's skirt. It is a wonderful juxtaposition of the hard and the soft, the permanent and the transitory, darkness and light.

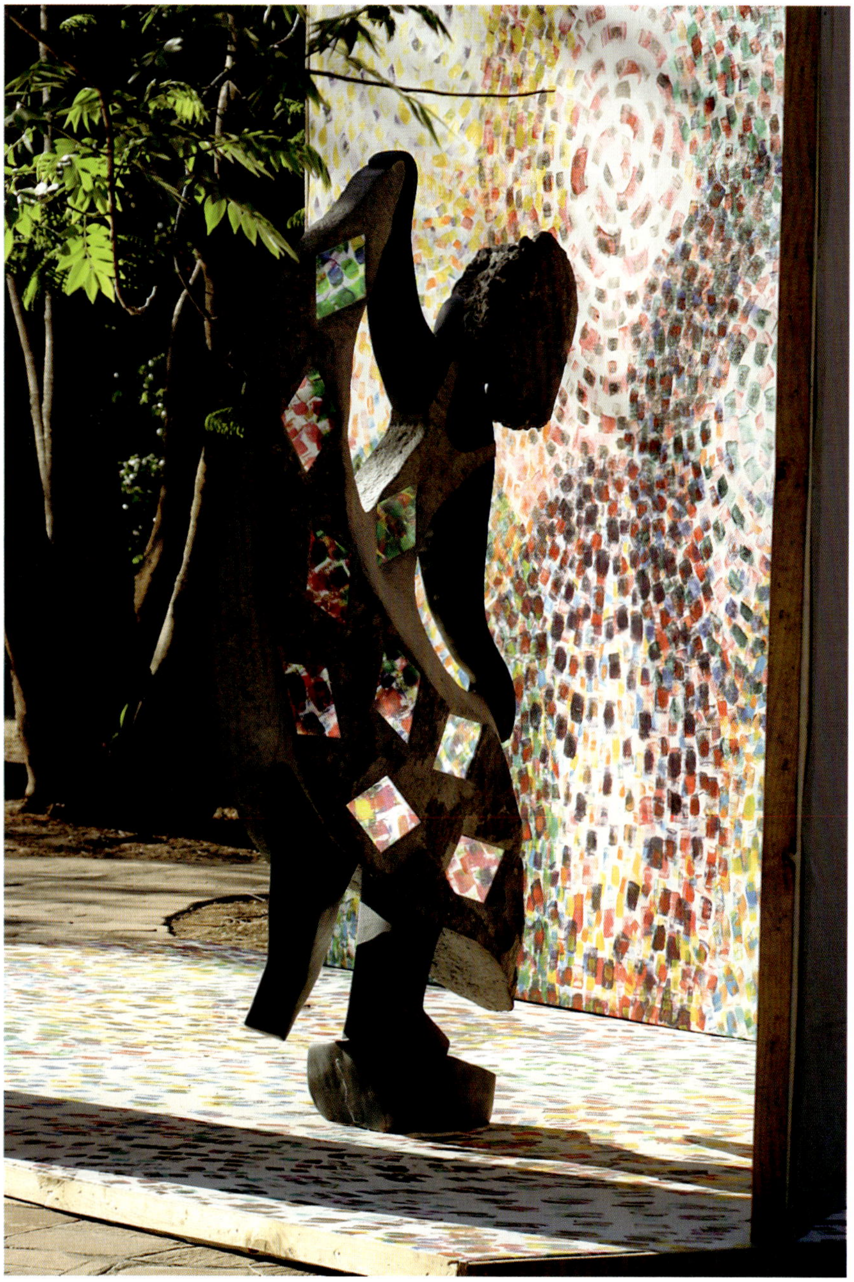

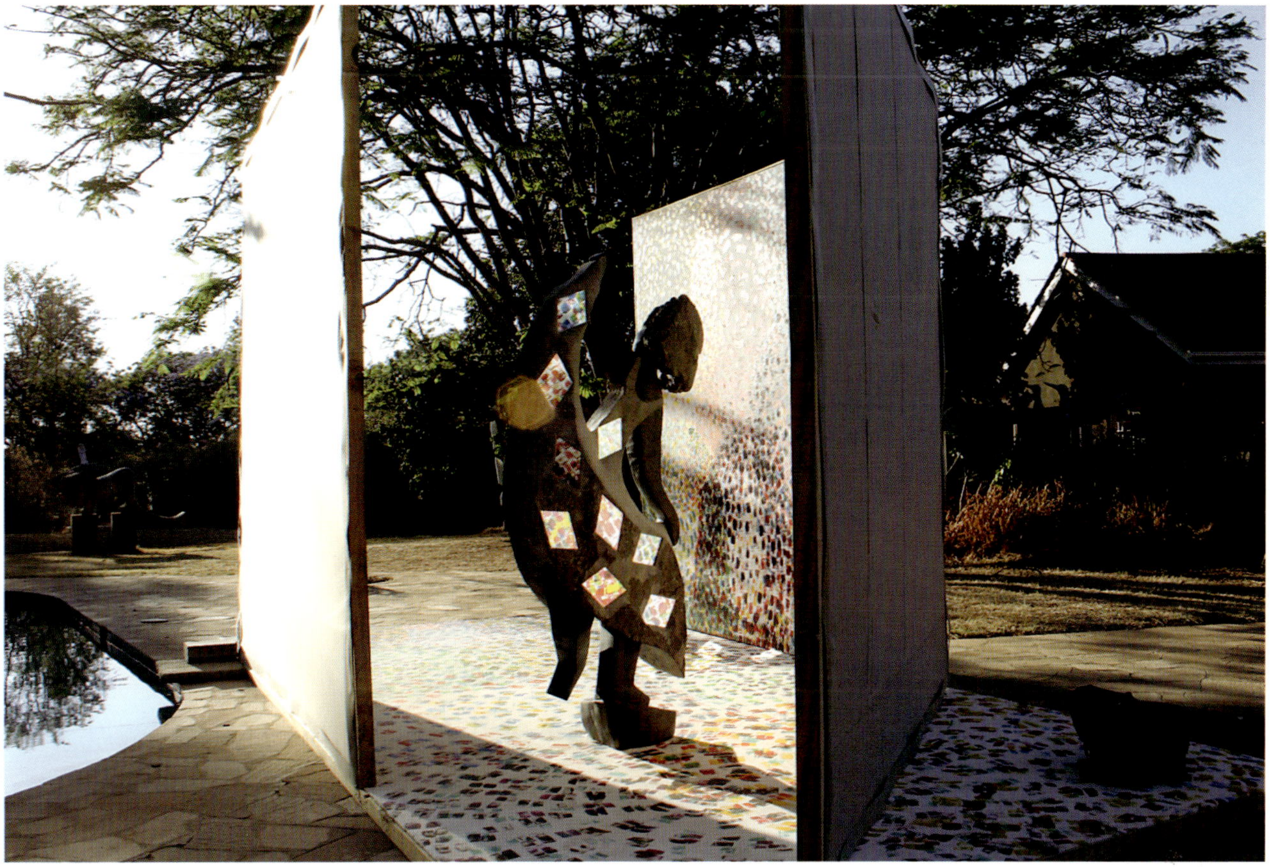

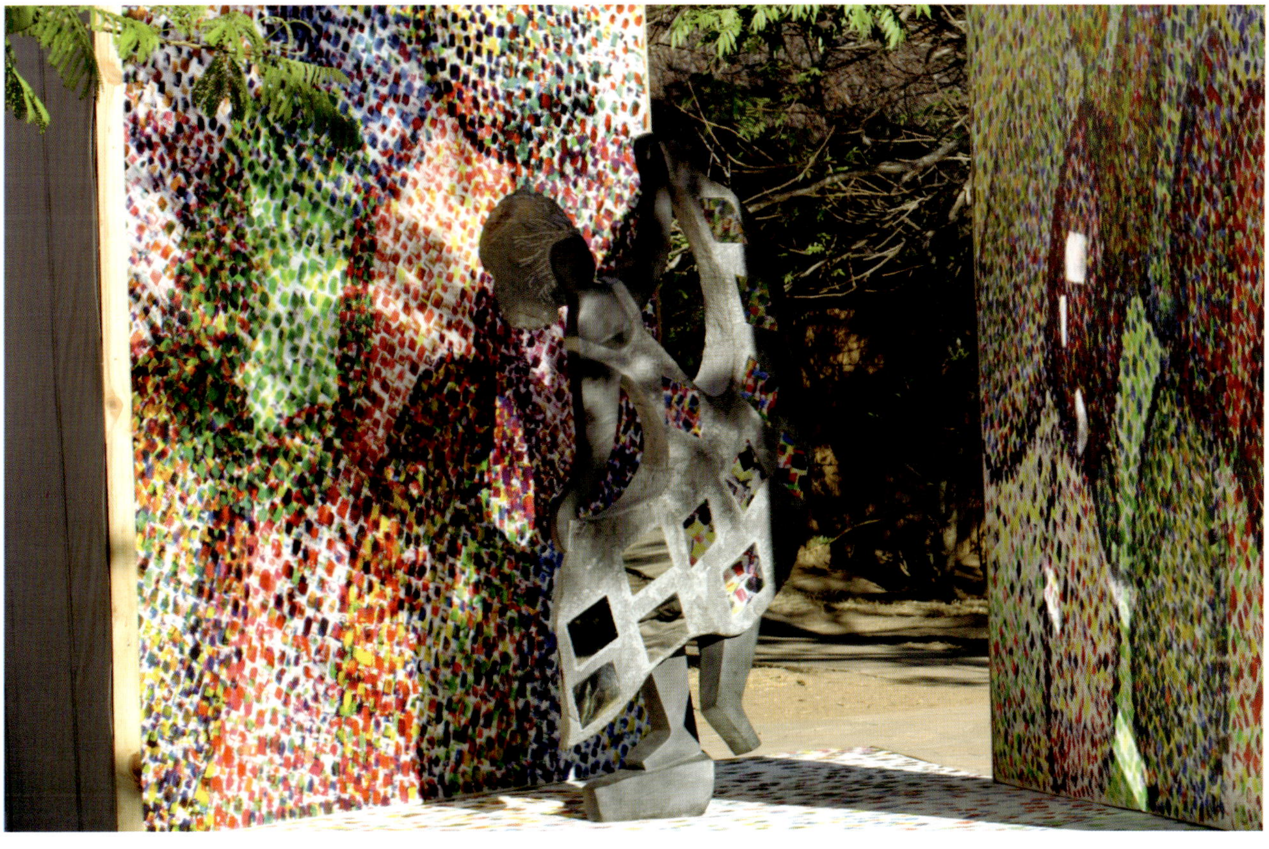

MARIO BENJAMIN
HAITI

Below *Untitled*, 2000.
Mixed media on canvas,
76.2 x 101.6 cm (30 x 40 in).
Private collection.

Bottom *Untitled*, 2005.
Mixed media on canvas,
76.2 x 76.2 cm (30 x 30 in).
Private collection.

Right *Untitled*, 2005.
Mixed media on canvas,
76.2 x 76.2 cm (30 x 30 in).
Private collection.

'I begin with a formal sketch. I deconstruct it until it is destroyed... and then it appears... within the light.' Mario Benjamin's paintings are like volcanic eruptions, his luminous colours forcing their way to the surface like molten lava through a suffocating mantle of darkness. In some ways they reflect the artist's own struggle to assert and maintain his own artistic identity.

Mario Benjamin was born in Port au Prince, Haiti, in 1964. He is a self-taught artist who initially made a name for himself as a photorealist portrait painter, but has since worked in a number of different media, including installation, performance and highly expressive painting and drawing.

Haiti is a country with a proud and tragic history. In 1791 Haiti became the first independent free black nation in the colonial world, following a successful uprising of its enslaved people under the leadership of Toussaint l'Ouverture. The pride that Haitians feel at this historical fact should be matched by the shame of the rest of the world for allowing Haiti to become the poorest country in the northern hemisphere.

When I met Mario Benjamin in London we talked about Haitian art and whether there was a recognizable movement or style that could be so described. 'All voodoo', he answered with a smile.

It was against this historical and socio-religious background that Benjamin began to practise his art, though from the start he was determined not to conform to what he saw around him. As Simon Njami acutely observed in his notes to Benjamin's 2007 solo exhibition at Afro-Nova, Johannesburg:

> *Mario Benjamin ...was born in a country where his experience of the absurd forced him into conflict with madness and he was obliged to recreate himself. He fashioned himself alone, far from a world in which he was unable to decently recognize himself.*

Benjamin is a generous supporter of young artists in Haiti. In 2006 he became artistic director of a project to create a 'Freedom' sculpture to mark the bicentenary of the abolition of the Atlantic slave trade in 2007. The sculpture will be on permanent display in the new International Slavery Museum, Liverpool, UK.

'For me it was very important to show that slavery has always been part of civilization. My ambition was that we would create something that is quite universal, that is about suffering, hoping, fighting, what humanity has been about all the time.'
Mario Benjamin

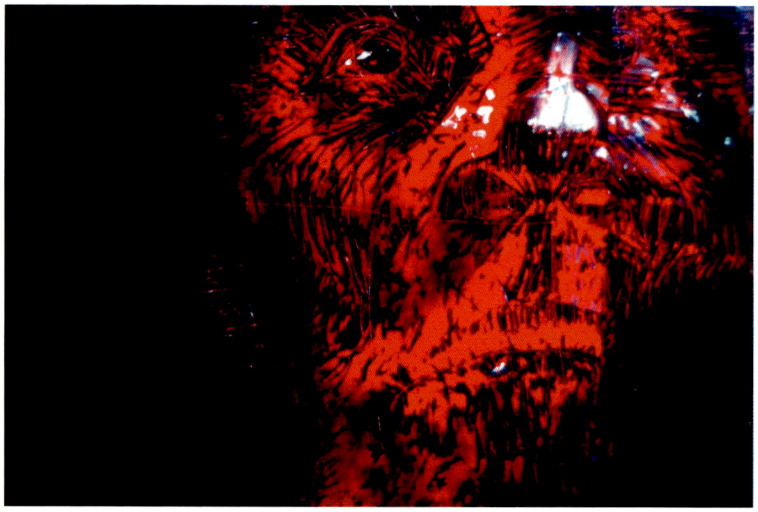

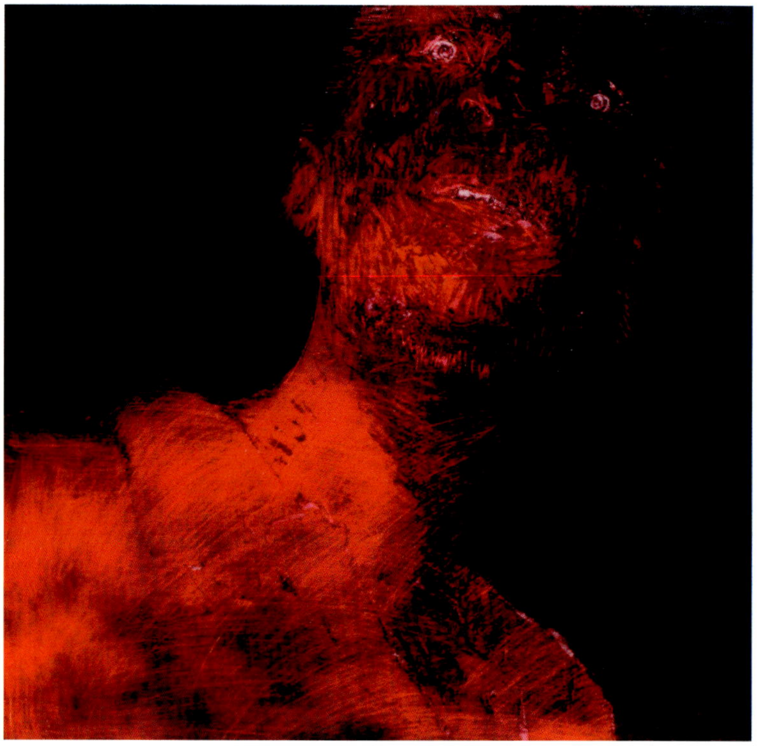

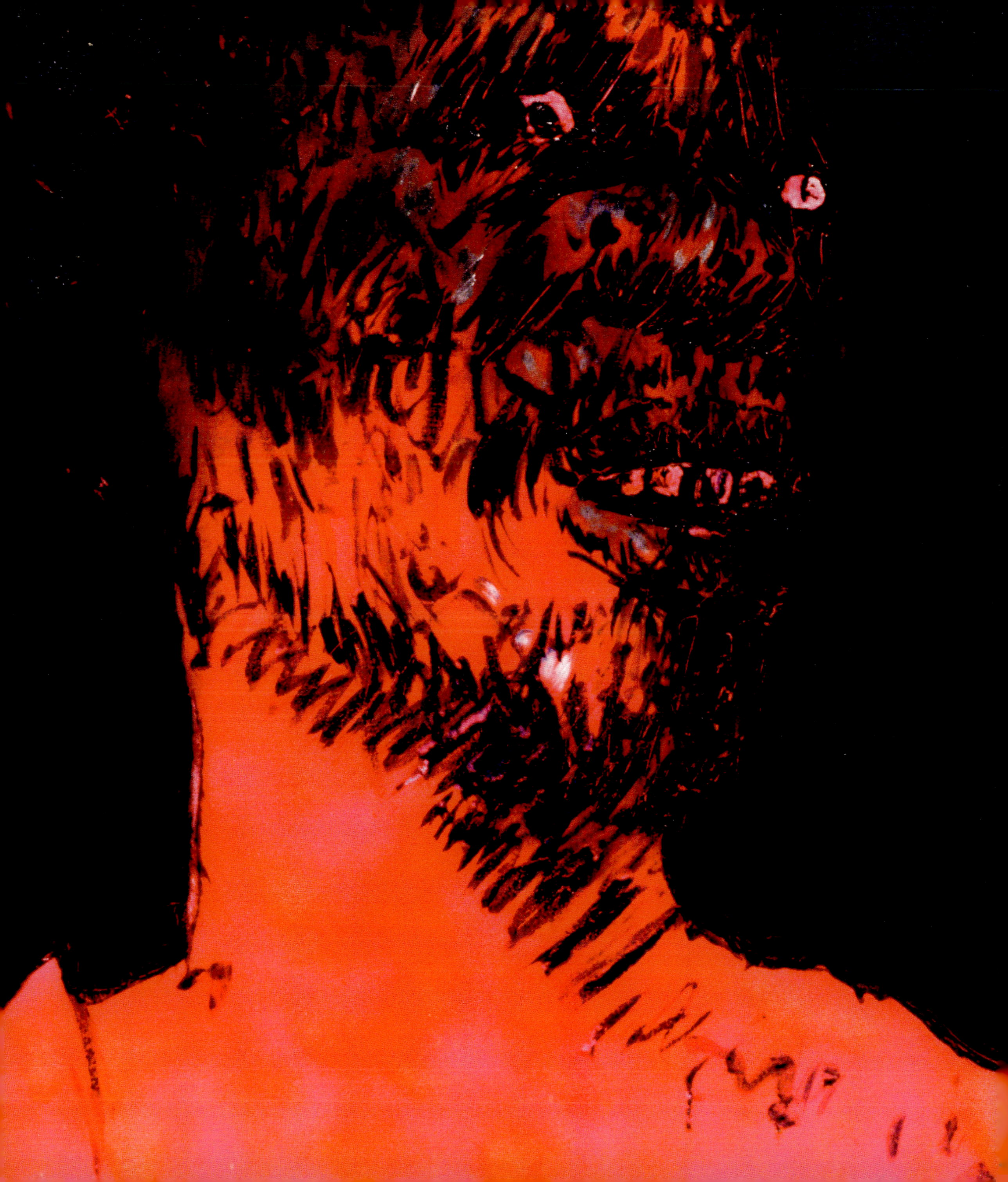

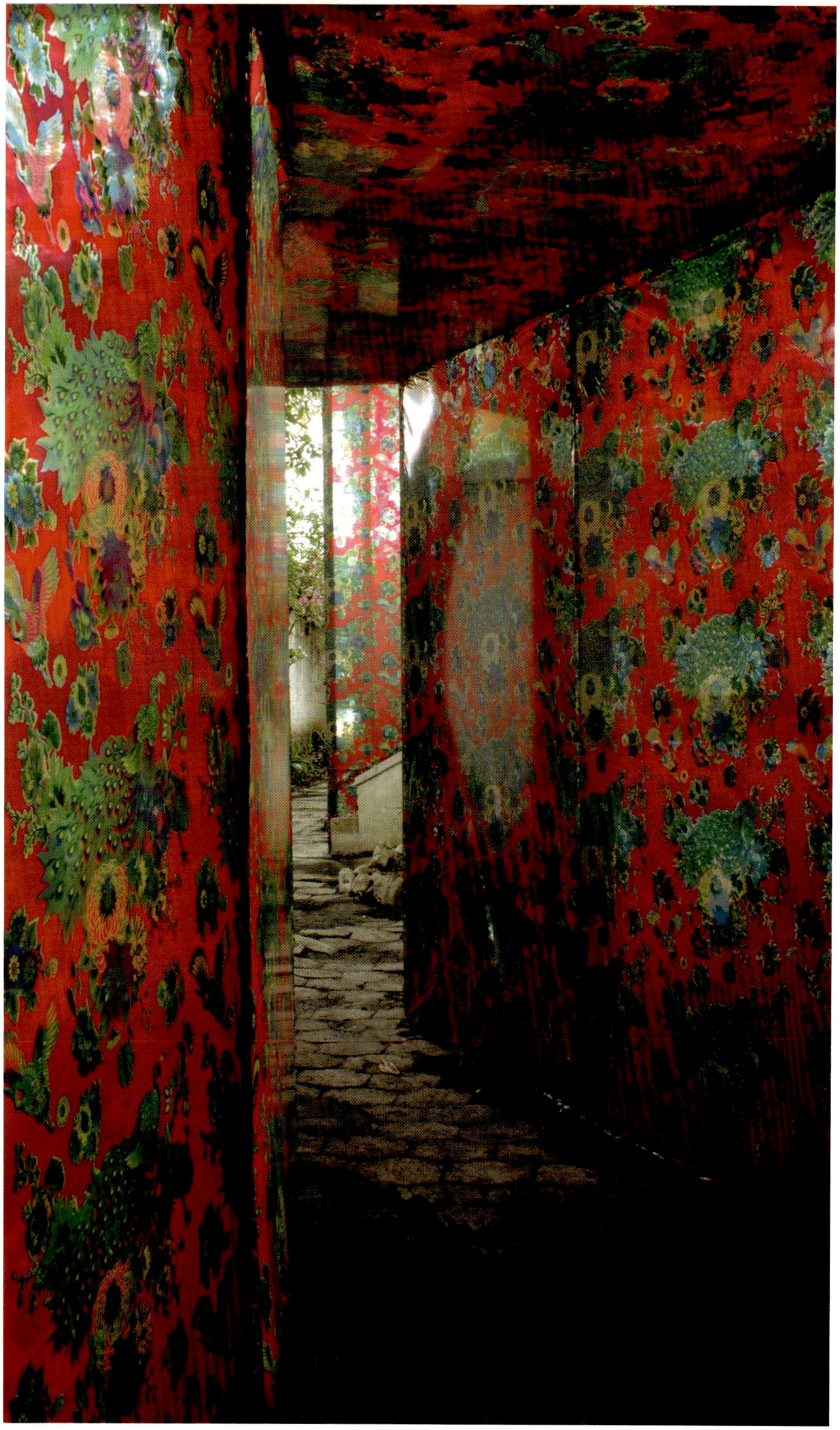

Left *Carte Blanche* (detail), installation at the French Institute, Haiti, 1992. Fabric, plaster, found objects, variable dimensions.
Benjamin often uses different materials to create walls, passages and staircases. Here he creates a maze of passageways from translucent, printed cloth through which the light and the world beyond are visible – but unattainable.

Right *Ministry of Culture Float* (details), 2006. Collective work by Mario Benjamin, Celeur, Guyodo and Eugene. 150 still drums.
A wall of oil drums, punched with holes and illuminated from within to create a mosaic of faces, masks, skulls and various magical and religious signs and symbols. Once again the theme of light trying to get out of – or into – a variety of different containers is an important recurring theme in Benjamin's work.

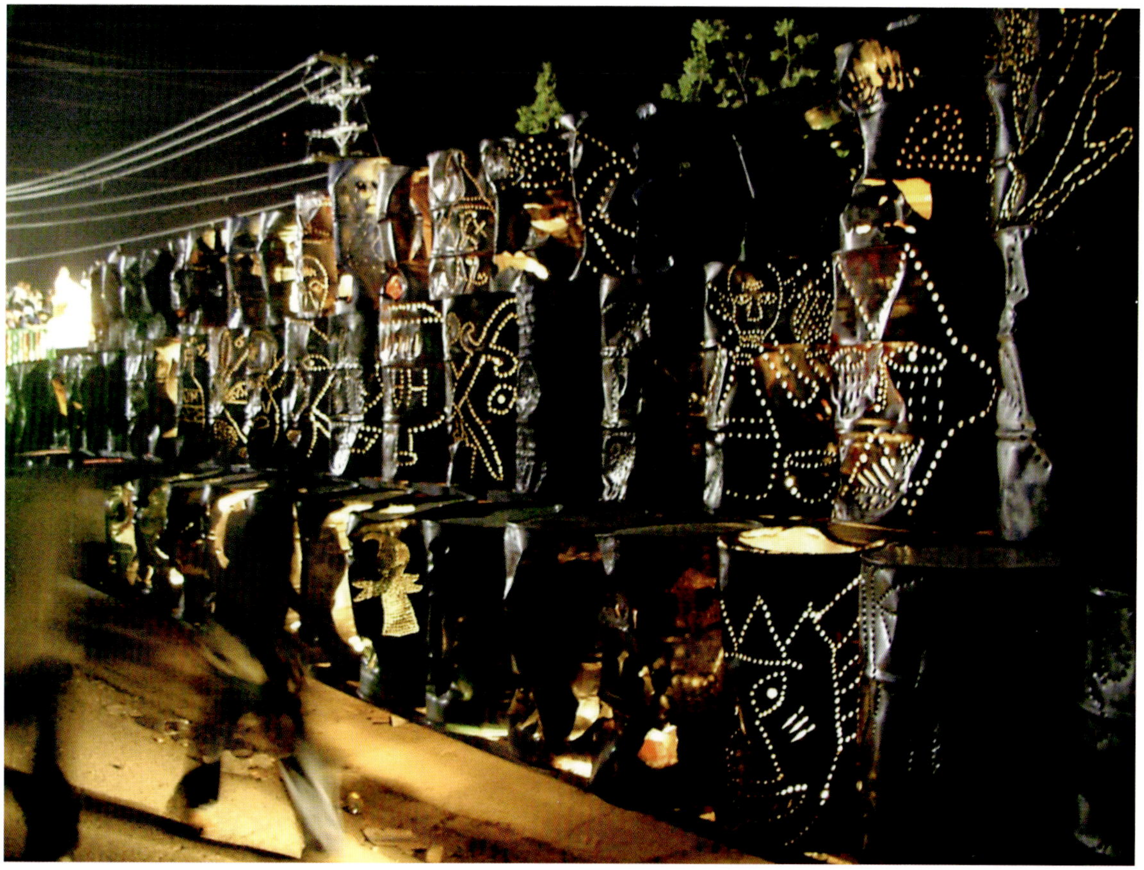

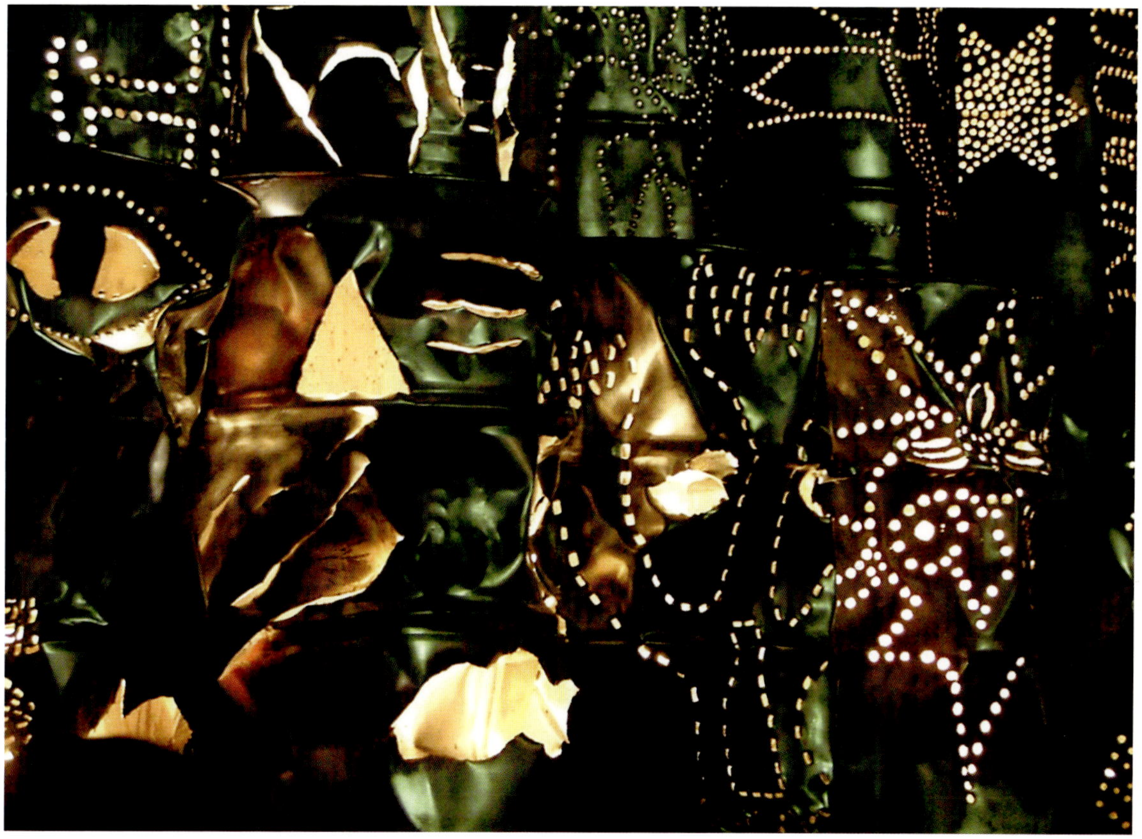

WILLIE BESTER
SOUTH AFRICA

This spread *Transition,* 1994 (details). Mixed media, 92 x 152 cm ($36\frac{1}{5}$ x $59\frac{4}{5}$ in). Private collection.

Willie Bester was born in Montagu, near Cape Town, in 1956. His father was Xhosa, his mother 'coloured', making him 'other coloured' in the obscene classification of apartheid. Bester was forced to endure the extreme racism, forced removals, segregation and oppression that were the lot of all South Africa's non-white citizens under the apartheid regime. Then, at the age of thirty, Bester attended classes at the famous Community Arts Project in District Six, Cape Town, a strongly political organization that aimed to empower black or marginalized visual and performing artists in the movement towards liberation. Here Bester's latent talent blossomed as he realized that his skills as an artist represented a means of fighting back:

> *I was angry... so I used my work as a tool against apartheid. I didn't care if it matched your curtains or not. My art was a chance to be heard.*

Although Bester's work could be described as 'resistance art', from the start it was complex both in its visual presentation and its iconography. While overtly resisting the system, Bester's art also championed the dignity, indomitable spirit and creativity of those who suffered at its hands. The abolition of apartheid did not signal the immediate end to all the evils it engendered, just as the abolition of slavery did not mark the end of the practice, but was simply a milestone in the long battle against it:

> *What I try to get behind is why it is so difficult for people to change from their old ways. People who thought they were superior before haven't really changed. I try to find out through studying history what gives people the right to think that way.*

Many of Bester's works are mixed-media collages mounted on board, often incorporating found objects together with his own photographs and scenes painted in oils or enamel. His work may be found in public and private collections all over the world, and remains as politically and socially committed as ever.

'I am sometimes tempted to go to the seaside and to paint beautiful things from nature. But I do not do it because my art has to be taken as a nasty-tasting medicine for awakening consciences.'
Willie Bester

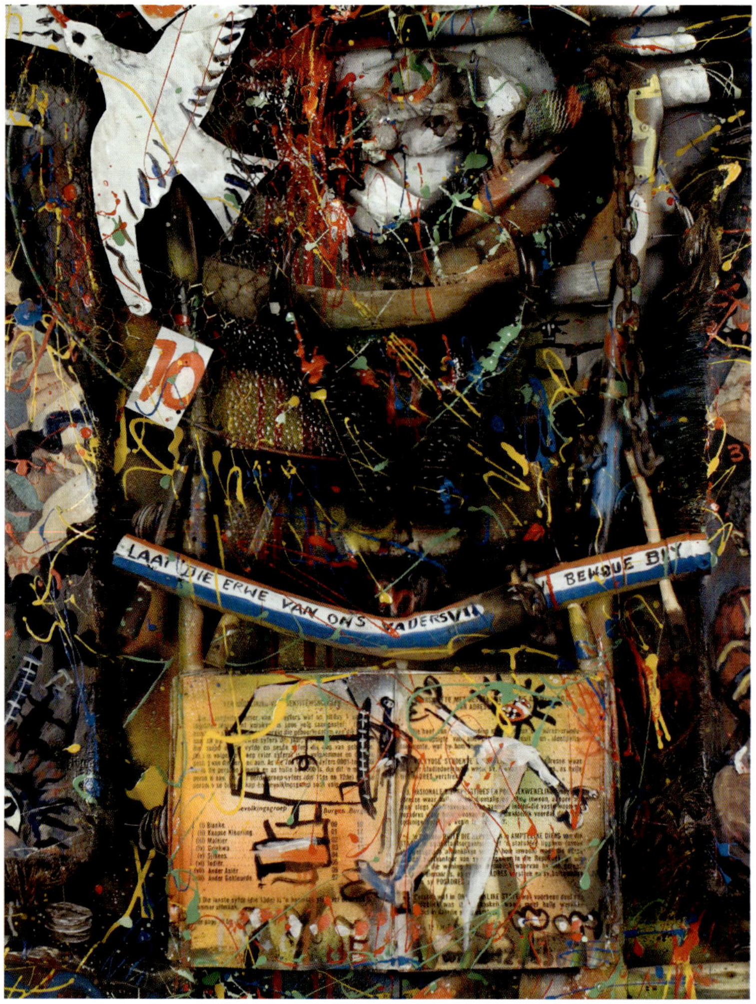

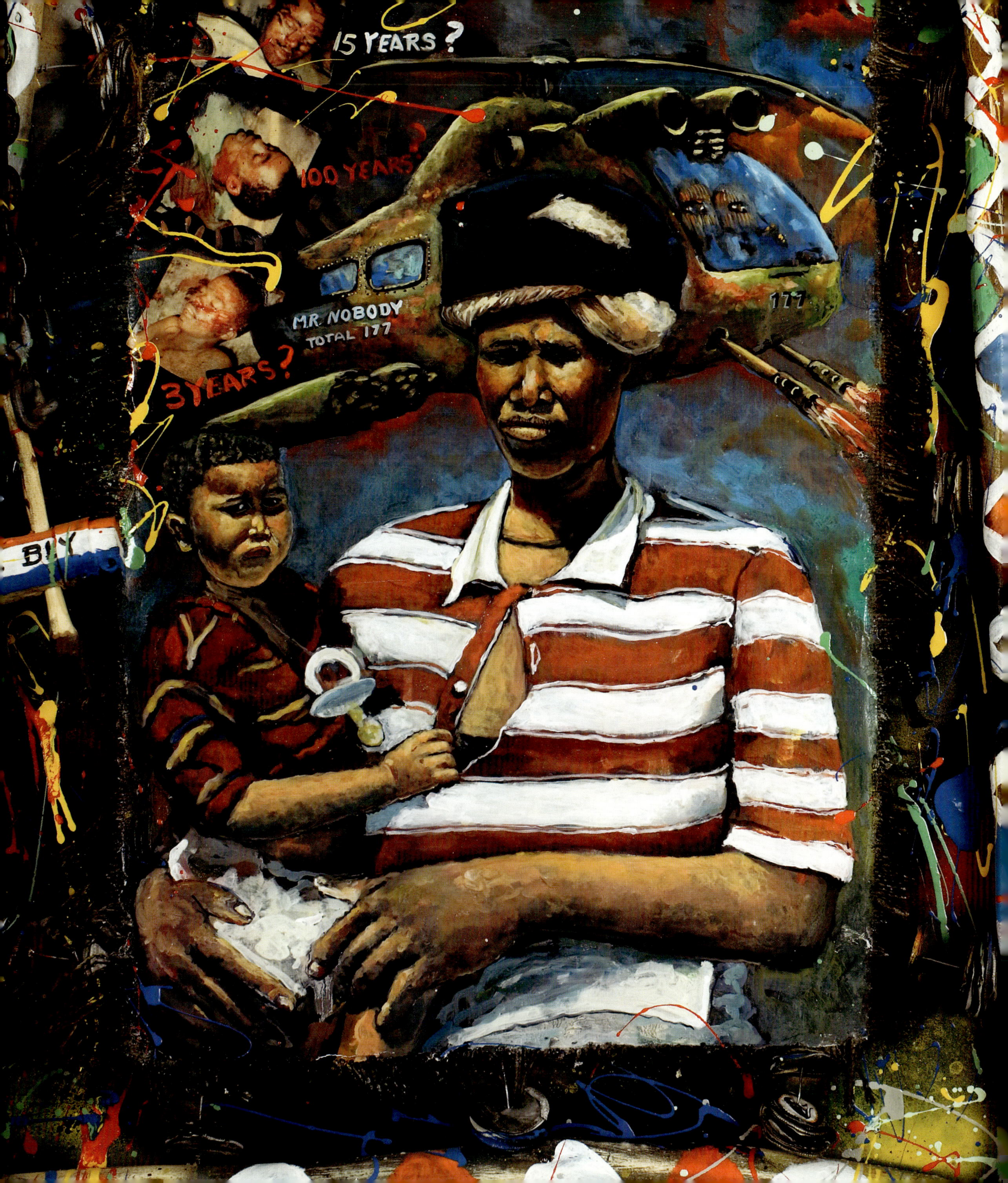
15 YEARS ?
100 YEARS?
MR NOBODY
TOTAL 177
3 YEARS?
177

Right *Transition*, 1994 (full image).
'My art is a means to give a more reliable expression of living conditions in the townships.' Bester includes a range of found and ready-made objects in his work, objects that in other circumstances might be considered rubbish but that here are elevated and dignified, as are the citizens of the townships that they represent.

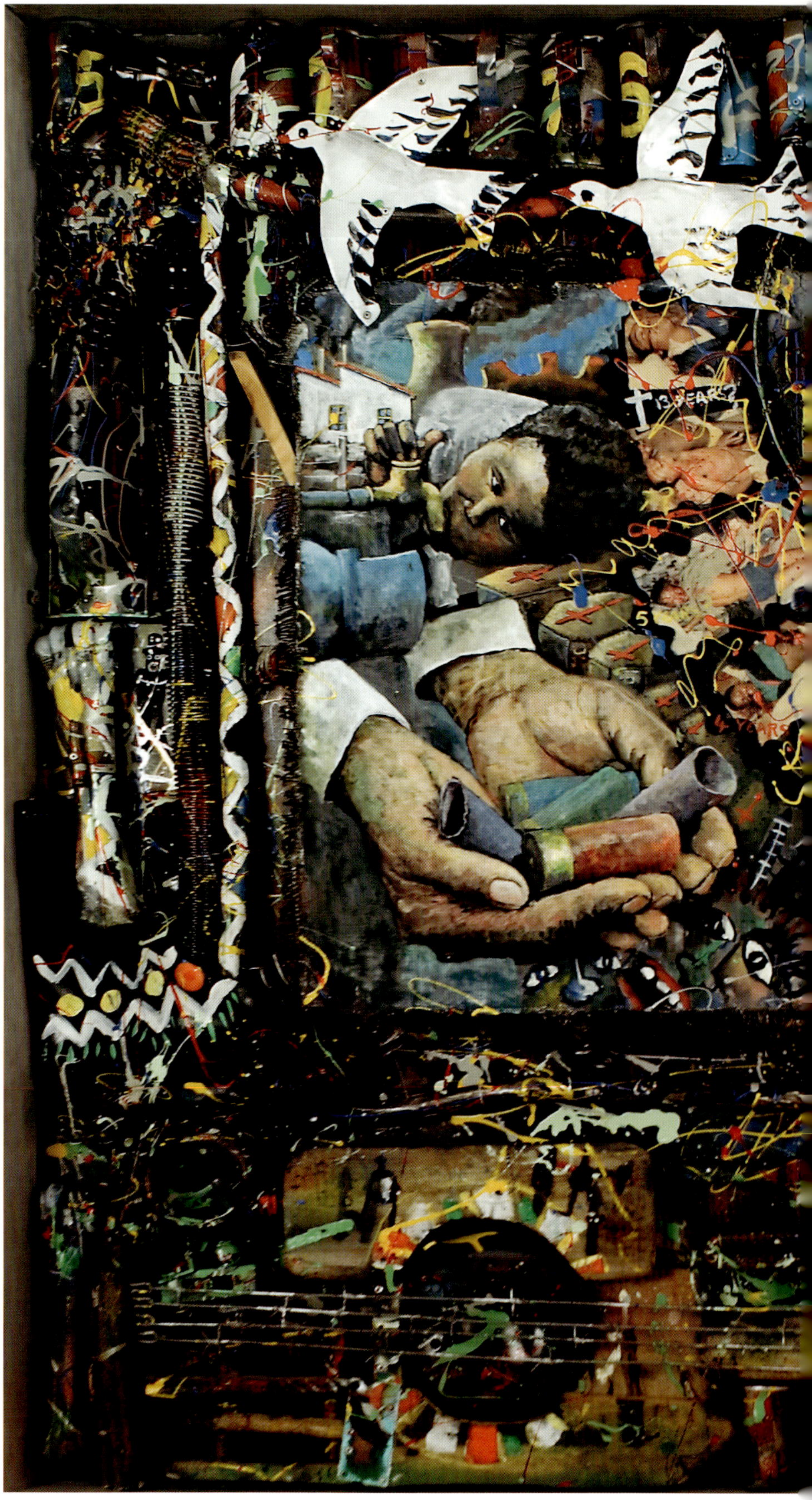

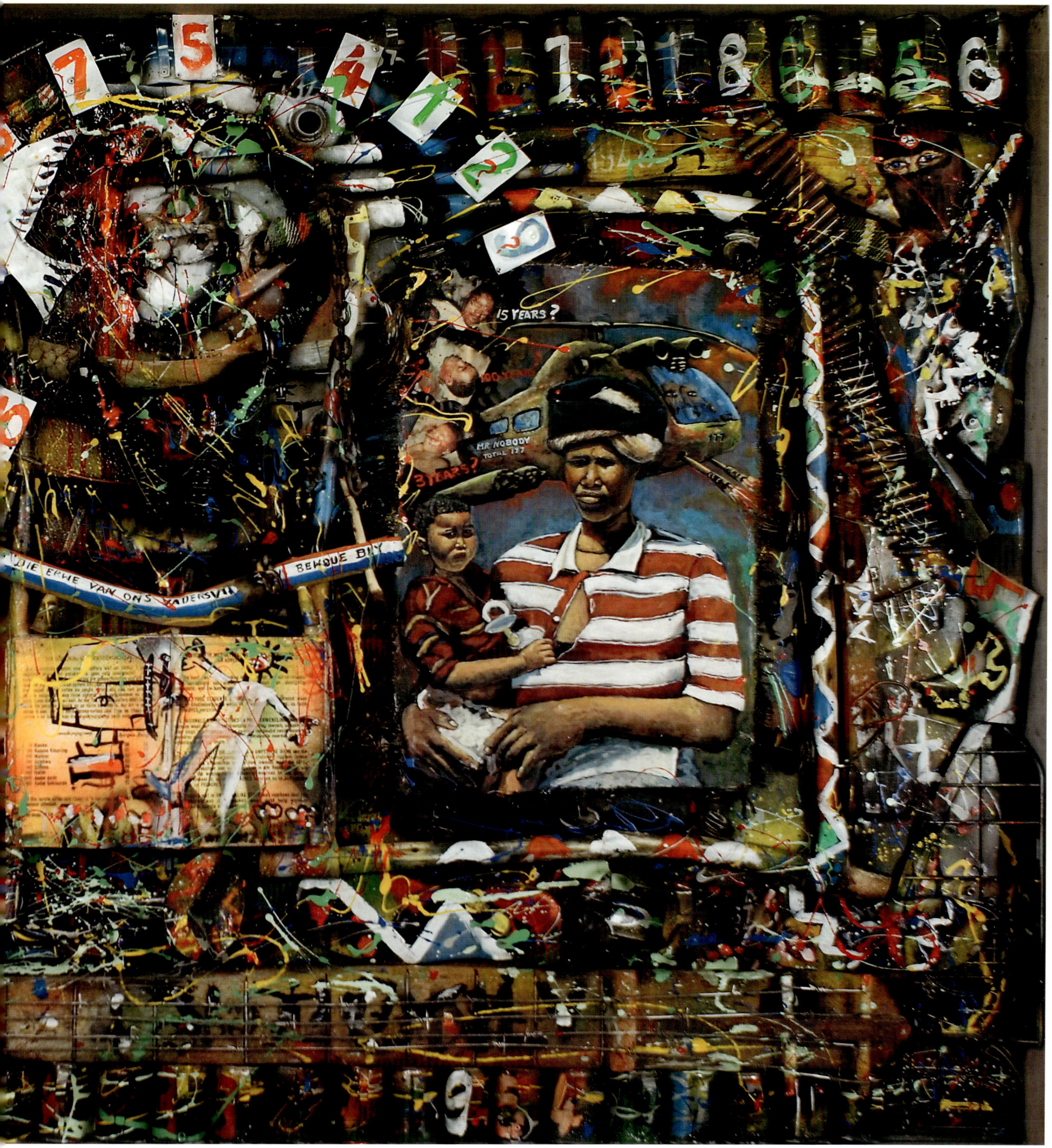
15 YEARS ?
MR NOBODY
TOTAL 177
3 YEARS?
BEHOUE BLY

Below and right *For Those Left Behind,* 2003. Recycled metal, 470 x 218 x 140 cm (185 x $85\frac{4}{5}$ x 55 in). Private collection. 'Whether established art circles like my work or not, I have embarked on a road that gives me personal satisfaction and depicts an era in our history that should be known by all.' Bester's menacing, spectral dog stands as an everlasting reminder of the brute force used to suppress the peoples of the townships during the apartheid years.

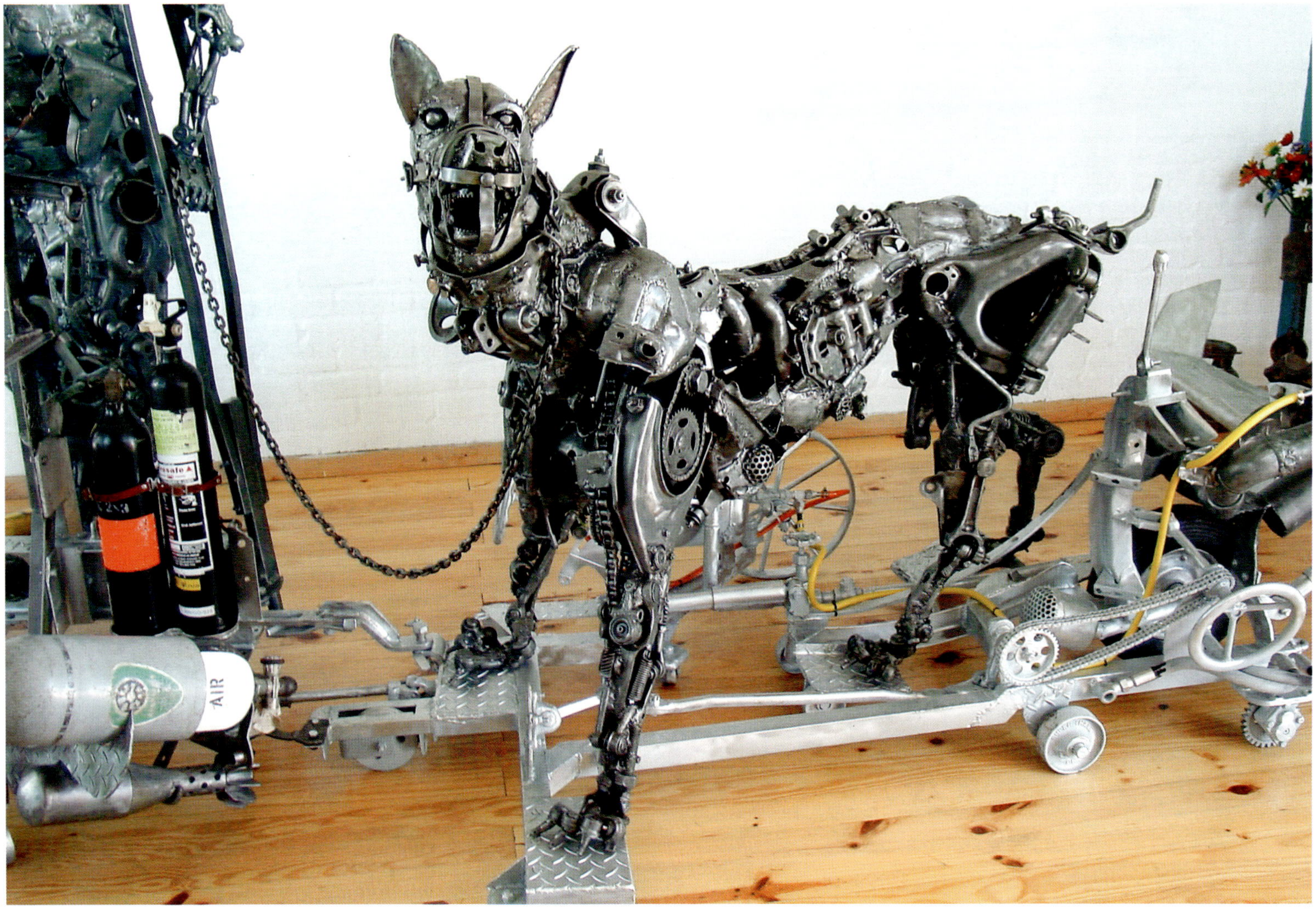

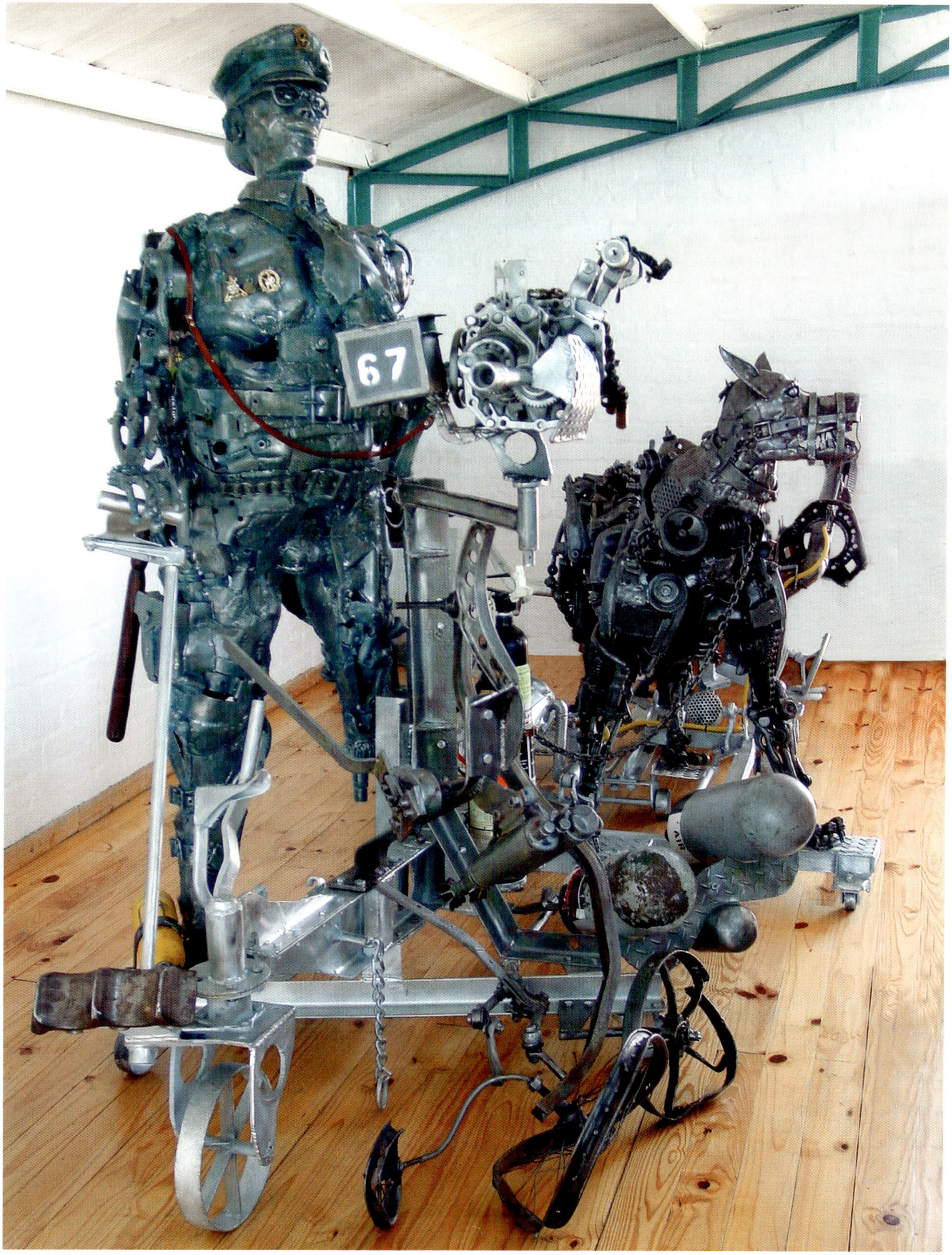
67

WIM BOTHA
SOUTH AFRICA

Below *Leda and the Swan*, 2005. Bone meal, marble, epoxy resin and webbing, 78 x 150 x 108 cm (30⅔ x 59 x 42½ in). gordonschachatcollection. The rape of the human Leda by the god Zeus in classical mythology is portrayed by Botha as the shattered dream of domination by one people over another – or perhaps not. Botha's works are often suspended in mid-air, a device that perhaps suggests the transitory nature of firmly held beliefs and monolithic institutions, as well as the artist's insistence that 'there is no one explanation for any particular piece.'

Right *Commune: Onomatopoeia*, 2003. Stained glass, wood, artificial marble, paper and water, dimensions variable. Tollman Family Collection. Onomatopoeia is essentially the imitation of a sound or a concept, in this case perhaps the idea of 'commune' – which is itself a play on words. 'The elements create a discourse of reflexive and interpolating references around the central theme while avoiding direct or didactic commentary, leaving the subject without a final conclusion.'

Wim Botha's work is full of subversive, ironical humour. He demands and feeds off the reactions of his viewers, delighting in *trompe l'oeil* and other visual and verbal subtleties. For example, four elements in his work *Commune: Onomatopoeia*, 2003, are rectangular, leaded glass 'windows' in a room. At first glance the image in the leaded glass seems to be that of a bald, bespectacled, egg-headed man with tufts of hair sticking out from behind his ears. Look again and you see that it is one of Botha's pseudo-heraldic crests, with the egg-headed man being replaced by two of the artist's signature hyenas, in profile, nose to nose. Botha seems to invite the viewer to add to the man the physical details he has omitted – eyes, nose, mouth – to colour in the sections of glass and to add a suitable motto in the empty scrollwork at the bottom. In common with all the other elements in the installation (table, sideboard, ceiling rose, mirror) save one, the windows are suspended on thin metal wires, so that the ceiling, walls and floor of the room become illusory. Water drips sporadically from the ceiling rose, echoing on the concave surface of the table before draining into a galvanized metal bucket, of the type used for rubbish, slops and so on, on the real floor beneath the suspended table. This water and the sounds it makes are the only 'real' elements of the installation. All the rest is an illusion, an imitation of the life force represented by the water – and thus an oblique reference to the title of the work *Onomatopoeia*.

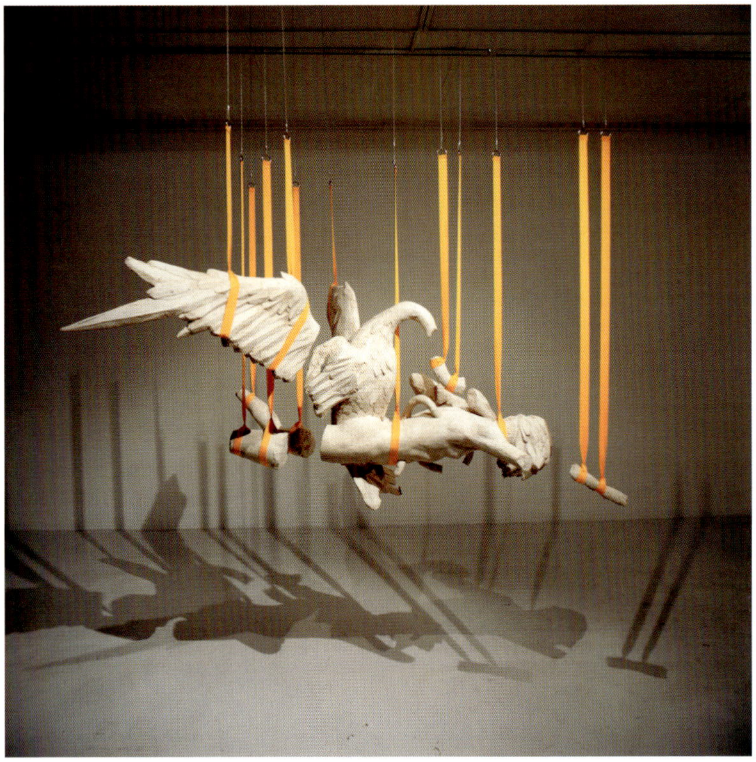

I believe this single example reflects many of the themes Botha is exploring in his art: the impermanence of grand institutions and people; the pomposity and pseudo-grandeur of the imagery used to maintain their memory and significance; the illusory nature of power and position in church and state. All this could, of course, be read as having a direct relationship with the apartheid regime in South Africa, but Botha's subjects are far more universal.

Born in Pretoria in 1974, Botha graduated from the University of Pretoria in 1996. He has won many awards for his art, including the Standard Bank Young Artist of 2005. Many of his works are created with great technical skill from unusual materials such as modelled maize meal or carved governmental documents, the nature of which adds significantly to the understanding of the artist's intention, inviting the viewer to participate in his debunking of many of society's sacred cows.

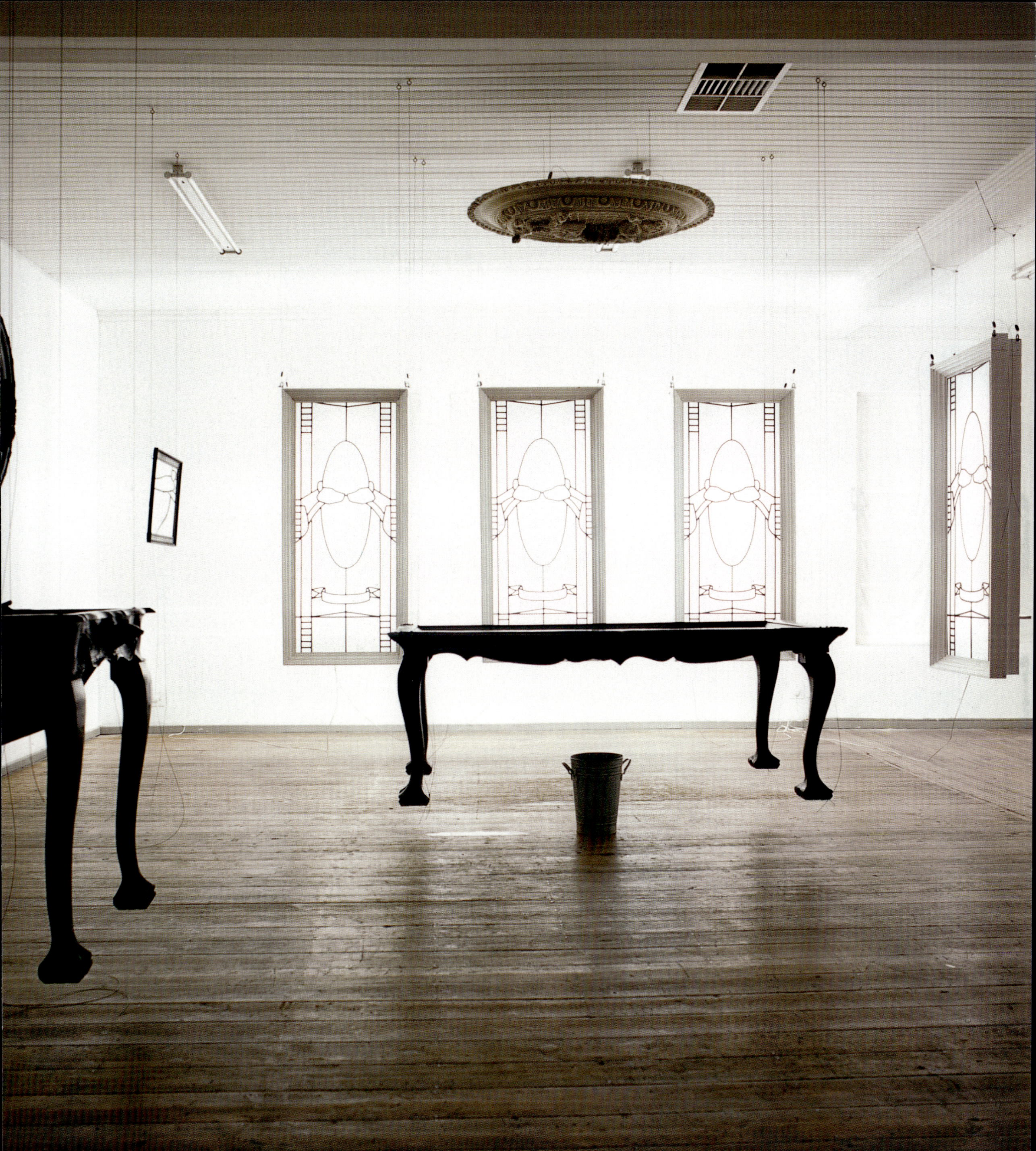

Below *Mieliepap Pietà (Maizemeal Pietà)*, 2004. Maize meal, epoxy resin mirrored replica, height 503 cm (198 in). Spier Estate Collection.
Botha has created a reverse or mirror-image of Michelangelo's famous Pietà which is in St. Peter's Basilica, Vatican City. Instead of carving the work out of white marble, Botha has sculpted his work from 'mieliepap', the maize meal that is the staple diet of millions of South Africans and of people throughout sub-Saharan Africa. *Mieliepap Pietà* was first exhibited in 2004 at the Cathedral of St. John the Divine, New York, where it was appropriated by worshippers as part of the fabric of the church.

Right *Premonition of War (Scapegoat)*, 2005. Eco-solvent inks on satin paper, burnt African hardwood, resin and gilt, sculpture: 188 x 152 x 64 cm (74 x 59⅘ x 25 in), installation: 202 x 653 x 64 cm (79½ x 257 x 25 in). gordonschachatcollection.
This work consists of a central figure of African hardwood, blackened and charred, to the left and right of which are six pictures of gathering clouds in gilt frames, each of which is composed of the numerous pieces of a completed jigsaw puzzle. It is a classic Botha image – enigmatic, provocative and beautifully crafted. The central figure may be read as the crucified Christ or Satan in the guise of the Goat of Mendes. The pictures may be seen as the twelve disciples, or perhaps the arrogant pretensions of humankind, attempting to contain the sky in elaborate gilded cages.

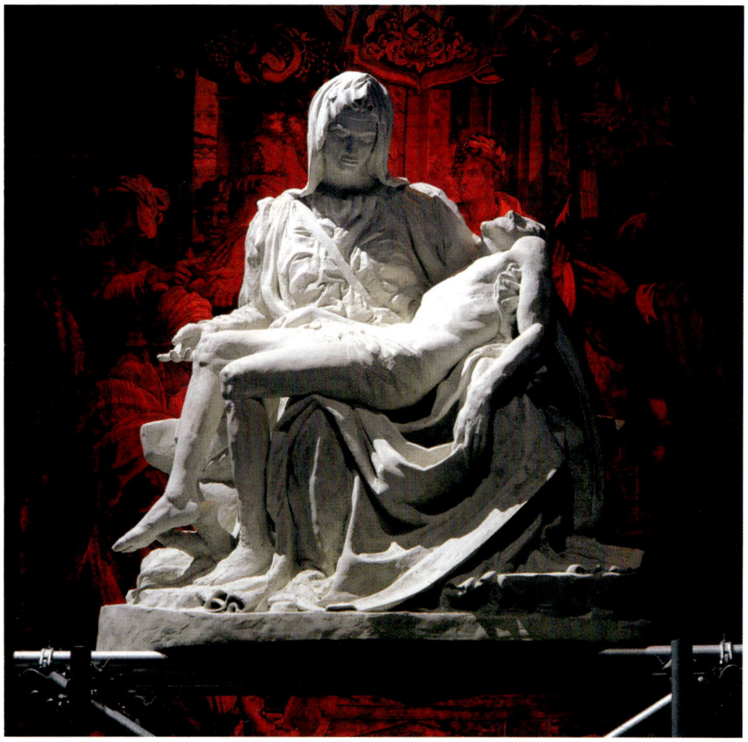

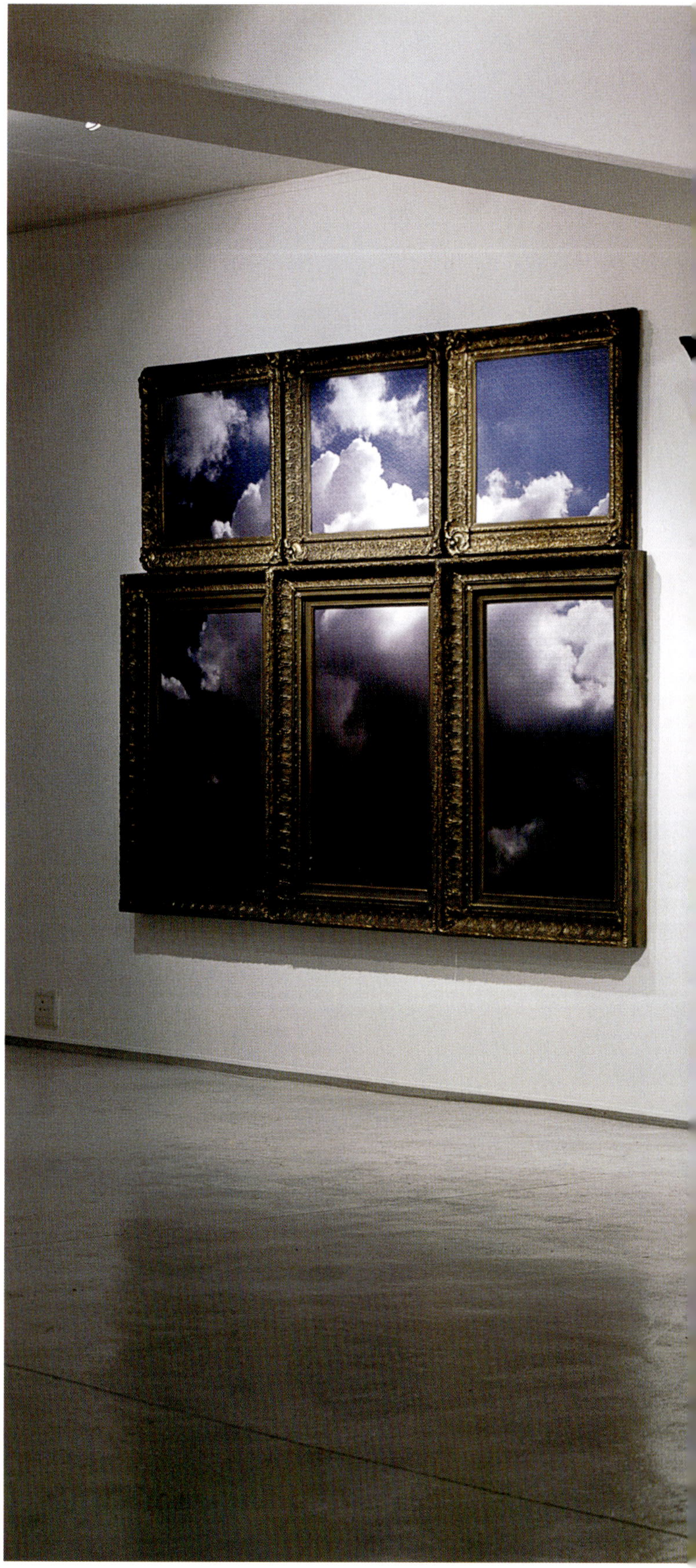

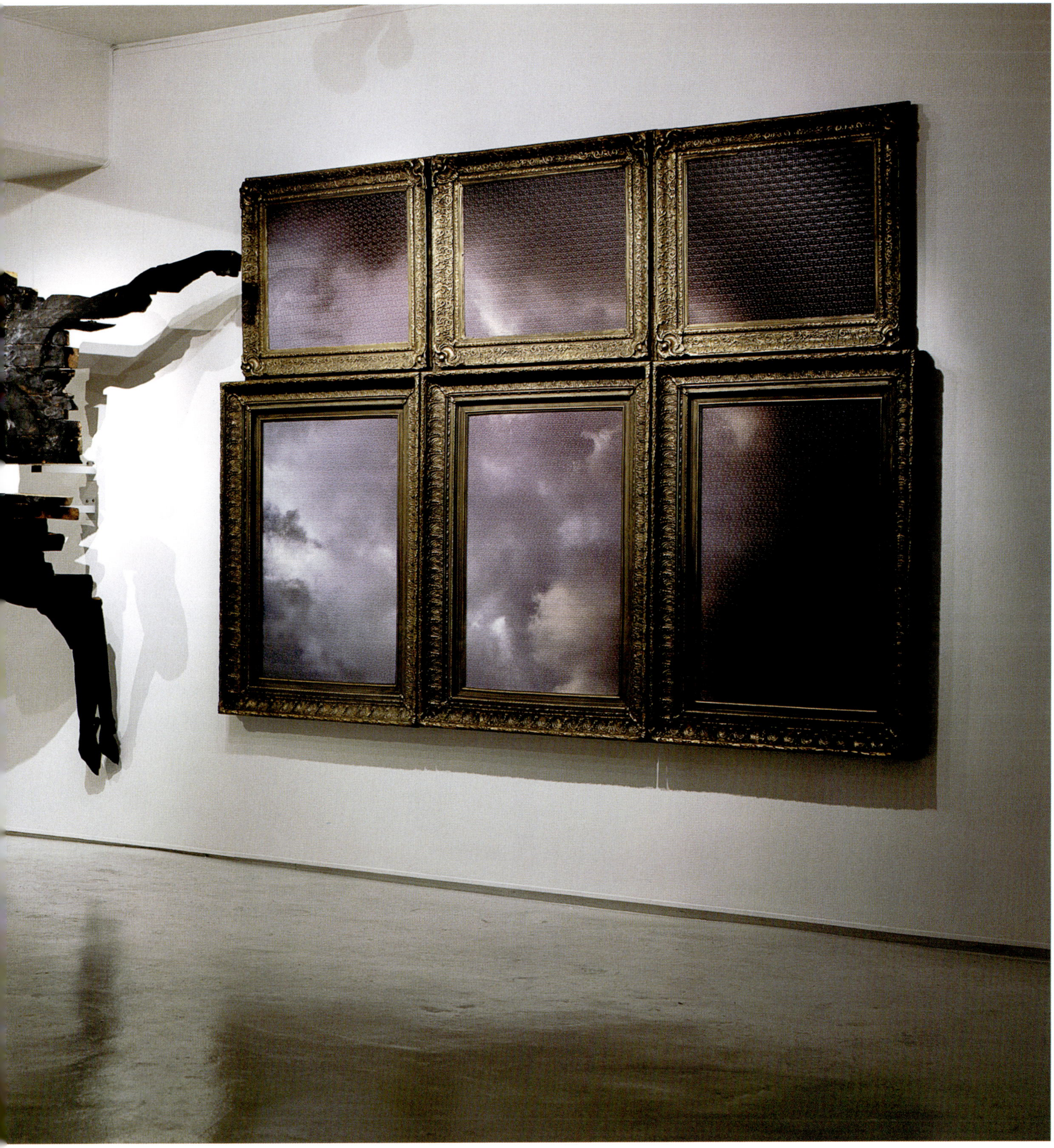

MOHAMED OMER BUSHARA
SUDAN/UK

This spread *Untitled*, 2007 (details). Collage, 110 x 120 cm ($43\frac{1}{3}$ x $47\frac{1}{4}$ in). Collection of the artist.
Much of Bushara's work seems to suggest conflict of some kind, a struggle between elemental forces. In this work that battle might be between creativity and its brutal opposite. The music of the violin and the intricate patterns on a piece of cloth are juxtaposed with images of violence – a gun and blindfolded captives. Yet Bushara is reluctant to talk about meanings in his work: 'It's very difficult to say, "this work means this".' While hinting at psychological depths of meaning, Bushara's works are full of a knowing wit and playfulness that is entirely in keeping with one of his primary aims in art, namely 'to enjoy myself'.

Mohamed Omer Bushara was born in Omdurman, Sudan, in 1946. He started to draw and paint from an early age with whatever materials he could find, a passion that was staunchly supported by his family. His father, a non-literate yet creative man, encouraged his eldest son's interest in art and literature: 'he provided me with painting materials which we really could not afford... it was strange behaviour, even to me. For a father to encourage his eldest son in the arts is very rare.' Unlike many of his fellow artists in Sudan, he studied geography at the University of Khartoum rather than fine art at the Khartoum Technical Institute. He continued to paint during his spare time, and finally won a scholarship in the mid-1970s to attend the Slade School of Art in London, where he studied printmaking with Barto dos Santos, Stanley Jones, Peter Daglesh and Antony Gross.

> *Once my working process is under way, ideas and images become woven together in a very personal language. Printmaking provides an ideal medium, as images can be modified and changed almost endlessly, and it allows play between representation and abstraction within the images: shapes coalesce to form figures, but then fall back out of focus, while a jagged line can form a mountain range yet remain a line.*

During much of his life in Sudan he worked under autocratic militaristic regimes, which in the end forced him into exile, first in Saudi Arabia and then in the UK. This process of dislocation, travel, denial and opportunity is mirrored in Bushara's work. A constant experimenter, his concern is with the process of creation rather than in striving towards a finished article. Whether witnessed at first hand or from overseas, Bushara's passionate involvement with the turmoil and upheaval that has afflicted his native land is powerfully reflected in his work.

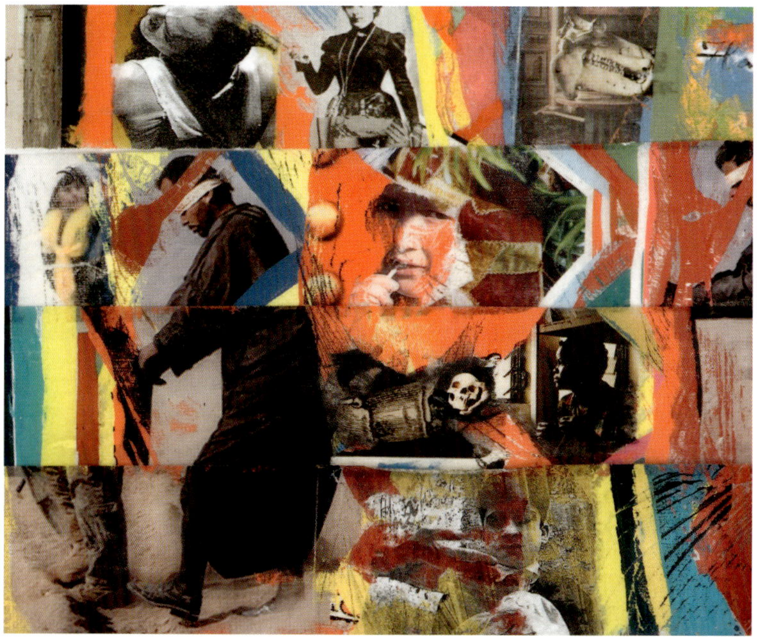

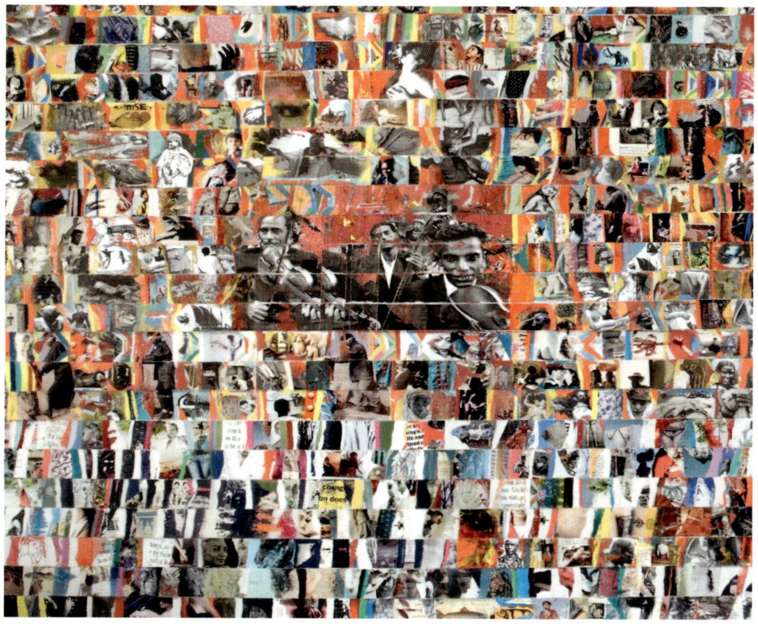

'I work from nowhere, without an idea. It is a feeling. I attack the surface, then the white is no longer neutral. There is a dialogue between the surface and myself. Ideas begin to build up. The more I work the more things develop, until I become in control of the image. The images are elusive. They are both free and entrapped at the same time.'
Mohamed Bushara

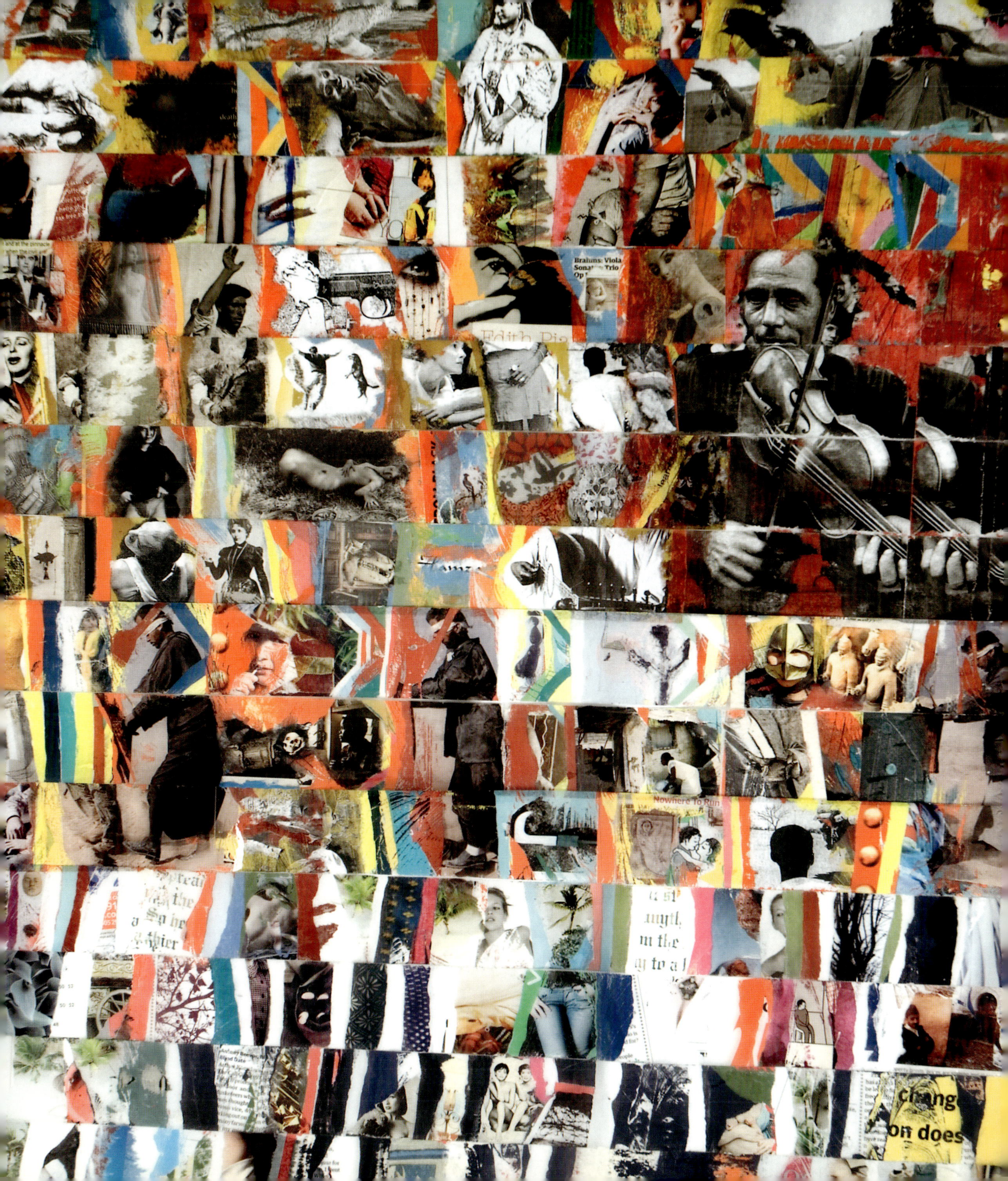
Brahms: Viola
Sonata Trio
Op
Edith
Nowhere To Run
on does

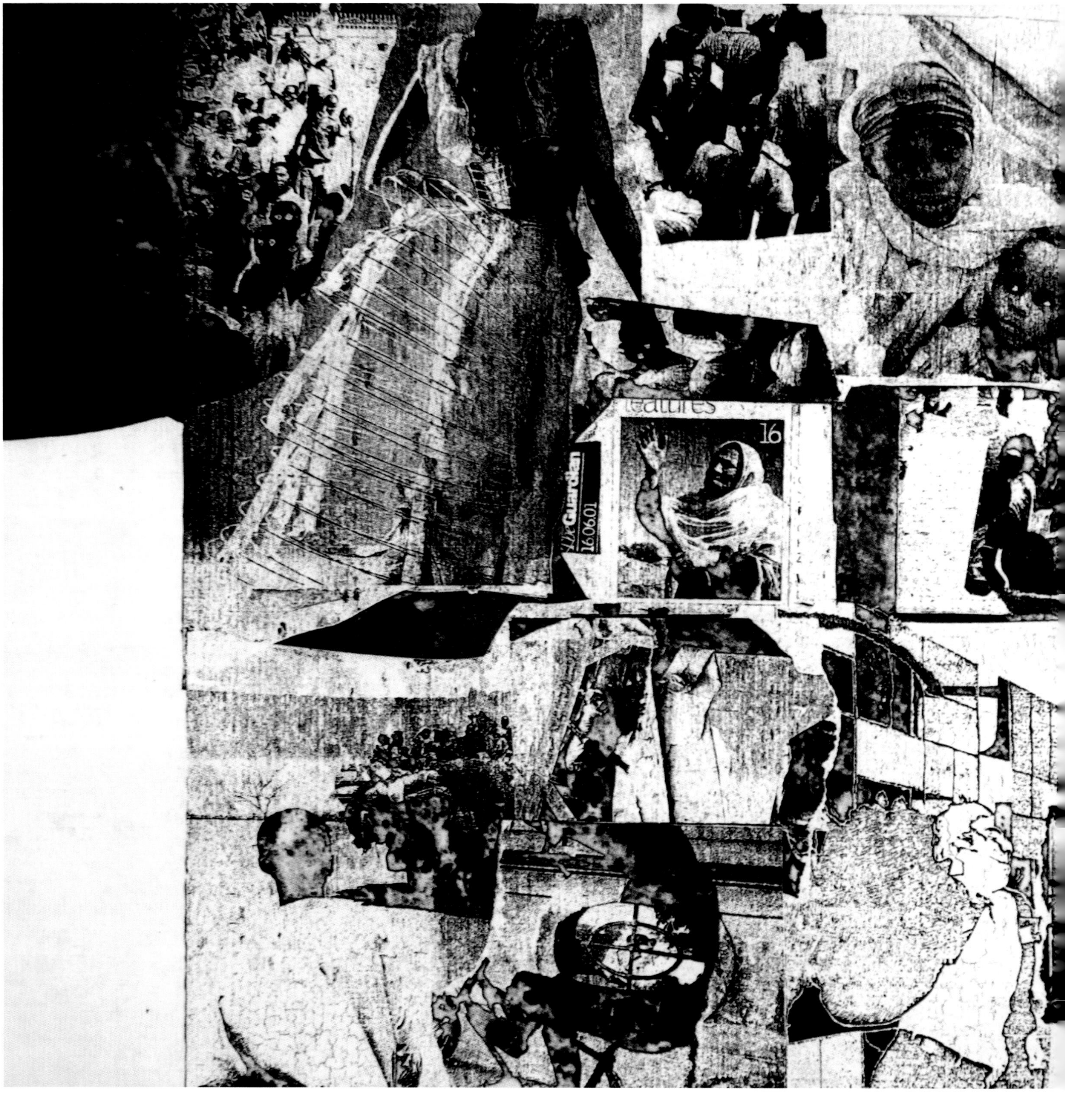
16
Guardian
16.06.01

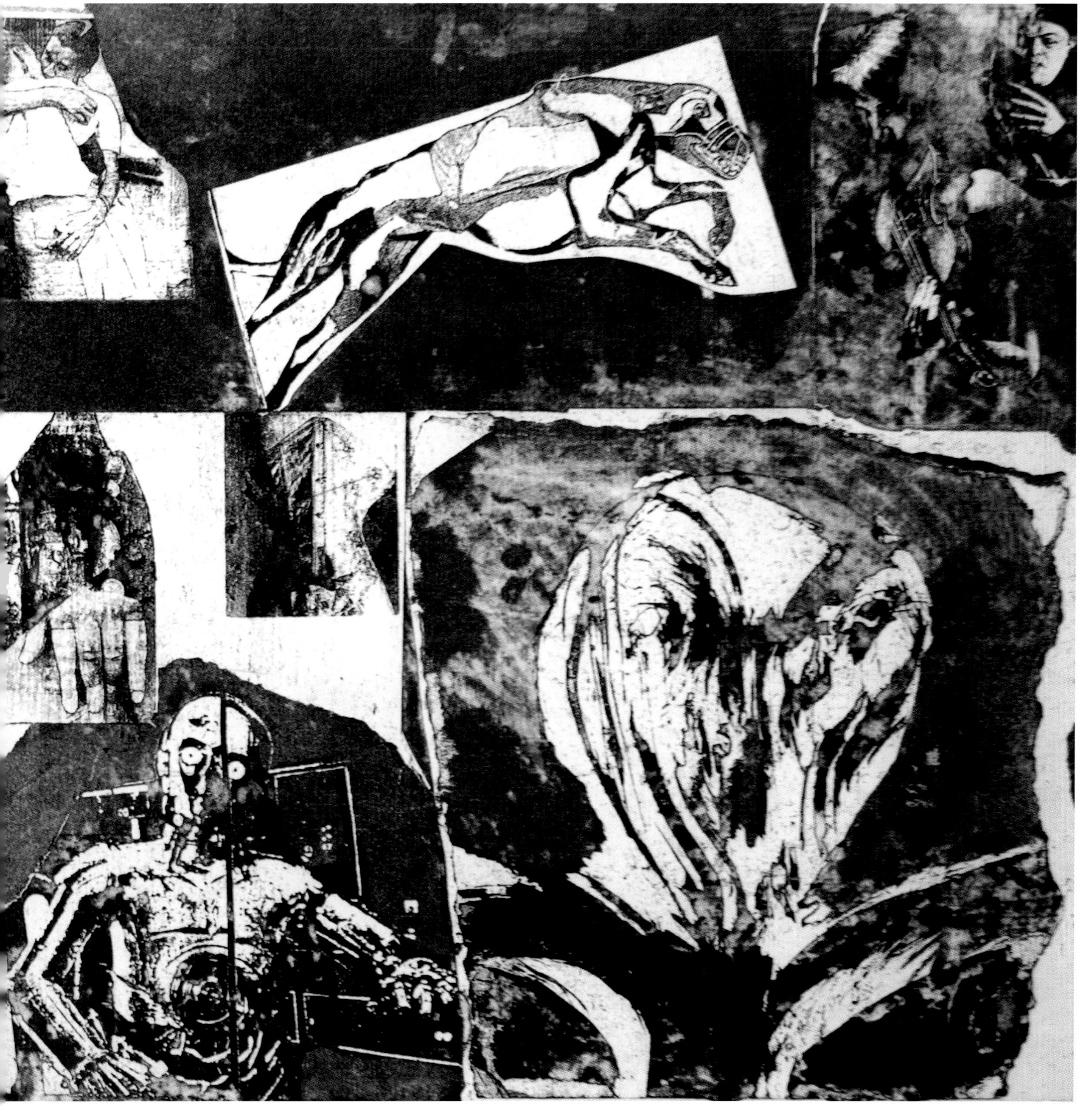

Previous spread
Untitled, 2006. 2 etchings: softground, each 34.5 x 69.2 cm (13½ x 27¼ in). Collection of the artist.

Below and right
Untitled, 2006–7. Etching (front and back): sugar lift, softground, Chine collé and aquatint, 49.1 x 49.5 cm (19⅓ x 19½ in). Collection of the artist.
Sometimes Bushara suggests conflict as a struggle between abstract forms, or between two contrasting styles of draughtsmanship. Here it is between expressive, complex gestures and broad areas of colour. He challenges the viewer to look closely at how he has created his images and their different components. 'The only way to see it is to look; anything in the work is significant, a part of the whole, as in music. For the audience it may be good to read both visually and intellectually.' In the image to the right, two individual forms – one of swirling but ordered patterns, the other of fragments of light and colour – are locked into the intense relationship with one another that is such an important characteristic of many of Bushara's compositions.

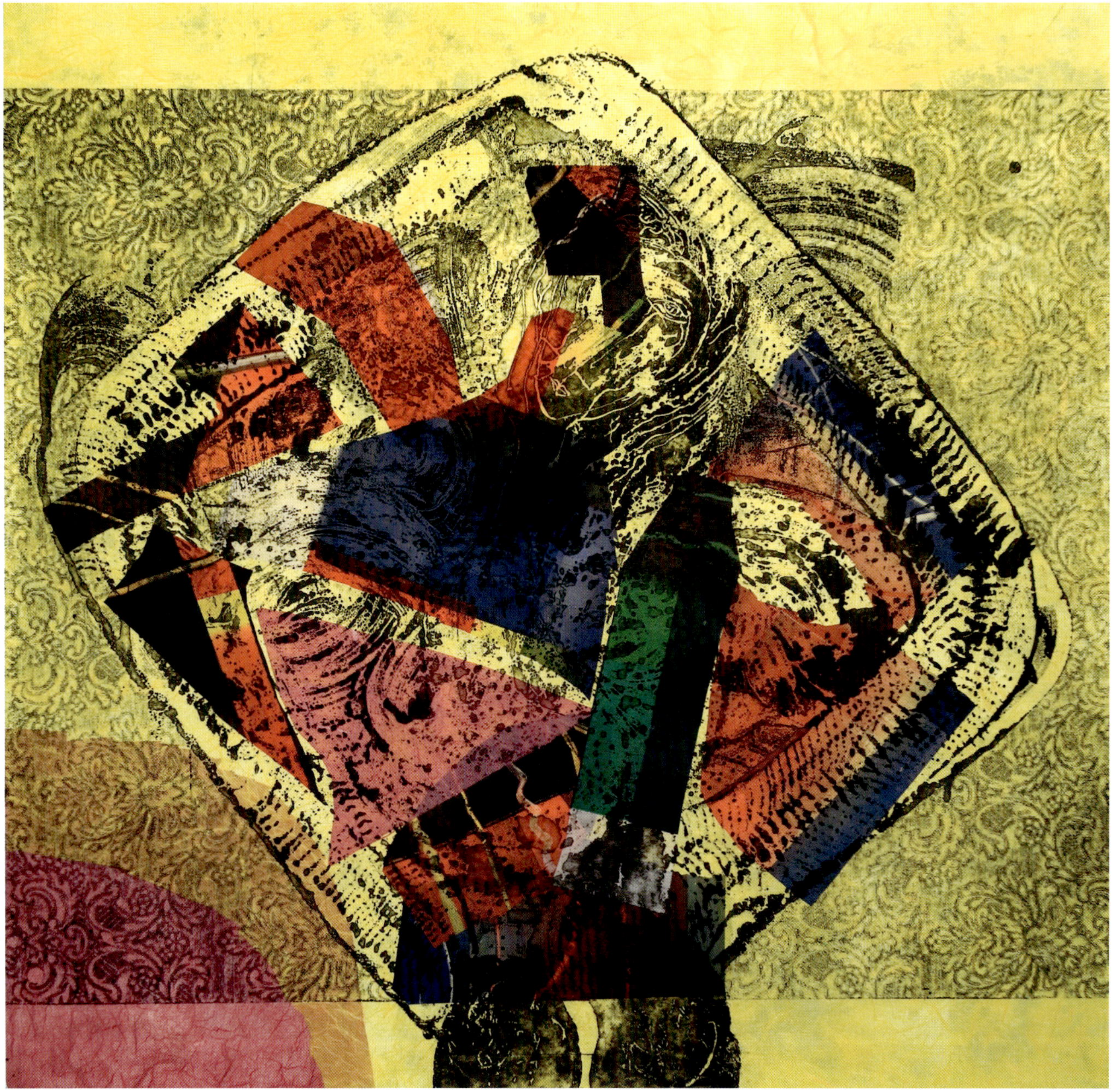

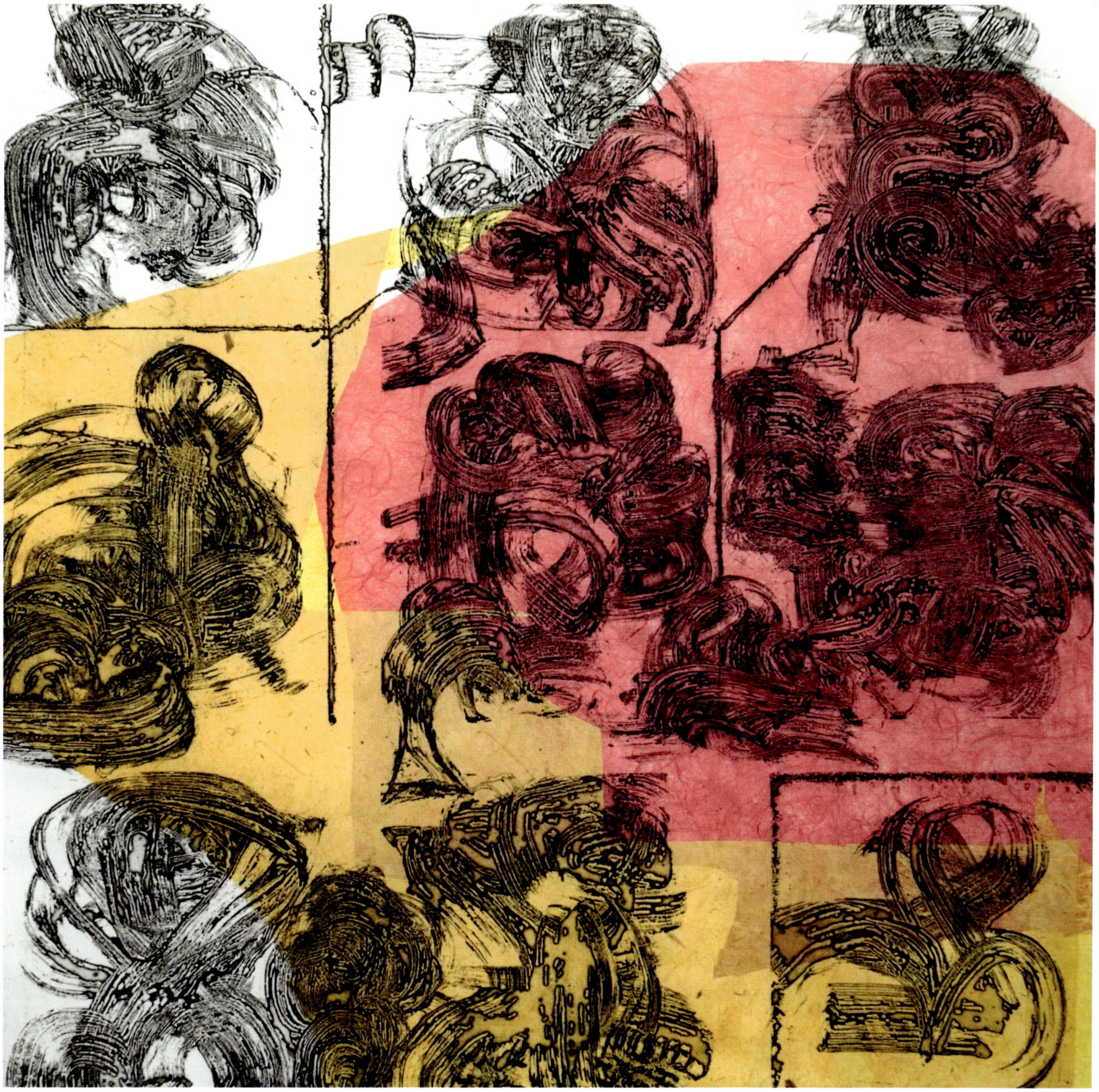

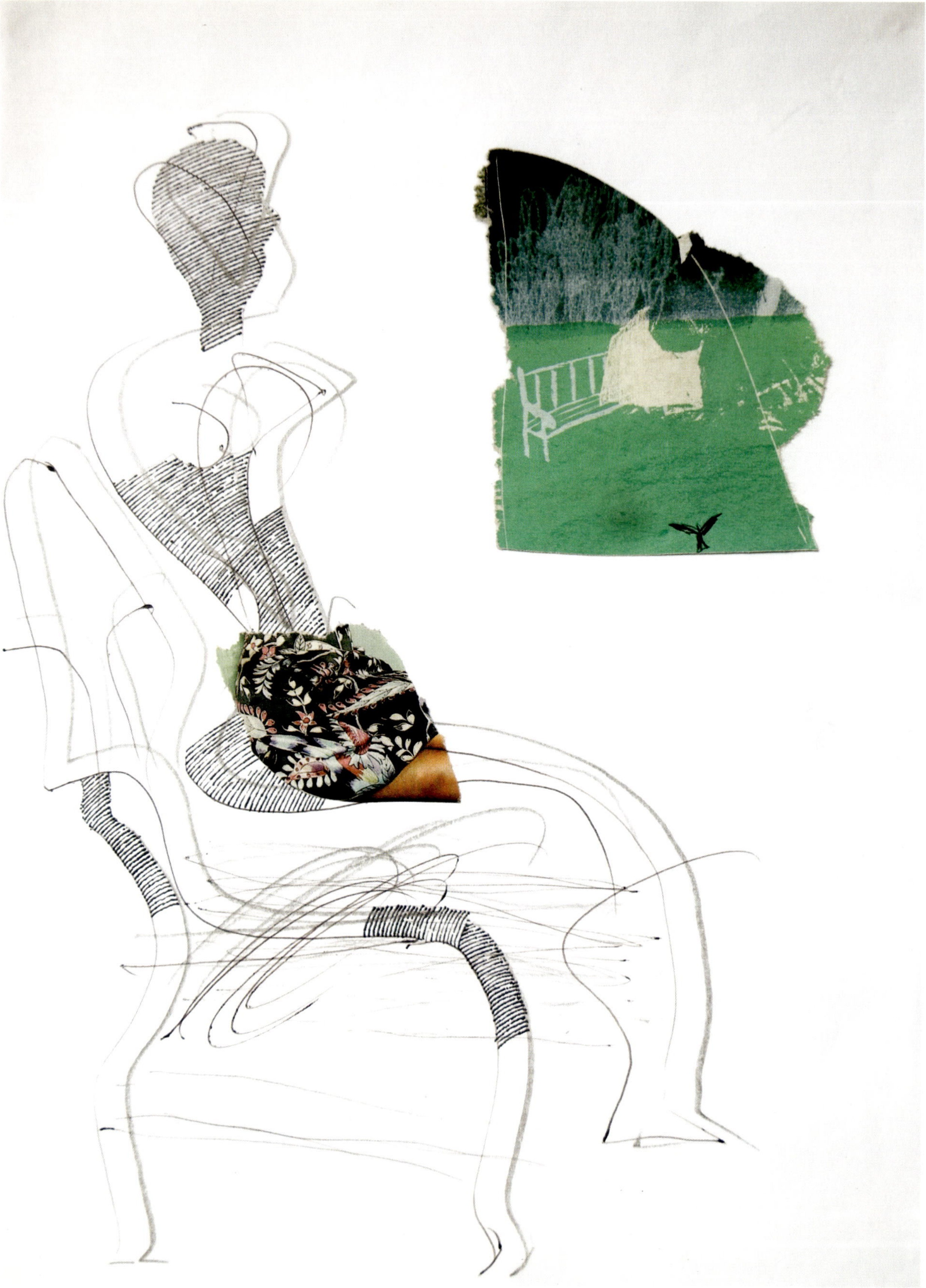

Left *Untitled*, 2007.
Pen and ink drawing and collage, 29.7 x 20.9 cm (11⅔ x 8⅕ in). Collection of the artist.
A lone figure, seated on a park bench, has been torn from the world it once inhabited; the place where it sat has been erased.

Right *Untitled*, 2006.
Etching: sugar lift, softground and aquatint, 14.5 x 10.3 cm (5¾ x 4 in). Collection of the artist.
When Bushara introduces colour to his work, it is often in the form of luminous, acidic primary colours that act as an extension of his theme of light and dark, attraction and repulsion.

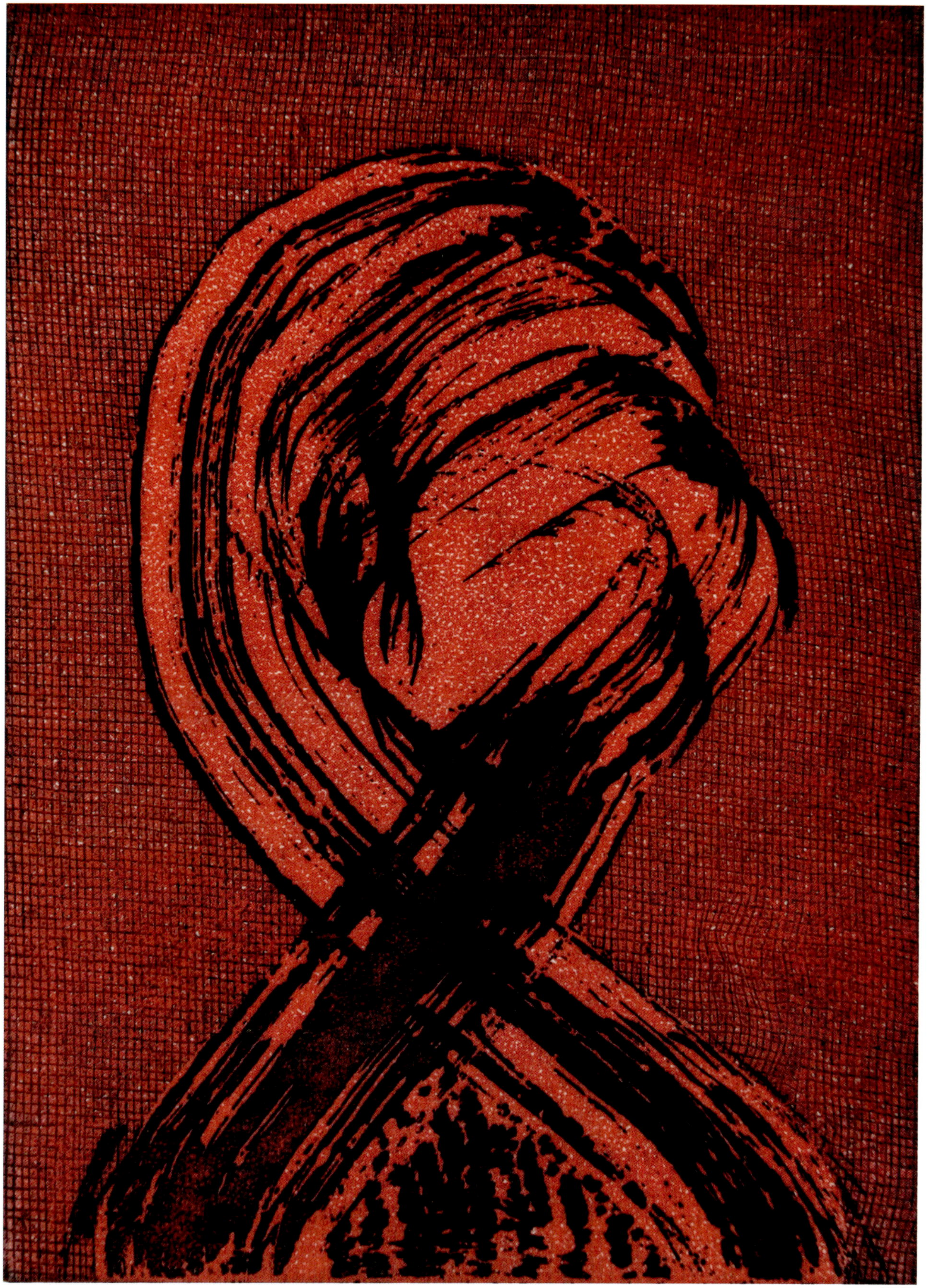

FLINTO CHANDIA
ZAMBIA

Below *Anvil*, 1995. Metal and wood, 140 x 95 cm (55 x $37\frac{2}{5}$ in). Private collection.
Created during the artist's residency at Gasworks Studios, London, this work illustrates Chandia's interest in combining different materials within the same form. The anvil, closely associated with masculinity and the 'cultural' world, is held within an organic wooden form representing the 'natural' and the feminine world.

Right *Elephant*, 1995. Stone, approximately 500 x 200 cm (197 x $78\frac{3}{4}$ in). BIAO Meridien bank, Lusaka.
The work was commissioned by the BIAO Meridien bank in Lusaka in 1991, and completed in 1995.

Flinto Chandia was born in Northe rn Province, Zambia, in 1953. Essentially self-taught, Chandia began his career as a graphic artist, getting a job with the Zambia Consumer Buying Corporation in 1976, where he learned the art of silk-screen printing, producing T-shirts and designing record sleeves for local bands. However, he began to concentrate more and more on sculpture, holding his first exhibition in Kitwe in 1978 and another the following year at the Mpapa Gallery in Lusaka.

In 1980, the British Council awarded Chandia a scholarship for a three-year City and Guilds diploma course in fine art. When he returned to Zambia from London in 1983 he began working full-time as a sculptor, exhibiting regularly. In 1991 he was commissioned by BIAO Meridien bank in Lusaka to make a series of sculptures, which culminated in one of his most important works, the life-size *Elephant*, completed in 1995. In 1993, while making this series of works, Chandia helped to organize the first Mbile Triangle Arts Trust artists' workshops in Zambia, which ran until 1998. During this time he also completed residencies at Gasworks Studios in London (1995) and at the Bag Factory in Johannesburg (1998).

Chandia has won a number of arts prizes and awards during his career, including the Zambia National Visual Arts Council best three-dimensional artist award in 1996 and the Ngoma award in 1998.

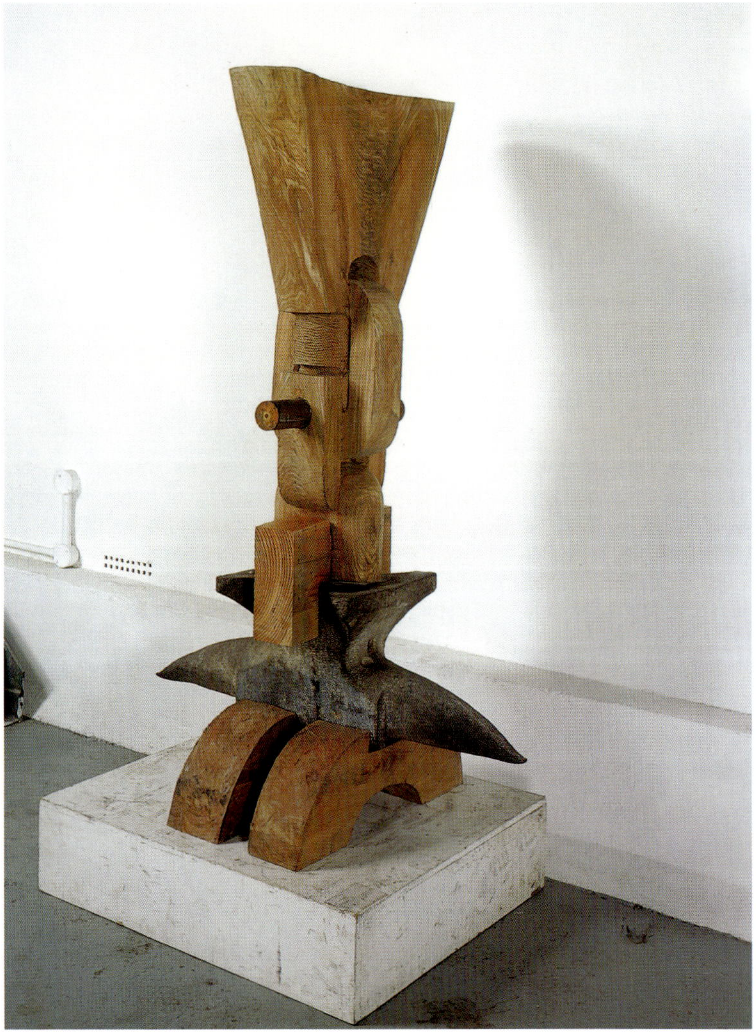

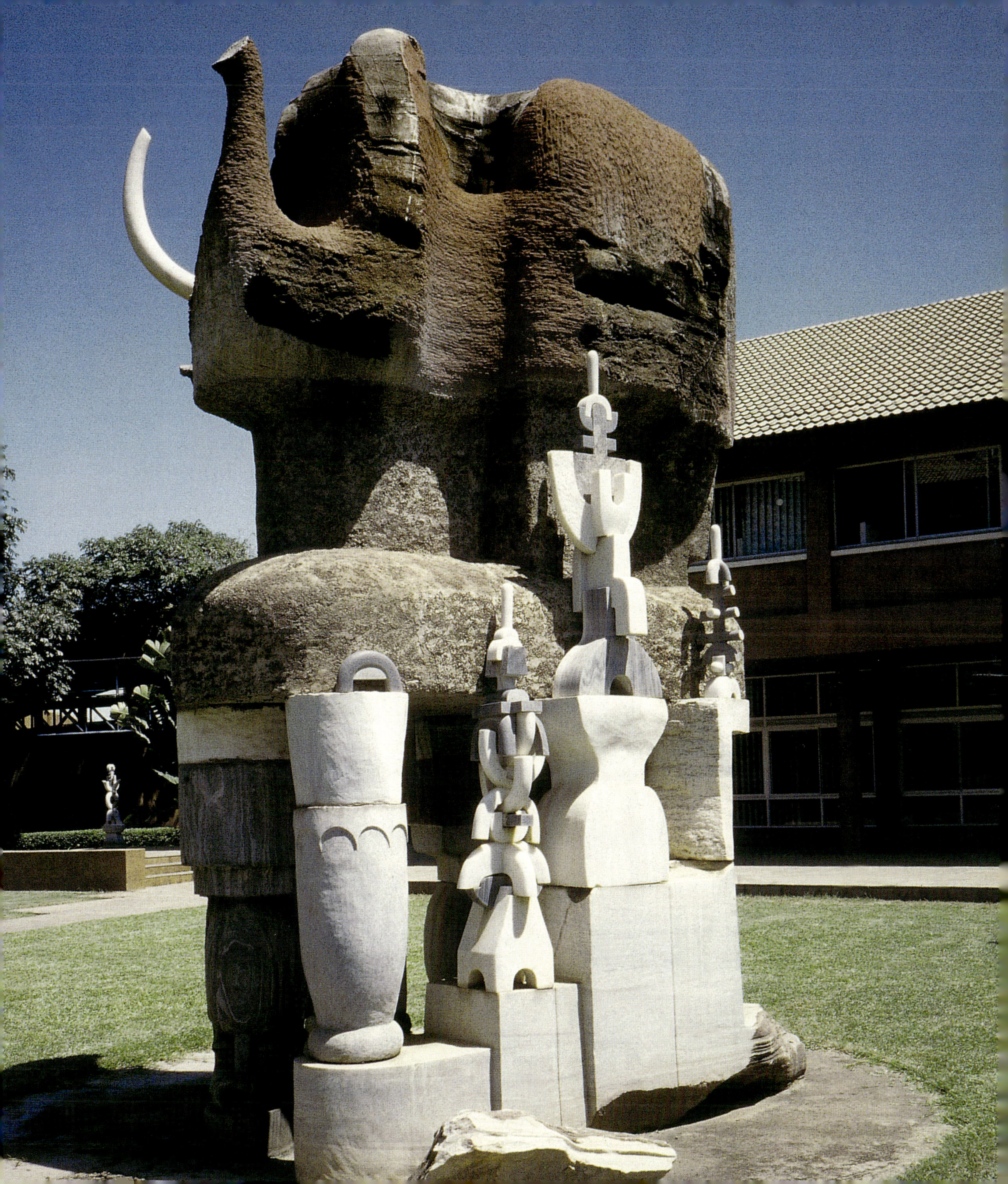

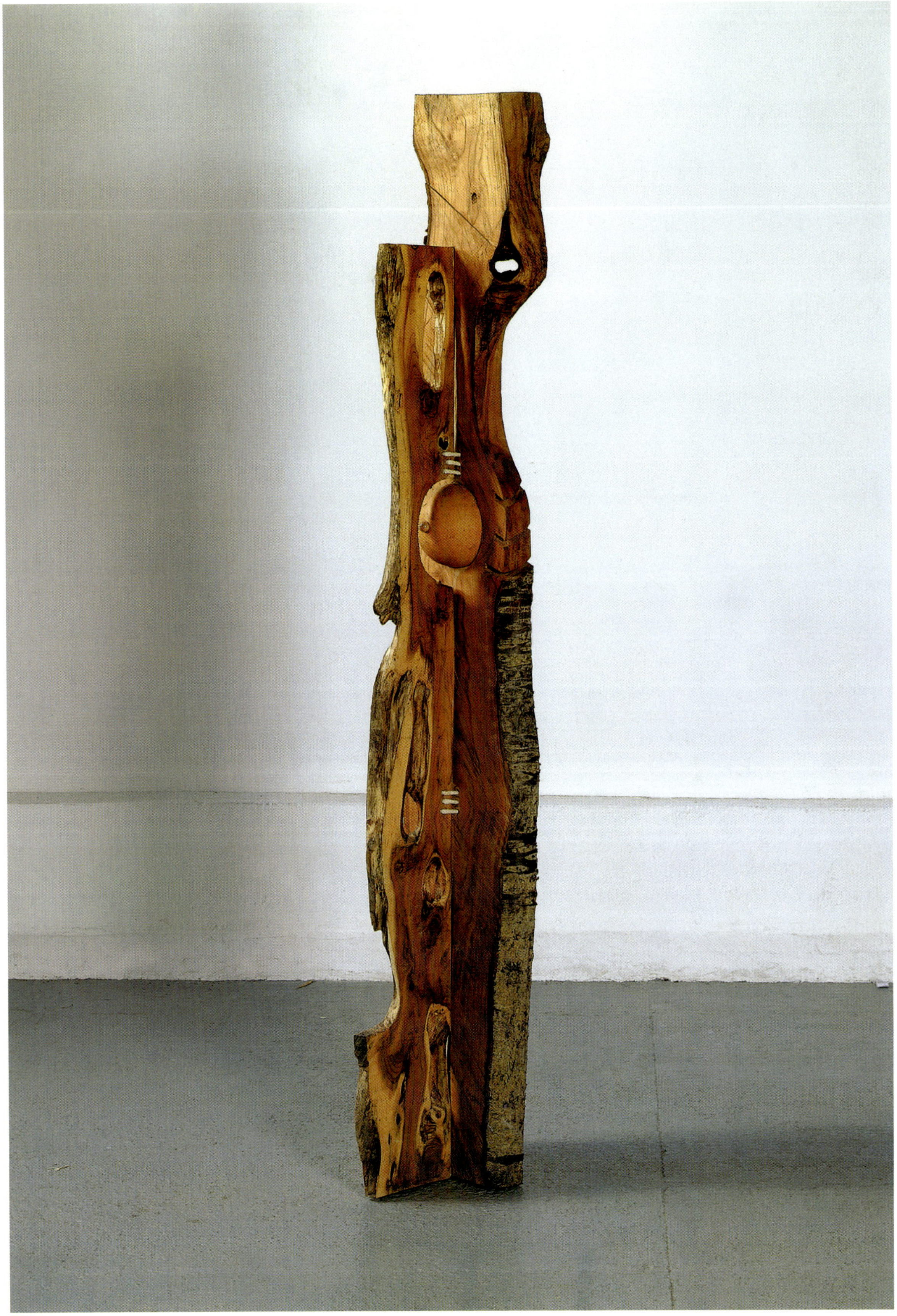

Left *Namumbi,* 1995. Wood and gourd, 190 x 30 x 30 cm (74 x 11½ x 11½ in). Private collection. Namumbi is a town in Senanga province, Western Zambia.

Right *Mumbi Lullaby,* 1995. Wood and gourd, 190 x 76 cm (74⅘ x 30 in). Private collection. This work is partly inspired by the *kalumbu,* a single-stringed Zambian chordophone with gourd resonator. One of the occasions on which it was played was when young men wanted to show off their readiness to marry.

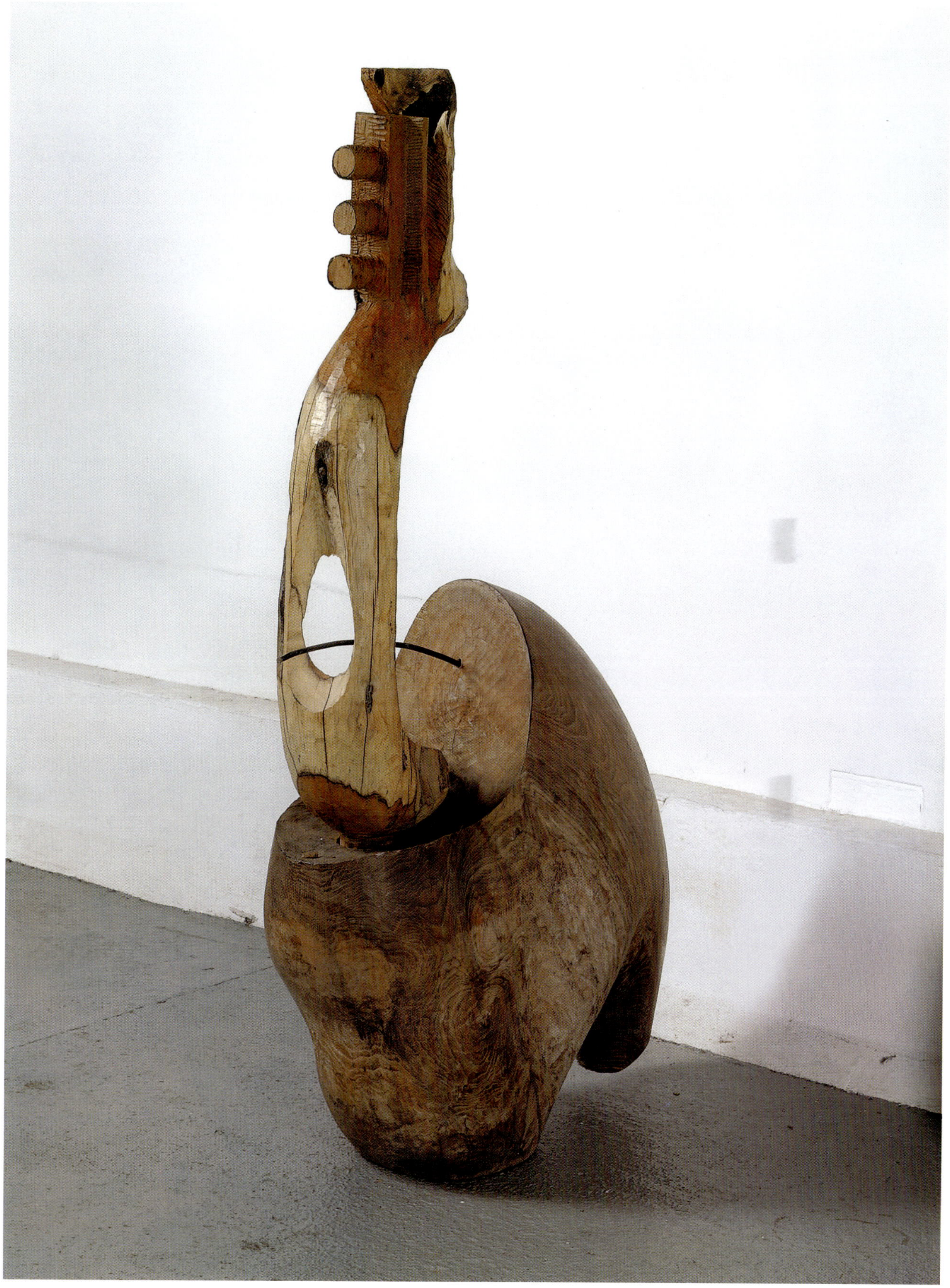

MOHAMEDI CHARINDA
TANZANIA

Below *Easy System to Cultivate with Irrigation*, 2007. Enamel oil paint on canvas, 60.9 x 121.9 cm (24 x 48 in). Collection of the artist.
This scene depicts the irrigating and growing of maize and watermelons with the help of a sprinkler system created from discarded plastic bottles.

Right *Drawing Water, Drinking Beer*, 2002 (detail). Enamel oil paint on canvas, 74 x 110 cm (29 x 43⅓ in). British Museum, London.
Two women stand beneath a sheltering cashew tree, distributing water from a standpipe. The cashew is a powerful symbol of wealth and fertility in eastern Africa.

Mohamedi Charinda was born in 1947 in Nakapanya village in the Tunduru district of the Ruvuma region in southern Tanzania. He attended school, followed by military service before moving to Dar es Salaam in 1972, where he worked for two years as a car mechanic. He became an apprentice to the artist Hashim Mruta in 1975, a first-generation painter of the Tingatinga Cooperative Society based at the Morogoro Stores in Oyster Bay, Dar es Salaam.

Working within the accepted collective conventions of the Tingatinga Cooperative (see introduction to this book), Charinda developed his own distinctive style of painting, as well as making technical innovations such as being the first artist to paint on canvas as opposed to the masonite board that the group's founder Edward Saidi Tingatinga and his fellow artists traditionally used. Charinda also developed a distinctive subject matter for his paintings, creating minutely observed narratives of rural life in Tanzania, often with an educational content, as well as portraying significant moments in the history of Tanzania.

Charinda has exhibited his work widely in Tanzania and has also had exhibitions in Europe; one of his works currently hangs in the Sainsbury African Galleries at the British Museum.

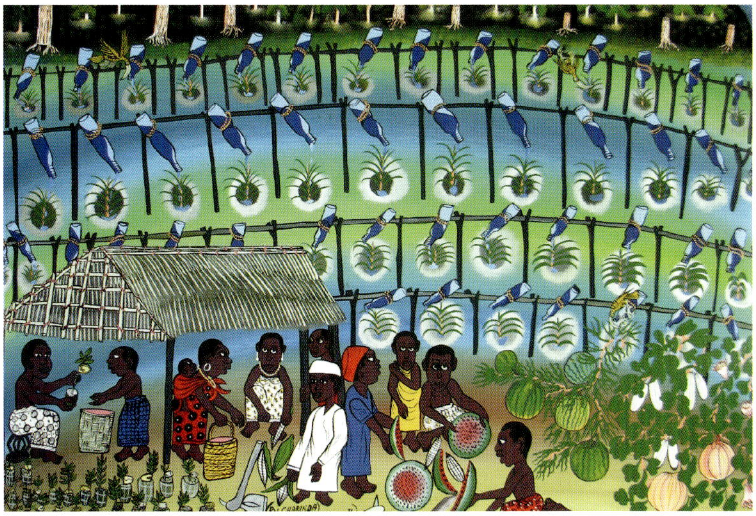

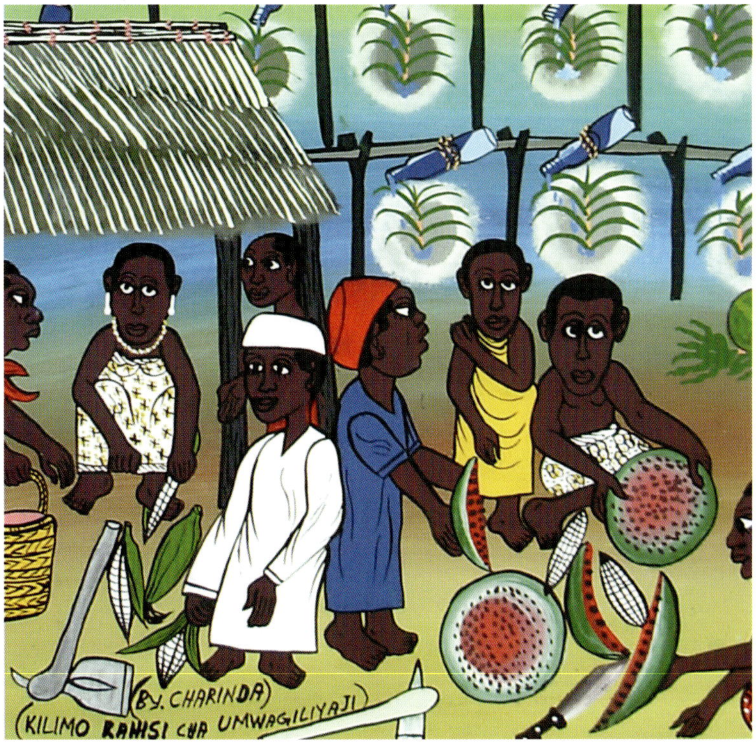

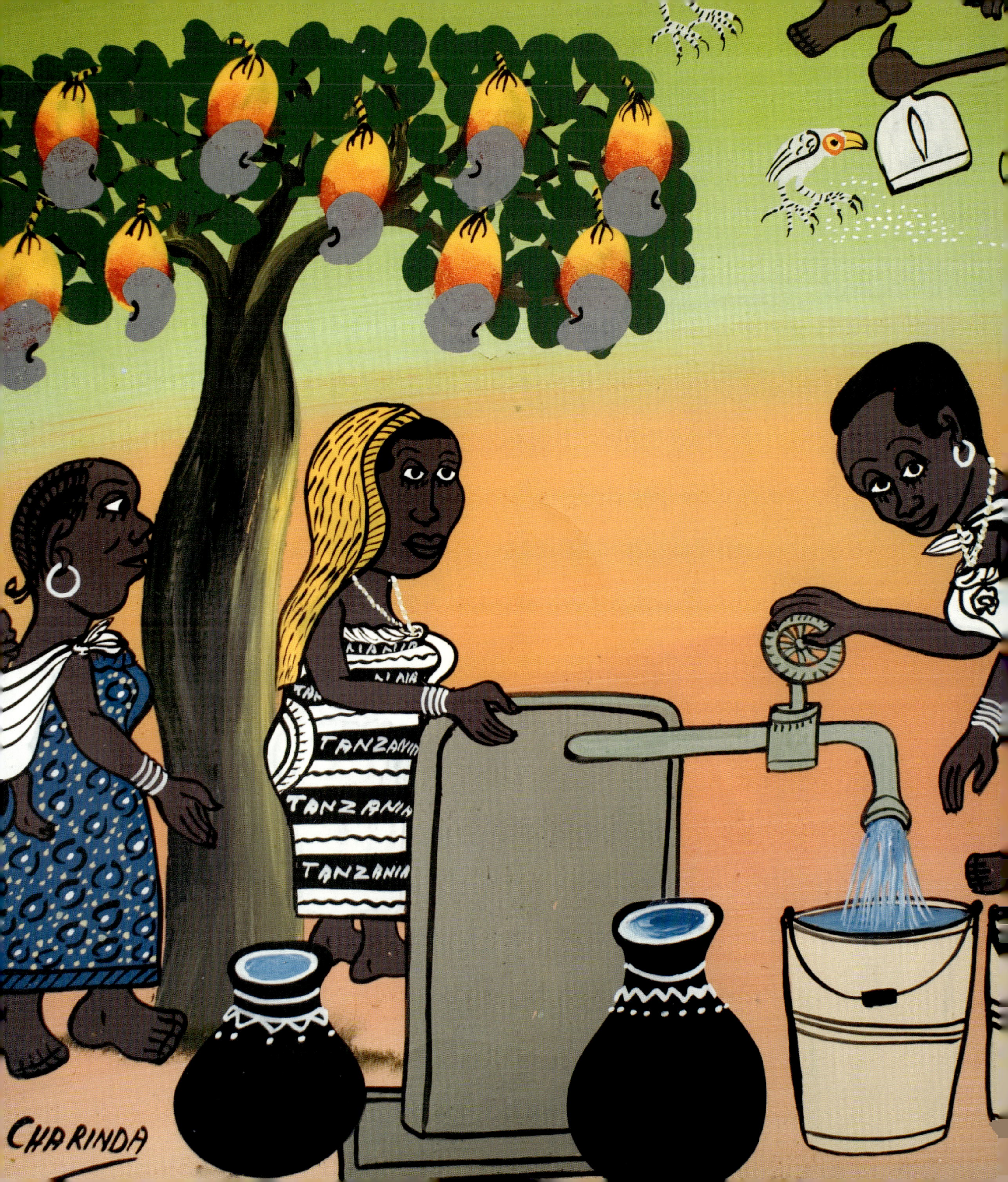
TANZANIA
TANZANIA
TANZANIA
CHARINDA

Right *Drawing Water, Drinking Beer*, 2002 (full image).
A rural village scene in Tanzania, with women collecting water from a standpipe, washing and drying *kangas*, and with men drinking beer with the head of the local community. The slogan on one of the drying *kangas* is 'JEMBENI – MALI', which translates literally as 'in a hoe – [there is] money'; this exhortation to work hard in order to prosper is the message of the whole painting, which is full of images of fertility and wellbeing.

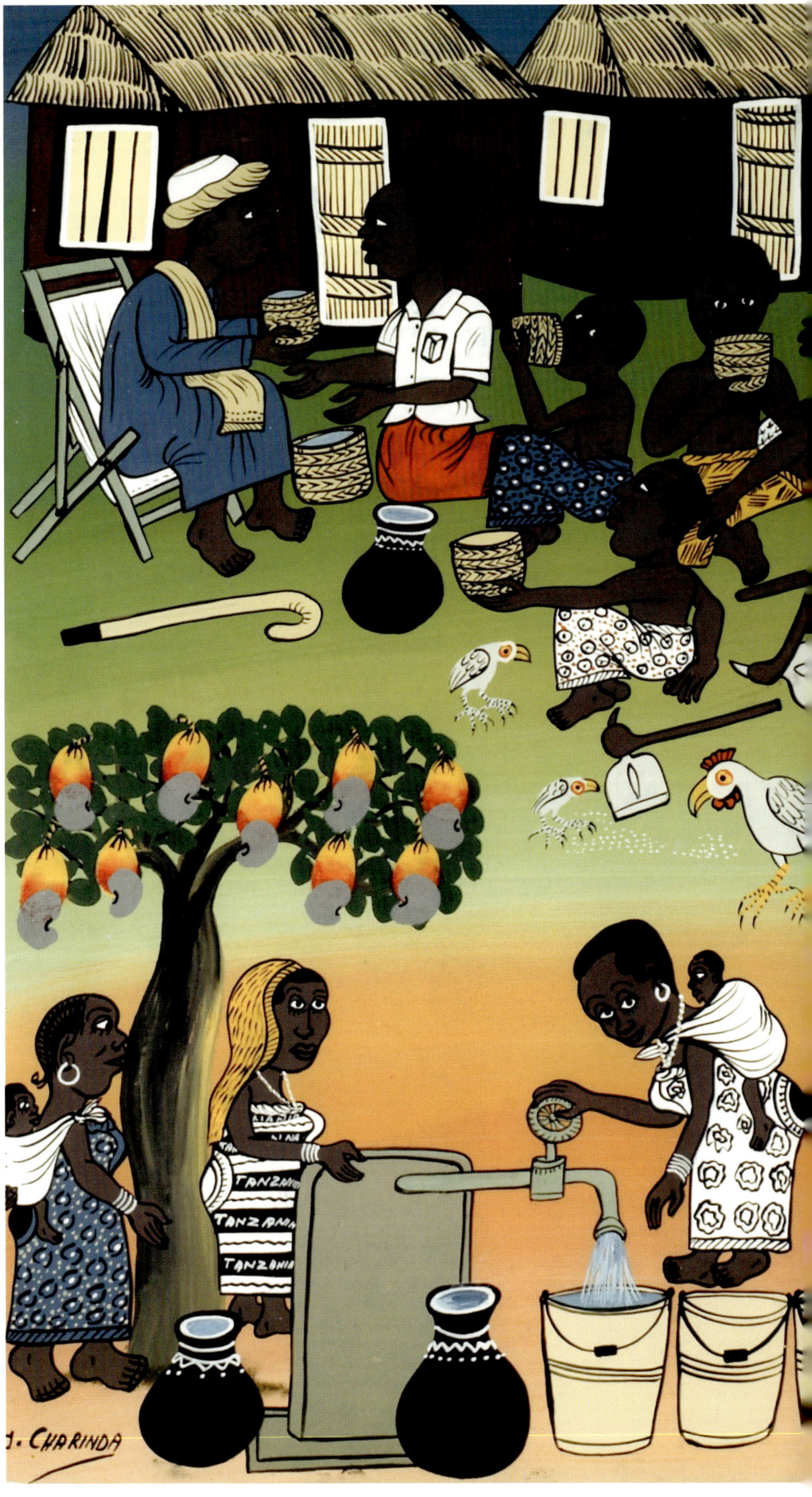

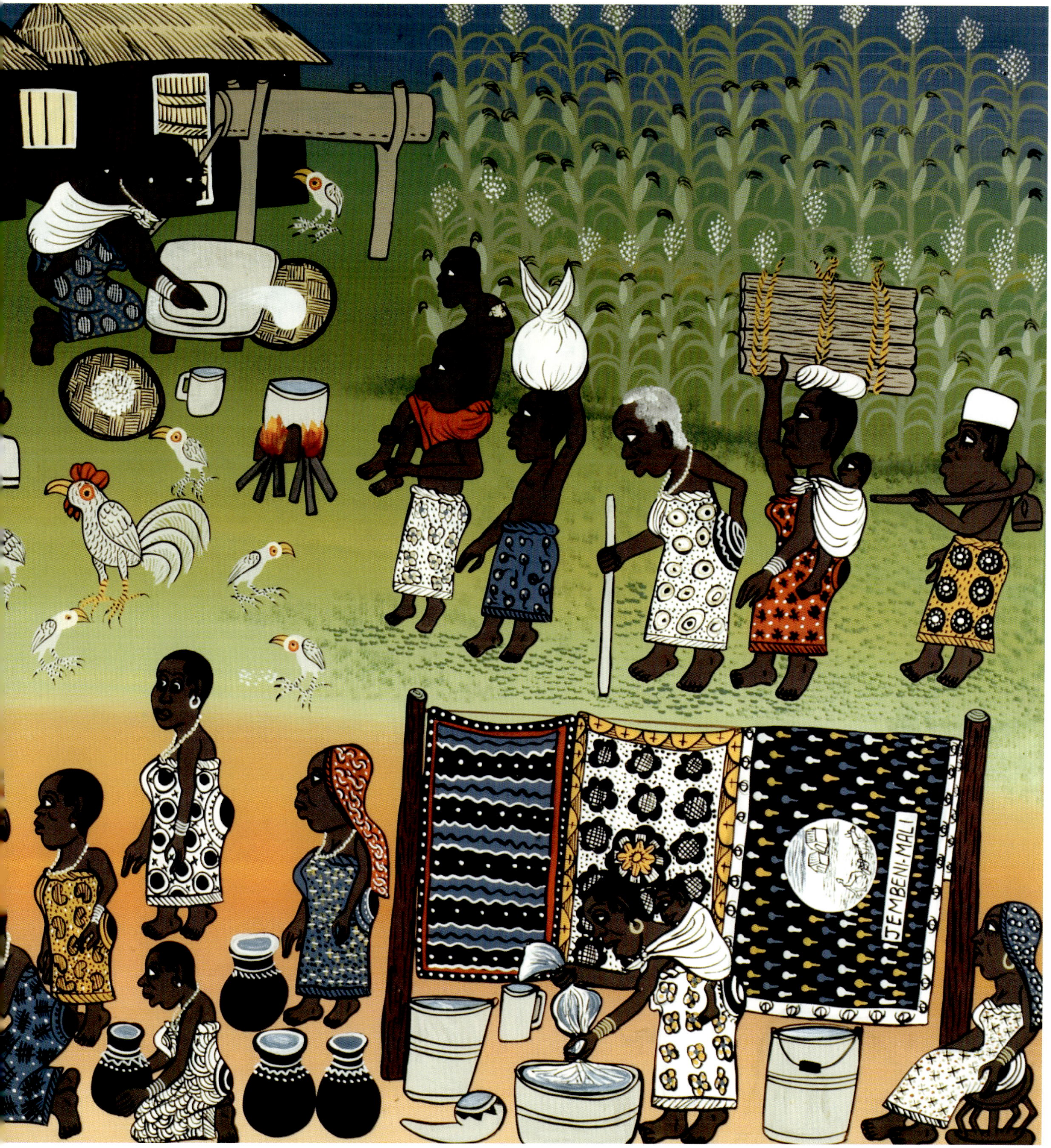
JEMBENI-MALI

JORGE DIAS
MOZAMBIQUE

This spread *Old Works in New Projects*, 1994–2007. Acrylic and collage on paper, dimensions variable. Alvaro Henrriques, Maputo. Dias has painted bold, calligraphic images on to heavy-gauge watercolour paper and other surfaces, then cut them out and reassembled them. He sometimes adds his trademark wire creatures, which are made in Maputo and sold in numerous venues around the town, including the shop at the National Museum of Art, where Dias is Curator.

Jorge Dias was born in Maputo, Mozambique, in 1972. He studied ceramics at the National School of Visual Arts in Maputo. In 2002 he achieved a Licentiate in Sculpture at the School of Fine Arts of the Federal University of Rio de Janeiro, Brazil. He is currently Curator of the National Museum of Art in Maputo.

Dias works in a variety of media, including sculpture, painting, photography, video and installation. He works with images from popular culture and the natural world, giving a spiritual dimension to everyday materials and situations. Together with Pompílio Hilário (Gemuce), he is one of the founders of MUVART, the Movement for Contemporary Art in Mozambique. He has curated a number of important exhibitions, including the Mozambique representation at Arco 2006 in Madrid and the 'Expo Arte contemporanea Mozambique-MUVART's Biennial' in Maputo in 2004 and 2006.

Dias has had a number of solo exhibitions, including 'Systems and Connections' at the Galeria Campus Avançado in Niterói, Brazil (2002), 'Zoologia dos tropicos' ('Zoology of the Tropics') at the Lago cultural centre in Portugal (2005) and has participated in group shows in Mozambique, Brazil, Portugal, Italy and Angola.

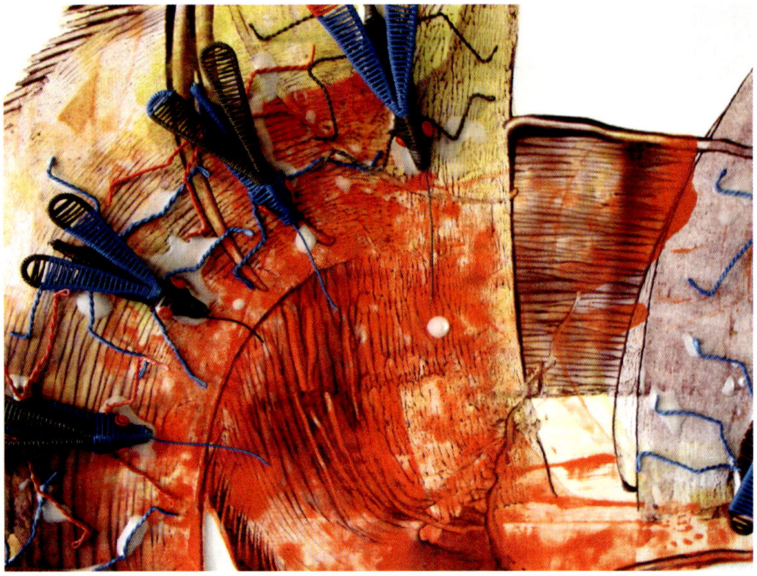

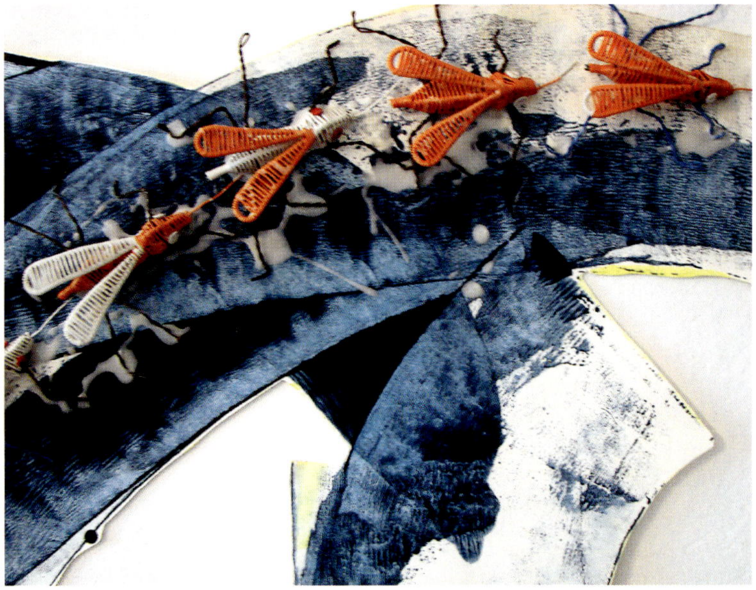

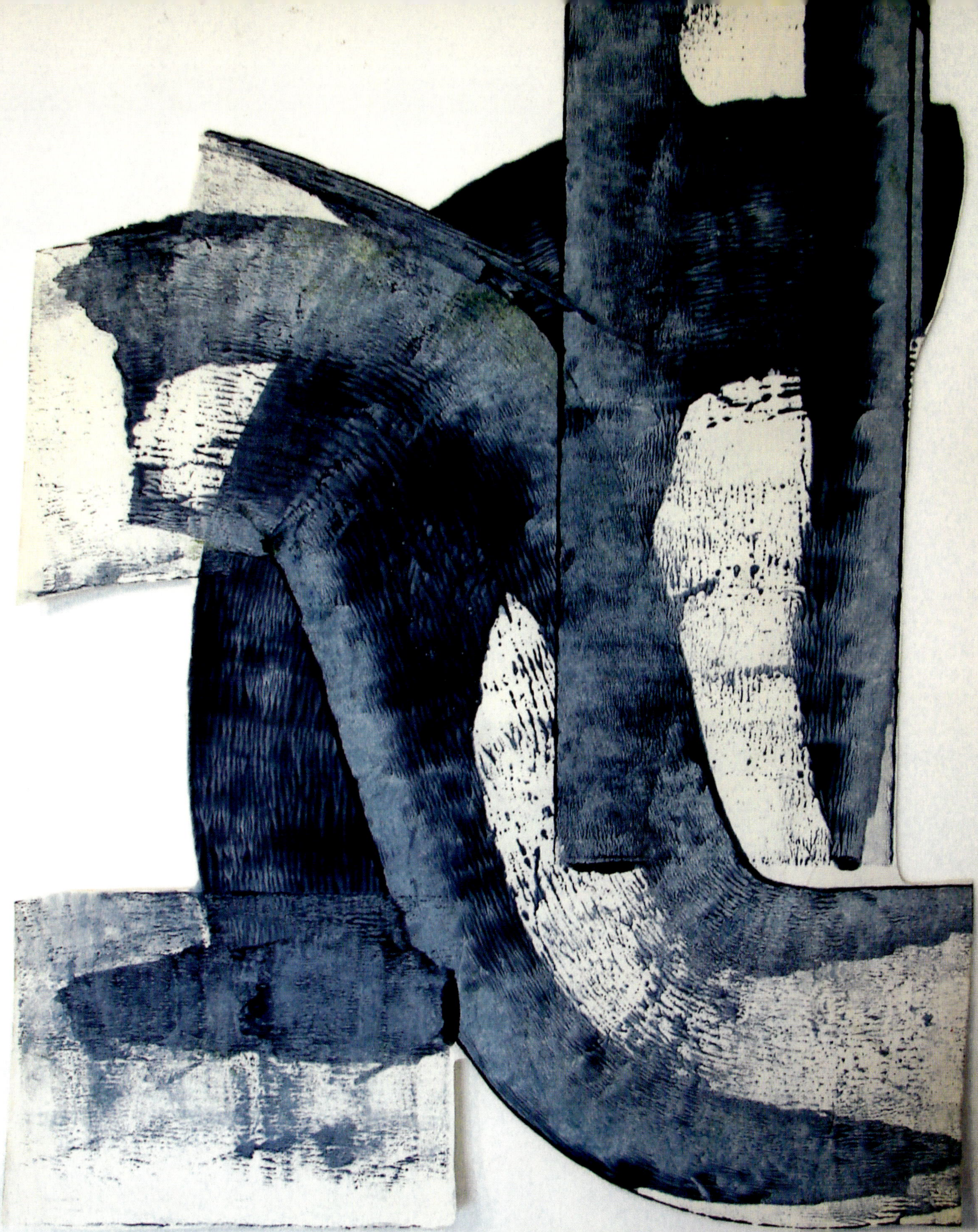

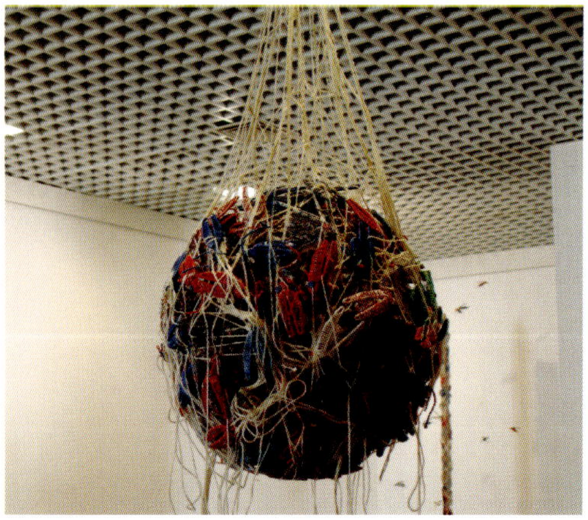

Left *Coisas Suspendidas (Suspended Things)*, 2005. Ceramic, wire insects, silicone and thread, 120 x 29 x 29 cm (47½ x 11⅖ x 11⅖ in). Mazambique-French Cultural Centre, Maputo.
Suspended in a net, as if it has been dragged up from the depths of the sea, is a ball of matter that has attracted more of Dias's wire creatures, which appear to be feasting on it.

Below *Spiritual Platform*, 2005. Ceramic, wire insects, shallow baskets and woodcraft, dimensions variable. Collection of the artist.
Large balls of ceramic and wood fragments stand on and around two platforms in the centre of the room, which are themselves covered in fragments. It is as if, rather like giant snowballs, they have gathered the fragments as they have moved across the surfaces of the platforms.

Right *Habitação ao Zero (Habitation to the Zero)*, 2005 (detail). Wire insects, shallow basket and painting, 80 x 180 x 12 cm (31½ x 71 x 4¾ in). Collection of the artist.
One of two large, shallow plaited baskets of the type used for winnowing grain. On the base of each basket Dias has attached numerous wire insects and lizards, which are converging on the central, circular image of a piece of bread in the form of a road sign. The sign, with its red line through the image of the bread, suggests that it is forbidden to eat.

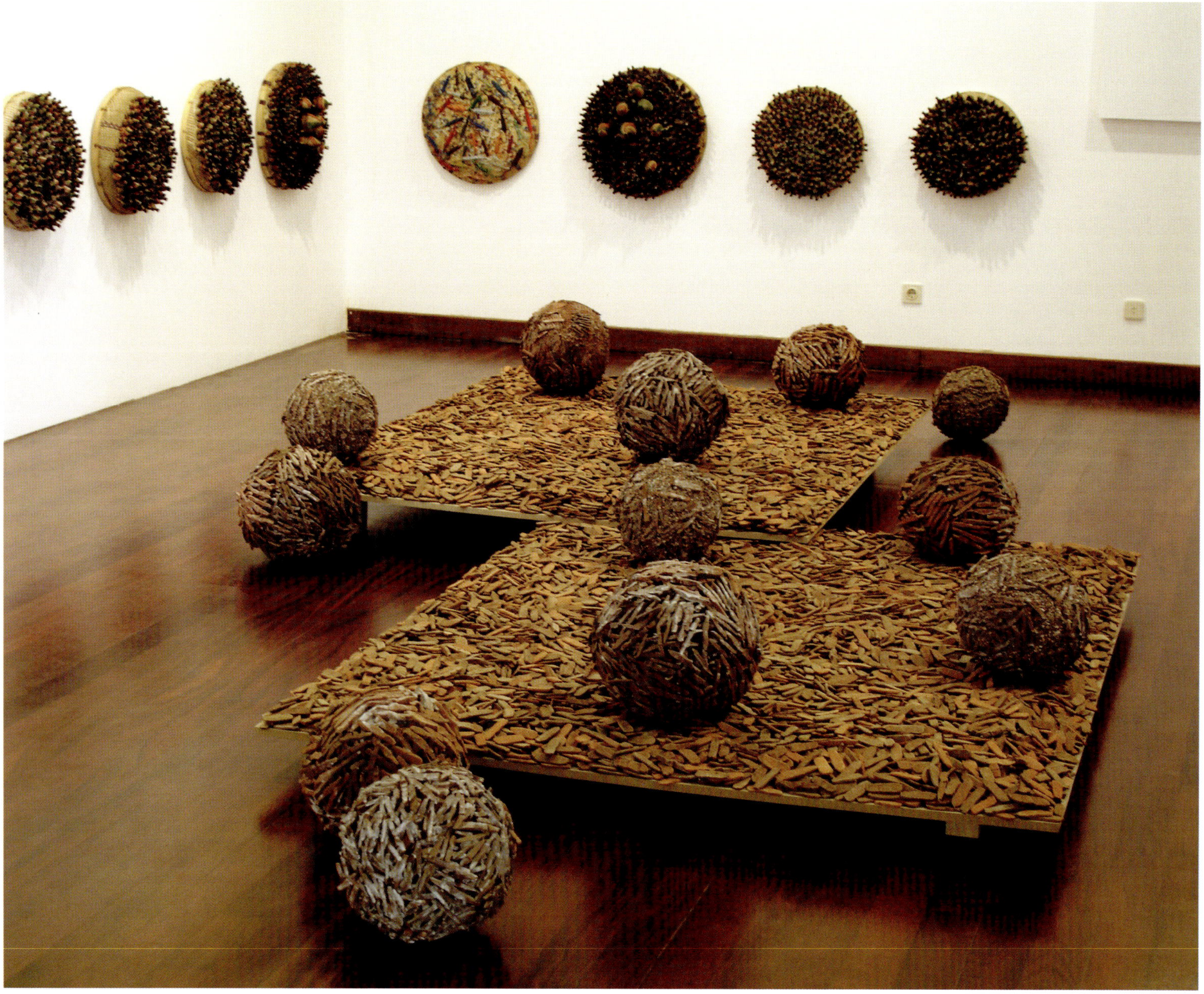

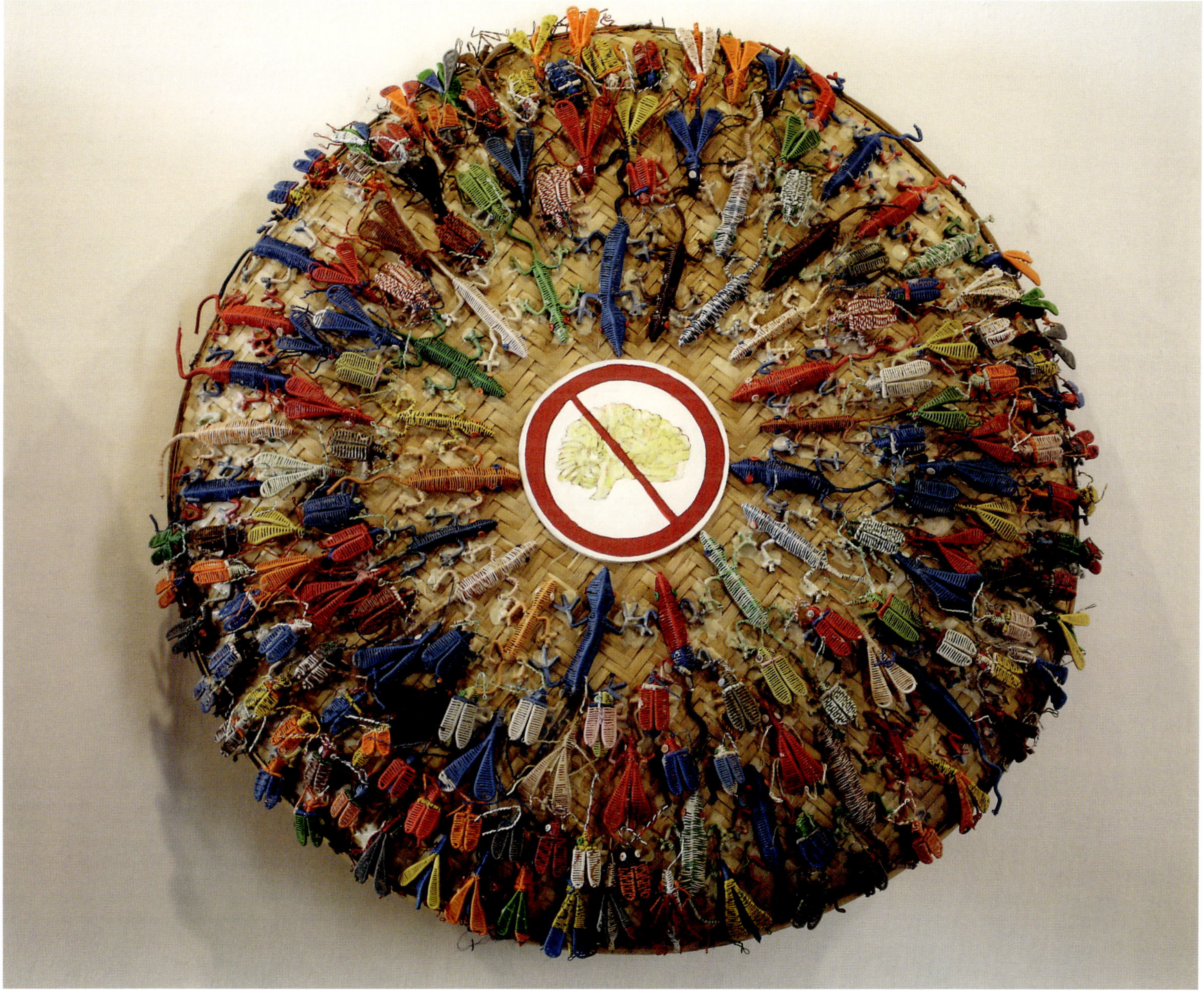

DILOMPRIZULIKE 'THE JUNKMAN FROM AFRIKA'
NIGERIA

This Spread *The Face of the City*, 2005. Junk, 182.8 x 365.7 x 121.9 cm (72 x 144 x 48 in). Collection of the artist.

'These firewood-like characters of a city – the African city, are made to retain their beings as used, abused but not in the least abandoned; for the big man needs them when the time comes to rig the elections. Then he shares tinned tomatoes and salt, and in return they do "things" that retain his "shit of power".'

Dilomprizulike ('The Junkman from Afrika') lives with his family in the Junkyard, an isolated compound on the fringe of Alpha Beach, Lagos. He has ambitious plans for the space:

> *It's a place where I want to build five small beautiful huts that are self-contained, for mostly local artists on residency programmes. Anything creative that you want to do and is not possible for you to do effectively in that madness outside, here is a place you can run into to do that. There should be a space like the Junkyard where authenticity, the true nature, the nakedness of what you call the creative instinct can manifest itself.*

Born in 1960 in Enugu, Nigeria, Dilomprizulike studied fine art at the University of Nigeria and at the University of Dundee, Scotland. He has exhibited widely in Africa and in Europe, where he has been artist in residence at a number of institutions including the Victoria and Albert Museum, London, the Scottish Sculpture Workshop, Lumsden and the Heinrich-Böll-Stiftung, Bonn.

Dilomprizulike is preoccupied with the explosive growth of African cities in the post-colonial period, scouring his home town of Lagos for 'junk', which he resurrects into startling tableaux of this urban landscape. He is acutely aware of the rampant consumerism, environmental degeneration, religious fundamentalism and moral decline that have led to 'the alienated situation of the African in his own society'.

He sees his studio as a kind of artistic hospital in which he, as a skilful and humorous surgeon, 'looks at these outcasts, bruised and battered from the battle, with abandon – and their innocent, bleeding wounds evoke compassion in me as I pick them, bathe them, give them a roof, nurse their wounds – rear them with the emotional touch of a mother.'

Born Dil Humphrey-Umezulike, Dilomprizulike's name, a little like his sculptures, is an assemblage:

> *It has an entity. It's very representational. It's an icon. An icon is defined as the significance or the meaning of a thing. And it's not a nickname. And you can't say it's a fake name; neither would you say it's a real name. It just stands out. It's a name that you see and you will never forget. Just like when you see me, you can never forget me.*

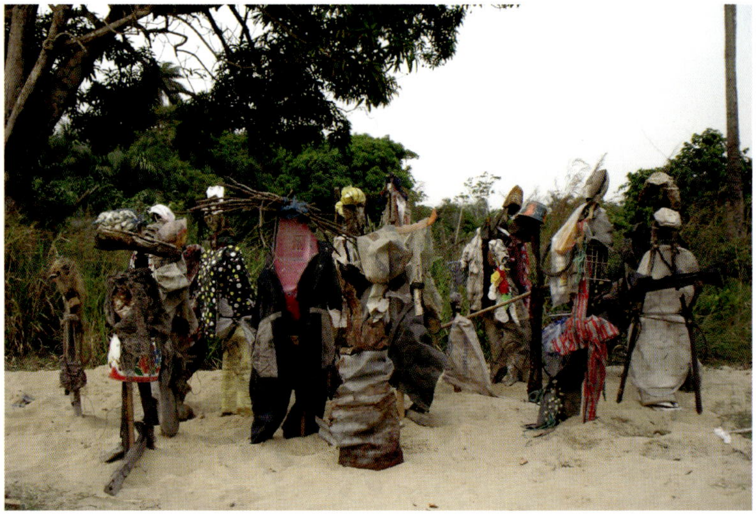

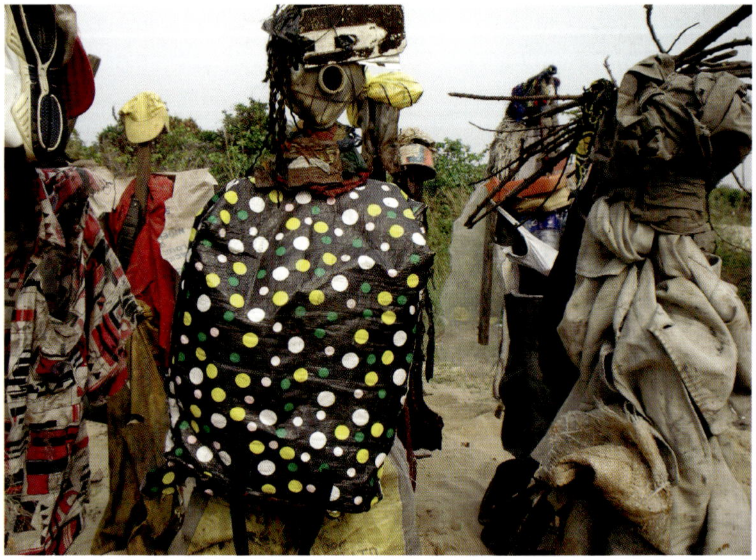

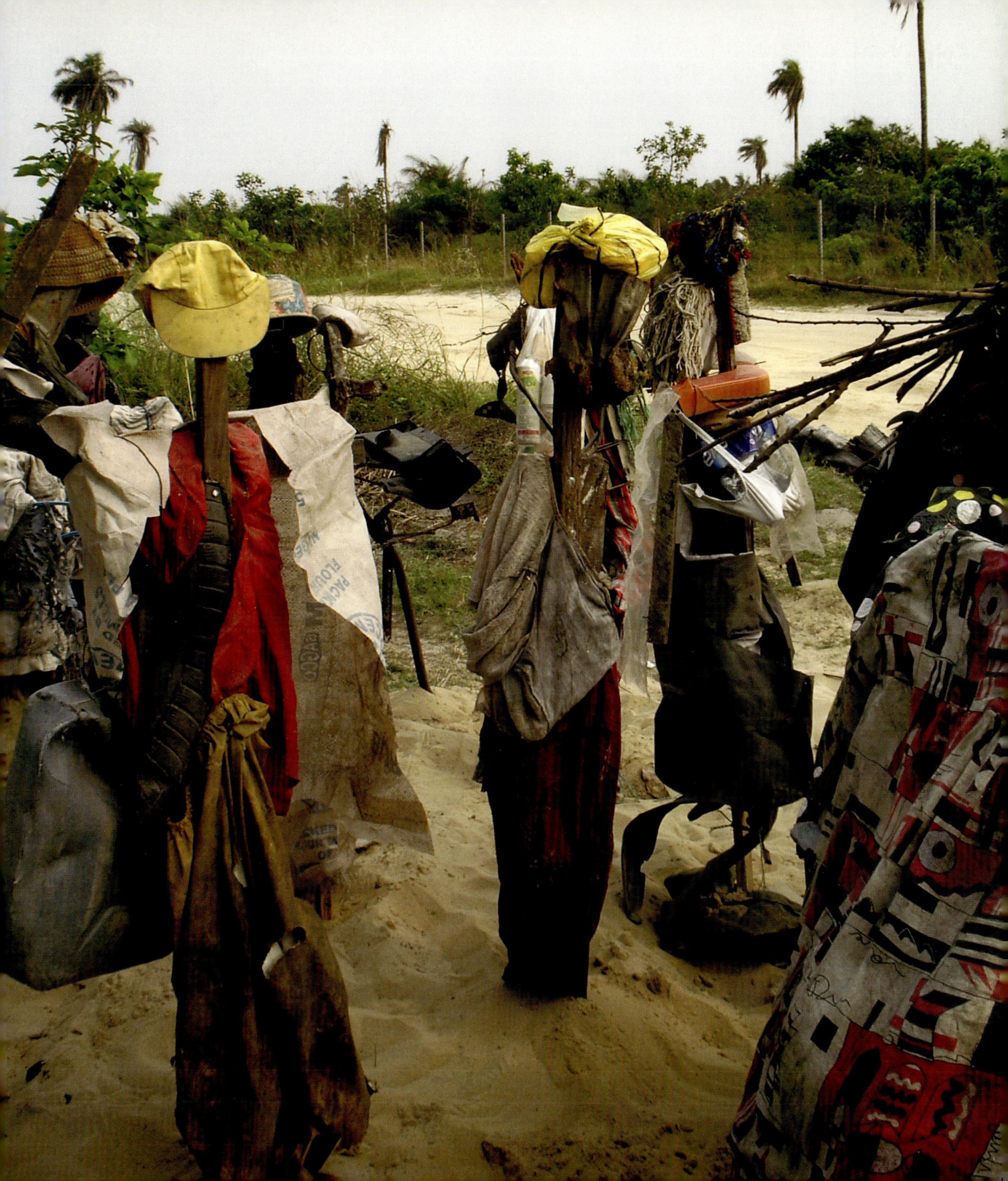

‘Junk keeps following me like a pilot fish, because I won’t let it rest. And toying with junk has taught me that reality lies within the property of the madman; and not in this “Plastic world” of the world.’
Dilomprizulike

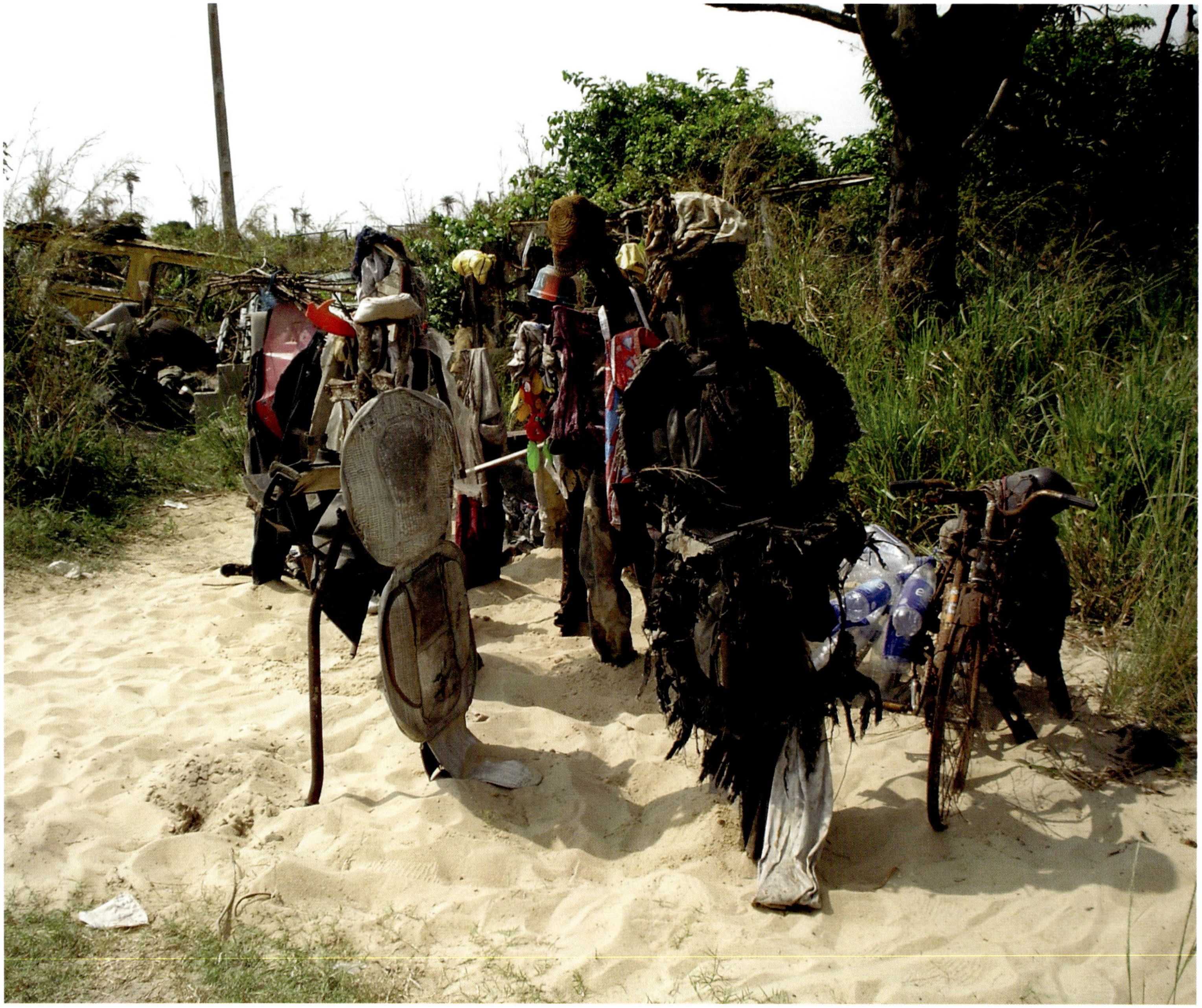

This spread *The Face of the City*, 2005.

'Vultures in the street, Saints in the church; these wet-wooded-fire-fanning-firewood-like creatures indulge dust at dusk and ashes at dawn. And still entangled in a web of their eventual complexities, they hurry to retain their space in a queue which neither moves nor scatters; returning a scratch of the back to them who scratched their backs while maiming and eliminating them who "stand in their way".'

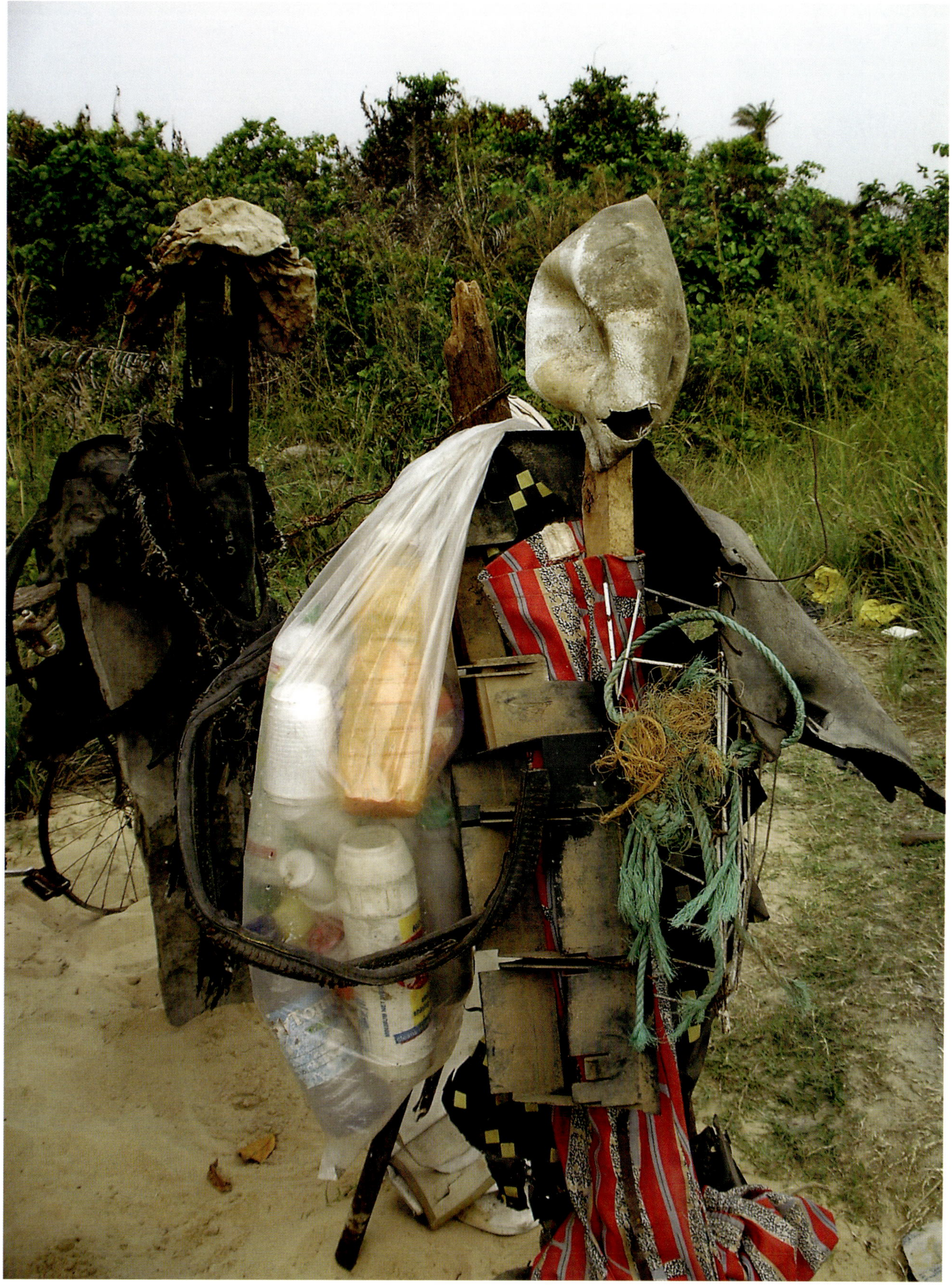

Below *Journey Out of Africa*, 2005. Junk, 182.8 x 365.7 x 121.9 cm (72 x 144 x 48 in). Collection of the artist.
A journey in a junked automobile that is going nowhere, but is itself crammed with the junk that takes the artist on his journey – complete with a triangular warning sign on the rear bumper: 'CAUTION slow down speed'.

Right *Waiting for the Bus*, 2003. Junk, approximate height 182.8 cm (72 in). Collection of the artist.
'We have henceforth resolved to wait for the bus which will take us to the promised land, since we have aided and abetted the burning down of our house. All roads lead to the BUS STOP. The traffic light has already turned to grin. Do not forget to gather your loins…'

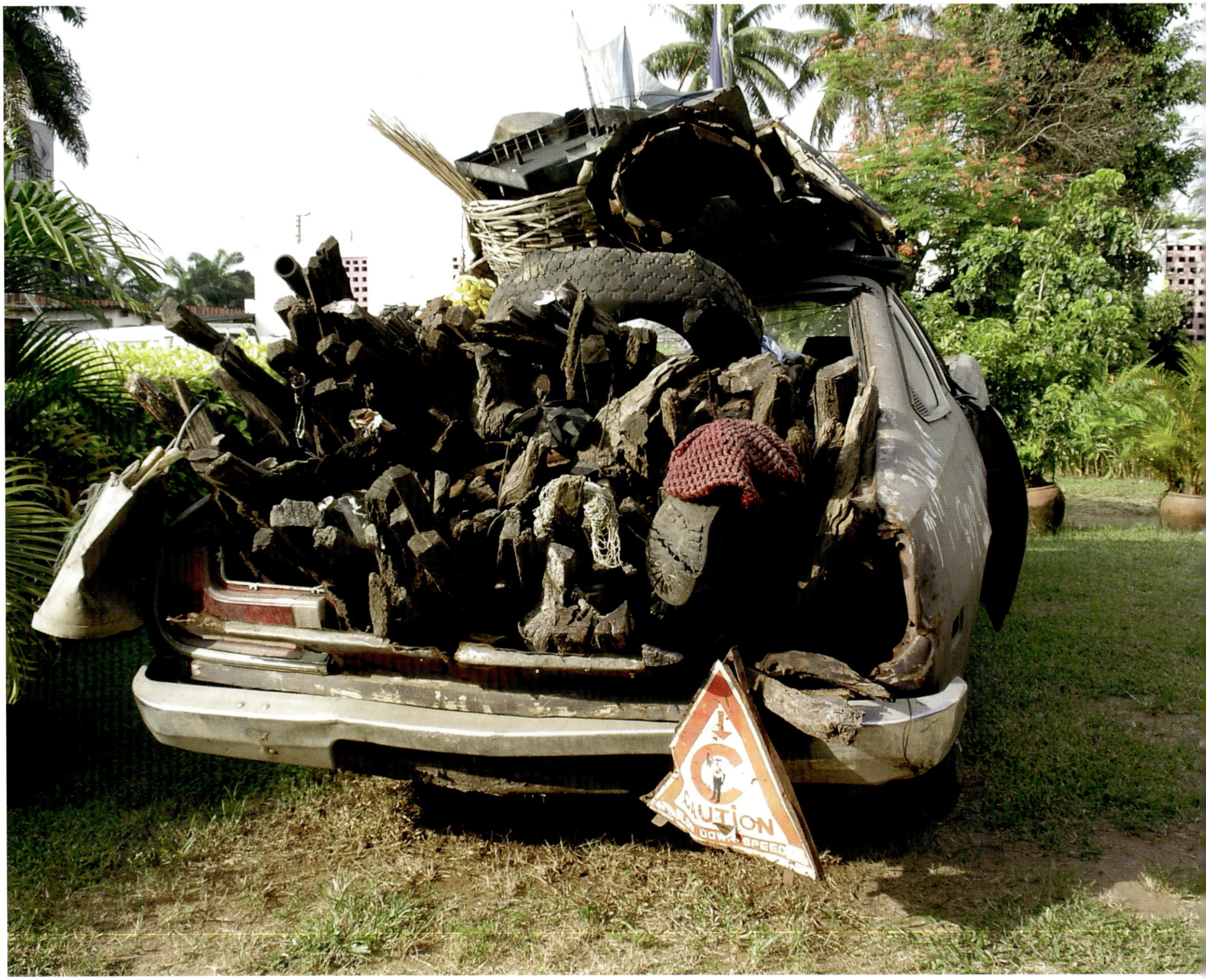

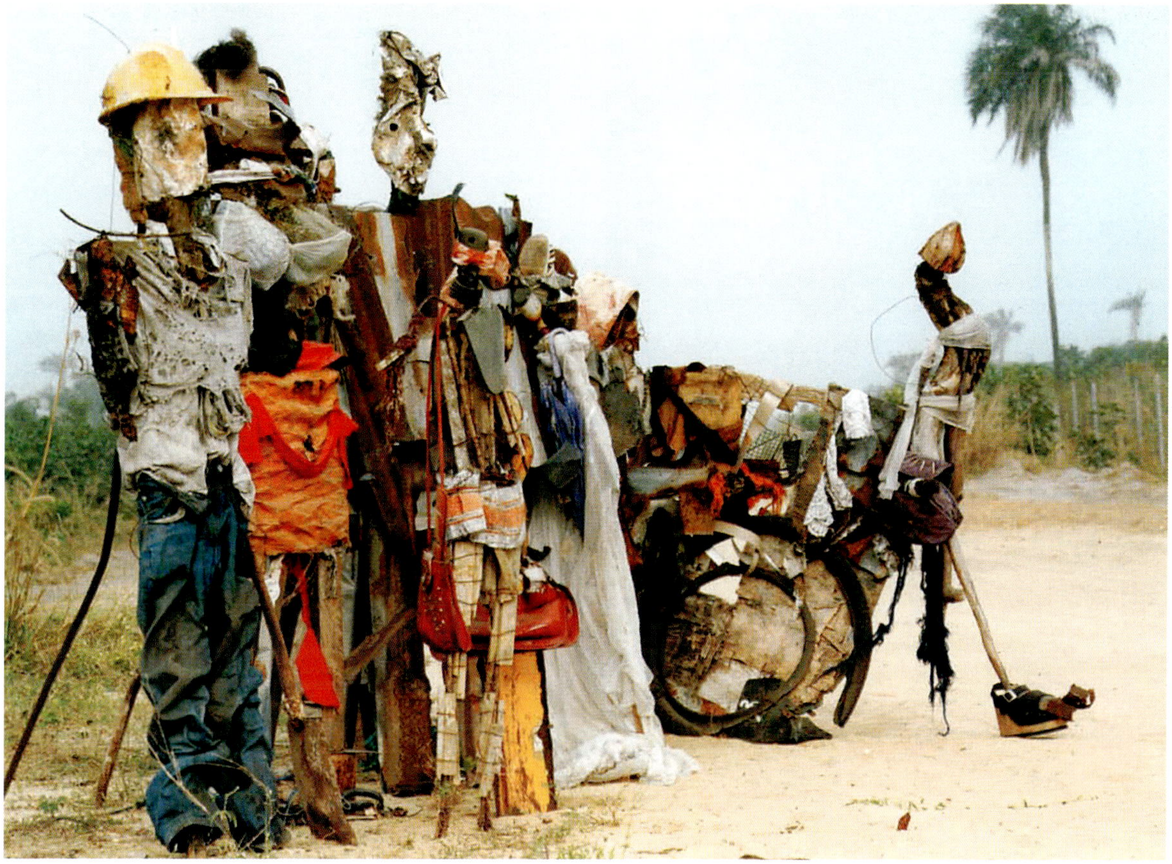

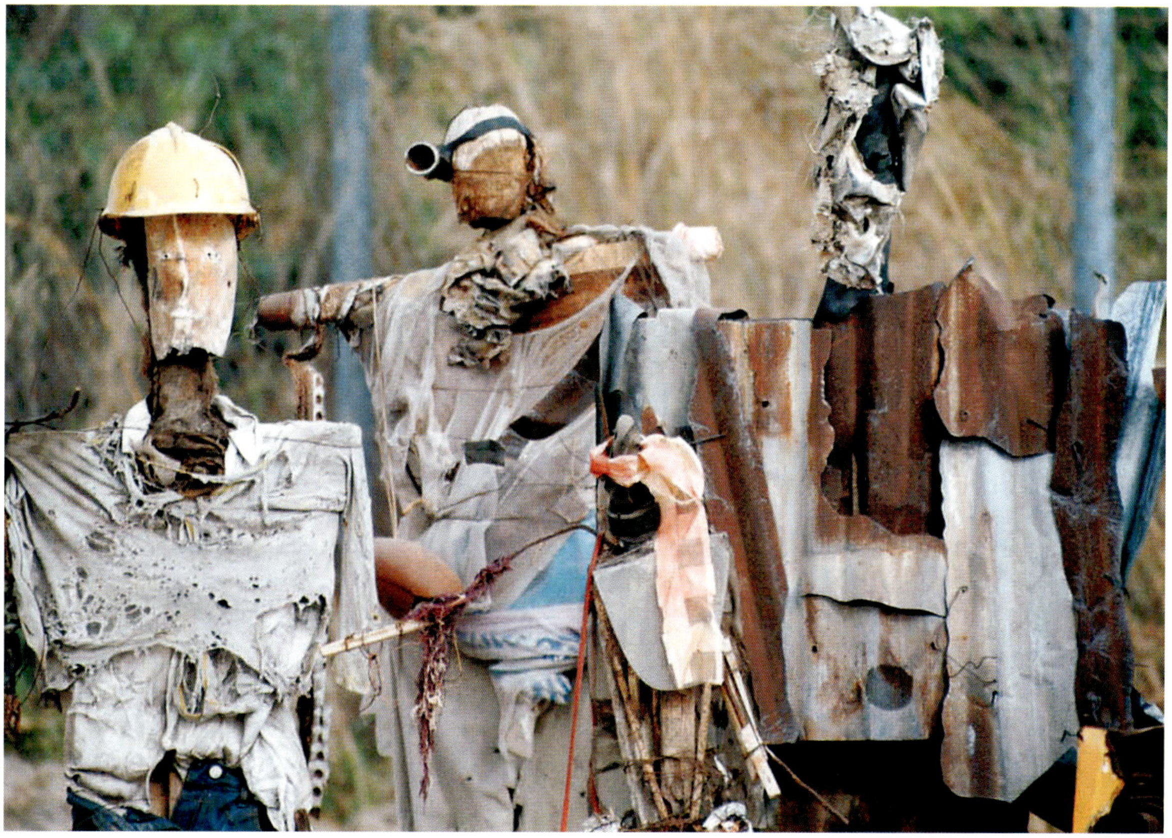

SOKARI DOUGLAS CAMP
NIGERIA/UK

Below *Teasing Suicide*, 2004. Steel, 190 x 60 x 100cm (74⅘ x 23⅗ x 39⅖ in). Collection of the artist.

Right *11th Commandment*, 2005. Powder-coated steel, 240 x 390 x 210cm (96 x 156 x 84 in). Southwark Council.
'The commission was for Channel Four, who wanted a permanent sculpture to travel around the country reminding people of their programme "The New Ten Commandments". I came up with this piece because I wanted a gesture that went with the words: "Treat others as you would be treated". There are three figures in the sculpture: two are throwing the word as if to cloak each other; the figure in front is waiting to receive his cloak, and he is red, to catch the viewer's attention. I chose the colours blue, pink and red, because of Renaissance religious paintings depicting people with cloaks and shawls (blue) touching angels (pink) and God (red).'

When asked about her future plans following her show 'Knots of the Human Heart' at London's Morley College in 2000, Sokari Douglas Camp replied, 'Being out there and being very loud!' She's been 'out there' for more than a quarter of a century now, and the volume is still increasing. During that time Sokari has created some of the most moving and remarkable memorial sculptures by any British artist, including *Cross We Bear* (1999) for the murdered teenager Stephen Lawrence and *Memorial Bus* (2006) for the executed Nigerian activist and writer Ken Saro-Wiwa, which is currently touring the UK. Sokari was on a shortlist of two to win the commission to create a memorial marking the bicentenary of the abolition of the Atlantic slave trade. The memorial, *The World is Richer*, will be on the Princess Diana Memorial Walk in London's Hyde Park. She lost this particular commission, but the maquette for her sculpture, entitled *The World is Richer*, shows what a powerful work it would have been – and she is hopeful that the commission may yet be realized elsewhere.

Sokari Douglas Camp was born in 1958 in Buguma, Nigeria, the cultural capital of the Kalabari people, who live on 23 islands in the Niger Delta. She moved to Britain as a child, her art education taking place in London at the Central School (1980–83) and the Royal College of Art (1983–86). 'My work is about what's going on in London', she says, though part of that is a celebration of her own Kalabari culture, a theme that occurs in different ways in her work. 'I live the reality of being both Nigerian and British, but feeling outside both cultures', Sokari admits, though perhaps being 'outside' allows her to observe both cultures with such extraordinary clarity.

Sokari has had more than 40 solo shows around the world and her work is held in many private and public collections, including the Museum of African Art in Washington, the Setagaya Art Museum in Tokyo, and the British Museum in London, where she created five galvanized steel figures of Kalabari women, the centrepiece for the Ground Force Africa Garden during the Africa '05 year of celebrations. Entitled *Asoebi – Lace, Sweat and Tears*, the sculpture displays the subtle combination of humour, wit and pathos that are the hallmarks of Douglas Camp's work. Ten years earlier, her exhibition 'Play and Display' at the Museum of Mankind, as part of the Africa '95 season, had set an important precedent for the display of contemporary African art in the British Museum.

Sokari was awarded a CBE in 2005.

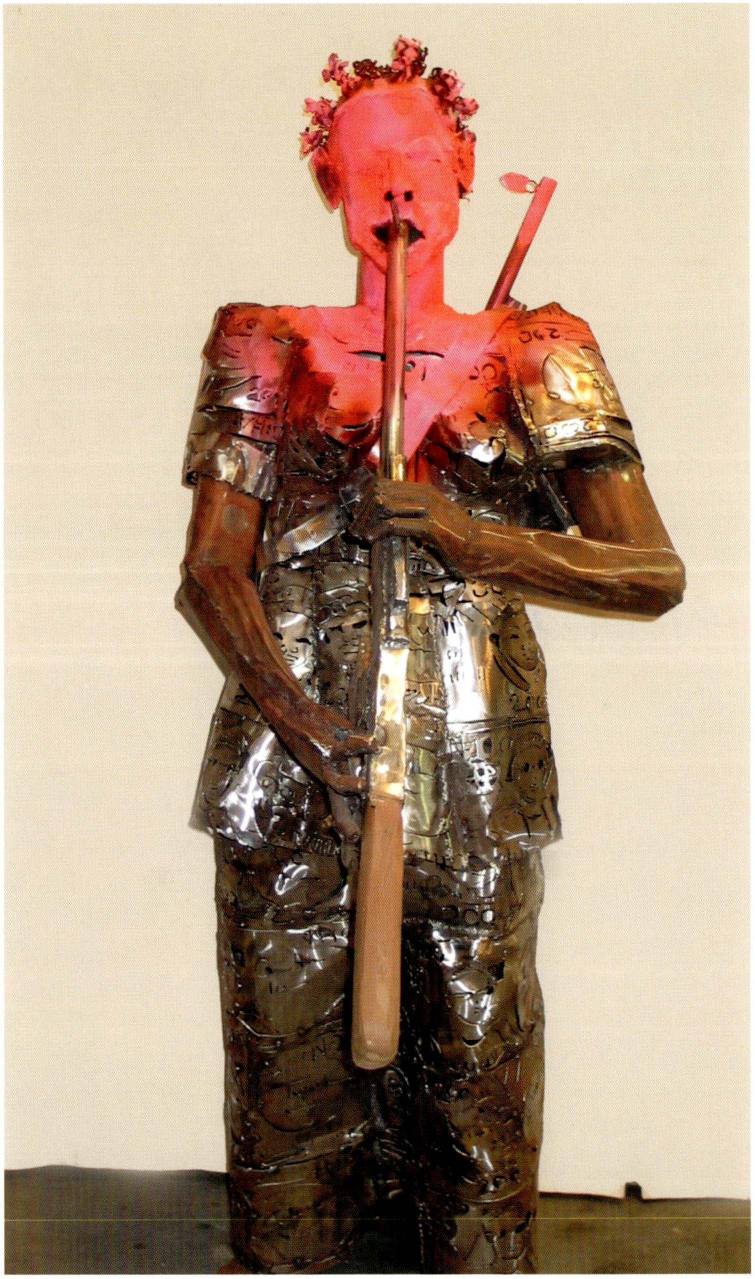

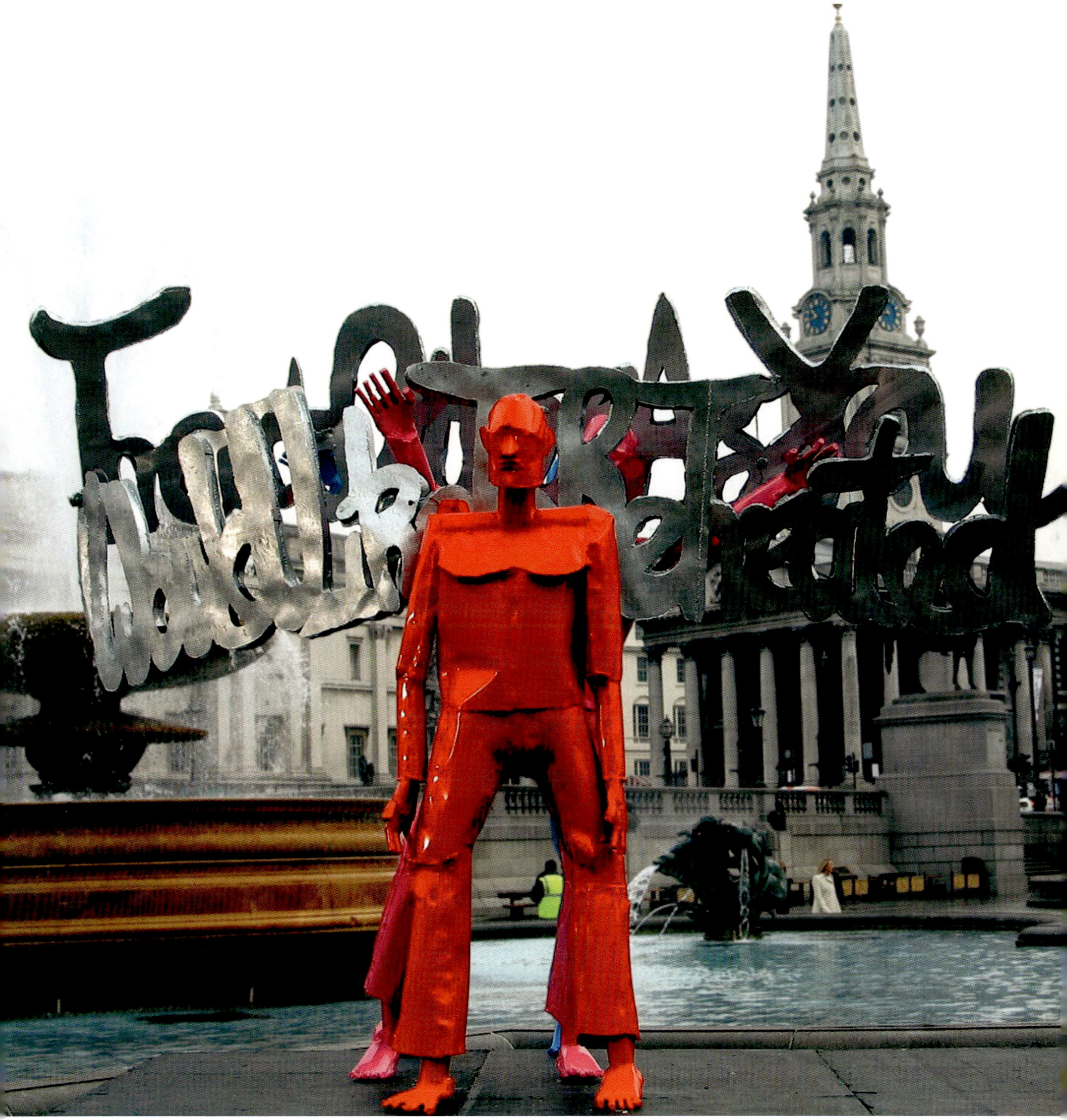

Below *We Were Brave…*, 2006. Steel, 23 x 120 x 63 cm (9 x 46½ x 24½ in). Collection of the artist.

The group of six figures represent different periods in the ongoing story of slavery and its legacy. Each figure throws a sculpted shadow, a line of words which together create a poem:

To Make a Few Rich
We were sold, bought and used
We Were Brave
We were strong
We survived
The World is Richer.

Right *Age Flame Head*, 2000. Plastic, glass, water and acetate oil, 103 x 28 x 36 cm (40½ x 11 x 14⅕ in). Private collection.

This work is a cry of protest against the damage done to people and to the environment by the petroleum companies in the Niger Delta, where Sokari's own Kalabari people live.

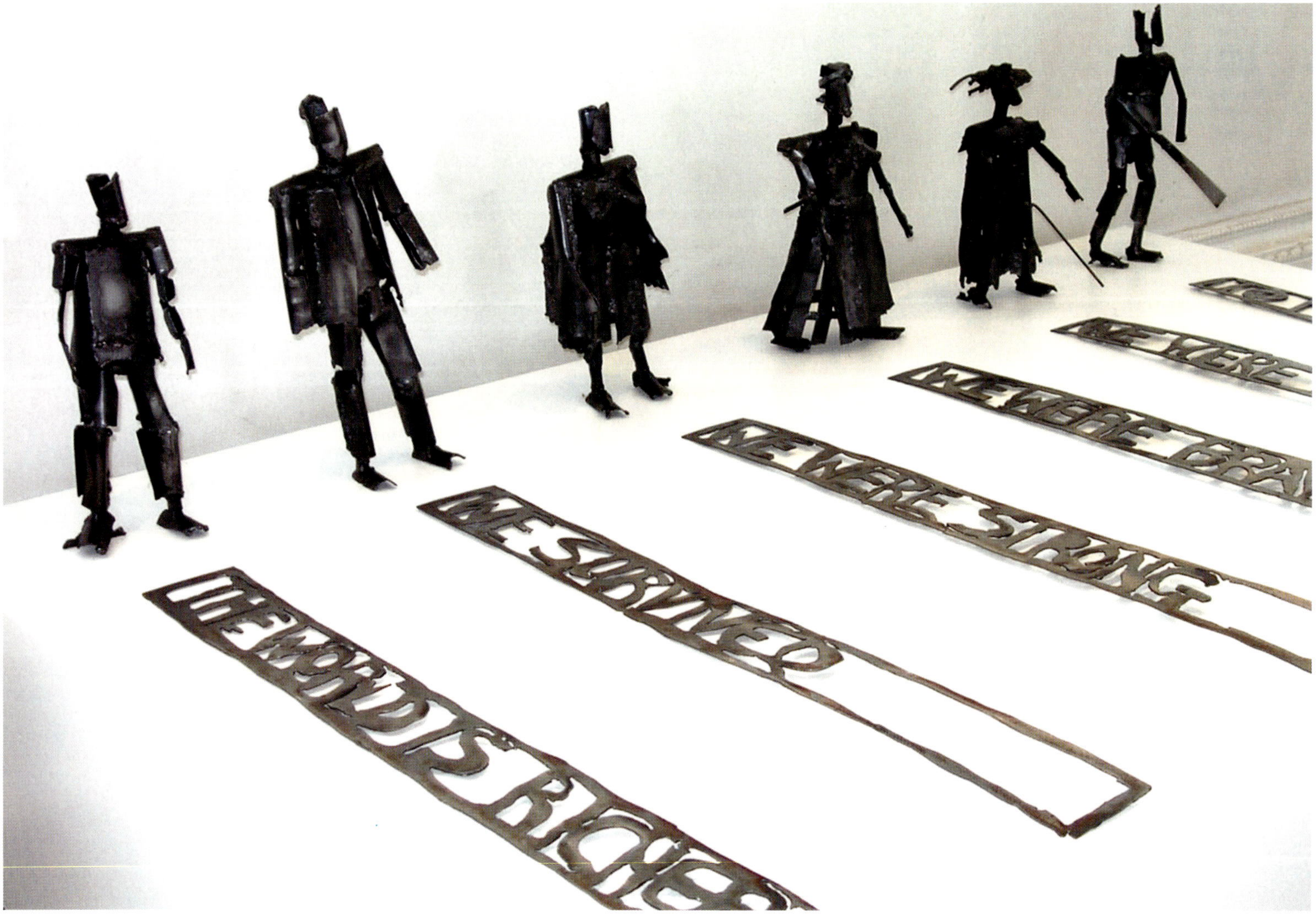

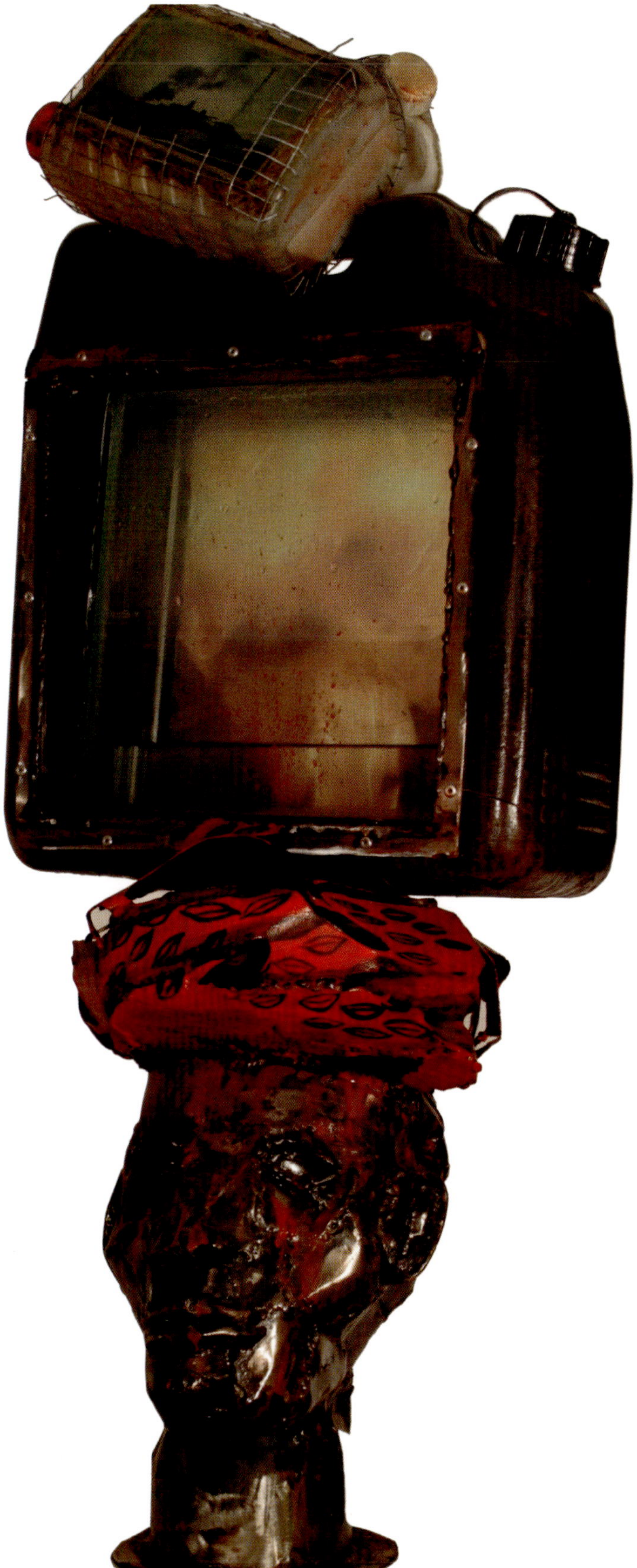

SAFAA ERRUAS
MOROCCO

Below *Broderie aux lames de rasoir* (*Razor Blade Embroidery*), 2004 (detail). Fragments of razor, embroidery wire, needles, gauze and cotton on fabric, 28 x 28 cm (11 x 11 in). Collection of the artist.
The surgeon's scalpel, the suturist's needles and the bandage to dress the wound are all suggested by this image.

Right *Untitled*, installation at the Torre de Puces, Castel del Denia, Spain, 2003. Gauze bandage and barbed wire, variable dimensions. Collection of the artist.
Exhibited in the old prison of the Castel del Denia, the delicate gauze and wire elements of Erruas's work are emphasized by the massive stone walls that surround them.

Safaa Erruas was born in 1976 and lives and works in Tétouan, Morocco. She graduated from the National Institute of Fine Arts, Tétouan, in 1998. She is a member of Appartment 22, a collective of contemporary artists based in Morocco. She has contributed to a number of exhibitions in Morocco, Senegal, France and the UK, including the Dak'Art Biennale in Dakar, Senegal (2002 and 2006) and 'Beyond the Myth: Contemporary Moroccan Art' at the Brunei Gallery, London (2003).

Erruas uses a combination of hard, sharp and extremely fragile material in her ethereal constructions, conjuring the eternal struggle represented in the children's game of scissors, paper, stone. She took part in the Wasla workshop, supported by the Triangle Arts Trust, in Nuweiba on the Gulf of Aqaba, Egypt, in 2003, shortly after the beginning of the second Gulf War. Only 250 miles from the Iraqi border, every night the Wasla artists could see the US aircraft flying over to drop bombs on Baghdad. Erruas wrote as follows about one of her pieces, created during the workshop:

Gaza, Stones, needles, gauze bindings
Desert...
Operational space
mental space
imaginary space
appropriable space... non-appropriable...
White.
white absent
shouting white of whiteness
and of absence

Razor blades
blades of memories
suspended
tended
remained unfinished...
coated out of white cotton
white present
soft, fragile, sharp-edged.
sometimes light... sometimes stable...
combined with the ground, the stone
with the Man, the skin...
Lived
adapted... non-suitable

(Translated from the French)

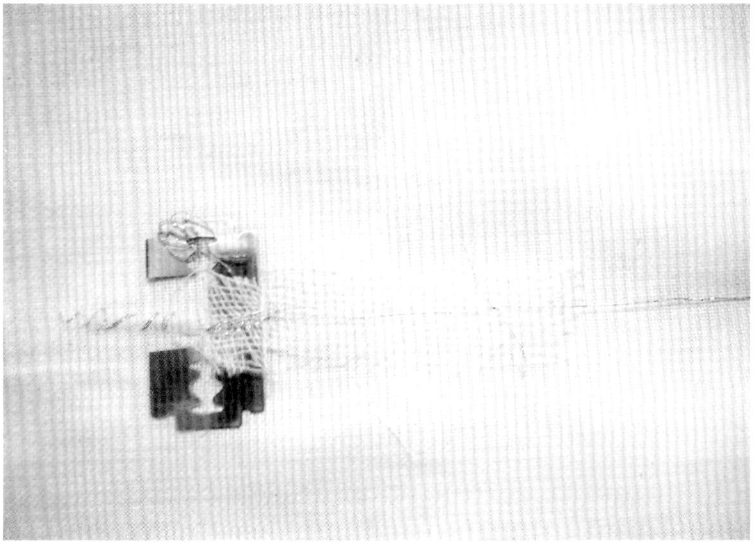

> 'White is not as neutral as it appears. Every colour conceals a message. White is a universal colour – the colour of peace, of Utopia. It feels immaterial to me, and allows the materials to be shown to better advantage.'
> *Safaa Erruas*

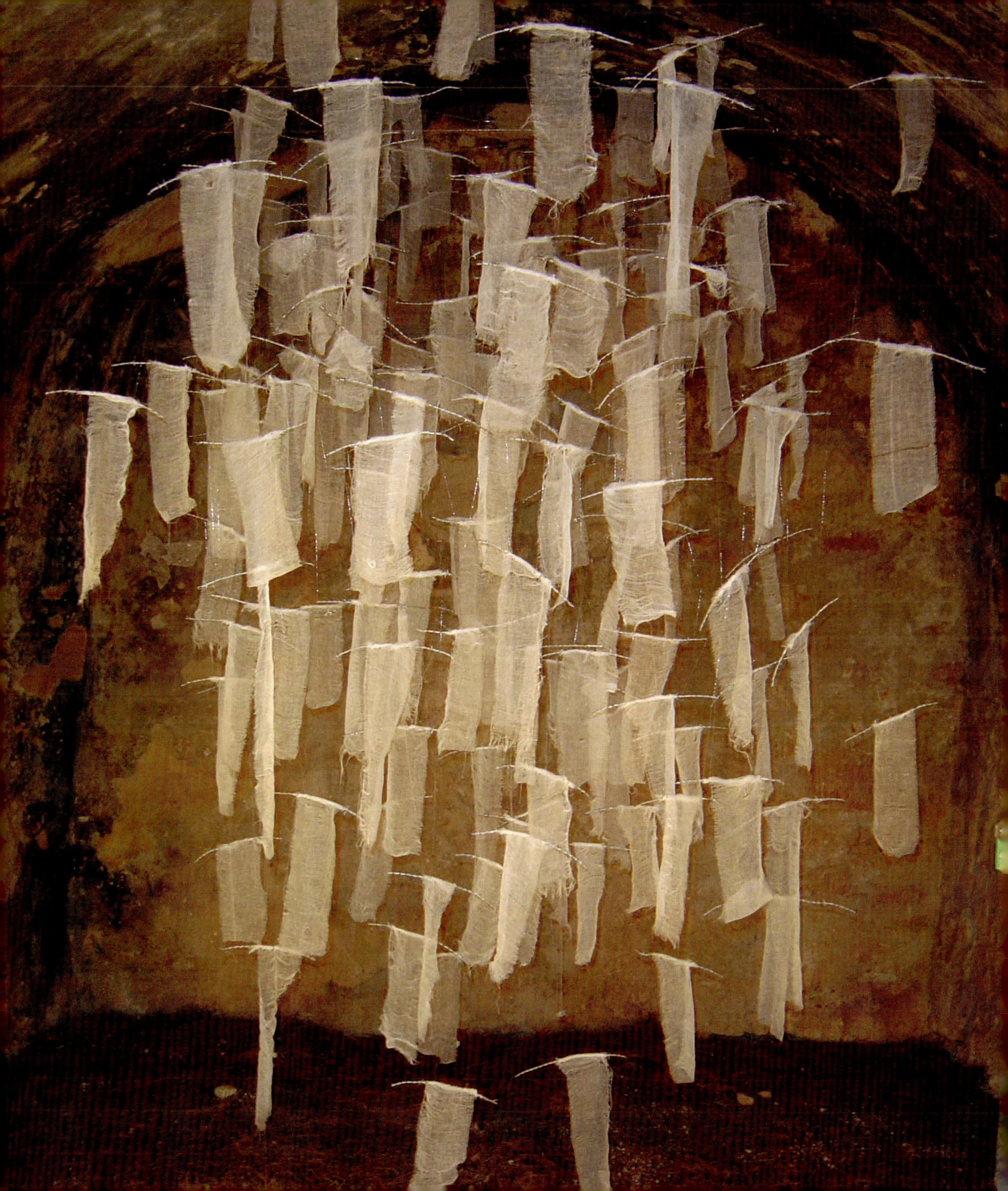

Below *Dress*, 2004. Plaster, gauze and needles on wood, 130 x 130 cm (51⅕ x 51⅕ in). Blachère fondation, France.
The title of the work suggests the art of dressmaking, but also the process of dressing a wound, an interpretation that is given weight by the plastered gauze and steel needles from which the piece is created.

Bottom *A Romantic Bouquet*, 2006 (detail). Porcelain and metallic wire, diameter 50cm (19⅔ in). Collection of the artist.
Porcelain, an extremely delicate material, is used here to create the feel of a bouquet of white roses – and perhaps the pure white wedding dress to follow.

Right *Talons Aigu* (*Stiletto Heels*), 2006. Porcelain and metallic wire, approximately 21 x 30 x 21 cm (8¼ x 11⅘ x 8¼ in). Collection of the artist.
These porcelain shoes evoke a complex range of associations: marriage, the sewing up of wounds, the shoemaker's craft and the slim stiletto of the assassin.

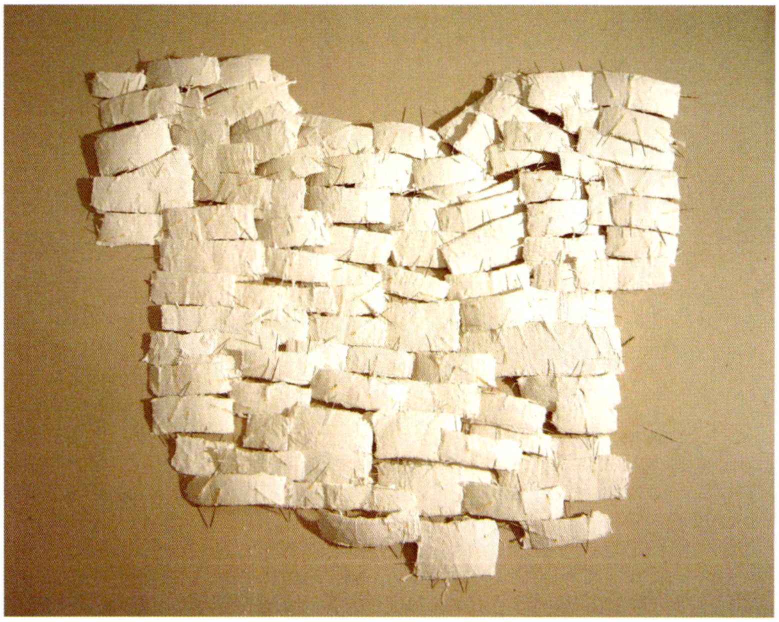

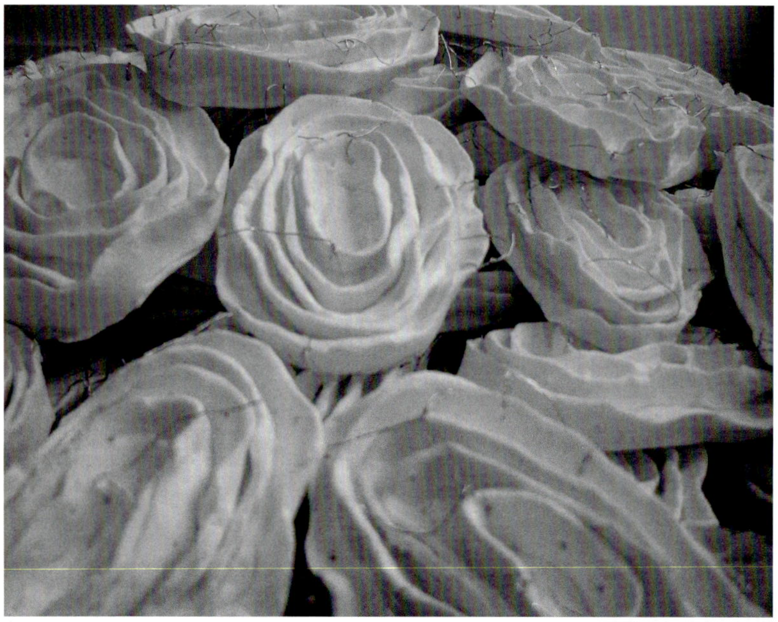

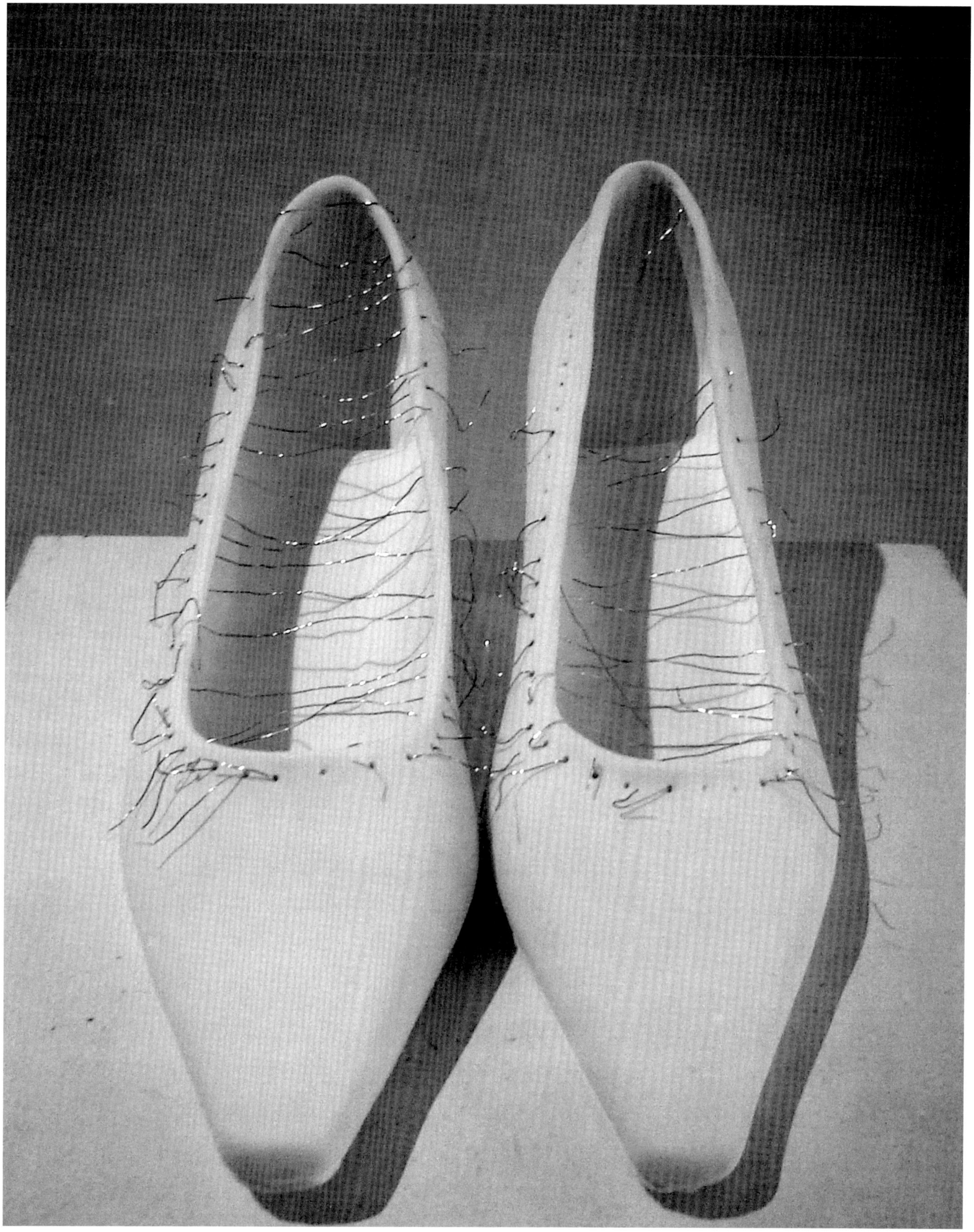

SAMUEL FOSSO
CAMEROON/CENTRAL AFRICAN REPUBLIC

Below *Self-Portrait*, 1976. Gelatin silver print, 50.8 x 50.8 cm (20 x 20 in). Jack Shainman Gallery, New York.

Right *Self-Portrait*, 1977. Gelatin silver print, 101.6 x 101.6 cm (40 x 40 in). Jack Shainman Gallery, New York.

Fosso began taking pictures of himself to send to his grandmother in Nigeria: 'I always got a photo to her every year, so that she would know I was alive, with a note saying, "I'm fine, I'm growing up!" I started taking photos as a way of watching myself grow up, but this turned into art and, consequently, a history of myself.'

It was St. Valentine's Day 2005, a day for falling in love – perhaps with a *Liberated American Woman* wearing stilettos, a white straw Stetson and looking good enough to eat on a red-and-white check table cloth, though maybe she'd already fallen for the dapper *Sailor*. Bewildered passengers on London's eastbound District Line train, on their way home peered out at the arty types on the opposite platform, sipping champagne and trying not to look too self-conscious. It was, after all, the most natural thing in the world to be standing on a freezing Underground platform in front of an eight-foot-high portrait of *The Chief: The One Who Sold Africa to the Colonial Powers*, resplendent in leopard skin, white-framed sunglasses and a bunch of sunflowers in his hand. In the world of Samuel Fosso, anything is possible. Samuel himself, casual, almost nondescript in jacket and jeans, beamed through his Private View, perhaps feeling closer to home than in the white-walled confines of a gallery. It was difficult to believe that Chief, Liberated Woman and Sailor were one and the same person – Samuel Fosso.

Fosso was born in 1962 in Kumba, Cameroon, but was brought up by his grandparents in eastern Nigeria. He was caught up in the Biafran war, and after several years of extreme hardship left Nigeria to join his brother, who had a furniture-making business in Bangui, Central African Republic. There he became an apprentice to a studio passport photographer, learned the trade and in due course acquired his own studio. He still runs his passport photo business, though they are photos with a difference.

In 1994, Fosso was 'discovered' by a French photographer organizing an exhibition. A series of shows in Europe and the USA followed. Fosso's photographs are all self-portraits, though he examines many issues through the guises that his persona adopts. His early black-and-white photographs, taken in the 1970s, are among his most powerful works and are a testament not only to his own talent, but also to the extraordinary vitality and originality of the studio photography tradition that has been flourishing in many parts of Africa for more than a century. *The Chief* became one of the iconic images of Africa '05.

'When I look in the mirror, I am not looking to find out if what I see is an Ibo, a Central African or even a black American. The only thing I can see is Samuel Fosso, who is trying to make himself as handsome as possible before taking a self-portrait.'
Samuel Fosso

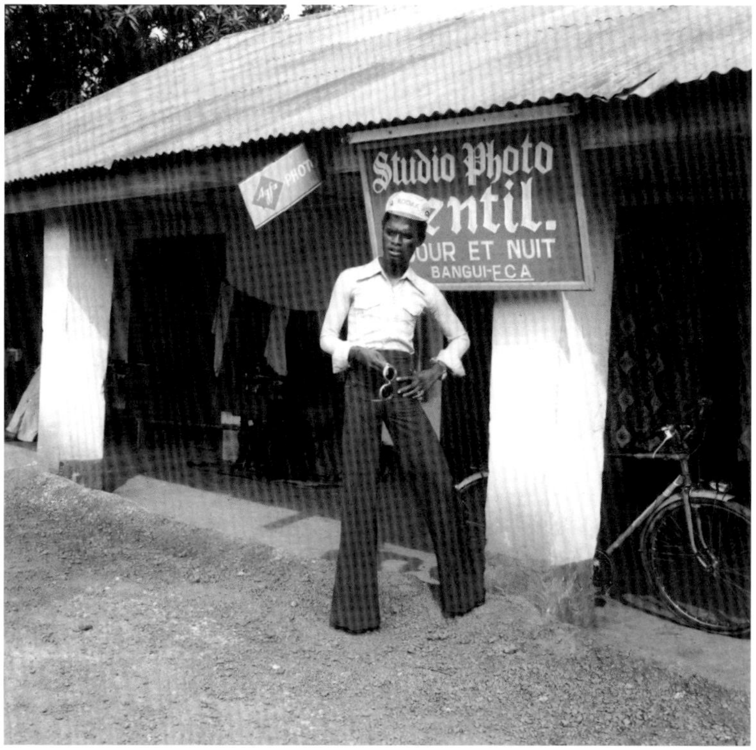

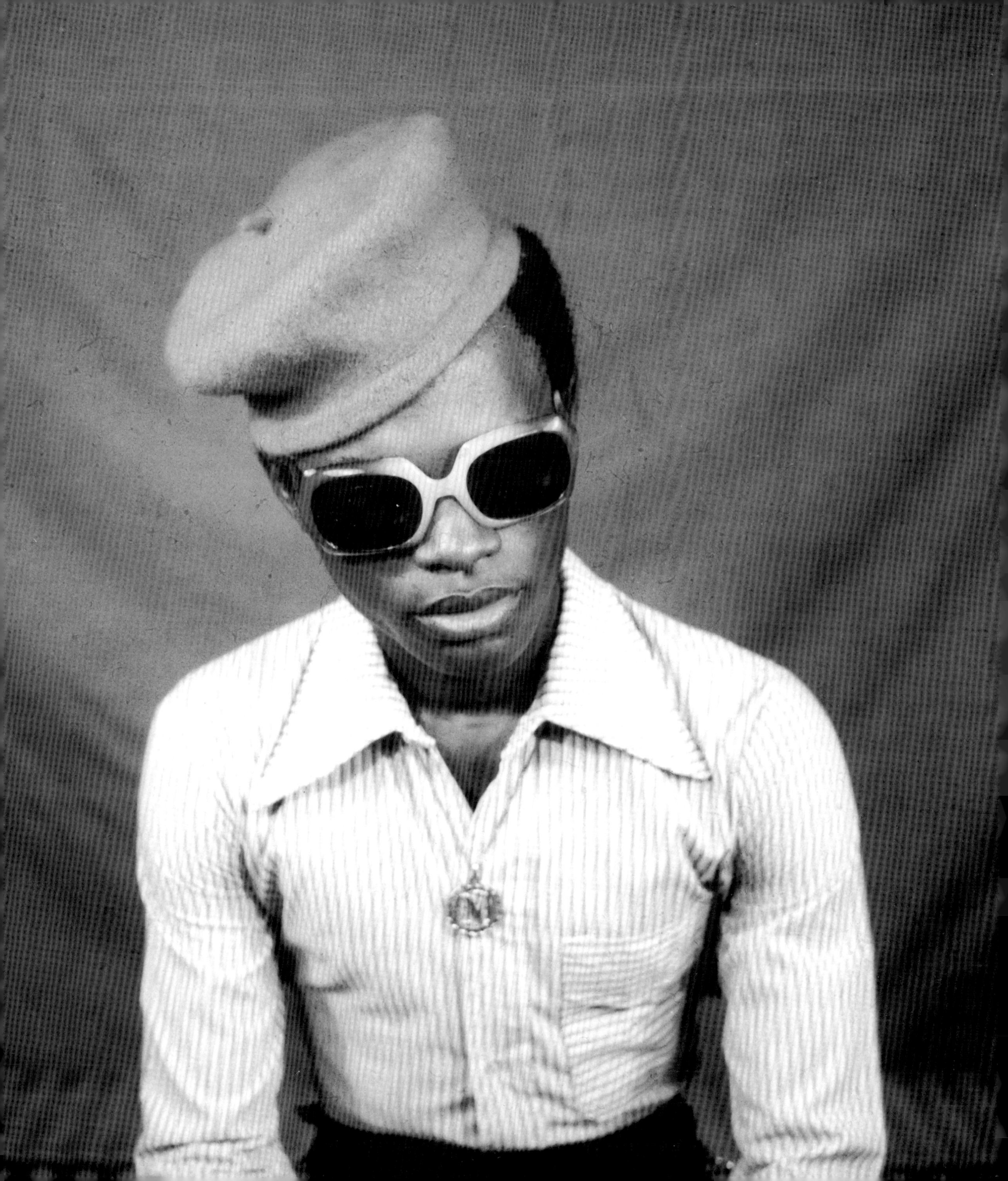

Below *Self-Portrait*, 1977. Gelatin silver print, 101.6 x 101.6 cm (40 x 40 in). Jack Shainman Gallery, New York.
'When I'm taking a self-portrait, I'm not looking to find out more about Samuel Fosso. I'm searching first of all to see my beauty. That's how I started.'

Right *Le marin (The Sailor)* from *Série Tati*, 1997. C-print, 144.7 x 101.6 cm (57 x 40 in). Jack Shainman Gallery, New York.
'Who decides what the mainstream is? I want to get my work across to as wide an audience as possible. But I'm not interested in being a part of a mainstream that doesn't reflect the reality of where I live.'

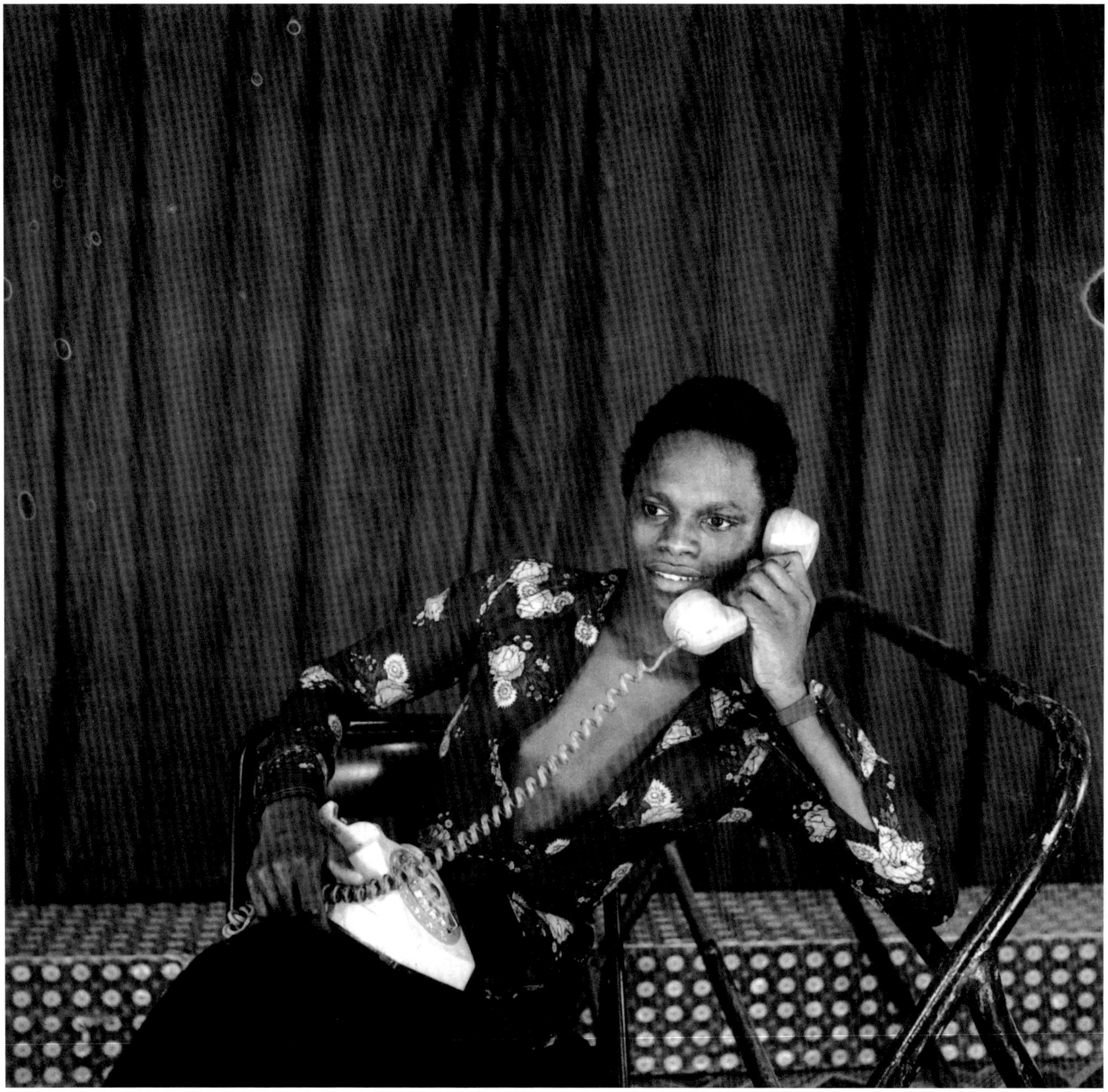

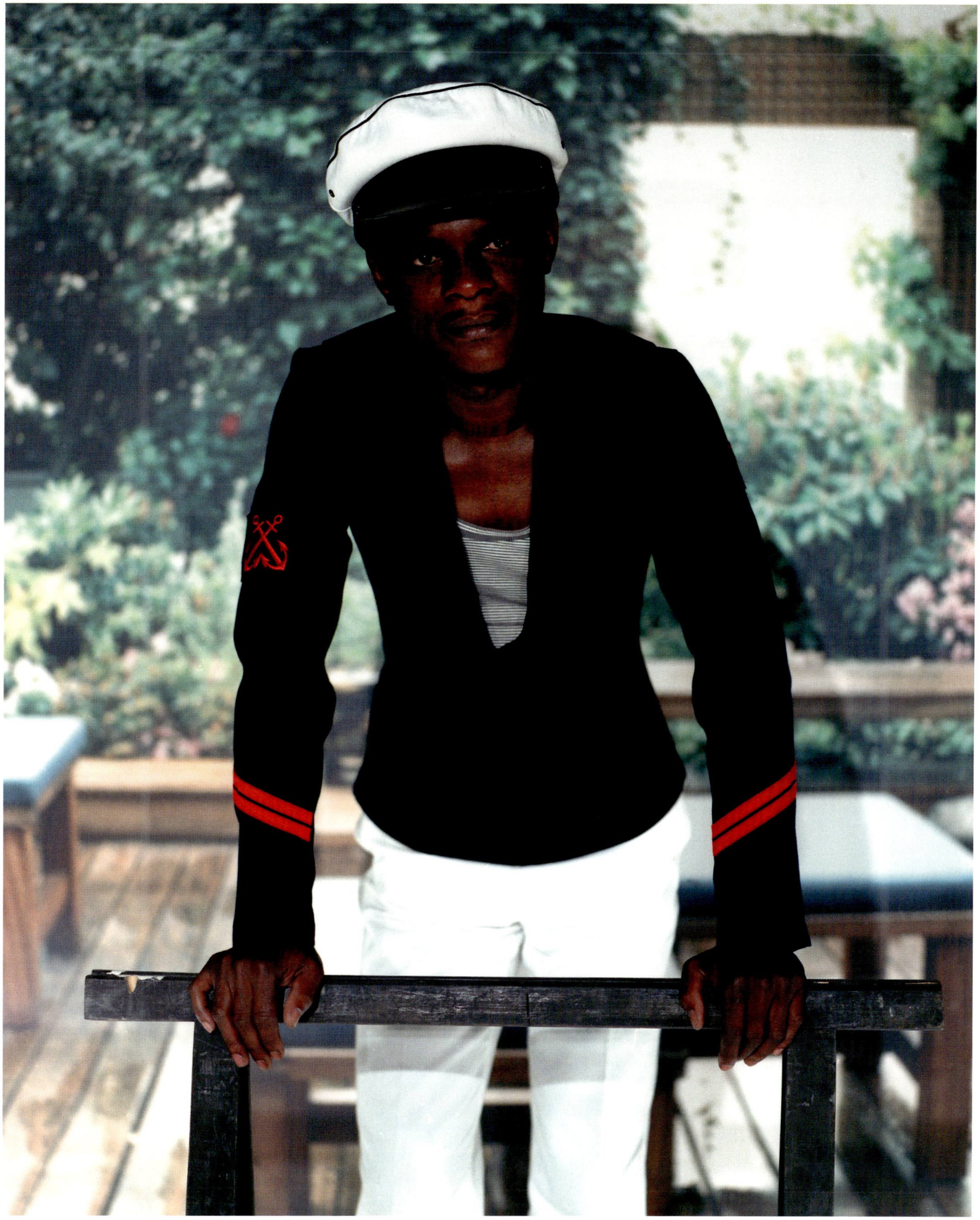

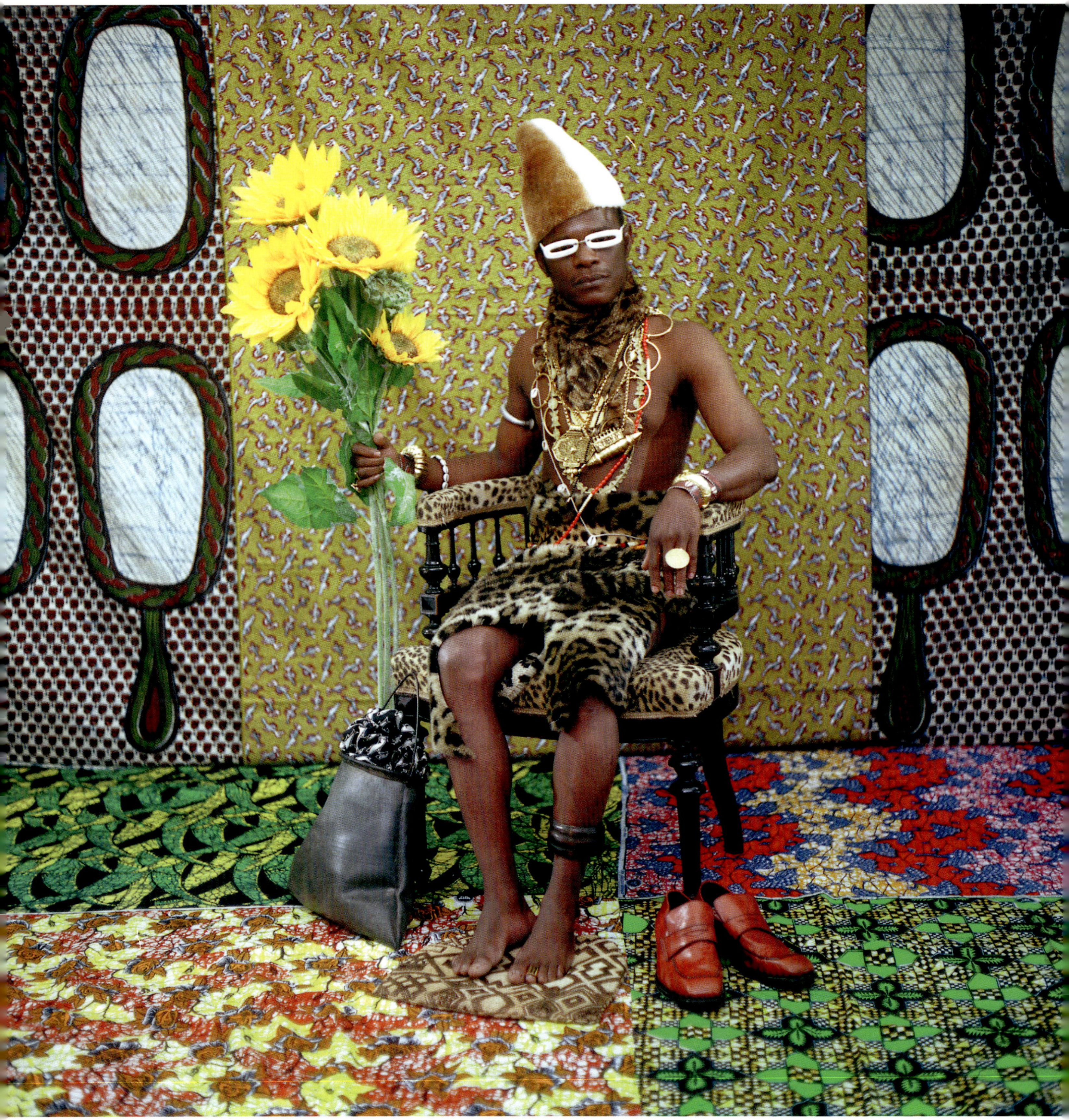

'The way I take photographs and the way that I use backdrops in order to pose people for their pictures is all about transporting them, taking them to places where they don't go.'
Samuel Fosso

Left *Le chef: celui qui a vendu l'Afrique aux colons (The Chief: The One Who Sold Africa to the Colonial Powers)* from the series *Série Tati*, 1997. C-print, 144.7 x 101.6 cm (57 x 40 in). Jack Shainman Gallery, New York.
'With this photo I wanted to say to Westerners, "Look, we had our own democracy before you came, we had our own rulers, our own presidents, but it was our ruler that you came and got rid of, and in his place you set up your hierarchies, your systems".'

Below *La femme américaine libérée des années 70 (The liberated American Woman of the 1970s)* from the series *Série Tati*, 1997. C-print, 144.7 x 101.6 cm (57 x 40 in). Jack Shainman Gallery, New York.
'Would I ever leave Africa for Europe? No, absolutely not.'

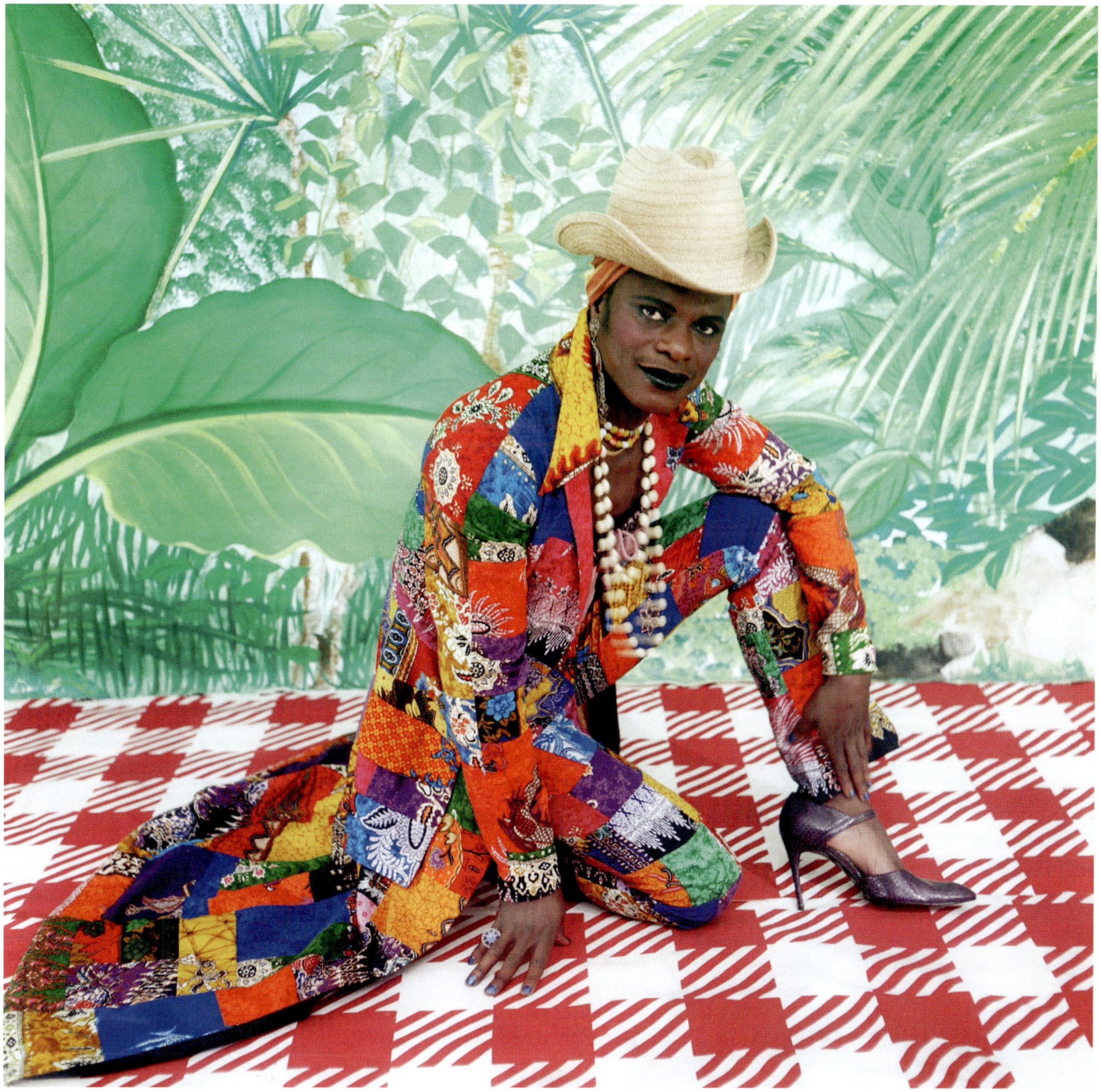

ASSEFA GEBREKIDAN
ETHIOPIA

Below and bottom *Coming Out*, installation, c. 2005 (details). Mixed media, variable dimensions.
'Light and sound lines mainly dominate my works. My works are full of power and motion. I use wires... these wires create different lines and satisfy my drawing thirsts'.

Right *A Glimmer of Hope*, installation at the Camden Arts Centre, 2005 (detail). Mixed media, variable dimensions.
Part of Gebrekidan's installation at Camden Arts Centre, in which he used plastic containers and other familiar objects from the marketplace and transformed them into constructions that were by turns delightful and sinister.

Born in Axum, northern Ethiopia in 1973, Assefa Gebrekidan now lives and works in Addis Ababa, where he has his own studio. Gebrekidan trained at the Addis Ababa University School of Fine Arts and Design, graduating in 1996. Among his early influences were the works of Russian constructivist sculptors such as Vladimir Tatlin, as well as the wider international constructivist movement led by sculptors such as Naum Gabo with their emphasis on kinetics, modern materials including plastic, planar and linear forms and the importance of space as opposed to mass. Some of these influences can be clearly seen in Gebrekidan's work, particularly his exhibition 'A Glimmer of Hope' (2005) at the Camden Arts Centre in London, his first international solo show. The vitality of his vision, particularly in the use of colours and forms, and the application of his ideas within a distinctively Ethiopian cultural context, make the work a remarkable achievement. From a combination of brilliantly lit plastic vessels and sounds produced by various kinetic devices, Gebrekidan evokes the quiet echoes of an Ethiopian Orthodox church, combined with the vibrant colours of a marketplace and the disturbing forms of missiles and bombs.

Gebrekidan taught at the Mekele Fine Art School in northern Ethiopia for several years after graduating. During this period he created and photographed substantial clay sculptures, before destroying them. It was not until he returned to Addis Ababa that he began to experiment with the effects of light and darkness within different containers and spaces, resulting in his exhibition 'Light and Dark' at the Zoma Contemporary Art Centre, Addis Ababa, in 2003. The following year he exhibited at the Dak'Art Biennale in Dakar, Senegal, and in 2005 took up a two-month residency at Camden Arts Centre, London.

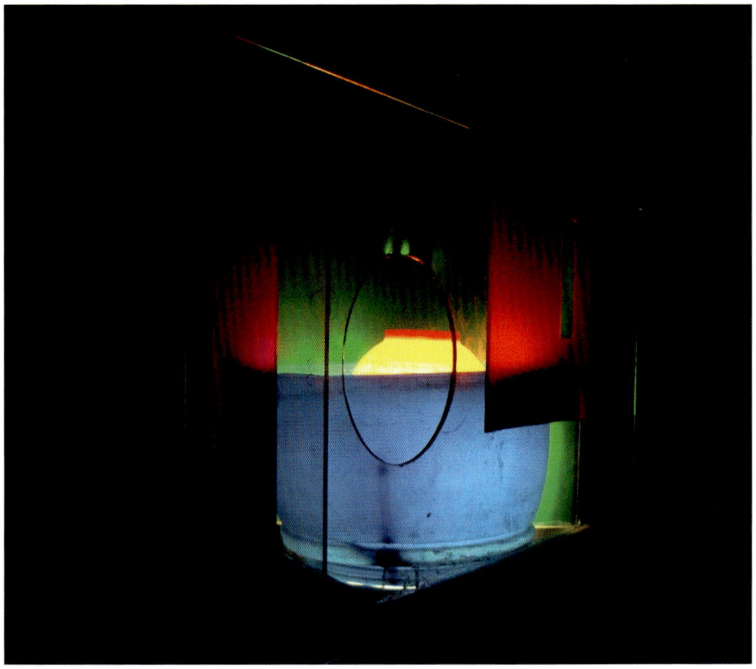

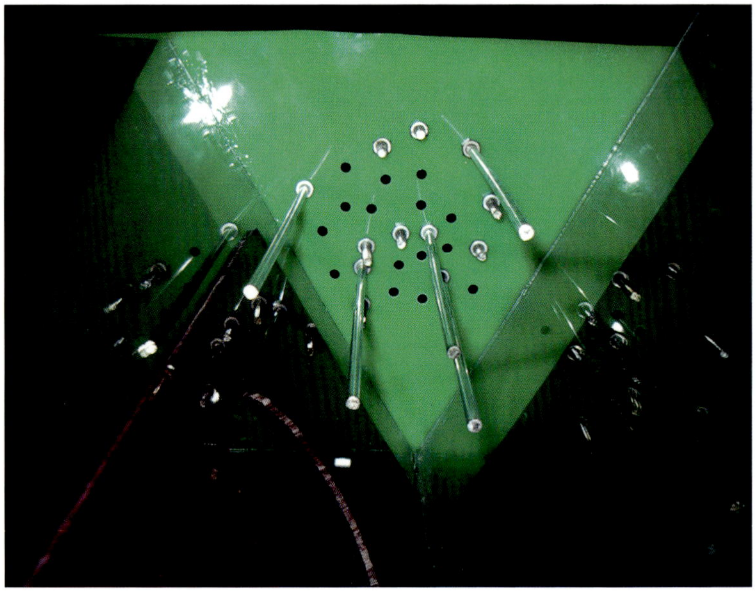

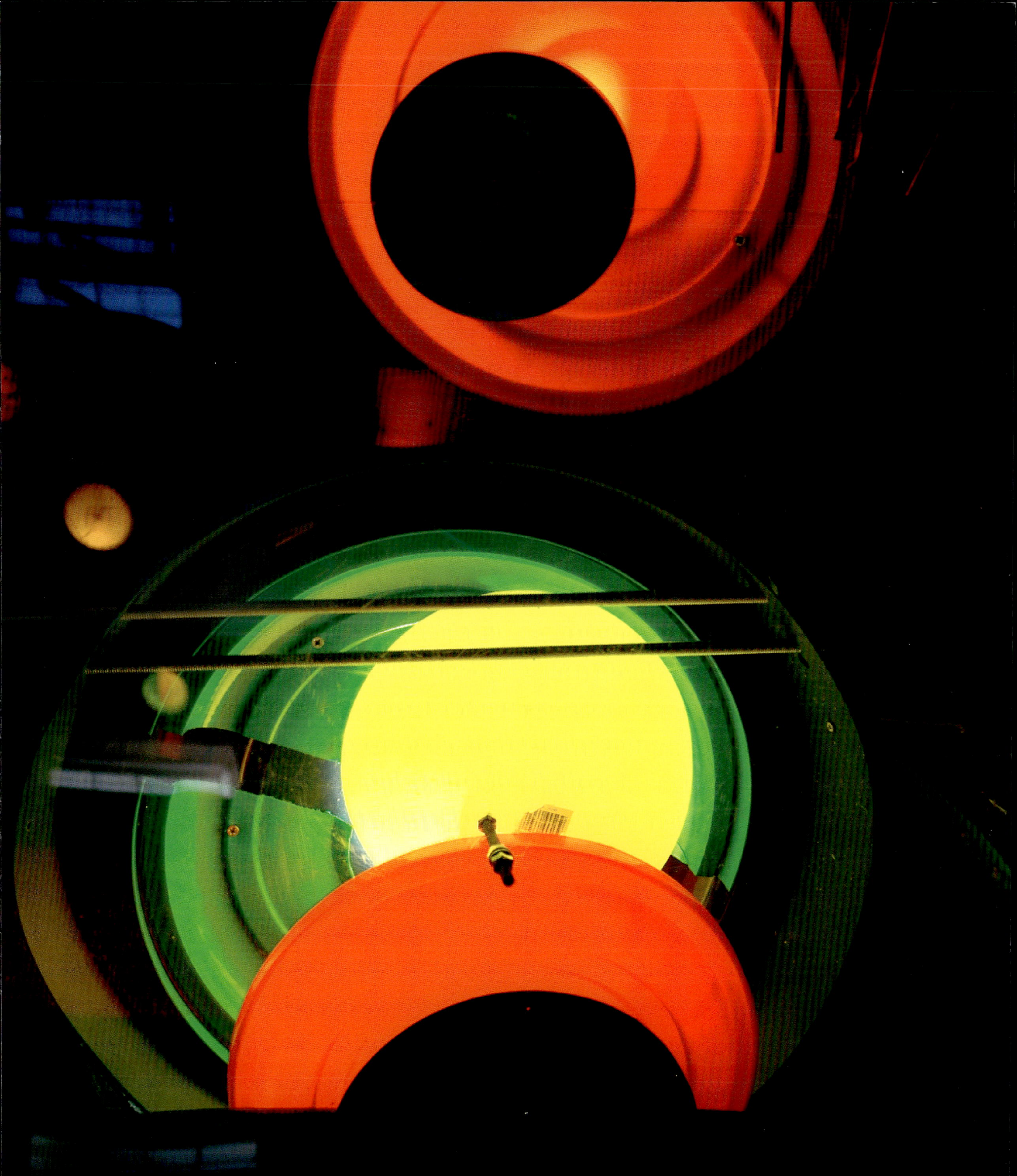

Below *Inner Power,* installation, 2004 (detail). Mixed media, variable dimensions.

Right *A Cracking Night,* installation, 2004 (detail). Mixed media, variable dimensions.

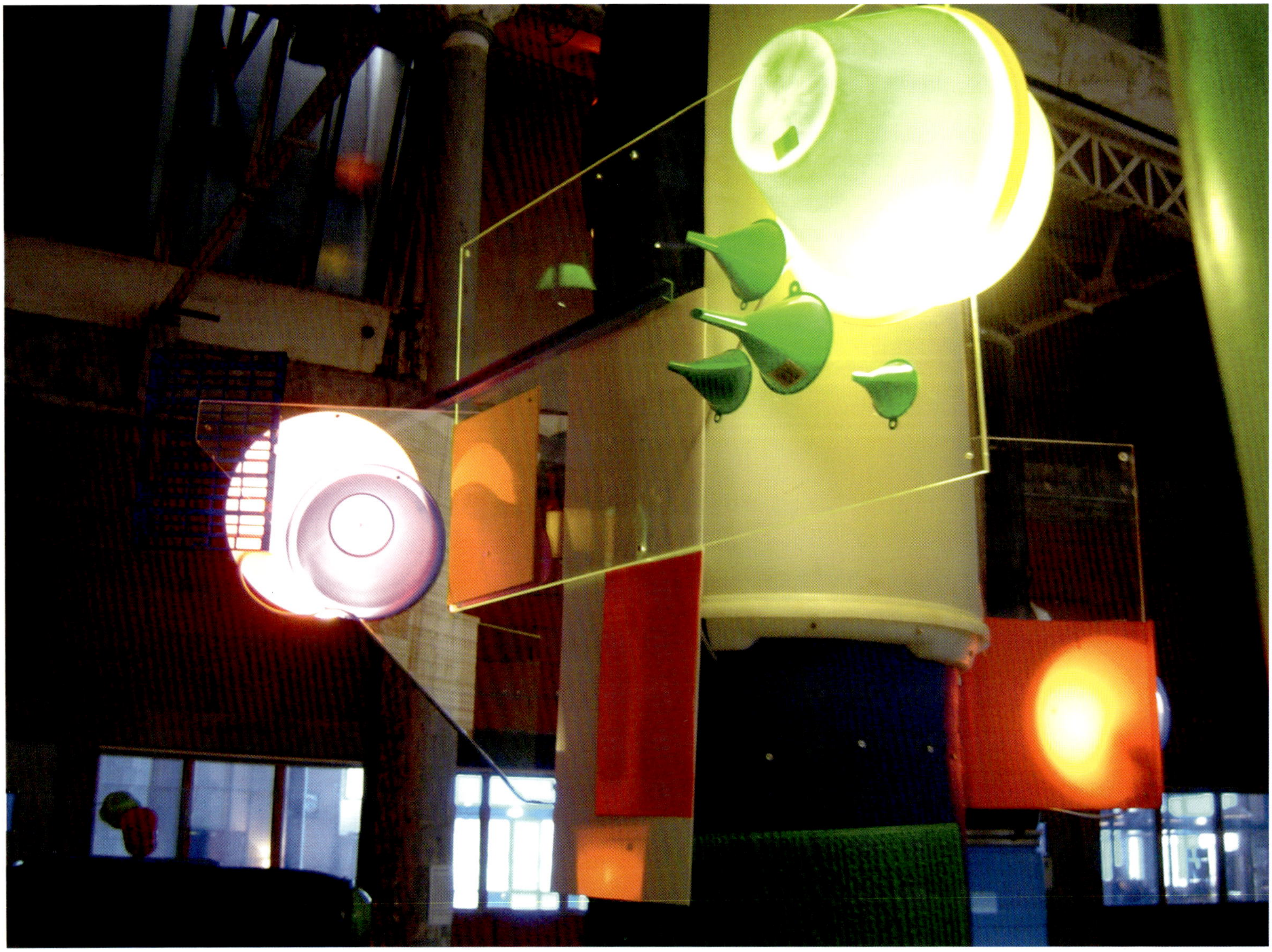

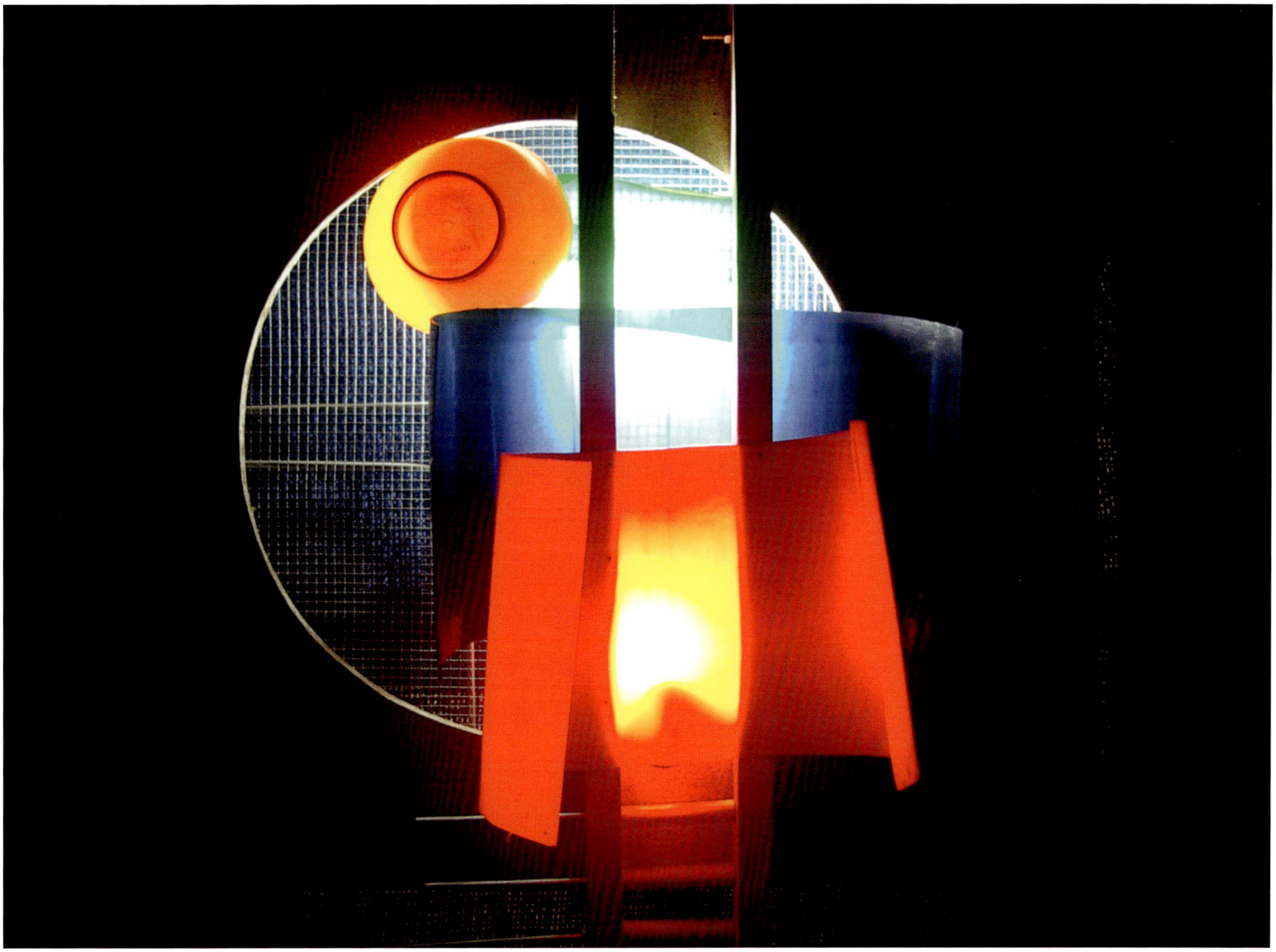

POMPÍLIO HILÁRIO (GEMUCE)
MOZAMBIQUE

Below *Democracy Game*, installation at MUVART Biennale, Maputo, 2005. Gameboard and pieces, diameter 50 cm (19⅔ in). Interactive work that reflects on social anxieties and their potential solutions. 'Homo Sapiens? Maybe. More likely Homo Ludens. Are we simply in a game? Can we rewrite the rules?'

Bottom *Letting Things Go*, installation at MUVART Biennale, Maputo, 2005. Mixed media, variable dimensions. A multimedia installation consisting of figures of women coming and going, dressed in *capulanas* (printed cloth) and other clothes typical of those worn by Mozambican women. Other elements include a video and soundtrack of walking feet, and a wall made of zinc plates and other material.

Right *Grandmother and Granddaughter*, from the series *No Mystery*, 2007. Oil on canvas, 120 x 150 cm (47¼ x 59 in). Collection of the artist.

Gemuce, intellectual and founder of MUVART (the Movement for Contemporary Art in Mozambique), considers contemporary art as 'a challenge of intelligence'. The artist must be an observer, an investigator and an inquisitor, constantly assessing the political and social situation. Given the late twentieth century history of Mozambique and the wars, floods and famine that have plagued the country, it is impossible to overestimate the level of responsibility the artist accepts.

Gemuce was born in Quelimane, Mozambique in 1963. He completed a course in ceramics at the School for Visual Arts in Maputo, Mozambique (1983–85) before studying for a Licentiate at the Institute of Fine Arts in Kiev, Ukraine (1990). He then completed a Masters in mural painting at the Academy of Fine Arts, Ukraine (1993), followed by a Masters in the conception and management of cultural projects at the Faculty of International Cultural Training in Paris (2000–1). He currently lives and works in Maputo.

Gemuce has exhibited widely in Mozambique and in Europe. In 2006, he participated (with Malangatana and Mieke Oldenburg) in a three-artist show at the French Cultural Centre in Maputo, 'Sonata for Three Hands'. Later that year his *Democracy Game* was one of the talking points of the 2006 Dak'Art Biennale in Dakar, Senegal. Since 1993, he has taught at Maputo's National School for the Visual Arts, and assisted in the planning and organization of the touring exhibition '"Replica and Rebellion": Plastic Arts of Mozambique, Angola, Cape Verde and Brazil' in 2006.

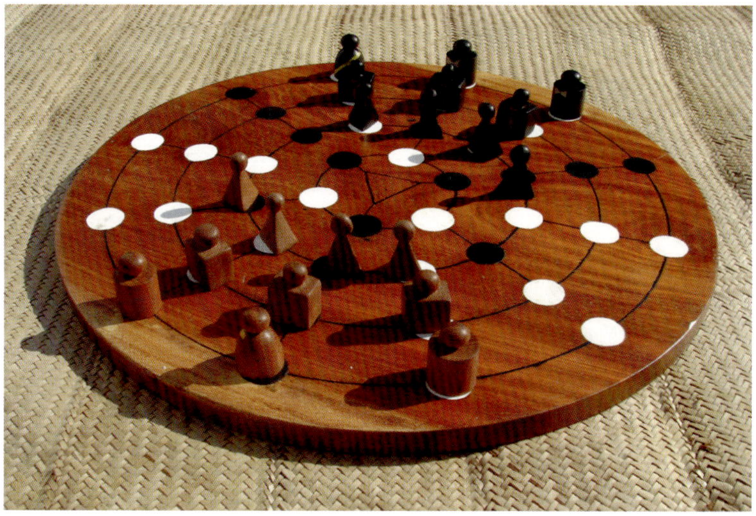

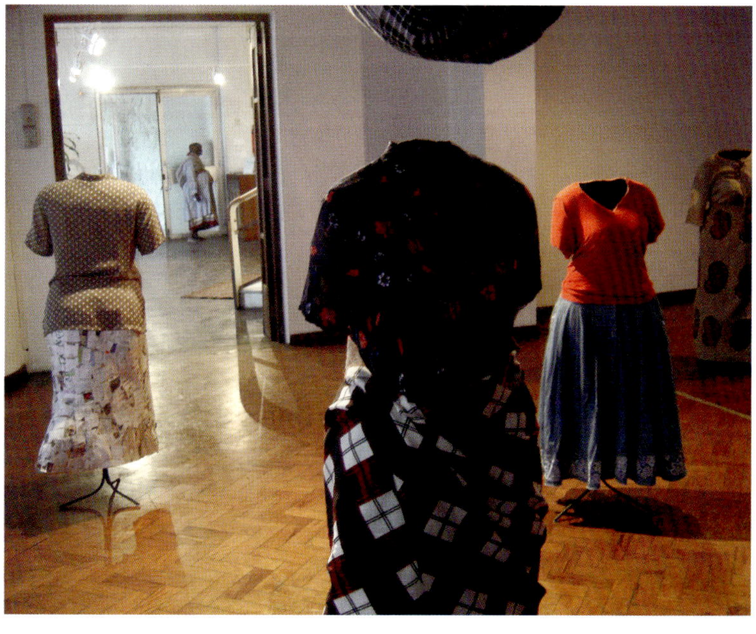

'On a Saturday in April 2005, in one of the quarters of Catembe, I recorded in my subconsciousness women in motion. I recorded feet hurrying and crossing, going in all directions, as if they were saying to each other "let me walk". I also recorded walls made of a lot of different materials in the road margins and on a zinc plate the inscription "let go". These elements appeared to be details from the current Mozambican reality and signs of the everyday struggle for survival and for a better life...'
Gemuce on his 2005 installation Letting Things Go

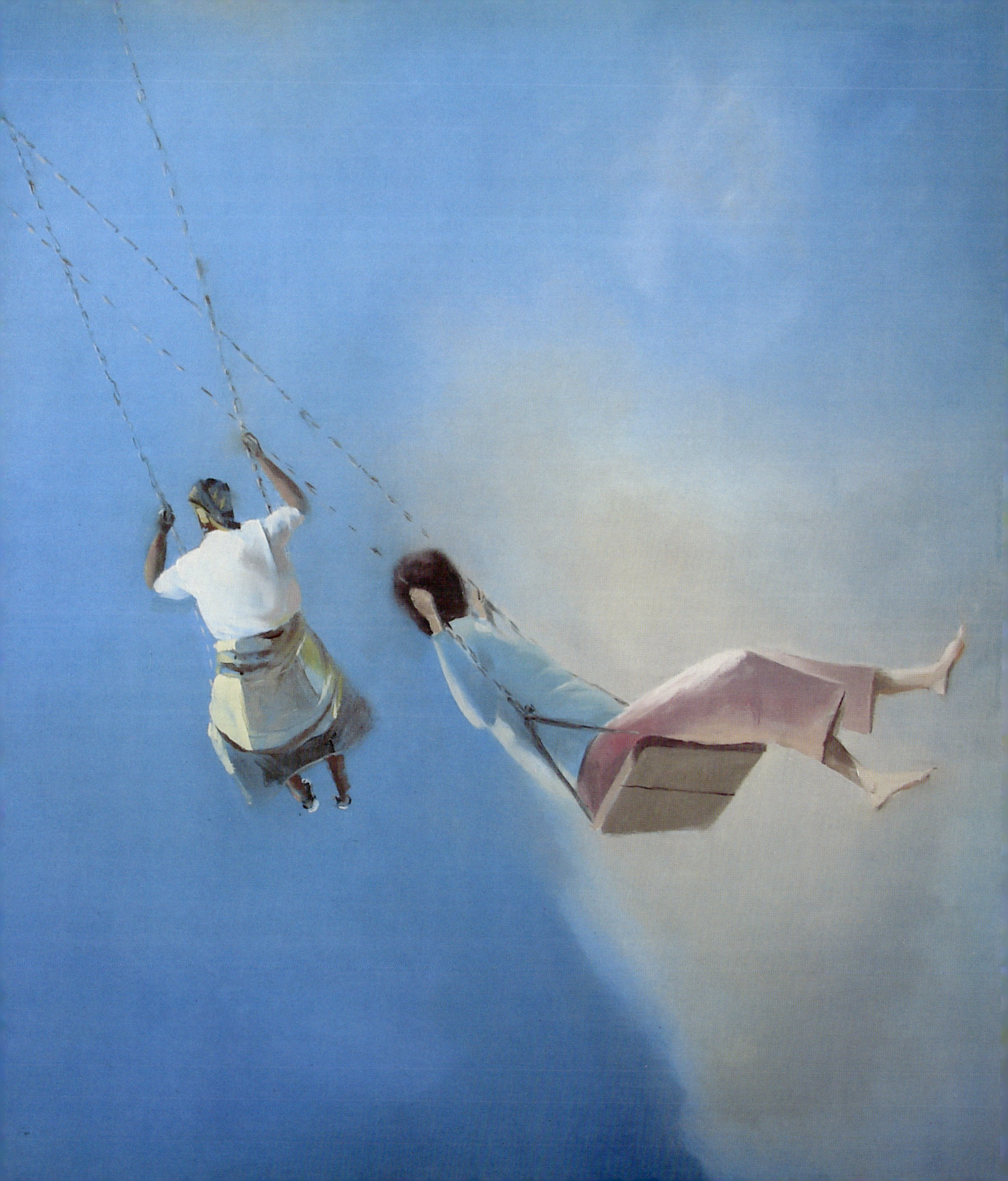

Below *The Sex of Butterflies*, from the series *No Mystery*, 2007. Oil on canvas, 120 x 150 cm (47¼ x 59 in). Collection of the artist.

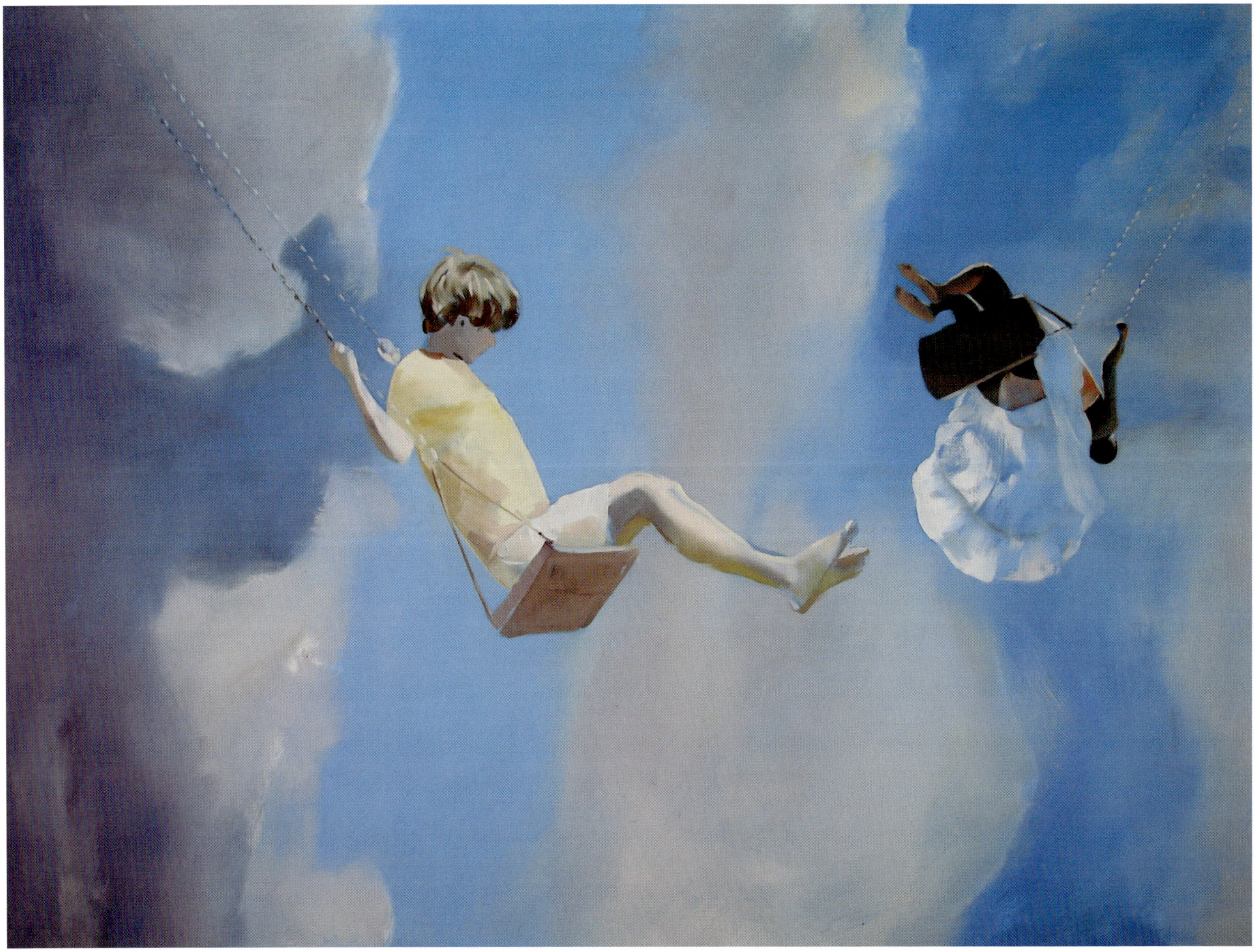

Below *Manoeuvre of Guelegule*, from the series *The Human from Here*, 2007 (detail). Set of seven pairs of men's and women's underwear on wheels. Collection of the artist.
The Human from Here is a new project between the Mozambican writer Daniel da Costa. The idea behind the first project in the series, *Manoeuvre of Guelegule*, is to represent the problems of sexuality, corruption and poverty in Maputo city life.

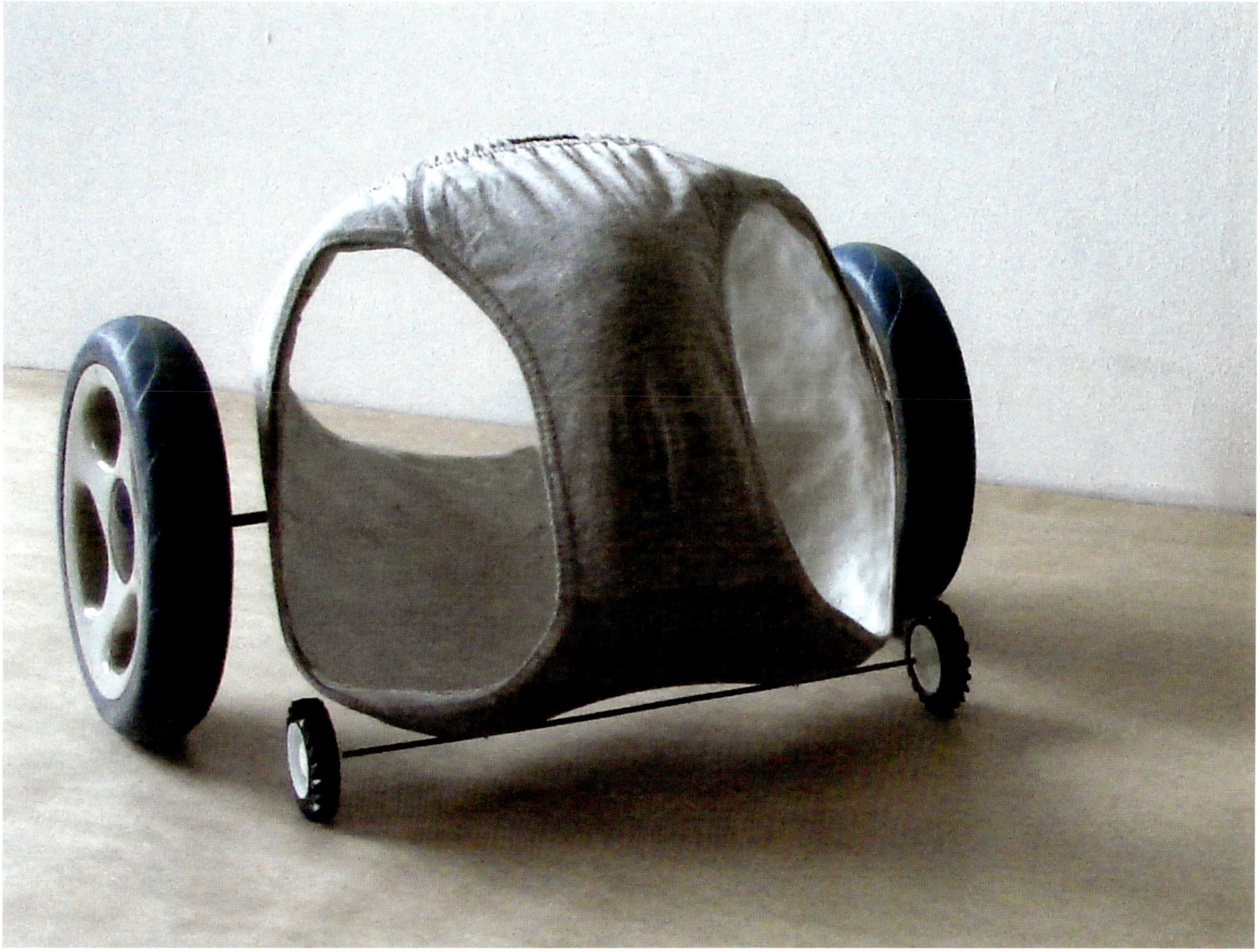

TAPFUMA GUTSA
ZIMBABWE/AUSTRIA

Below *Embrace*, 2002. Serpentine, *kudu* horn and cow horn, approximately 195 x 48 x 40 cm (76¾ x 19 x 15¾ in). Collection of the artist.

Right *Corpse*, 1993. Wood, mask and scarf, 63 x 123 x 23 cm (24⅘ x 48⅖ x 9 in). Private collection. The figure is similar to those created by Gutsa for his work *African Genesis* in 1995.

'The forms are corpses: there is a shedding of life in death to make way for new birth. Or they are sleeping forms waiting for life. There is genesis – creation – death and recreation and regeneration all the time, at every moment.'

Tapfuma Gutsa, perhaps more than any other of the 'second generation' of Zimbabwean stone sculptors, has broken free from the traditions already established in this young movement. Often using a combination of materials, including stone, metal, wood, horn, wire, paper and string, he strives to express contemporary as well as traditional ideals to a local as well as an international audience. He has exhibited his work all over the world and currently lives and works in Vienna, Austria.

Born in Harare, Zimbabwe in 1956, Gutsa studied art at the Dreifontein Mission School where he joined the woodcarving workshop taught by the respected sculptor Cornelius Manguma. Gutsa became the first recipient of a British Council scholarship to study at the City and Guilds School of Art in London in 1982–85. On returning to Zimbabwe he held his first one-man show, 'Utonga', in 1987. He was later approached by Robert Loder and Di Mitchell to discuss the possibility of holding a Triangle Arts workshop at Murewa; under Gutsa's leadership this became the first of the Pachipamwe series of workshops, which ran in Zimbabwe from 1988 to 1994. In 1997 Gutsa opened the Surprise studio space in Zimbabwe, bringing together younger and more established artists. In common with many artists in Zimbabwe, the deteriorating situation forced him to leave, though he is upbeat about the future:

> *The good people who have left will one day bring back their experience to their homeland and this will fertilize the local context and will merge with it.*

'Objects such as buffalo horns are used by medicine men to empower and strengthen the warrior before battle – in this sense the shaman creates an object that can acquire meaning and influence people, just as an AK47 or a bible can wield influence and power. I am, therefore, interested in creating enigmatic forms that are intrinsically functional, in the sense that medicines or weapons are functional. It is a kind of alchemy.'
Tapfuma Gutsa

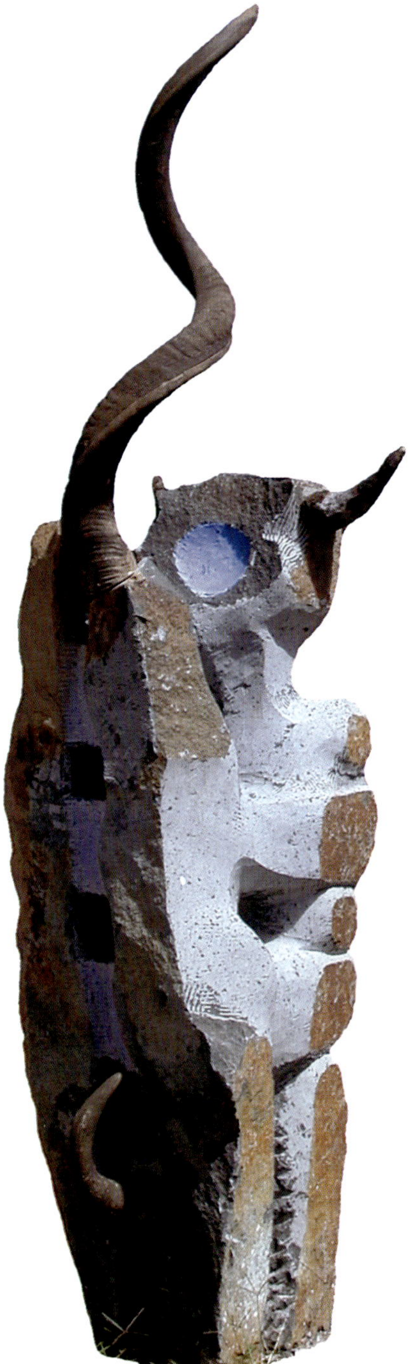

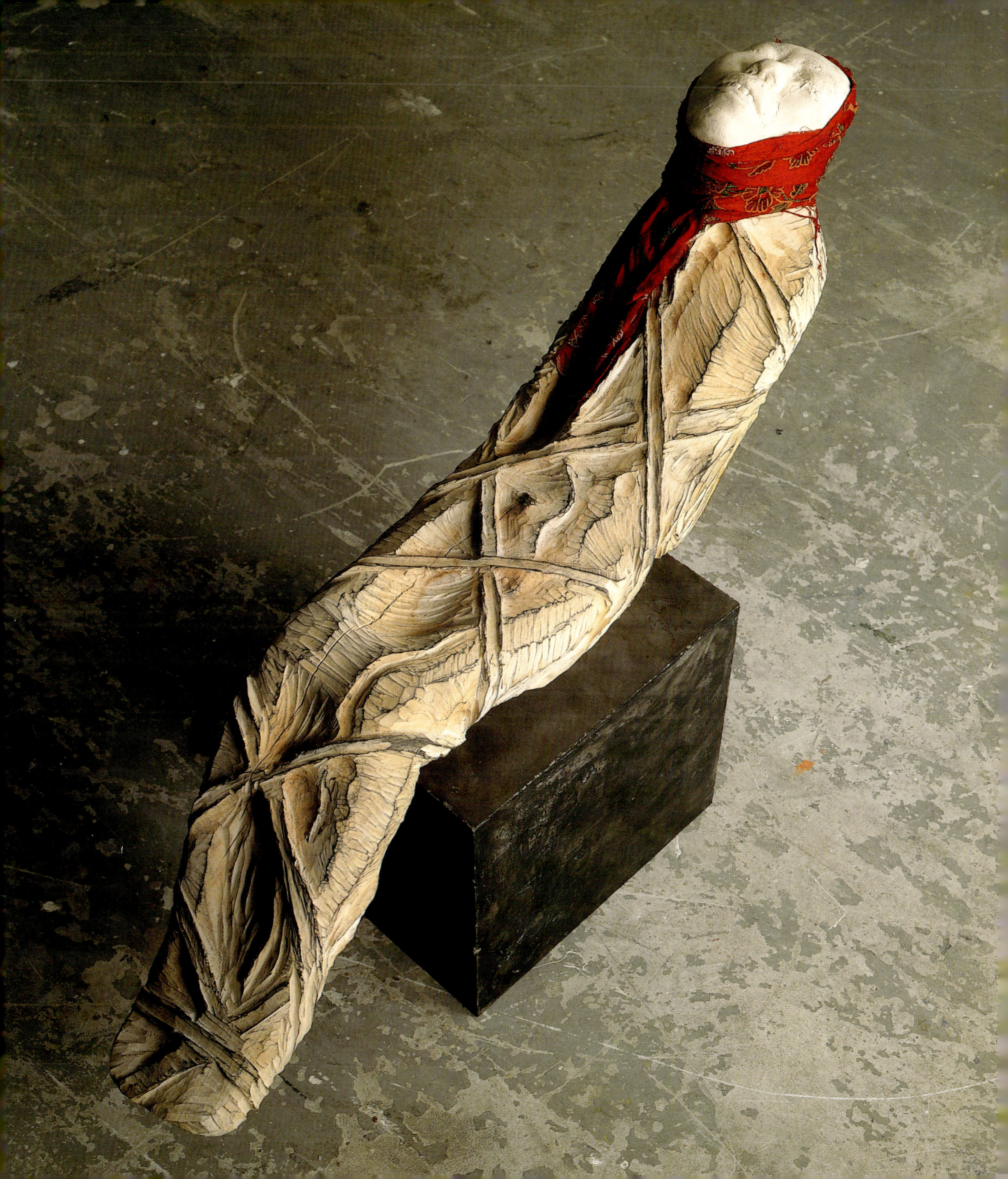

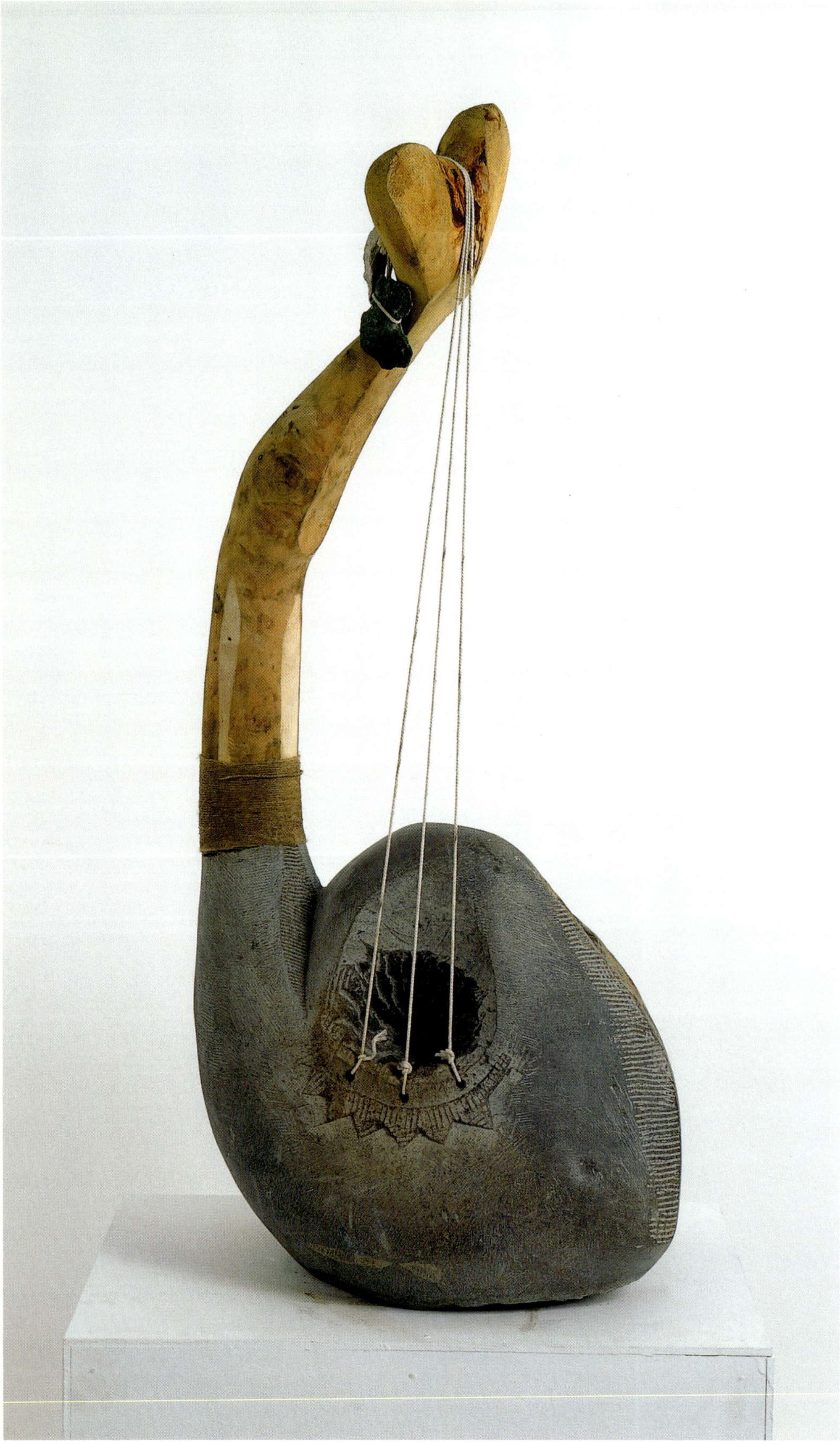

Left *String of My Heart,* 1989. Stone, wood and string, 103 x 45 cm (40½ x 17¾ in). Private collection. From the series *Gadgets of Influence*. 'To each his gadgets.'

Right *Tribute to Sango,* 2005. Granite and calabash, 123 x 100 x 25 cm (48⅖ x 39⅖ x 9⅞ in). Private collection. 'I made *Sango* in Zimbabwe and was trying to work granite without the folly of trying to dominate the stern material, hence the delicate balance meant to lend the piece a feeling of lightness.'

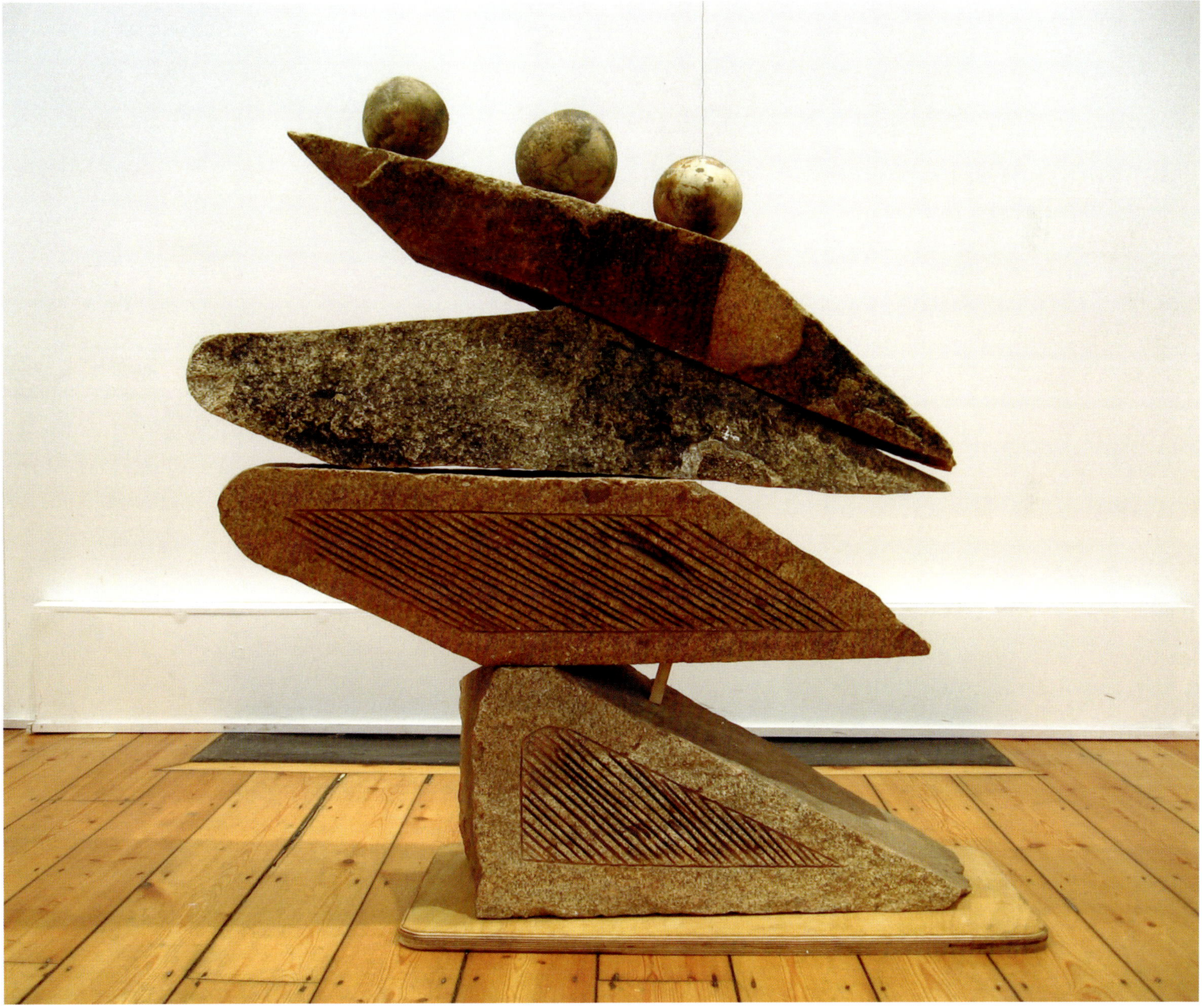

ROMUALD HAZOUMÉ
REPUBLIC OF BENIN

Below *The Last Moines*, 2003. Found objects, 40 x 18 x 16 cm (15¾ x 7 x 6⅓ in). Collection of the artist.

Right *La Bouche du Roi*, 1997–2005 (detail). Petrol cans and various found objects, 1000 x 290 cm (393⅔ x 114⅙ in). British Museum, London. *La Bouche du Roi* is a meditation on human greed and exploitation: the Atlantic slave trade of the past, as well as the different forms of oppression that continue today.

'They didn't know where they were going, but they knew where they had come from. Today they still don't know where they are going, and they have forgotten where they come from.'

Hazoumé has worked with many different media throughout his career: paint on canvas, video, photography and artworks composed of various found and ready-made objects. He is particularly fascinated by the anthropomorphic forms of certain plastic canisters and vessels, which he transforms into his signature 'masks'.

Hazoumé is of Yoruba ancestry, and his work is profoundly infused with the Yoruba religion and way of life, known as *Ifa*, which is itself based on the *Odu Ifa*, a vast body of oral literature containing the collective wisdom of the Yoruba people. Individuals may access this wisdom by bringing their problems to priests who consult *Ifa* on their behalf. Many of Hazoumé's works, particularly the plastic petrol can masks in his monumental installation *La Bouche du Roi* (1997–2005), carry small objects or other symbols that relate to particular Yoruba gods, *orisha*, or to the many different signs used in *Ifa* divination.

Romuald Hazoumé was born in Porto Novo, Republic of Benin, in 1962, and he continues to live and work there, though he travels around the world as a Yoruba itinerant artist (*are*). Originally, he wanted to dedicate himself to a medical career, then he contemplated becoming a professional sportsman before he turned full-time to art in the early 1980s. Hazoumé recently collaborated in founding a gallery and cultural centre, the Fondation Zinsou in Cotonou, Benin, with the specific aim of promoting contemporary African and world art. In the words of Marie-Cécile Zinsou, 'Art today is the best metaphor of Africa tomorrow. Nothing is more urgent than to access it. Let's look at ourselves in the mirror that Romuald hands us.'

In addition to the exhibitions of *La Bouche du Roi* at the Menil Collection, Houston (2005), at the Musée du Quai Branly, Paris (2006), and at the British Museum and various UK venues (2007–9), Hazoumé has had more than a dozen solo exhibitions since 1989. He contributed to 'Africa Remix' at the Hayward Gallery, London, as part of Africa '05, and created a monumental commissioned piece for the Victoria and Albert Museum's 'Uncomfortable Truths' exhibition in 2007. He was awarded the prestigious Arnold Bode-Prize at Documenta 12 in Kassel, Germany in 2007.

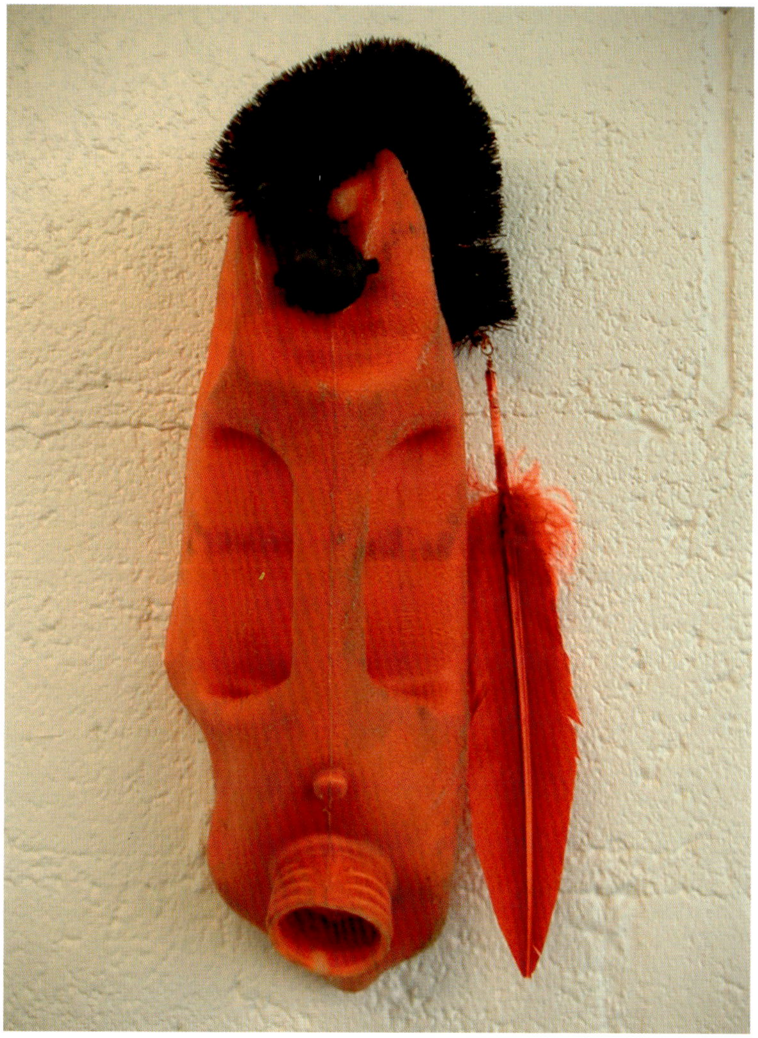

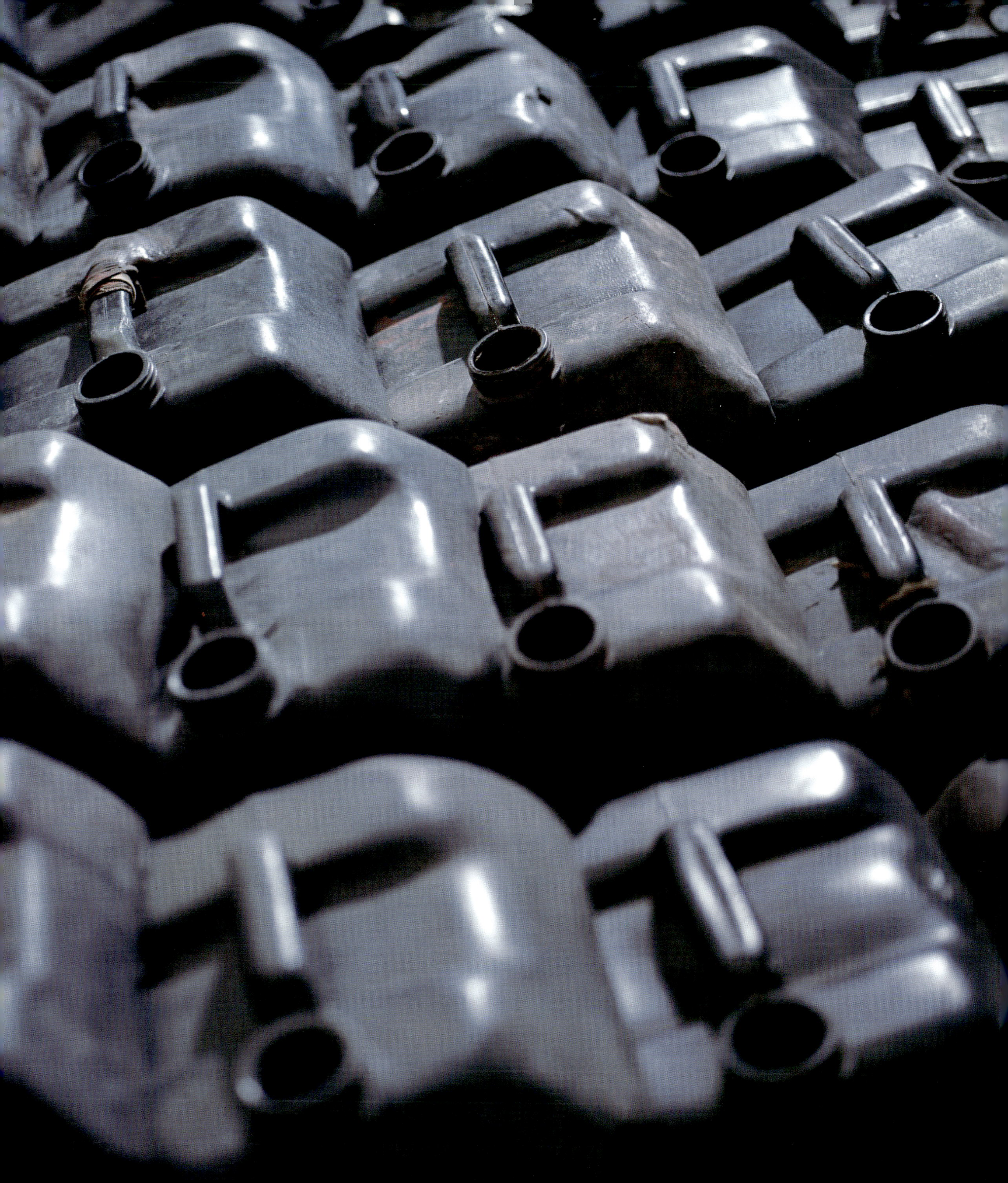

'Materials are a way of connecting with people's lives... Everything we use says something about us, and all the things we reject and throw away are still part of us, part of our lives in a way... My work is like a kind of modern-day archaeology.'
Romuald Hazoumé

Below *La Bouche du Roi*, 1997–2005 (full image). *La Bouche du Roi* is named after a place on the coast of the Republic of Benin from which slaves were transported for hundreds of years. It is a multimedia installation, though its principal components are 304 plastic petrol can 'masks' arranged in the form of the famous print of the Liverpool slave ship *Brookes* (**right**), which was used by the abolitionists in the late eighteenth century. Every mask represents a person, each one given a voice by hidden microphones through which the slaves call out across the centuries. The print of the *Brookes* was designed to demonstrate the appallingly inhumane conditions on board ship, though its deliberately schematic style has since been seen as unacceptably negative in its portrayal of African people as passive victims, stripped of all individuality and culture. *La Bouche du Roi* challenges this European perspective and aims to restore the identities of the enslaved people.

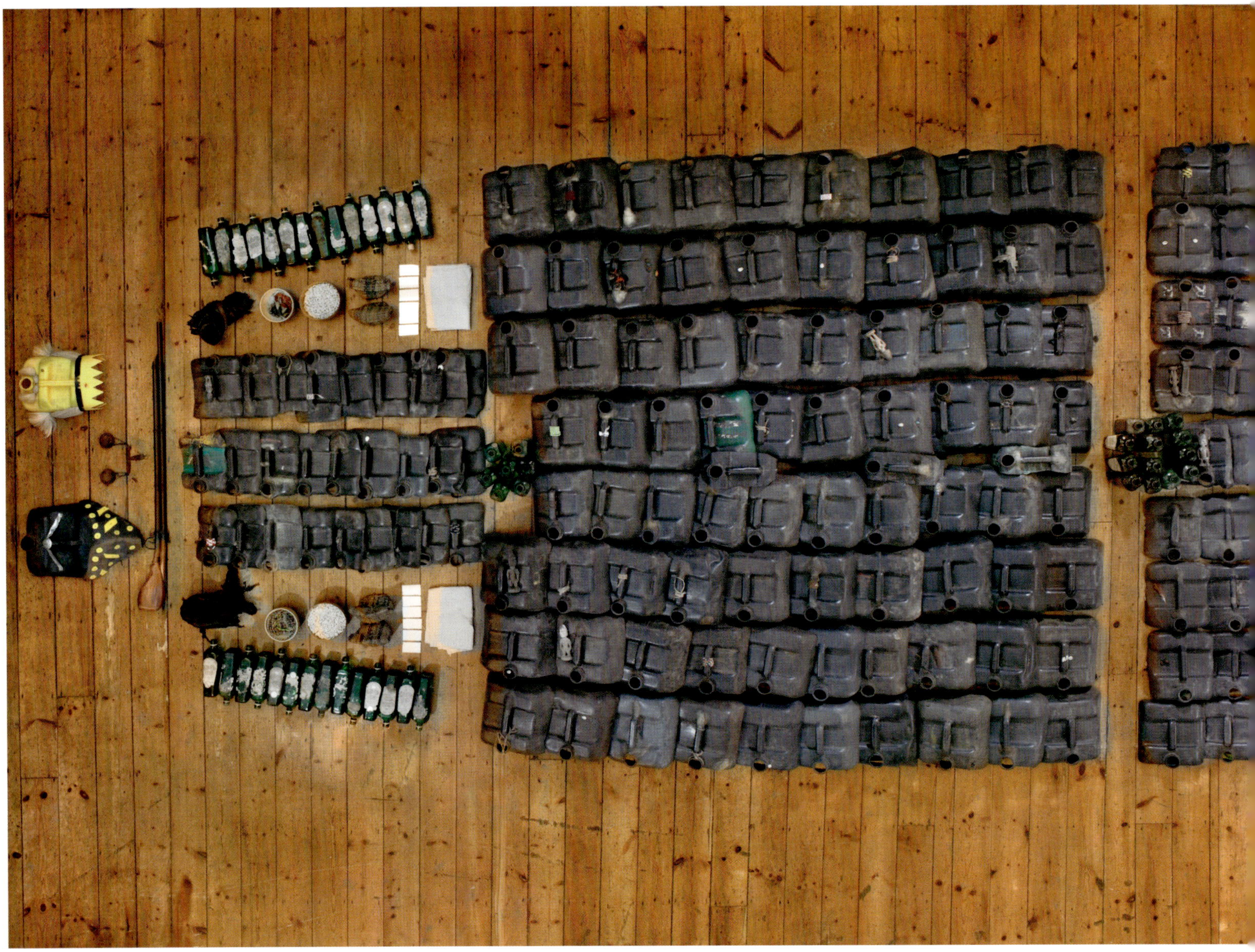

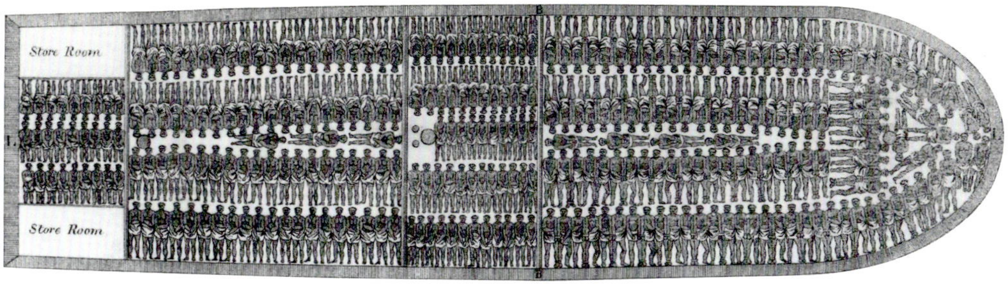
Store Room
Store Room

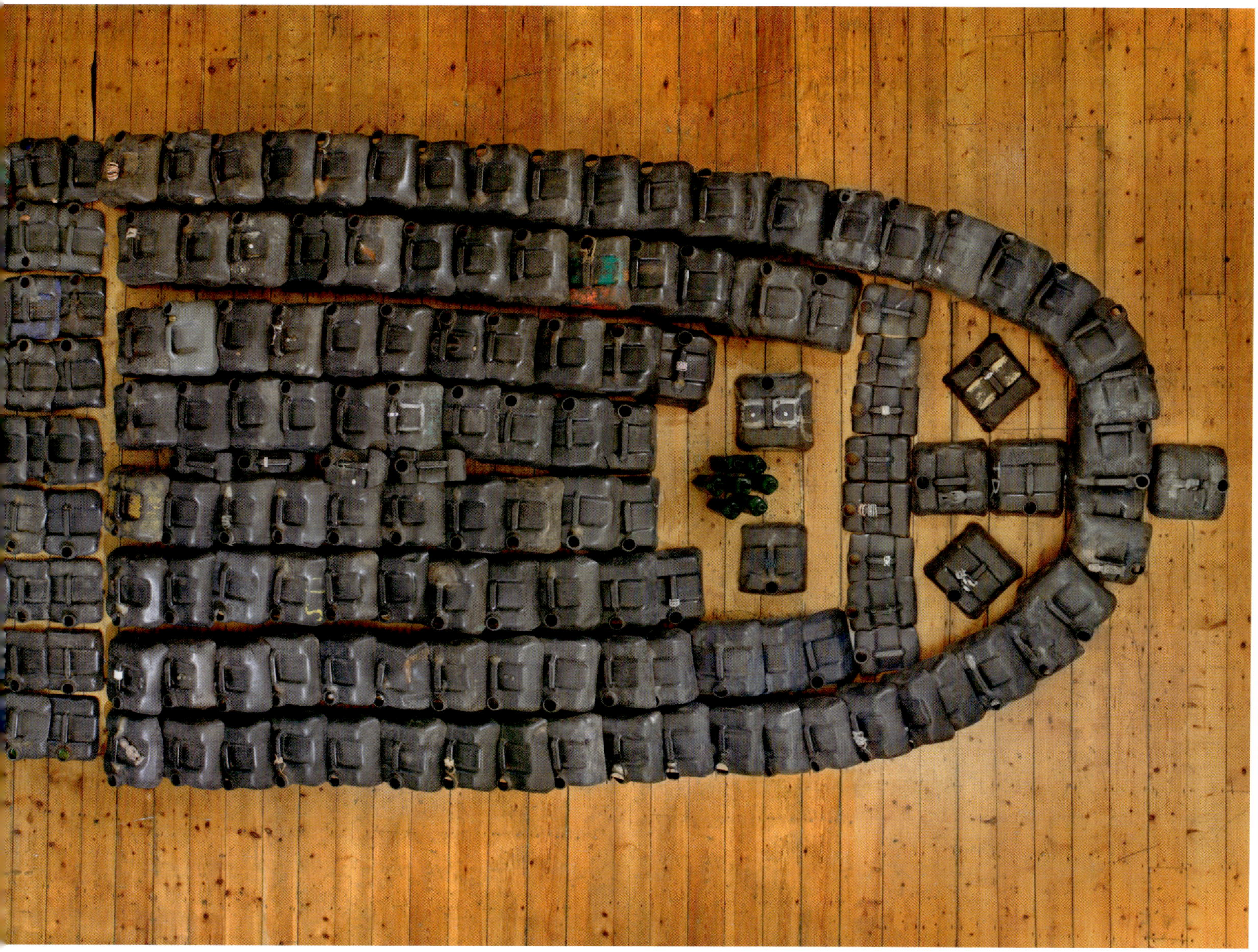

Below and right
La Bouche du Roi,
1997–2005 (details).
The air is filled with the aroma of tobacco and spices, which blend disturbingly with the terrible smells of a slave ship. On the ship you can also see liquor bottles, beads, shells, mirrors, cloth and a musket, all of which were taken to African countries by Europeans to barter for slaves. Slave traders tried to remove all traces of African life and culture from their captives; the process of resistance to enslavement began with the slaves' refusal to give up their religions, language, music and other forms of cultural life. The objects attached to many of the masks symbolize personal connections with many of the gods of Benin. Two large masks, one yellow the other black, represent the European ruler imposed during colonial times and the rightful king of Benin; the scales between them represent the balance of blame between Europeans and some African rulers for the slave trade and its ongoing legacy.

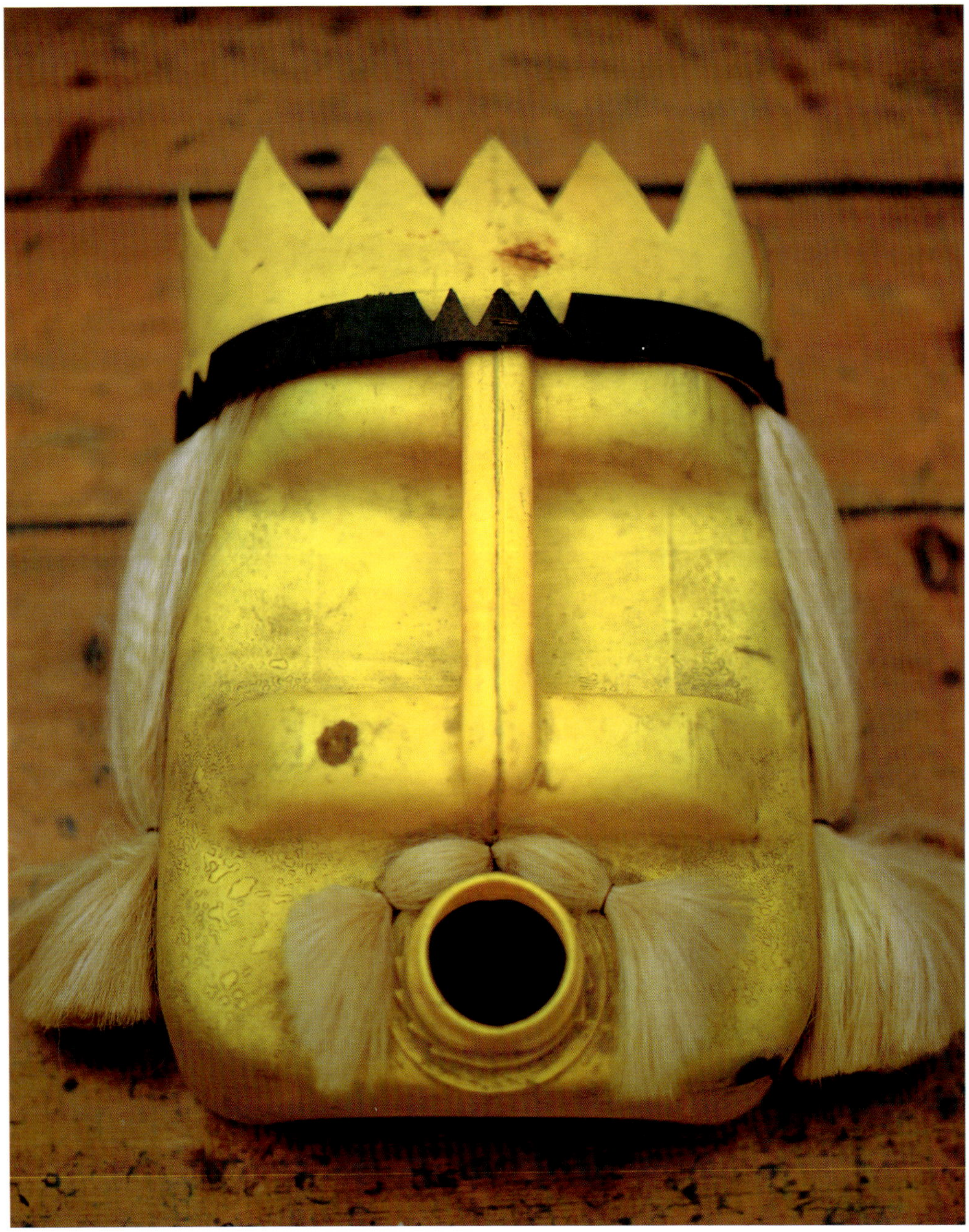

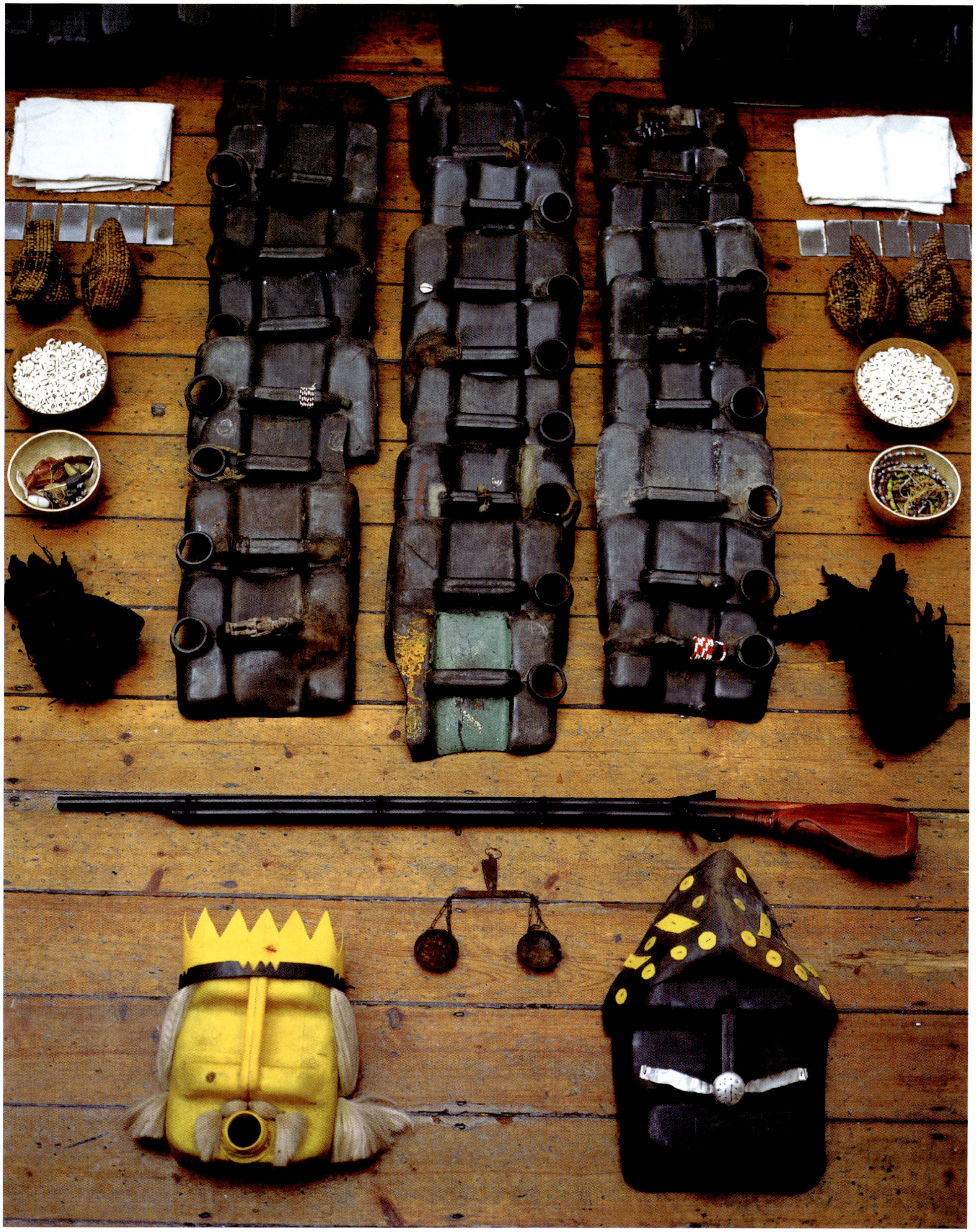

Below *ARTicle 14,* 2005 (detail). Trader's cart and found objects, various dimensions. Collection of the artist.
There is a hypothetical clause, ARTICLE 14, enshrined by popular imagination in many African constitutions, which reads 'figure it out for yourself'. It is a way of life that depends on a talent for survival and in which nothing is wasted.

The handcart at the installation's centre is typical of those found on every street in southern Benin. Hazoumé has festooned the cart with the detritus of UK society, collected by schoolchildren in 2005. In this way he links the people of London with those of Benin, and both with the commercial exchange which for so many centuries has represented the main point of contact between Europe and Africa.

Right *Cargo,* 2006. Metal and plastic, 130 x 484 x 186 cm ($51\frac{1}{6}$ x $190\frac{1}{2}$ x $73\frac{1}{3}$ in). Private collection.
Inspired by the Benin motorcyclists laden with cans of black market petrol, Hazoumé has created his own humorous version of the ingenuity of the motorcyclists in loading their flimsy vehicles to capacity.

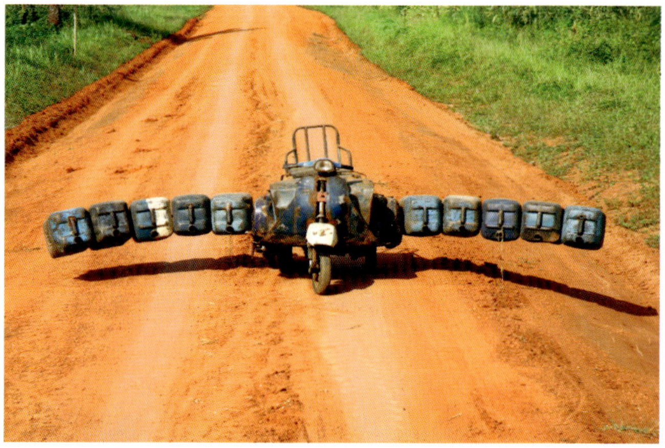

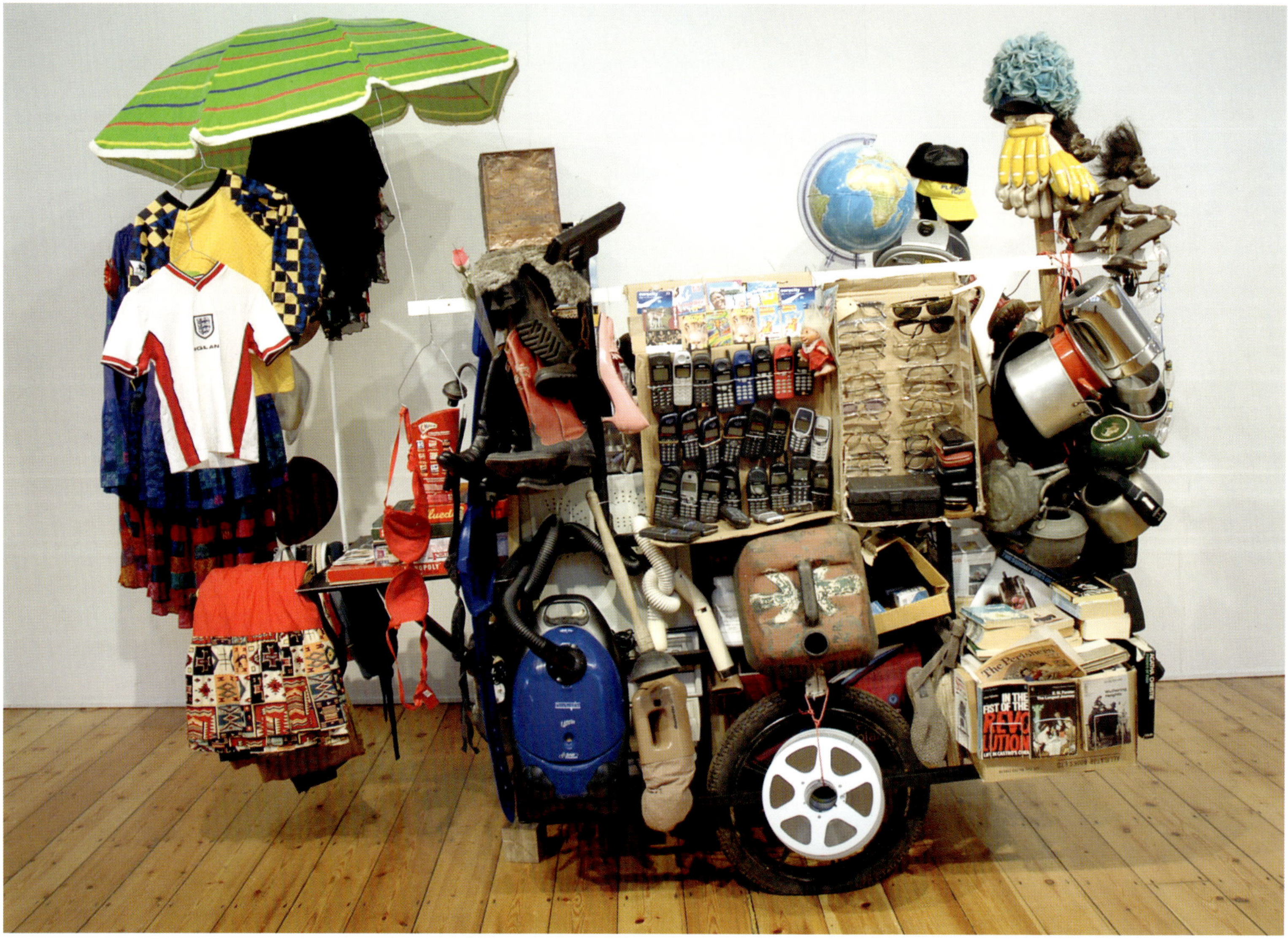

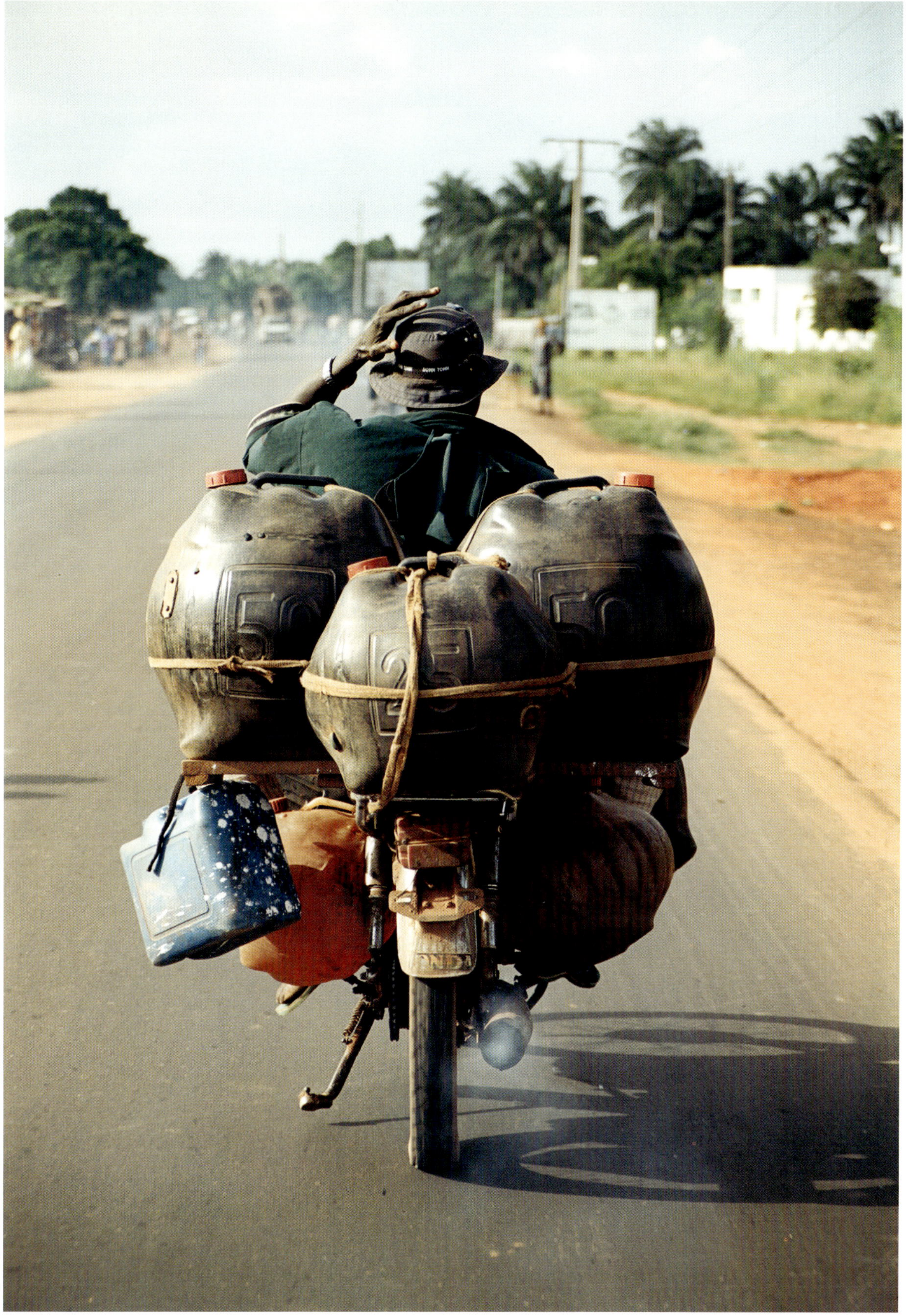

Right *Bidon Armé*. Photograph from the publication accompanying the 2005 exhibition of *La Bouche du Roi*.

La Bouche du Roi also includes a film and still photographs by Romuald Hazoumé of motorcyclists who run black market petrol between Benin and Nigeria. The plastic cans they carry – worked to breaking point then discarded – signify enslavement. Though unable to escape the economic circumstances that force them to pursue their hazardous existence, the cyclists themselves signify resistance to oppression, clawing back some of Africa's natural resources, which make fortunes for a few while leaving the majority in desperate poverty.

'In many ways slavery has never ended – many people live in the same kind of conditions, bound to work their whole lives for rich bosses who use them without regard for their humanity, and who then throw them away, like refuse.'

JACKSON HLUNGWANI
SOUTH AFRICA

Below *Christ with a Football*, 1992. Wood, height 210 cm (82⅔ in). Private collection.
'The night had come and I was lying down, thinking of the coming day and what I was going to do (commit suicide), when suddenly Jesus appeared. Actually there were three persons. They came from the northern horizon, the Kalanga country.'

Right *Ngungungyani Warrior*, before 1985. Wood, height 78 cm (30¾ in). Private collection.

In 1978, Jackson Hlungwani was on the point of taking his own life when he had a profoundly powerful vision of Jesus; not only was he healed, but he started to create a series of unique, visionary sculptures. These sculptures were first displayed to the South African public in the ground-breaking 'Tributaries' exhibition of 1984–85, curated by Ricky Burnett, at which the work of both white and black South African artists was displayed. For the first time, black artists showed work that had been produced outside the formal system of art education, which at that time was only available to white students under the apartheid regime. Hlungwani's work caused an instant sensation.

Jackson Hlungwani was born at Nkanyani, Northern Province in 1923. As a boy he herded his father's cattle and became a close observer of the natural world around him. As a young man he was sent to work in Johannesburg but he came home after losing a finger in an accident. He joined the African Zionist Church and was ordained as a minister in 1946. Together with some of his followers he began to construct a hilltop complex of buildings and stone enclosures, which he called the New Jerusalem; his wood sculptures became an integral part of the complex.

'I first saw the work of Jackson Hlungwani at the "Tributaries" show,' recounts Robert Loder, 'and faced by his crucifix shown there, realized that this was a major talent that embraced local formal tradition but was also contemporary and relevant in feeling. No representation of work from South Africa can be without reference to Jackson's work. It is entirely *sui generis* but, at the same time, an assertion of the common humanity of all the diverse peoples that make up South Africa.'

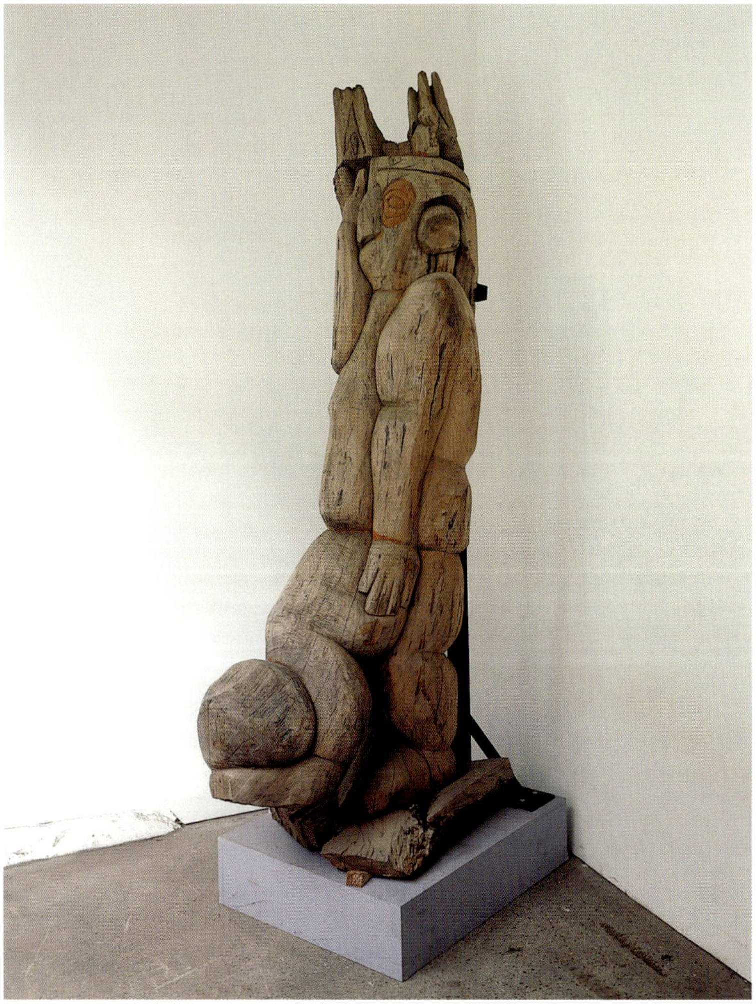

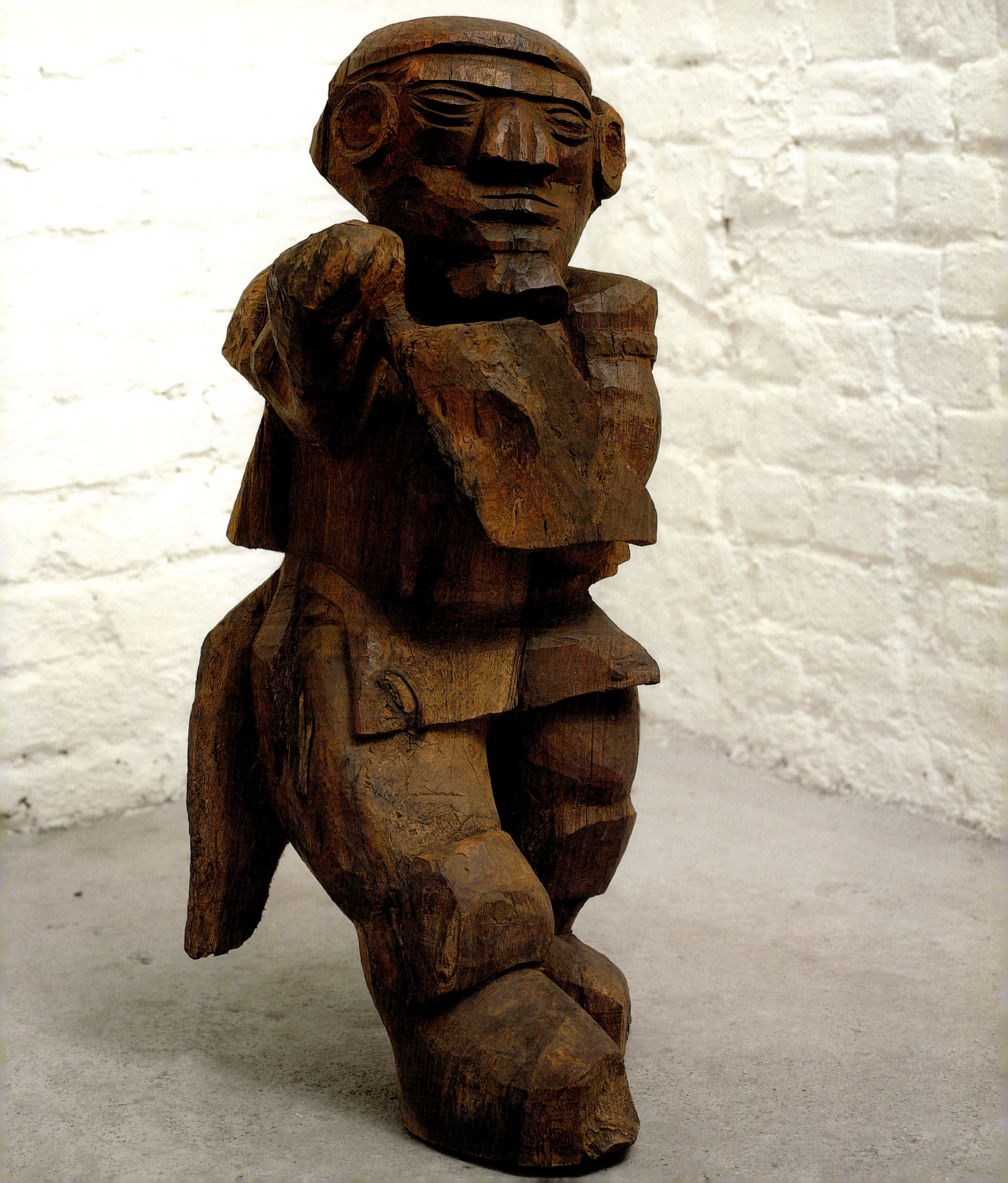

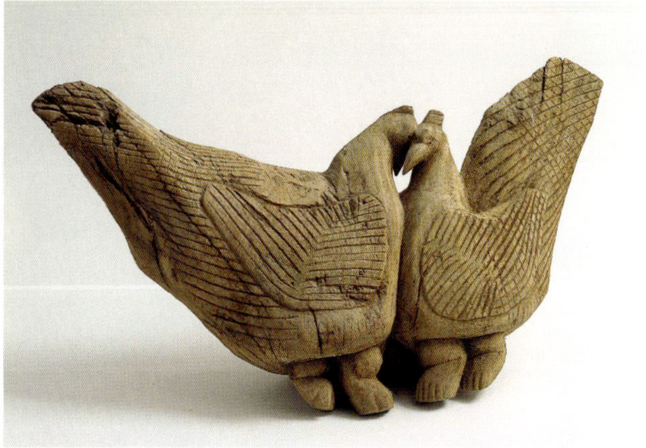

Left *Two Chickens*, 1992. Wood, 40 x 70 cm (15¾ x 27½ in). Private collection.

Below *Fish*, 1990. Wood, 170 x 126 cm (67 x 49⅗ in). Private collection. Hlungwani frequently carves a fish, symbol of Christ, in all shapes and sizes. 'Fish don't fight, fish are happy, fish teach, I teach.'

Right *Son of Adam*, 1990. Wood, height 66 cm (26 in). Private collection.

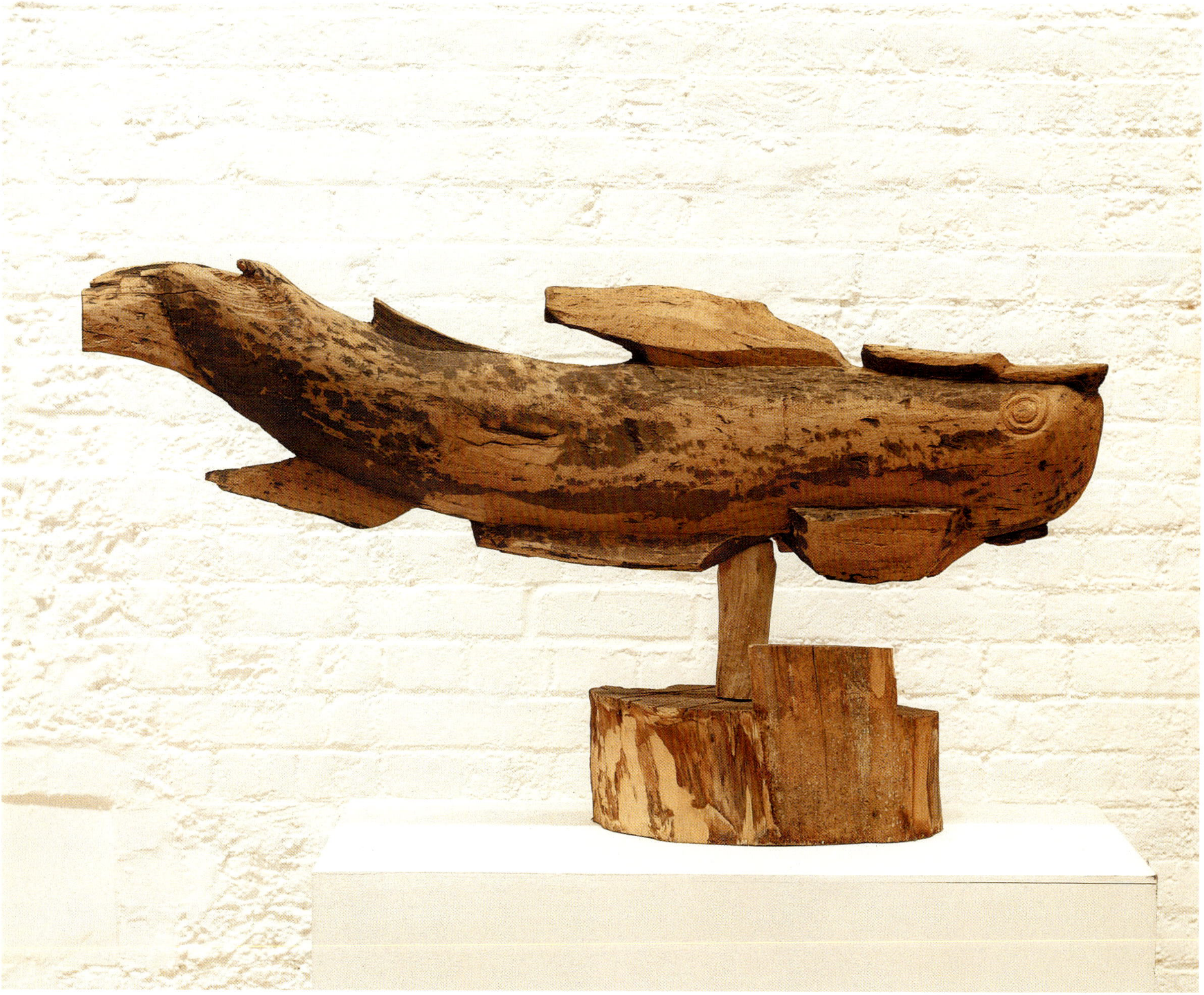

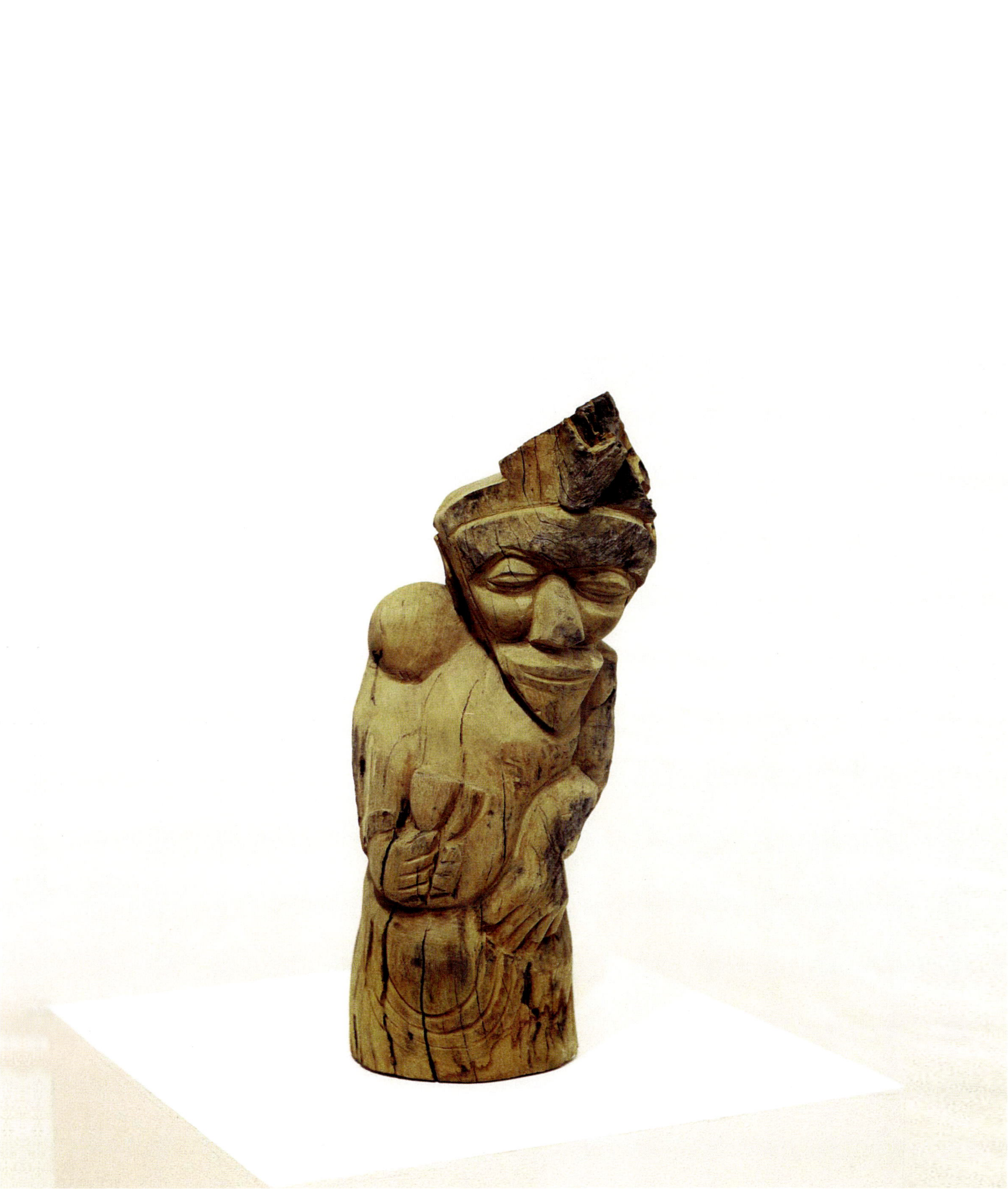

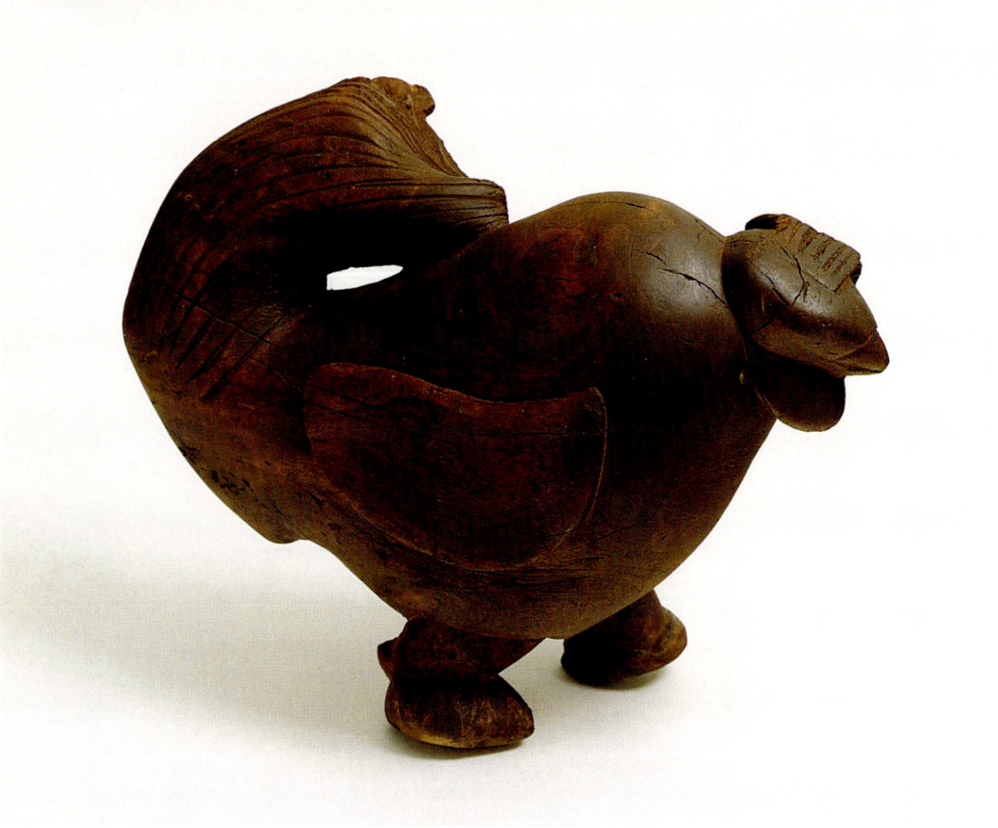

'Jesus stretched out his right arm and grasped my right hand. Number one he said: "You see, today you are healed, you will not die." Then, number two: "You will serve God for your whole life." Number three he said: "You will see God himself. Look over there." I did not, in fact, see God's full stature. I only saw his legs, from the knees down. I watched the legs passing by, going in the direction of KwaZulu. Then Jesus ceased holding my hands.'
Jackson Hlungwani

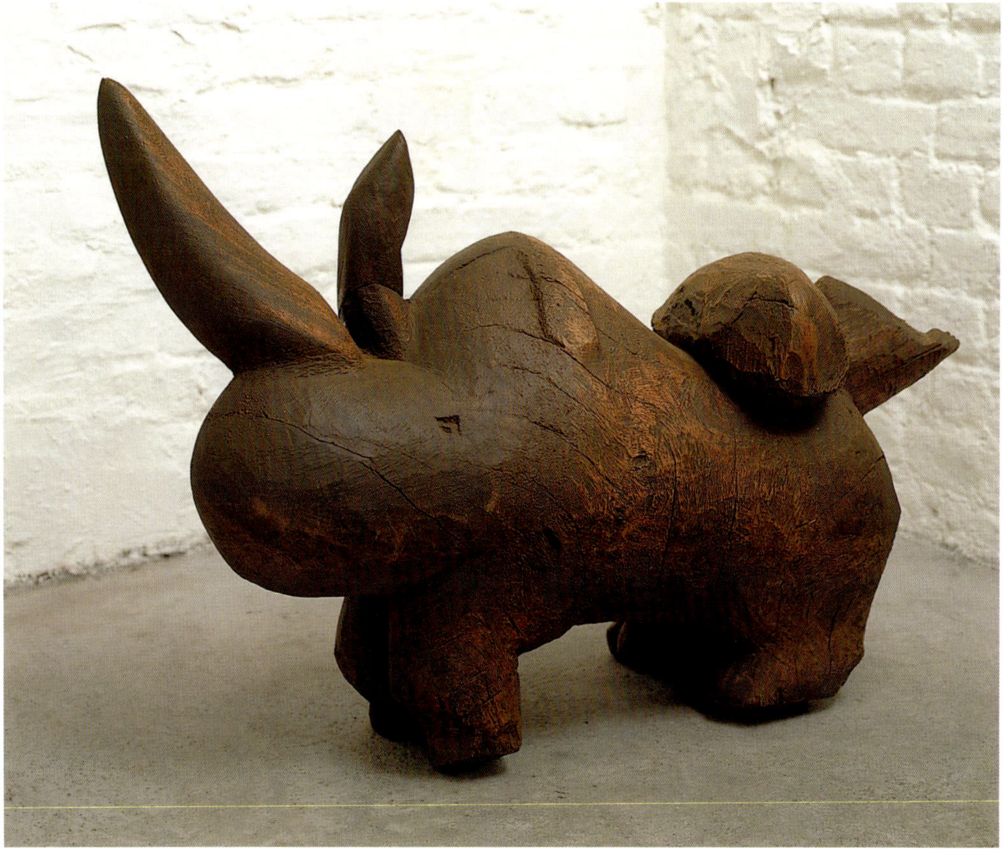

Top left *Chicken*, before 1985. Wood, height 31 cm (12⅕ in). Private collection.

Below left *Rhino*, before 1985. Wood, height 59 cm (23⅕ in). Private collection.

Right *Very First Gabriel*, before 1995. Wood, height 185 cm (72⅘ in). Private collection.

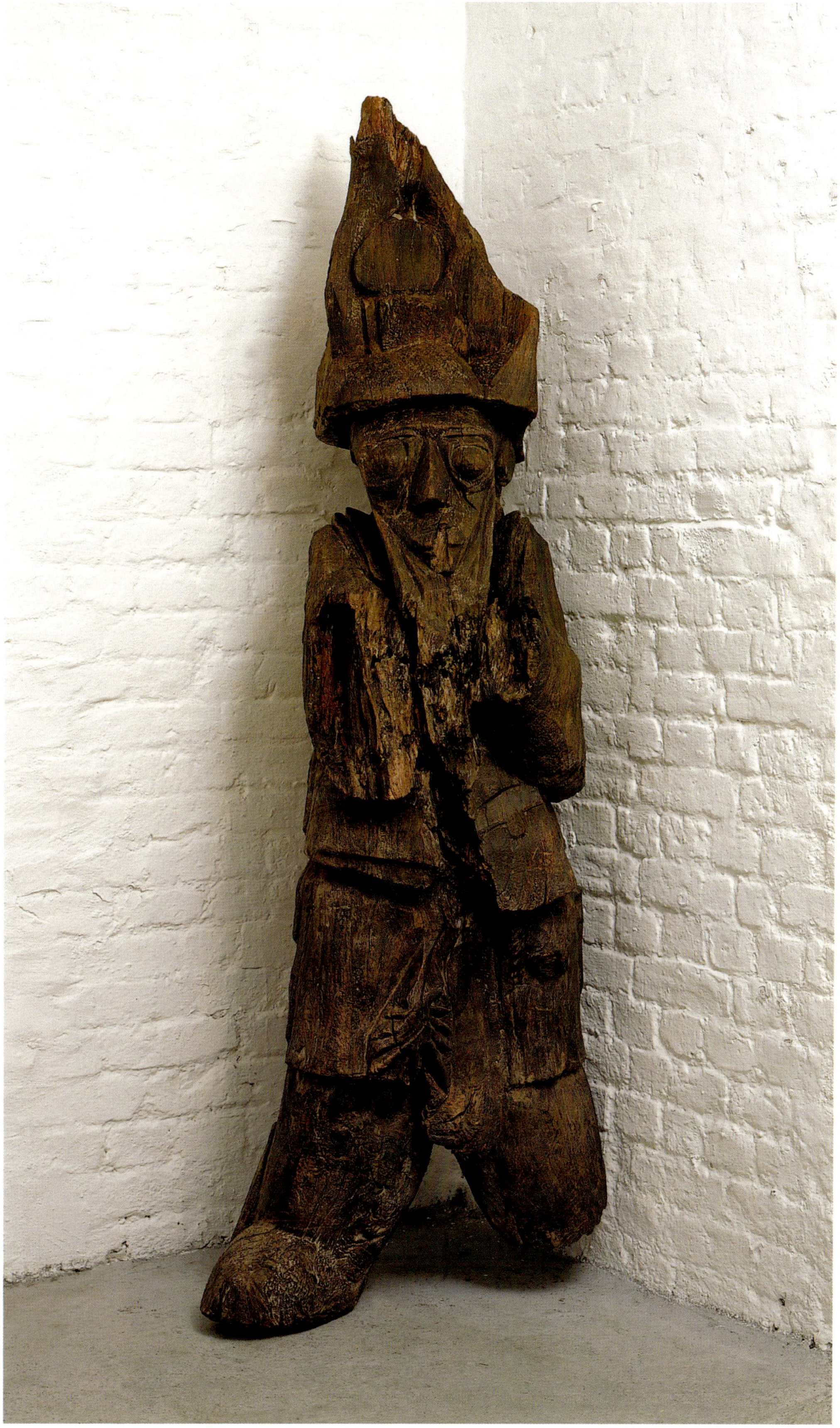

JAK KATARIKAWE
UGANDA

Below *Princess Bagaya of Toro*, 1974. Oil on board, 63.5 x 51 cm (25 x 20 in). Stadt Frankfurt am Main Museum der Weltkulturen.
The princess, a Cambridge-educated lawyer, was foreign minister in Idi Amin's regime. 'She tried to work, to help Uganda. I think Idi Amin was in love, but she is very strong. She knows what she is doing. She looks very, very far.' This early portrait perfectly captures the qualities of the princess at the same time as indicating the weight of her responsibilities.

Right *The Dreams*, 1989. Acrylic on paper, 68 x 53 cm (26¾ x 20⅘ in). Private collection.
The central figure is king, politician, artist – the 'Big Man' of the community. The butterfly motif on his jacket and in the top right of the picture symbolize sexual satisfaction; the pink, skewered pieces of meat evoke the pleasure of eating. He is surrounded by an unruly, yet largely adoring assortment of cattle, which represent the poor people of rural Uganda, and specifically of the artist's homeland in the lakes region, where cattle are an integral part of the community.

Jak Katarikawe was born in *c.* 1940 in Kabale, Kigezi region, southern Uganda. He grew up on his parents' farm without any formal education, though he was inspired both by his mother's paintings on the walls of their house and by the murals in the Catholic cathedral at Rushoroza. He returned periodically to Kigezi throughout his life. In 1963, Jak moved to Kampala and became a driver for David Cook, a lecturer at Makerere University, who encouraged him to paint. Jak held two exhibitions in Kampala in 1965 and 1966. In 1967 he came to the attention of the Tanzanian painter Sam Ntiro, who taught in the Arts Faculty at Makerere and became an important influence on Jak's career. In 1981 he moved to Nairobi, Kenya, where he now lives and works.

Although Jak has spent much of his life living in big cities, his paintings are almost always set in the country, though they are not necessarily 'about' rural life. Animals, particularly cattle, feature strongly in his work. Elsbeth Court has noted that: 'He is convinced – through his experiences and observations when herding cattle – that cows watch people, imitate them and express feelings just as much as humans do.'

Jak lived through an extremely turbulent time in Uganda after Idi Amin's coup in 1971, and counts himself lucky to have survived. His strong Christian faith has supported him throughout his life and is an important element in his art: 'Me, I trust God. I know one day we'll be okay. Always I pray to God.' He has exhibited widely, particularly in eastern Africa and Germany, and has been an inspiration to generations of young artists:

> *Art is your passport; your talent is your treasure. When you go to a foreign country you cannot sell your shirt because in Europe and America they make better shirts. But they don't create paintings or sculptures as we do here... Angels of creation, be on your guard!*

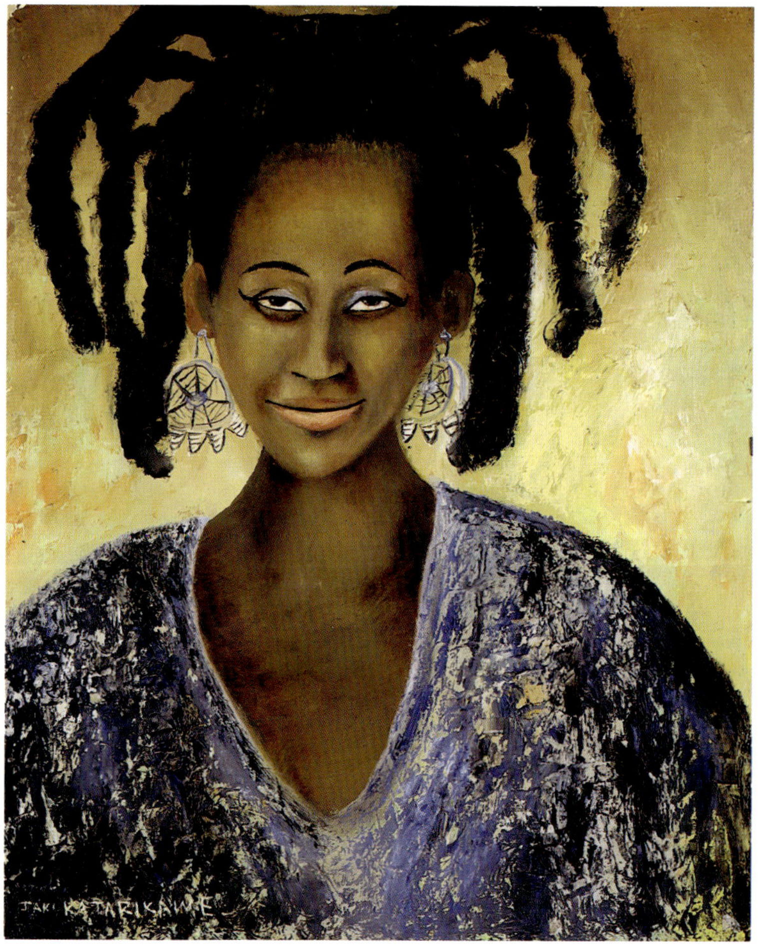

'When I remember or listen to a good story, I laugh at it, and then later, translate it into a painting. I do the same thing with dreams. I awake from a dream and begin to paint my story right away before I forget it... all my pictures are dreams.'
Jak Katarikawe

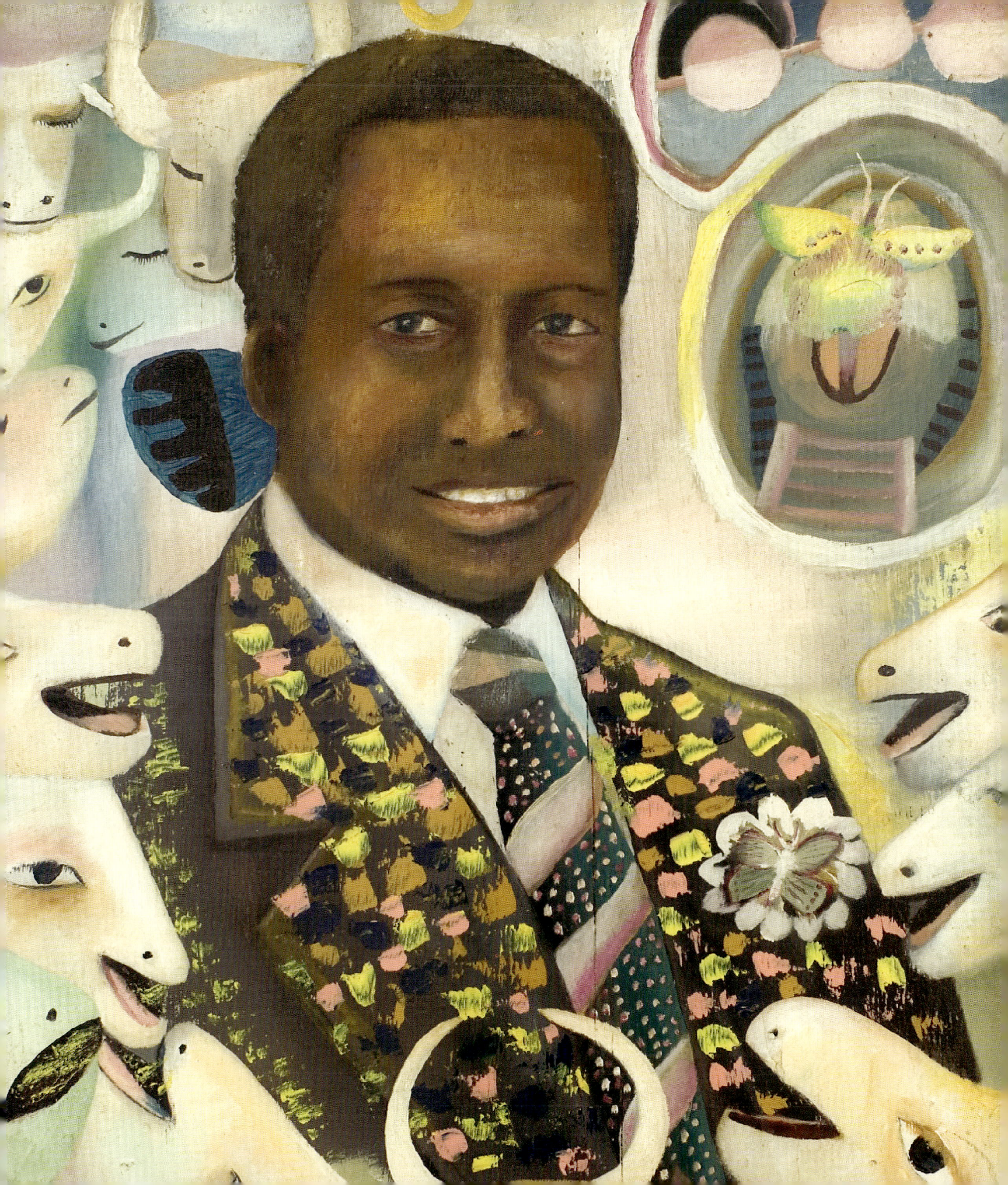

Below *Kigezi, c.* 1965–67. Watercolours on board, 45 x 58.5 cm (17¾ x 23 in). Stadt Frankfurt am Main Museum der Weltkulturen. This is the wistfully evoked landscape of Kigezi, the artist's homeland.

Right *This is the Wedding, c.* 1965–67. Watercolours on board, 45 x 58 cm (17¾ x 22⅘ in). Stadt Frankfurt am Main Museum der Weltkulturen.

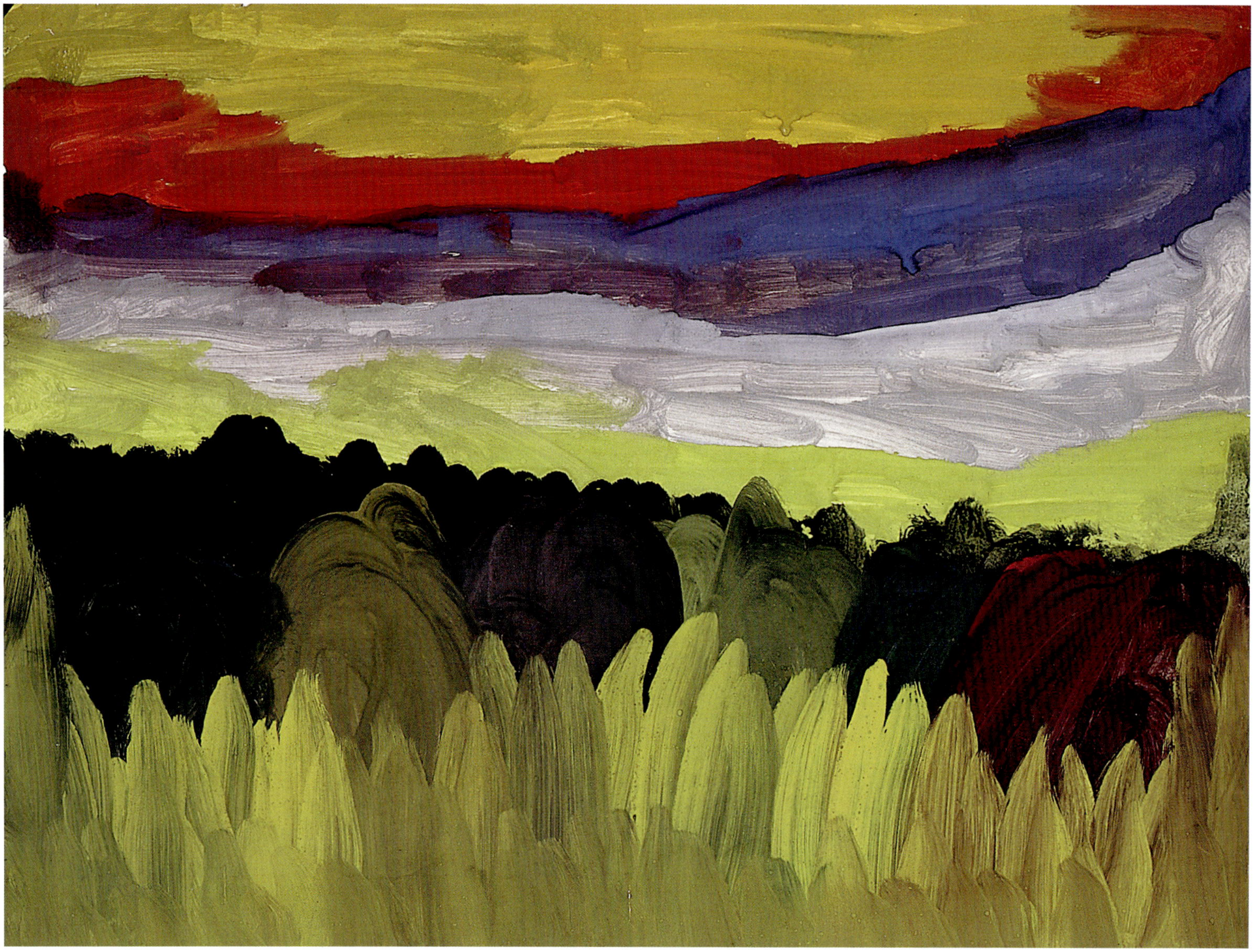

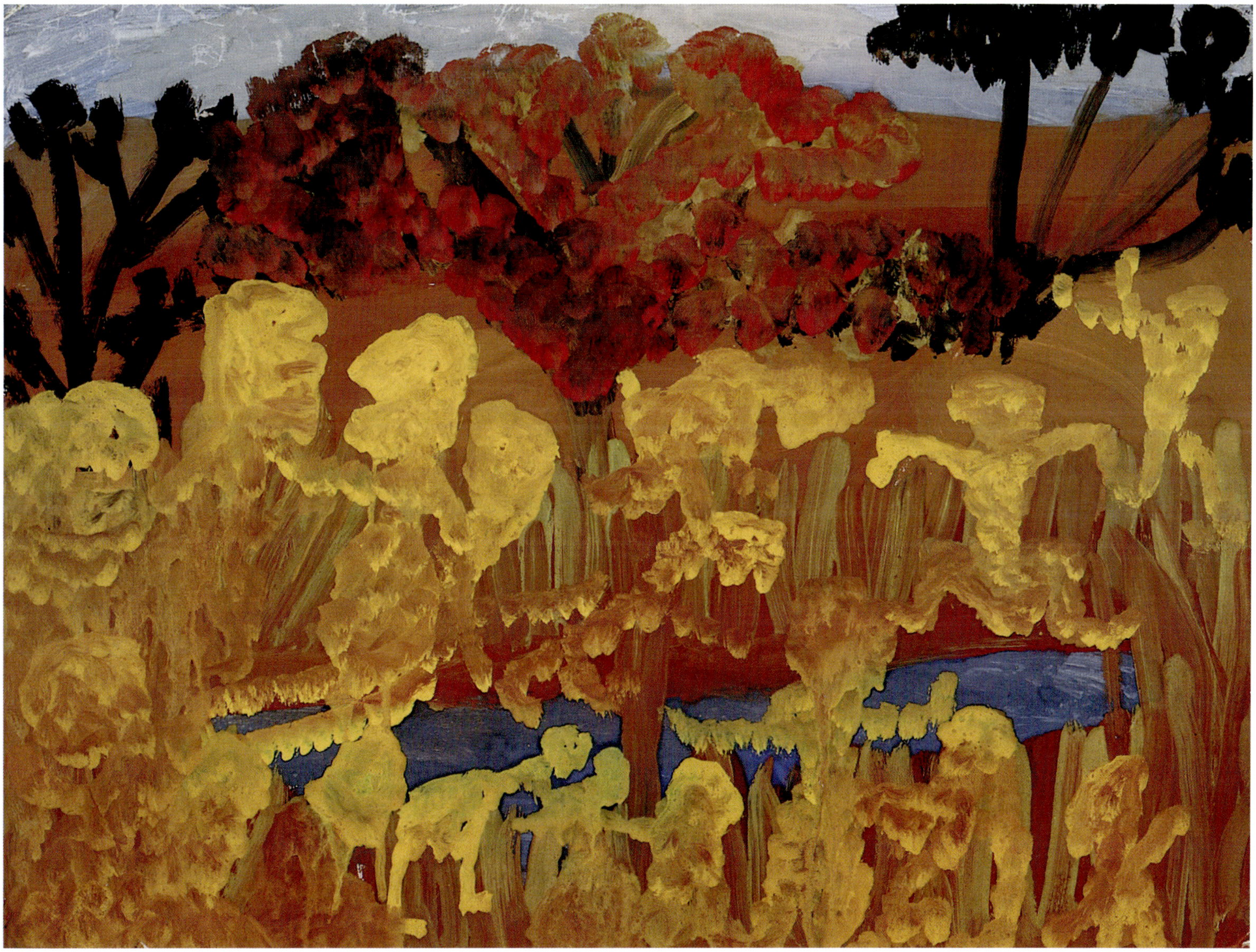

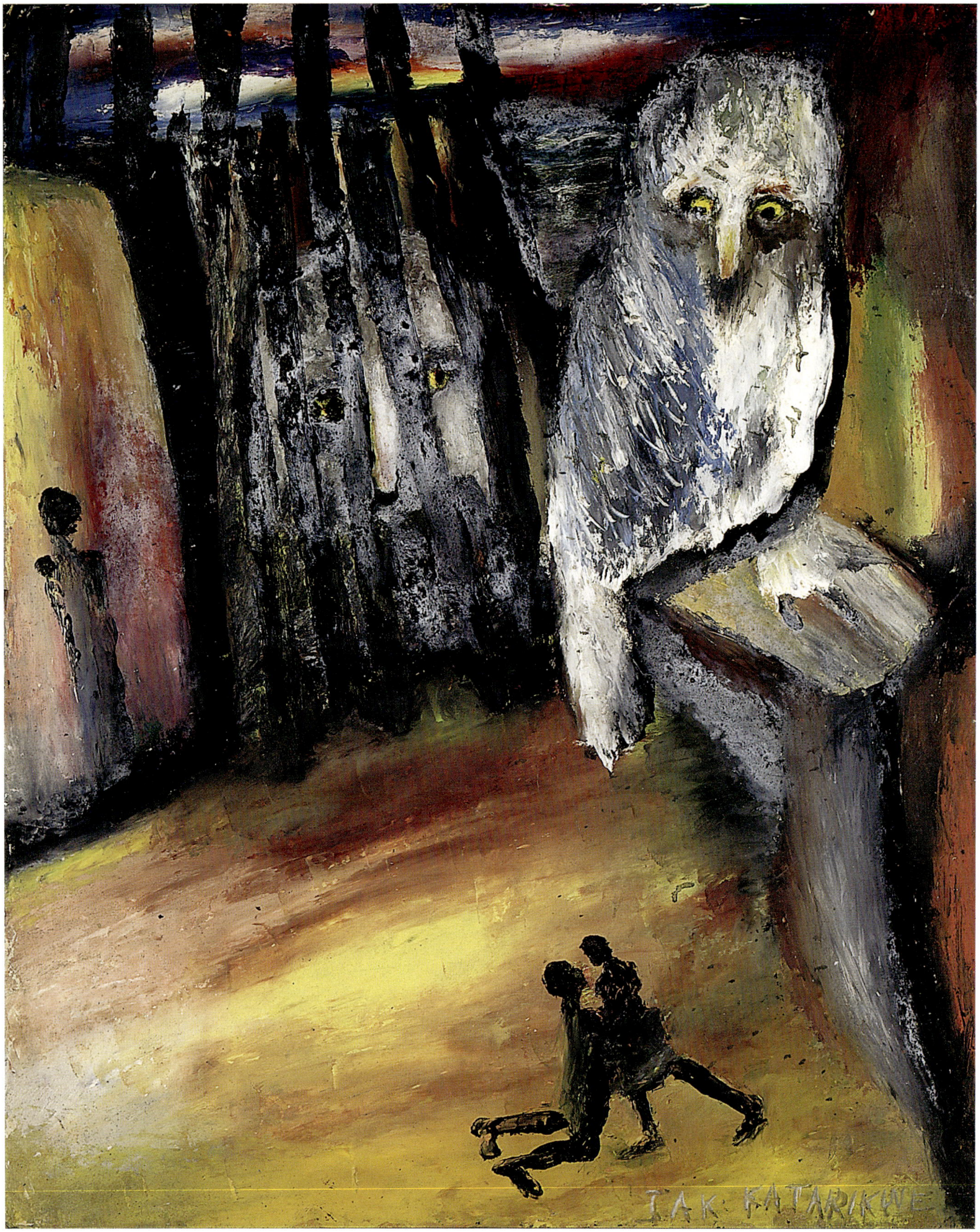
JAK KATARIKWE

Left *A Very Good Angel*, no date. Oil on board, 64 x 51 cm (25⅓ x 20 in). Stadt Frankfurt am Main Museum der Weltkulturen.
Birds are often messengers in Katarikawe's art, as they are in the folklore of many societies around the world: 'This man married. When the woman was getting a baby he ran away and got another one. He is catching another one here. She says: "You don't have a wife?" – He says: "No, no, no." Now this bird he says: "No, he is telling you lies." He is a very good angel.'

Below *Mountain of Love (Mlima na mapenzi)*, 2006. Oil on board, approximately 76 x 92 cm (30 x 36⅕ in). Private collection.
In Katarikawe's narrative paintings cattle and people live together virtually as one community, sharing many of the same thoughts and desires. Here the artist depicts a couple lying beneath a patchwork quilt of dreams, surrounded by the cattle/people that they love – and who love them in return.

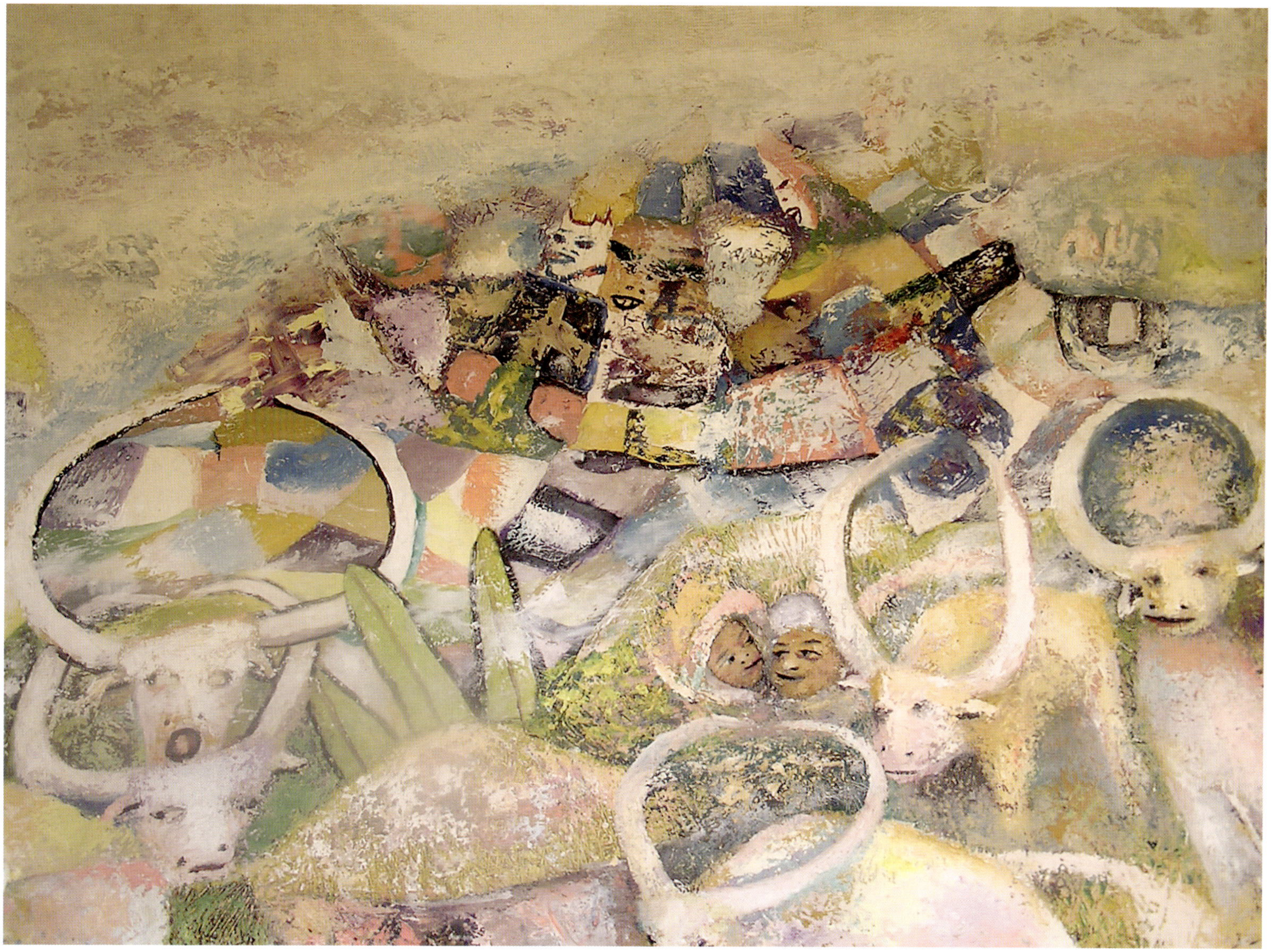

WILLIAM KENTRIDGE
SOUTH AFRICA

This spread Images of two of the miniature theatre models for *Black Box/ Chambre Noire*, 2005. Installed in the artist's studio with projections and mechanical prototypes.
'I'm playing with three sets of associations in *Black Box*. The first is the black box of the theatre. The installation consists of a model of a theatre, which houses projections and characters... The second... is the *chambre noire* – the central chamber of a camera between the lens and the eyepiece, into which light enters and a kind of meaning is created... The third reference is to the flight recorder that is used to trace the last moments before an airline disaster. And the disaster I will be referring to... is the German massacre of the Herero people in southwest Africa.'

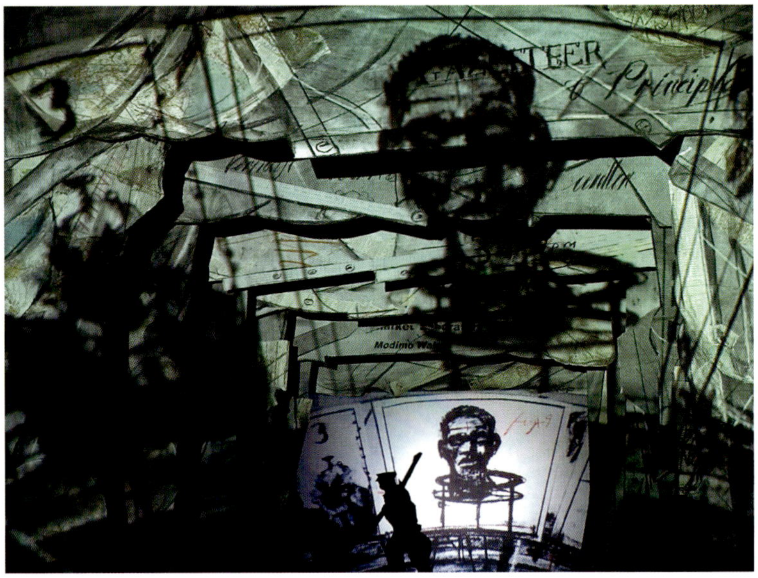

I was six years old and my father was one of the lawyers for the families who had been killed [in the Sharpeville massacre]. I remember once coming into his study and seeing on his desk a large, flat, yellow Kodak box, and lifting the lid of it – it looked like a chocolate box. Inside were images of a woman with her back blown off, someone with only half her head visible.

To William Kentridge the box became a perfect metaphor for South Africa's recent history. As an artist and film-maker, his life and career have been spent constantly contemplating and re-examining South Africa's recent history, the light and darkness that are both outside and within it and the essential incompleteness of its victims and of those who observe or engage in this victimization.

Kentridge was born in 1955 into a wealthy Johannesburg family, descendants of Jewish refugees from the purges and pogroms of Russia and Europe. For generations the family had been deeply involved in politics and human rights issues in South Africa.

Kentridge studied politics and African studies at the University of Witwatersrand (1973–76), art at the Johannesburg Art Foundation (1976–78) and mime and theatre at the Ecole Jacques Lecoq in Paris (1981–82). He was a member of the Junction Avenue Theatre Company (1975–91) and since 1992 has worked with the Handspring Puppet Company in Johannesburg. 'I have never been able to escape Johannesburg, and in the end all my art is rooted in this rather desperate provincial city.'

A consummate draughtsman, Kentridge's animated films depend for their effect on the technique of altering, erasing and adding to a few drawings, rather than running together hundreds of 'frames', each consisting of a slightly different complete drawing.

Kentridge is fascinated by the physical and metaphysical qualities of light, dark and shadows, using them as ways of thinking about the world and about perspectives gained or lost through the passage of time. Two of his most recent projects, *The Magic Flute* (2005) and *Black Box* (2005), look at the historical and philosophical Western concept of the Enlightenment, and how this justified European attempts, through force of arms if necessary, to bring light to the 'Dark Continent' of Africa.

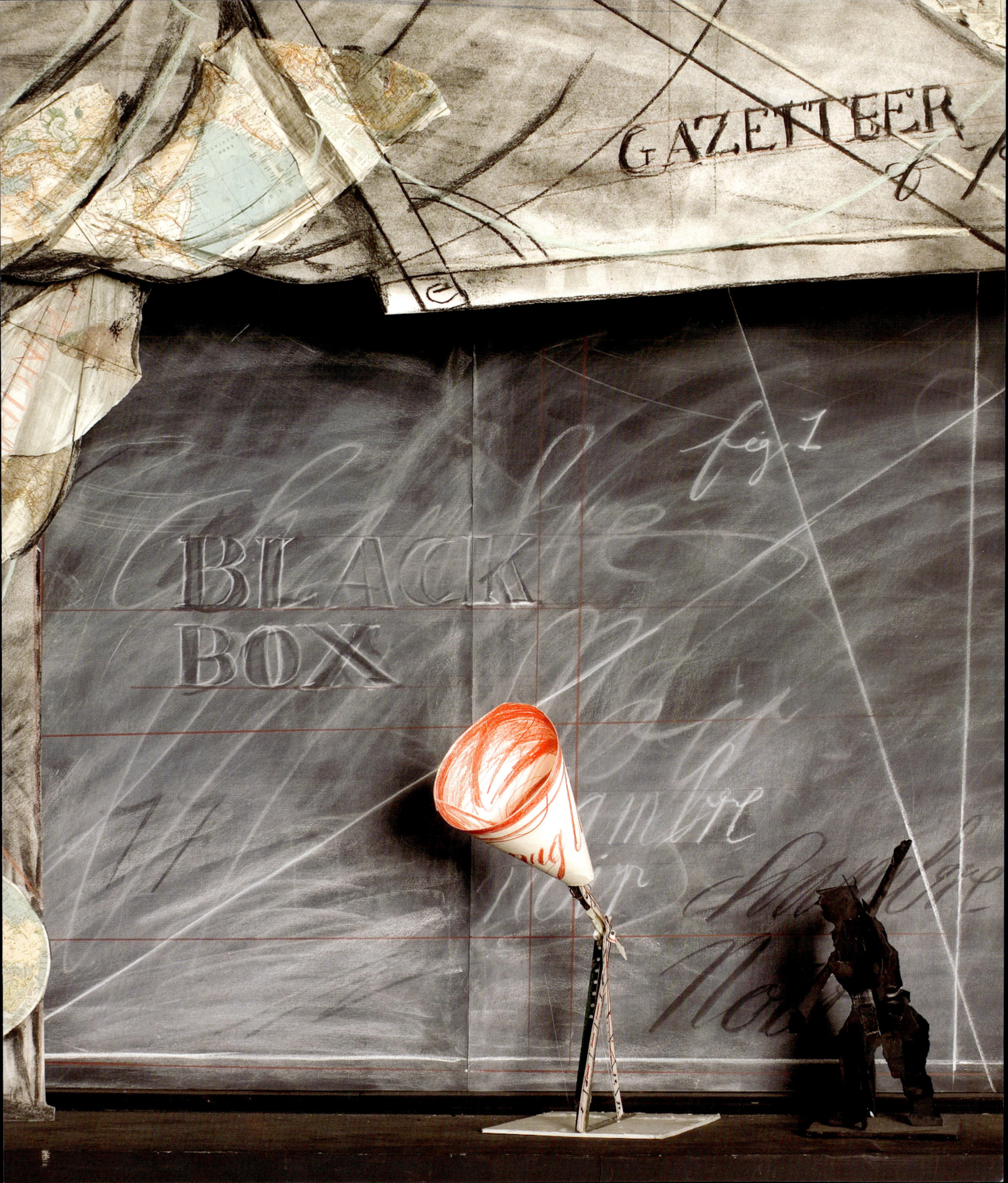
GAZETTEER
BLACK
BOX
fig 1

'Much of what I will be discussing here has to do with the nature of shadows, which I see as an important preliminary consideration for *Black Box*. One of the metaphors I'm playing with is that of the illuminating shadow. If you have an image, and a shadow across it, you invert what is light and what is dark, and the shadow itself functions as a kind of spotlight... If the *Magic Flute* represents the Utopian moment of the Enlightenment, *Black Box* represents the other end of the spectrum.'
William Kentridge

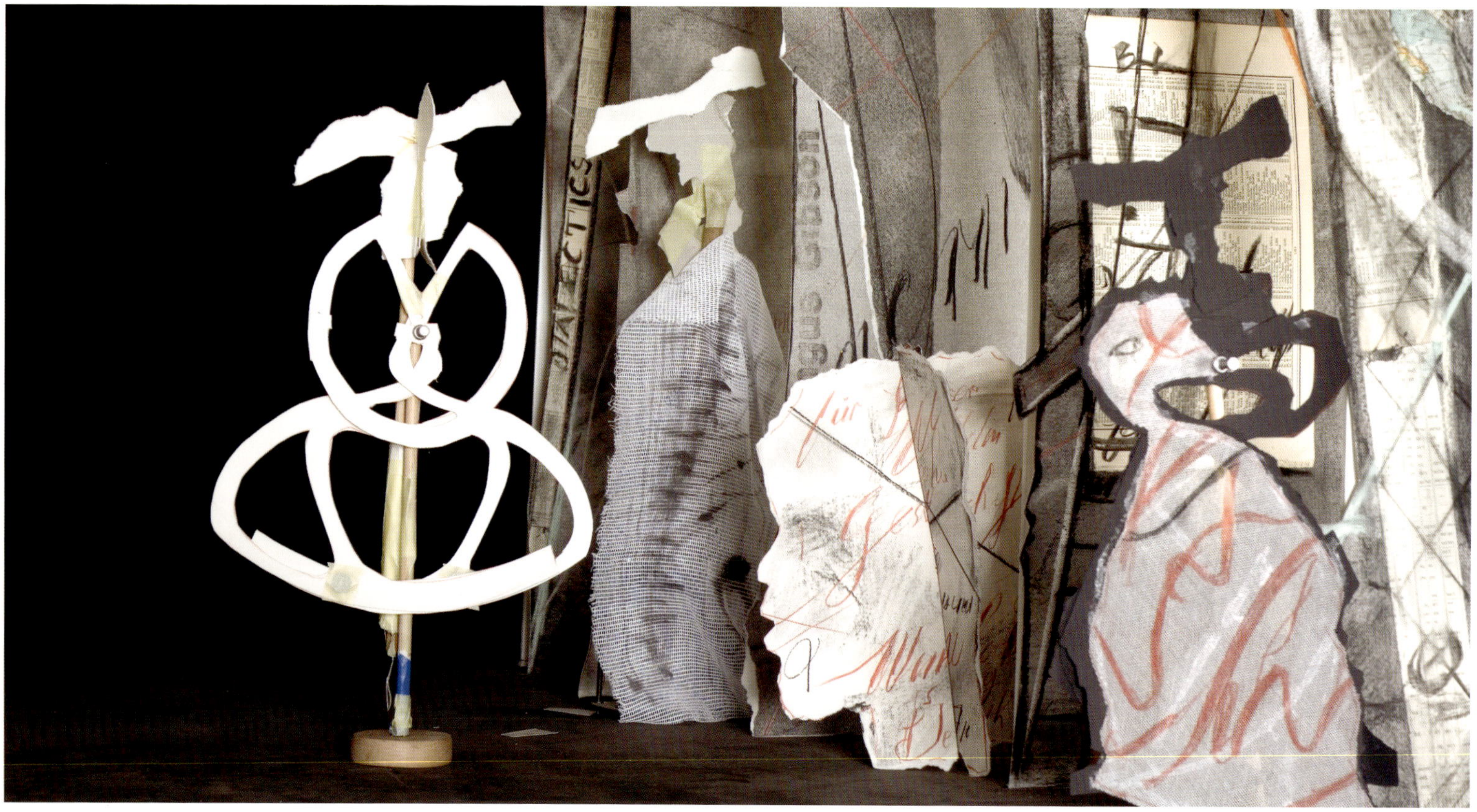

This spread Images of two of the miniature theatre models for *Black Box/ Chambre Noire*, 2005. 'Approximately two years ago a solar eclipse could be seen in southern Africa... While looking at the eclipse I became very aware of the process of looking – of being made conscious of the nature of light... The second thing the eclipse made me consider was a question: what is the nature of the meeting point between the individual receiver of images and the broad projector of them?... I ask this question not only in terms of looking, but also in terms of our direct experience in the world. What parts of the world do we have some control over? What parts are utterly beyond us?'

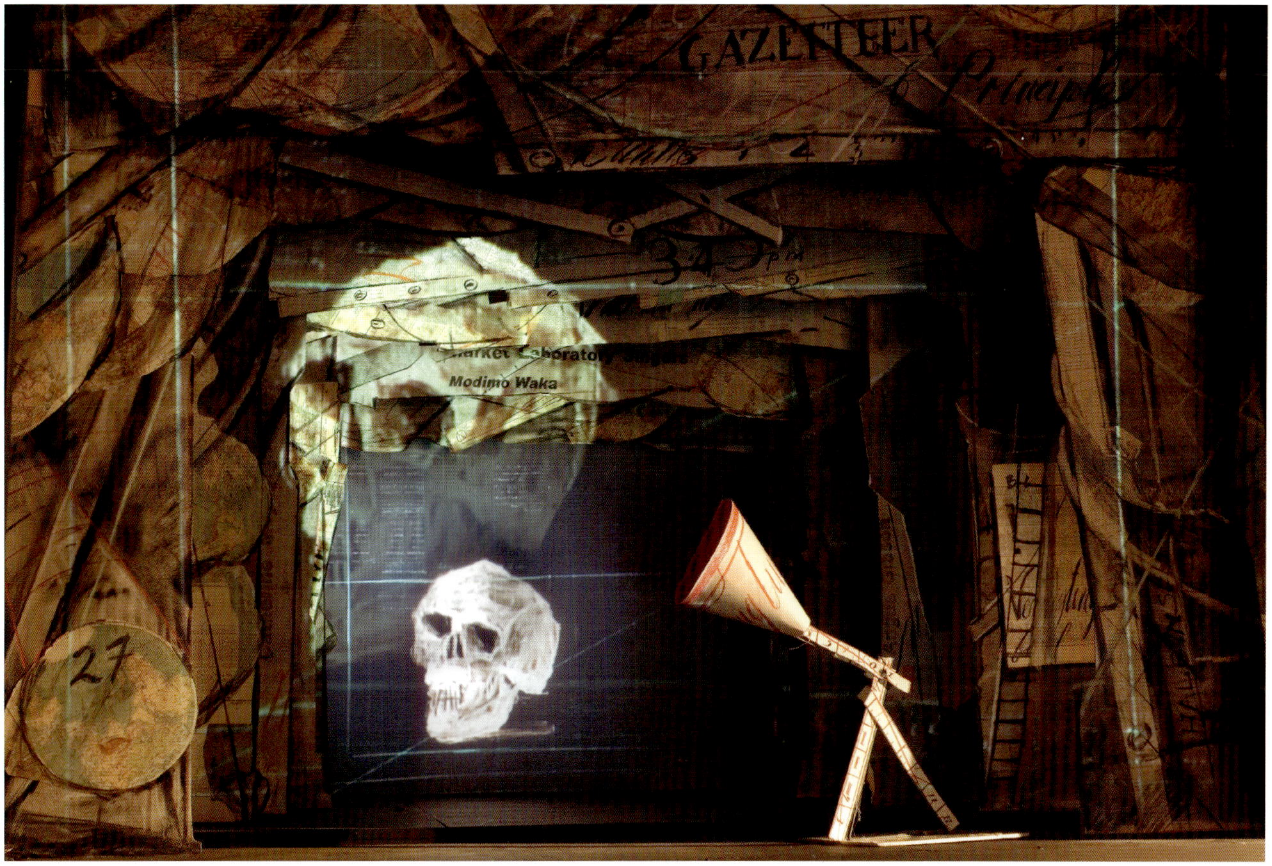
GAZETTEER
Modimo Waka

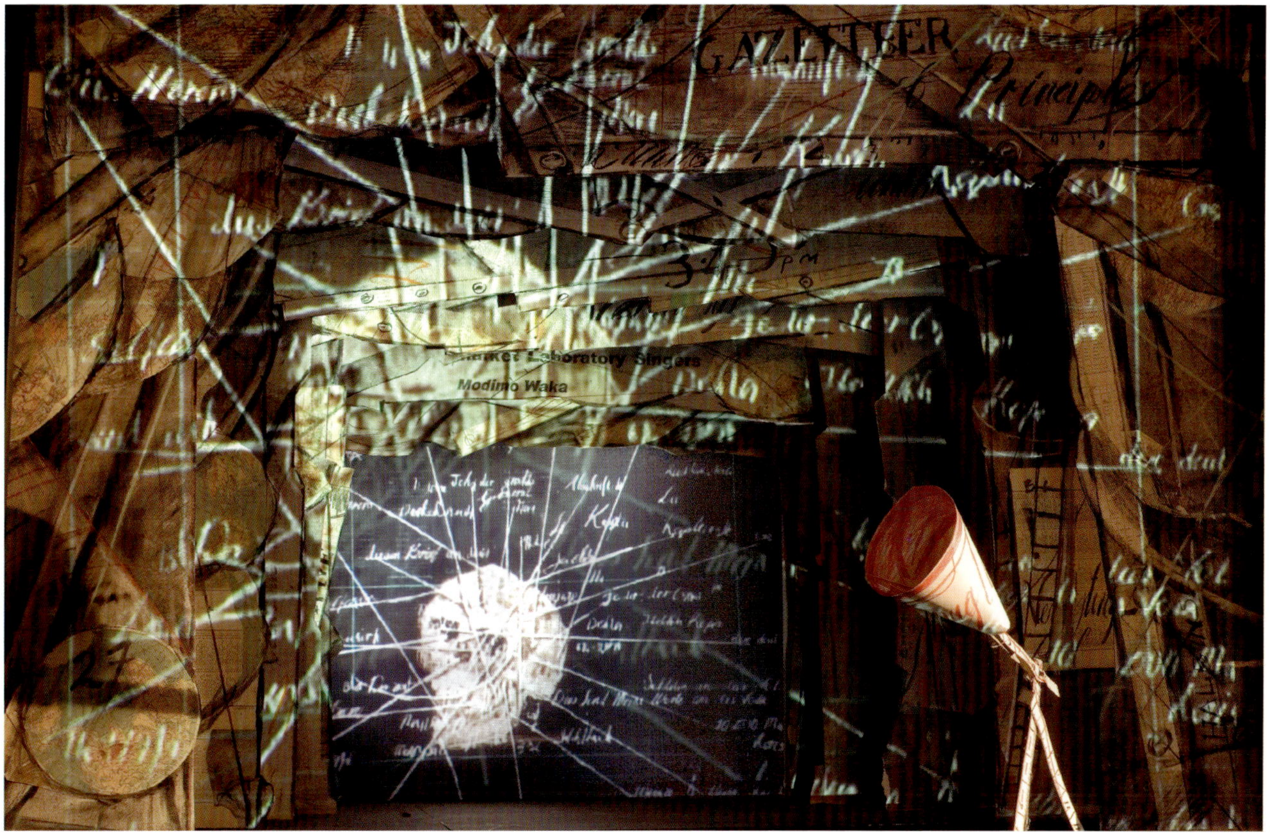
GAZETTEER
Modimo Waka

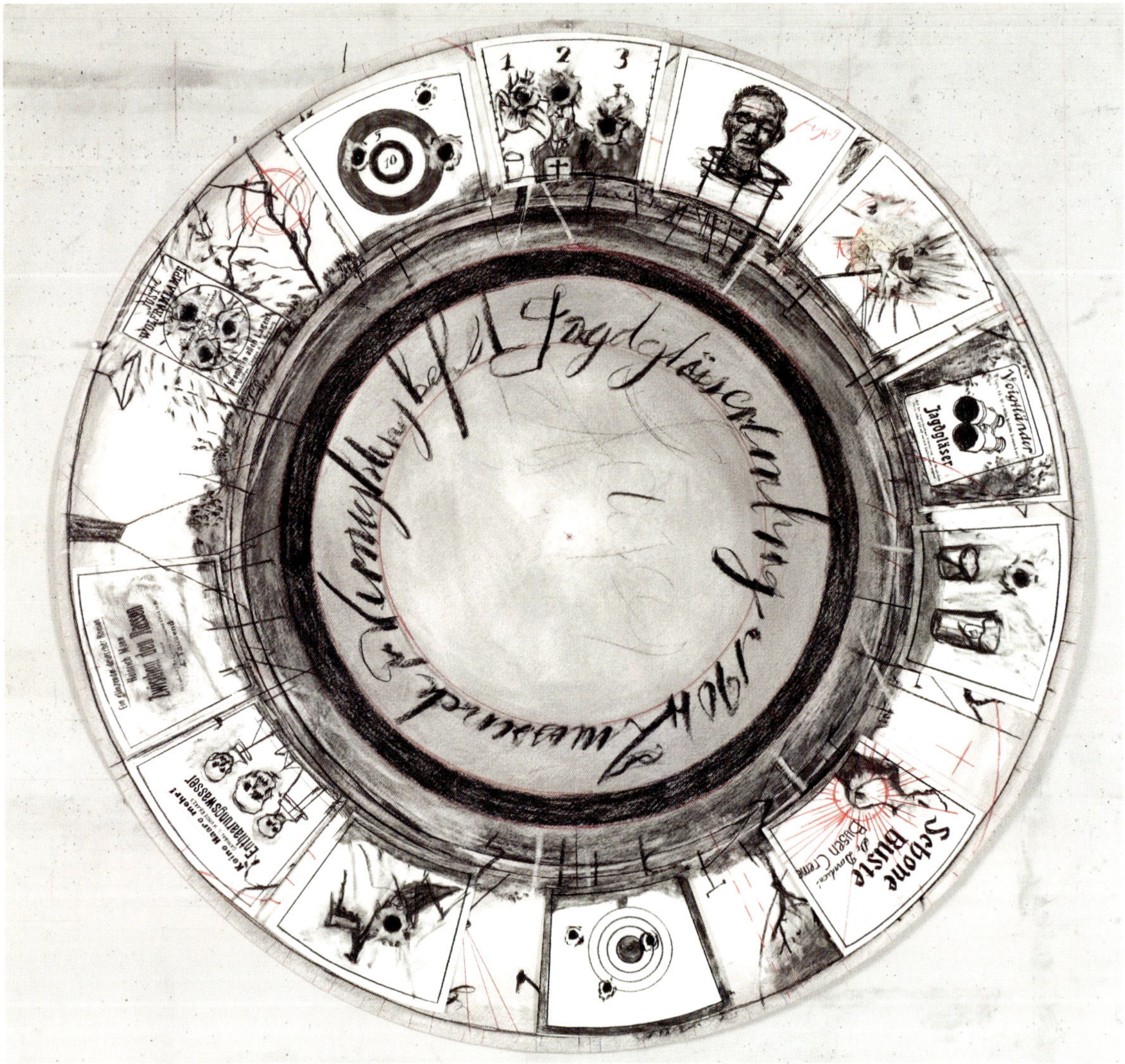

This spread Drawings for *Black Box/Chambre Noire*, 2005. **Left:** collage of charcoal sketches, collage and coloured pencil on paper, diameter 115 cm (45¼ in). **Below:** charcoal and coloured pencil on paper, 60.5 x 320 cm (23⅘ x 126 in). **Right:** charcoal and coloured pencil on paper, 120 x 160 cm (47¼ x 63 in). Collection of the artist.

'The idea of colonialism, and Europe's justification of its actions, have much to do with both *The Magic Flute* and Plato – of bringing light to what was called the 'Dark Continent'... In the first years of the twentieth century there was an enormous massacre, primarily of the Herero tribe, in southwest Africa. Although it is now mainly forgotten, overshadowed by other German massacres and genocides later in the century, there are many ways in which the mechanisms of those later European massacres were already underway in southwest Africa.'

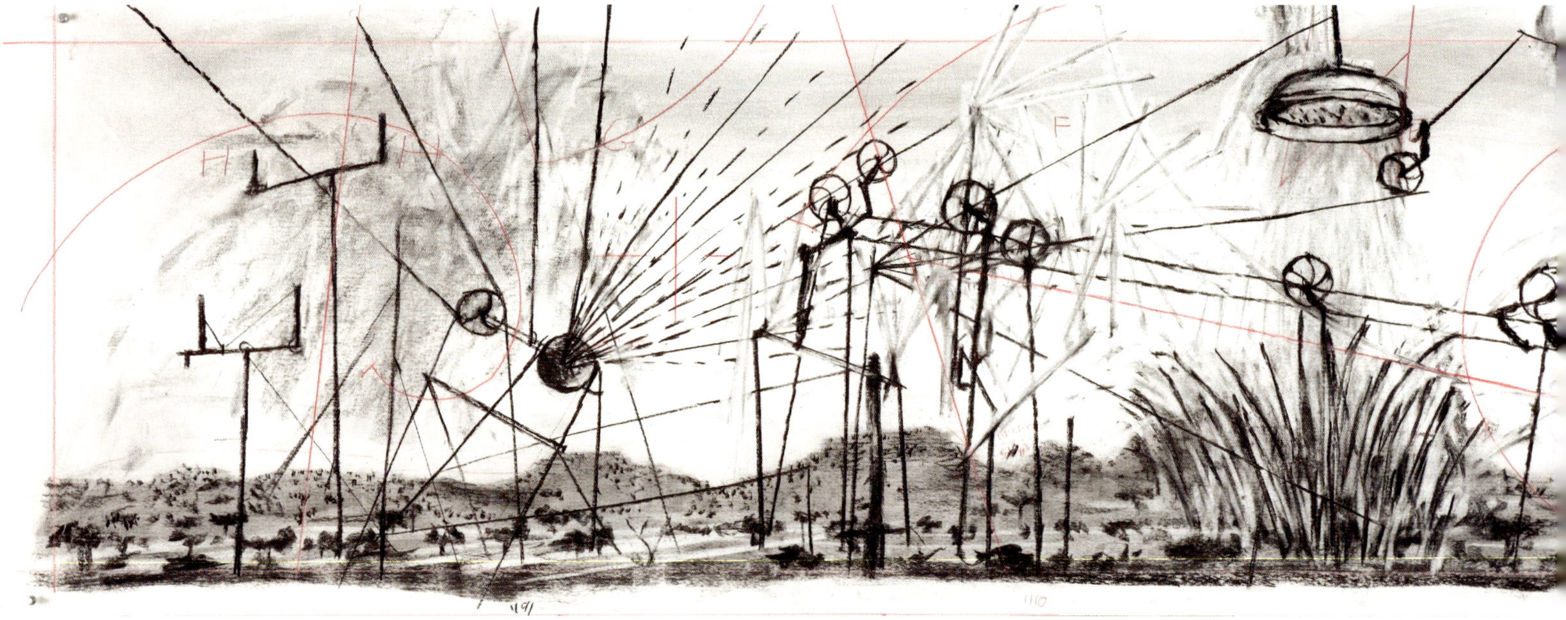

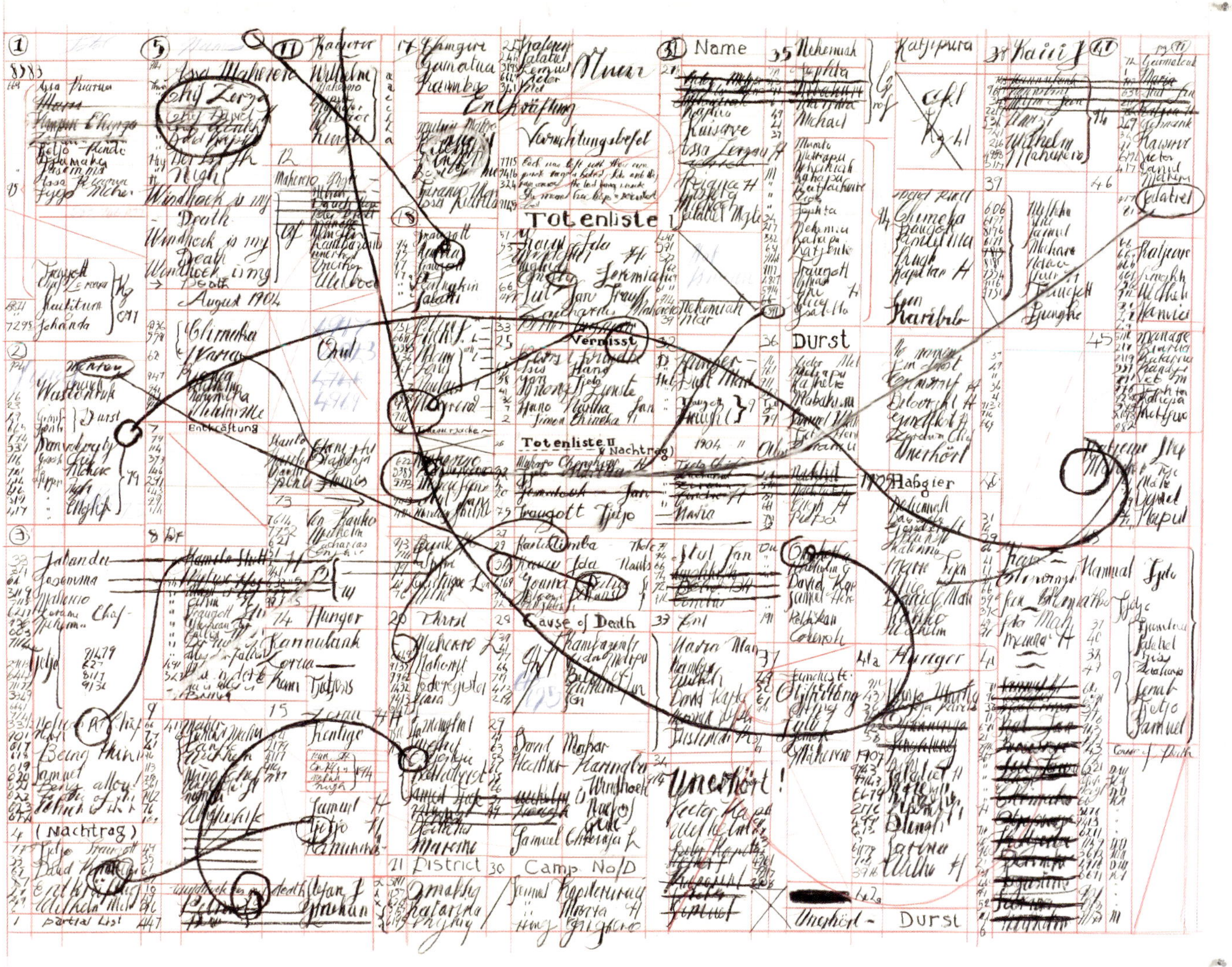
Name
Totenliste I
Vermisst
Durst
Totenliste II
Nachtrag
Habgier
Hunger
Cause of Death
District
Camp No/D
Unerhört
Unerhört - Durst
August 1904

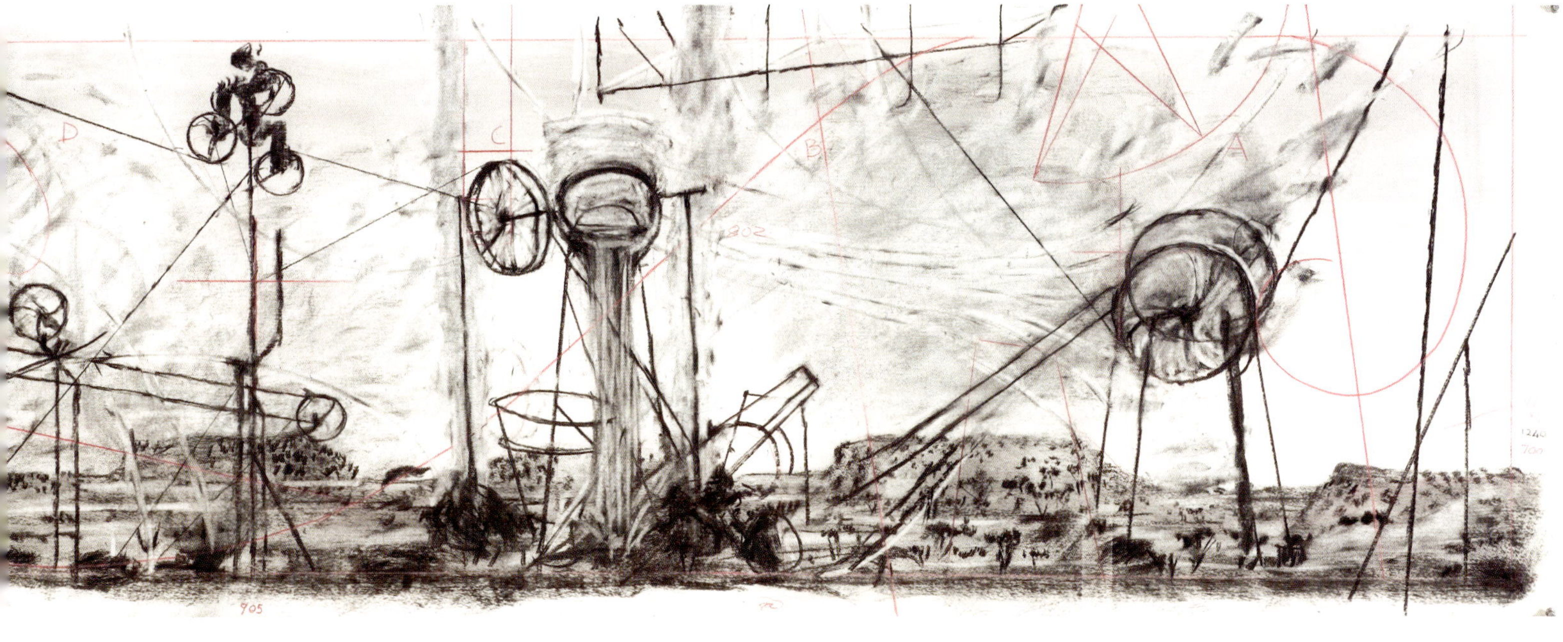

KESTER, DOS SANTOS, NHATUGUEJA, MATÉ
MOZAMBIQUE

Below *Digging Up Guns*, 2004.
'Some people think that peace can be achieved by using guns. No! Real peace will never come until guns have been destroyed.'
Kester

Right Kester, *Throne of Weapons*, 2001. Recycled guns, 101 x 61 cm (39¾ x 24 in). British Museum, London.

In 1995, Bishop Sengulane initiated the Swords into Ploughshares project in Mozambique as a way of trying to rid the country of the seven million guns that had accumulated via the international arms trade during the bloody war that ended in 1992. The NGO Christian Aid began to support the project in 2000, and in 2002 held an exhibition in London of the sculptures that had been created by a group of Mozambican artists out of the weapons yielded up in exchange for more useful hardware – hoes, sewing machines, bicycles, and so on. I bought one of those sculptures, the *Throne of Weapons* (2001) by Cristóvão Canhavato (Kester), and determined to find out more about the project and to commission a work for the African galleries at the British Museum. This became the *Tree of Life* (2004), a collaborative project undertaken by four artists.

These four artists had originally come together to work on the Swords into Ploughshares project, which was initially based at the Núcleo de Arte in Maputo, one of the oldest art schools in Africa. All are members of the Núcleo, though their backgrounds and training are quite different.

Kester (b.1966) had no formal art education but came to the Núcleo from a career in technical engineering. His sculpture, *Throne of Weapons*, toured more than 30 venues in the UK during 2005–6.

Fiel dos Santos (b.1972) is a versatile sculptor in stone and metal, and also a ceramicist and painter. He learned the techniques of stone carving and metalworking in Zimbabwe and South Africa, respectively, and has exhibited in Japan, the UK, Portugal and South Africa as well as in Mozambique.

Hilário Nhatugueja (b.1964) studied ceramics at the Escola de Artes Visuais in Maputo, where he is now a teacher. He has exhibited in the UK, Zimbabwe and South Africa and has worked with street children to create murals in Maputo.

Adelino Maté (b.1973) was taught by the sculptors Ndlozy and Zaqueu, who themselves had been pupils of Alberto Chissano, arguably the greatest Mozambican sculptor of the twentieth century. Maté has exhibited in the USA, Swaziland and the UK, and was recently commissioned to produce a public sculpture in Maputo symbolizing the Mozambican struggle against HIV/AIDS.

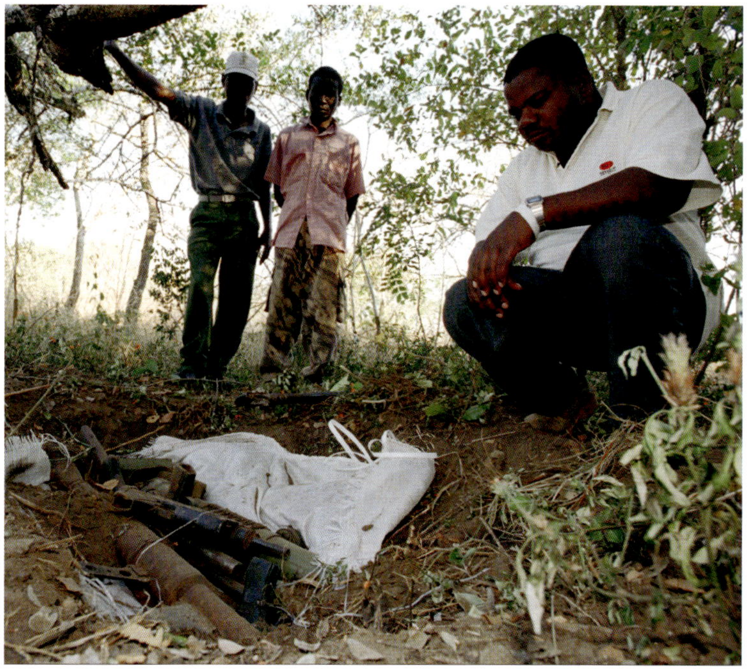

'You dismissed lives
Your prowess broken
Impotent arms, prick backs, elbows
A monument of silence
To those who never heard your thud.'
Nkosana Mpofu (Zimbabwean poet)

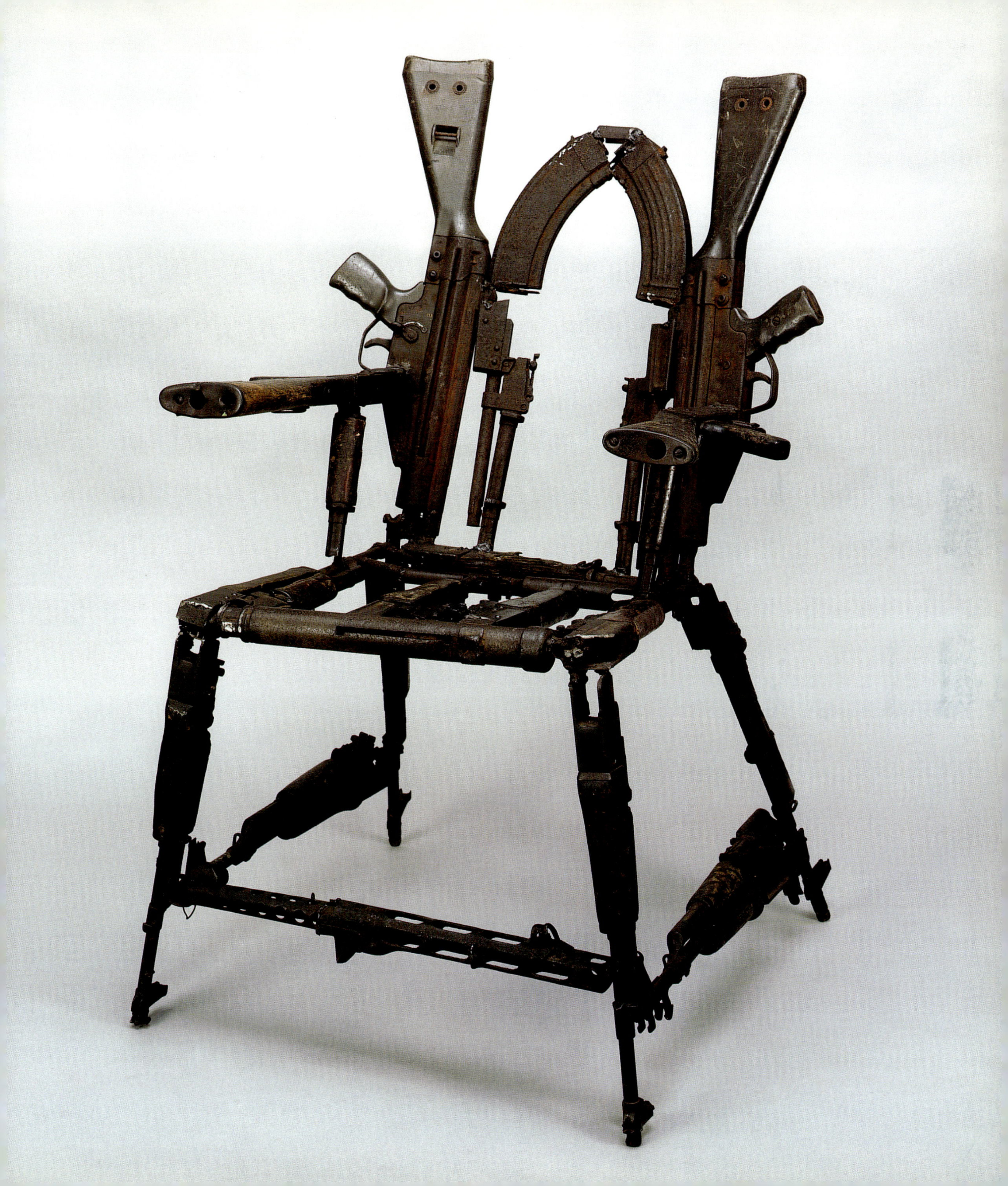

Right *The Tree of Life*, installation view in Peace Park, Maputo, 2004. Recycled weapons, 300 x 250 cm (118 x 98⅖ in). British Museum, London.
'We artists want to turn the situation around, change the story. Changing these instruments of death into hope, life and prosperity, the tree symbolizes life, symbolizes a future, symbolizes hope.'
Hilário Nhatugueja

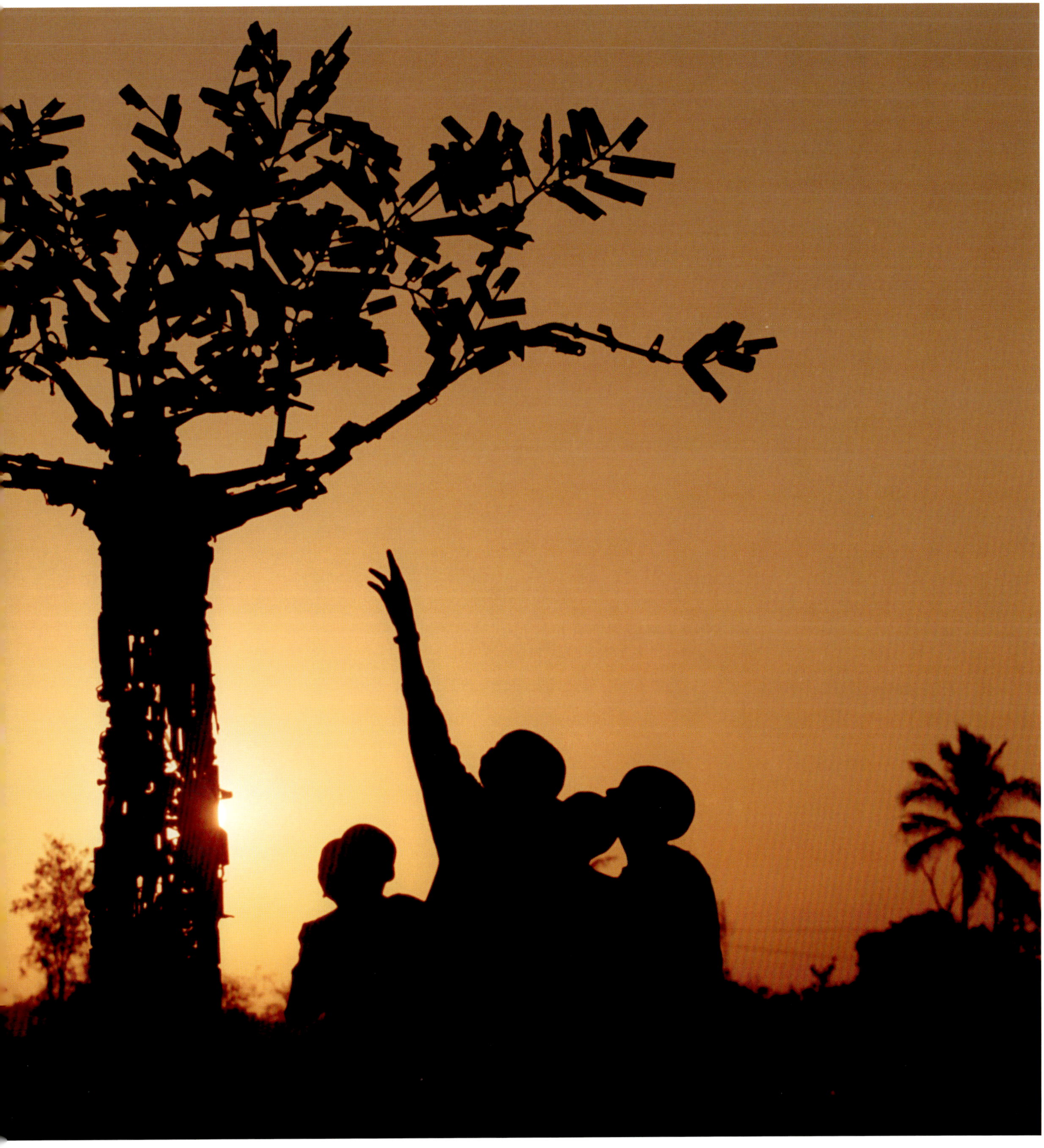

Below and below right Creating the *Tree of Life*, Maputo, 2004.

'We all know what a tree looks like, but we had to work out how to construct it. Then we started to work. As for the foliage, that was another discussion. We had to find light pieces. Then we found the part of the AK47 that sits above the barrel.'
Adelino Maté

Right Children around the *Tree of Life*, Peace Park, Maputo, 2004.

'When I was thirteen years old they recruited me to be [a] child soldier... then they requested me to kill.'
Albino Forquilha, project coordinator

'We had some sad moments, thinking of what those guns did. They killed people, children, old people, women.'
Fiel dos Santos

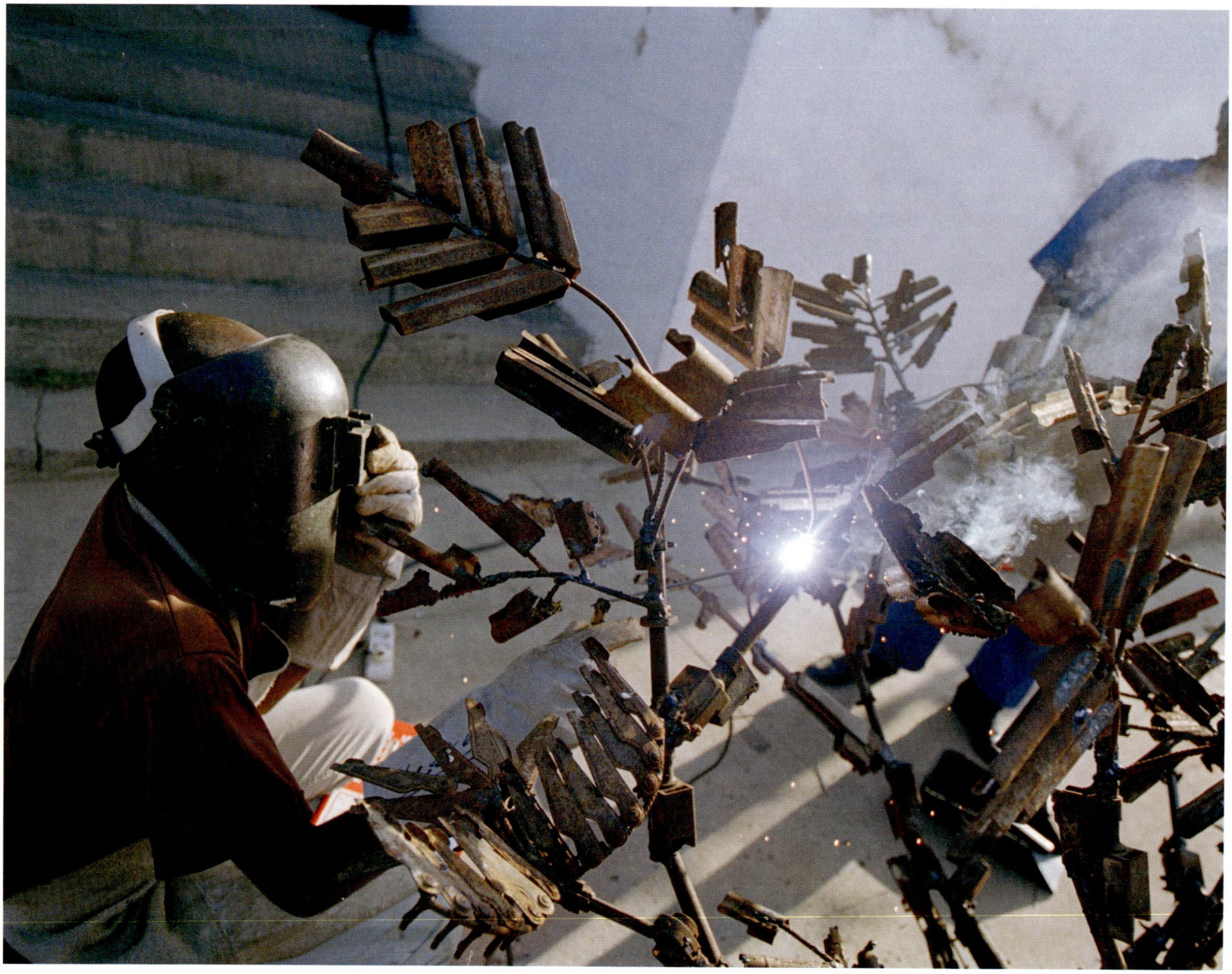

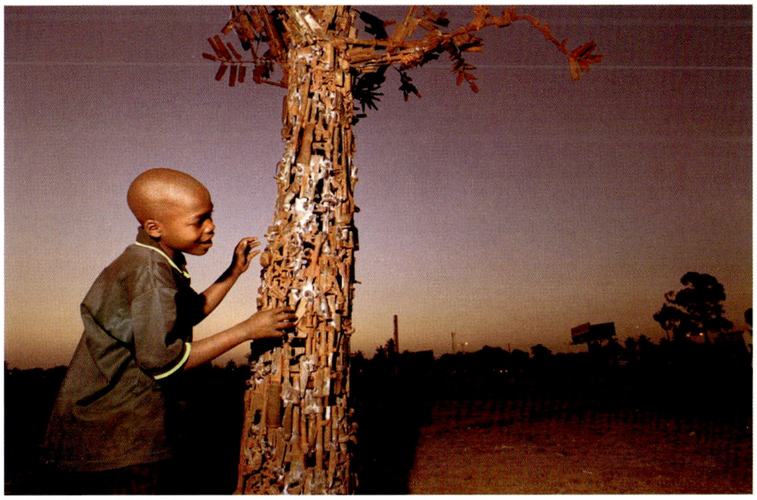

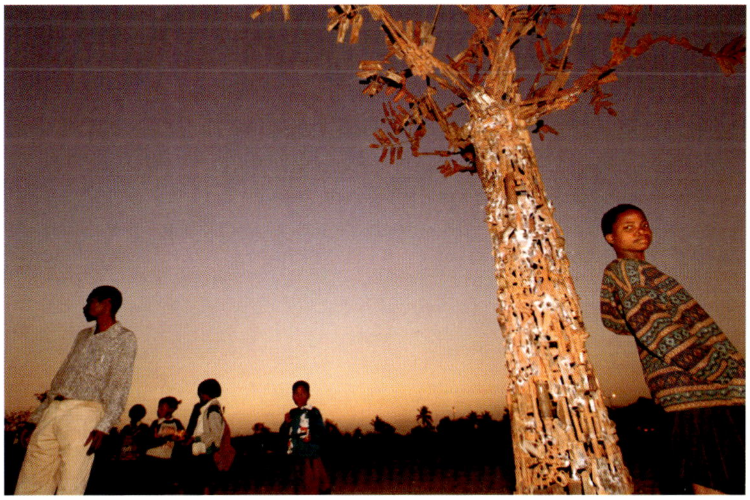

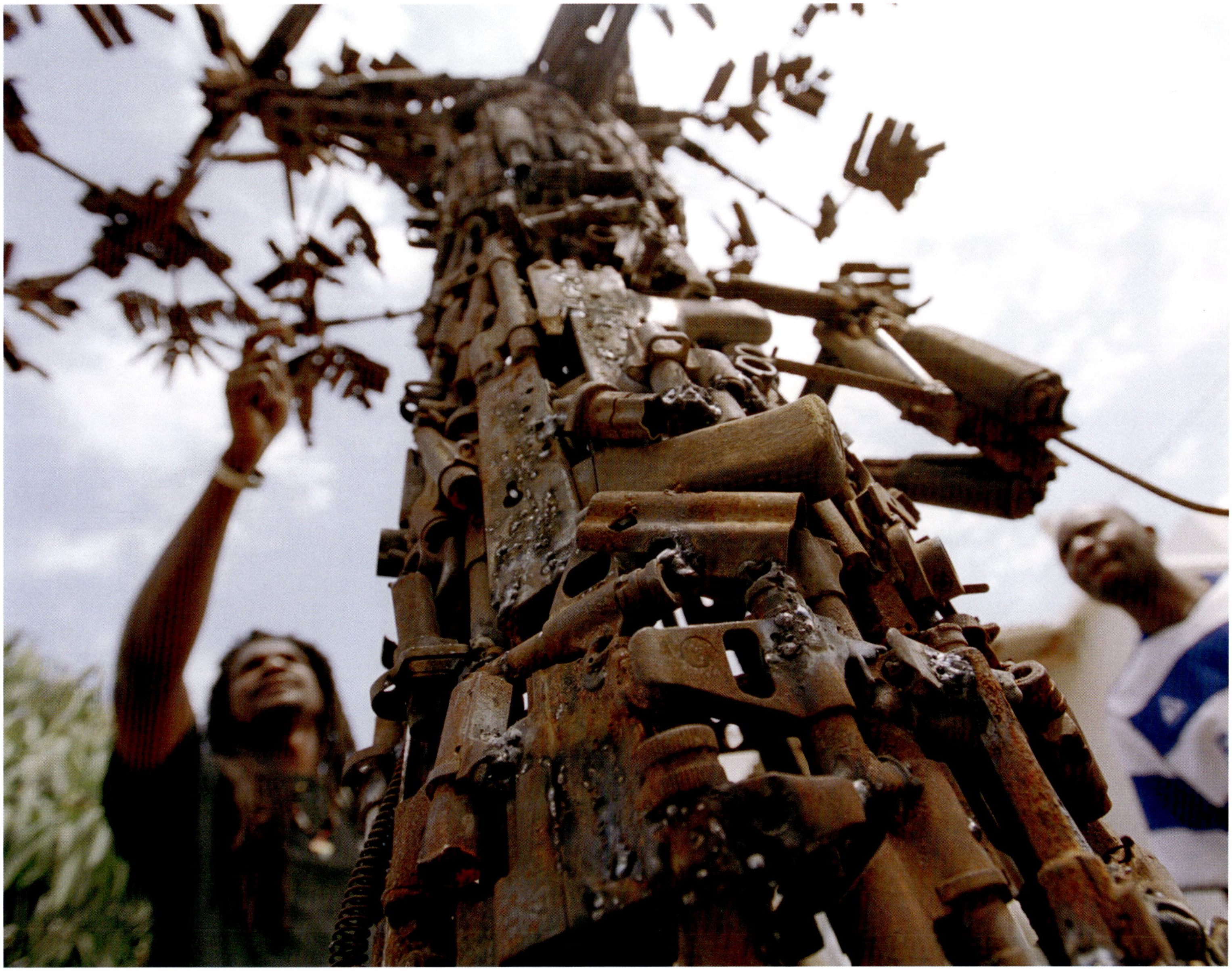

'I tell people that sleeping with a gun in your bedroom is like sleeping with a snake – one day it will turn round and bite you. We tell people we are not disarming you. We are transforming your guns into ploughshares, so you can cultivate your land and get your daily bread.'
Bishop Dom Diniz Sengulane

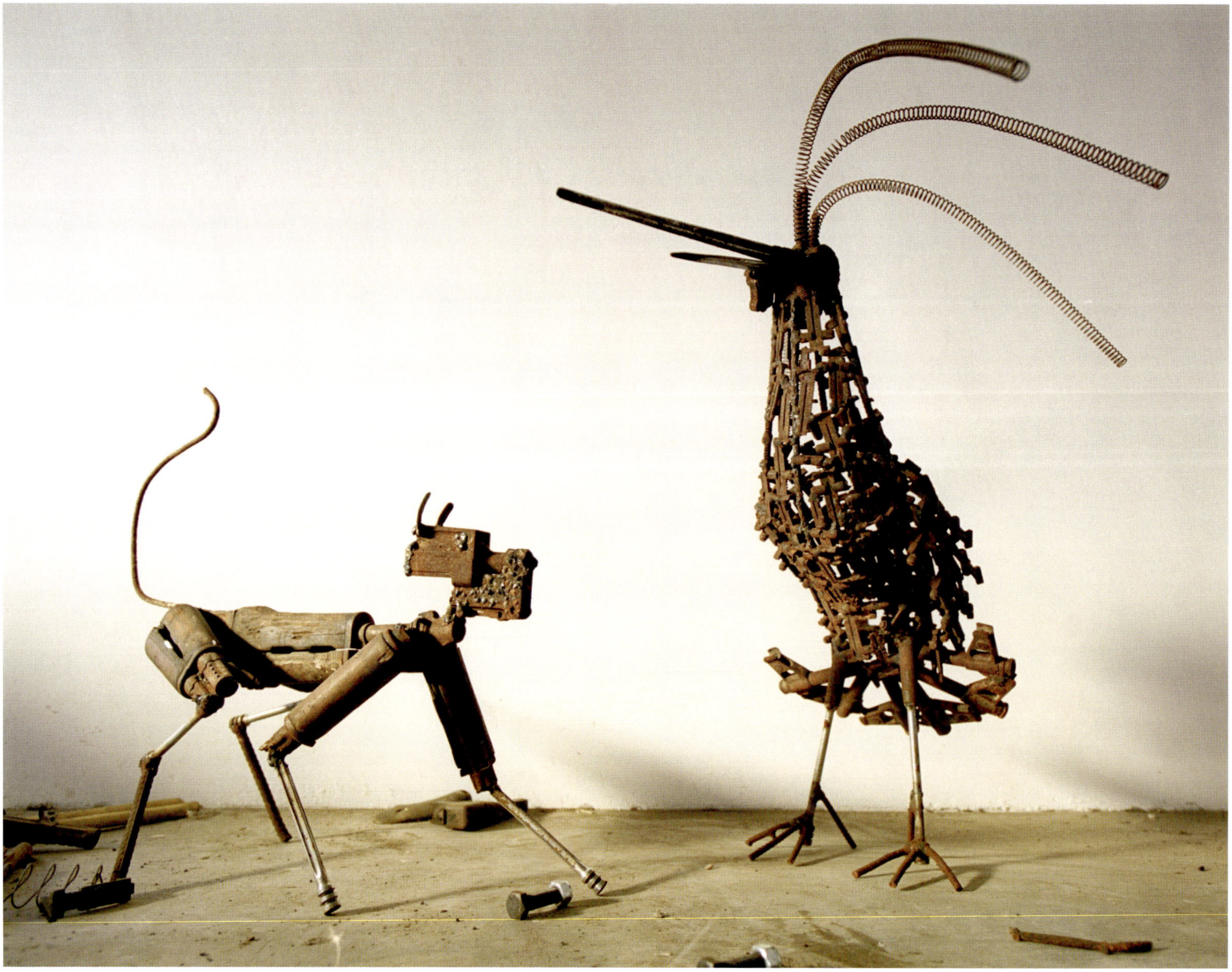

Below left Kester, *Monkey* and Fiel dos Santos, *Bird*, 2004. Recycled weapons, monkey: 30 x 45 x 15 cm (11⅘ x 17¾ x 6 in), bird: 70 x 50 x 30 cm (27½ x 19⅔ x 11⅘ in). British Museum, London.
The creatures that are associated with the *Tree of Life* are an integral part of the sculpture – they walk in its shade, feed off its fruit and nest among its branches.

Right Adelino Maté, *Man with Briefcase* and Fiel dos Santos, *Flautist*, 2004. Recycled weapons, man: approximately 85 x 40 cm (33½ x 15¾ in), flautist: approximately 75 x 50 cm (29½ x 19⅔ in). Collection of the artists.

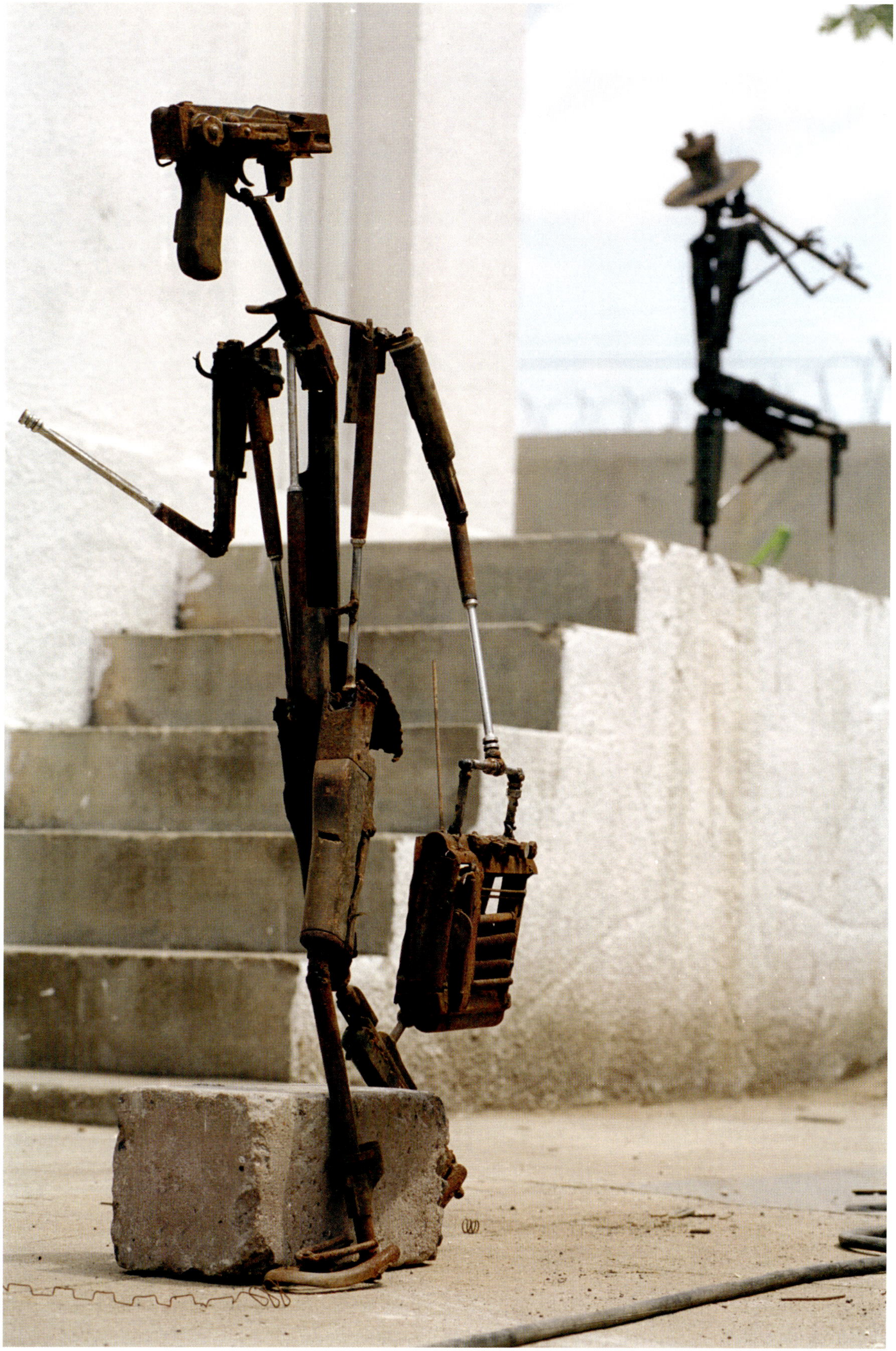

DAVID KOLOANE
SOUTH AFRICA

Below *Three Dogs*, 1988. Acrylic on canvas, 26 x 186 cm (10¼ x 73¼ in). Collection of the artist.
These sinister and enigmatic street dogs, often portrayed in groups of three, have become Koloane's artistic signature. He has a sneaking admiration for them, perhaps seeing their independence and talent for survival as in some ways reflecting his own struggle as an artist.

Bottom *Coca Cola Moonlight*, 1999–2001. Acrylic on canvas, 176 x 273 cm (69⅔ x 107½ in). Hollard Insurance Company, Johannesburg.

Right *Dusk*, 1996. Acrylic on canvas, 133 x 133 cm (52⅓ x 52⅓ in). Private collection.
'The commuters... leave their homes against a mist of brazier fire, smog and industrial emissions. They return at dusk under a blanket of dark and ominous layers, which hover over the township so much that shape and form become blurred.'

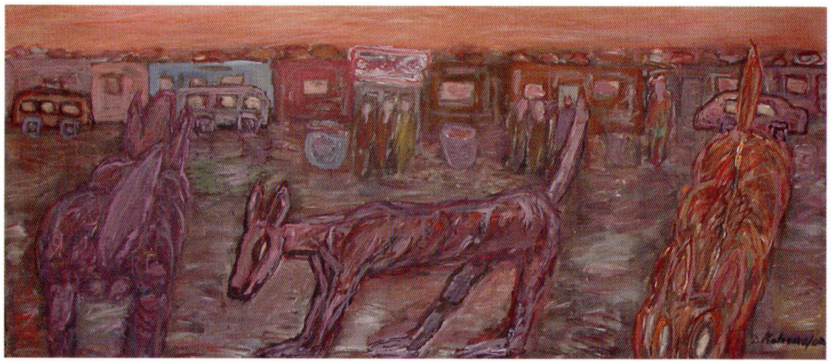

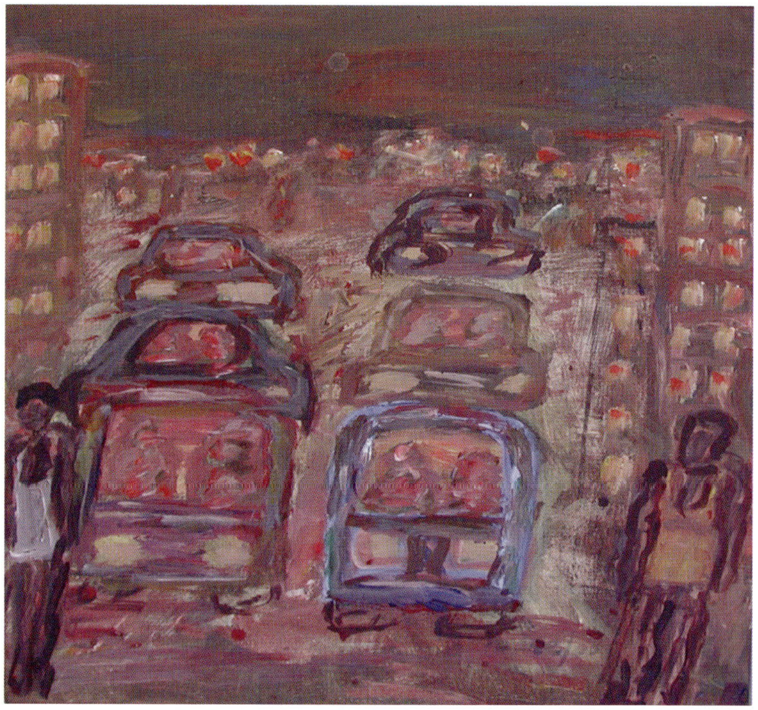

David Koloane was born in 1938 in Alexandra, Johannesburg. As one of the older generation of black South African artists he has experienced at first hand the daily struggle simply to survive, let alone to practise his art. Writing in 1989, he asked:

> *...how effective a role can the artist play within the community; in an environment devoid of any creative infrastructure such as museums, galleries, tuition institutions; where all such facilities for enriching the artist's heritage are located in the affluent and privileged section of the spectrum in a racially divided society? Creative activity has often been viewed by the community as a pariah activity, suitable for providing necessary therapy to social misfits.*

Koloane developed his skills between 1974 and 1977 at the studios of the visionary artist and educator Bill Ainslie, who encouraged him to explore his inner self through his art: 'I want to be in a position of not knowing rather than knowing – to have a burning curiosity.' The following year, at the height of repression in the apartheid regime, Koloane was involved with Ainslie and others in founding FUBA (the Federated Union of Black Arts) in Soweto 'to alleviate the virtual absence of formal tuition in the communities.' Koloane is now an internationally acclaimed curator, critic and artist, whose works are held in public and private collections throughout the world.

Koloane's early abstract paintings are remarkable, but through his figurative work he has become one of the truly great interpreters of city life, developing a palette that is as warm and rich as that of Bonnard, but deployed in a way that brings a suffocating and oppressive intensity to his subject. Yet, as Robert Loder observed:

> *...unlike much graphic work produced by artists in South Africa during the apartheid years, [his] work stands by itself and is not overwhelmed by the weight of guilt which lies so heavily on some South African art.*

Koloane is one of the founder members (with Robert Loder) of the Fordsburg Artists' Studios, aka the Bag Factory, which, at the time of its creation in 1991, provided the only dedicated space for black South African artists in downtown Johannesburg and Soweto, and it still plays a vital role.

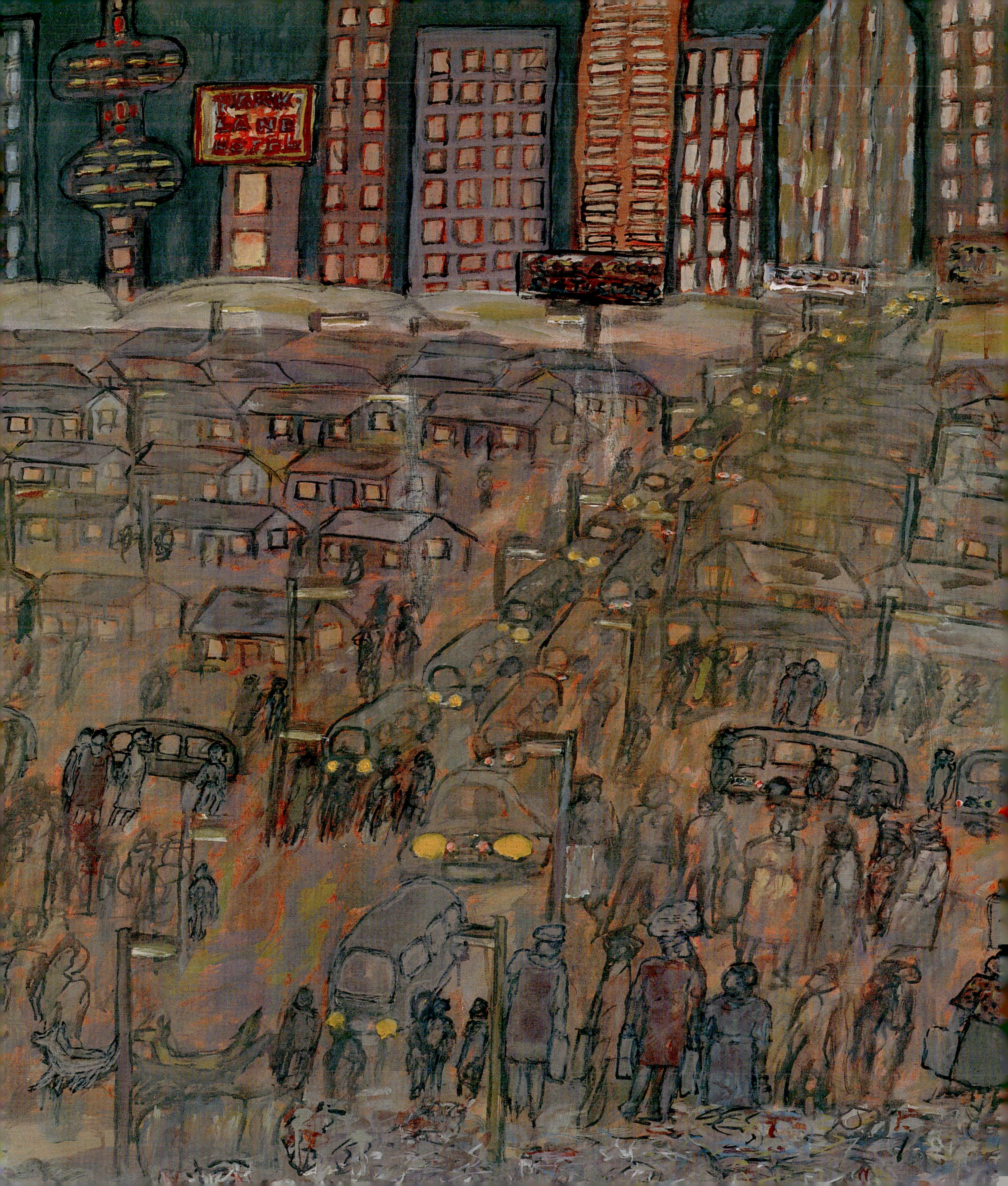

'Their [street dogs'] existence is almost a minute-to-minute feat of survival. The dogs move about in packs like hyenas and can be just as vicious. They drift around waste dumps, garbage cans, wedding and funeral ceremonies.'
David Koloane

Below *Night Dogs*, 2005. Acrylic on paper, 70 x 100 cm (27½ x 33⅖ in). Collection of the artist.

Right *Man Reading*, 2001. Acrylic on canvas, approximately 60 x 45 cm (23⅗ x 17¾ in). Collection of the artist.

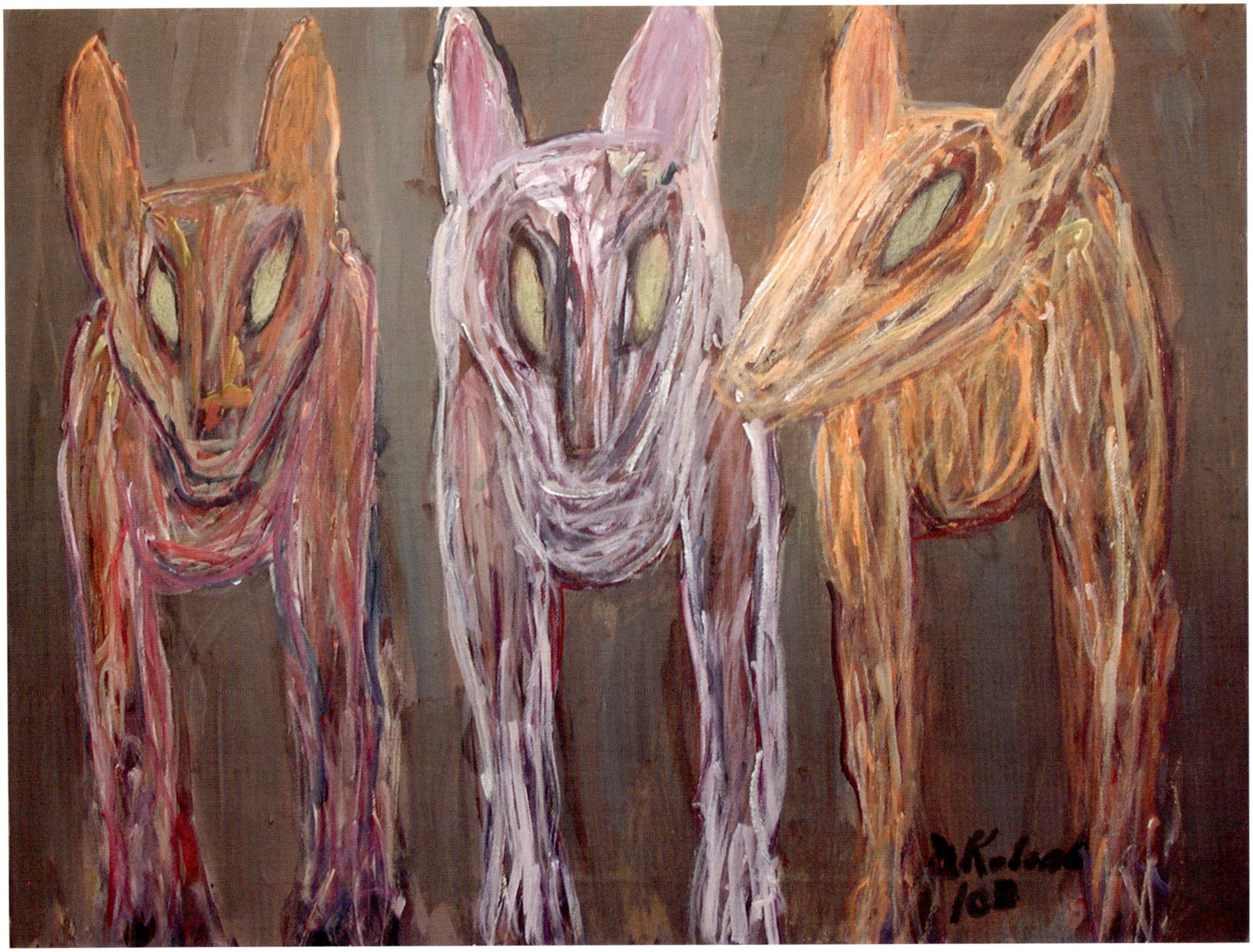

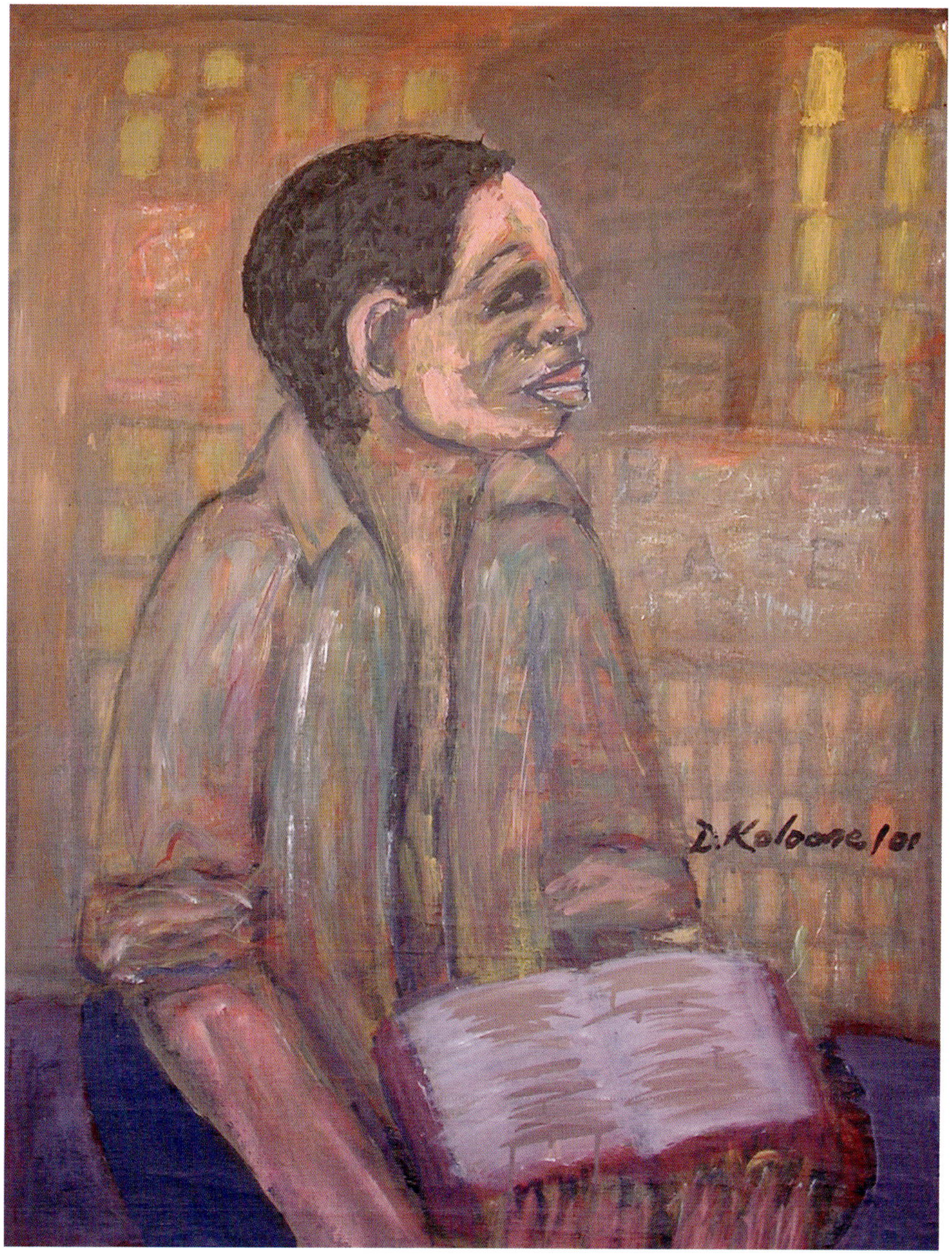
D. Koloane / 01

Below *Lovers*, 2005.
Acrylic on canvas, 60 x 45 cm ($23\frac{3}{5}$ x $17\frac{3}{4}$ in).
Nandos Collection.
Although Koloane's vision of the city may sometimes seem gloomy and pessimistic, he is also a believer in the power of human relationships to rise above the hardships that confront them – and the buildings that surround them.

Right *Celebration*, 2005.
Acrylic on canvas, 60 x 75 cm ($17\frac{3}{4}$ x $29\frac{1}{2}$ in).
Collection of the artist.
The four figures at the bar seem trapped between a row of bottles and the faceless wedding couple, presumably celebrities of some description, on the TV screen behind them. The gaze of the drinkers is focused obliquely and vacantly at something undisclosed.

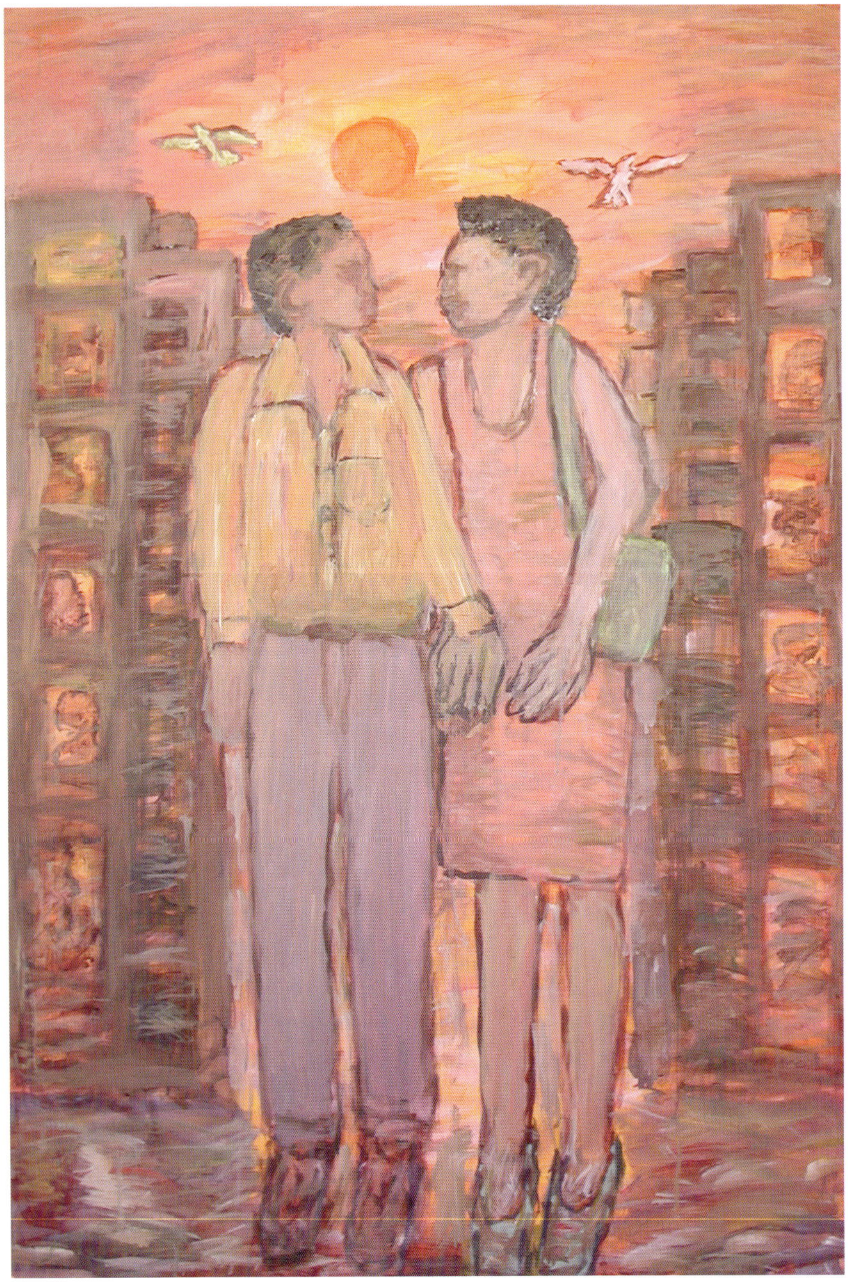

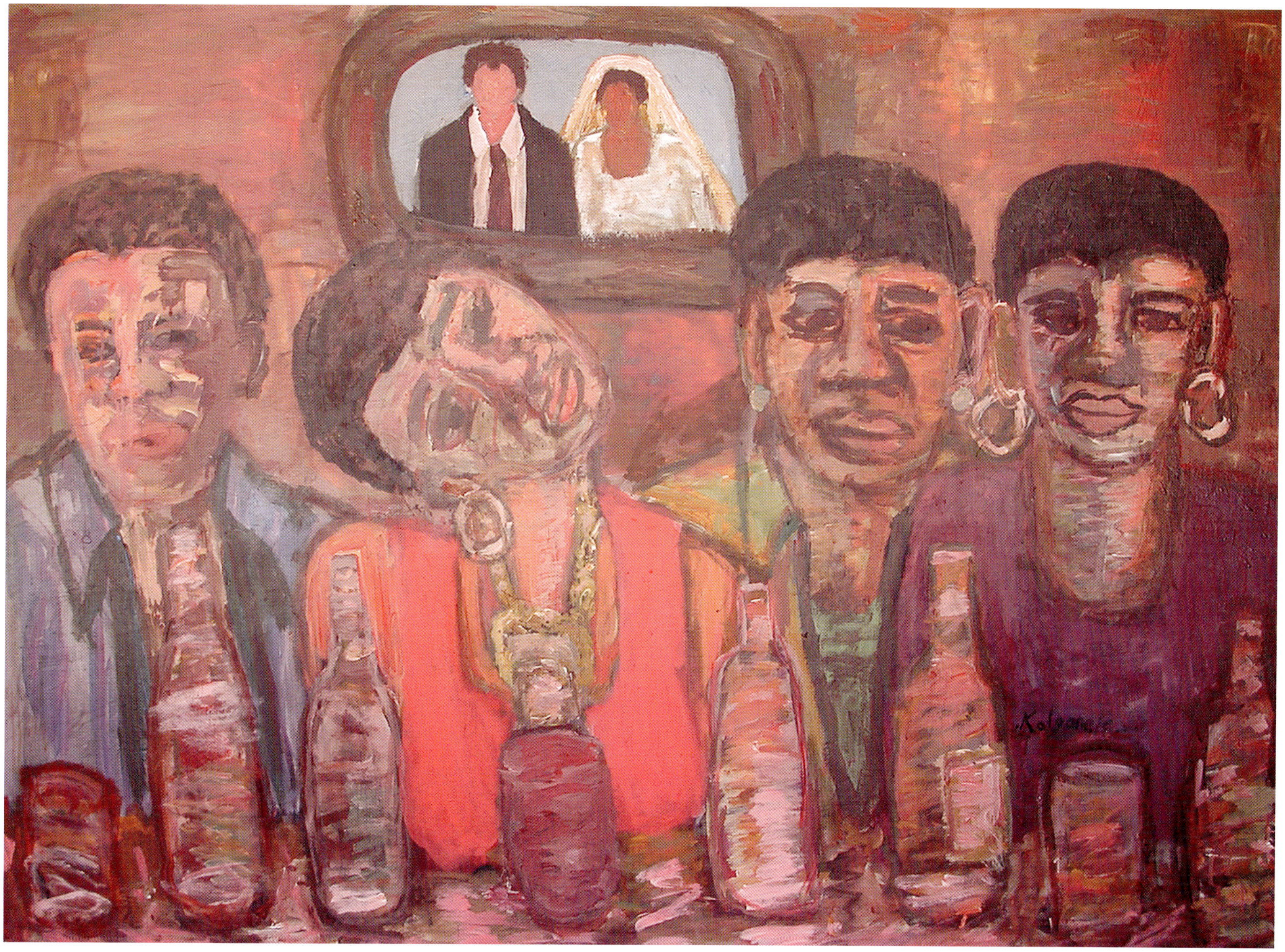
Koloane

ABDOULAYE KONATÉ
MALI

Right *L'Initiation*, 2004 (detail). Installation in 7 parts, mixed media, each part 265 x 180 cm (104⅓ x 71 in). Private collection. The artist's impassioned cry for global peace and international understanding and cooperation is given powerful voice in this work. The title refers to that elemental rite of passage, changing from one state to another, which will be necessary to achieve these goals.

The works of Abdoulaye Konaté, whether in paint, in installations of found or ready-made objects, or in his extraordinary textile creations, are all infused with a sense of serenity and of profound wisdom. This is not to say that the subjects he confronts in his work are serene: HIV/AIDS, worldwide conflict, environmental degeneration. Konaté's works regularly reference various cultural traditions of the Bamana people of Mali in particular, though he himself is quick to point out the narrow perspective of the colonial 'tribal' definitions of the past: 'I am a Bamana, but here one does not always think about such a distinction.'

Abdoulaye Konaté was born in 1953 at Dirë in Mali. He studied painting at the National Institute of Arts in Bamako, 1972–76, then at the Higher Institute of the Visual Arts in Havana, Cuba from 1978 to 1985. In 1996, he won the prestigious Leopold Senghor prize at the Dak'Art Biennale in Dakar, Senegal and he has exhibited widely in Africa and around the world. In Cuba, Konaté became familiar with the works of the great Cuban painter Wilfredo Lam, whose deep knowledge and appreciation of the Santería religion and its African roots had become integral to his artistic vision. On returning to Mali, Konaté continued to work at the National Museum of Mali, as well as acting as Director of the Palais de la Culture, of the Rencontres de la Photo de Bamako and of the Conservatoire des Arts et Métiers Multimédias Balla Fasséké Kouyaté at various points in his career. Recently asked whether these responsibilities interfered with his career as an artist he replied: 'Yes, I sometimes ask myself the same question but, on the other hand, they allowed me to help others'.

Konaté's quiet but passionate altruism is directed not just towards his own country and people, but also towards the people of the world. Far from diminishing his stature as an artist, a lifetime of working towards greater local and international understanding on a range of issues has given his work a profound stature and gravitas.

'All my work is informed by my culture. I worked for 20 years with the National Museum of Mali and this helped me towards a deeper understanding of my cultural and linguistic heritage. I use this knowledge to develop the artistic and aesthetic elements of my work.'
Abdoulaye Konaté

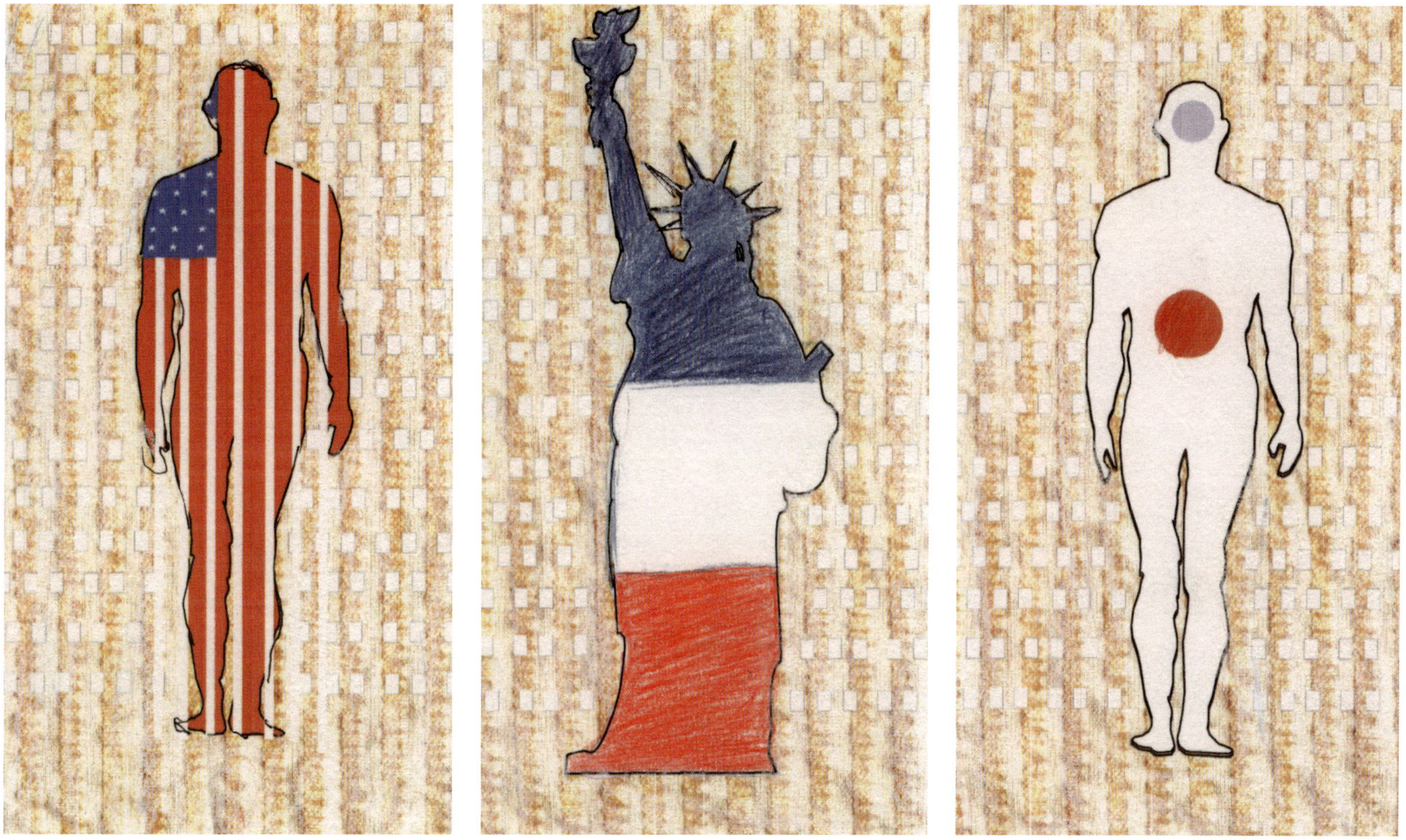

Below *L'Initiation*, 2004 (detail).

Right *Gris-gris blancs*, 2005. Textile, 230 x 500 cm (90½ x 197 in). Jean Paul Blechère Collection. Konaté has a deep knowledge of, and admiration for, the way of life of the Mandé hunters of Mali. In common with many of the peoples living inthe Sahel region to the south of the Sahara, Mandé hunters wear tunics covered with charms (*gris-gris*) to protect them from harm. *Gris-gris* can take many forms, though usually the object of power and protection is wrapped or contained in some way. Konaté's accumulations of these packages are both visually intriguing and emotionally intense – and are also a very real extension of an ancient tradition through the medium of contemporary art.

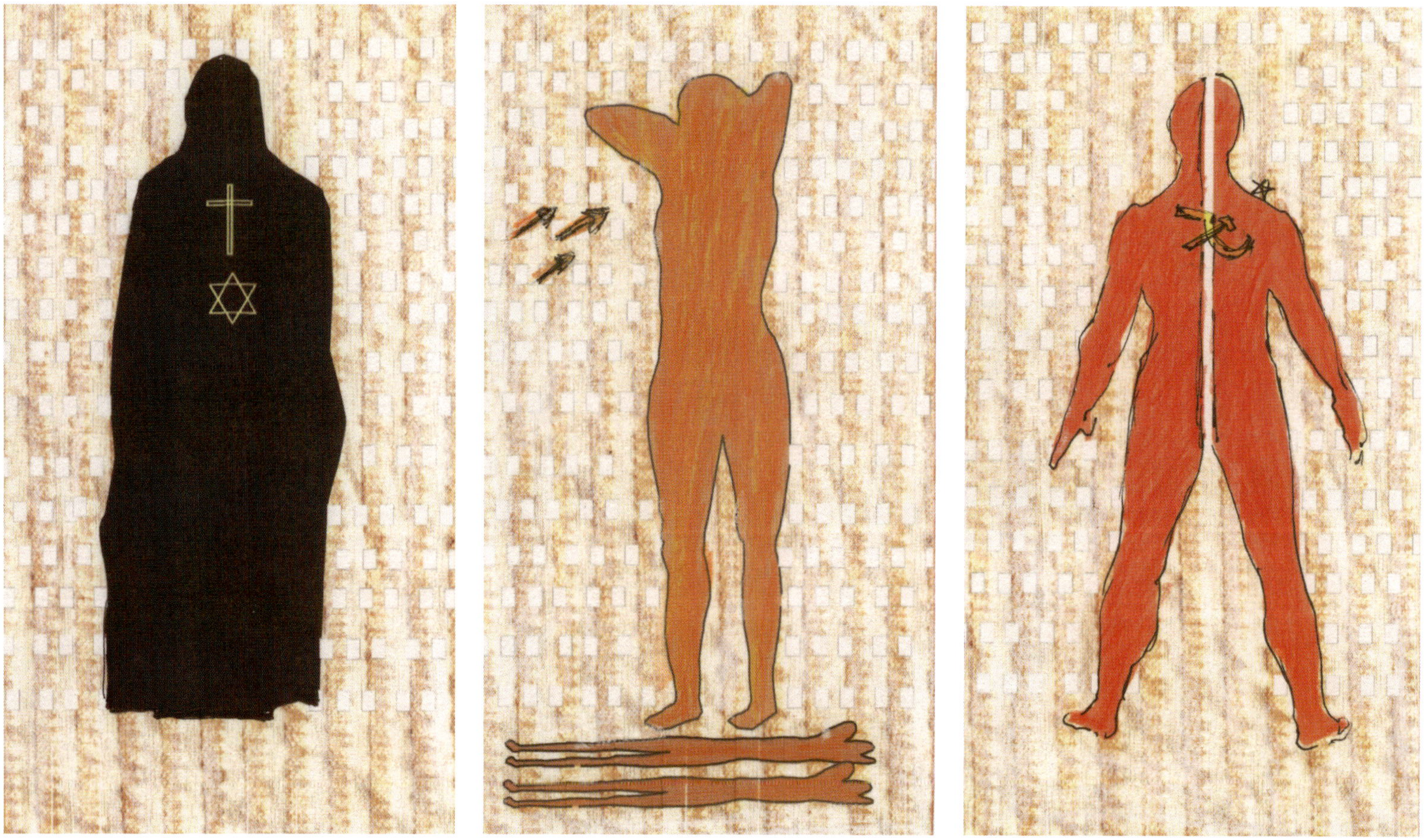

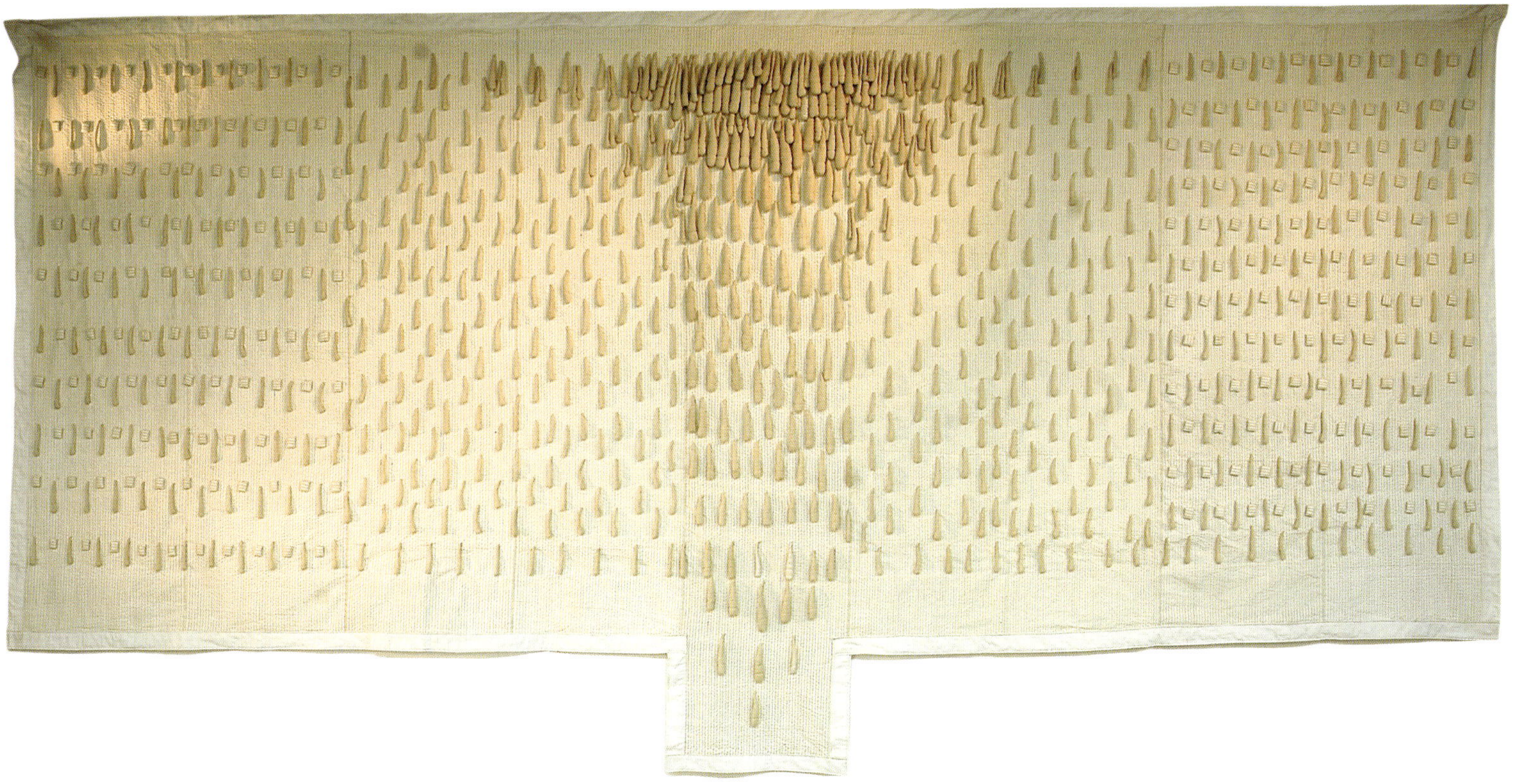

RACHID KORAÏCHI
ALGERIA/FRANCE

This spread *Tapisserie*, 2004. Silk and wool, *technique d'Aubusson*, 277 x 170 cm (109 x 67 in). Collection of the artist.
Koraïchi's work incorporates a range of magical and protective signs and symbols from North and West Africa, together with Arabic and Berber letters and numbers, as well as cryptograms of his own inspiration. The banner emphasizes the cultural diversity of this region of Africa, but also suggests a common magical and symbolic language.

Born in Ain Beida, Algeria in 1947, Rachid Koraïchi now lives and works in Paris. His artistic training includes a diploma from the Higher Institute of Fine Arts, Algiers, and from the National School of Decorative Arts and the School of Urban Studies, both in Paris. He is passionately involved in the struggle for democracy and freedom of speech in North Africa and the Middle East, drawing on the profoundly humanistic and enlightened traditions of true Sufism.

Koraïchi works in many media, including ceramics, textiles, poetry, calligraphy, light and paint. Born into an ancient Sufi family in Algeria, Koraïchi's work is intimately informed by the numerology, signs and ethos of Sufi mysticism and reflects the unique contribution of Africa to Islamic culture and philosophy. He has developed his own lexicon of signs and symbols based on Arabic, Berber, Chinese and Japanese characters and figures, as well as 'cryptograms' of his own invention.

One of his major installations, *The Path of Roses*, is a homage to Jalal ad-Din ar-Rumi, the thirteenth-century mystic and poet, and in particular to his physical and spiritual journey of enlightenment across the Mediterranean to meet his fellow traveller and Sufi mystic, Ibn el Arabi. The work comprises embroidered silk textiles, steel sculptures and ceramics and explores the Sufi concept of *safar* (travel and transcendence). The individual elements of the installation were made in Tunisia, Morocco and Syria with the advice of local ironworkers, weavers, embroiderers and ceramicists, with whom Koraïchi shares a close kindred.

While Koraïchi's aesthetics are deeply rooted in his multicultural Algerian heritage, he is a truly cosmopolitan artist, who speaks to a global audience. His works were included in the international touring exhibition 'Short Century', the 47th and 49th Venice Biennale and may be found in public and private collections worldwide.

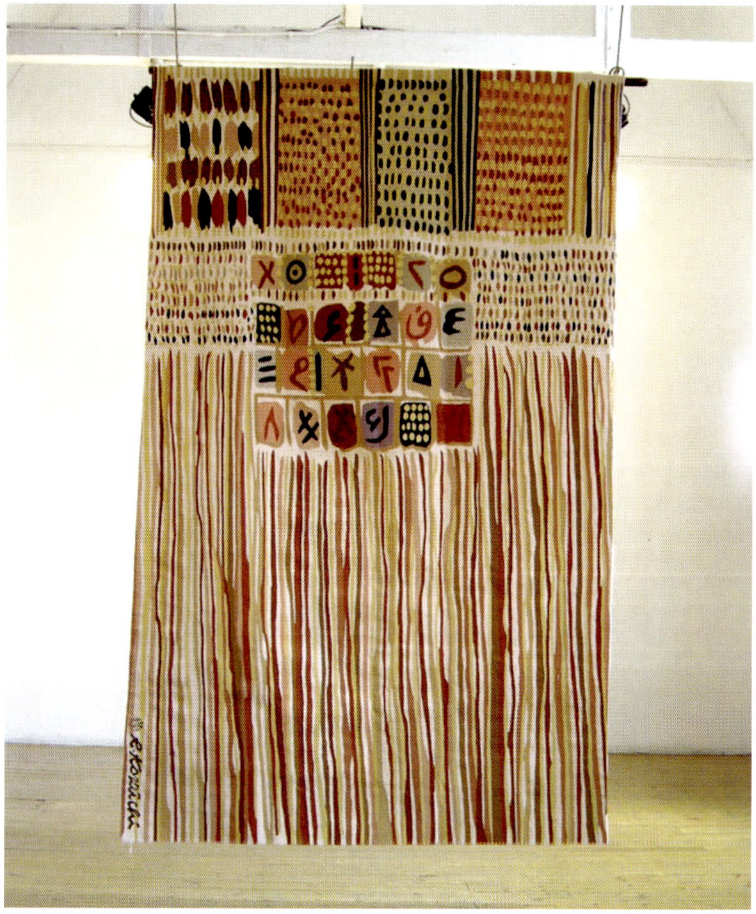

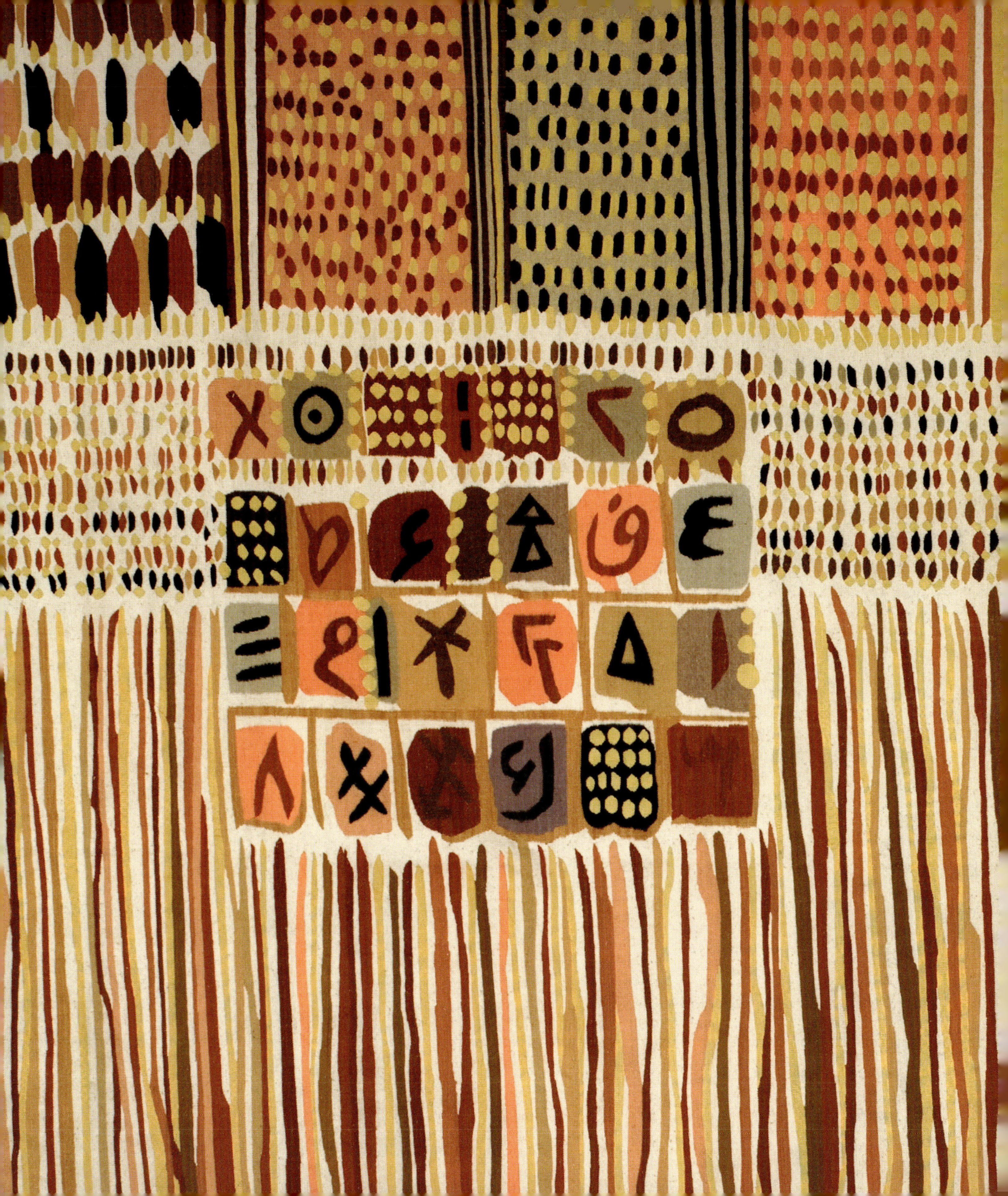

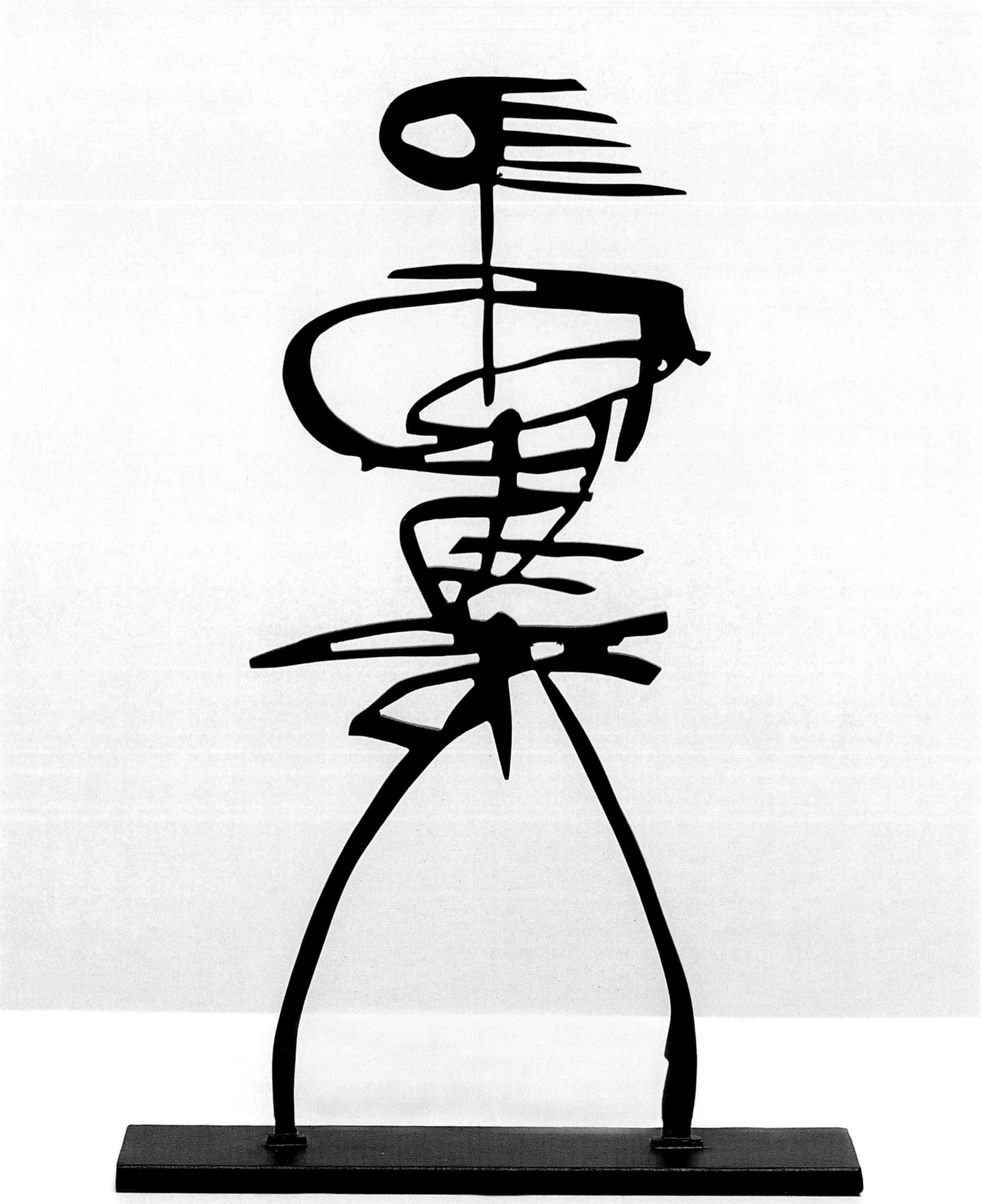

Left *Calligraphic Figure*, from the *Path of Roses* installation, 2001. Painted steel, 32 x 22 cm ($12\frac{3}{5}$ x $8\frac{2}{3}$ in). British Museum, London.
This anthropomorphic figure is part of the multimedia installation entitled *Path of Roses*, a homage to the thirteenth-century Sufi mystic Jalal ad-Din ar-Rumi.

Below *At Nightfall*, views of light installation, Quai de L'Isere, Grenoble, 2002.
Koraïchi's cryptograms projected on to the walls of the embankment beside the Rhône in Grenoble, France.

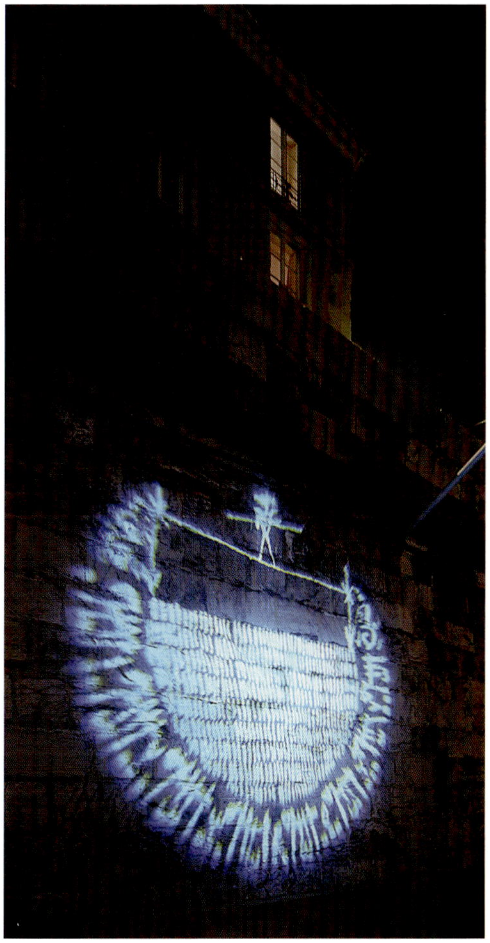

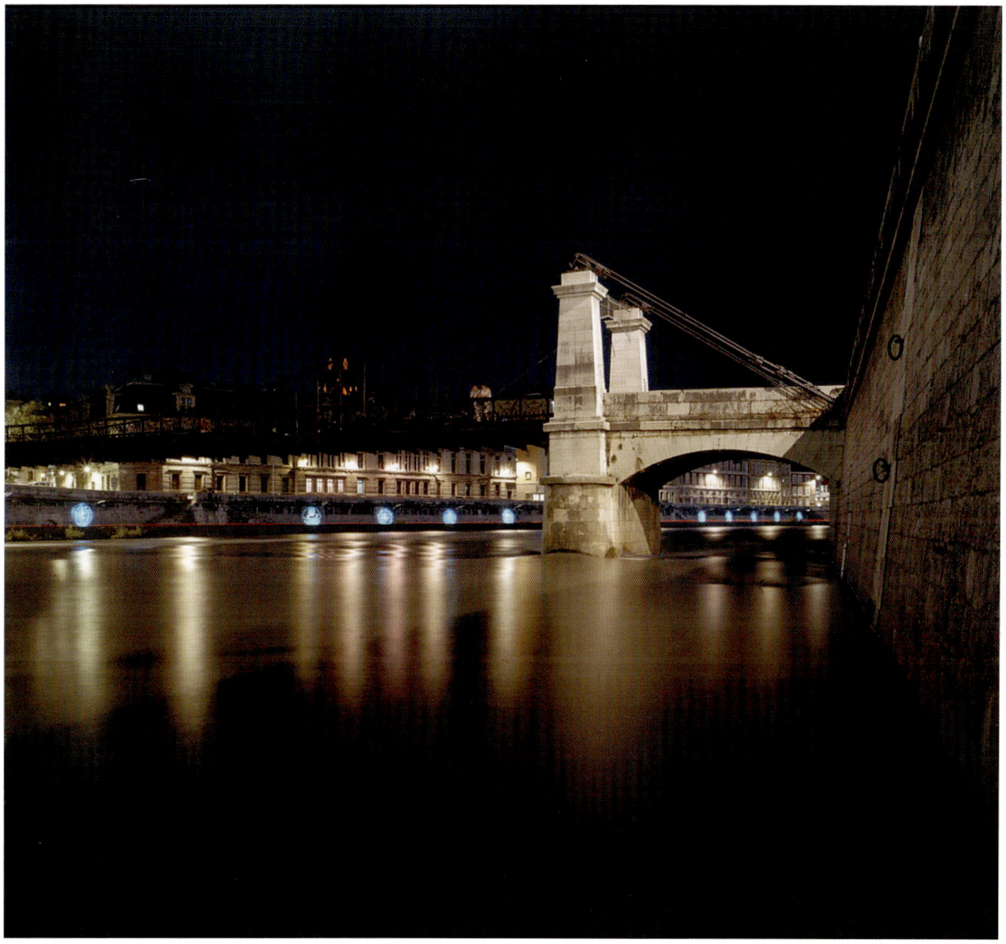

This spread *Banners*, from the *Path of Roses* installation, 2001. 4 gold-embroidered silk banners, each 23 x 96 cm (9 x 37⅘ in). British Museum, London.

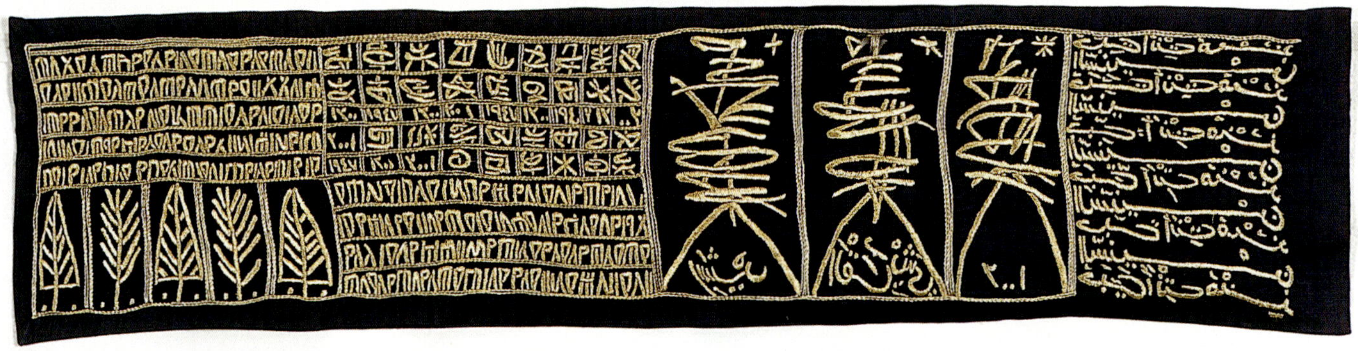

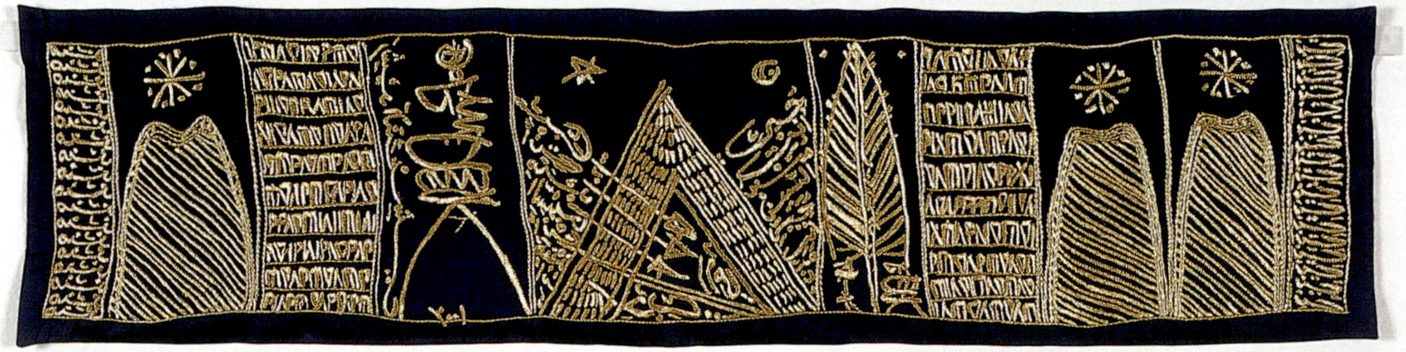

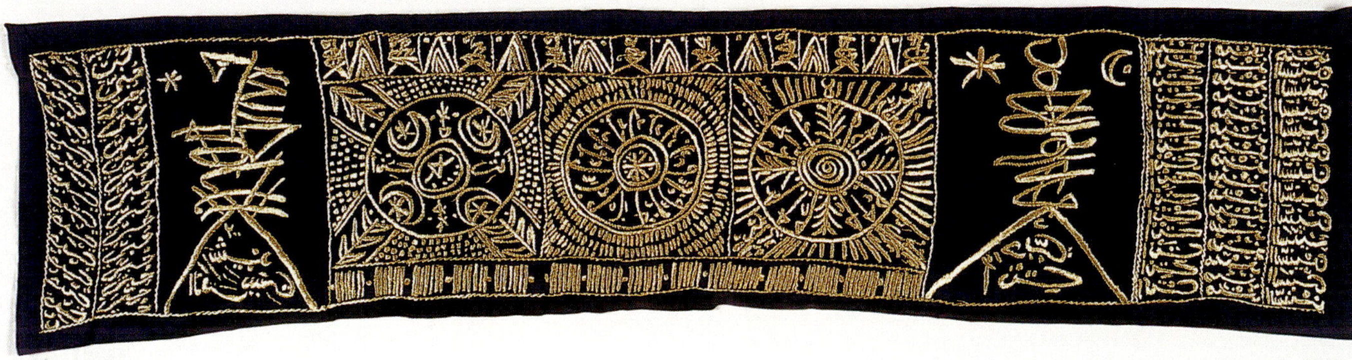

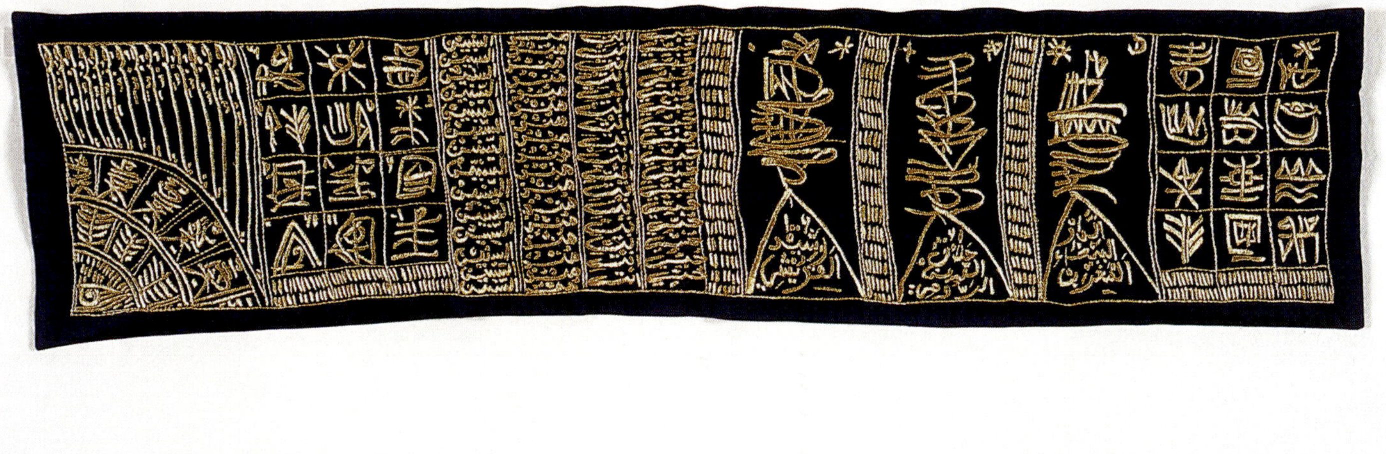

ATTA KWAMI
GHANA

Below *Bosoe*, 2000. Acrylic on canvas, 42 x 35 cm (16½ x 13¾ in). Collection of the artist.
Bosoe is the name of a popular musical style in Ghana.

'I have focused on colour as subject matter, perhaps taking me back to what I started with as a child, in my mother's studio; the perception of colour-tablets in tins. My mother's paints and her textiles were a good resource.'

Right *Kokrobitey*, 2007 (detail). Acrylic on canvas, 146.5 x 165 cm (57½ x 65 in). Collection of the artist.
Kokrobitey is the name of a small coastal village about an hour from Accra. The Kokrobitey Institute offers a retreat for students to come and learn about Ghanaian and African culture.

'In recent works I have pursued the use of the imaginary grid as a matrix for emotion. This structure is a smokescreen within which to create something new. Working in different places requires an ever-present preparedness to take the work wherever it demands to go.'

One of Atta Kwami's earliest memories is of the tablets of brilliantly coloured paint in his mother's studio. Two other aesthetic and intellectual influences from the rich visual environment of the town of Kumasi have had a profound effect on him: the textile tradition and the art of commercial sign-painters. 'The starting point of my inspiration is my environment. Many of my images have been shaped by my experiences of Atonsu Agogo, a commercial/workshop area in Kumasi, close to my studio.

Atta Kwami was born in Accra, Ghana in 1956 and now lives in Kumasi where he was formerly head of the Department of Painting and Sculpture at the College of Art and Curator of the Knust Museum. Of his working practices, Atta Kwami states: 'I use oil on canvas, inks and acrylics on paper to portray a relationship between textiles, vision, time and the visual arts.' He is impatient with the inadequacies of the critical criteria with which artists, whose work has a superficial similarity, are compared and judged. 'Although I find my work being compared with the work of other painters, surely that suggests only that several artists internationally are working in comparable ways? Yet my work is the outcome of a series of engagements with practices, forms and visual environments that are specific to me in Ghana.'

Atta Kwami has exhibited in Africa, Europe, Australia, the USA and Mexico. His exhibition 'Kumasi Junction', in which he showed his work alongside that of 11 street painters from Kumasi, toured the UK in 2002–3. He has lectured widely and participated in numerous workshops and residencies around the world. In the catalogue to his exhibition at the Beardsmore Gallery, London in 1995 he commented:

> *All too often, opinion-makers from the West see their own art in innovative terms, while African art is inauthentic unless it can be seen to be rooted in tradition. Why not reverse the assessment and judge Western art by its authenticity and African Art by its originality?*

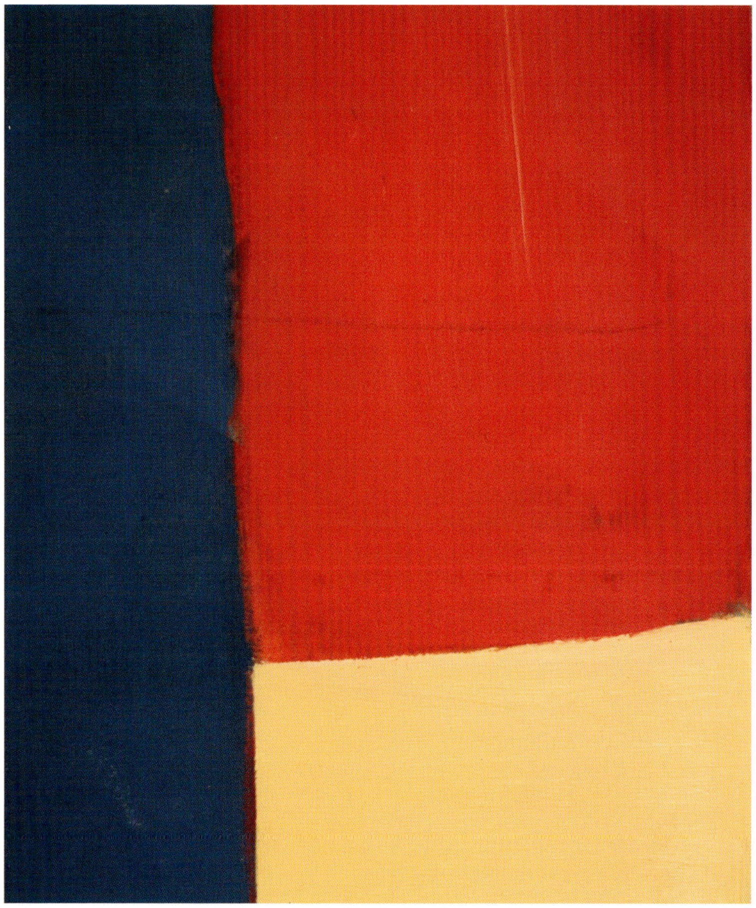

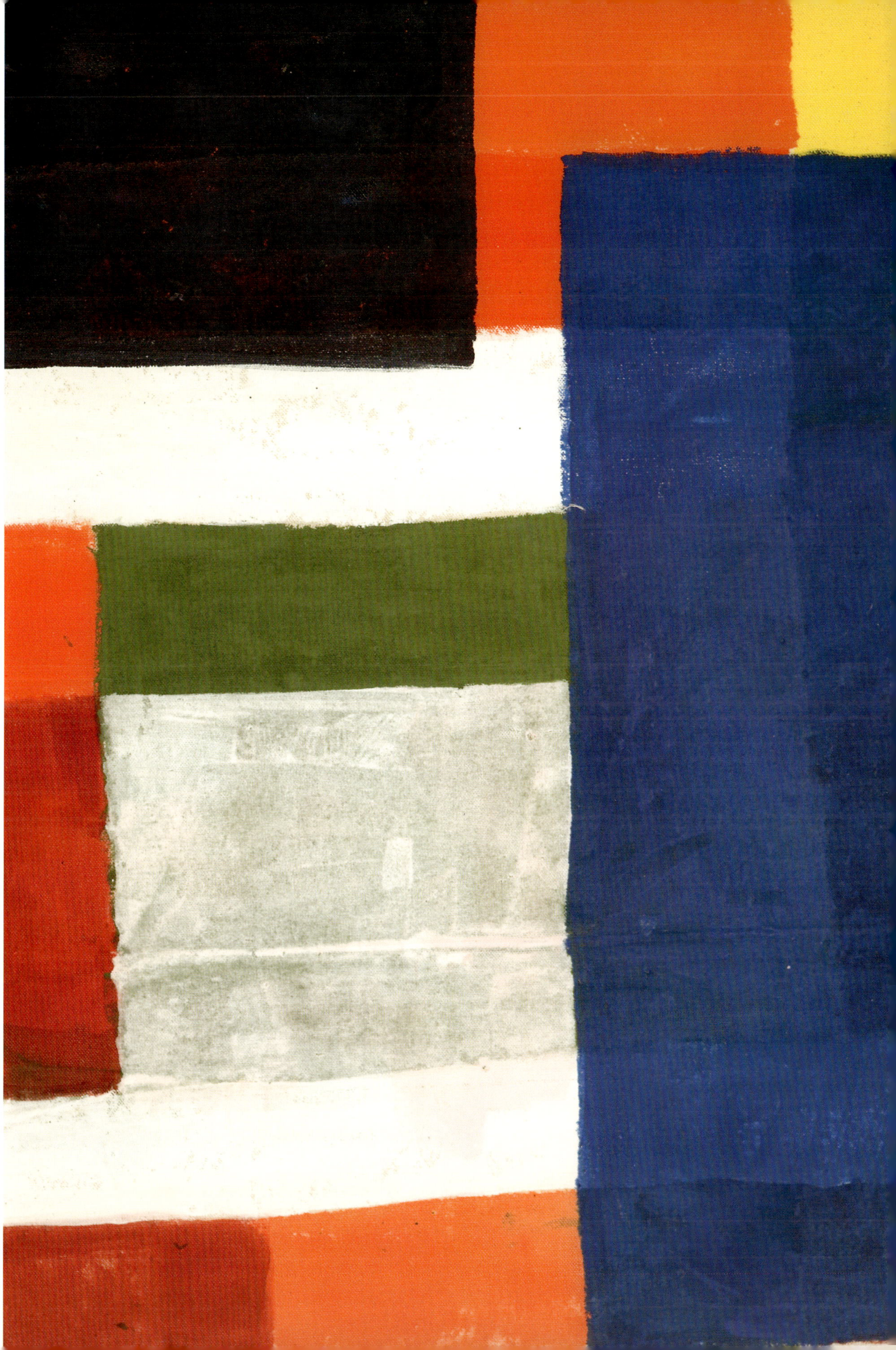

Below *Amamu*, 2007. Acrylic on canvas, 40 x 40 cm (15¾ x 15¾ in). Collection of the artist. Amamu is the hero of the 1971 novel *This Earth My Brother* by the Ghanaian writer Kofi Awoonon.

Right *Kokrobitey*, 2007 (full image). 'My work is described, conventionally as "abstract", given that there is a very precise, knowable set of resources at the back of it. I would describe it rather as schematic; not like a map, but like a reaction to or interpretation of a map. It is about ownership, a way of finding myself, where I am. In that sense my work enhances a viewing of Kumasi and Ghana.'

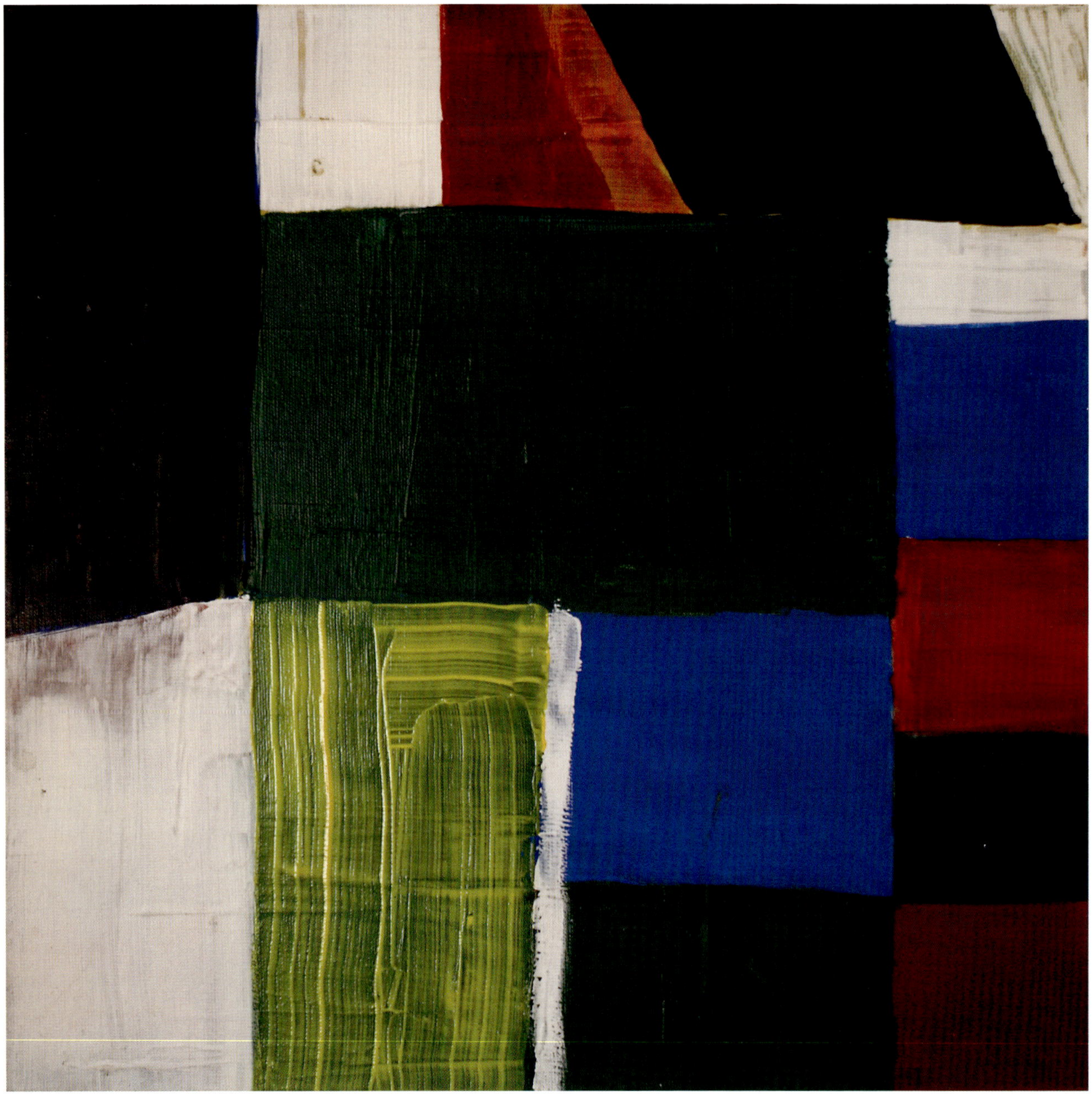

'Wherever I go I take my world with me; this implies the memory that I carry with me.'
Atta Kwami

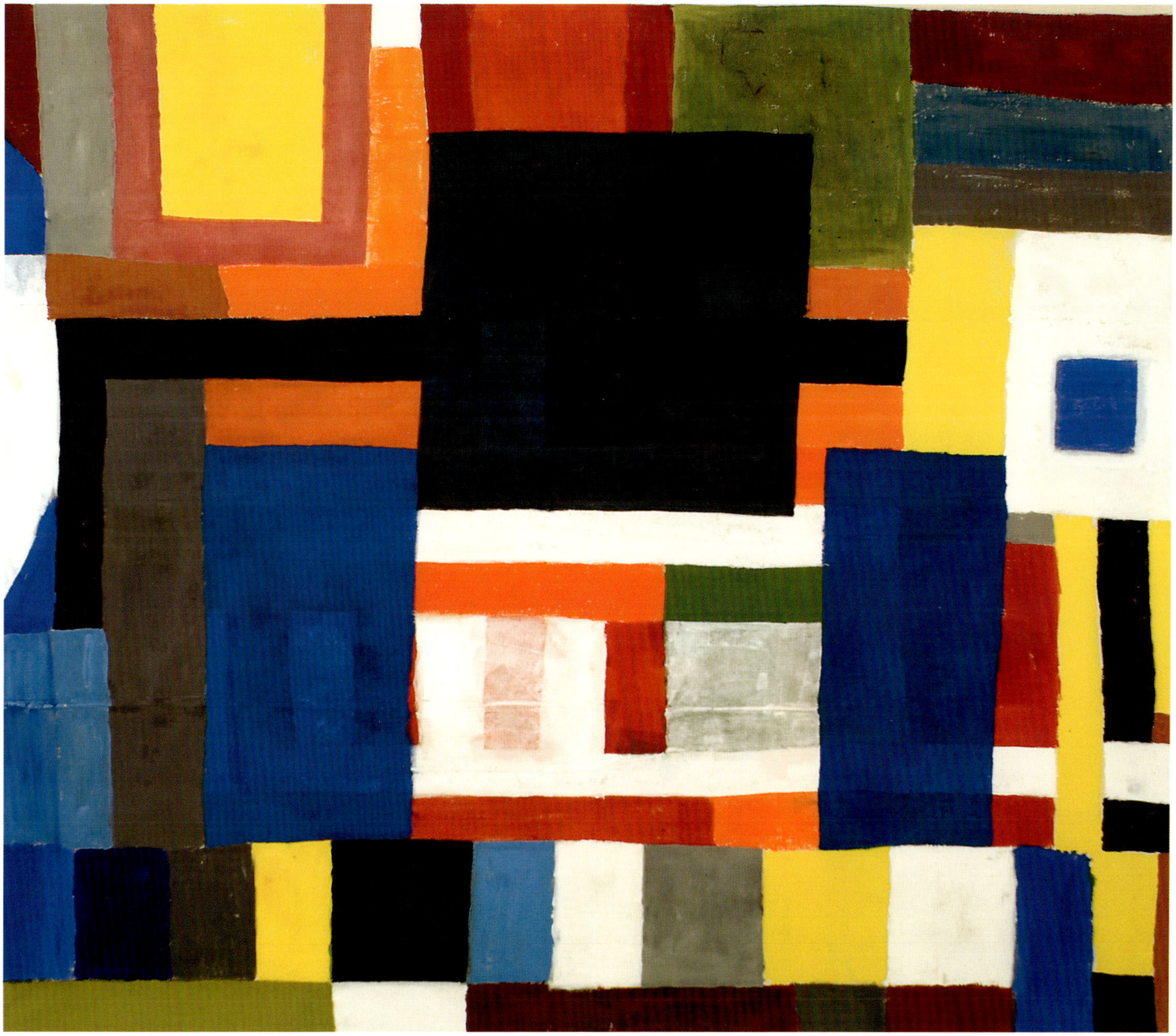

NJA MAHDAOUI
TUNISIA

This spread *Drum*, 1998. Wood, skin, pigment, synthetic material, metal, 67 x 47.5 cm (26⅓ x 18¾ in). British Museum, London.
'In response to the essential nature of this drum, I have modified its traditional appearance by physically inscribing free calligraphic signs on the two blank, circular membranes. I decided to conceptualize it as a silent, sculptural object and intentionally transposed its original role as the sonorous accompaniment of an oral tradition. Consequently, this drum has taken on a new physical presence. From a conceptual point of view it is a new, three-dimensional installation; from a functional point of view its two voices have been silenced by its re-contextualization as a work of art.'

Nja Mahdaoui was born in 1937 in Tunis, Tunisia. While studying painting and history of art at the Carthage Museum, he came to the attention of the Director of the Italian Cultural Centre in Tunis, who encouraged him to take a diploma in painting and philosophy at the Santa Andrea Academy in Rome (1966–68). From there he moved to Paris where he attended courses at the Department of Oriental Antiquities, École du Louvre (1968).

Together with a generation of North African artists who emerged in the 1960s, Mahdaoui began to push the boundaries of acceptable practice in using calligraphy as an art form. While always mindful of its sacred role recording and revealing the word of God as set down in the Qu'ran, Mahdaoui and others began to explore the artistic potential of the forms rather than the literal meaning of these words and letters, and of the radically different types of script that had been developed by calligraphers over the centuries.

Mahdaoui experimented not only with his own personal 'calligrams' on conventional surfaces, such as paper and parchment, but also embellished a range of other materials, such as melamine, brass, aluminium, denim, as well as other forms including costume, musical instruments, buildings, the human body and even a jet aircraft.

Mahdaoui has lectured and exhibited all over the world, winning many prestigious awards, including the UNESCO Crafts Prize for the Arab States in 2005. His works are held in many museums and public institutions around the world, including the National Museum, Tunis, the British Museum, London, the Smithsonian Institution, Washington, the National Library, Paris and the Museum of Modern Art, Kuala Lumpur.

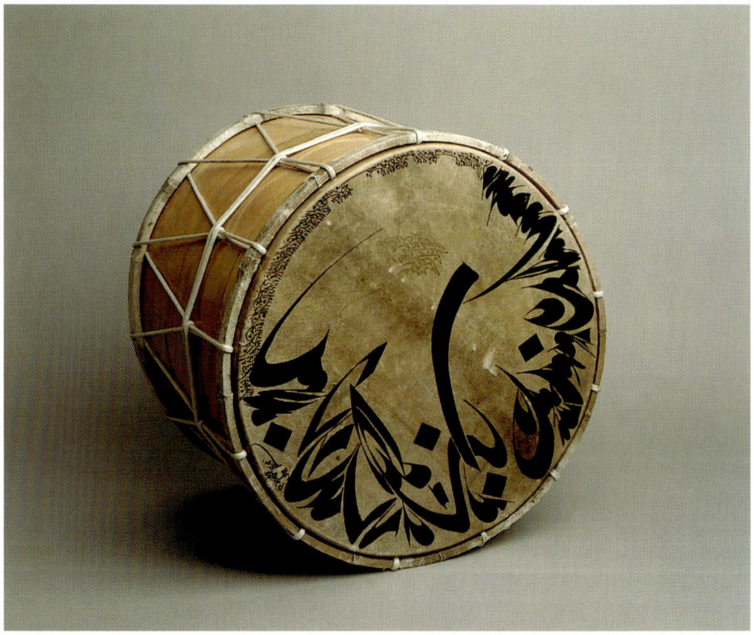

'This drum, transformed into a silent sculpture, has temporarily ceased to be an instrument; it simply exists. Its cultural function – as a catalyst to the senses articulated through formal and improvised melody – has been interrupted. More importantly, it has renounced its particular voice as part of a collective artistic performance. Instead, with its multiplicity of resonances, it has become a dynamic symbol of cultural pluralism, a kind of "total art" to which people throughout the world can respond in a myriad different ways.'
Nja Mahdaoui

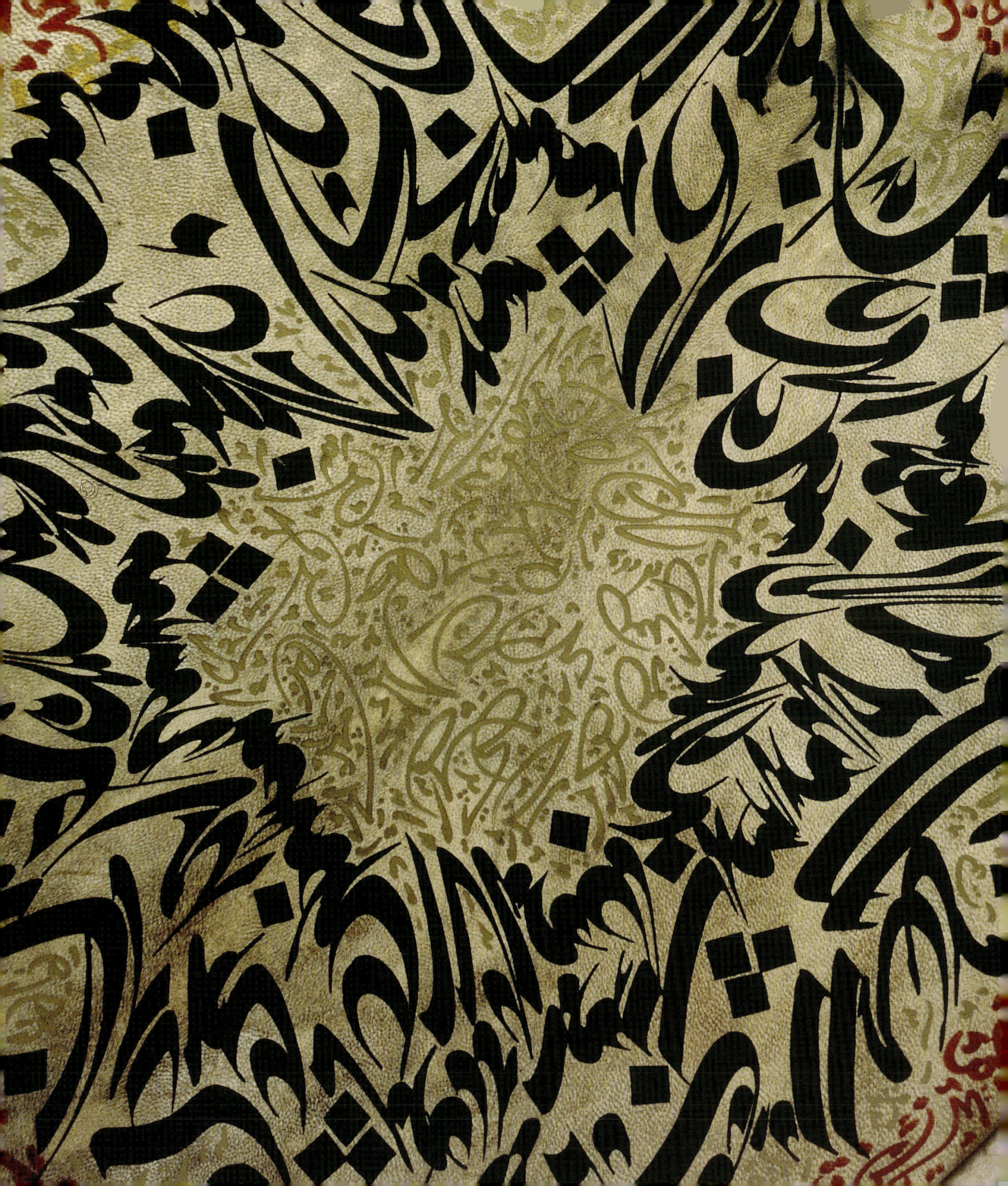

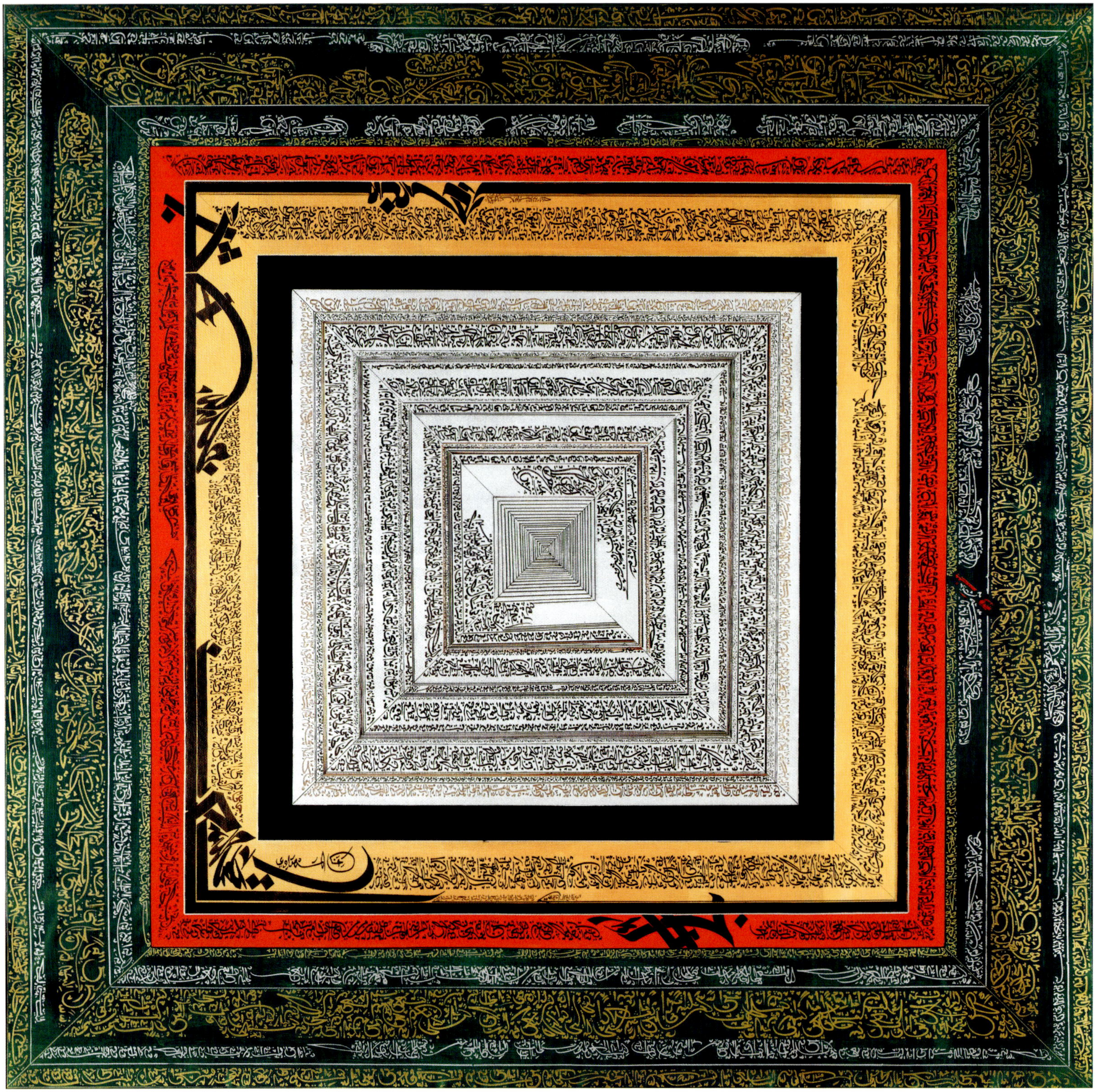

Left *Midoun*, 2002–7. China ink, acrylics, oil paint, gold and silver on linen canvas, 150 x 150cm (59 x 59 in). Private collection.

Below *Walegh Triptych*, 2002–7. China ink, acrylics, oil paint, gold and silver on linen canvas, 100 x 150cm (39⅖ x 59 in). Collection of the artist.

Mahdaoui is not concerned with the meaning of words – 'words restrict meaning' – but rather with transforming them into 'calligrams' of his own invention. By this means he releases their potential, in combination with colour, to evoke a range of sensations, from intense visual pleasure to the melodies and rhythms of music and the collective passion of religious devotion.

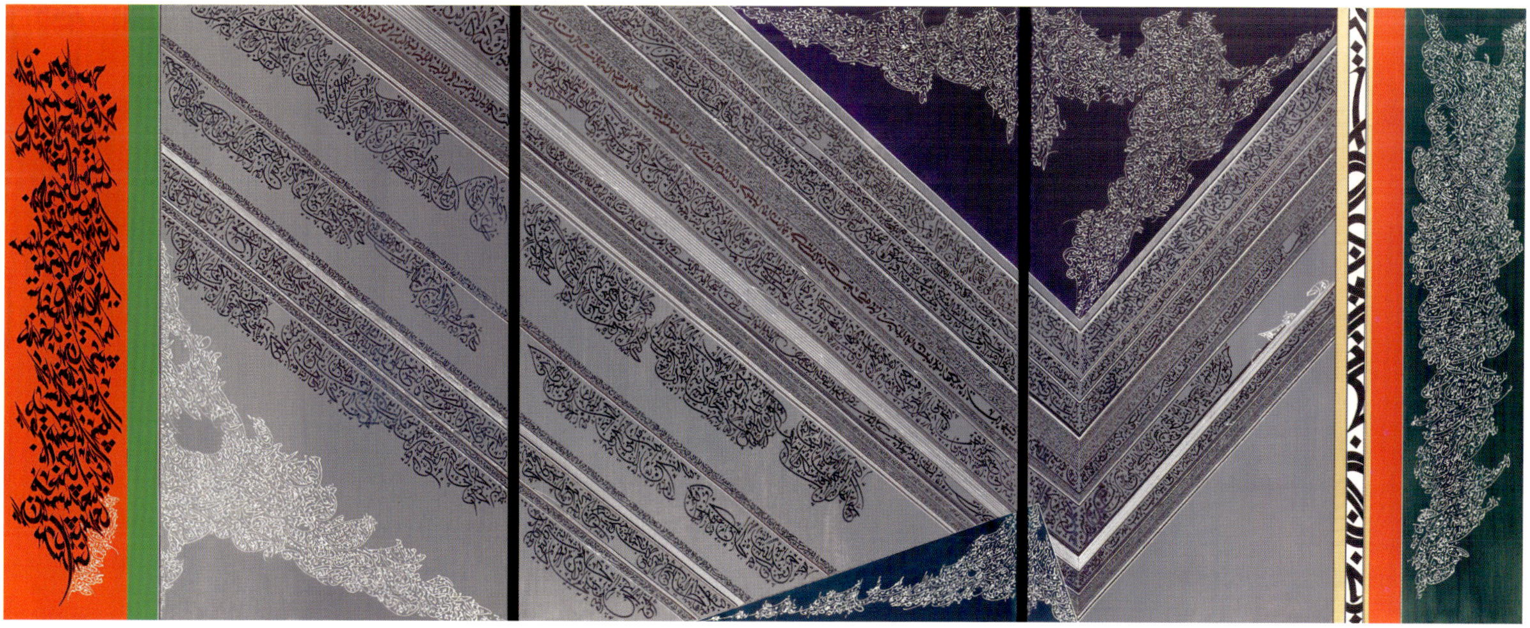

MALANGATANA VALENTE NGWENYA
MOZAMBIQUE

Below *Untitled*, 1994. Ink on paper, 43 x 31 cm (17 x 12⅕ in). Private collection.
'For me, beyond the aesthetic composition and expression, art is without doubt a musical instrument full of messages. These are messages that the artist selects to "put together" in front of humanity.' Flute players appear regularly in Malangatana's work.

Right *Untitled*, 1982 (detail). Mural on boundary wall of Natural History Museum, Maputo. Pigments on concrete.
One of Malangatana's finest works is his mural on the walls of the garden of the Natural History Museum in Maputo. Here his signature patterns of eyes and limbs combine with colours to create an orchestral piece celebrating the harmony between humankind and the natural world. The work changes miraculously as the sun moves across the sky, casting shadows from the surrounding trees and bushes.

Malangatana is a painter, poet, sculptor and musician, who has spent his life fighting injustice, war, poverty and his own personal demons with whatever means his prodigious talents provided for him. Mozambique and its people endured great suffering during Malangatana's lifetime, and he has been instrumental in helping to bring the country to the period of peace and redevelopment that it currently enjoys.

Born in 1936 in Matalana, a village in southern Mozambique, Malangatana sought his fortune in the capital, Lourenço Marques (now Maputo) at the age of twelve. He did various jobs, including being an apprentice to a traditional healer or *curandeiro*, and attended classes at night, through which he developed an interest in art. He began to draw and paint, encouraged by Augusto Cabral (later Director of the Natural History Museum in Maputo) and the architect Pancho Guedes. He also attended functions at the Núcleo d'Arte, the long-established art school in Maputo, and held his first solo exhibition in 1961. This was quickly followed by group exhibitions in countries outside Mozambique, including France and the USA, drawing the following assessment from the German curator and advocate of African arts Ulli Beier in 1962: 'Malangatana is one of the few really original painters to be found in Africa today'. It is part of Malangatana's achievement that today he is just one of thousands of 'original painters' in Mozambique alone.

Malangatana used his art and growing international reputation to fight for Frelimo against the colonial regime in Mozambique, then after independence in 1975 against the Western-backed Renamo rebels, who were armed by the apartheid regime in South Africa. His paintings, poems and vast murals depicted oppression in various forms and fanned the flames of resistance leading to liberation and to the end of the 'civil war' in 1992. He helped to found the National Museum of Art in Maputo and to turn the Núcleo d'Arte from an exclusively white institution into a thriving focus for young black Mozambican artists. He is also a passionate advocate of the rights of children, and has collaborated with UNICEF for many years.

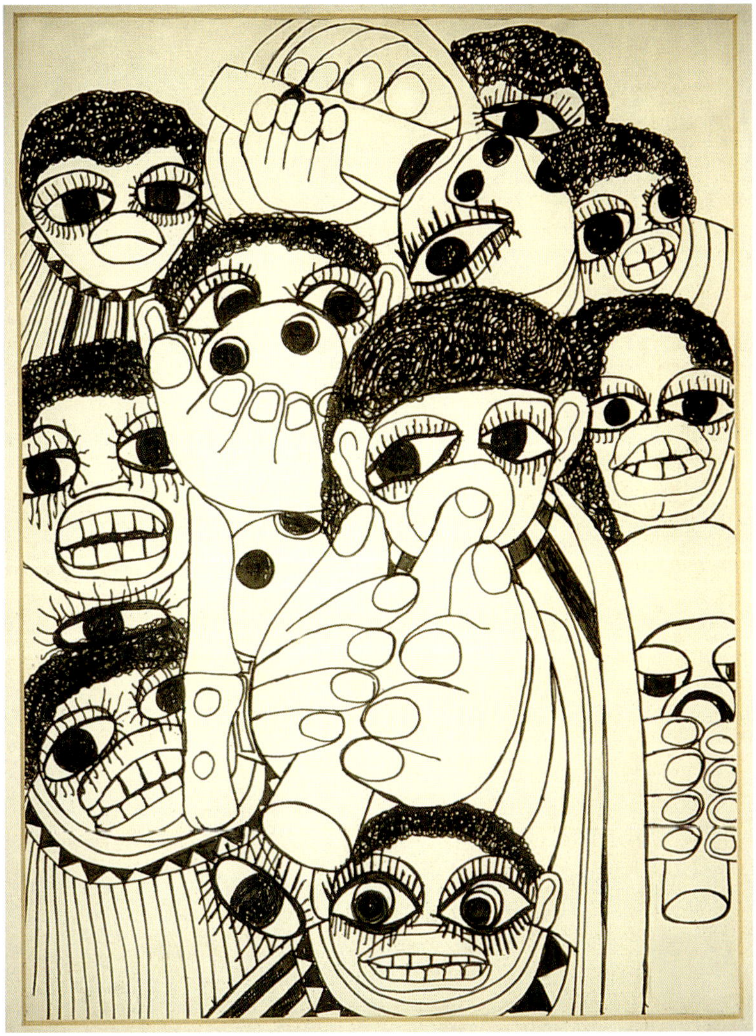

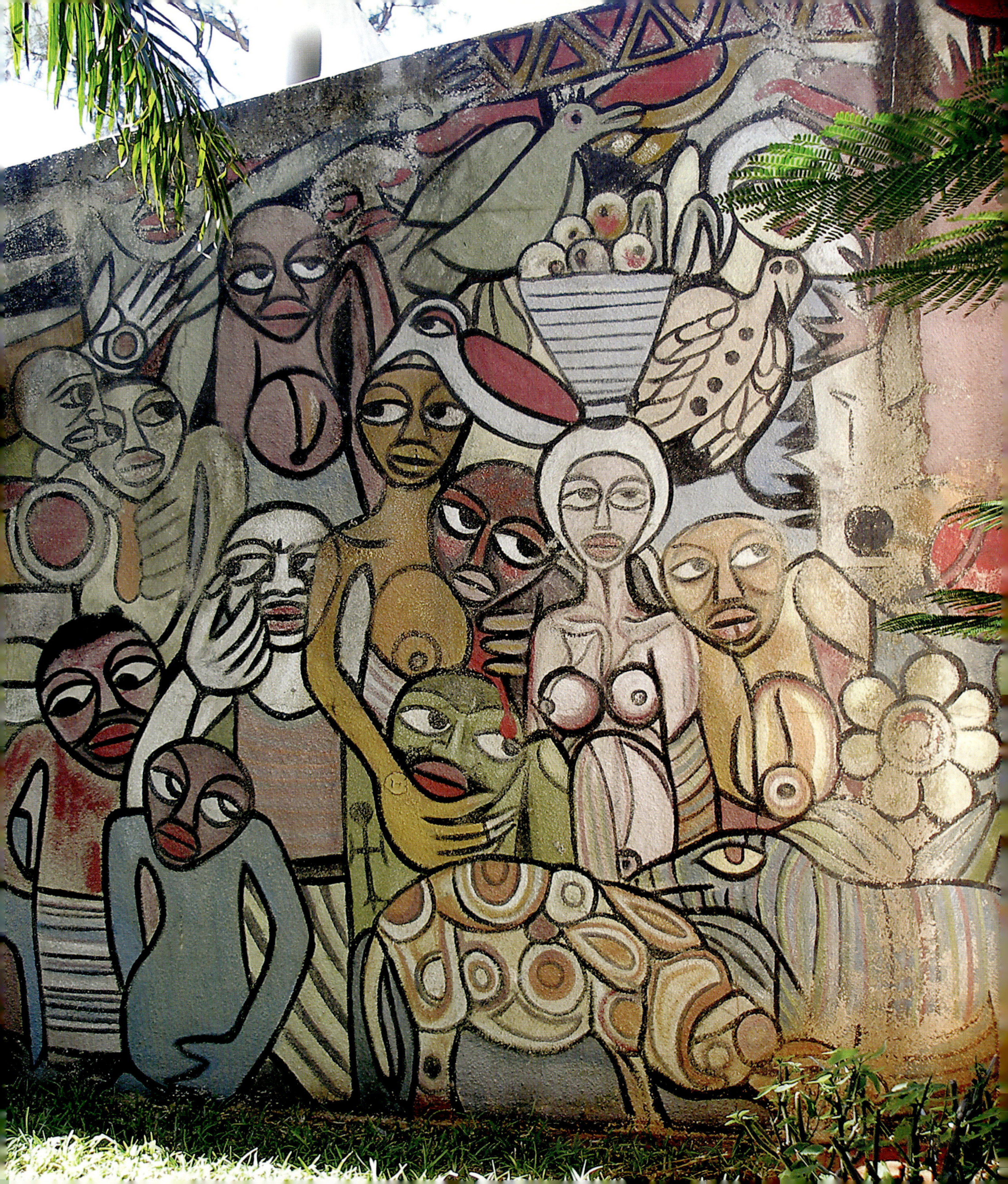

Below *Untitled*, 1992.
Oil on board, 47 x 98 cm (18½ x 38⅗ in). Private collection.
Malangatana uses teeth as a recurring motif in his paintings, usually symbolizing monsters and savagery. Another of his paintings is entitled *The Only Way to Destroy a Monster Is to Pull Out His Teeth.*

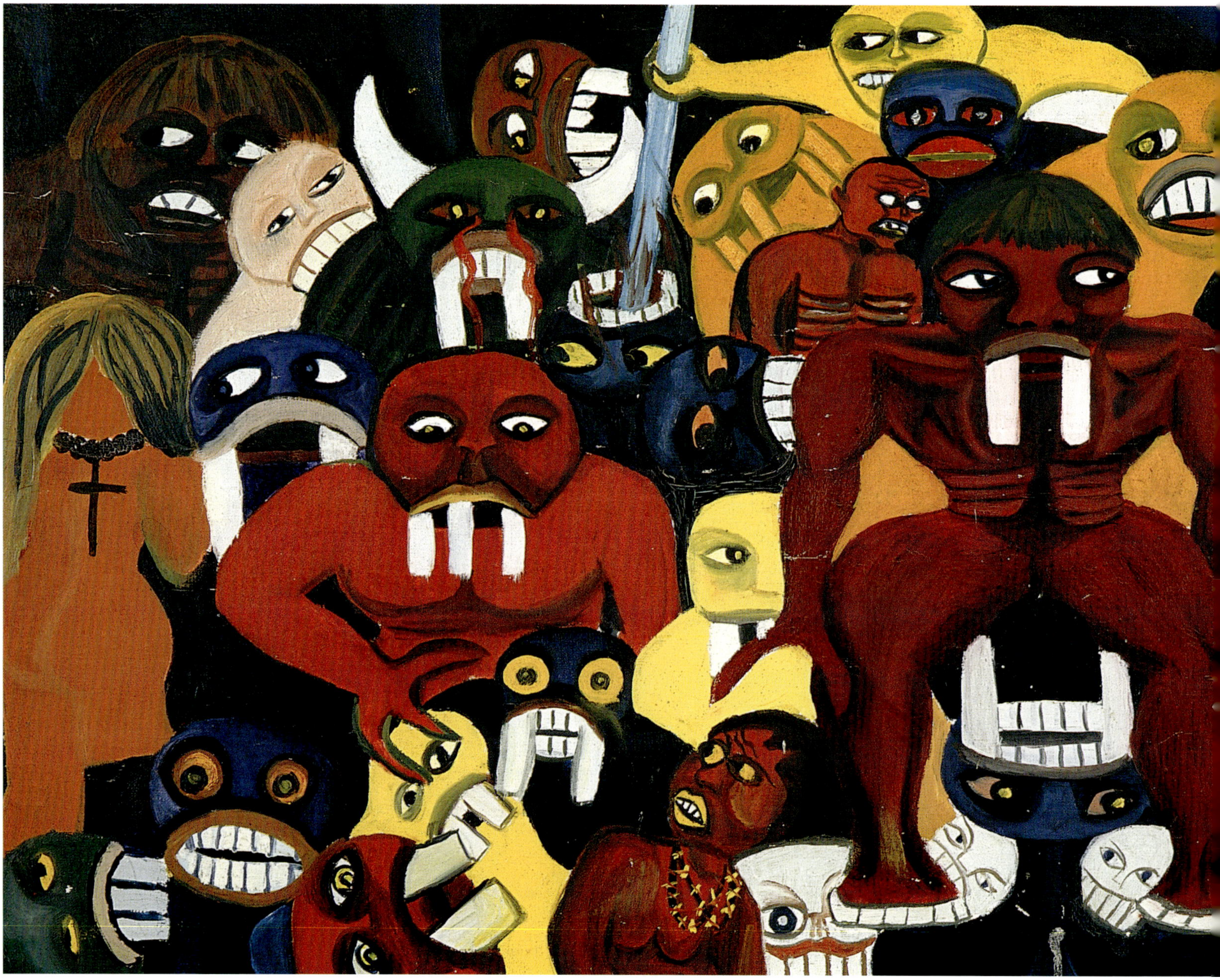

'The owl augurs for me
and tells me that I'll never arrive
beyond where desire leads me
and thus the dream evaporates.

I am struggling with myself alone
it is impossible to conquer the waves
scratched over me through witchcraft
by the owls, cats and drums.'
Malangatana Valente Ngwenya

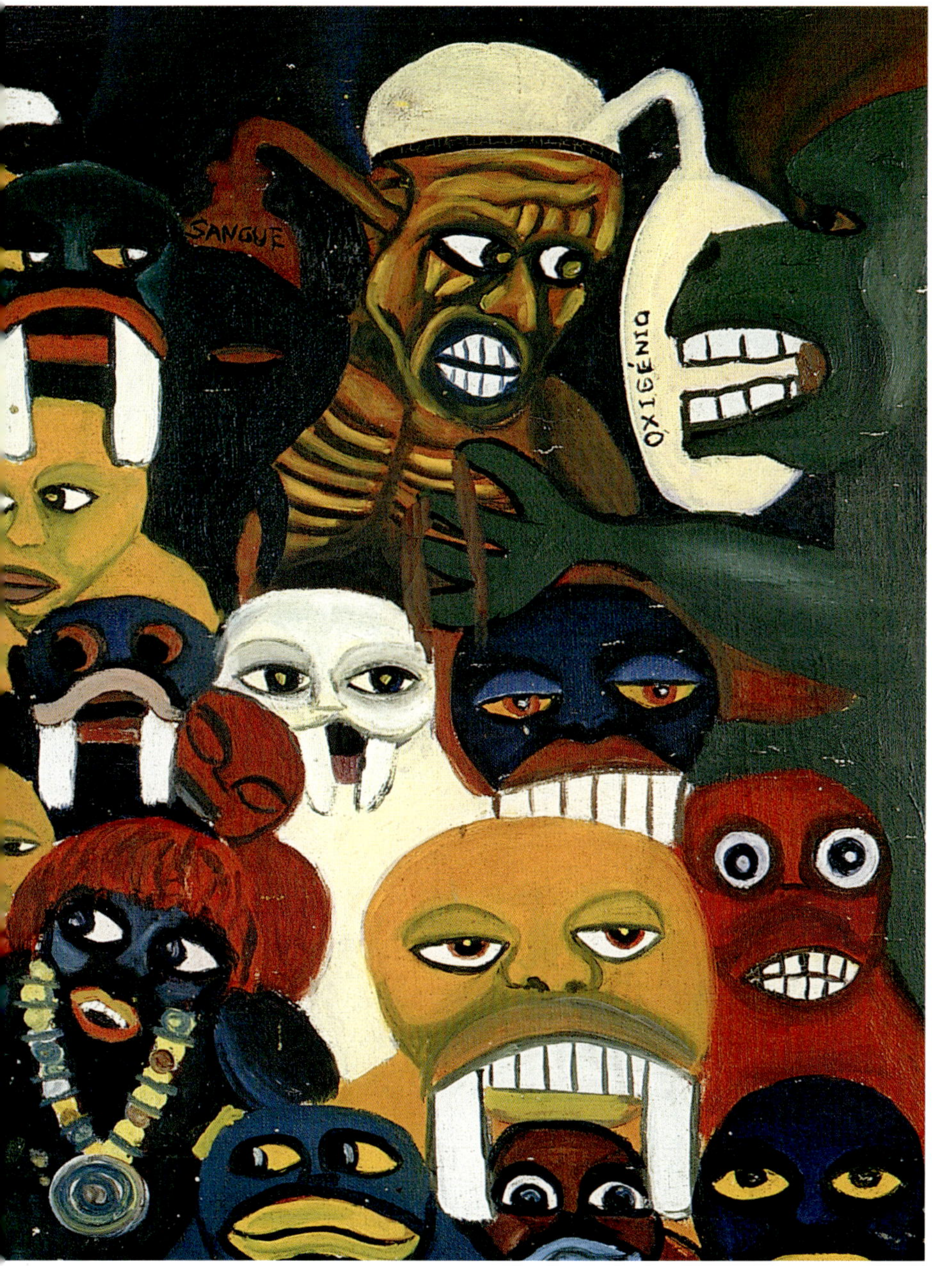

TASLIM MARTIN
UK

Below *Icosahedral*, 2004. Stainless steel, diameter 300cm (118 in). Cambourne Business Park, Cambridge, UK.

Bottom *Kente Day Couch*, 2007. Upholstery, stainless steel and recycled plastic, 42 x 215 x 91.5cm (16½ x 84⅔ x 35⅘ in). Private collection.
'The upholstery in these works is very similar to a fabric used on the London Underground... Many of the classic Enid Marx designs for the London Underground are easily recognizable as being derived from *kente* cloth from Ghana.'

Right *Portrait-head Meiko*, 2007. Cast iron, life-size. Private collection.
'Inspired in part by the classical style of Ife heads of the Yoruba people... the intention here is to hint at what lies beneath the skin, and to question preconceptions about portraiture in African art.'

Taslim Martin was born in London in 1962. His father is from Nigeria, his mother from St Lucia in the Caribbean. 'I suppose that some might think that that would give you something of a crisis of identity', says Martin, 'but I see it more as giving you choices. It's the same with my work; you have the option of various cultures to choose from.'

He obtained a City and Guilds certificate in carpentry and joinery at Southend College of Art and Technology in 1981, and pursued a career as a carpenter for the next 13 years before going to art school in 1991, first in Southend, then in Cardiff and finally in London, graduating from the Royal College of Art in 1998.

Martin's creative output ranges from figurative sculpture to public art commissions and furniture. Craft skills are very important in his work, and through these he examines the idea and the reality of cultural identity.

> *I first seriously considered the notion of cultural identity in my work after Africa '95 and the Royal Academy show 'Africa: the Art of a Continent'. I happily call myself an African artist; does this prescribe the kind of work I should make? Is there such a thing as an appropriate artistic response to one's cultural background?*

Martin's work was featured in the 'Mixed Belongings' touring exhibition, which was curated by the artist Raimi Gbadamosi at the Crafts Council, London in 2005. In this show and in his solo exhibition 'Contemporary Primitive' at the 198 Gallery, London in 2007, Martin continued his theme of investigating cultural identity, 'how cultures give meaning to objects and how objects often define cultures', and 'how Africa gave modernity to the world through the iniquities of the slave trade'.

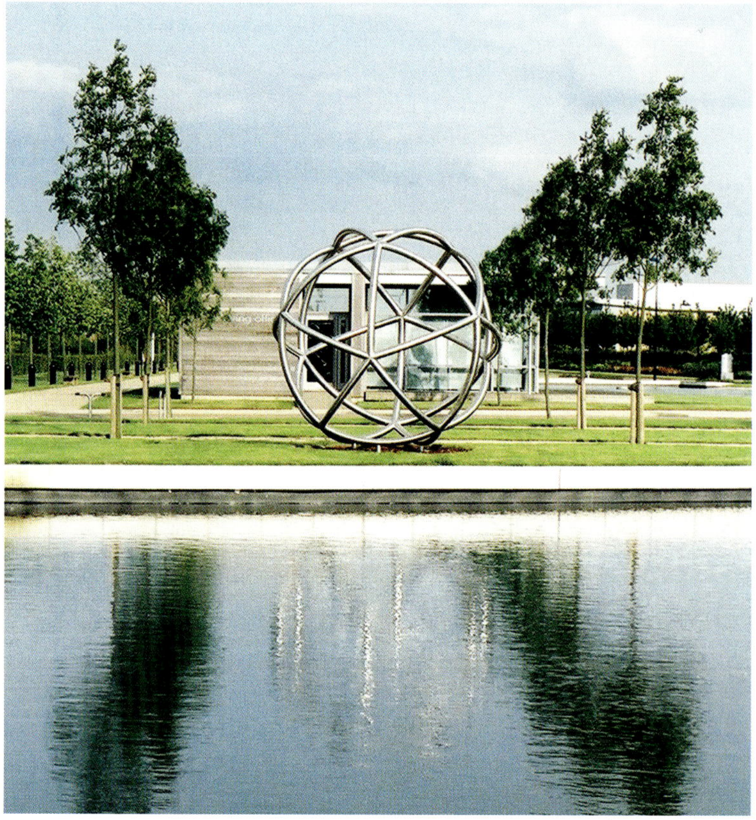

'I am very interested in what people imagine constitutes African art; whether the art itself should visually be apparent as produced by an African or coming from Africa. I've asked many people, educators and artists in Africa and in Britain, and there's a real confusion; it's not clear at all, and I think it's interesting to have the debate...'
Taslim Martin

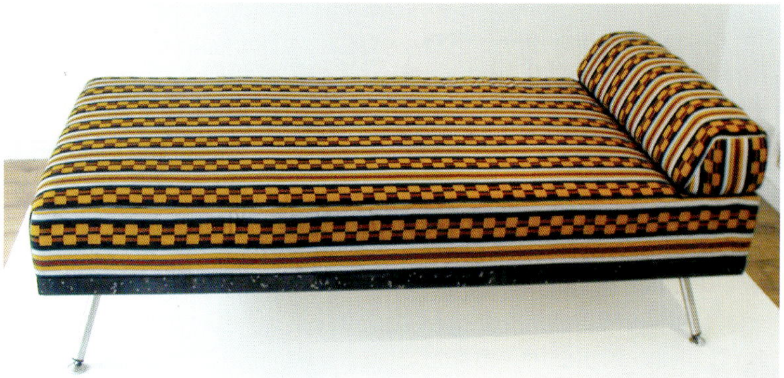

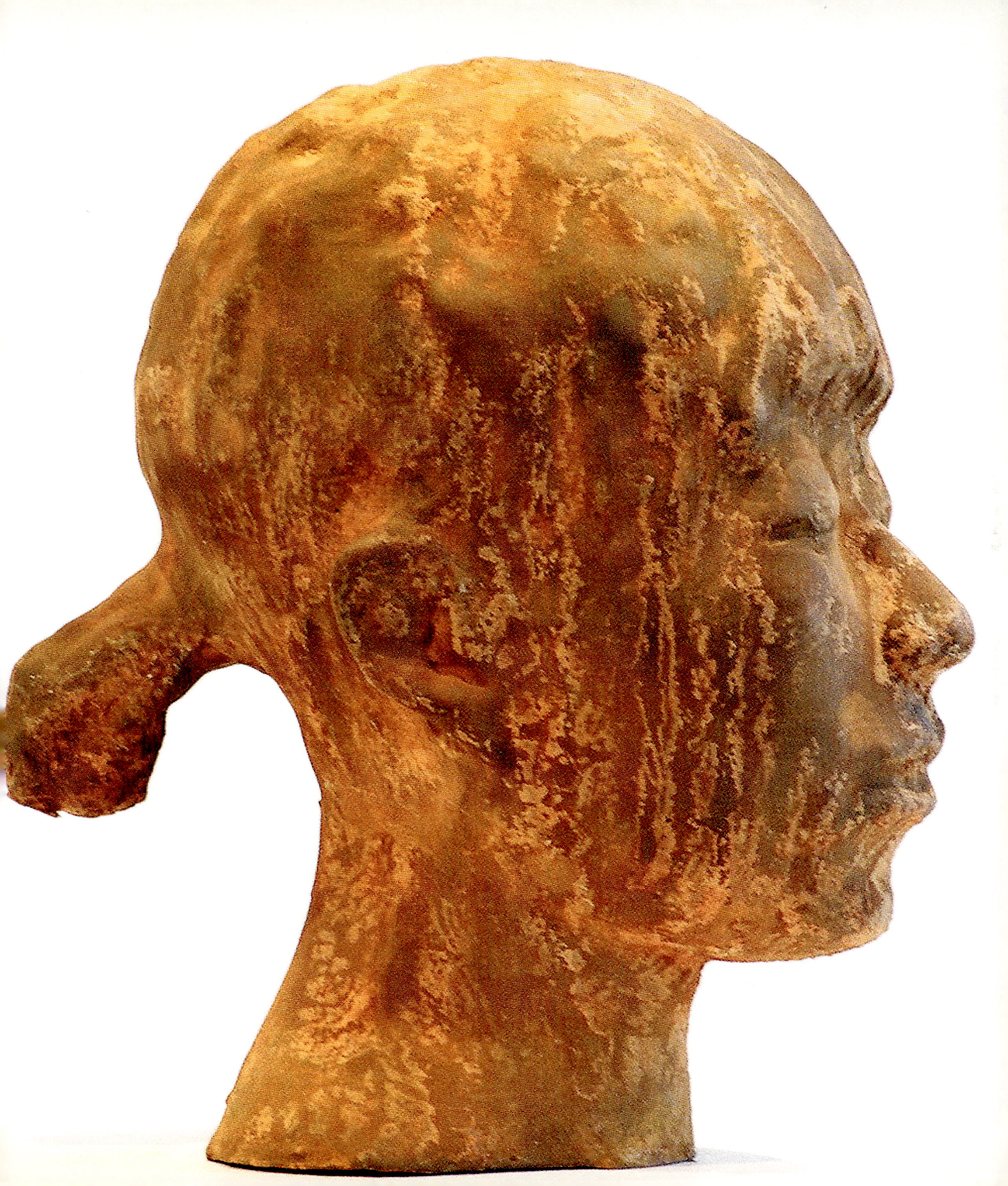

Below *Secret Dovetail*, 2005. Cast aluminium, 42 x 40 x 24cm (16½ x 15¾ x 9½ in). British Museum, London.
'This work takes as its starting point the carved wooden stools of the Ashanti and Yoruba peoples of West Africa. However, the choice of material and finish also references the craft of coach building for the car industry. A butterfly dovetail extrusion on the underside of the stool locks the three pieces in place; this detail is not visible and that gives the work its title.'

Right *Secret Dovetail*, with *Clay Drawing*, from an installation at 198 Gallery, London, 2007.
'Besides the strong artistic influences, trans-Atlantic slavery is the other cross-cultural exchange between Africa and Western societies, which allowed the development of modernity in the West. In this series of two drawings, using the most "primitive" form of mark-making, the most humble material, I have chosen to draw the symbolic imagery of economic power and nationhood, and to refer to slavery as the moment in history when Modernity began.'

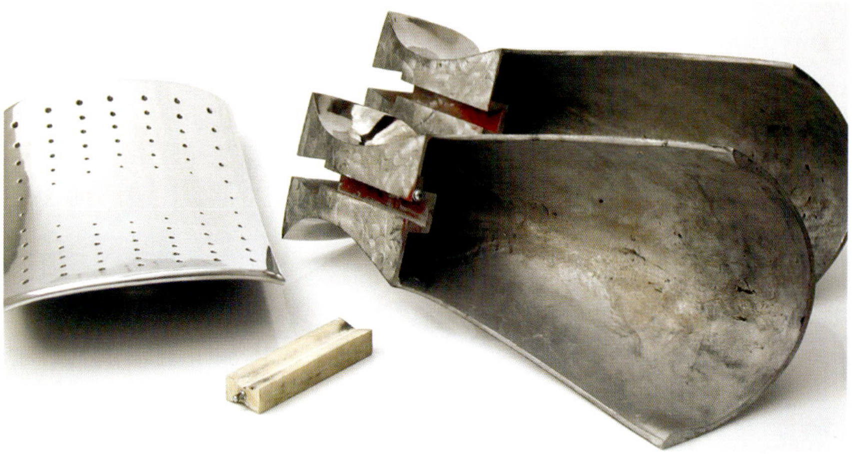

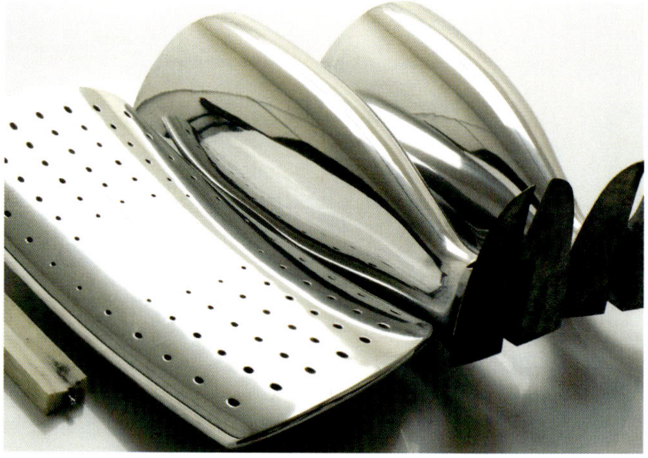

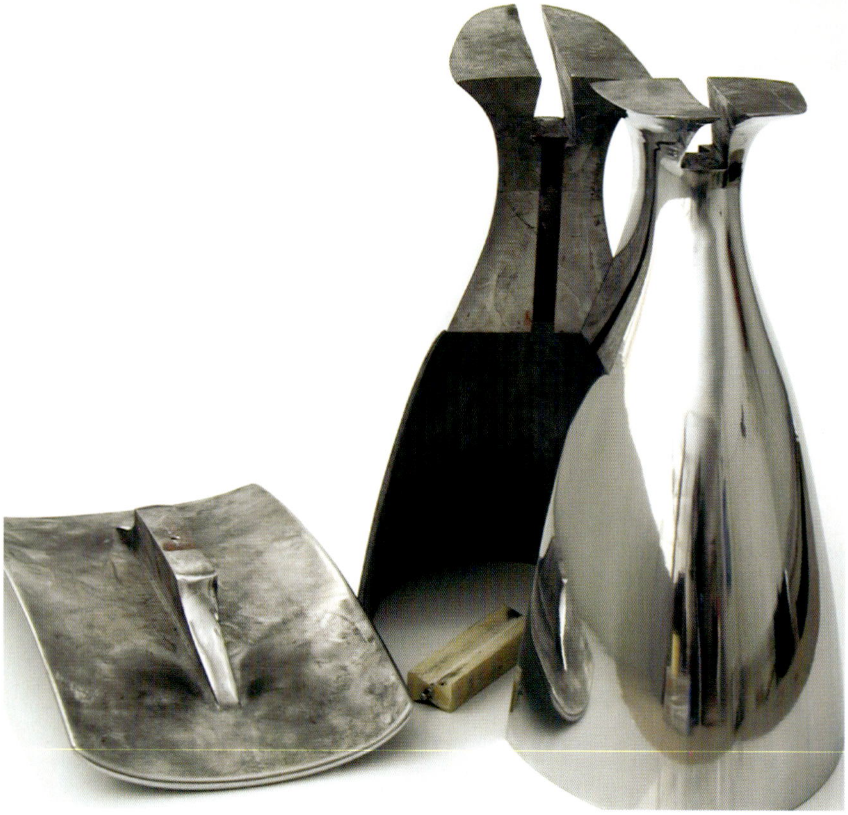

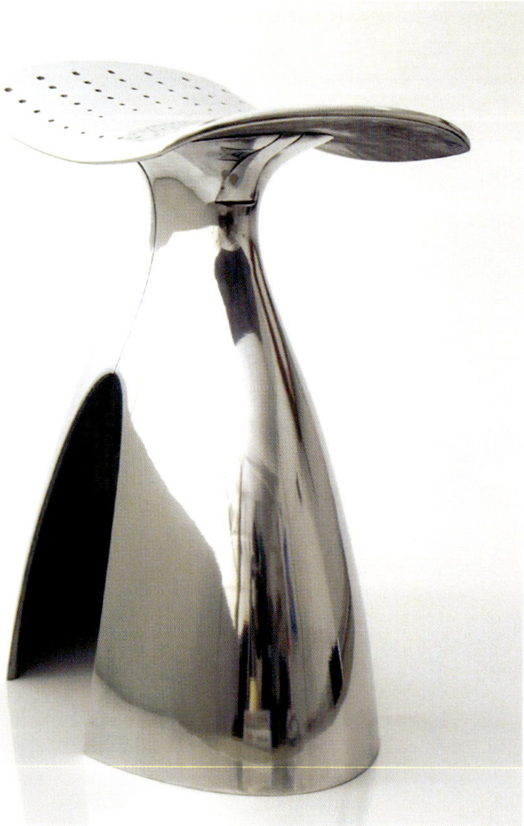

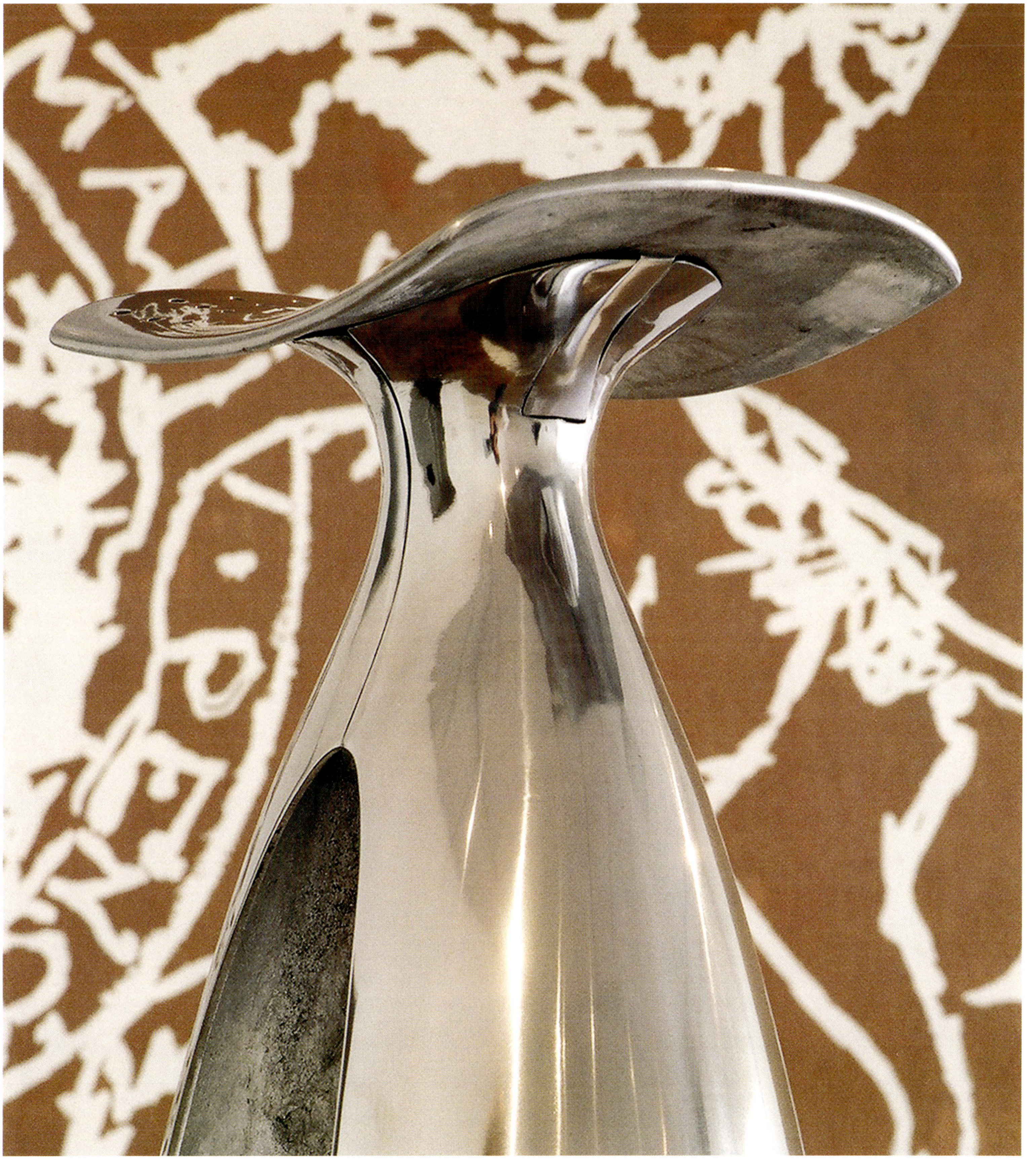

JULIE MEHRETU
ETHIOPIA/USA

This spread *Easy Dark*, 2007. Ink and acrylic on canvas, 274.3 x 183 cm (108 x 72 in). Collection Louisiana Museum of Modern Art.
Despite the apparent chaos they depict, Mehretu's works are precisely mapped and architecturally constructed. She refers to them as psychogeographic paintings.

'I'm interested in describing this as a system... a whole cosmos, and that is the overall painting, while the minute detailed marks act more like characters, individual stories.'

Julie Mehretu was born in Addis Ababa, Ethiopia, in 1970. She grew up in Michigan, USA, studying at Kalamazoo College, then at the Cheik Anta Diop University, Dakar, Senegal, and at the Rhode Island School of Design, USA. Her father is Ethiopian, her mother a white American; she now lives and works in New York.

Mehretu's paintings seem to tell of an ordered, precisely mapped universe in which anarchy has been suddenly unleashed – but it is always an ordered anarchy, as if the previous order was questionable and ready to collapse, and a new order about to be created. She uses the precise, technical drawings of town planners and architects as a metaphor for the old order, overlaying and invading them with a mass of disparate forms, colours and shapes.

> *I like the idea that everything fits into a structure with a map or an architectural plan, but part of it is also about mapping who I am. I come from two different realities and I'm trying to locate myself, ... trying to make sense of the version of history and reality that my whole family in Ethiopia is living in, and another one that exists here with my parents and my grandmother – and yet another one that I experience.*

Mehretu has been the recipient of many prestigious grants and fellowships; she was the artist in residence at the Walker Art Center, Minneapolis in 2003 and won the American Art Award at the Whitney Museum of Art, New York in 2005. Her two major solo exhibitions 'Black City' and 'Heavy Weather' have been on tour in the USA and Europe in 2006–7.

'All this stuff is layered inside me, all these parts of who I am. Two sides of me do battle: the conceptual side and the visual side.'
Julie Mehretu

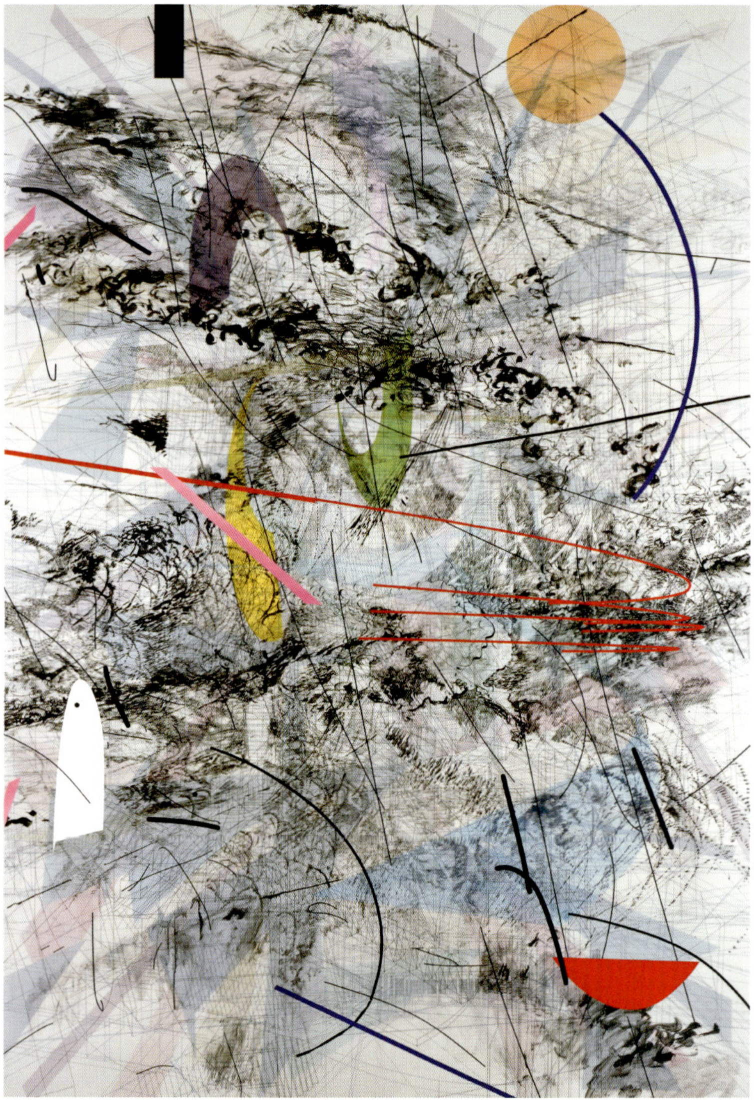

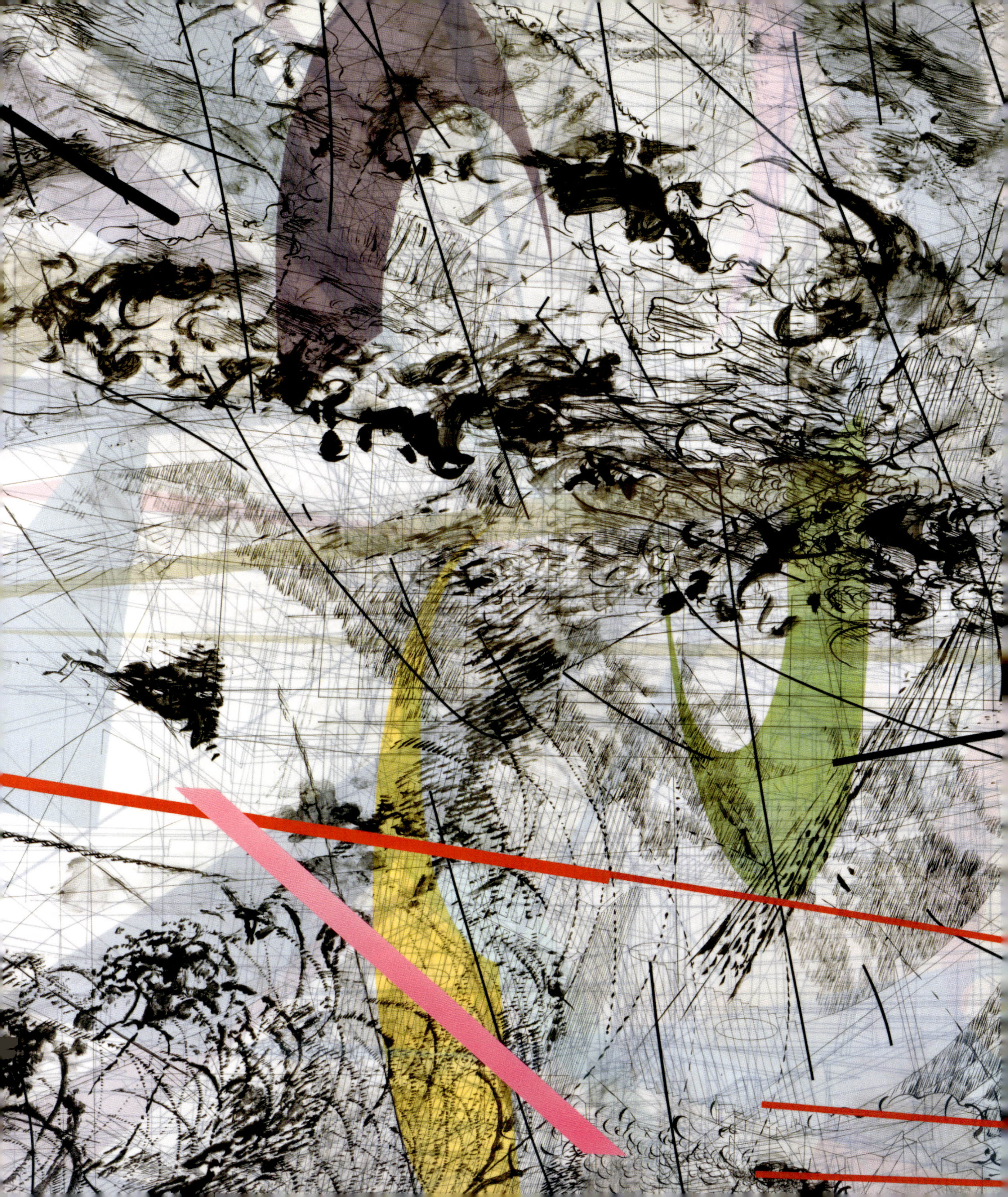

Below *Transients*, 2006. Ink and acrylic on canvas, 123.2 x 153.7 cm (48½ x 60½ in). Private collection. Mehretu's own complex family history, 'the multifaceted layers of place, space and time that impact the formation of personal and communal identity', are reflected in the personal narrative of her paintings.

Right *Zero Canyon (a dissimulation)*, 2006. Ink and acrylic on canvas, 304.8 x 213.4 cm (120 x 84 in). Collection MUSAC – Museo de Arte Contemporáneo de Castilla y León. 'Painting is more of a representation of something else, a metaphor. Of course, it has agency in a certain sense, but it's not an active agent in the same way that I think the drawing is.'

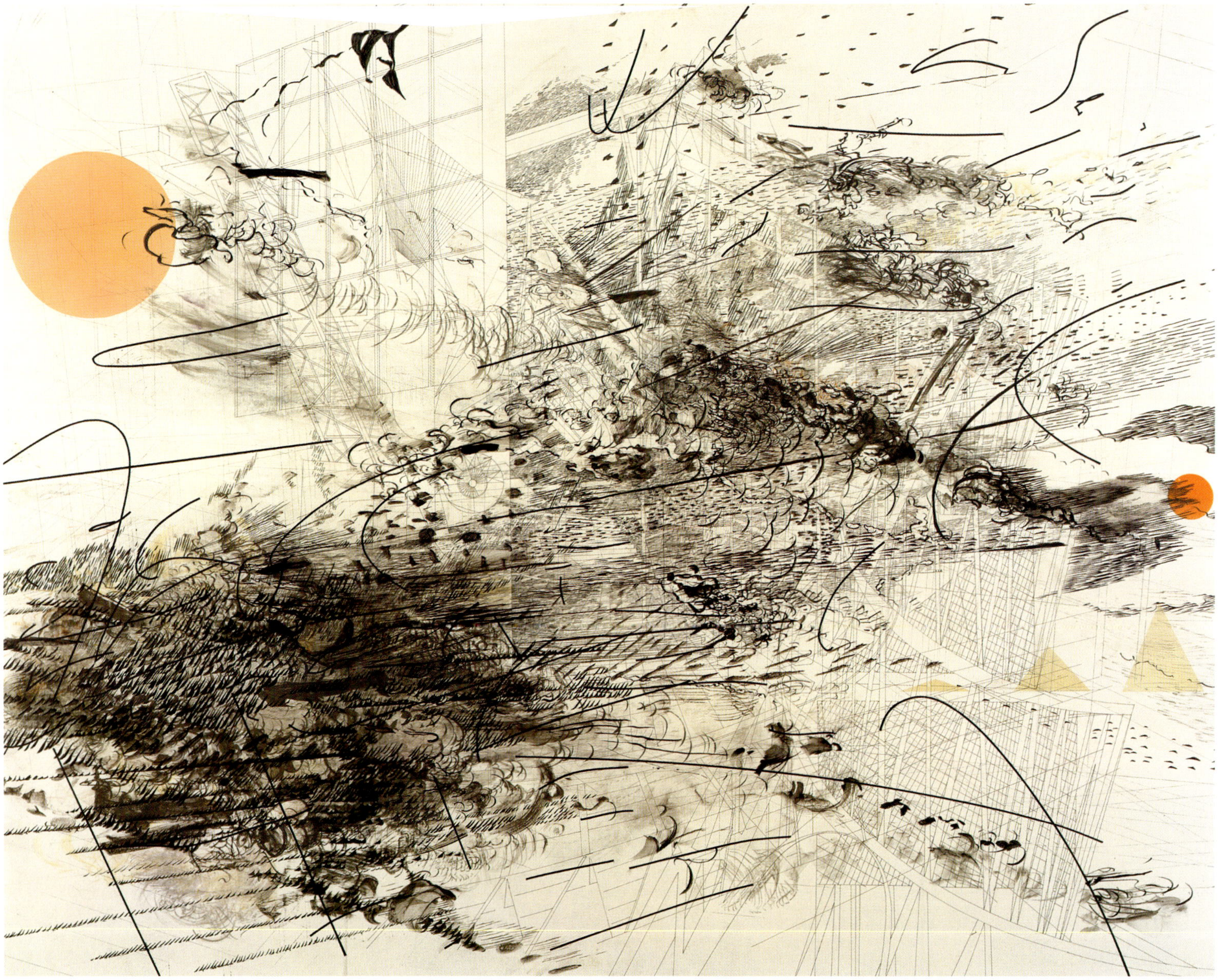

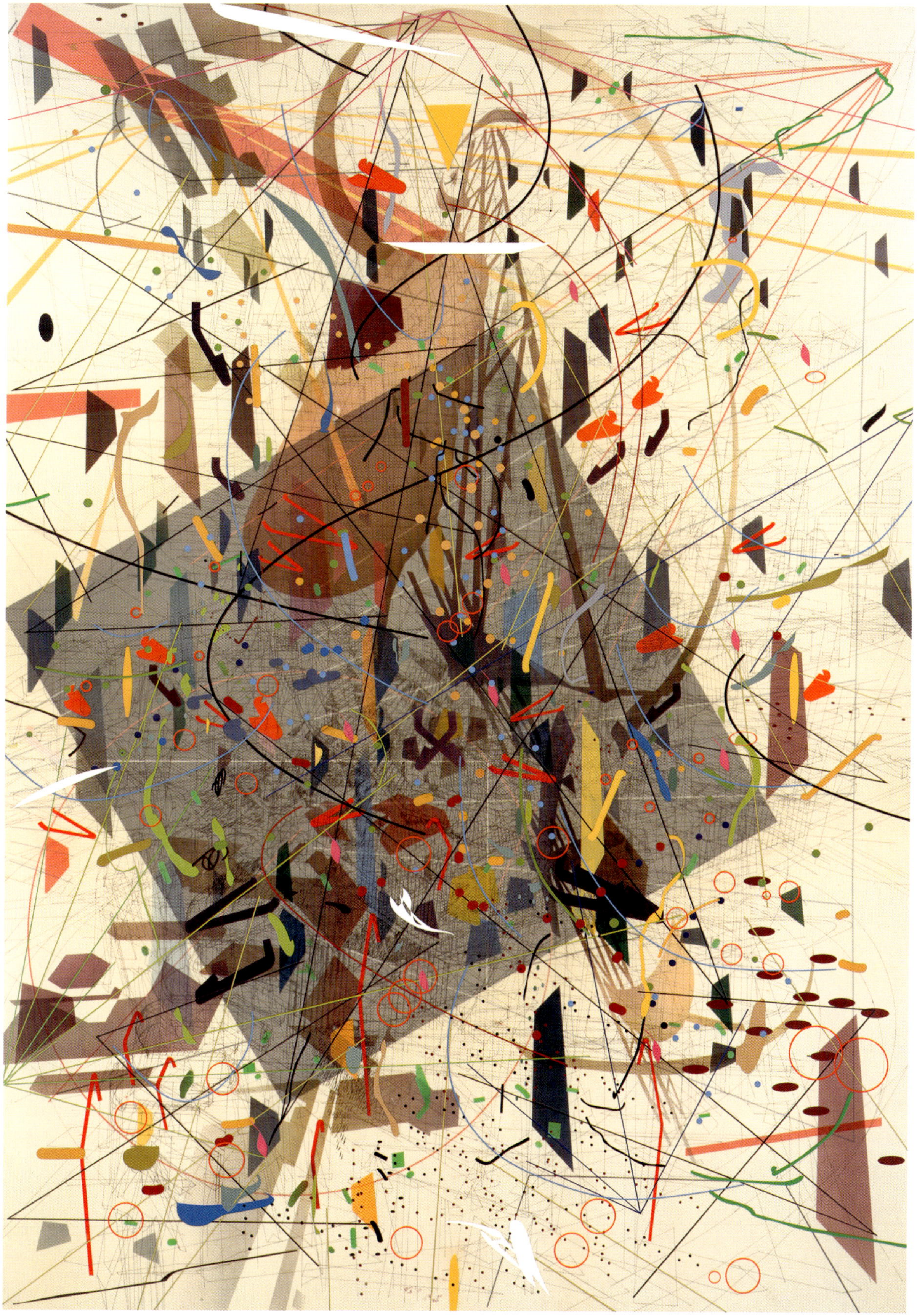

MANUEL MENDIVE
CUBA

Below Performance at FIAC (Foire Internationale d'Art Contemporain), Paris, 1999.
Performance art and body painting are important elements in Mendive's art, referencing the complex traditions of masquerade among the Yoruba people of West Africa.

Right *Elleguá lo museve todo* (*Elleguá Moves Everything*), 2004.
Gouache on canvas, 41 x 42 cm (16⅙ x 16½ in).
Orlando Borges Collection.

In the late 1970s a group of artists and intellectuals, many of them Afro-Cubans, began meeting in Havana and exhibiting their work under the name *Grupo Antillano* (the Antilles Group) in order to acknowledge their solidarity with other Caribbean artists. Manuel Mendive, already an established artist, exhibited his work with this group, whose unofficial, yet deeply felt, manifesto was expressed by their leader, Rafael Queneditt:

> *We all wanted to express the depth and profundity of our history. We were not at all interested in making little dolls with large mouths or big black women with big asses. We were more interested in colour and form, and a certain concept of movement. One didn't have to paint black people in order to grasp our history. We were interested in expressing the black side, but also the Spanish side.*

Although the group dissolved in the mid-1980s, many of its members, including Manuel Mendive, continued to work and vigorously explore its original aims. Mendive first travelled to Africa in 1982–83, an experience that profoundly affected his work.

Manuel Mendive Hoyo was born in 1944 in the Luyanó district of Havana to parents of Yoruba ancestry. In 1959, he enrolled in painting and sculpture classes at the San Alejandro Visual Arts School, and in 1964 held his first solo exhibition at the Havana Art Center; since then he has exhibited worldwide and won numerous awards for his art. Mendive is a practitioner of the syncretic religion Santería, which is based on the Yoruba *Ifa* and its pantheon of gods (*orisha*). Mendive draws heavily on Santería imagery and iconography in his work.

Mendive works in a variety of media, including performance art in which he paints the bodies of dancers from the National Folklore Troupe who enact scenes related to Mendive's Yoruba ancestors and to the Atlantic slave trade that brought them to the Caribbean.

'You ask why I chose the Yoruba theme for my work. Well, I'll tell you... African traditions that have so influenced our culture have been the medium that has enabled me to express my life experiences.'
Manuel Mendive

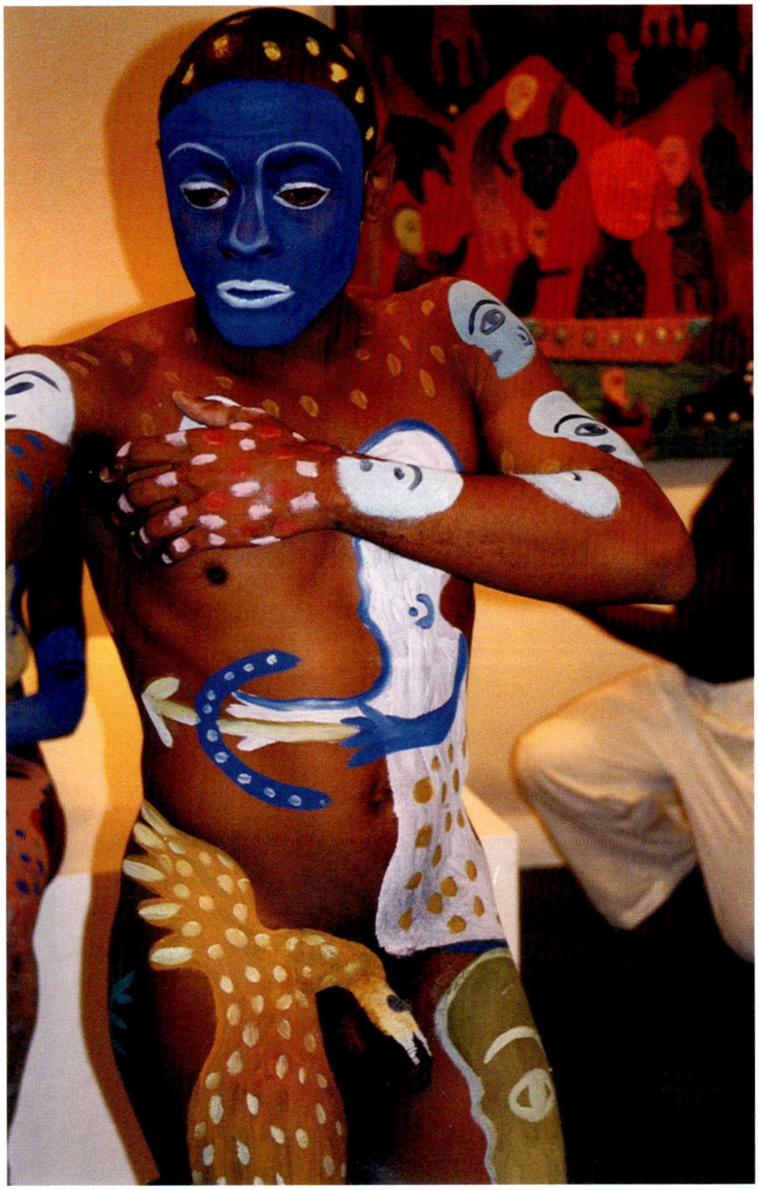

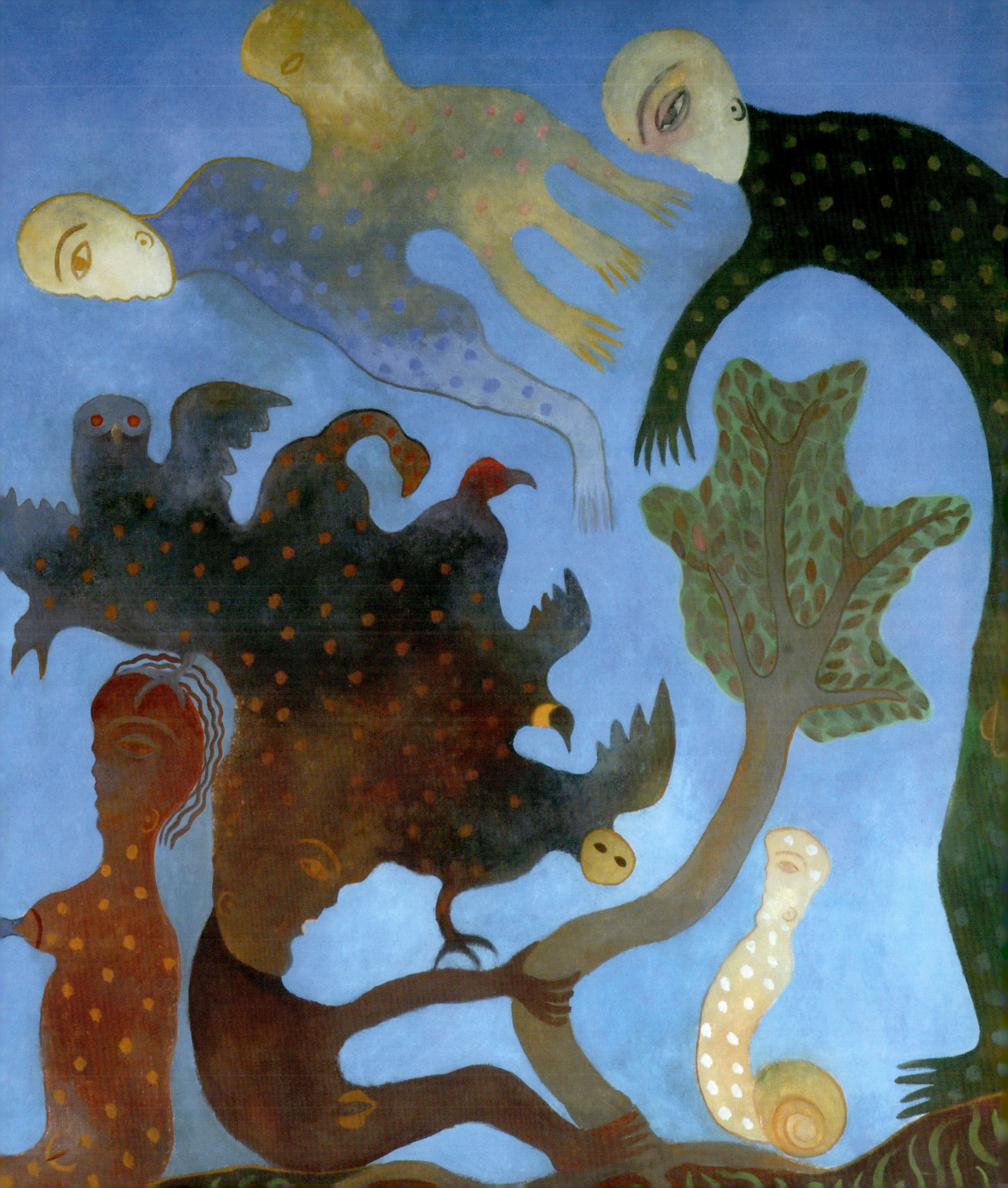

Below *Los ibeji y el tomeguín del pinar* (*The Ibeji and Tomeguín del Pinar*), 2006. Acrylic on canvas, 198 x 248.5 cm (78 x 97⁴⁄₅ in). Orlando Borges Collection.

Right *Los hijos de Oggún* (*The Children of Oggún*), 2006. Acrylic on board, 123 x 123 cm (48²⁄₅ x 48²⁄₅ in). Orlando Borges Collection.
Mendive depicts the spirit world, where humankind and animals share many common features, with tenderness and affection. He shares his home with a menagerie of creatures sacred to the various gods (*orishas*) of the Yoruba pantheon.

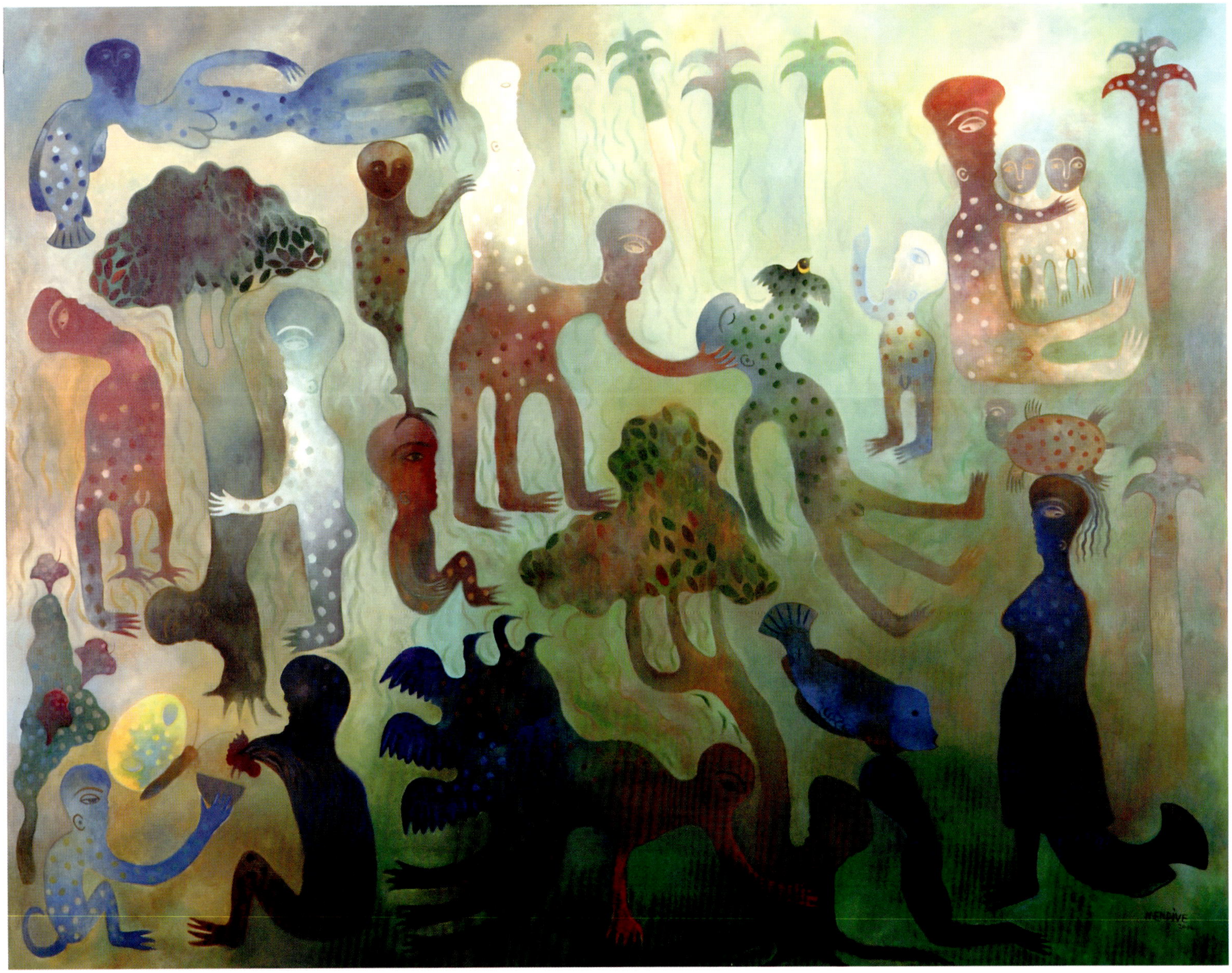

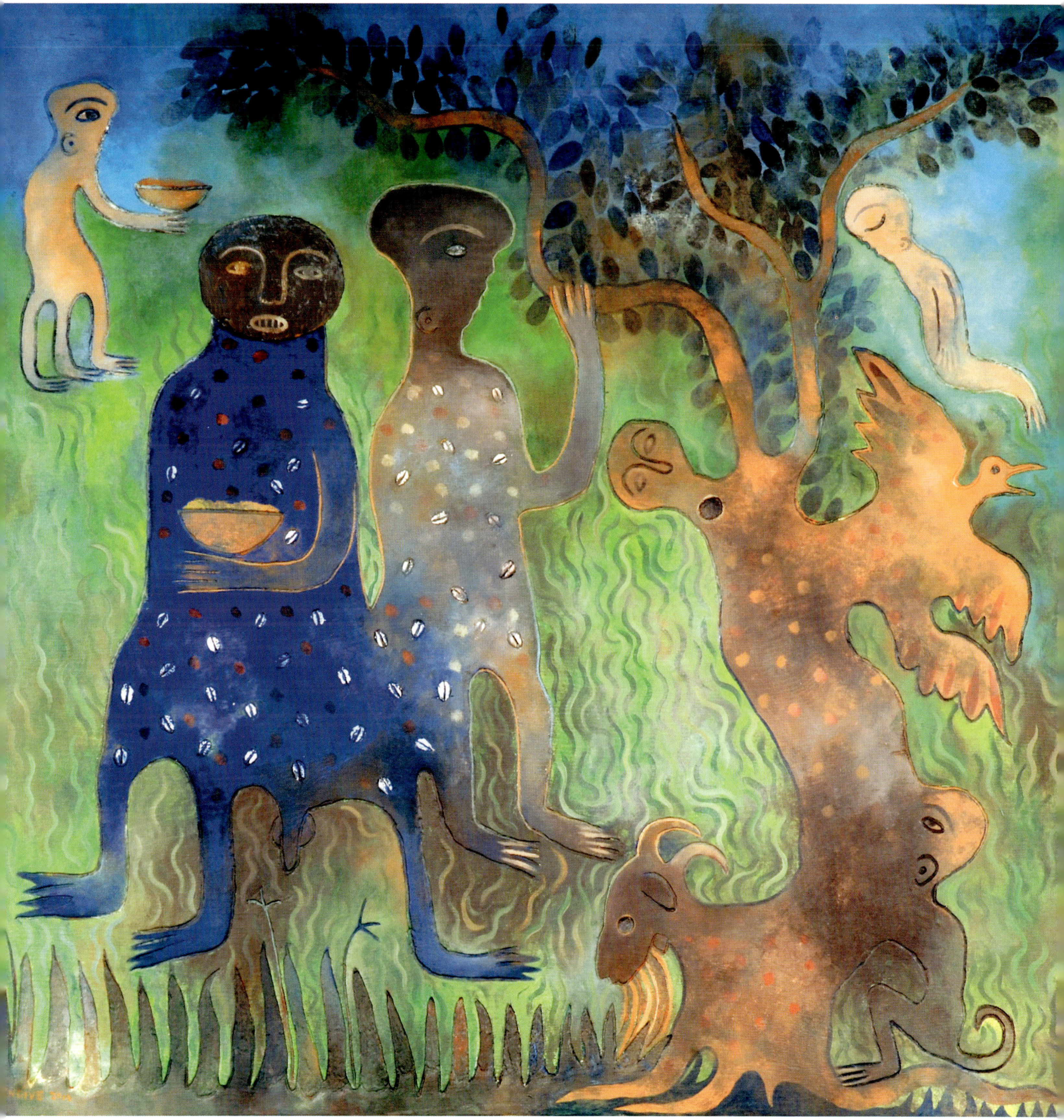

PETRONA MORRISON
JAMAICA

Below *Assemblage V*, 1993. Metal, length 261 cm (102¾ in). Collection of the artist.
'Petrona's scavenging and assembling is a process of reclaiming and pronouncing this lost heritage, while her interest in the geometric, symmetrical aspects of these forms reflects her inner striving for balance and providing a point of equilibrium between two cultures.'
Petrine Archer-Straw, October Gallery, London, 1994

Right *Reality: Representation*, 2004 (detail). Photographic installation at the National Gallery of Jamaica, Kingston.
Morrison's installation seeks to define personal, physical and historical identity and the ways in which these may be manipulated and misrepresented. This installation was featured in the 'Curator's Eye' exhibition, 2004, curated by Lowery Stokes Sims at the National Gallery of Jamaica.

Petrona Morrison was born in Manchester, Jamaica in 1954. She was educated at MacMaster University, Hamilton, Canada (BA Fine Arts, 1976) and Howard University, Washington DC (MFA 1986). She is the head of fine arts at the Edna Manley College of Visual and Performing Arts, Kingston, Jamaica.

Morrison works primarily with found and ready-made objects, transforming them into monumental sculptures reminiscent of shrines and altars. She is concerned with an exploration of the past as a means of restoring and re-evaluating history, written and unwritten, and thus beginning a process of healing – many of her recent works, such as *Reality: Representation* (2004) and *South African Diary II* (2005) employ photogaphy to this end. Morrison spent a year in Kenya as a post-graduate exchange student, becoming deeply immersed in African art history and the connection between her own art-making practice and her historical roots as part of the African diaspora. Morrison believes passionately in the importance of workshops and residencies as a way of engaging in the process of art-making with fellow artists in different parts of the world, and she is concerned with the relentless emphasis on selling her profession.

Morrison was artist in residence at the Studio Museum in Harlem, New York (1995), and took part in the Thapong workshop (1996), one of a series organized in Botswana through the Triangle Arts Trust. Morrison's experience on a two-month residency in 2004 at the Bag Factory (Fordsburg Artists Studios) in Johannesburg inspired her to create *South African Diary II* for the 198 Gallery in Brixton, London in 2005, looking at 'the inconsistencies and disparities of today's South African society.' She has exhibited widely in Jamaica, the UK and the USA.

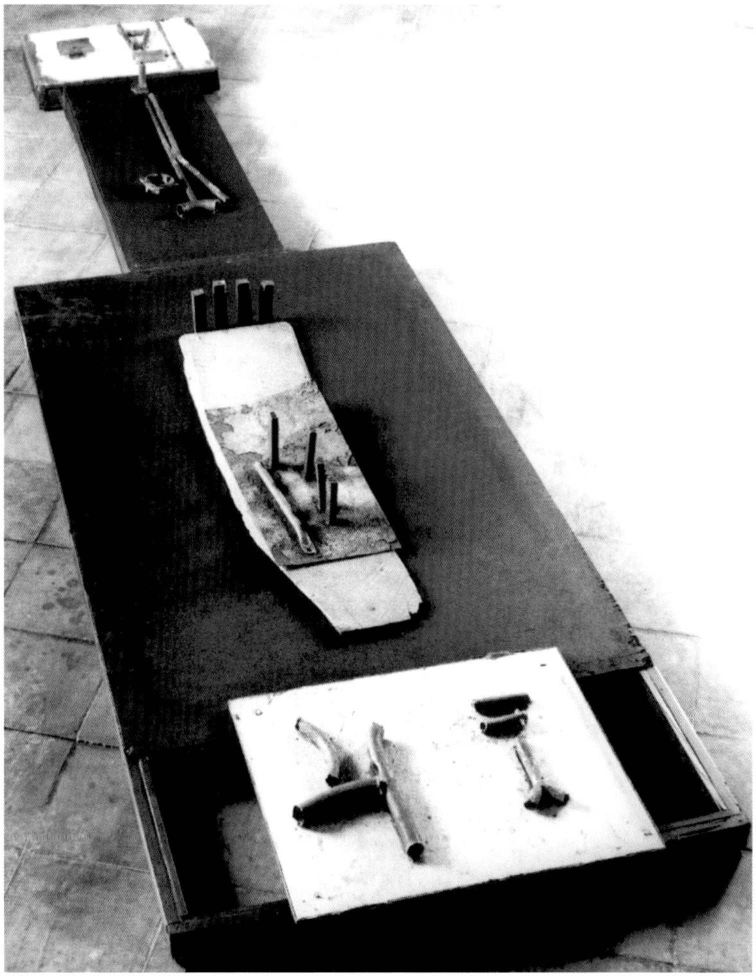

'No one asks "how is your work coming along?" They ask "how is your work selling?". Galleries churn out shows that are essentially marketing pitches, so there is a lot of work that lacks integrity.'
Petrona Morrison

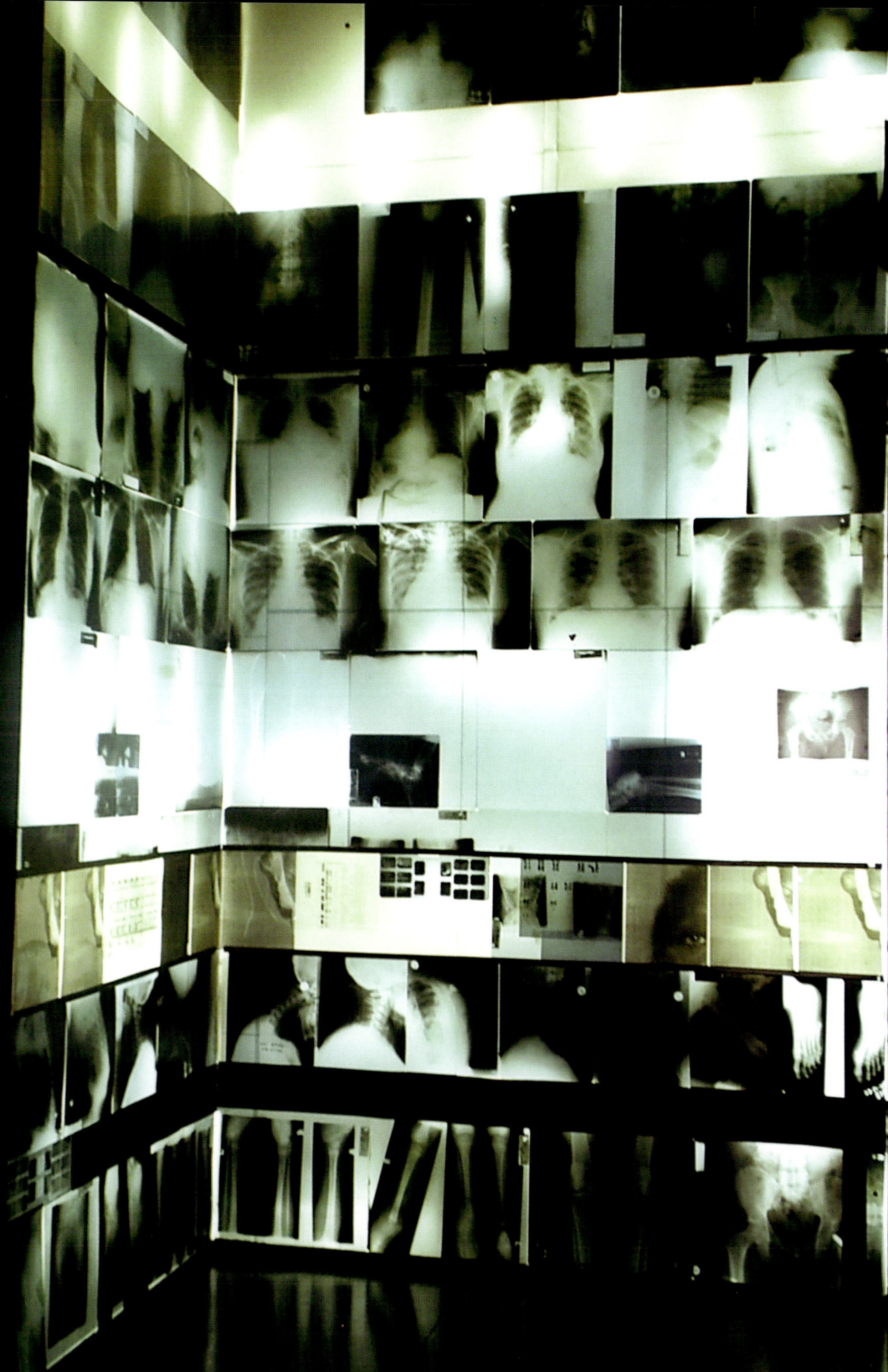

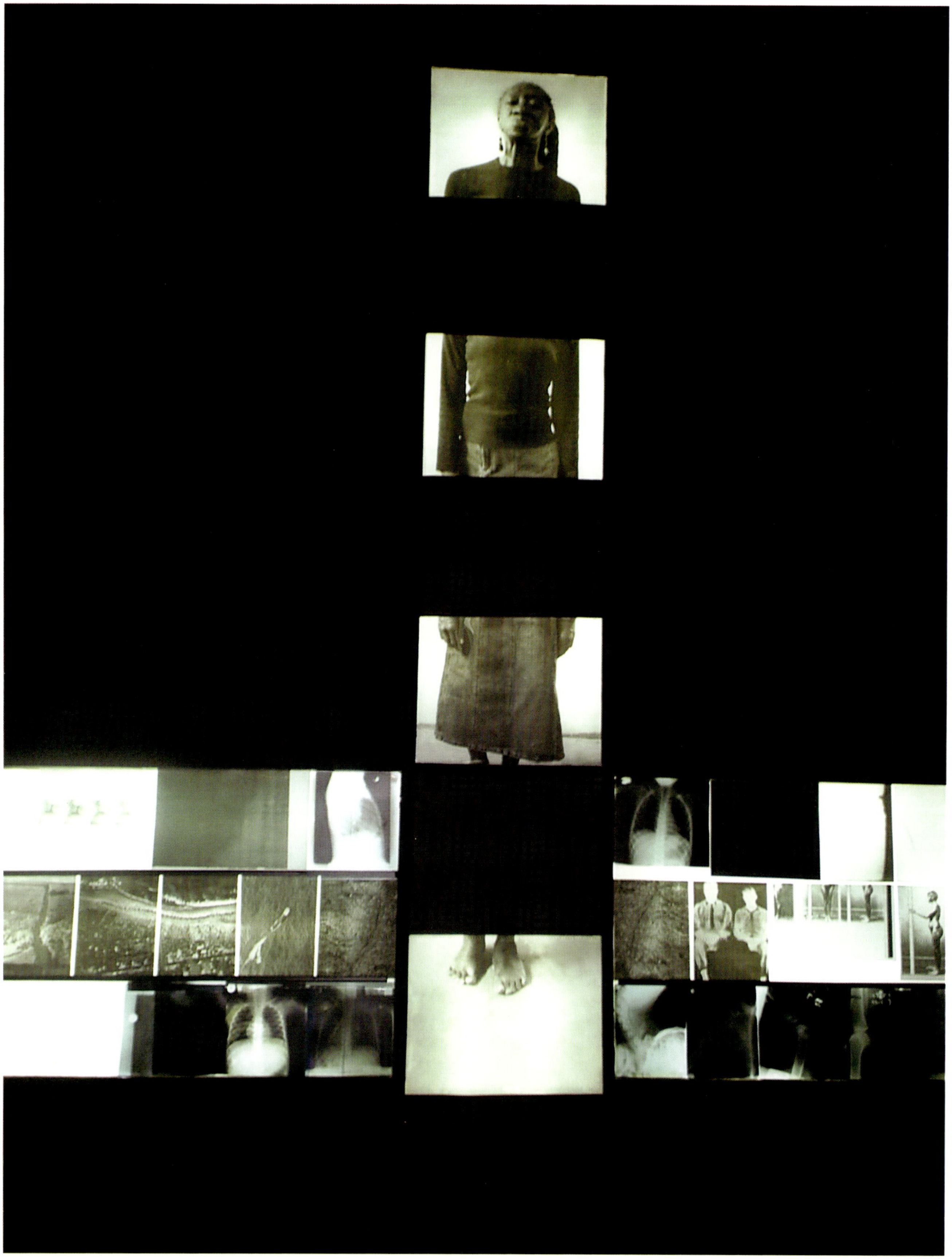

This spread *Reality: Representation*, 2004 (details).

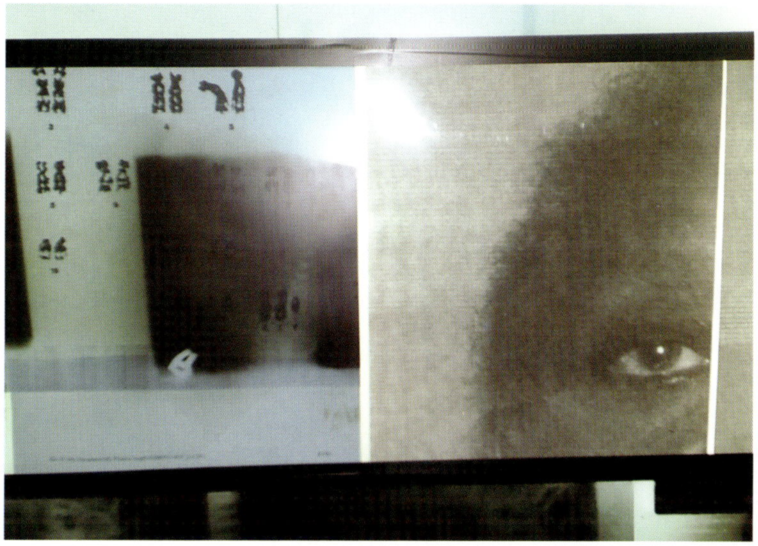

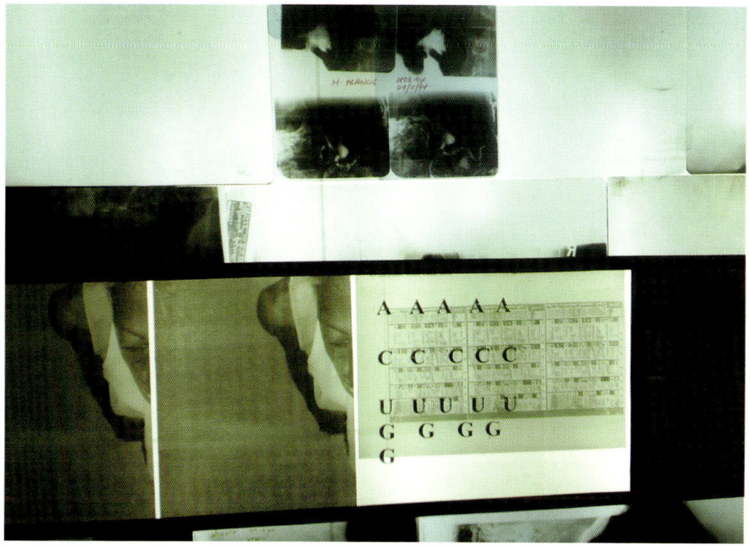

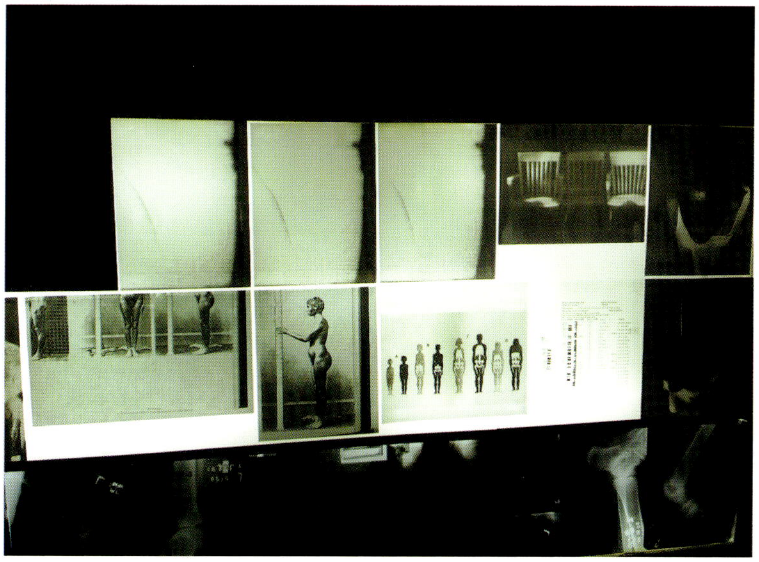

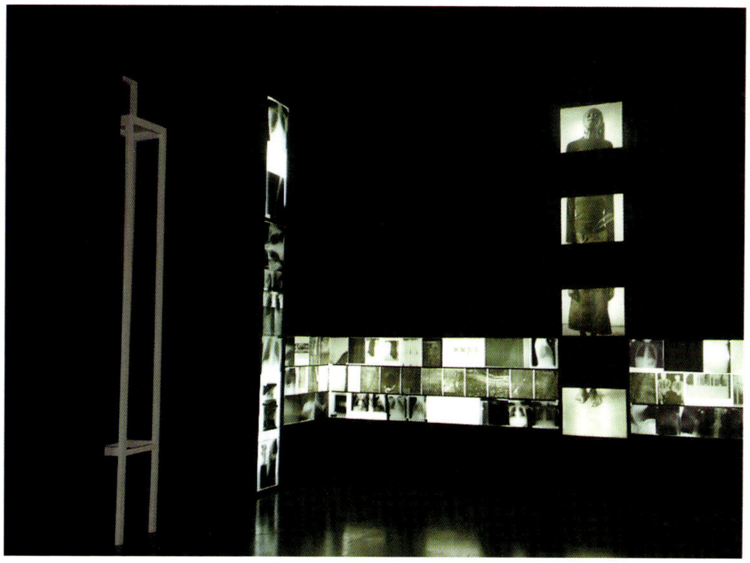

ZWELETHU MTHETHWA
SOUTH AFRICA

Below *The Schemer*, 2006. Pastel on cotton paper, 70 x 46cm (27½ x 18 in). Everard Read, Johannesburg.
Many of Mthethwa's portraits are of black migrants moving from rural to urban areas in search of work and decent living conditions. Sometimes they are driven to desperate measures if their search is unrewarded.

Right *The Artist*, 2006. Pastel on cotton paper, 71 x 57cm (28 x 22⅖ in). Everard Read, Johannesburg.
'If you look at the light in South Africa it's very different from that in America or Europe, so it influences the colours in the landscape.'

Through photography and luminous pastel images, Zwelethu Mthethwa examines the post-apartheid situation of black South Africans, in particular those for whom the old divisions in society have not materially changed and for whom the distinctions between the 'haves' and the 'have-nots' have, if anything, been heightened. One thing that has changed is the freedom of a black artist to portray these divisions to a global audience and more importantly, to convey the immense dignity and humanity of his subjects in a way that restores the respect so brutally removed under apartheid.

Zwelethu Mthethwa was born in Durban, KwaZulu-Natal in 1960. He went to the Open School in Cape Town, one of the very few schools admitting black students to study fine arts. His education there enabled him to join the Michaelis School of Fine Art at Cape Town University, from where he graduated in 1985. He won a Fulbright scholarship in 1989 to the Institute of Technology in Rochester, USA, gaining an MA that enabled him to return to the Michaelis School as a lecturer in 1994.

Mthethwa enjoys the versatility afforded him through working in two different media, frequently overturning or interchanging the conventions of painting and photography so that his paintings have the feel of snapshots or television stills, whereas his photographs are meticulously posed and constructed. Yet they are two sides of the same vision:

> *It's a window to my immediate world. It's personal but public. It's stories about people. As you see things you digest them and tell it in your own style. It's stuff that's around us all the time.*

Within the past five years Mthethwa has had 15 solo exhibitions in South Africa and around the world. He has shown at the Venice Biennale (2005) and his work has been included in the major touring exhibitions 'Short Century' and 'Africa Remix'.

'I always say that the word "artist" is not an appropriate one. Art refers to the author, to ownership, it puts you above culture. I would like to be seen as an image-maker. Art is never about one's experiences in a vacuum, but about life at large...'
Zwelethu Mthethwa

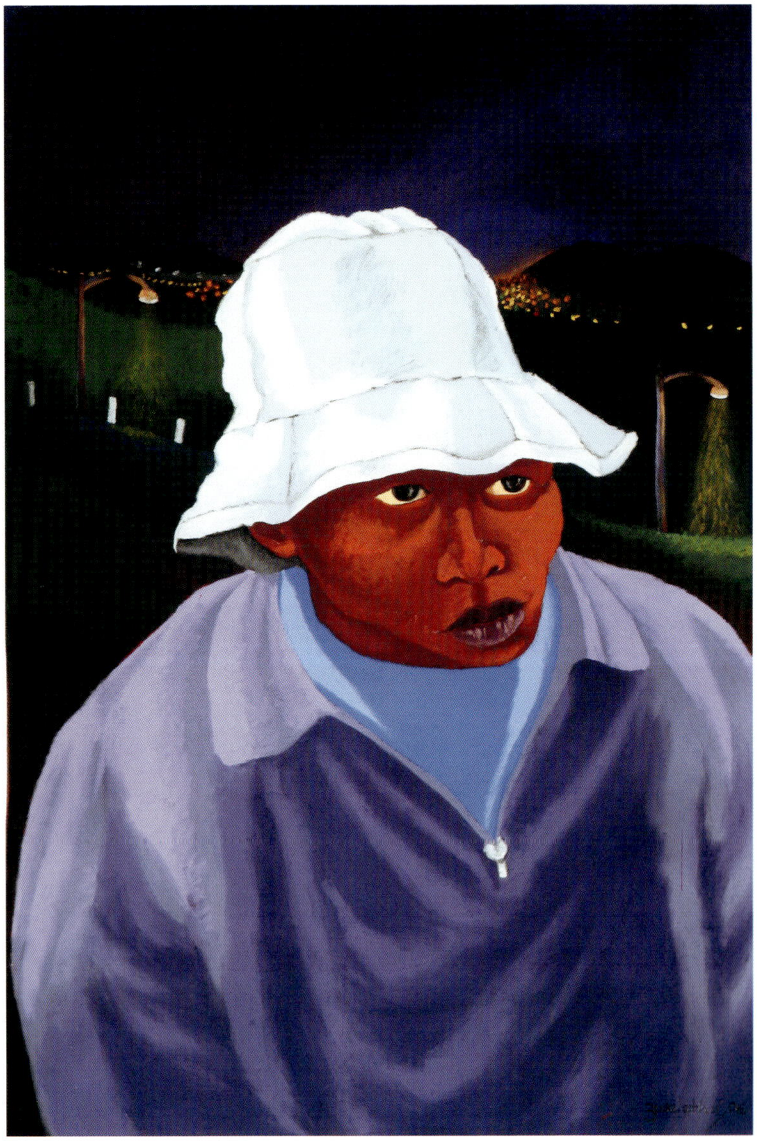

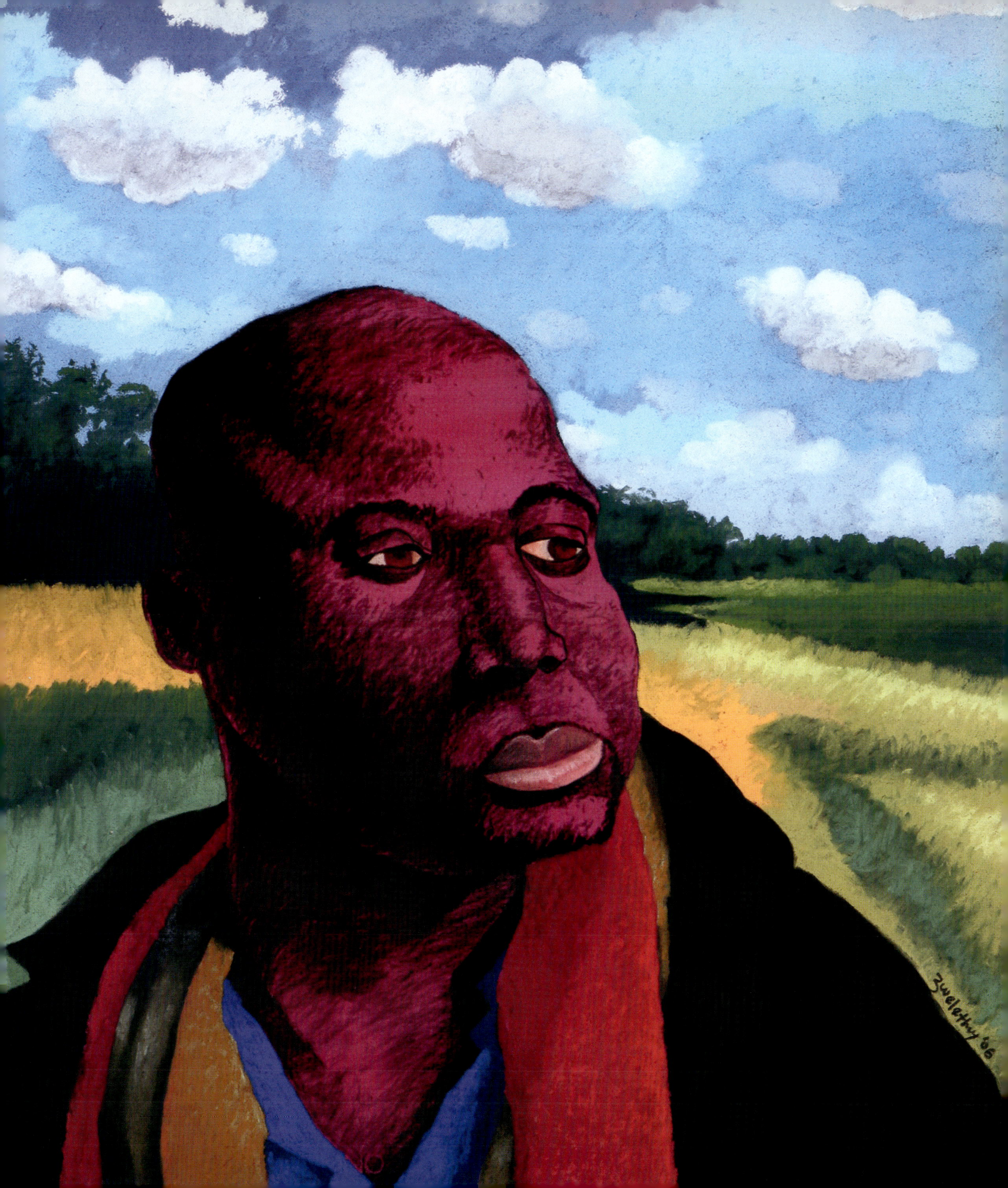
Zwelethu 06

Below *Ball Game*, 2006. Pastel on cotton paper, 70 x 100cm (27½ x 39⅖ in). Everard Read, Johannesburg.
It's a game, but it doesn't look much fun. The woman carrying her sleeping son stares accusingly at the viewer, as if the weight of the world is on her back. It's a picture full of portent, but it's also beautifully structured: 'It is imperative to engage with the formal visual language of my paintings, what the colours do and why, how the elements are arranged – their composition and structure. Each work is constructed through a ratio of colours, composition and rhythms, and these qualities are as pertinent to the meaning of the work as the iconography.'

Right *Private Meeting*, 2006. Pastel on cotton paper, 100 x 70cm (39⅖ x 27½ in). Everard Read, Johannesburg.
A man in a straw hat is deep in conversation with two younger men wearing baseball caps. In the background is a landscape that is dominated by an overgrown, sloping sports field with ramshackle goal posts.

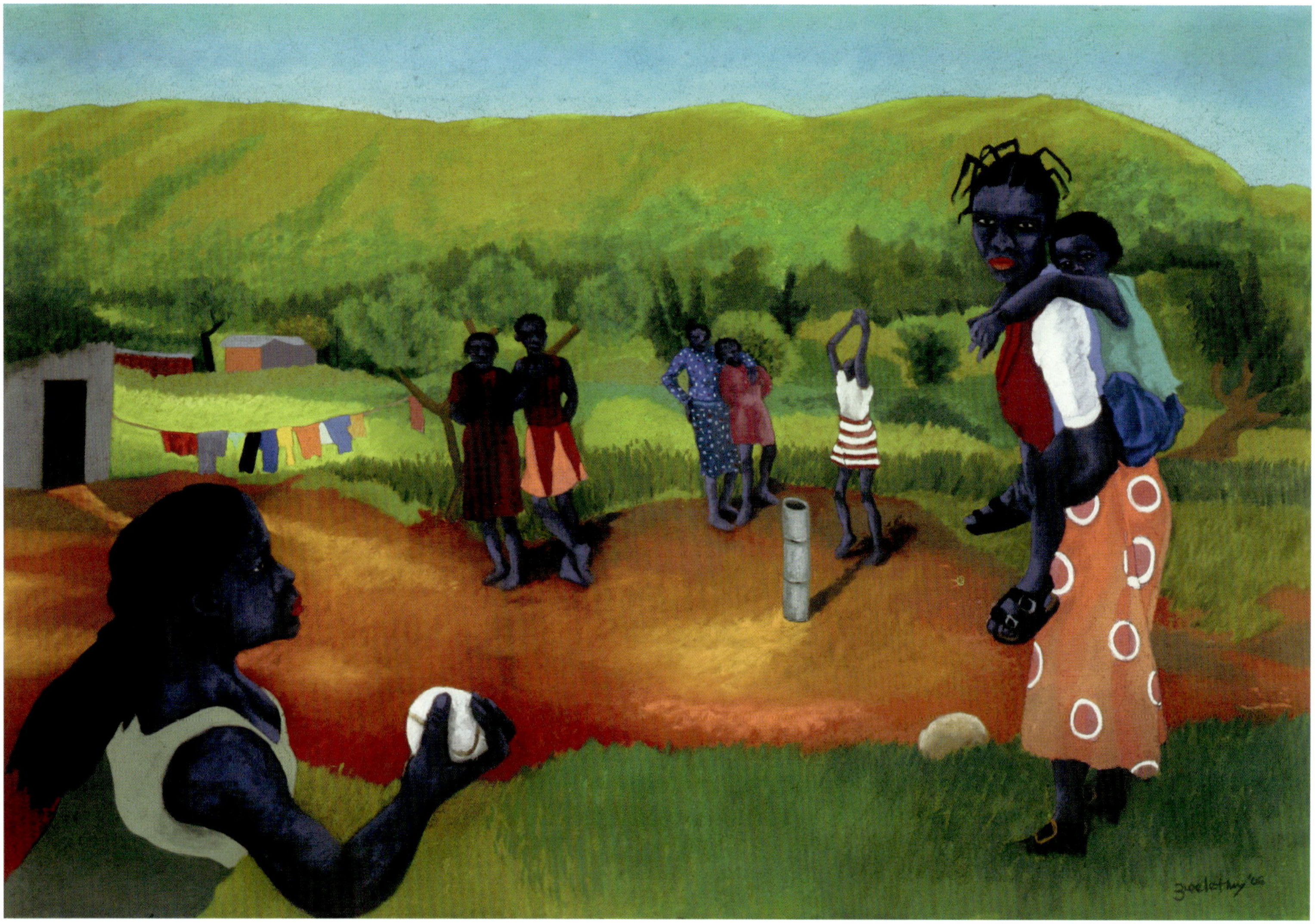

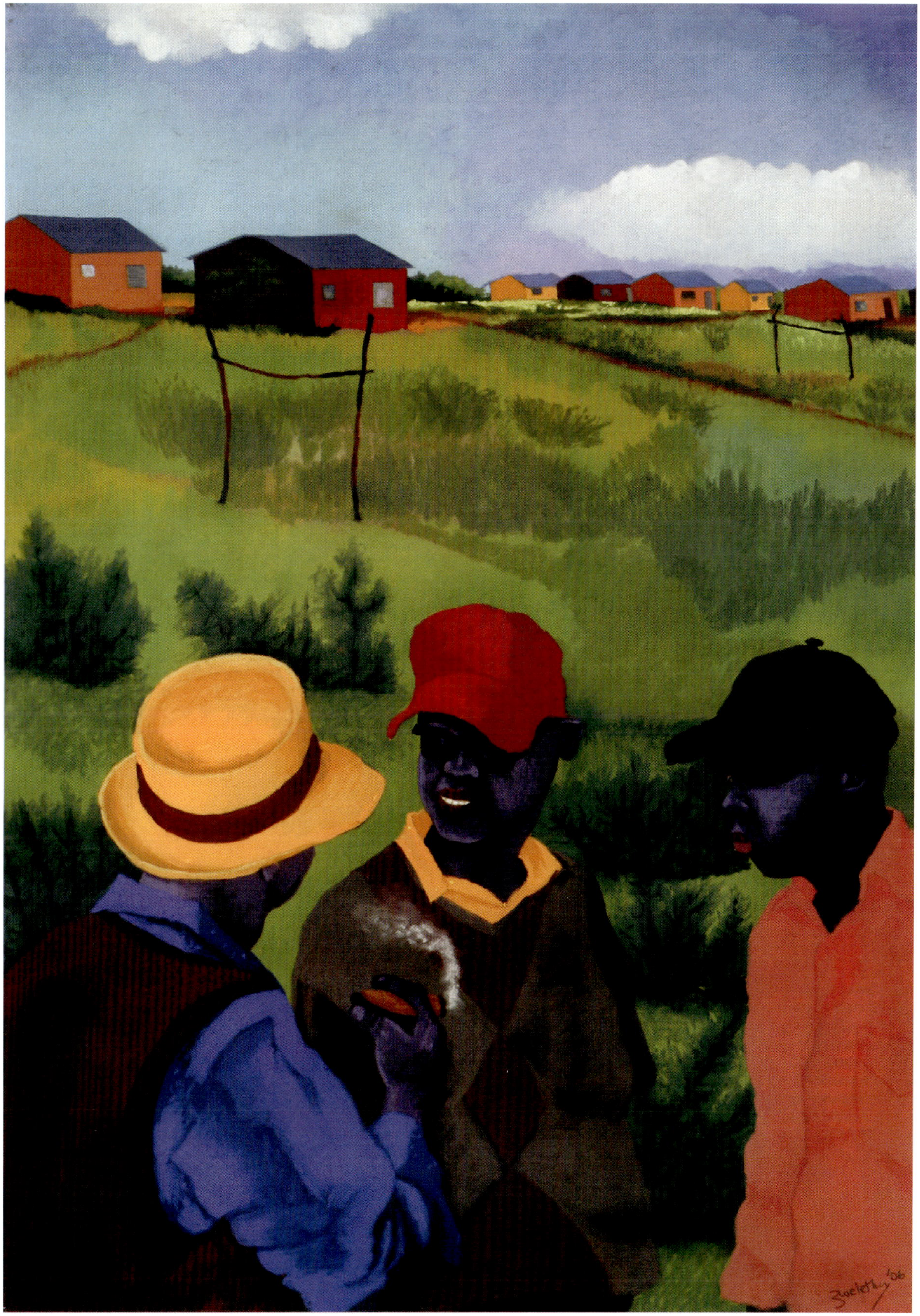
Zweletu '06

Below *Portrait I*, 2006. Charcoal, acrylic and ink on canvas, 76 x 99 cm (30 x 39 in). Everard Read, Johannesburg.
'The world is looking at how we nourish democracy. South Africa is a very new country. So the role of artists should be that of building or amplifying what is, or what is not, happening.'

Right *Sugar Cane Series*, 2004. C-prints, each 149 x 194.3 cm (59 x 76½ in). Jack Shainman Gallery, New York.
'I am exploring the parameters of men's relationships to one another and questioning how traditional environments view the role of men. How do they interact? How are they viewed? How are they revealed? The questions that I am asking, and will continue to ask, examine how capitalism has undermined traditional roles and the struggle for those caught in the crossfire as participants. My concerns are not only to display these dilemmas but to present a viewpoint that not only questions but educates.'

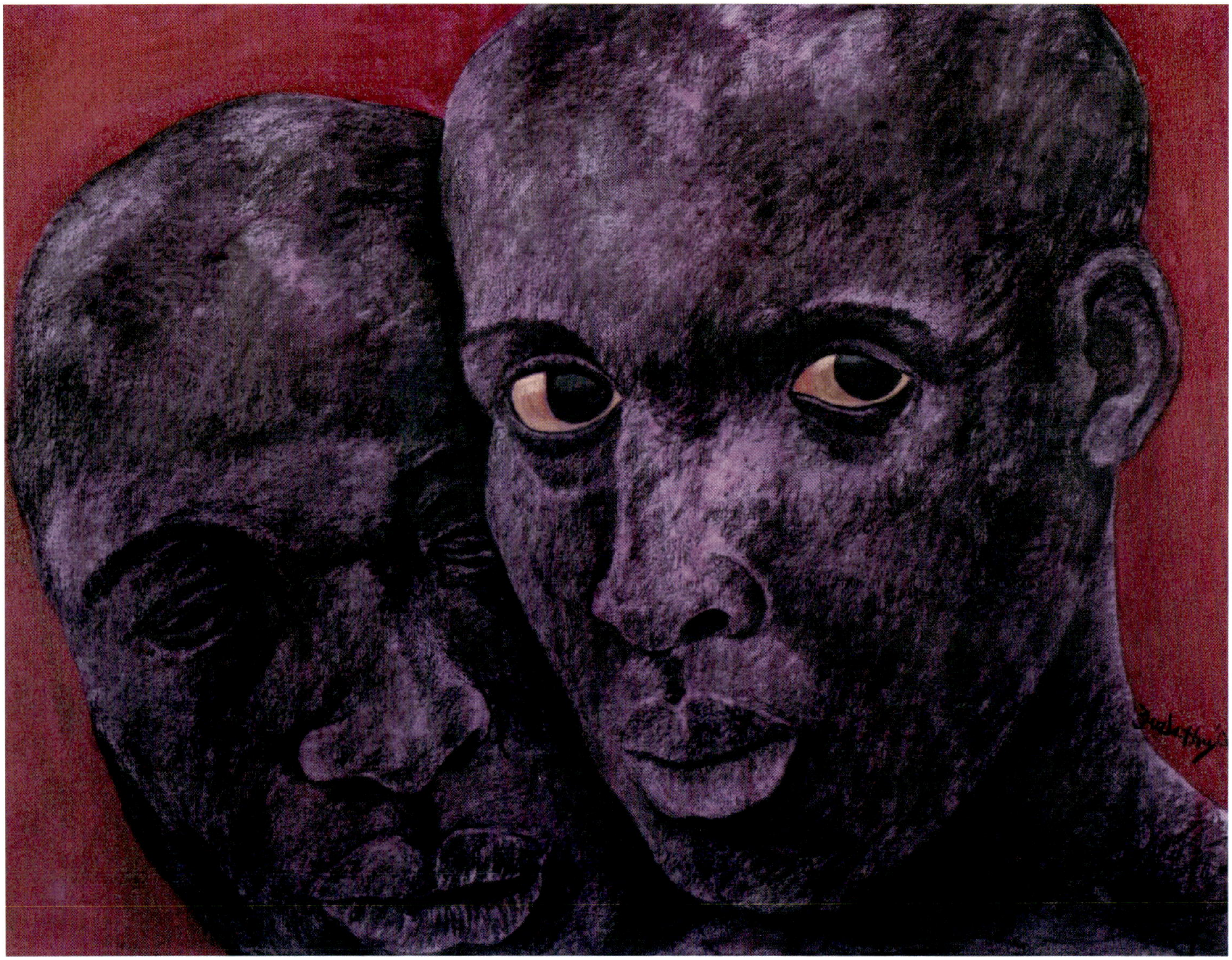

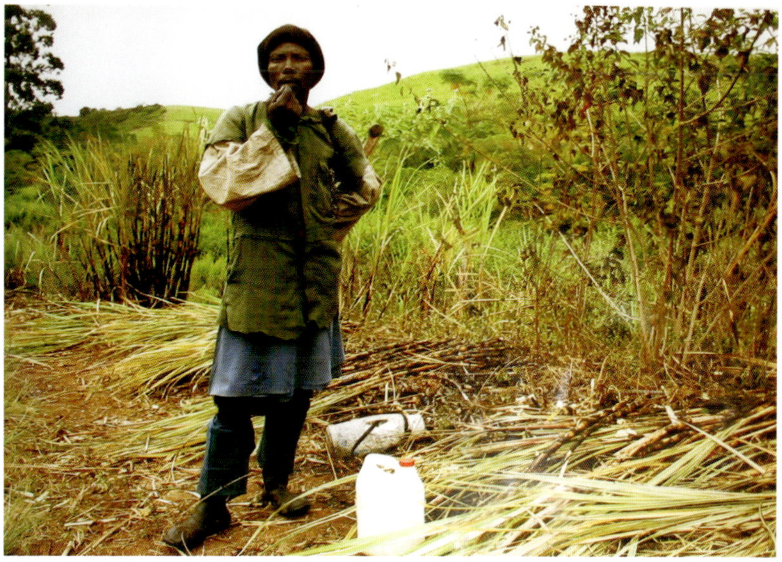

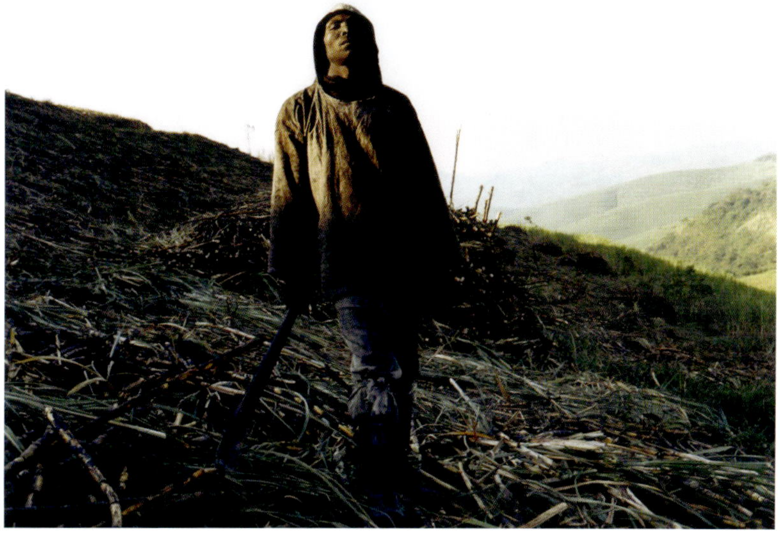

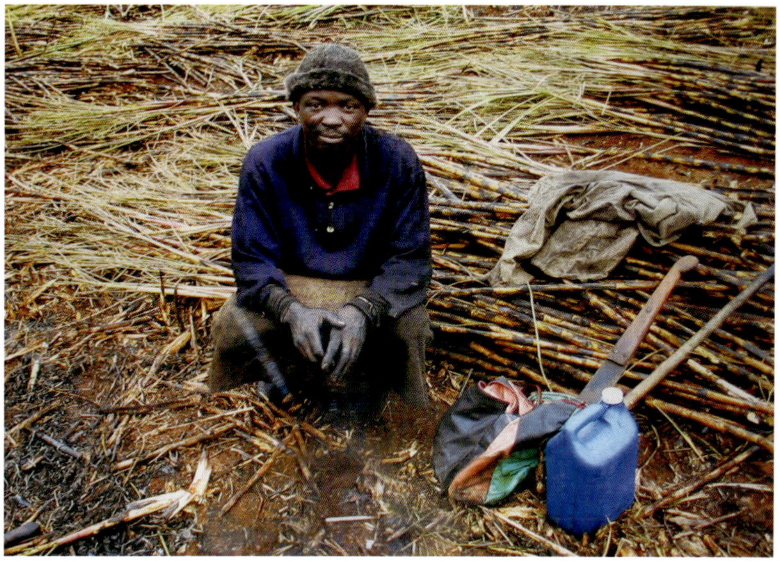

HASSAN MUSA
SUDAN/FRANCE

Below *Who Needs Bananas* in Ethiopia?*, 2002. Ink on cloth, 208 x 124cm (81 9/10 x 48 4/5 in). Private collection.
Painted and printed textile featuring the image of the American-born French entertainer Josephine Baker wearing her most famous costume – a skirt of fake bananas – for the *Danse Sauvage* at the Folies Bergère, Paris, in 1925. Baker was of African and Native American ancestry.

Right *Who Needs Bananas?* (Joséphine aux légumes)*, 2001 (detail). Ink on cloth, 208 x 124cm (81 9/10 x 48 4/5 in). Private collection.
Hassan Musa loves to subvert icons of European thought and culture. In this image Baker has shed her 'savage' banana skirt and is fleeing from a storm of very European vegetables. The final effect is, however, more exotic than any of Baker's performances on the stage in Paris.

*Bananas belong to the genus Musa.

Hassan Musa was born in El-Nuhud, Sudan, in 1951. He graduated from the College of Fine and Applied Art, Khartoum Polytechnic in 1976, moved to France in the late 1970s and studied History of Art at the University of Montpellier, obtaining his doctorate in 1990 and a teaching diploma in Fine Arts in 1995. He has had numerous solo shows and has participated in the Venice Biennale (1997) and important touring exhibitions such as 'Africa Remix'.

Musa is a painter, writer and performance artist, and an outspoken critic of the earlier generation of Sudanese modernist artists known as the Khartoum School, of which Ibrahim el Salahi is a leading light. Musa regards their work as a reactive rather than a proactive response to the West, and their approach to Sudanese cultural and artistic heritage as ahistorical, eclectic and uncritical. He also feels that he is held hostage and categorized by European notions of what constitutes 'African art', and that as an artist he has every right to make a critical choice about the world's cultural heritage to which he is an heir:

> *I think that what is called contemporary African art is just one of the possible evolutionary outgrowths of the European tradition... the whole European tradition is war booty in which I situate myself as a legitimate heir to all the human cultural fortune that the European tradition could encompass – including non-European traditions.*

Musa calls his performances, in which he invites the public to participate, 'Graphic Ceremonies'. They are intended to emphasize the importance of the creative act rather than the finished article, a vital ingredient that he feels is lost in the ritual of the gallery exhibition.

> 'To hell with African art. I have been forced – me, an artist from Africa! – to consider African art as a hindrance to my artistic projects rather than a favourable framework for their fulfilment. "But it's your identity and your roots" protested a Jamaican friend, who has always lived in London, when I suggested that there is no such thing as African art.'
> *Hassan Musa*

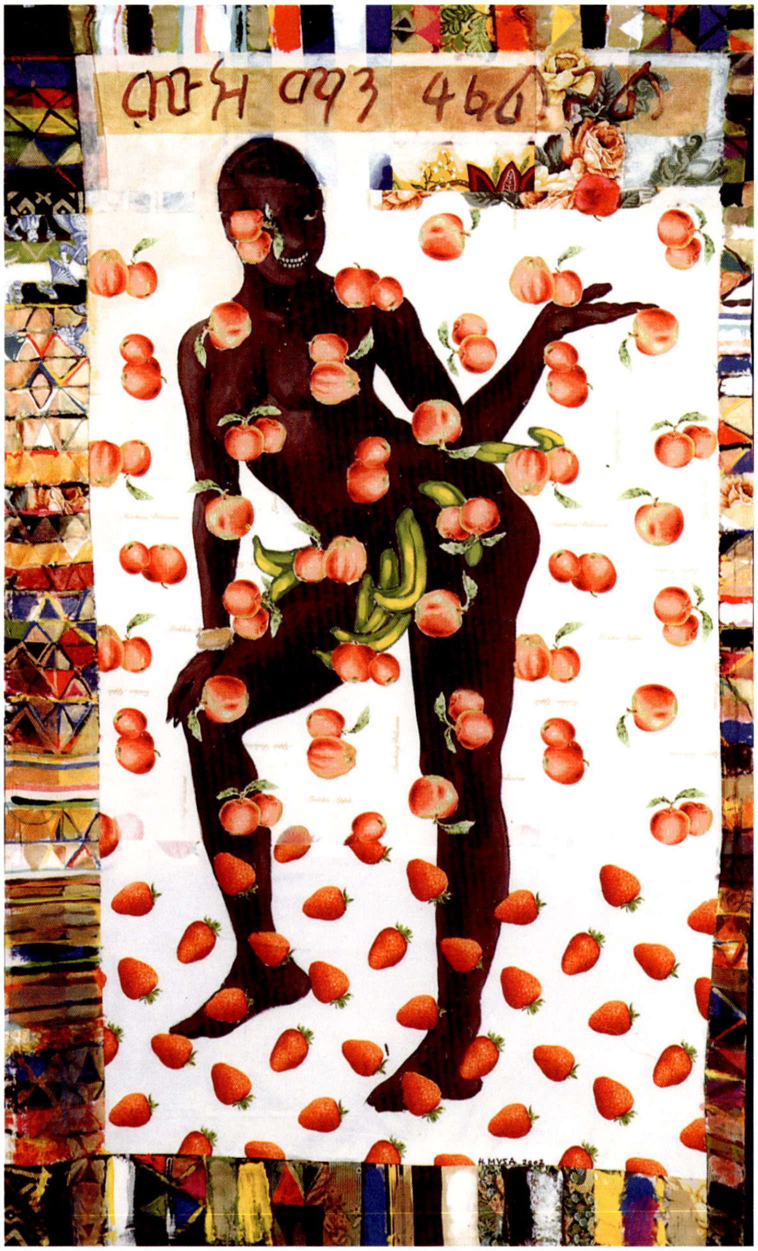

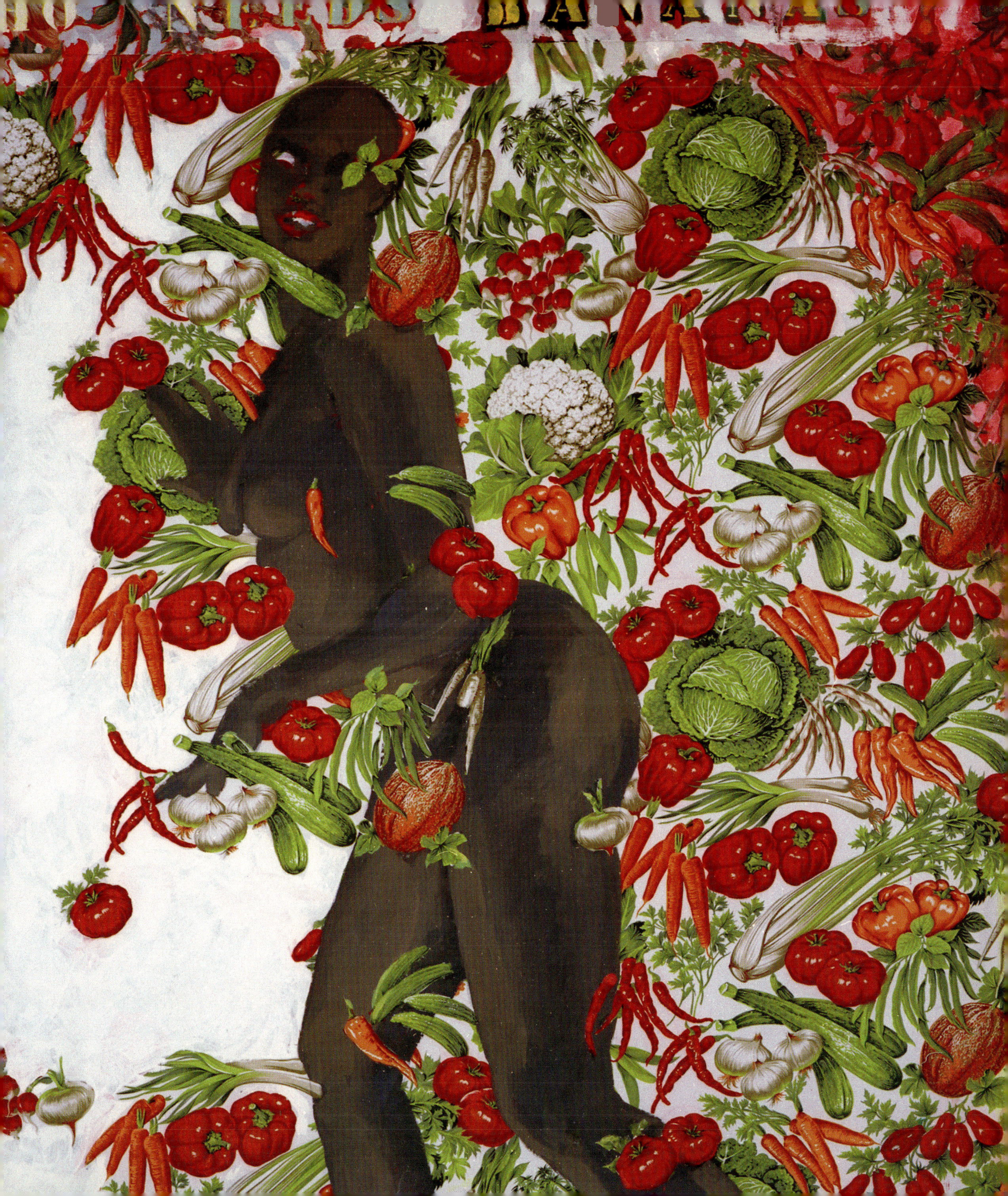

Below *Worship Objects*, 2003. Ink on cloth, 268 x 227 cm (105½ x 89⅓ in). Private collection.
A painted textile that is reminiscent of the *gris-gris*-covered textiles of the artist Abdoulaye Konaté. In place of Konaté's wrapped charms, the objects here are very visible – the material objects of a century ago, the antiques of today.

Right *L'art du déminage (The Art of Mine Clearance)*, 2004. Ink on cloth, 268 x 227 cm (105½ x 89⅓ in). Private collection.
Based on the famous celebration of the working class, Jean François Millet's *The Gleaners*, Musa has the women clearing mines in some undisclosed war zone. He has added a number of bandaged hands to those of the gleaners, whilst from the sky descends a blood red rain of fruit and vegetables.

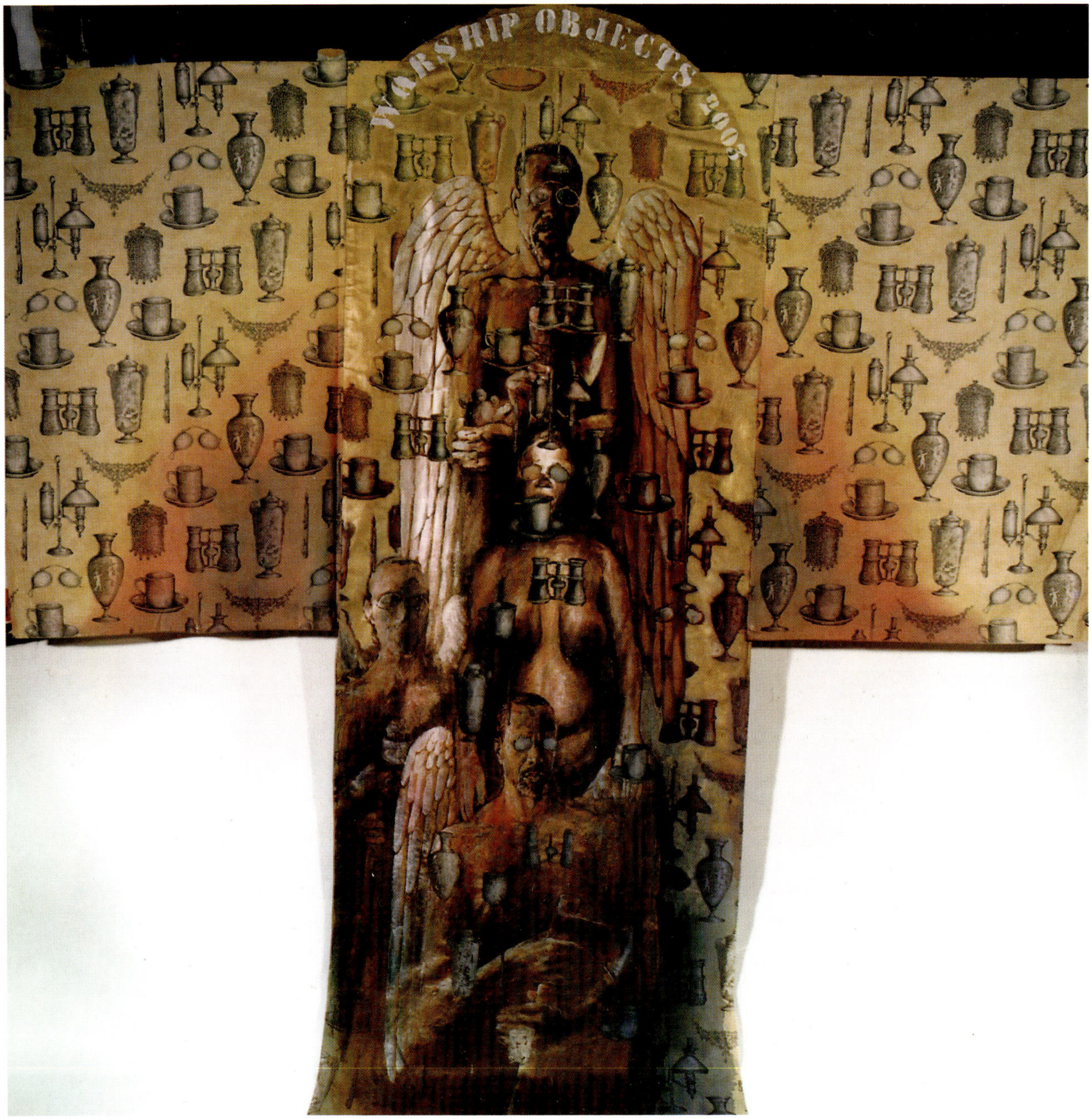

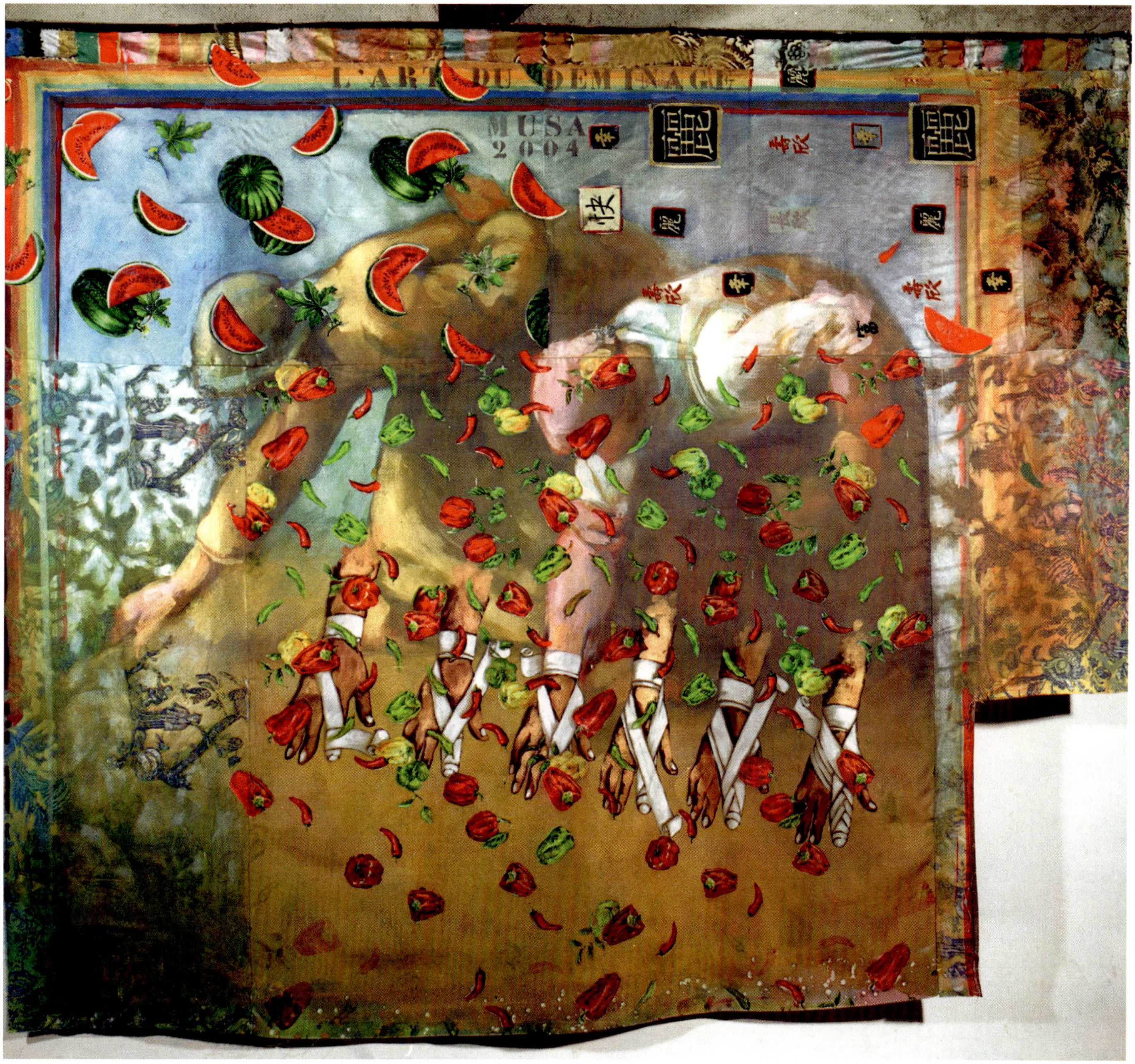
L'ART DU DEMINAGE
MUSA
2004

Below *Alien's Dream*, 2003. Ink on cloth, 459 x 247 cm (180⅔ x 97¼ in). Private collection.
Musa's version of the painting by Henri Rousseau has the eponymous 'sleeping gypsy' replaced by the slumbering Osama Bin Laden, grasping an AK47 rifle instead of a stick. He is being sniffed by a rather shabby American lion.

Right *The Great American Nude*, 2002.
Ink on textile, 204 x 357 cm (79½ x 139¼ in). Private collection.
'We get caught every day in the deluge of propaganda images invading our vital environment. I just can't close my eyes (even if I do I will keep seeing images!), so I keep my eyes open to each and every kind of image with the intention of rendering them back to the world, image for image, eye for eye.'

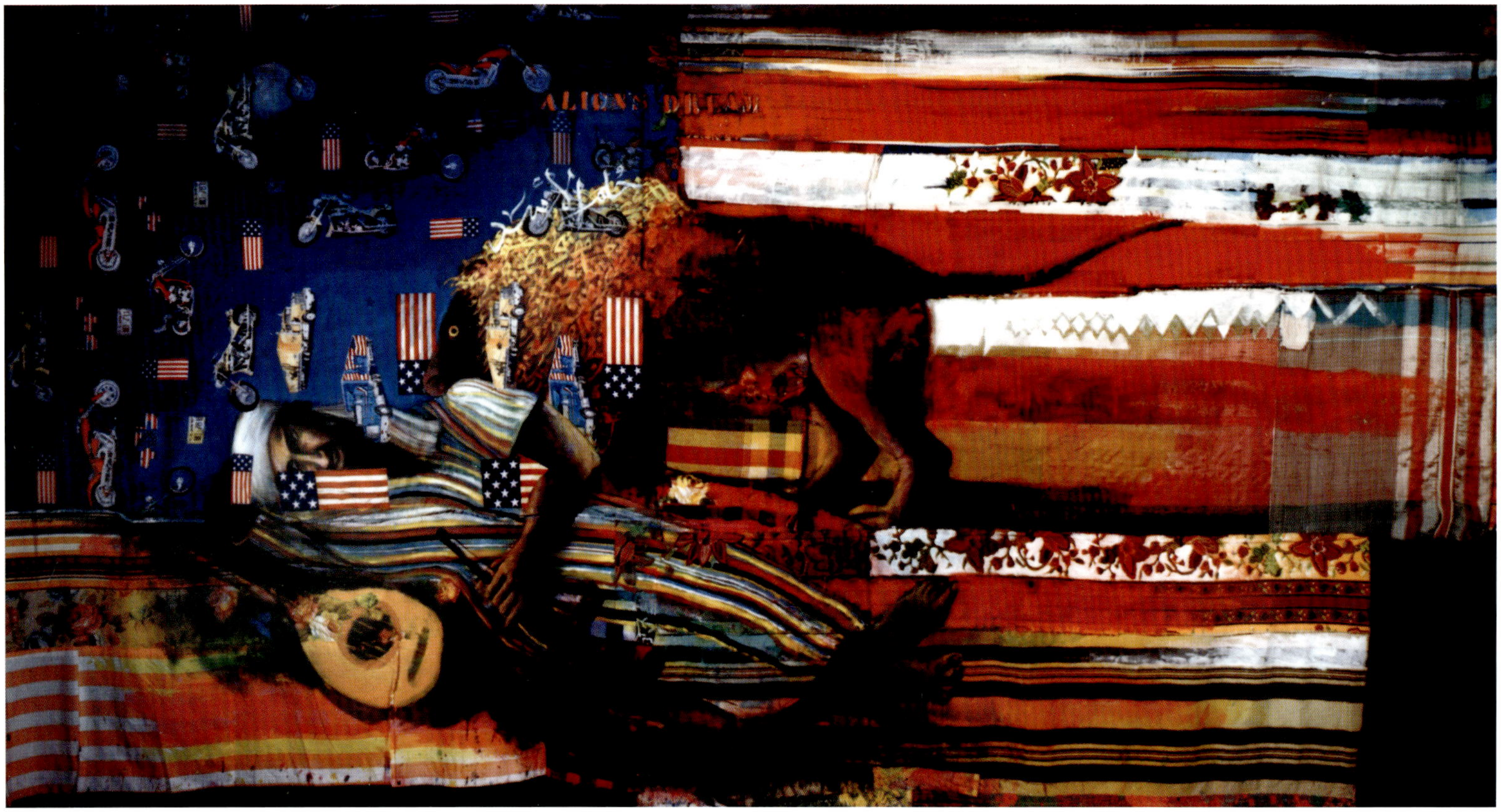

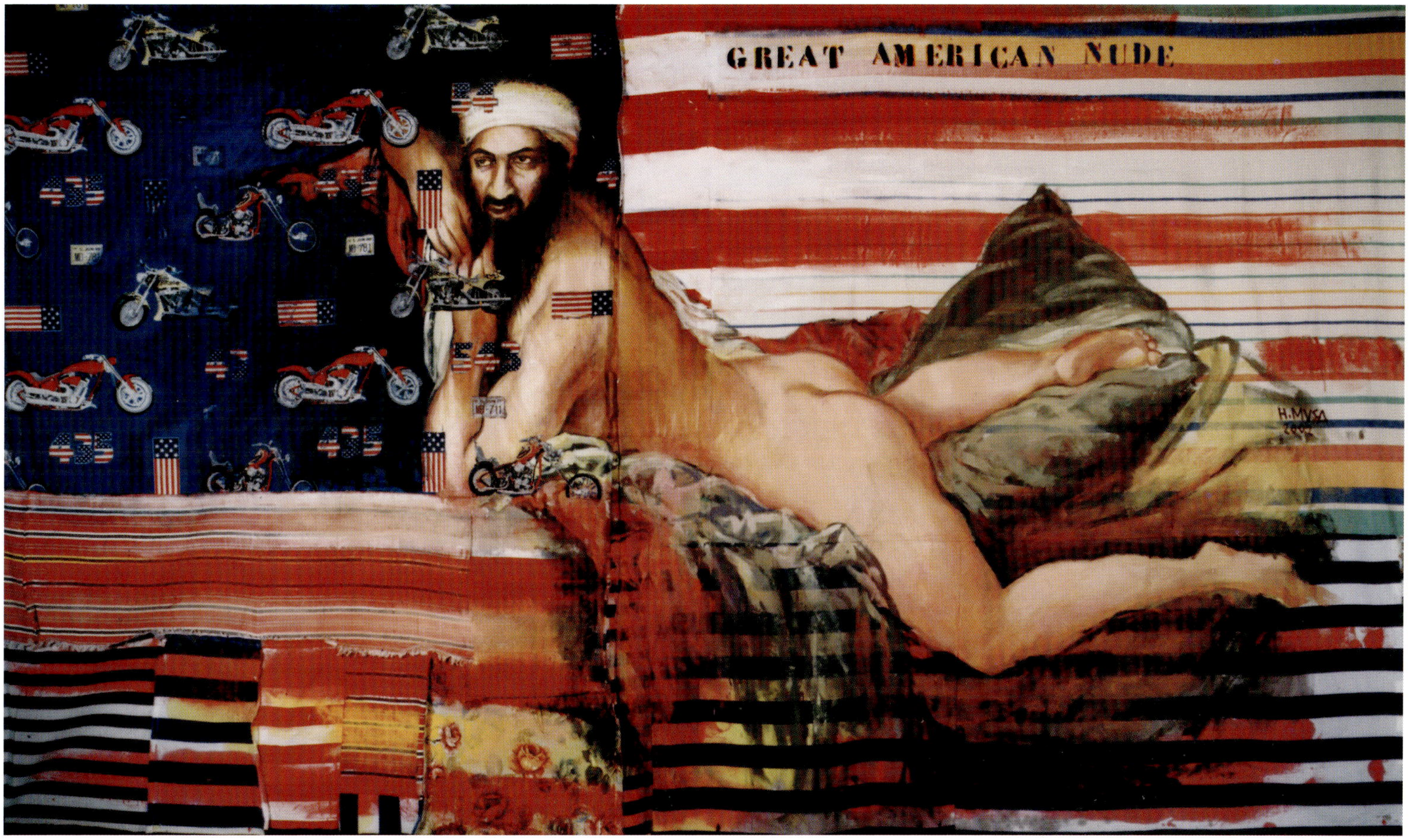
GREAT AMERICAN NUDE

MWANGIHUTTER
KENYA/GERMANY

Below *Being Bamako*, 2007. Single Channel Video.
'I meet another who is calling out to me. If I could see with his eyes and feel with his skin, I would arrive here.'

Bottom *In My House*, 2006. Video Installation.
'I dreamt I was in my house
There was a flood in the living room and a fire
An earthquake shook my bed
Smoke burnt my eyes
Something was going to happen.'

Right *Mzungu*, 2006. Video.
Mzungu is the KiSwahili word for a European; it also means 'something wonderful'. Here Robert Hutter has been kitted out in local costume by two Maasai men who think the end result is hilarious; the *mzungu* is not so happy. Would Europeans think the Maasai hilarious in jeans and shirt, or suit and tie? Probably not.

The artist collective MwangiHutter consists of Ingrid Mwangi, who was born in 1975 in Nairobi, Kenya and her husband Robert Hutter, born in Ludwigshafen, Germany in 1964. Mwangi's father is Kenyan, her mother German. Using their own bodies as canvases and sounding boards, their video and sound installations explore issues of identity, race and self-image with a mixture of humour, wit and pathos.

A recent collaboration between MwangiHutter and the Kenyan artist Jimmy Ogonga was presented in the show 'My Vision: Ideen für die Welt von Morgen' in which the artists create 'Blood Poems' by scarifying their own flesh with simple but profound words: 'you', 'alone', 'I will', 'embrace you', 'I cannot', 'die'. Commenting on the work, Ogonga states: 'It is important to note that multiculturalism is the product of a clash, not a comfortable convergence.'

Ingrid Mwangi and Robert Hutter return regularly to Kenya, contributing to a series of video workshops in various venues in Nairobi, including the National Museum and the Godown Arts Centre. One outcome of these workshops has been the video *Forward to Somewhere in Africa* (2006) on a group of Kenyan artists, many of whom had no experience of working outside painting and sculpture.

Individually and collectively, MwangiHutter have exhibited in numerous venues worldwide. *Down by the River* (2001) is part of the major touring exhibition 'Africa Remix' curated by Simon Njami, who says of Ingrid Mwangi, 'Her dual belonging is not only symbolic, but physical as well. It runs through her veins and is read on her body. And that richness, which makes her both from here and there, creates fragility in her, a prism through which she tries to see herself and see the world'.

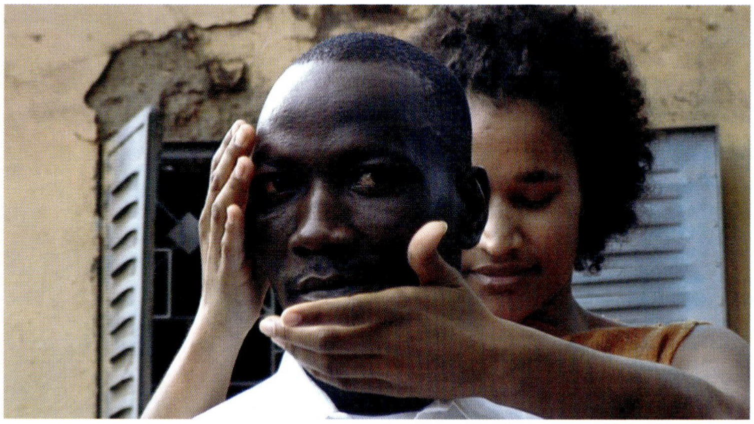

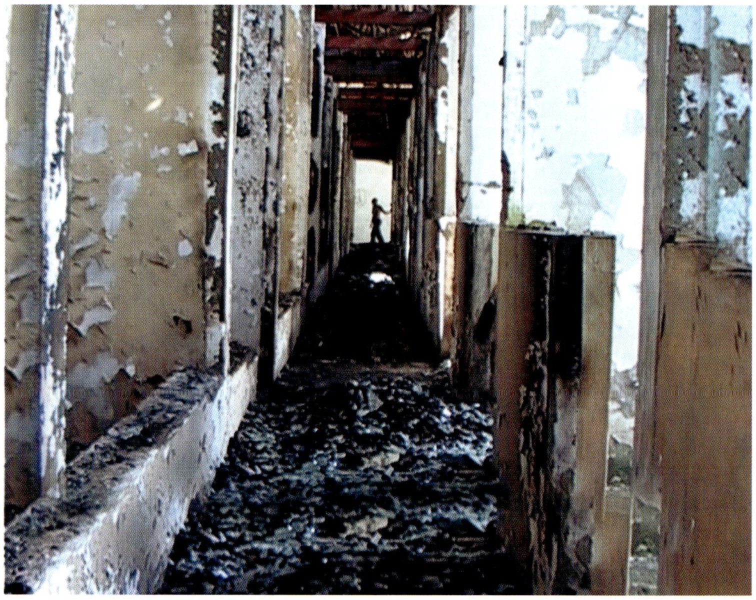

'Differences in culture, nationality, religion, gender, etc are often given as reasons to justify lack of understanding between people. It is deeply necessary to create meaningful exchange and tolerant discussion, not by ignoring the differing factors, but rather by allowing them to exist, without elevating their significance.'
MwangiHutter

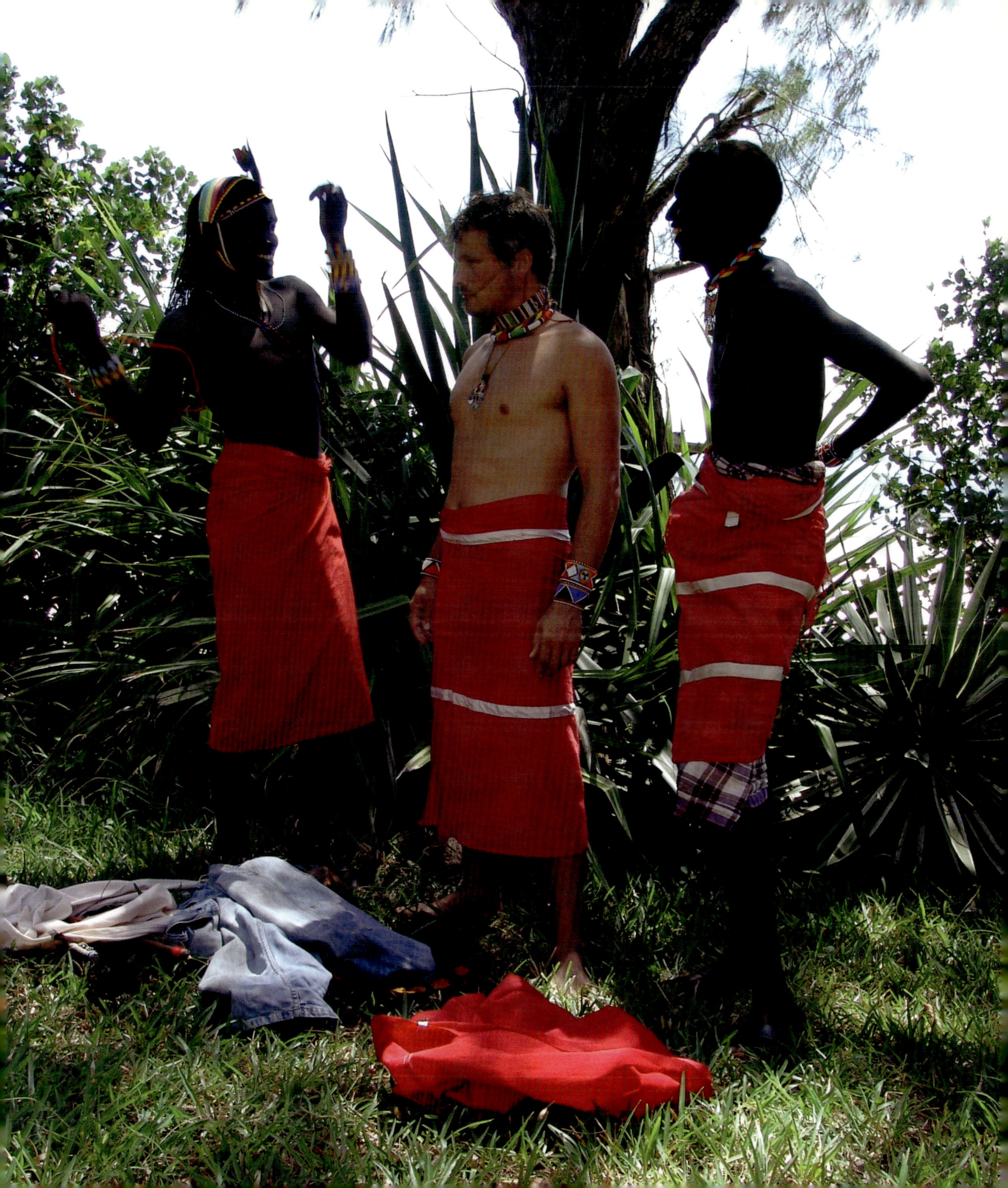

Below *If*, 2003.
Digital photography, 125 x 165 cm (49⅕ x 65 in). Collection of the artist.
'The presentation of a rejuvenated and modernized Hitler breaks with a quasi taboo of binding the infamous personage to a best-forgotten past. It opens up the context to an awesome and frightening thought: how would Ingrid Mwangi and Robert Hutter have related to each other only seven decades ago? And how far have we reached in overcoming this history?'

Right *Splayed*, 2004. 3 channel video installation.
The words 'monogamous polygamy' are cut into Mwangi's forearms as the video progresses; her face shows no pain. 'The self-contradictory phrase physically and painfully marks the artist as a sexual body, the conflicting ground on which a clash of oppositional cultural and moral views takes place.'

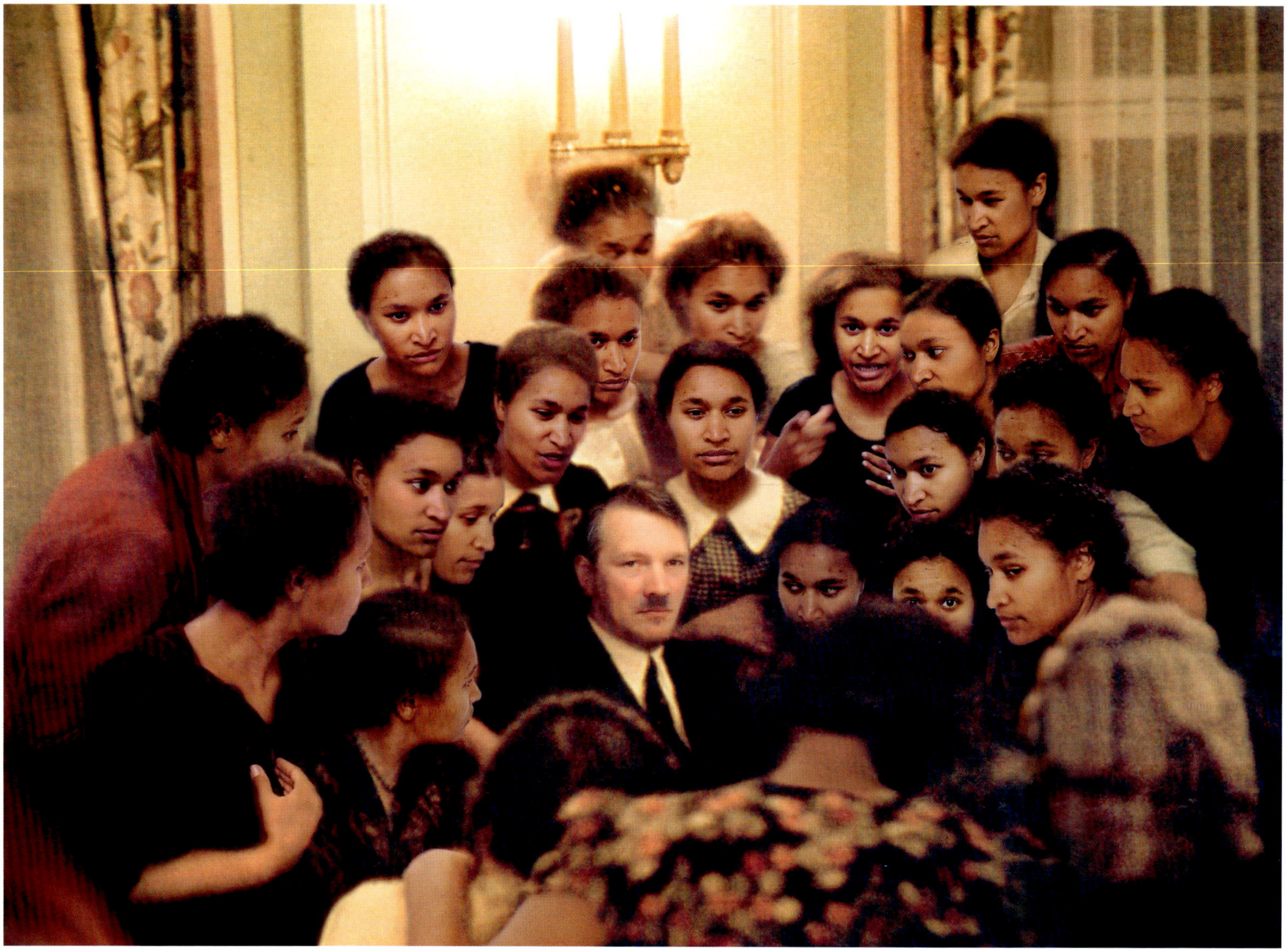

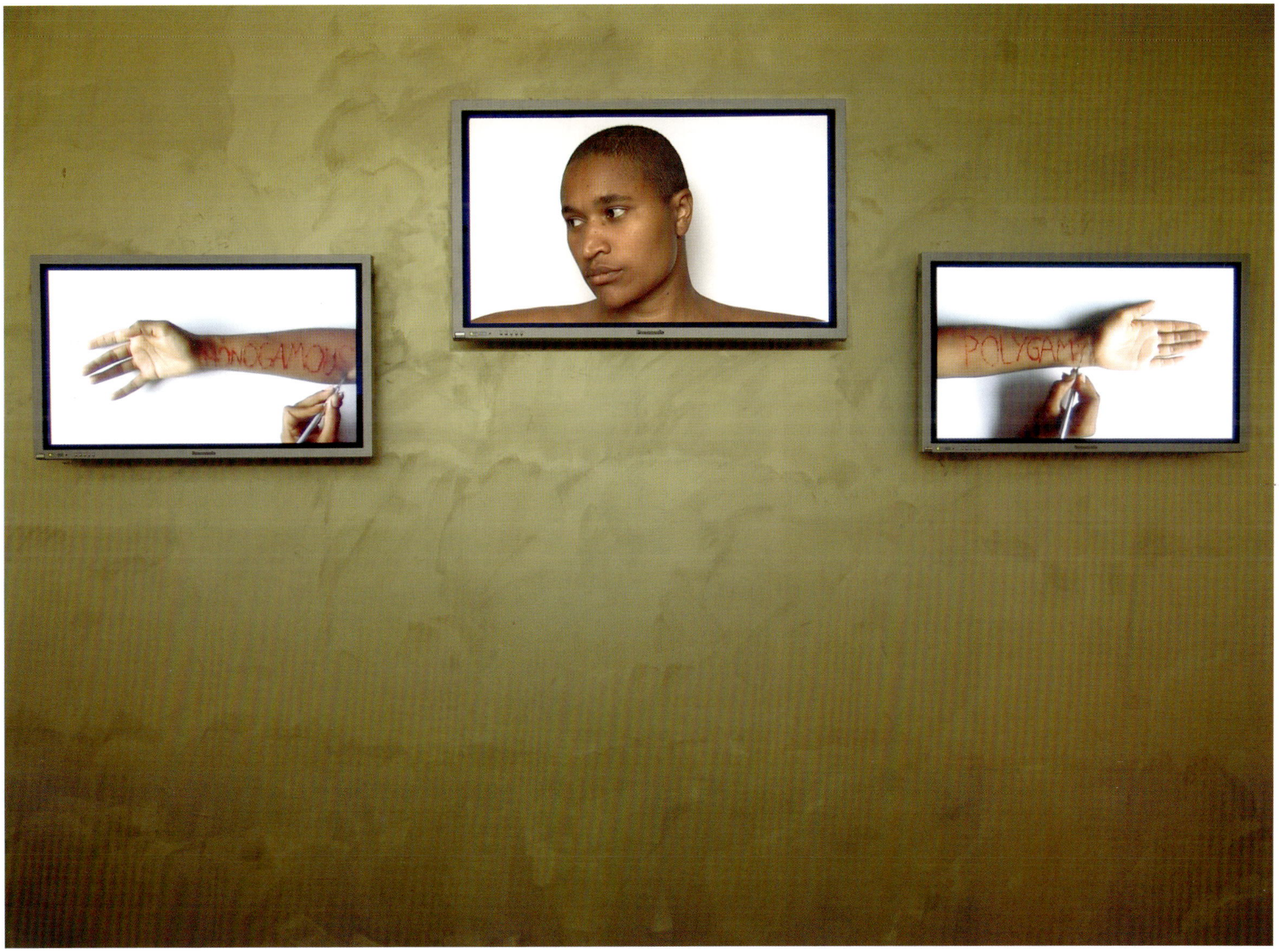

MOATAZ NASR
EGYPT

Below *The Echo, Parts I and II*, 2003. Video installation. The famous 1968 film by Youssef Shahine of Rahman El Sharkawi's novel *El Ard* (*The Earth*) is set in the Cairo of 1933. The main character complains at how passive Egyptians are in the face of the indignities of British occupation. Seventy years later the storyteller Chirine Al Ansary repeats the words in a Cairo coffee shop. Nothing has changed; people are still 'living in words, nothing but words.'

Right *Tabla*, 2003. DVD projection and c.100 *tablas*, variable dimensions.

Moataz Nasr, born in Alexandria, Egypt, in 1961, is a self-taught artist, best known for his multimedia installations and video work, though he is also a painter. 'Painting is a different story... a different language. You can't speak two languages at the same time. Installation is a language of expression I feel comfortable with, but painting is a language requiring another mood altogether.' In 2003, Nasr created two multimedia installations, *The Echo* and *Tabla* , which in their different ways both express the artist's frustration at the inertia he sees and feels all around him, not just in Egyptian society, but globally. 'The message is simply "we shouldn't just sit and complain, we should do something." We are doing nothing and it's something international.'

Tabla was first shown at the Venice Biennale in 2003 and is part of the large touring exhibition 'Africa Remix'. In the installation a large group of simple pottery drums stand in front of a video screen on which a much larger and more elaborately decorated drum of the same type is played by an anonymous, faceless musician. The work references the old saying, 'Empty vessels give a louder sound', as well as the folk story *Kalila Wa Dimna* (*The Fox and the Drum*). In the latter, a large drum hangs in a tree being played by the fingers of the branches blowing in the wind. A greedy fox leaps up to grab the drum, mistaking its loud sound and bulbous form for a tasty meal. The drum falls to the ground and shatters to dust. As Simon Njami said, writing about the work in 2003:

> *Here Nasr brings the drama of power back to centre stage. As I write these words, with Eastern and Western nations vying in the clamorous rhetoric that presages war, it is impossible not to project oneself beyond the national frontiers of Egypt.*

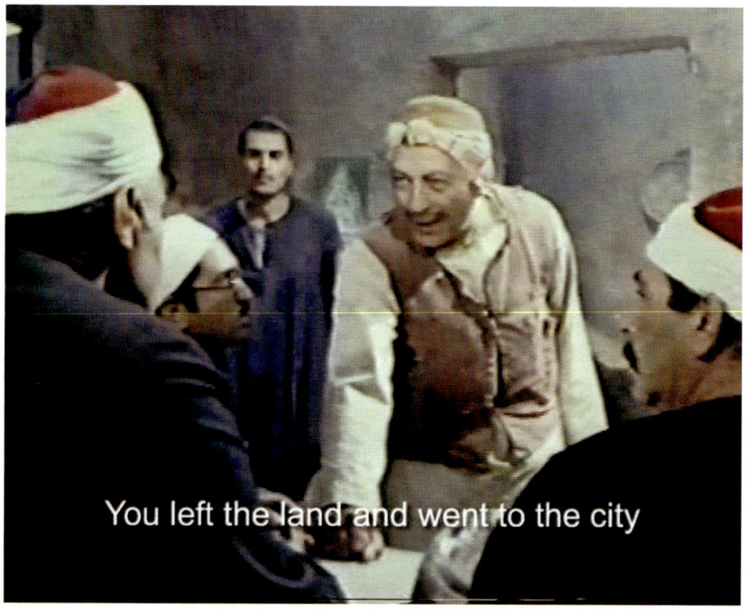

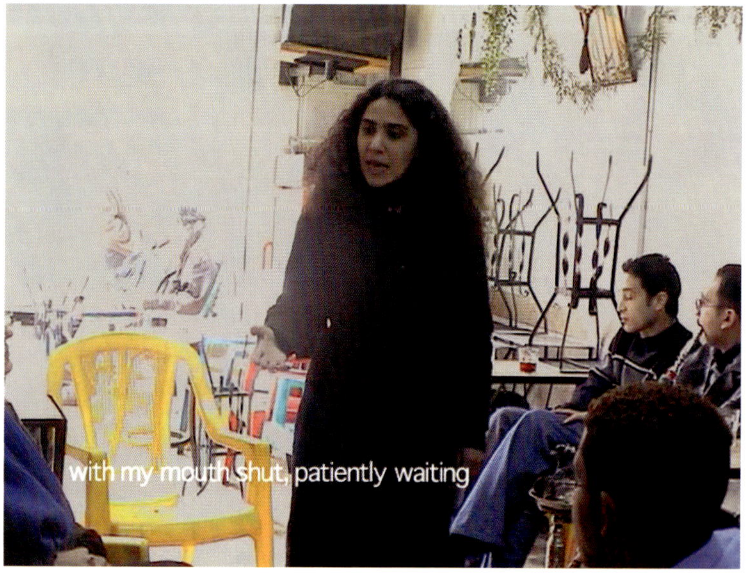

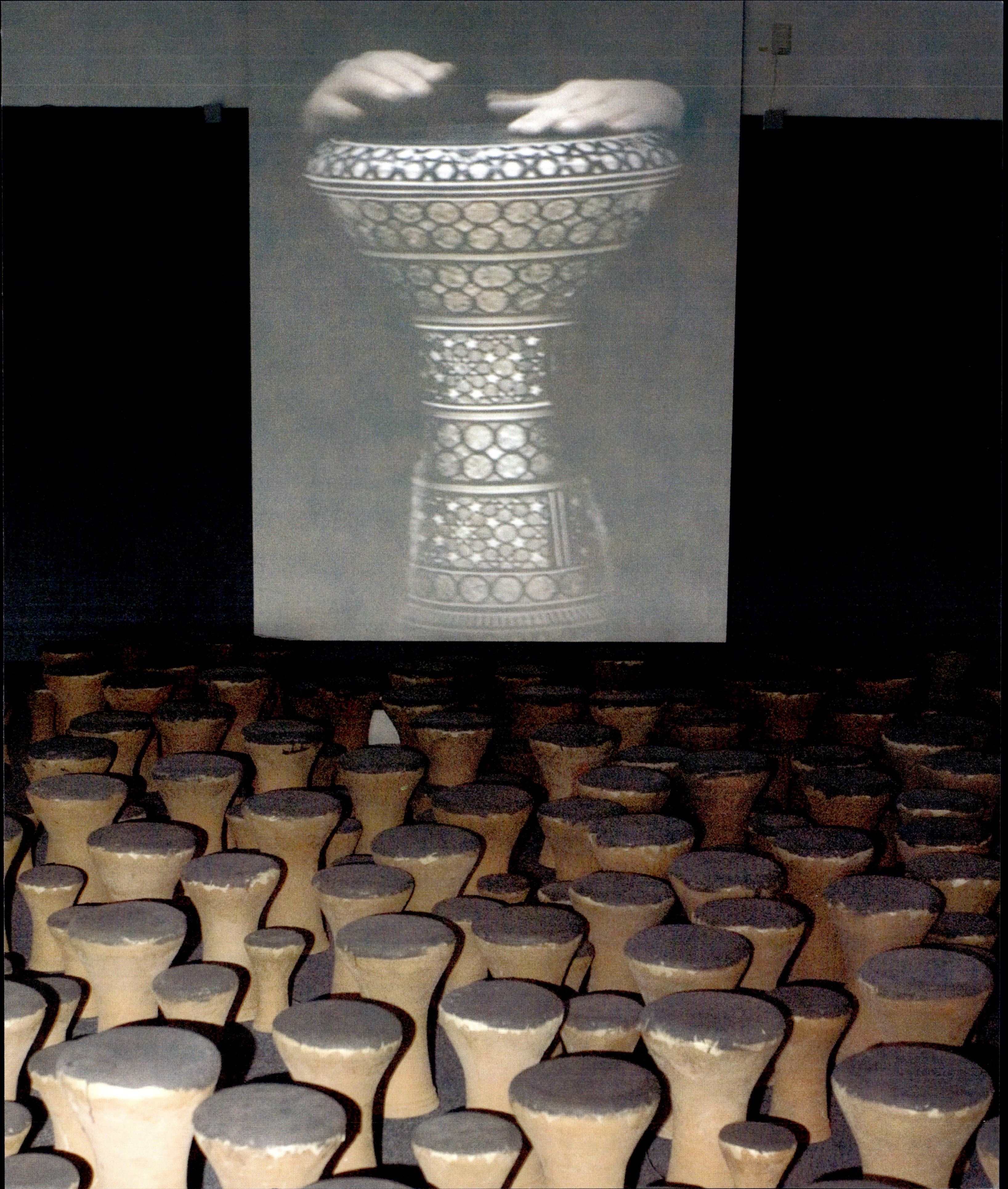

'It's our life in Egypt. You can't draw away from it. You open the newspaper and you read (about) elections, corruption, the Iraqis, the Americans. These really are the worries of the people... apart from football.'
Moataz Nasr

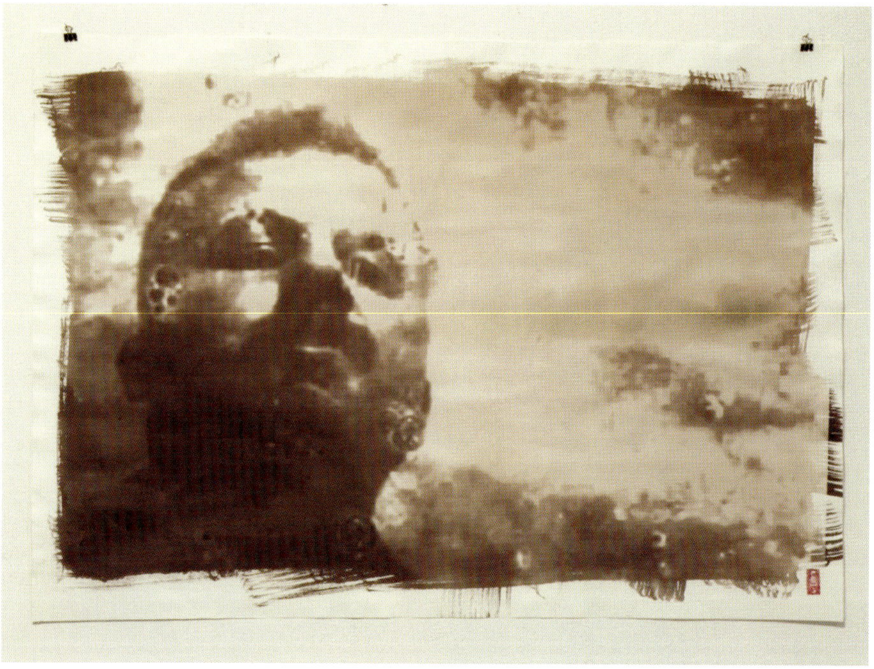

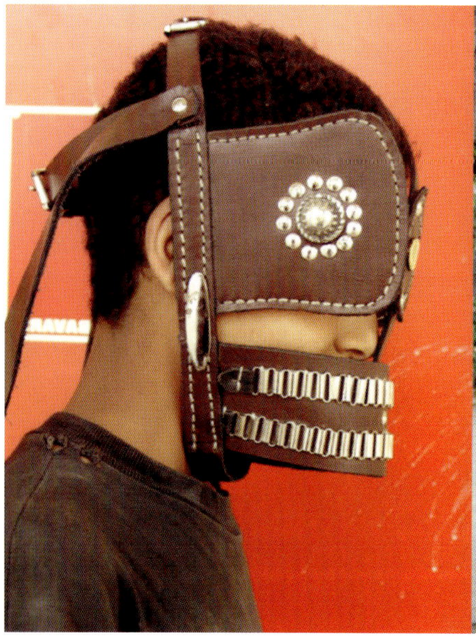

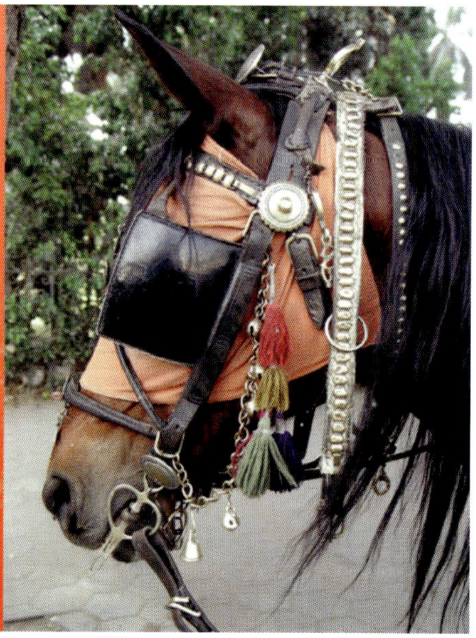

Top left *Insecure*, 2006. Hand-made sun print on paper, 72 x 100cm (28⅓ x 39⅖ in). Collection of the artist.
One of a series of large prints in which the negative is transferred on to photographic paper, then left in the sun until the image begins to develop. The portraits are 'of people but also portraits of society', and represent 'human security, the instability of our existence and the impossibility of recognizing and being ourselves.'

Bottom left *Man-Made*, 2006. Diptych, C-print on Dibond, shin mask and copper, 100 x 150cm (39⅖ x 59 in). Collection of the artist.
Nasr compares the blinkers, bridle and bit worn by a horse with 'the human inability to relate in a concrete and active way to the political and state system'.

Right *Tears*, installation at the church of Sant Agostino, Siena, Italy 2004. Crystal, sound, water, various dimensions.

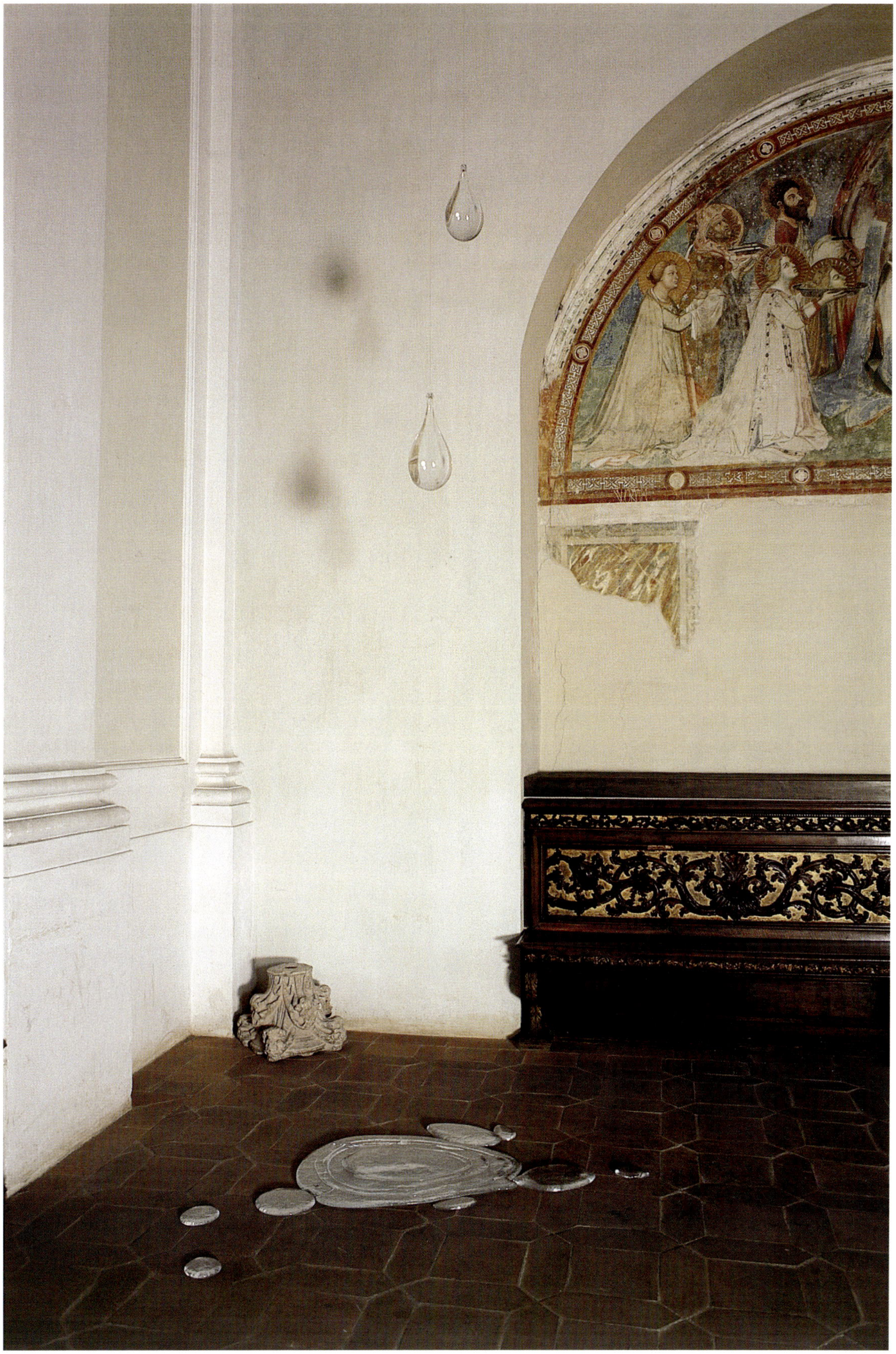

OWEN NDOU
SOUTH AFRICA

Below The brothers Owen and Godwin Ndou with their sculpture of Nelson Mandela and F.W. de Klerk cutting the ropes of apartheid. Venda, South Africa, 1994.

Right *Oxford Man*, 1992. Carved and painted wood, height 135 cm (53⅛ in). Private collection.

Owen Ndou was born in 1964 in Gwamasenga, Venda, part of the Northern Province of South Africa. He began to produce wood sculpture shortly after leaving school and had his first exhibition in 1988, three years after the 'Tributaries' exhibition in Johannesburg, which, for the first time, showed sculpture by black artists from rural apartheid South Africa (including Jackson Hlungwani) alongside white and black artists from urban environments. Owen persuaded his older brother Godwin (b. 1954) to become a sculptor, and together they worked on a number of pieces; today they work as individual artists, though still collaborating closely.

There is an old Venda saying: 'Human beings are like elephants; they eat many trees.' 'Ndou' means 'elephant' in Venda, and together the brothers must have 'eaten' many trees in producing their wood sculpture. Although they are essentially rural artists and have no intention of moving to the city, their subjects often take a new slant on urban/political life. Together they produced the sculpture of Nelson Mandela and F.W. de Klerk 'cutting the ropes of apartheid'.

In 1992 Owen created *Oxford Man*. Ironic, humorous, enigmatic and elegiac, the sculpture comments on changing cultural values, identities and sources of wisdom, and perhaps also questions the validity and meaning of terms such as 'African' and 'African art'. The sculpture was created two years after the groundbreaking 'Art from South Africa' exhibition at the Museum of Modern Art in Oxford, UK, and two years before the election of Nelson Mandela as President of South Africa. There is something of both those events contained within this monolithic figure – whether he is black or white – jealously guarding his book of knowledge and his briefcase, which bend him almost double with their weight.

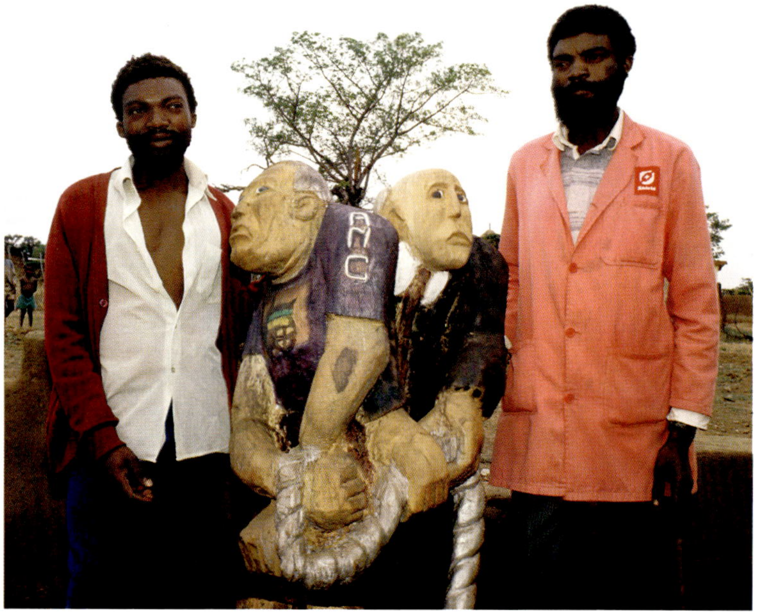

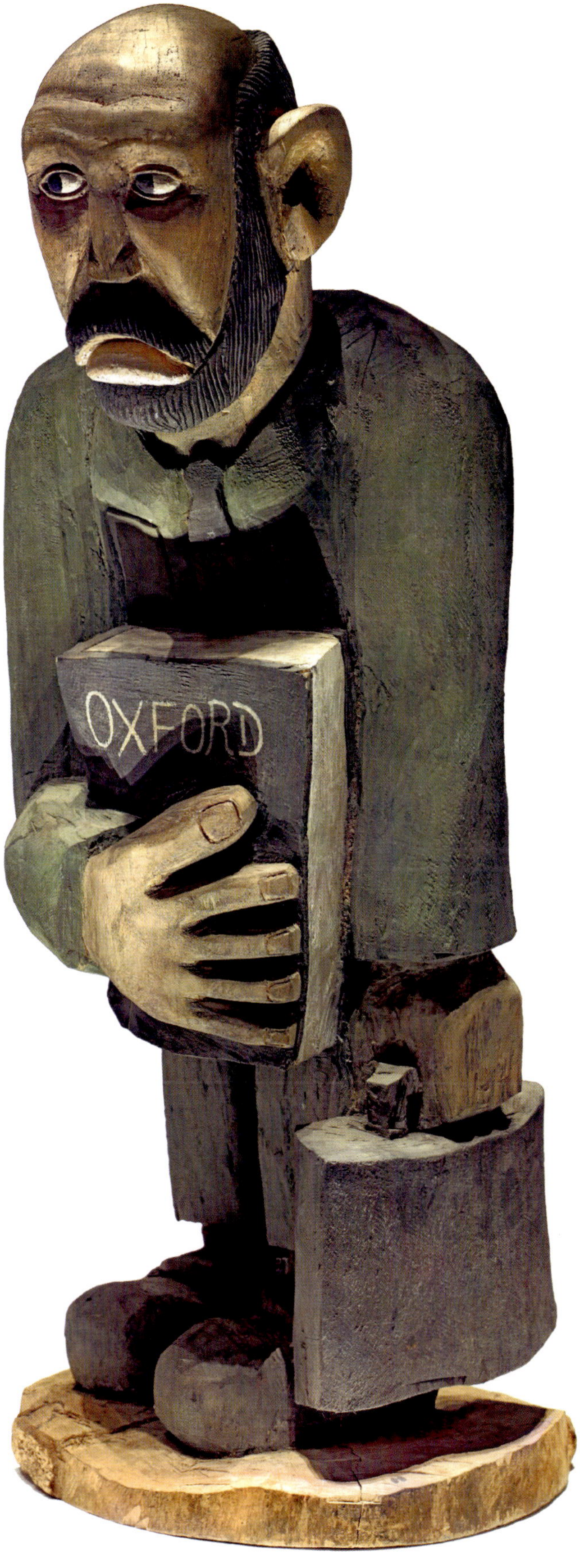
OXFORD

KAREL NEL
SOUTH AFRICA

Below *Stellar Grammar,* 2007. 540 million-year-old carboniferous dust and salt from the Atlantic ocean on a wooden base, 243 x 241 cm (95⅔ x 95 in). Collection of the artist. Nel's large, folding screen refers to the evanescent images approaching us from deep space.

Right *Stellar Grammar,* 2007 (detail). Nel captures these images and interprets them in a more permanent form by using primordial substances: white salt crystals from the evaporated water of the Atlantic ocean, and 540 million-year-old black carboniferous dust from Gondwanaland before the splitting of the continents.

Karel Nel was born in 1955 in Pietermaritzburg, South Africa. He gained a BA in Fine Art from the University of Witwatersrand (1973–77), then studied at St. Martin's School of Art, London before returning to teach at Witwatersrand, where he is currently Associate Professor of Fine Art. Nel is in many ways the direct opposite of his compatriot Jackson Hlungwani, yet like Hlungwani is not so much concerned with the ongoing political and social environment of pre- and post-apartheid South Africa as with the universal spiritual and metaphysical condition of all human beings.

Nel has travelled widely, researching and collecting, particularly in the Pacific where his Gauguinesque wanderings have taken him on the trail of the early navigators to some of the remotest islands of the world. He is particularly fascinated with traditional forms of currency, such as the giant stone discs still revered on the island of Yap. His collection of currencies formed part of his recent exhibition 'Lost Light' (2007), the title of which 'alludes to the fugitive images from deep space – images and ideas which have informed my long-standing interest in cosmology.' Nel is currently the resident artist on the COSMOS project, in which 30 astronomers attempt to map two square degrees of the universe.

> *Much of my drawing and environmental artwork explores the external and internal phenomena we call reality and, in my work, I draw on both artistic and scientific ways of making the world.*

Nel's two other major ongoing projects are *The Status of Dust,* in which he looks at the forensic nature of our time in relation to site-specific dusts collected from significant places in the world, including Ground Zero in New York, and *Elegies to the Forests,* a long-term reflection on the fragility of life and of the plant kingdom on the planet.

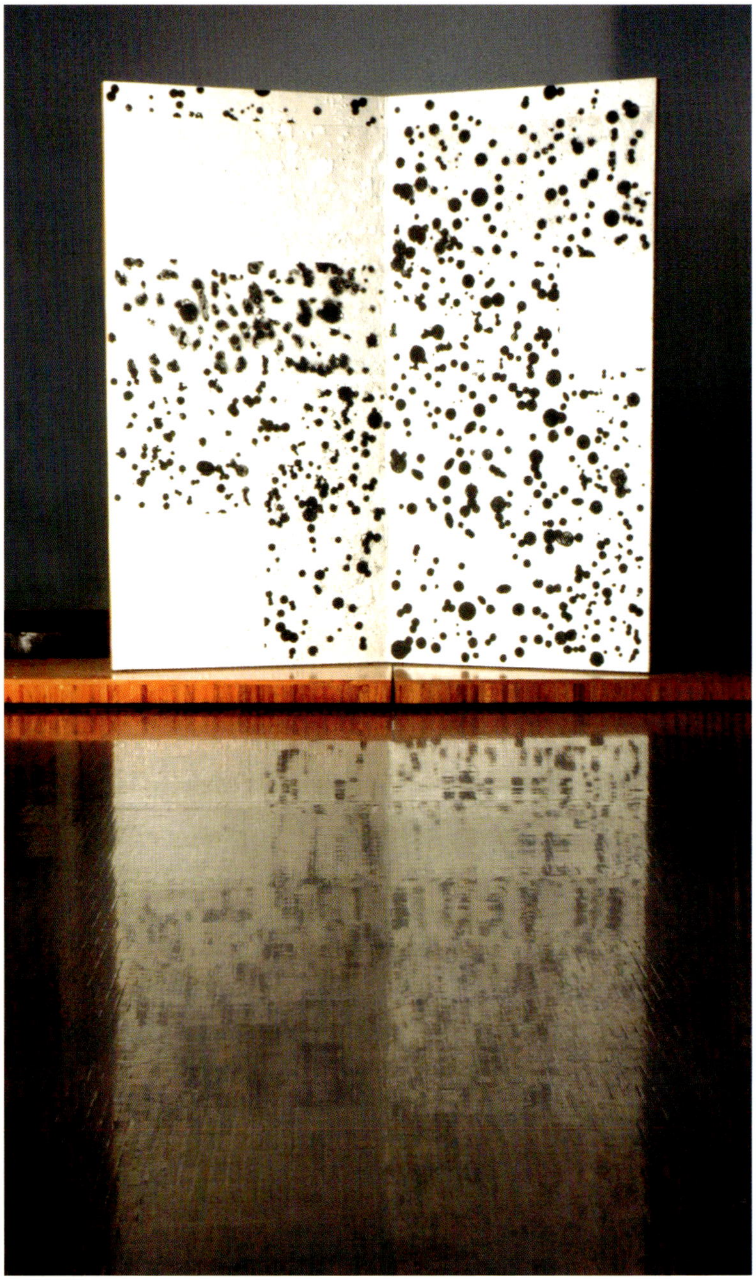

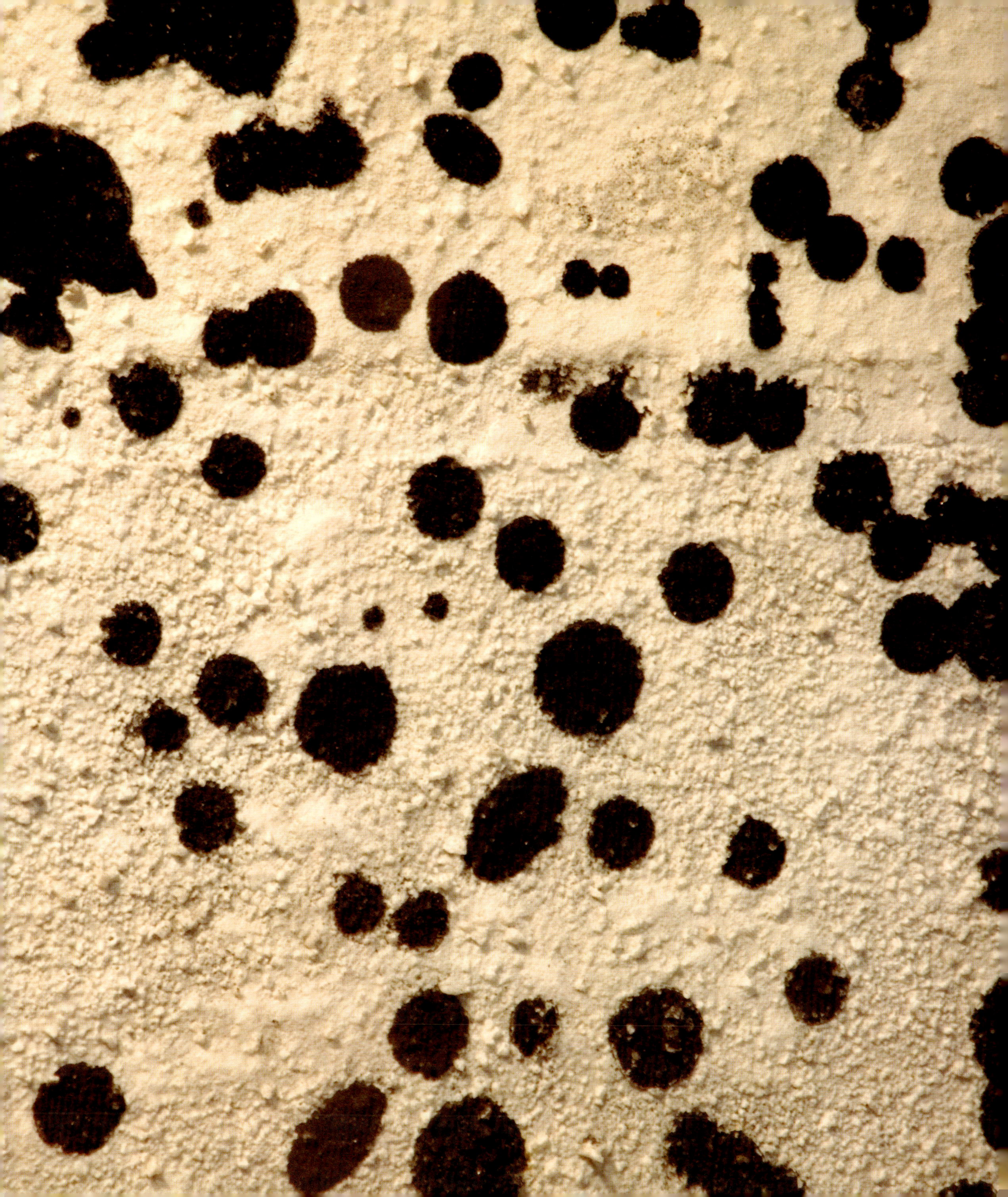

Right View of the installation *Lost Light* at the Standard Bank Gallery, Johannesburg, 2007. Three screens, from left to right: *Cypher, Stellar Grammar* and *Blind Swimmer*. Each: carboniferous dust and salt on a wooden base, 243 x 241 cm (95⅔ x 95 in).

'Much of Nel's most recent work is informed by vast, faint emanations from deep space, transient but long-lived images of light, infrared, radio or X-ray which left their sources millions of years ago, and which are now captured by telescopes as they approach our earth and pass it by, becoming lost again forever to our gaze.'
Emile Maurice

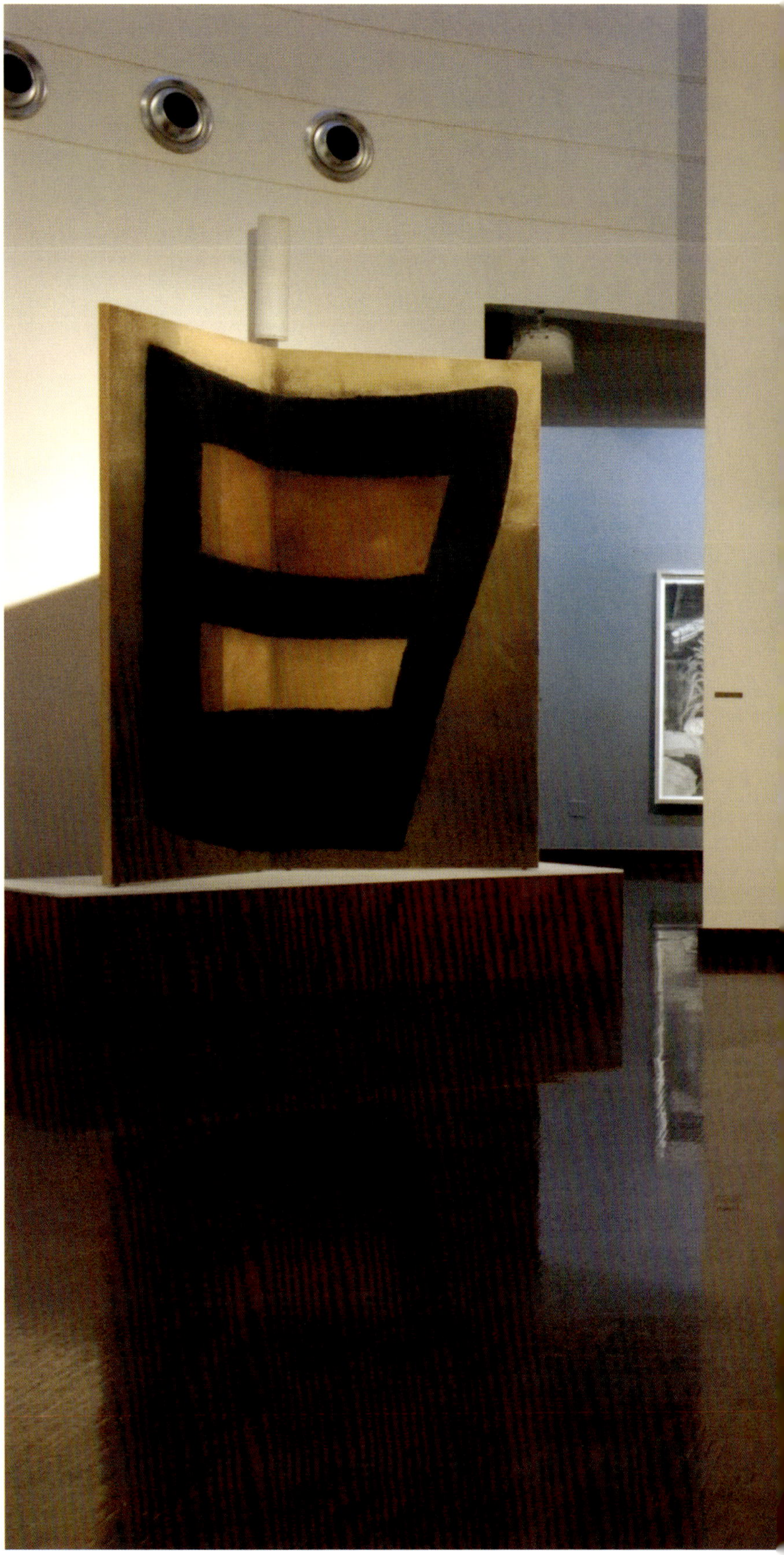

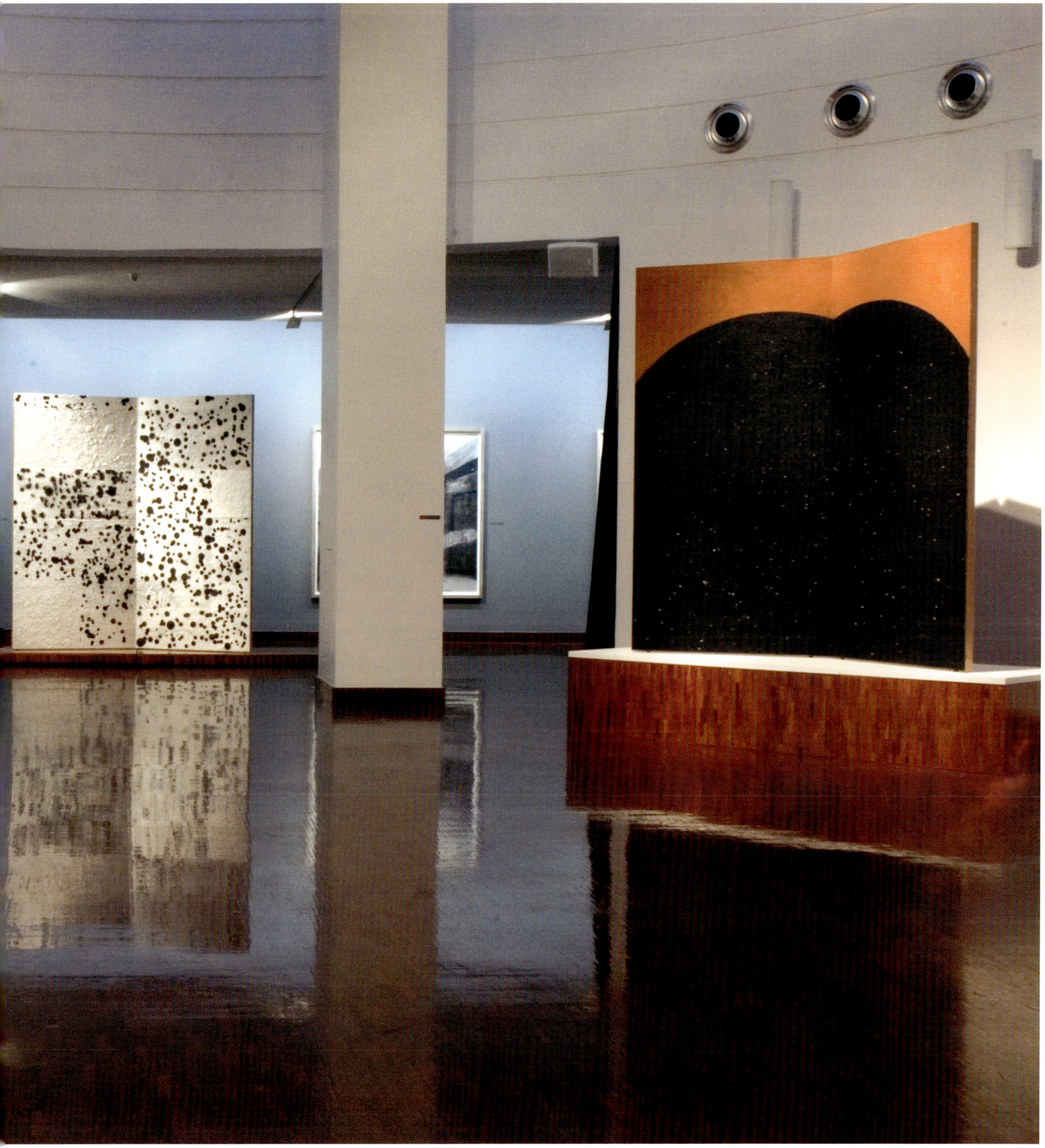

'For me art-making has always been a kind of reconnaissance, a means to explore and make sense of the world around me. Over many years, I have attempted to carefully document my "mind's eye" perceptions. The complex and often subtle interface of the inner and outer worlds has stimulated me to attempt to understand the primary mechanisms of perception – the inner vision from the mind's eye and the outer world using the physical eye.'
Karel Nel

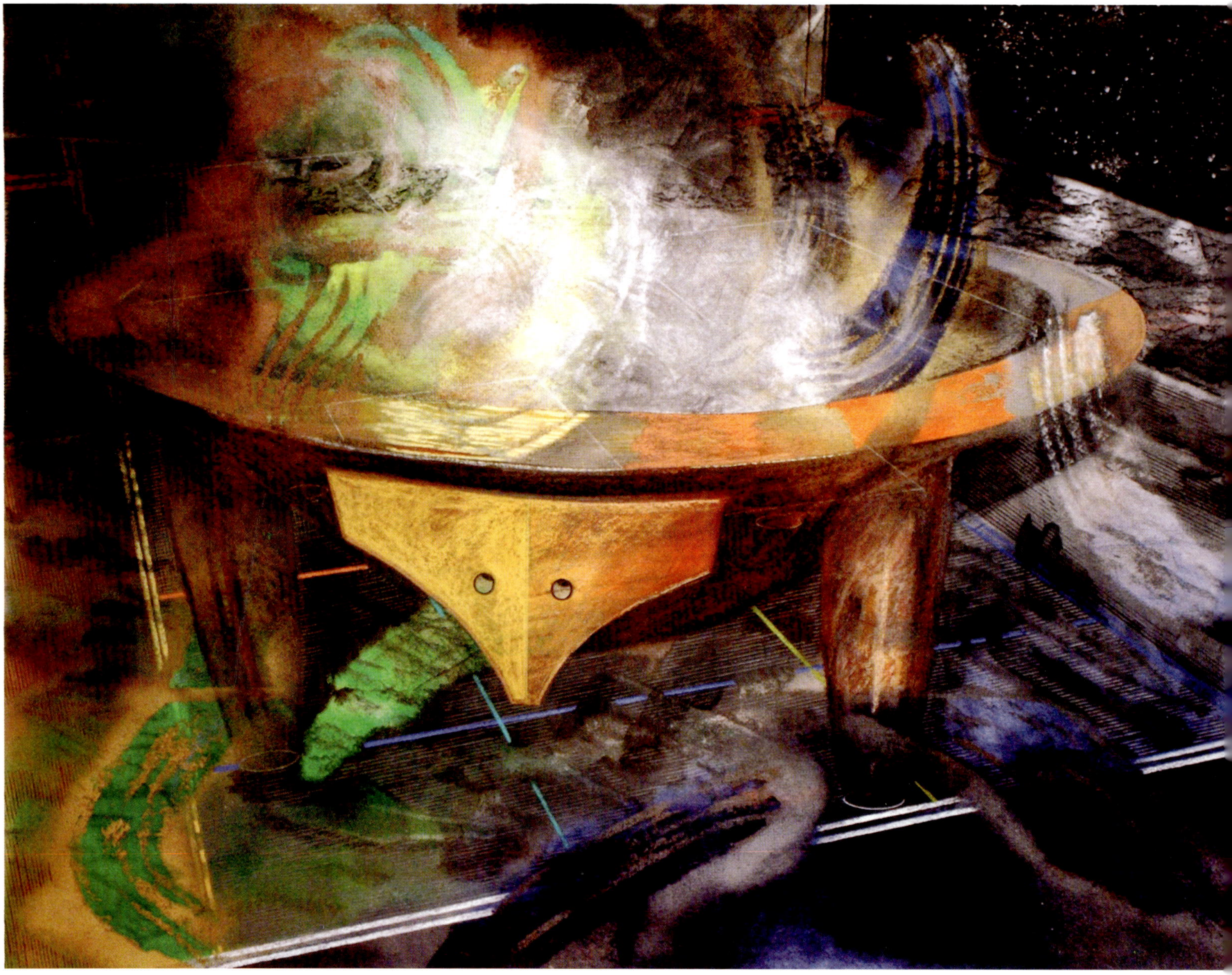

Left *Luminescence*, 2007. Pastel, dry and sprayed pigment on bonded fibre fabric, 230 x 179 cm (90½ x 70½ in). Collection of the artist.
The wooden bowl from which the ceremonial liquid *kava* is drunk in the Tonga archipelago of the Pacific is portrayed by Nel as a creature that bears this ancient ritual on its back. Its significance leaps from the floor of each Tongan home to the vast expanse of the universe beyond.

Below *Wayfarer* (*Mudif*), 2004. Pastel and sprayed pigment on bonded fibre fabric, 193 x 193 cm (75¼ x 75¼ in). Barlow World Collection.
The vast leaf of the coco-de-mer palm of the Seychelles, drawn in Nel's studio, Mudif, in Johannesburg. Two wooden stools of the Asante people of Ghana stand before the leaf as testament to the enforced exile of Asantehene (king) Prempe I to the Seychelles by the British in the late nineteenth century.

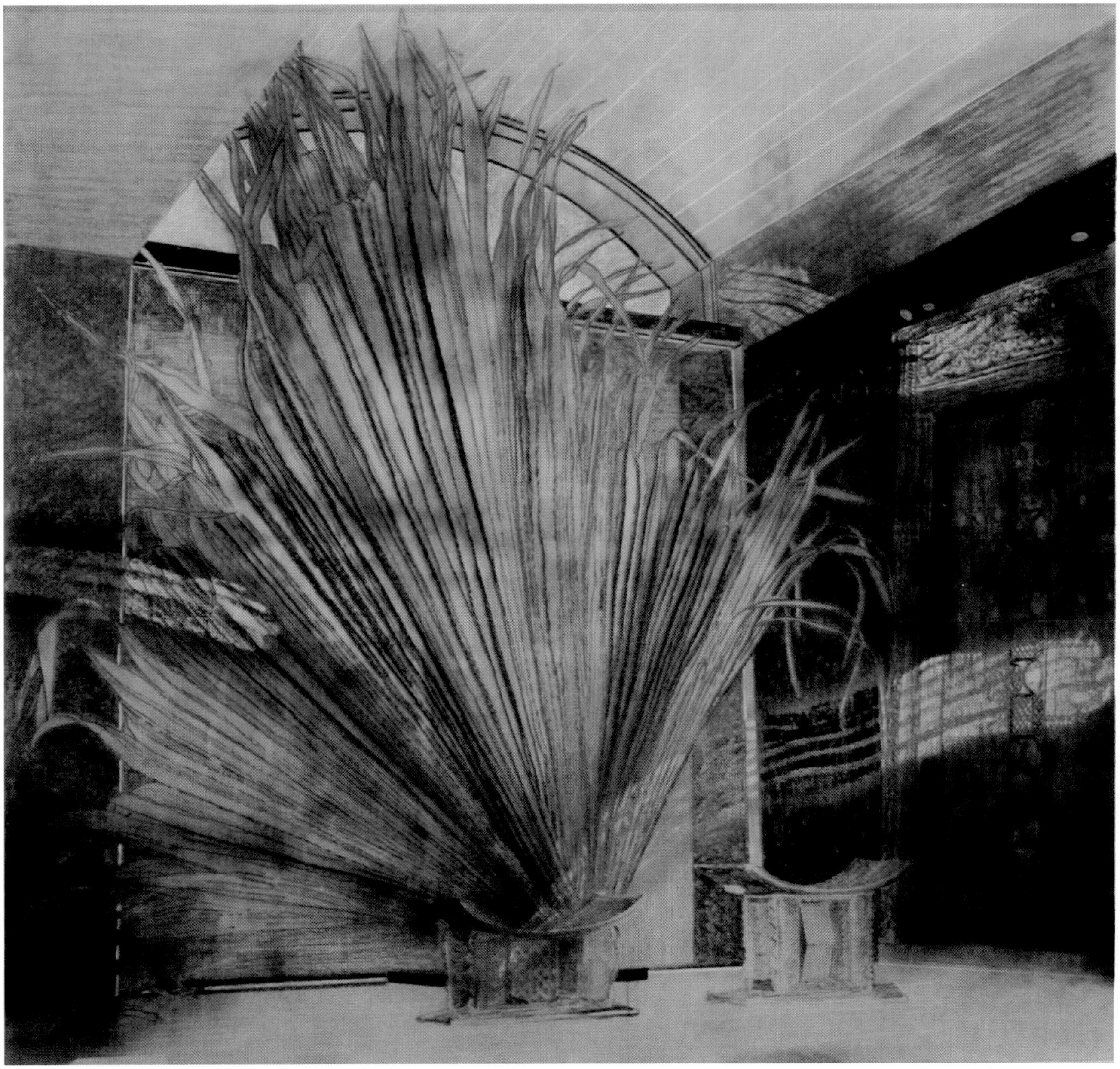

ROBINO NTILA
TANZANIA

Below *Untitled*, 2002. Etching, 39 x 29 cm (15⅓ x 11⅖ in). British Museum, London.
Women in a village in Tanzania pound and grate cassava. They are dressed in printed cloth, *kanga*, of various colours and patterns.

Right *Education in Tanzania*, 2002. Etching, 39 x 29 cm (15⅓ x 11⅖ in). British Museum, London.
This etching was commissioned for the cover of the book *Higher Education in Tanzania* (Mkude et al., 2003). The figures are sheltered beneath the distinctive umbrella-shaped roof of Nkrumah Hall in the University of Dar Es Salaam. According to Ntila:

'Tanzanian parents do everything they can in order to send their children to school and on to university. In return, their children come back with the fruits of their education and promote better health care and technological development. It is like a wheel – giving and getting.'

Robino Ntila was born in Ndanda, Mtwara region, southern Tanzania in 1953. Two years after the foundation in 1973 of the Nyumba ya Sanaa ('The House of Arts') arts centre in Dar Es Salaam, Ntila joined the organization, and has been associated with it throughout his career – first as student artist, then as teacher and later as chief coordinator. During that time he has exhibited and studied abroad, particularly at the International Academy in Salzburg, Austria where he learned various printmaking and bronze-casting techniques. He has gained wide recognition for his work as artist, curator and teacher, holding numerous printing workshops in Tanzania, Kenya and Zimbabwe. He has also acted as a cultural ambassador, promoting the arts of Tanzania in Kenya, South Africa, Europe and the Americas.

Equally inspired by 'traditional' and 'modern' life in urban and rural Tanzania, Ntila's etchings and paintings often humorously emphasize how artificial these categories seem to Tanzanians. He has curated exhibitions in India, Austria, Tanzania, South Africa and Senegal and has also organized international workshops and residencies both in eastern Africa and abroad – most recently the Rafiki and Wasani International Workshops that took place at the Nyumba ya Sanaa in 2007.

Ntila has exhibited widely in eastern and southern Africa, as well as in Europe and the USA.

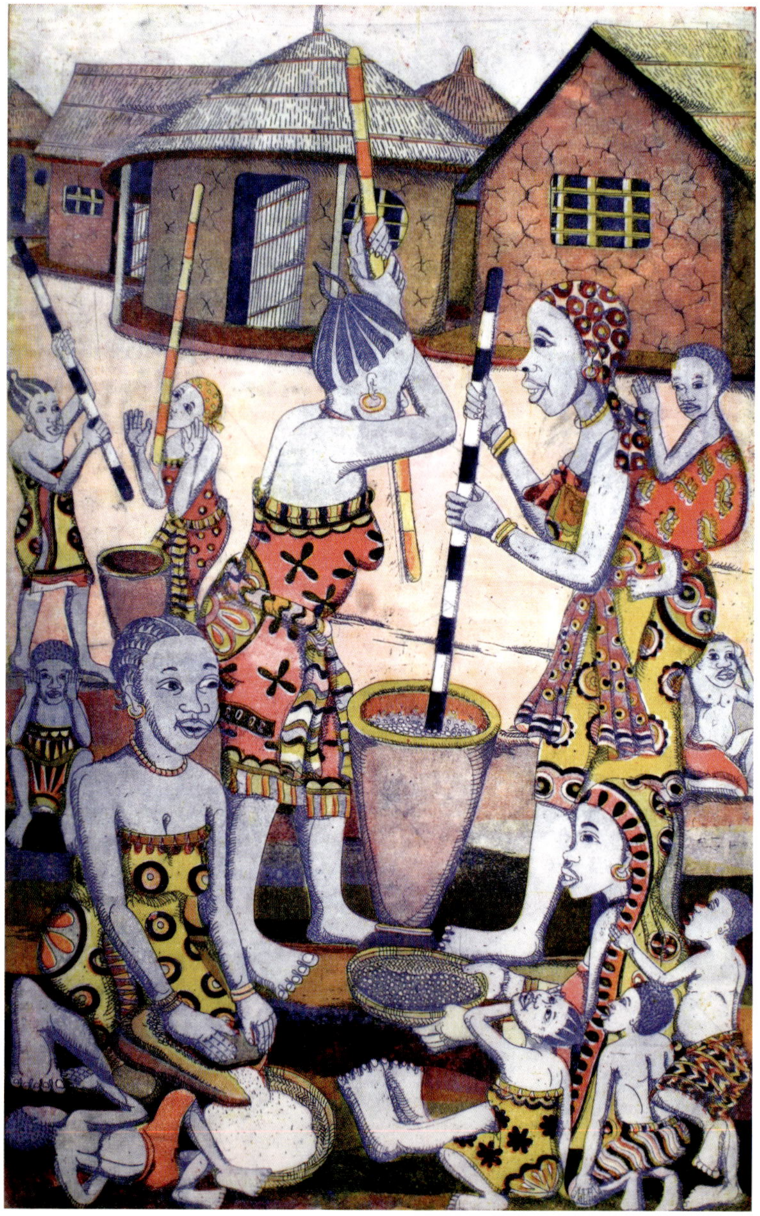

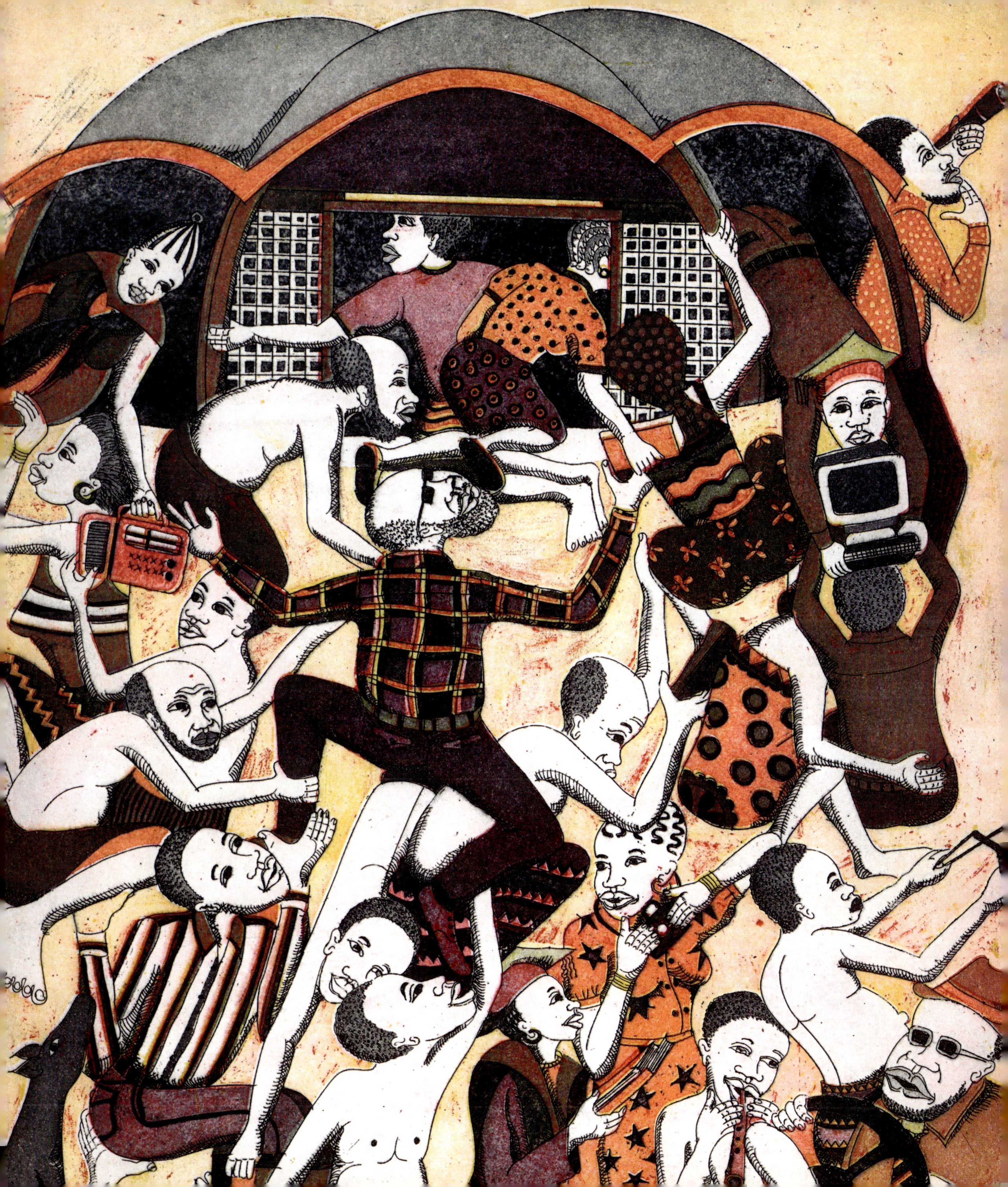

Right *Makonde Sculptor*, 2002. Etching, 24 x 39 cm (9⅖ x 15⅓ in). Private collection.
A sculptor of the Makonde people of southern Tanzania and northern Mozambique is seated beneath a sheltering cashew tree carving a complex ebony figure. The cashew nut symbolizes fertility, wealth and good fortune. It is a recurring motif, in stylized forms, on various objects including the printed textiles (*kanga*) worn by Tanzanian women.

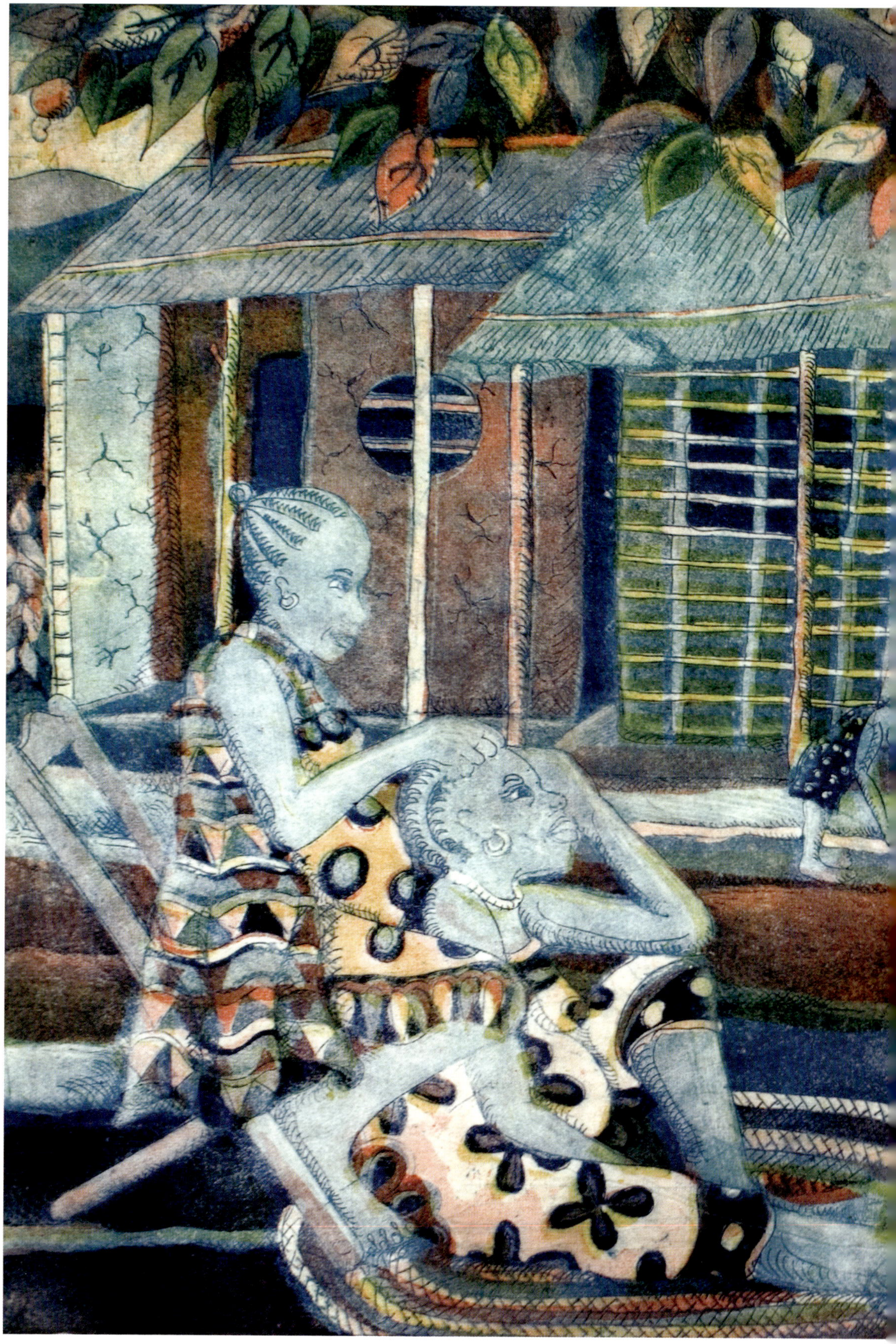

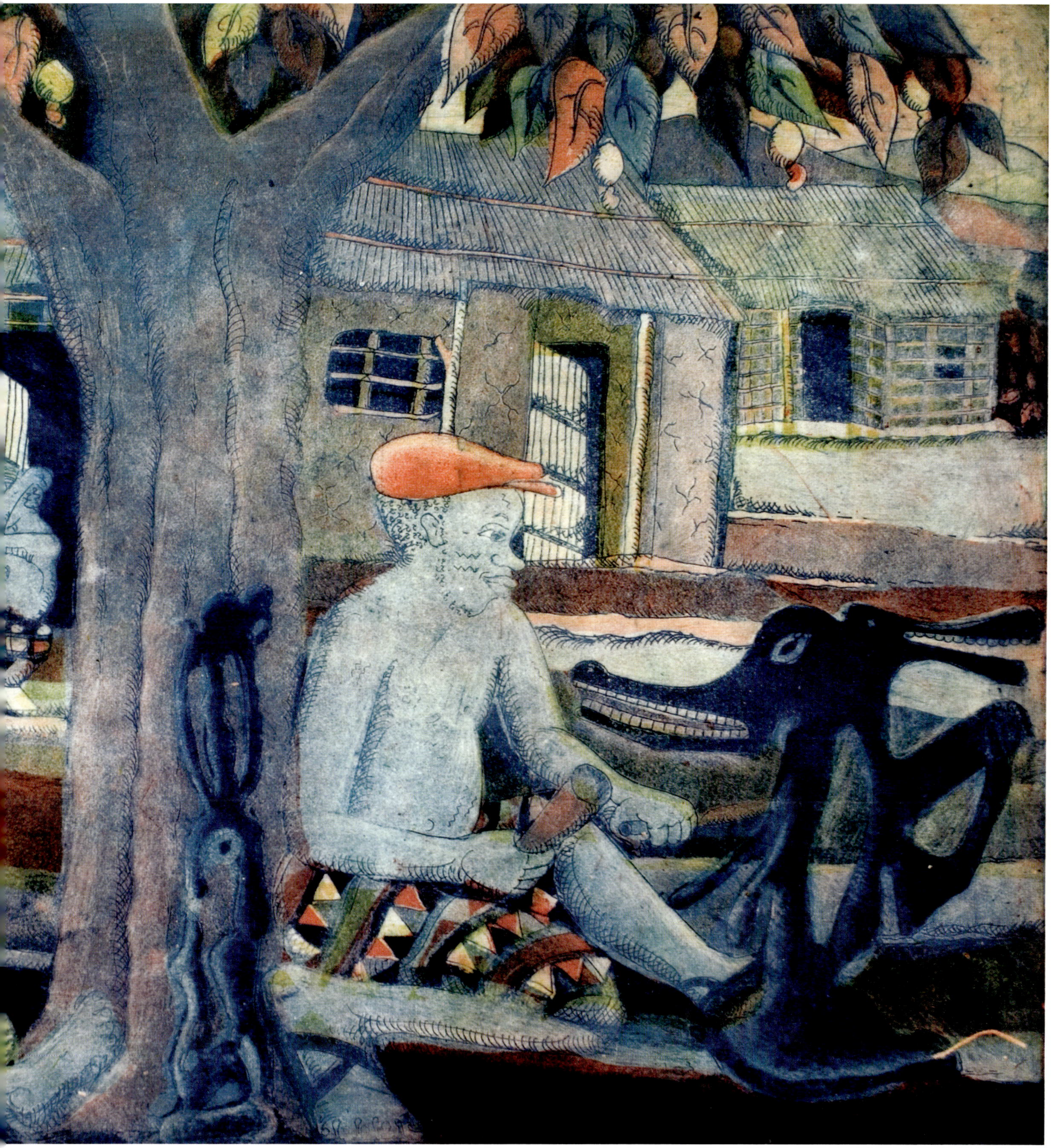

MAGDALENE ODUNDO
KENYA/UK

Below Drawing from sketchbook, no date. Pen and Indian ink on paper 58.5 x 41.4 cm (23 x 16¼ in). Collection of the artist.
'My ceramics have always been very personal and [the products of] a very personal engagement.'

Right *Vessel Series I, no. 5*, 2005–6. Red clay, carbonized and multi-fired, 45.4 x 29 cm (18 x 11½ in), signed under base. Collection of the artist.
'The vessel as a concept has always represented a search for humanity in my work – what they can't and don't contain, their function or non-function have never been issues for me; their presence, however, has been essential.'

'It is a form of alchemy', Odundo says in describing the technical processes involved in firing her ceramic vessels, yet through her art she has created the immortality that medieval alchemists strove for, but failed to achieve. Each of her vessels is a human being (mostly women, but some men I like to think), whose essence she has captured and to whom she has given eternal life. 'They look as if they might laugh out loud', Marina Vaizey remarked of some of the works in Odundo's show at Blackwell in 2001.

Magdalene Odundo was born in Nairobi, Kenya in 1950. She came to the UK in 1971 to study graphics at the Cambridge College of Art, but it was the pottery classes that caught her imagination. She studied ceramics at the West Surrey College of Art and Design in Farnham (1973–76), during which she spent time in the Pottery Training Centre at Abuja, Nigeria, set up by Michael Cardew. She then taught at the Commonwealth Institute, London (1976–79) before taking an MA at the Royal College of Art, London (1979–82) where, as well as gaining expertise, she also 'learnt to think' as she puts it. Today, Magdalene Odundo is Professor of Ceramics at Farnham; her works have been exhibited all over the world.

Odundo has travelled widely in Africa, gaining a deep knowledge and appreciation of African ceramics, how they are made and what a crucial part they play in so many aspects of life. Yet she is equally conversant with the art of other cultures and times, from pre-Columbian pots and ancient Cycladic figurines to Euro-American modernism – the highly personal experiment with form by sculptors such as Arp, Brancusi and Giacometti. 'I have become obsessed by form. What was once an embellishment has now become an engagement.'

Odundo is drawing constantly while working on her ceramics, several of which may be developing at the same time. Her drawings are breathtakingly beautiful, capturing those keenly observed moments that are painstakingly distilled in the exquisite forms of her ceramics: 'The unfurling of a plant, the fall of an Elizabethan sleeve, the momentary stillness of a dancer's pose or the silhouette of a Kenyan woman bound in layers of cloth.'

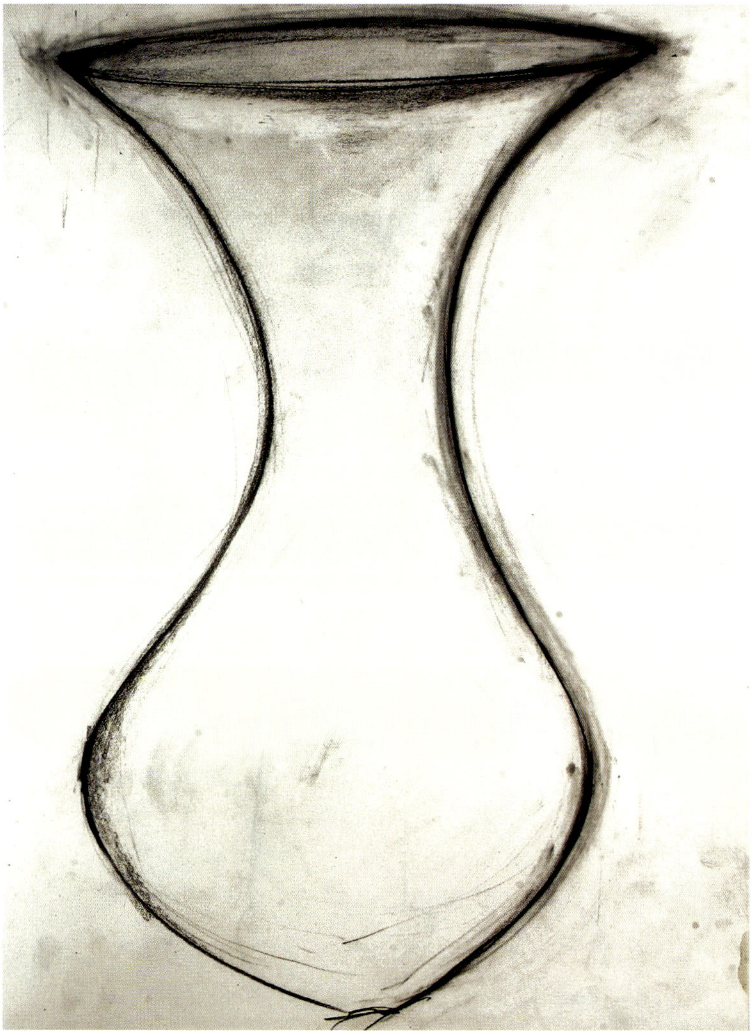

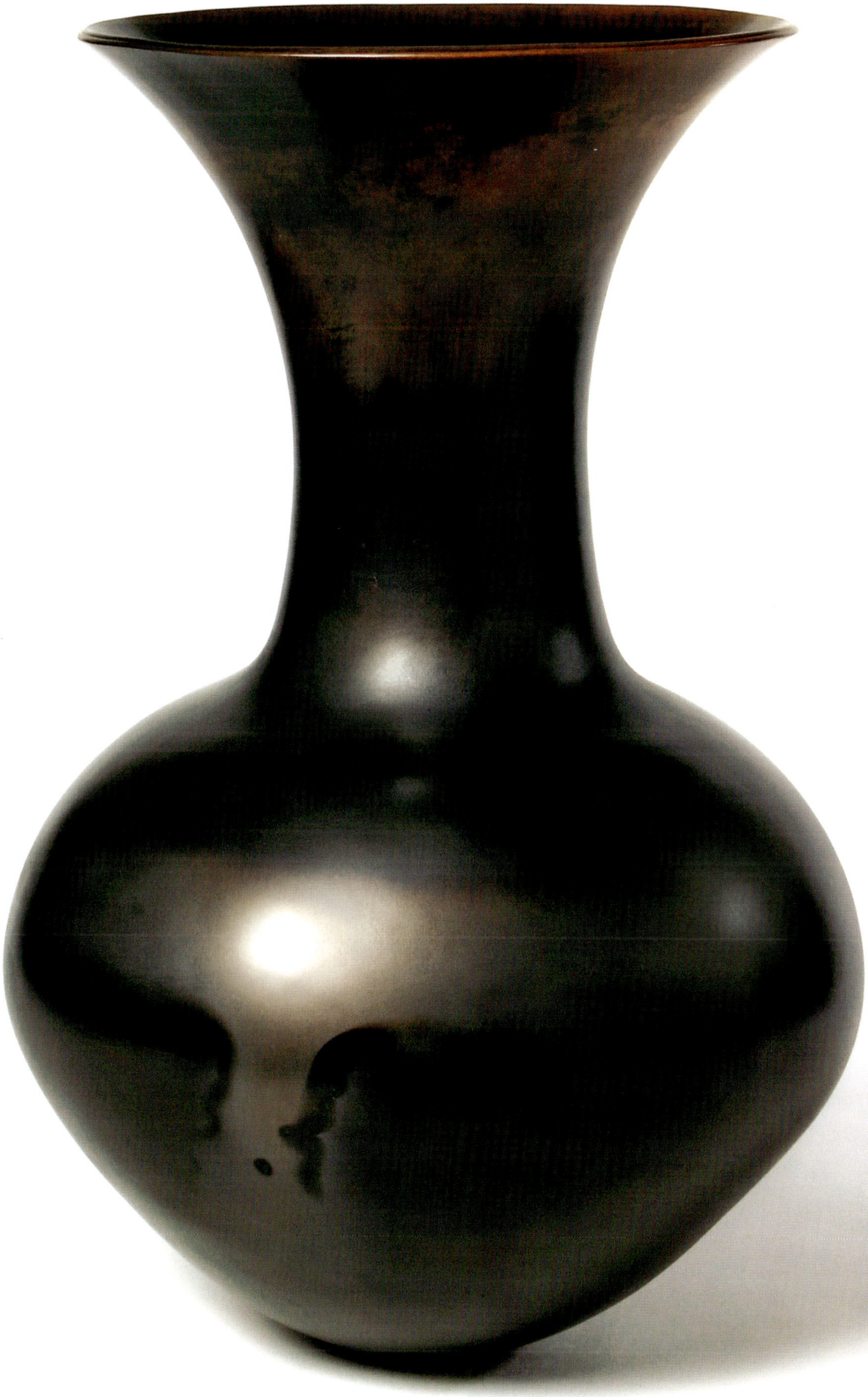

Below *Vessel Series IV, no. 1*, 2006. Red clay, carbonized and multi-fired, 27.5 x 36 cm (10³/₅ x 14¹/₈ in), signed under base. Private collection.
'I try to control it [the firing of her work], but I know that, and hope that, I will be surprised. There is an element of knowing and trusting, and an element of faith...'

Right *Vessel Series II asymmetrical, no. 1*, 2005–6. Red clay, carbonized and multi-fired, 56.4 x 29.7 cm (22 x 11³/₄ in), signed under base. Maxine and Stuart Frankel Foundation for Art.
'An object and vessel made in clay has nuances and gestures, which evoke emotions sometimes sensual, sometimes not.'

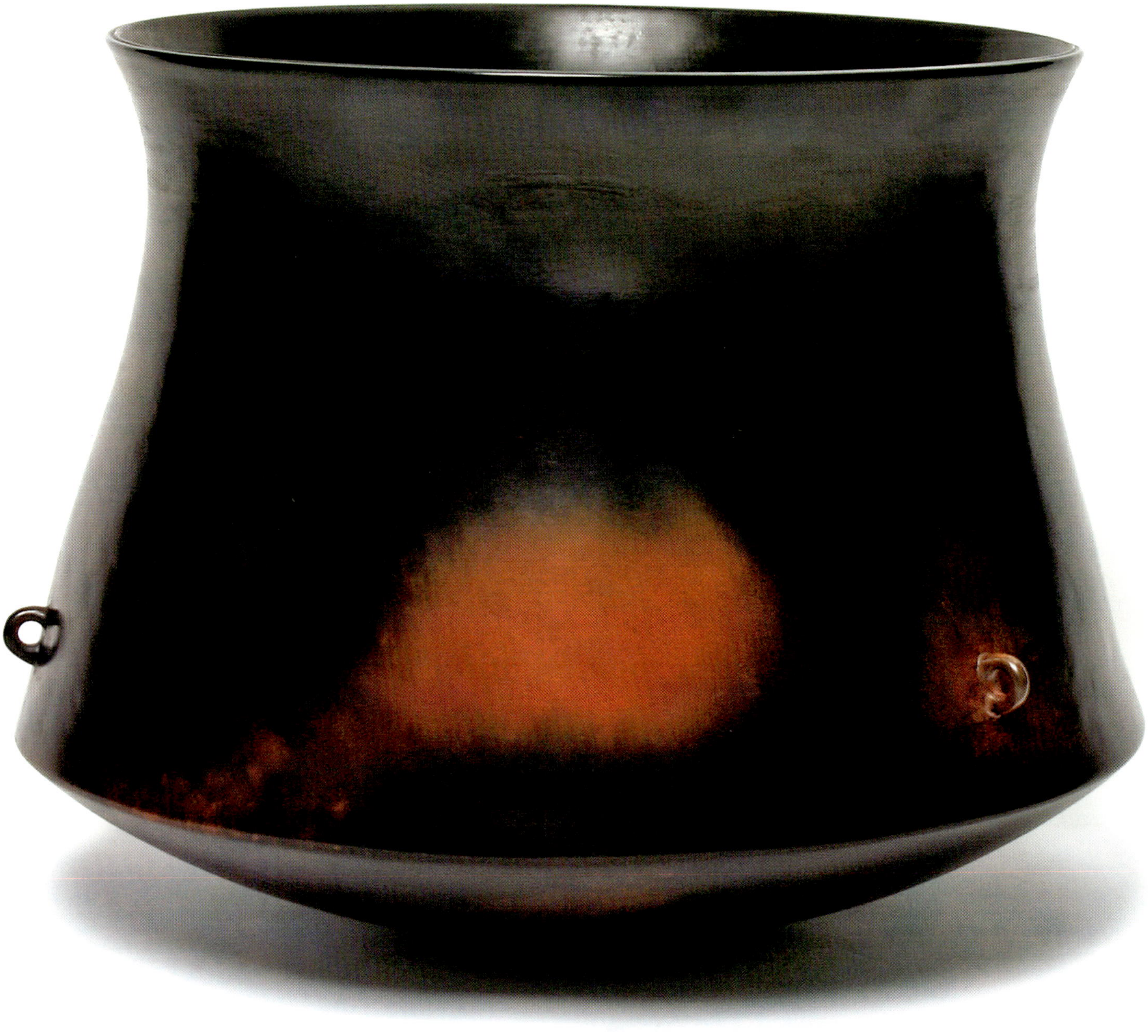

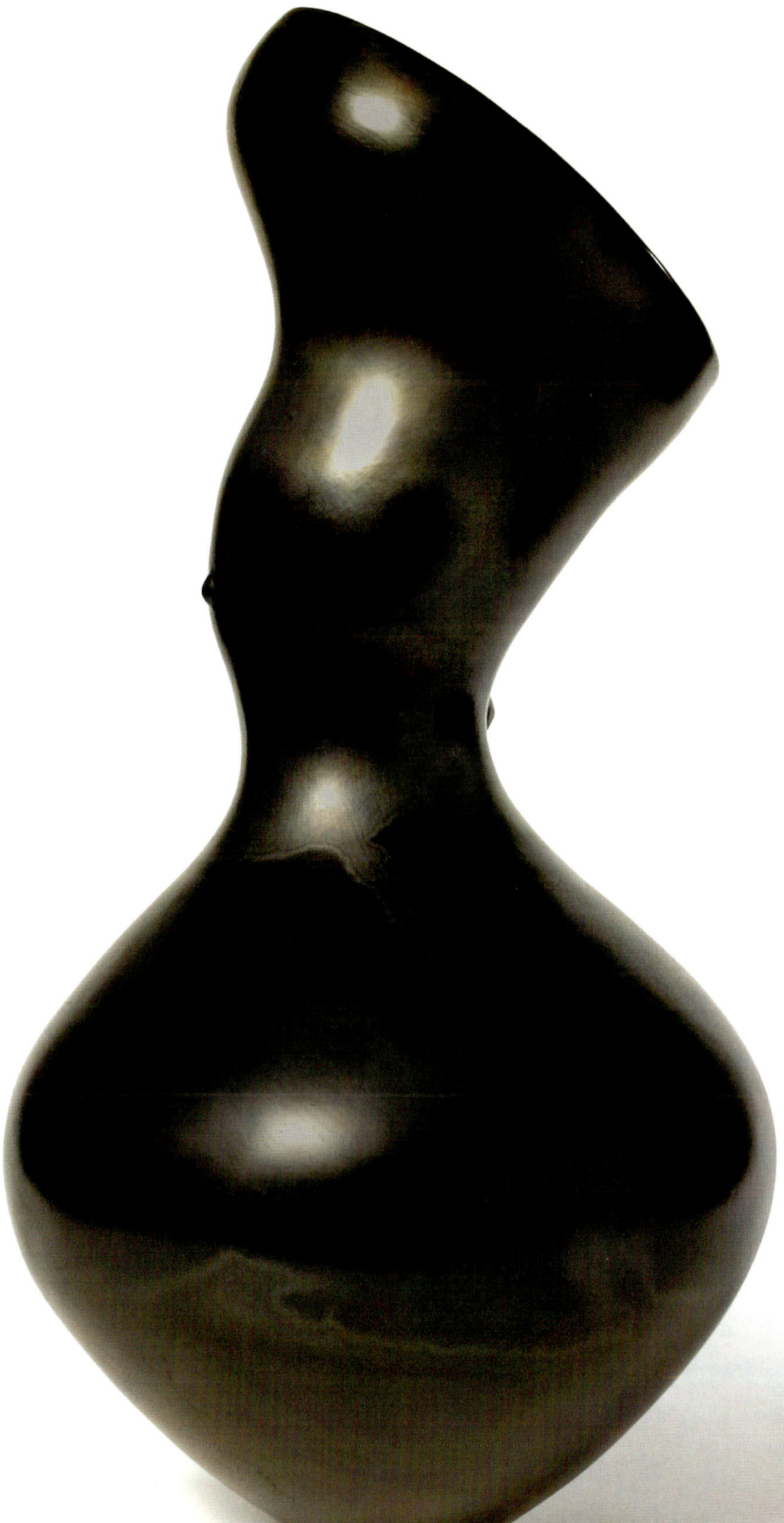

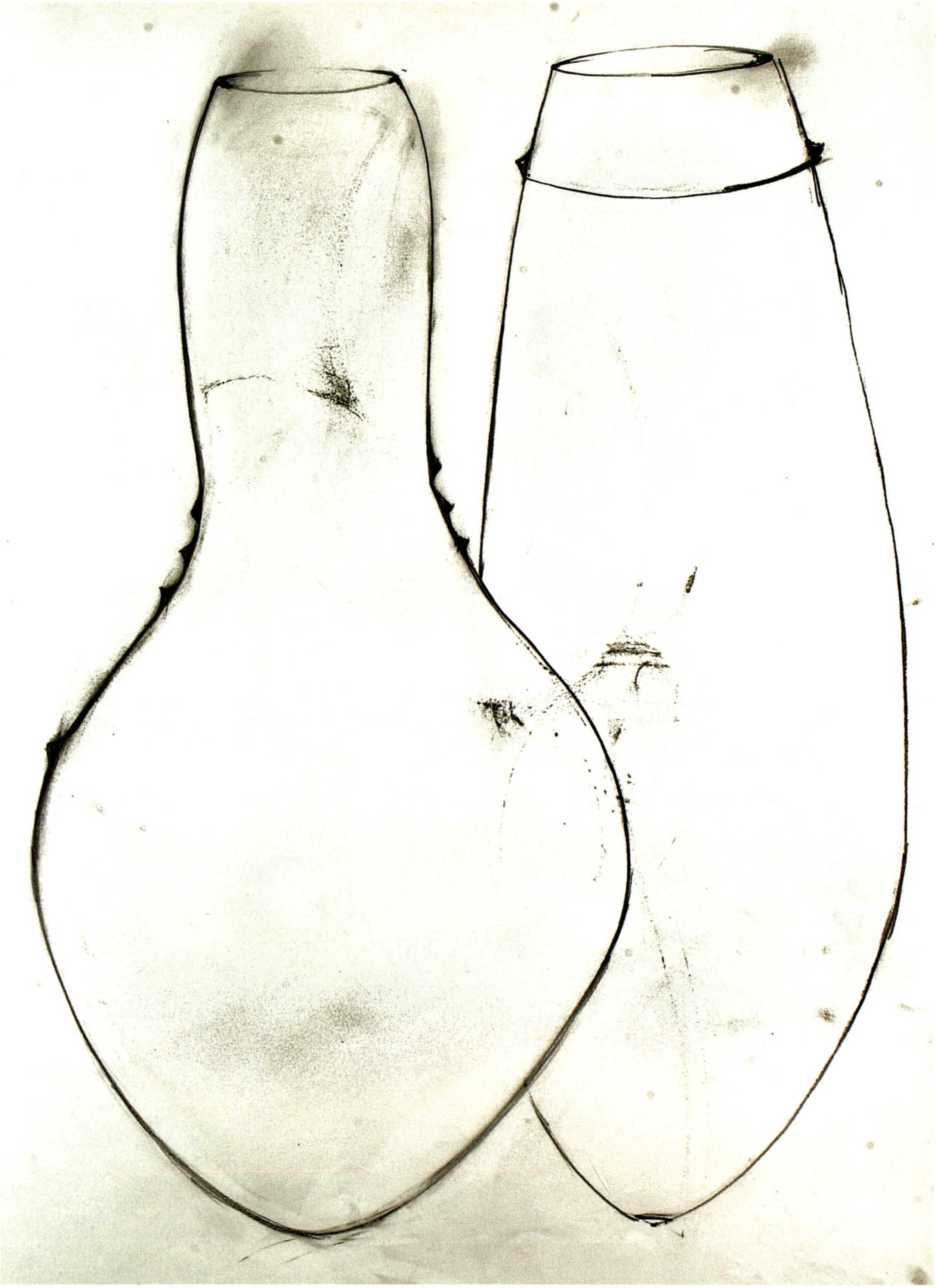

Left Drawing from sketchbook, no date. Pencil on paper, 58.5 x 41.5 cm (23 x 16⅓ in). Collection of the artist.

'When I begin to build a structure, I do a lot of drawing, in between, refining, revising, reworking, abstracting ideas from what is there... For all the drawing, planning and saying that I am going to create a certain kind of shape, it never actually gets realized.'

Right *Vessel Series III, no. 2*, 2005–6. Red clay, carbonized and multi-fired, 53 x 24 cm (20¾ x 9½ in), signed under base. Collection of the artist.

Far right *Vessel Series III, no. 3*, 2005–6. Red clay, carbonized and multi-fired, 51.2 x 24 cm (20⅛ x 9½ in), signed under base. Collection of the artist.

'After months of investment the firing is such a final moment, you want to prolong it. It is like life; you want it to go on and on. I enjoy making much more than finalizing the piece.'

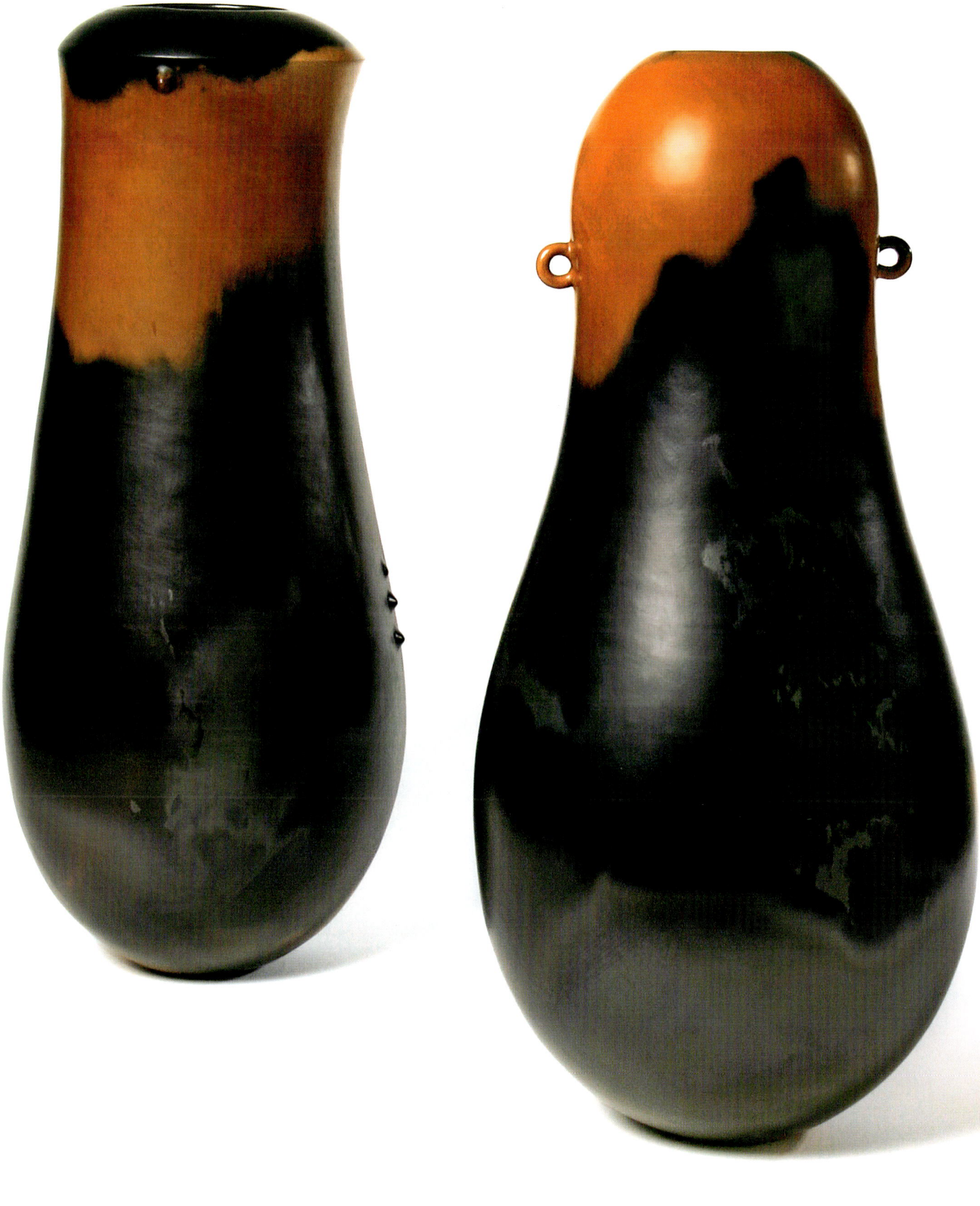

CHRIS OFILI
UK

Below *Mono Oro*, 1999–2002. Oil paint, acrylic paint, ink, gold leaf, polyester resin, glitter, map pins and elephant dung on linen with two elephant dung supports. 243.8 x 182.8 cm (96 x 72 in). Tate Gallery, London.

'The rhesus macaque is not just another monkey. Although most people have never heard of the species by name, there are many ways in which the rhesus macaque, or rhesus monkey, *Macaca mulatta*, is THE monkey.'
Dr Susanna Paisley, conservation biologist

Right *Mono Oro*, 1999–2002 (detail).

Chris Ofili
The artist was born in 1968 in Manchester, UK. He lives and works. (Biography in the catalogue of the The Upper Room, part of his exhibition 'Freedom One Day' at the Victoria Miro Gallery, London, 2002.)

Ofili studied at the Chelsea School of Art (1988–91) and at the Royal College of Art (1991–93). In 1992, he won a scholarship which allowed him to join the Pachipamwe workshop in Zimbabwe organized through the Triangle Arts Trust. There, he worked with artists from Zimbabwe and the international community. 'Pachipamwe has been a unique opportunity to develop and push myself and my work into a fresh area.'

Ofili's paintings are packed with images and allusions to race and religion, black popular culture and music. They may seem diffuse and confusing at first, but they are all painted with a precise and knowing composition that perfectly balances their component parts of colour, material and subject matter. They are all, in their different ways, expressions of the same love affair.

Chris Ofili won the Turner prize in 1998, worked with the architect David Adjaye on *The Upper Room* at the Victoria Miro Gallery in 2002 and repeated his collaboration with Adjaye at the Venice Biennale (2003), where he represented Britain.

Ofili is one of the team behind the Freeness project (www.freeness.co.uk), which is dedicated to finding and supporting new music, particularly that of black, Asian and other minorities. 'Creative genius often lives and dies in bedrooms, headrooms and other private spaces, but we want it out of the bedroom and into the sound system.'

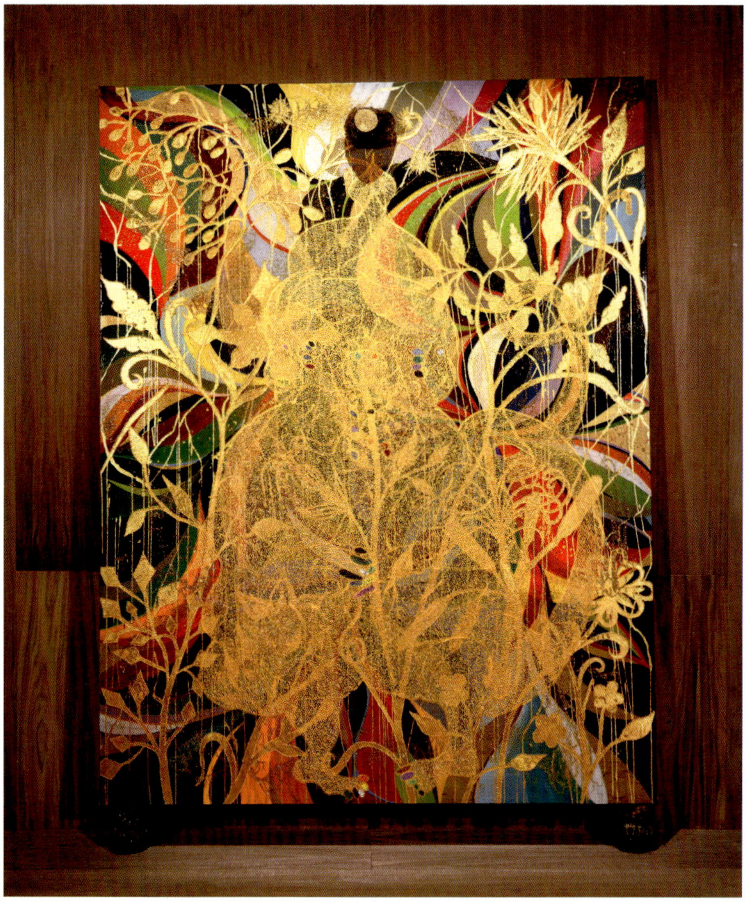

'The way I work comes out of experimentation, but it also comes out of a love of painting, a love affair with painting.'
Chris Ofili

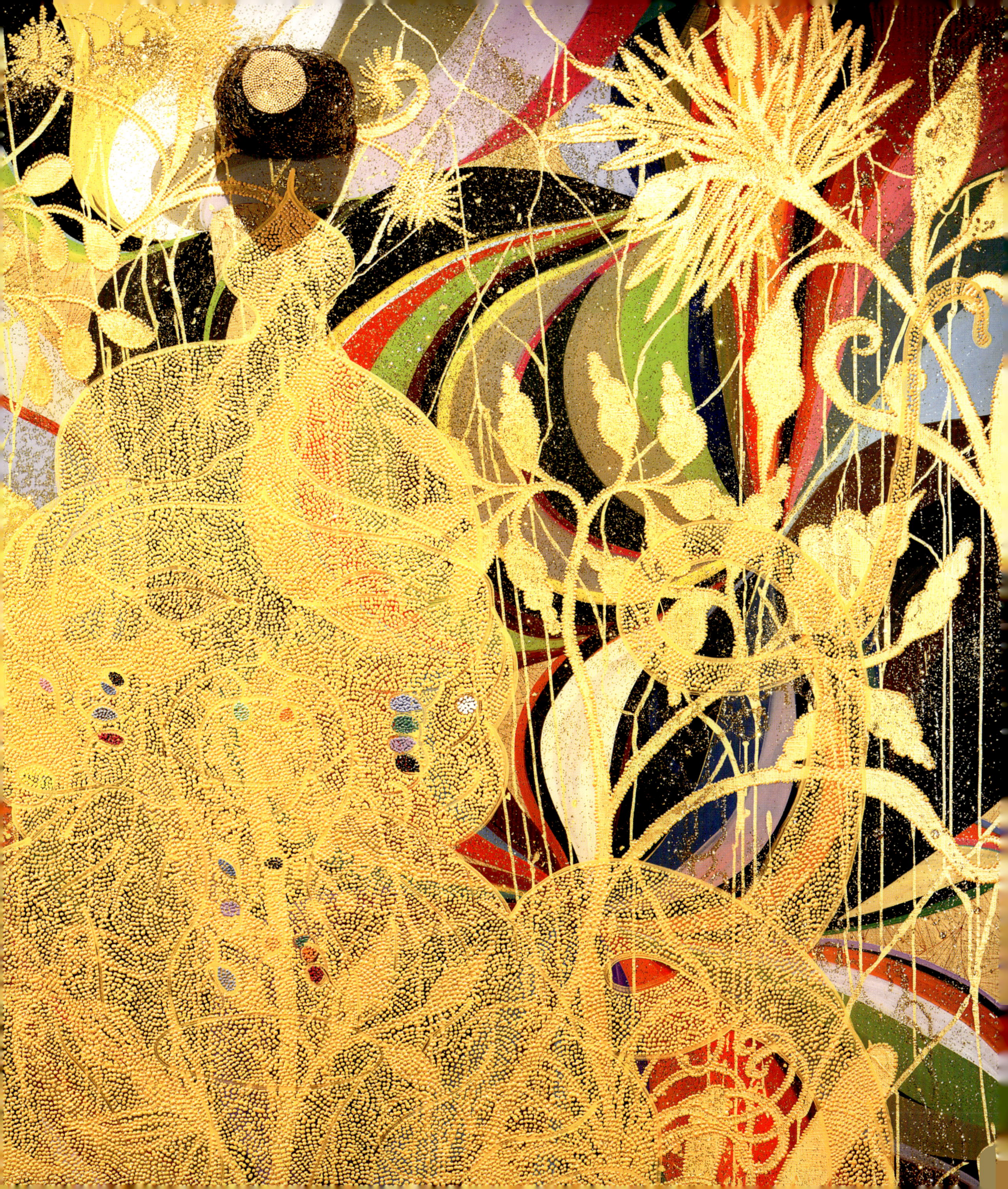

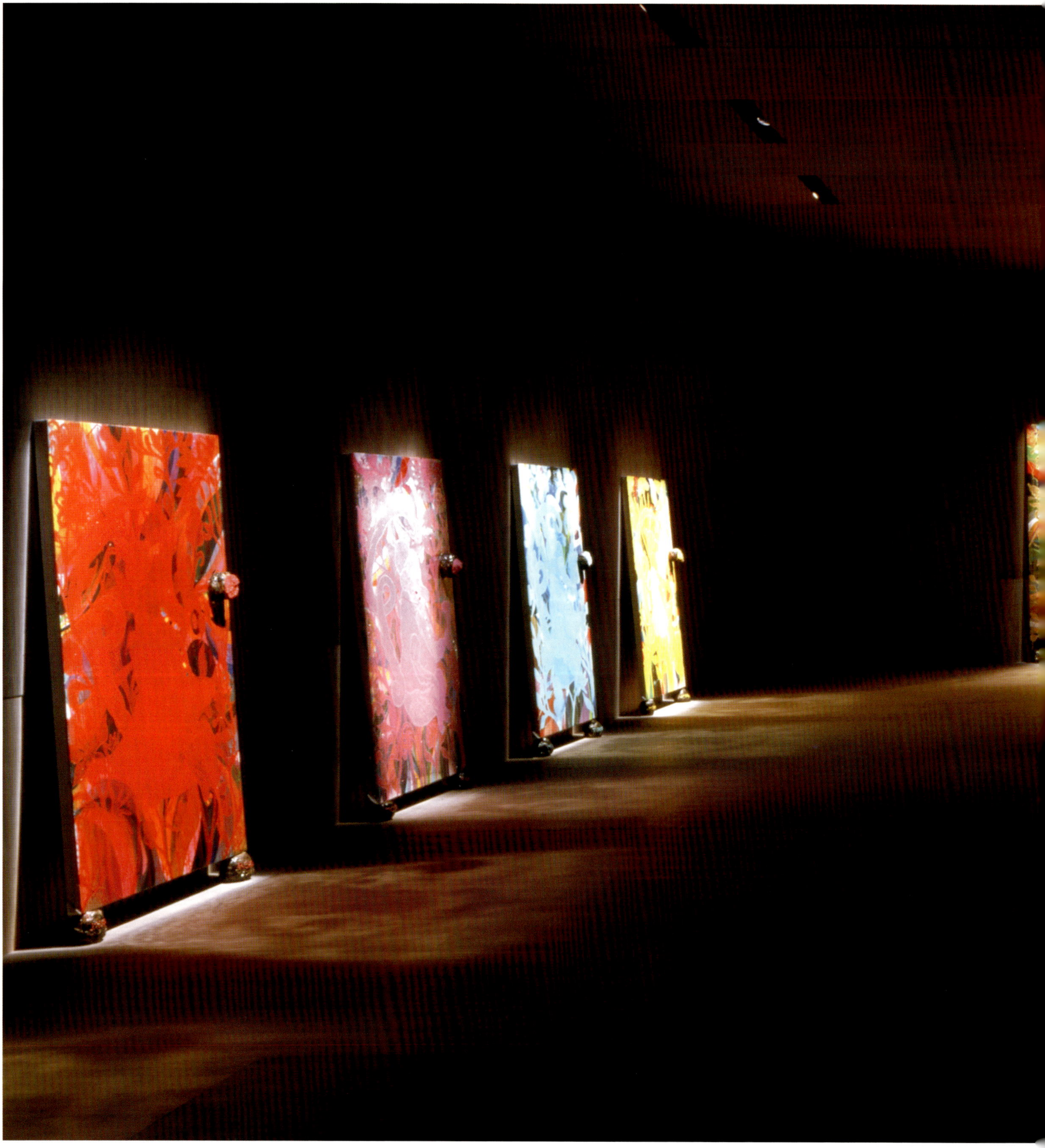

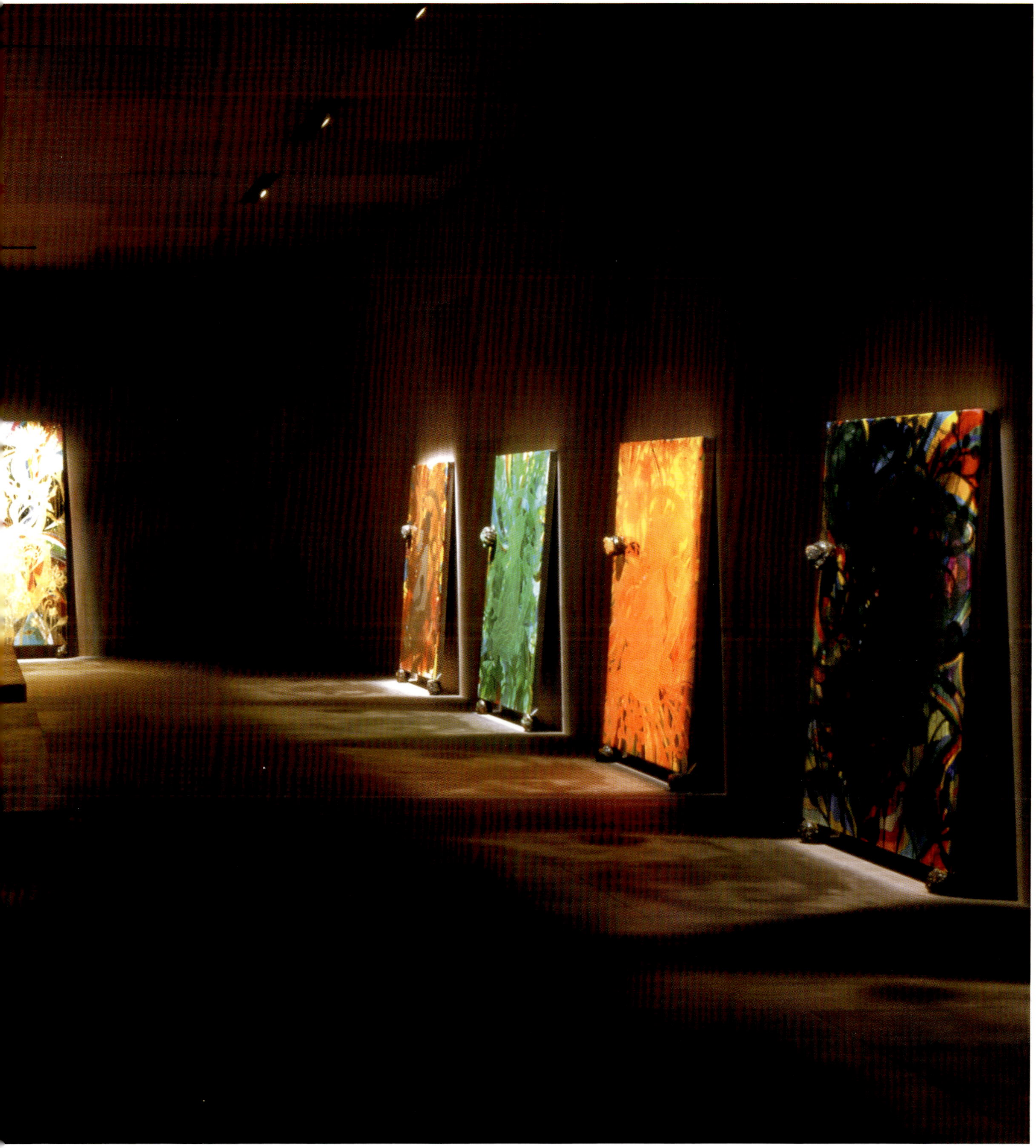

Previous spread *The Upper Room*, installation of 13 canvases at the Victoria Miro Gallery, 2002. The paintings are angled, in such a way as to cast reflected shadow images of each on to the floor.

Below *Mono Turquesa* 1999–2002. Oil paint, acrylic paint, pencil, polyester resin, glitter, map pins and elephant dung on linen with two elephant dung supports. 182.8 x 121.9 cm (72 x 48 in). Tate Gallery, London.

Right *Mono Marron* 1999–2002. Oil paint, ink, polyester resin, glitter, map pins and elephant dung on linen with two elephant dung supports. 182.8 x 121.9 cm (72 x 48 in). Tate Gallery, London.

Dr Susanna Paisley's essay in the catalogue to *The Upper Room* compares rhesus society with that of human beings. She also notes humans' different perception of monkeys. 'Monkeys do not share this special position within the Judeo-Christian tradition. The simple inclusion of monkeys in Veronese's painting of the *Last Supper* was one of the reasons why the Inquisition threatened to brand him a heretic, resulting in the giant masterpiece being renamed *A Feast in the House of Levi*.'

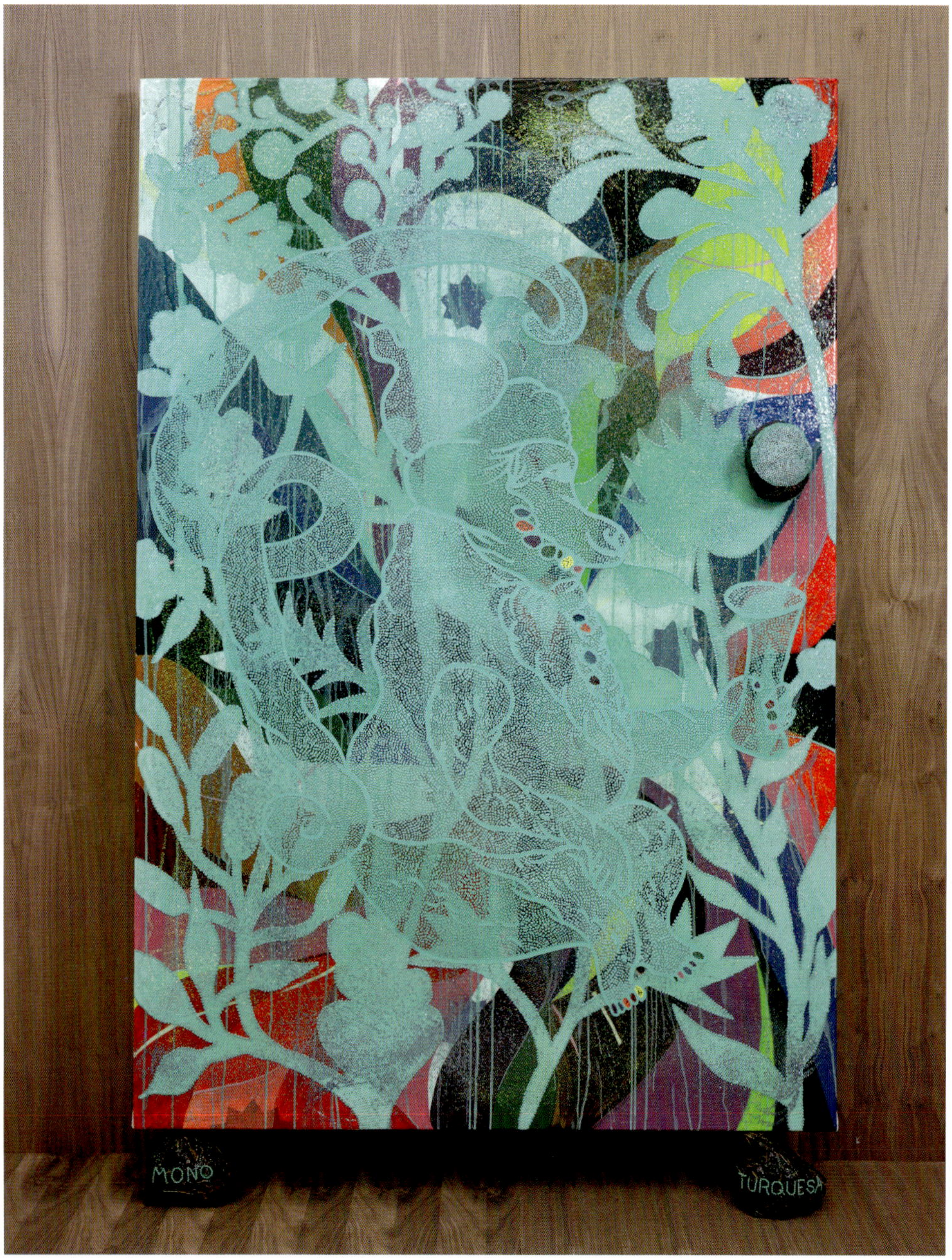

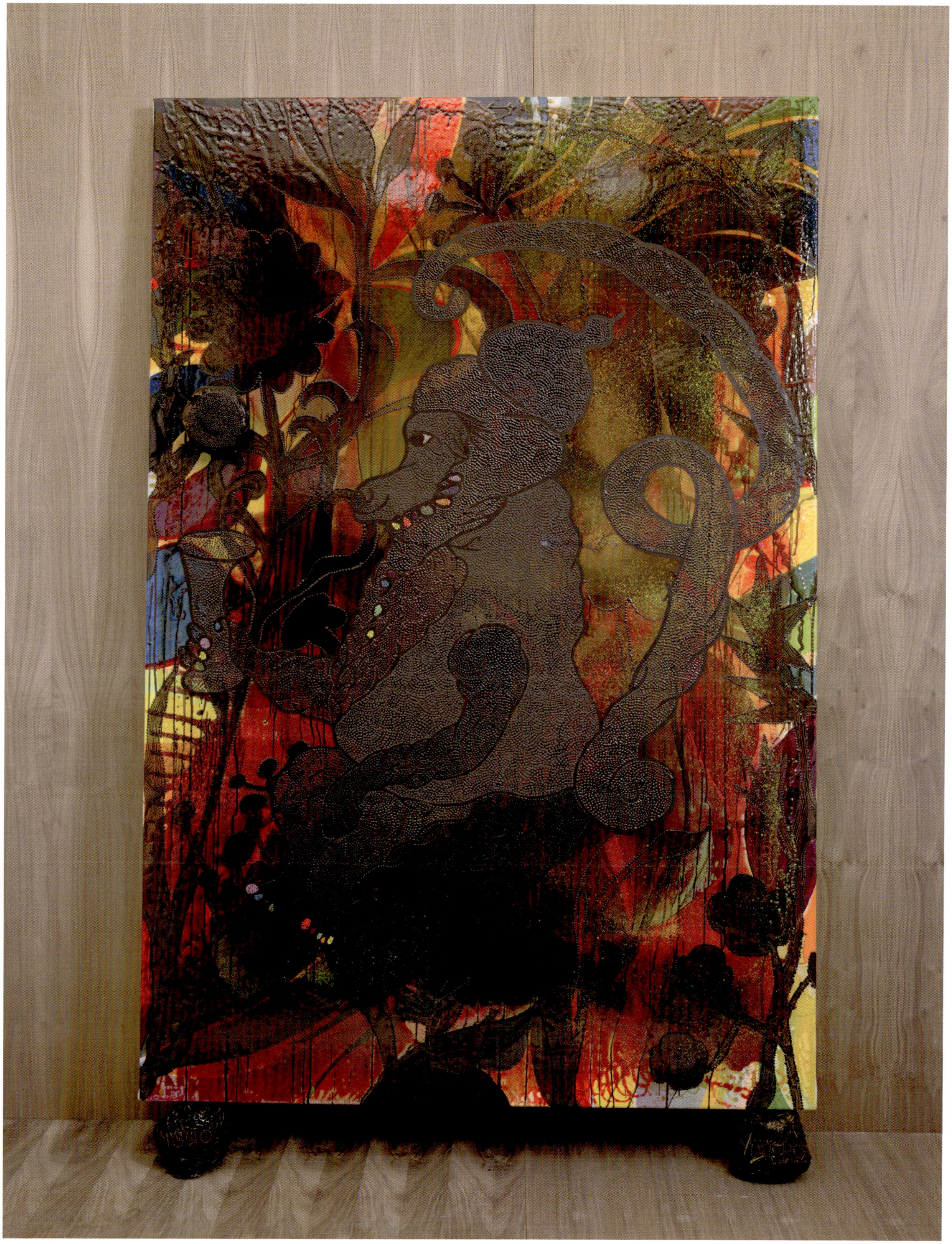

BRUCE ONOBRAKPEYA
NIGERIA

Below *Scavenging in a Lost Paradise*, 2006. Mixed media installation, 220 x 120 cm (86³⁄₅ x 47¼ in). Niger Delta Cultural Centre, Nigeria. Onobrakpeya articulates through his work concepts drawn from mythology, folklore, nature, religion and the environment. He is fascinated by the grouping of artefacts in shrines constructed by followers of traditional religions in various parts of Nigeria.

Right *Erheren* (*Ant Hill*), 1972 (detail). Plastograph, 61 x 45.8 cm (24 x 18 in). Niger Delta Cultural Center, Nigeria. Onobrakpeya pioneered a range of printing techniques which he originally discovered through a process of exploration. This led him to discover the possibilities inherent in a variety of techniques and materials.

Bruce Onobrakpeya's artistic influences are as varied as his knowledge and appreciation of Nigeria's many physical environments and the cultures of the people who live there. He is an Urhobo from the Niger Delta, but he spent his childhood in Benin – the famous sixteenth/seventeenth century cast brass 'plaques' (the so-called Benin Bronzes) of the ancient kingdom of Benin are often referenced in his work. Onobrakpeya then studied in the northern Nigerian city of Zaria, giving him an insight into the arts of the Hausa and Fulani people. Finally, his time in Lagos helped to familiarize him with Yoruba culture, in particular the various methods employed by the Yoruba in printing the indigo-dyed cloth *adire.*

Onobrakpeya is an artistic inventor and experimenter, constantly on the lookout for new technologies and techniques, particularly in printmaking. He is also a passionate defender of the natural environment, whether under attack from the desertification in the north or from the indiscriminate exploitation of oil and other natural resources, particularly in his homeland in the Niger Delta. This sets up a dynamic tension and potential source of conflict in his work.

Using a razor blade or a knife, I carved out my name on a tree thorn which I then inked and pressed onto my (school) readers and notebooks.

Born in 1932 in Agbarha-Otor, Delta State, Onobrakpeya is among the most successful artists to have emerged in West Africa during the twentieth century. In the late 1950s and early 1960s, he was a prominent member of the group of young artists (including Uche Okeke and Demas Nwoko) popularly known as the Zaria rebels at the College of Arts, Science and Technology, later the Ahmadu Bello University. They developed the art form, born out of local aesthetics but merged with appropriate Western technologies, which became known as Natural Synthesis and which Okeke described as 'the fertile fusion of the best in the old and the new cultures'.

Onobrakpeya initially studied painting, but he later developed a strong interest in printmaking, including conventional methodologies such as woodcut, linocut and etching. In due course he invented techniques of his own, including the bronzed lino relief, the plastograph and the plastocast relief.

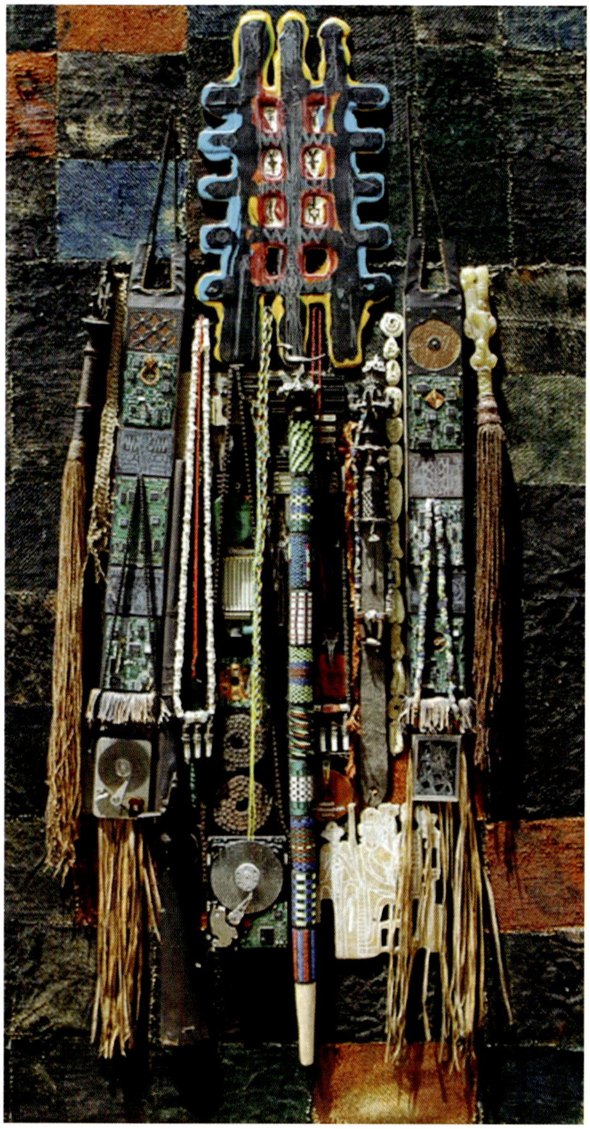

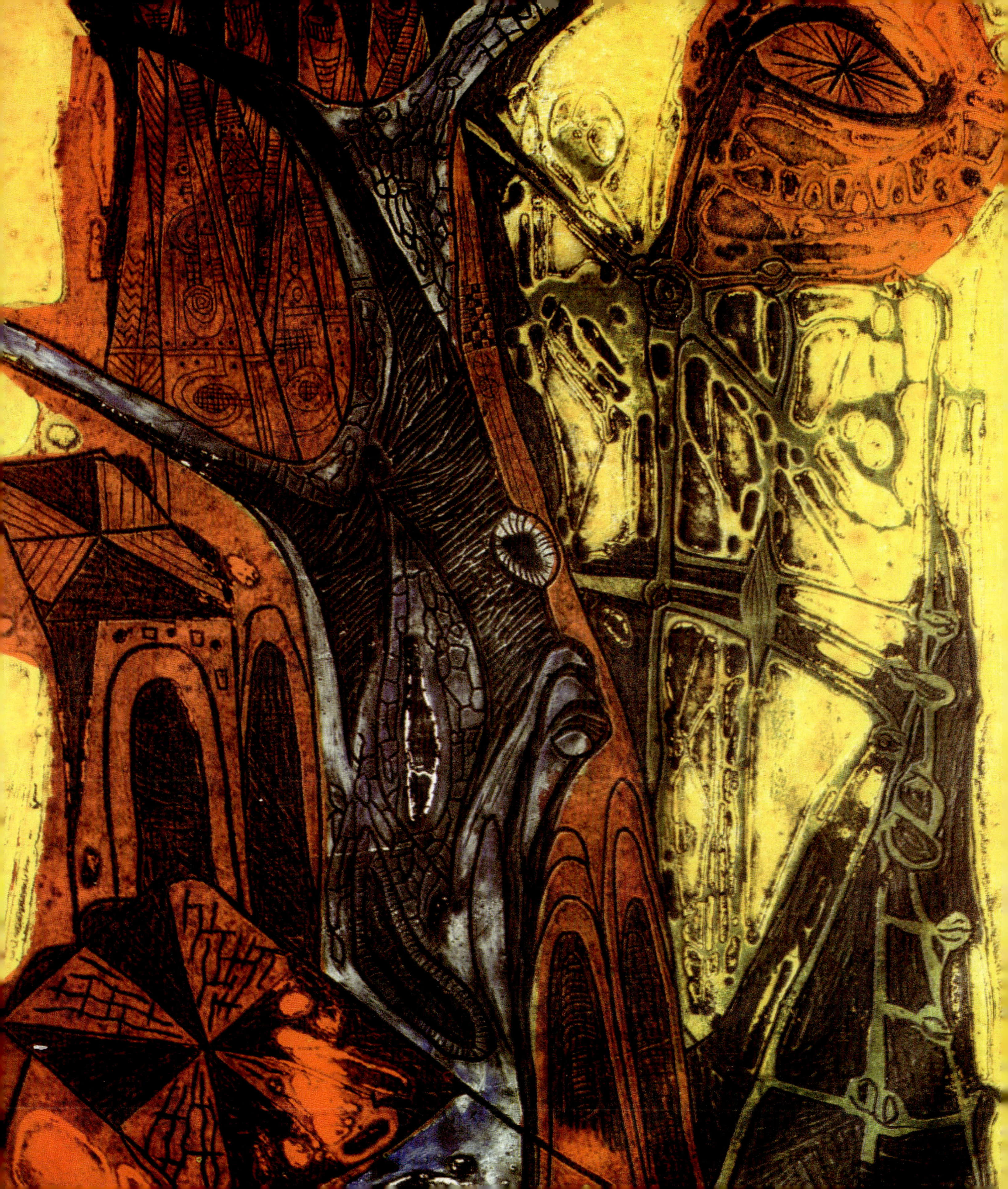

Below *Erheren* (*Ant Hill*), 1972 (full image).

Right *Environmental Regeneration*, 2005 (detail). Mixed media installation, 153 x 196 cm (60¼ x 77⅙ in). Niger Delta Cultural Centre, Nigeria.
This mixed-media work comprises discarded computer parts, bones, beads, small etching plates and incised metal panels arranged on perpendicular jute-fibre strips to suggest a formal connection with the numerous narrow-strip weaving traditions of Nigeria in particular, and of West Africa in general. The work draws attention to the erosion of culture, but also to the regenerative powers of ancient traditions.

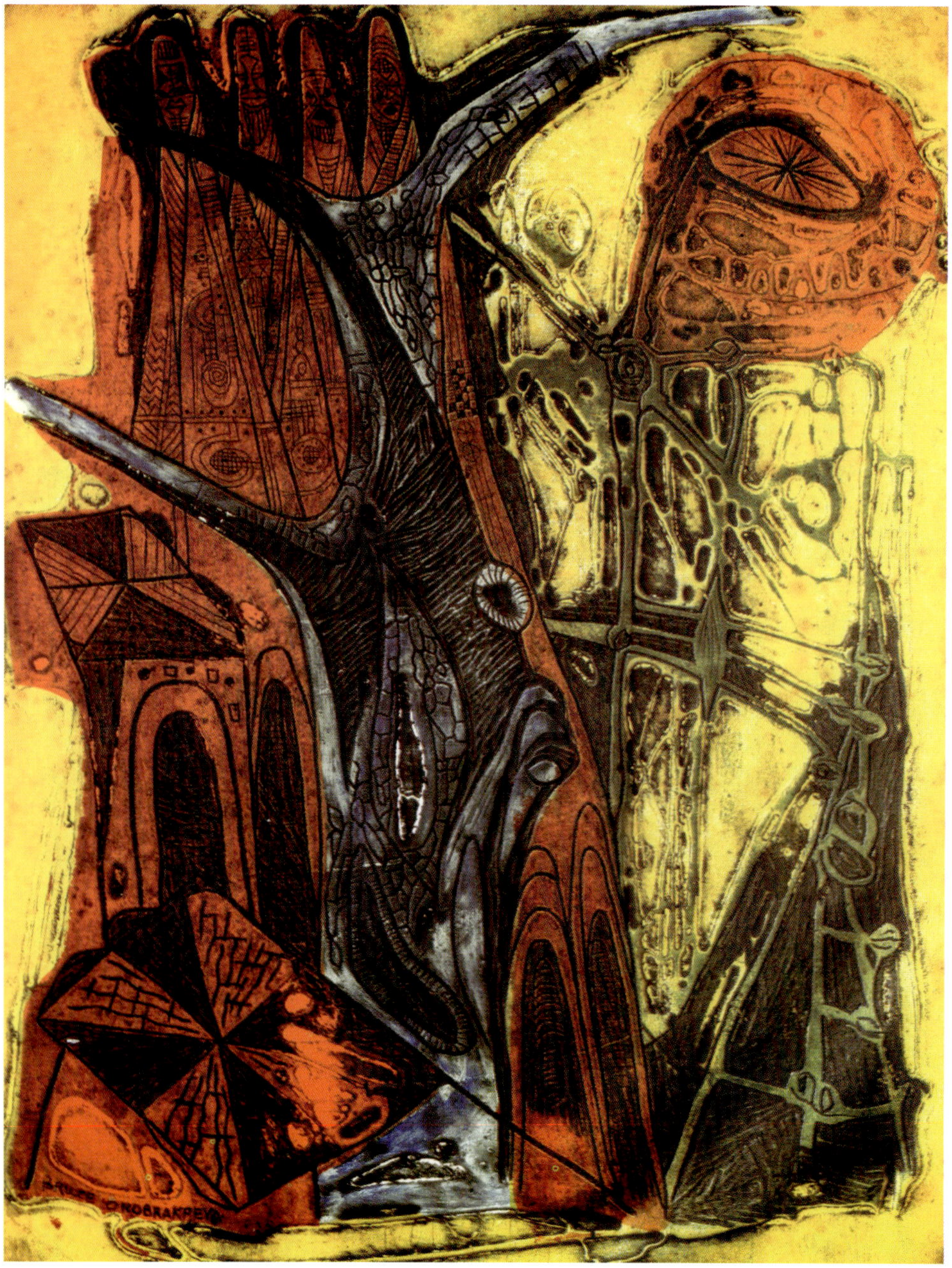

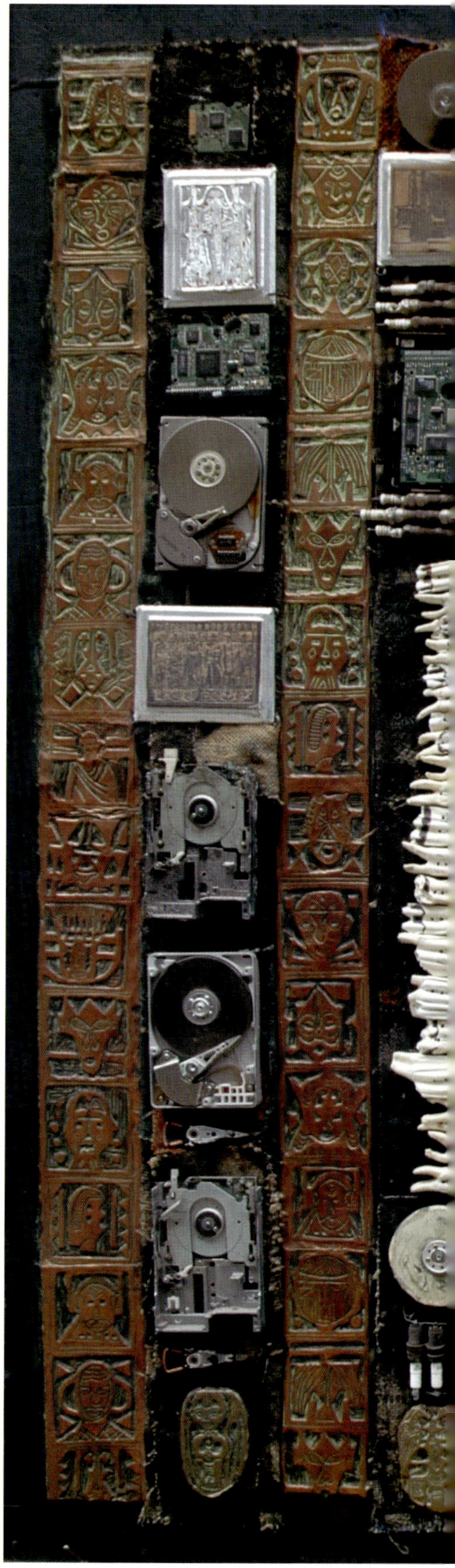

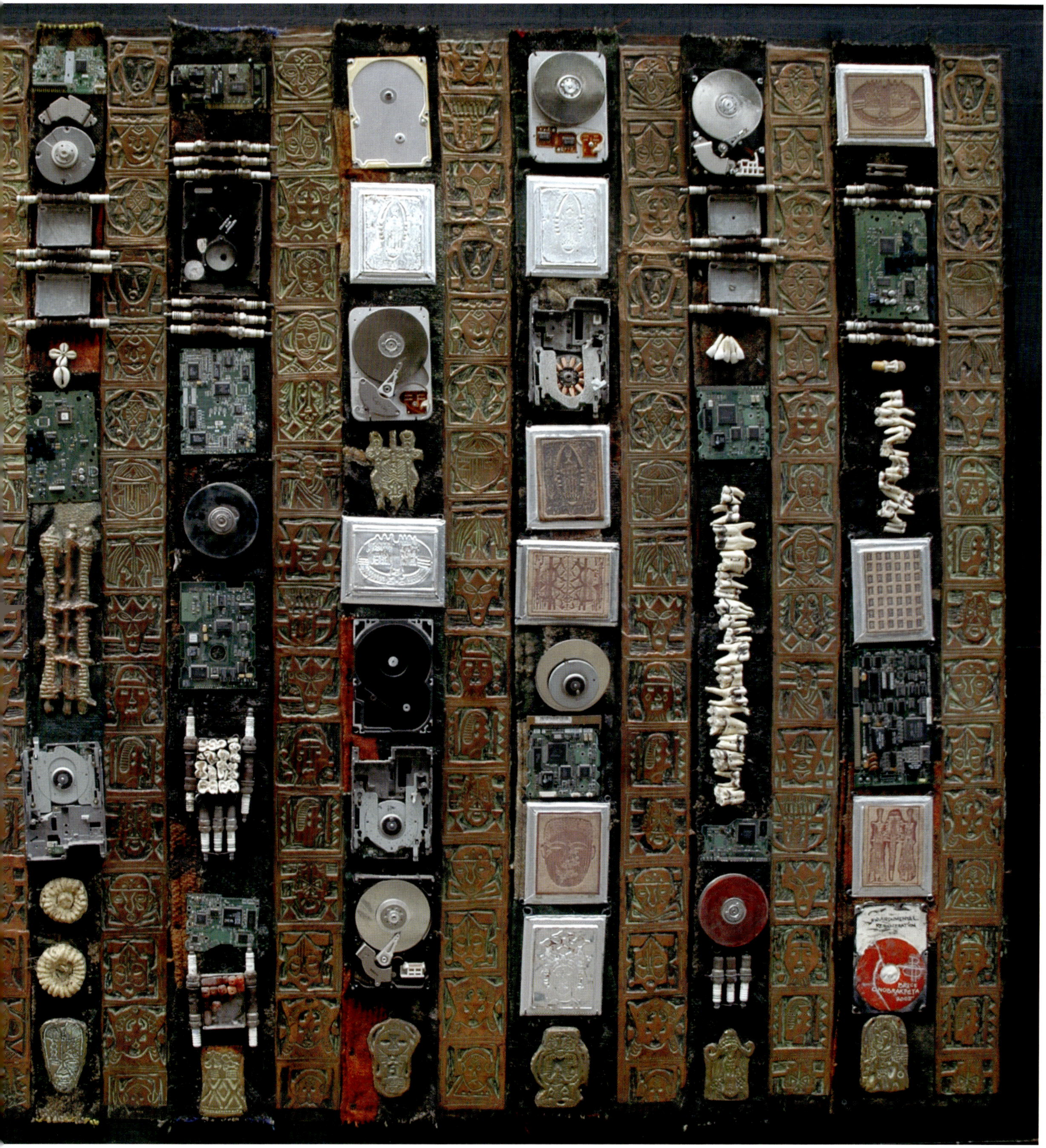

'The burning crescent dunes of the desert are forcing their way through lush grass and giant trees towards the surf-ridden sand shores of the Atlantic as if to become one and the same with their kinsfolk.'
Bruce Onobrakpeya

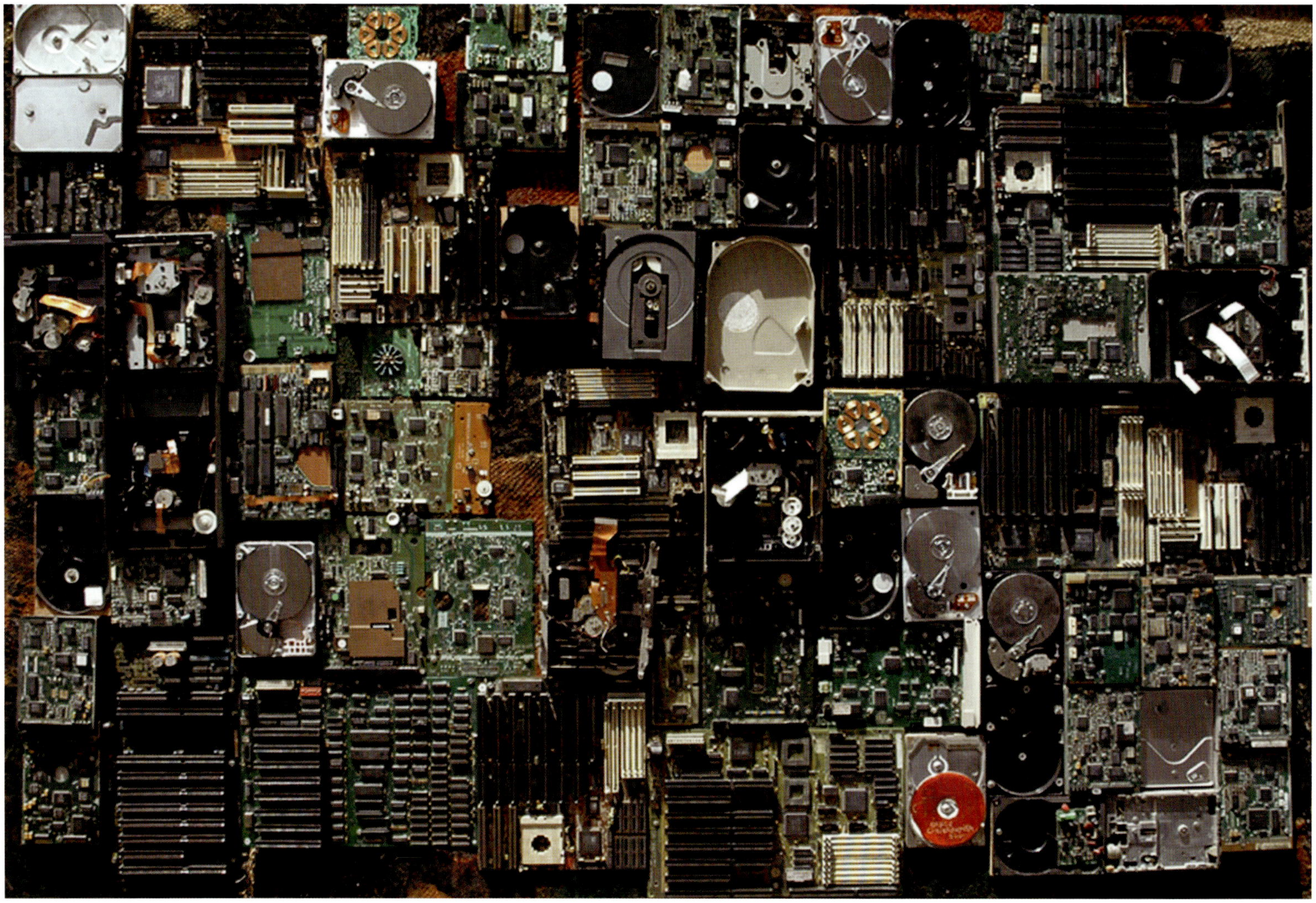

Left *Aerial Landscape*, 2006. Mixed media, 127 x 180 cm (50 x 70⁴⁄₅ in). Niger Delta Cultural Centre, Nigeria. Onobrakpeya draws comparisons between the intricacies of Yoruba beadwork, the complexities of computer circuitry and the patterns of human agency revealed by aerial photography.

Below *Totems of the Delta*, 2004. Copper foil relief, 153 x 209 cm (60¼ x 82¼ in). Niger Delta Cultural Centre, Nigeria.

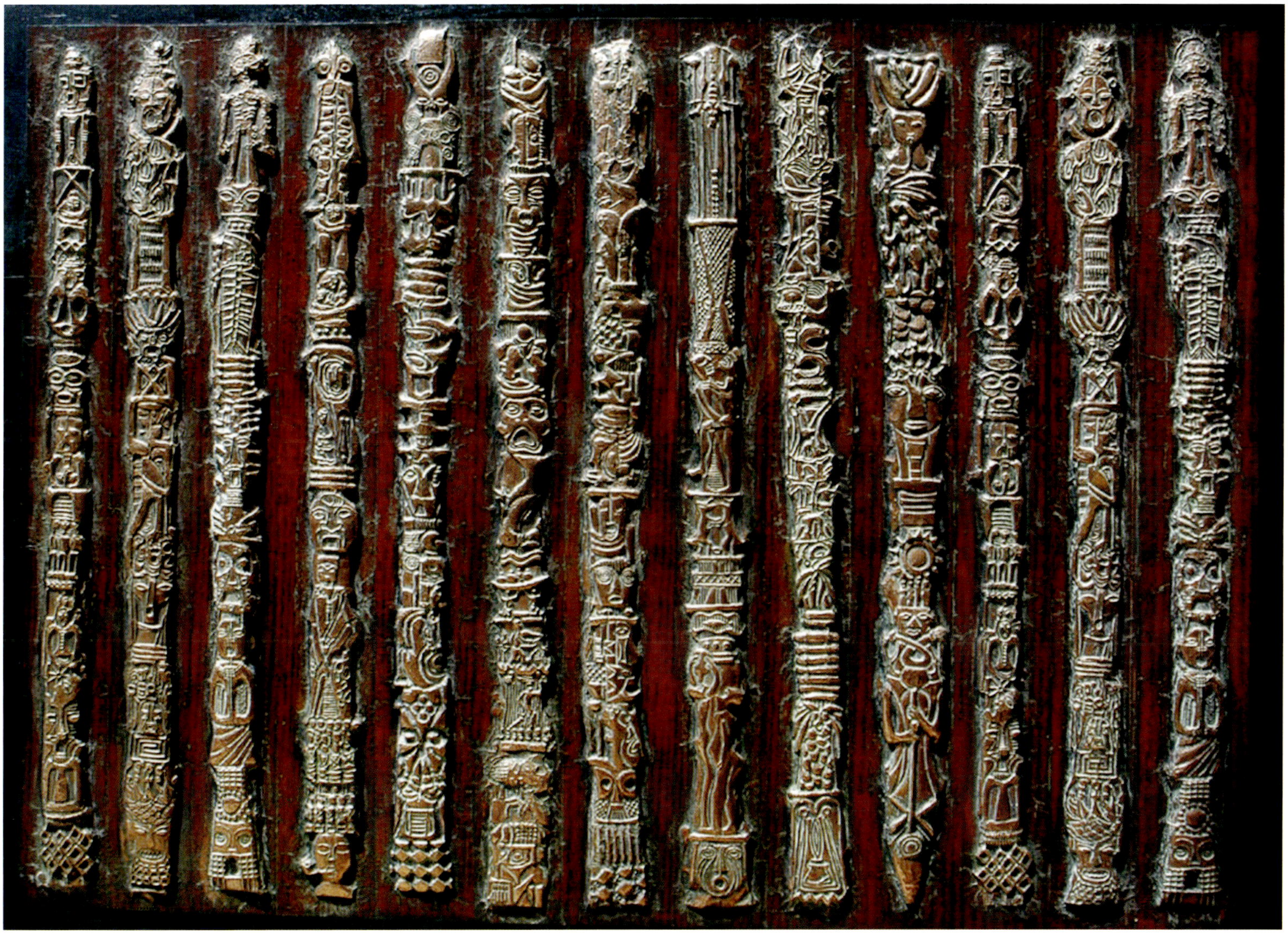

OWUSU-ANKOMAH
GHANA/GERMANY

Below *Heavenly Messenger*, 1997. Acrylic on sailcloth, 180 x 150cm (64½ x 58½ in). ARTCO Gallery, Herzogenrath, Germany.
'I see movement as an important principle of life, an authentic human principle. Life is in constant motion, from the cradle of the human race and culture in Africa up to modern times.'

Right *Free*, 2006. Acrylic on canvas, 150 x 200 cm (59 x 78¾ in). Collection of the artist.
'The figure in *Free* is caught in a moment of transcendence. Close observation might remind the viewer of two monumental sculptures, one found on each of the American continents: the Statue of Liberty in New York, and that of Christ the Redeemer in Rio de Janeiro.'

Owusu-Ankomah was born in Sekondi, Ghana in 1956, a year before independence from British colonial rule. He studied at the Ghanatta College of Art in Accra before moving to Bremen, Germany in 1986, where he now lives and works.

His paintings depict a spiritual world, without shadows, occupied by people and symbols. The way in which people and symbols co-exist in his paintings has moved through several distinct phases that reflect Owusu-Ankomah's own spiritual journey. His early work drew heavily on the ancient traditions of masquerade and rock painting in Africa; then his figures seemed to shed their masks and body painting to become boldly, unashamedly visible. In his most recent works his figures, though still bold, naked and powerful, are painted with complex symbols which make them almost invisible against a backdrop of the same symbols.

Owusu-Ankomah is profoundly influenced by the works of Michelangelo, 'This unbound energy, abounding with power, an exploding human adventure', and also by the philosophy of his own Akan-speaking peoples of Ghana. Owusu-Ankomah invests his figures with the almost divine energy of Michelangelo, then paints their bodies with the collective wisdom of the Akan people in the form of *adinkra* symbols, each of which represents a particular concept or proverb.

Yet he leavens the traditional lexicon of *adinkra* with Chinese calligraphy and well-known popular logos, as well as with symbols of his own invention. In his painting *Free* (2007), one of a series to mark the bicentenary of the abolition of the Atlantic slave trade, Owusu-Ankomah has created a symbol on the chest of the central figure which he describes as, 'An emanation from his inmost being which cries out "I am open, talk to me! My heart is receptive, I am full of love!" To me this is the message that most needs to be spread around these days, for with it we can change the world.'

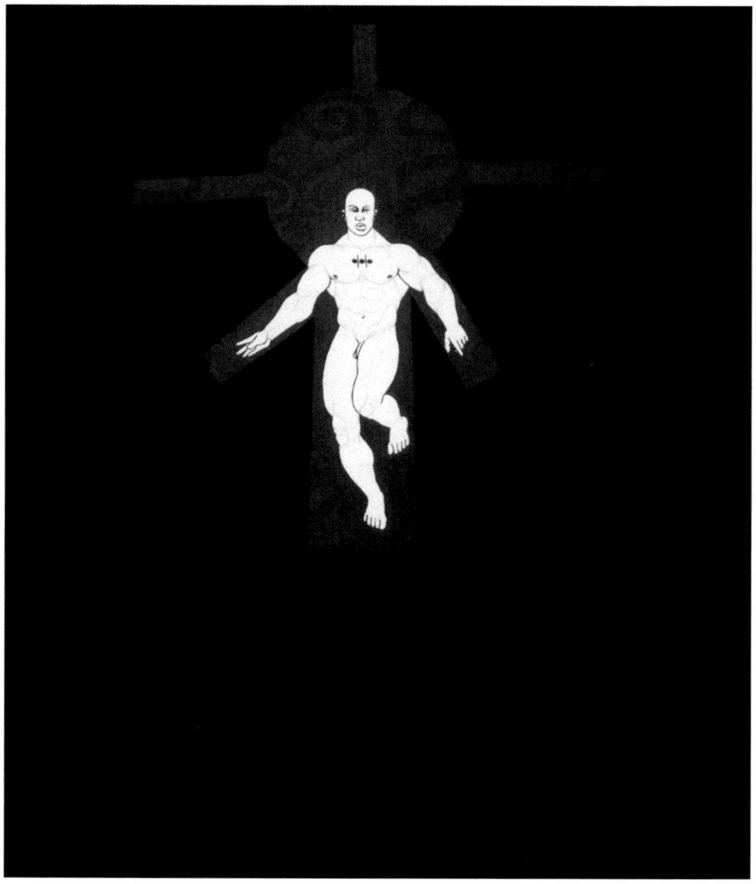

'I'm an artist who paints for humankind and who just happens to come from Africa.'
Owusu-Ankomah

Below *Future*, 2006. Acrylic on canvas, 150 x 200 cm (59 x 78¾ in). Private collection.
'The Sankofa symbol occurs twice in this painting, first as the bird looking back over its shoulder, and then, in its other form, above the star, as the sign to which the figure points. The meaning of this sign is crucial – we need to remember the past in order to live consciously in the present and to ensure a positive future.'

Right *Somehow Different*, 1992. Oil on nettle fabric, 150 x 200cm (58½ x 78 in). ARTCO Gallery, Herzogenrath, Germany.
The picture was painted as a reaction to the xenophobic attacks taking place in Germany at the time.

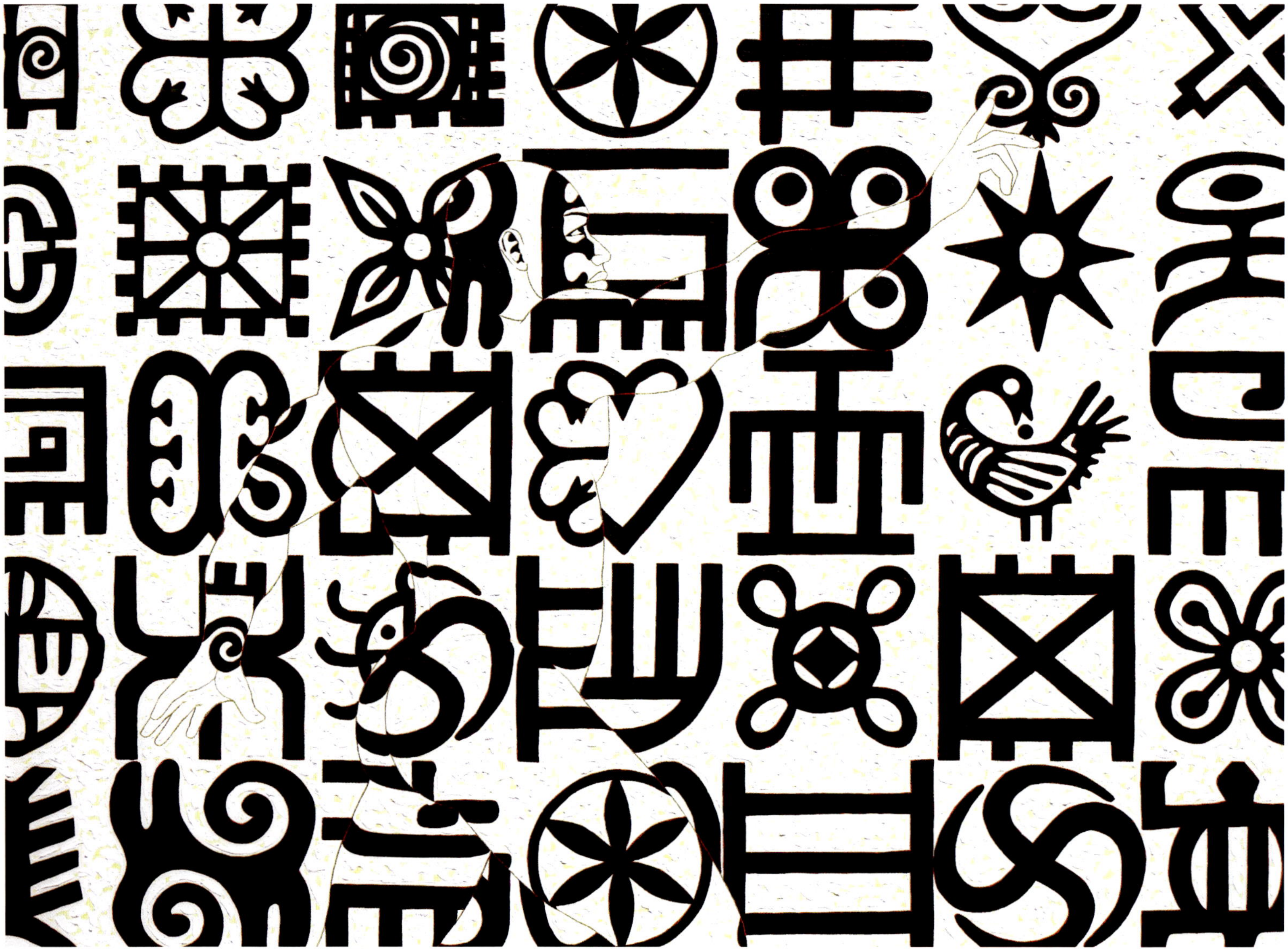

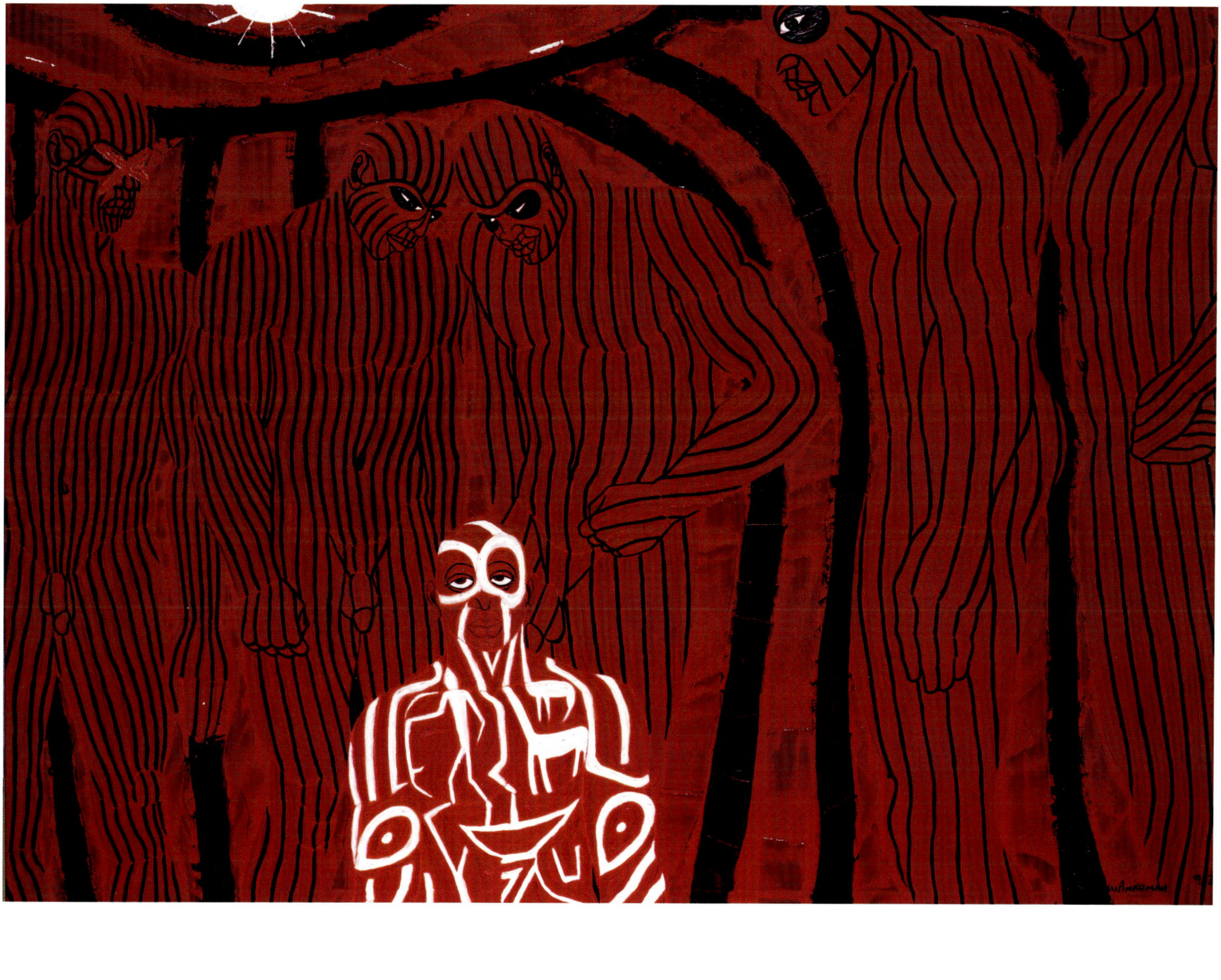

Right *Red Dancer*, 1992. Oil on nettle fabric, 126 x 160cm (49 x 62½ in). ARTCO Gallery, Herzogenrath, Germany. The two masked figures feel their way forward as if through a mystical red mist of emotions.

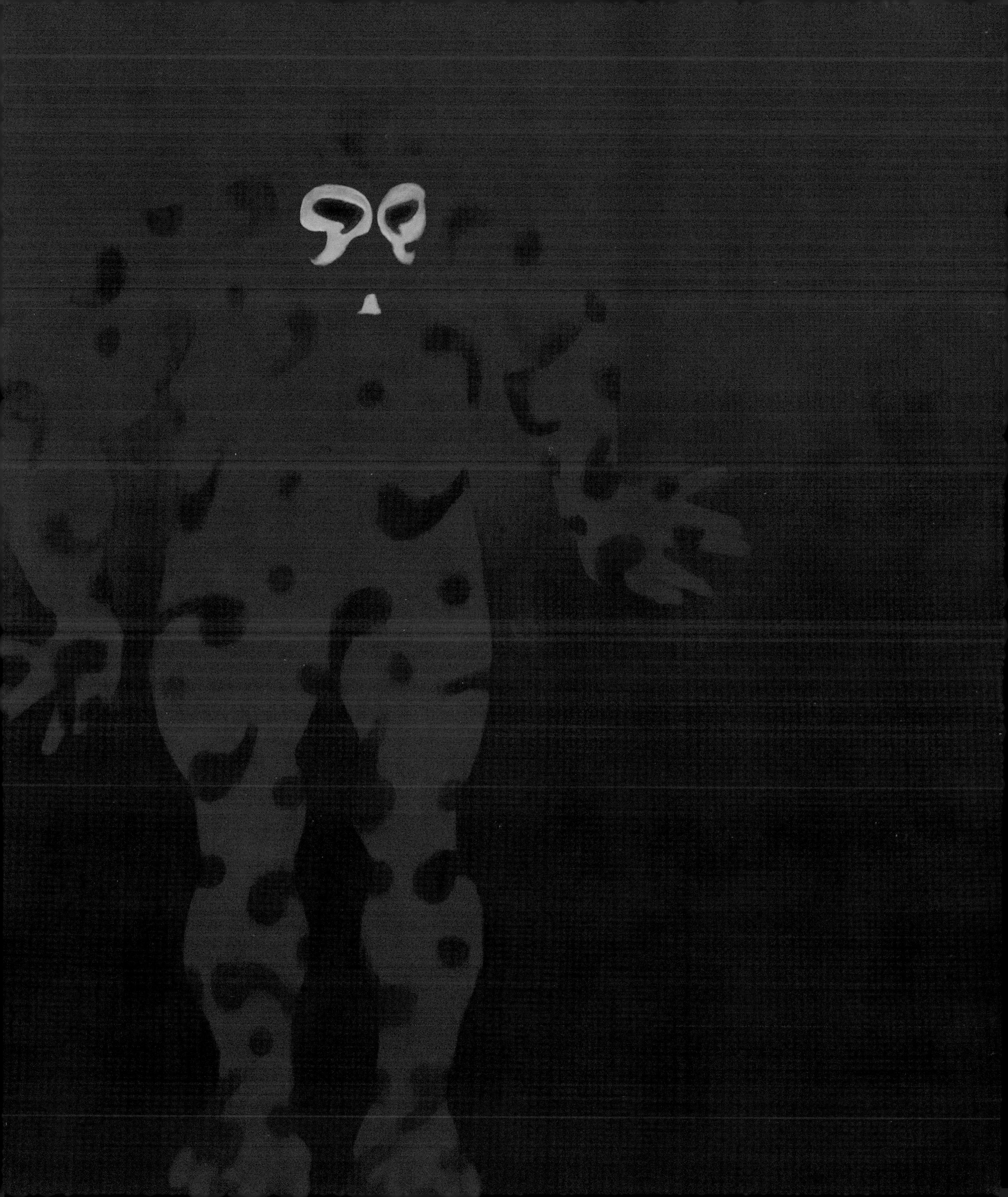

EUGENE PALMER
JAMAICA/UK

Below *In the Garden*, 1992 (part of diptych). Oil on canvas, 168 x 128 cm (66⅙ x 50½ in). Collection of the artist.

Right *Mr Palmer Senior*, 2003. Oil on canvas, 192 x 136 cm (75⅗ x 53½ in). Collection of the artist. Although Palmer's earlier work used photographs (often of members of his family) as a source to begin the composition of a painting, from the mid-1990s he began much more directly to reference photography. The photos were still of his family, but were rendered in a monochromatic, photorealist style of portraiture, which questioned notions of sameness, identity and representation.

Palmer's paintings, like their subjects, are dignified, restrained and cerebral. The people in his paintings do not have to ask questions by opening their mouths; likewise, the colours and tones of his paintings subtly question perceptions of light and dark, shadow and shade.

I need to and want to participate in the collective memory of slavery to fill out the experience of what it is to be black. 'Blackness' can be perceived in very narrow and impoverished terms, but it isn't like that.

Palmer was born in Kingston, Jamaica in 1955 and came to the UK with his family in 1966. Photographs of members of his family are often the starting point for his paintings; sometimes he paints what appears to be the 'same' portrait many times, though in fact each painting is completely different from the next. This is one of the ways in which Palmer questions notions of identity, of personal and cultural stereotyping.

In recent years my practice has involved me in a continuous examination of modes of representation related to cultural history and cultural identity. I am interested in the ways in which identity can be constructed.

Palmer studied at Wimbledon School of Art and at Goldsmiths College, London. He has had numerous solo exhibitions, including those at the Norwich Gallery (1993), the Threshold Gallery, Bath (2000), Victoria Street, Bristol (2001–2) and the Wolsey Art Gallery, Ipswich (2004). He is a member of the London Group.

'Painting for me is like exploration or little journeys, finding out what it feels like to create sensation. I think it's also a process of demystification. It's like passive aggression, being assertive, without shouting.'
Eugene Palmer

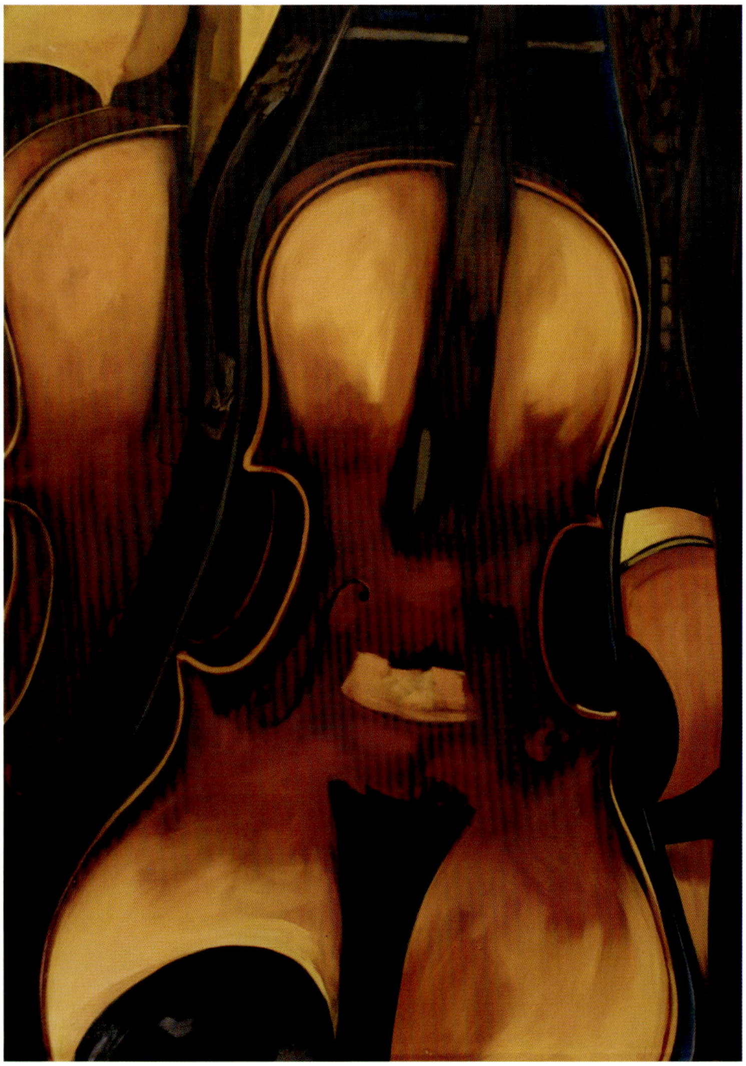

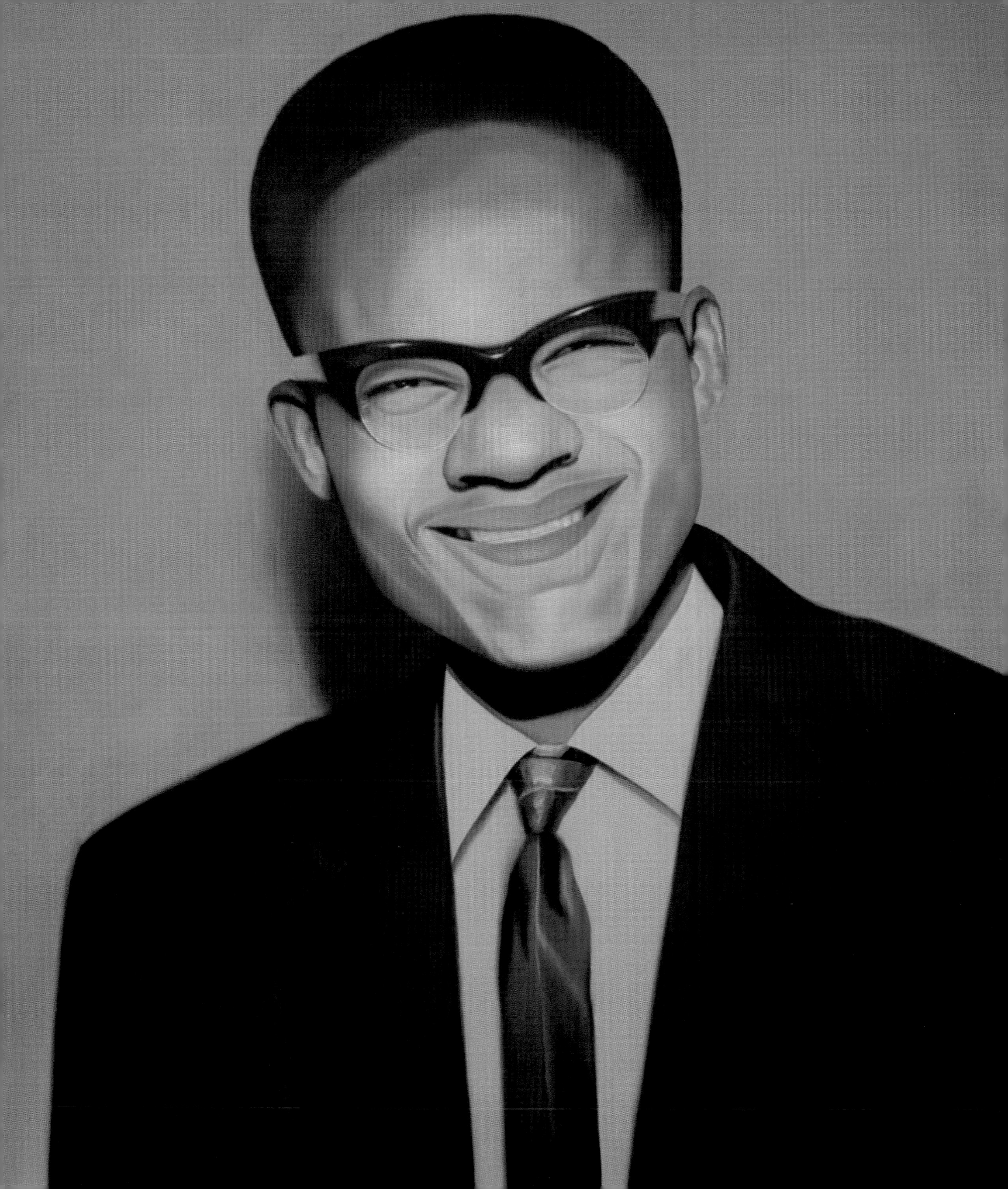

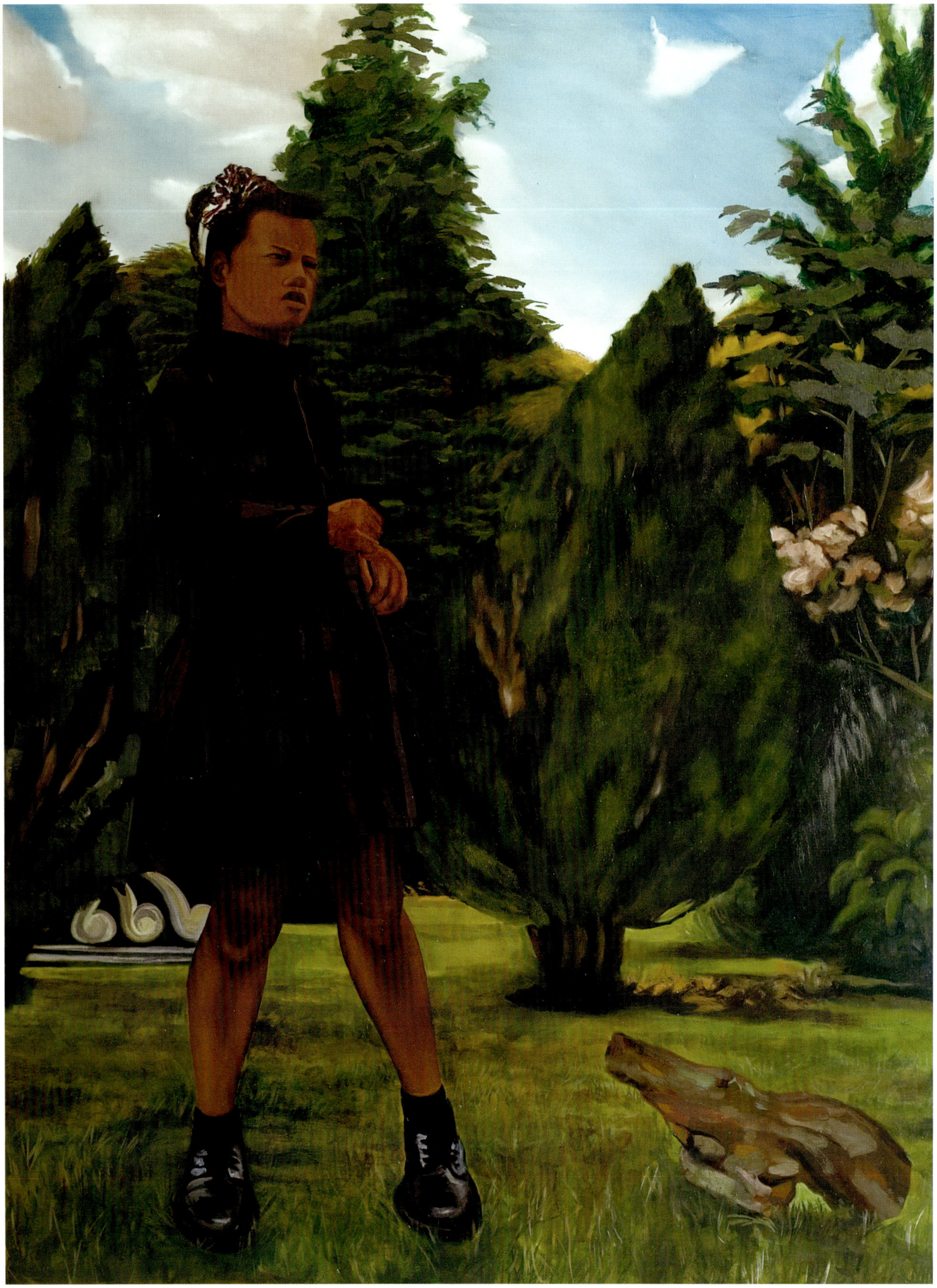

Left *Duppy Shadow*, 1993. Oil on canvas 213 x 152 cm (83 x 59¼ in). Wolverhampton Art Gallery, Wolverhampton, UK.
Duppy is a Jamaican patois term for 'ghost' or 'spirit'. The girl in the painting seems like a lost spirit, unsure of herself and her identity in the alien landscape that surrounds her. Yet she faces it with courage and dignity.

Below *In the Garden Alone*, 1992. Oil on canvas, 128 x 174 cm (50½ x 68½ in). Collection of the artist.
'My reference to the Western tradition is to do with quotes of style, like the "old masters" style. It is meant to recede into the background and to become a support. The whole tradition becomes a platform for the black subject which it can never usurp. Instead it is more in service to it, which is much more the way I feel.'

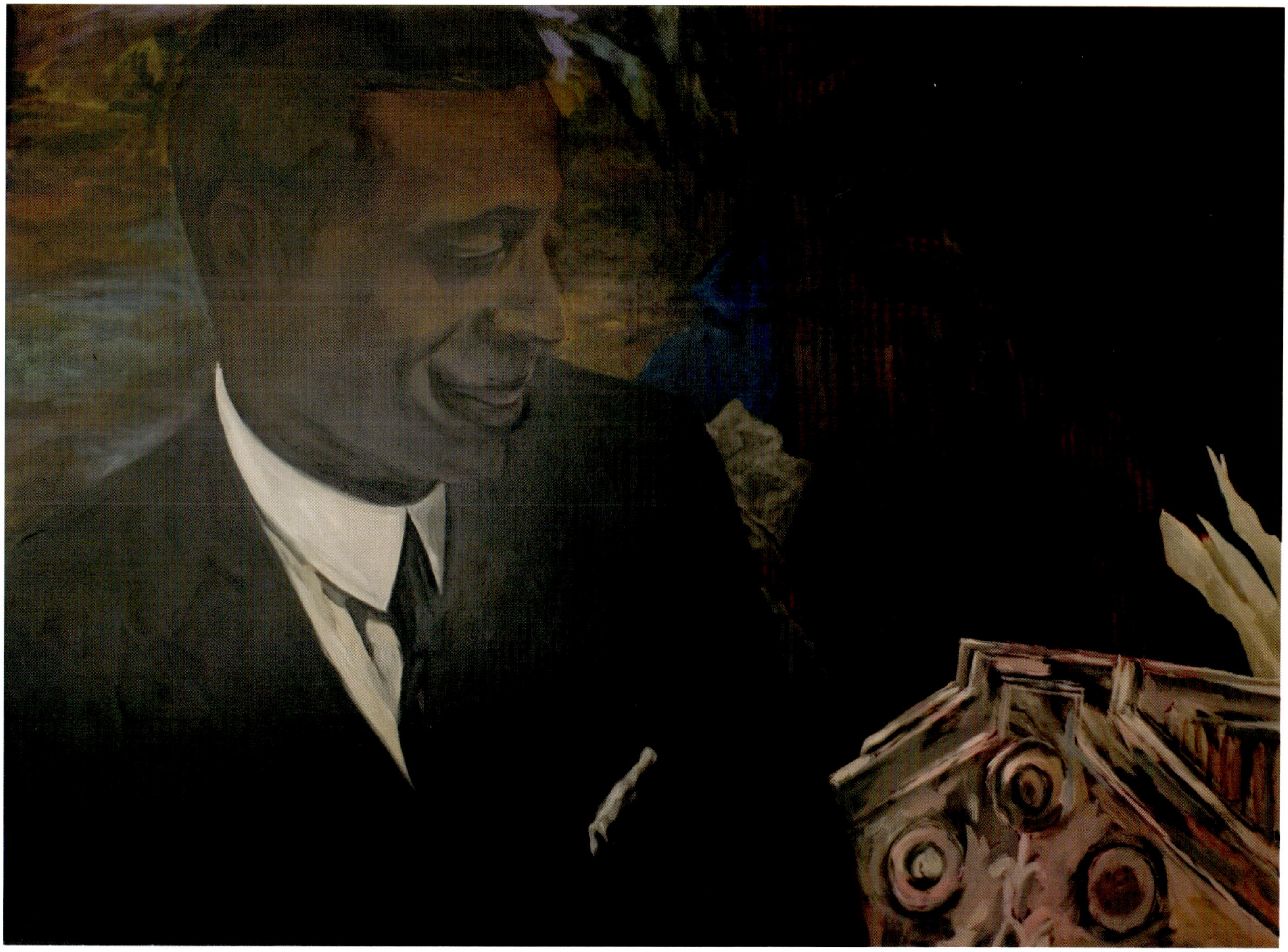

MARTA MARÍA PÉREZ BRAVO
CUBA

Below *Quiero pro techo el cielo* (*I Wish I Had the Sky as a Ceiling*), 1995. B&W photographic print, 100 x 80cm (39⅖ x 31½ in). Private collection.
'Black and white photography is capable of giving the whole an oneiric feeling, of producing associations with apparitions and other aspects that do not belong to a concrete reality.'

Right *Ebbo de Pensamiento* (*Sacrifice of Thought*), 1997. B&W photographic print, 100 x 80cm (39⅖ x 31½ in). Private collection.
'The aesthetics of sacred and cult objects that are made reference to can be extremely appealing in terms of colour; yet this appeal often distracts from, or dilutes, the true meaning of the objects. But that, the meaning, is precisely what I am interested in: I want to bring out the very essence of the object I create, without adulteration.'

Pérez Bravo's art is one of devotion. She uses her body as a living shrine to her faith in Santería, an Afro-Cuban syncretic religion that has its roots in beliefs brought to the Caribbean island by enslaved Yoruba people from Benin and Nigeria during the Atlantic slave trade. The way of life, the religion, the system of beliefs known as *Ifa* – with its pantheon of 256 gods (*orisha*) – is still widely practised among the Yoruba. Slave owners tried to remove all traces of it, and when they failed to do so it was demonized in the European/Western imagination. Yet it is a testament to its resilience and to the bravery of all its adherents down the centuries that, in its different forms, *Ifa* is a vital and growing religion today in many parts of the world.

Marta María Pérez Bravo was born in Havana, Cuba in 1959. She studied at the Instituto Superior de Arte, Havana, then at the San Alejandro Academy of Fine Arts, from which she graduated in 1979. In the 1980s she began a series of photographs each of which is a carefully set up symbolic scenario representing a particular aspect or facet of her faith. Since then she has had more than 50 solo exhibitions around the world. Although the colours of some of the materials and objects she uses in these scenes are important to her and her faith, the photographs themselves are always in black and white.

'I choose to use black and white photography for my work because it is the aesthetic resource which comes closest to documentation. Paradoxically, however, every religious object I use is made of specific materials and colours, although the observer can only distinguish shades of grey. In terms of concept, the private ritual is also part of the work – the use of colours is part of the meaning. It is a kind of moral compromise with the subject.'
Marta Maria Pérez Bravo

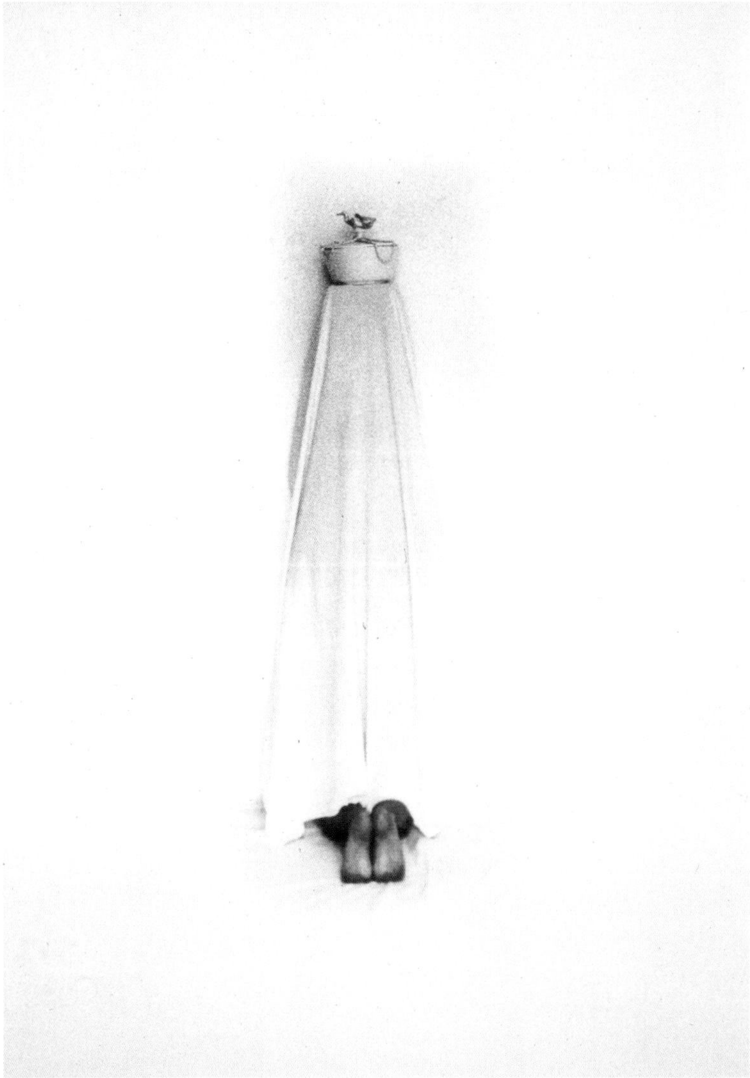

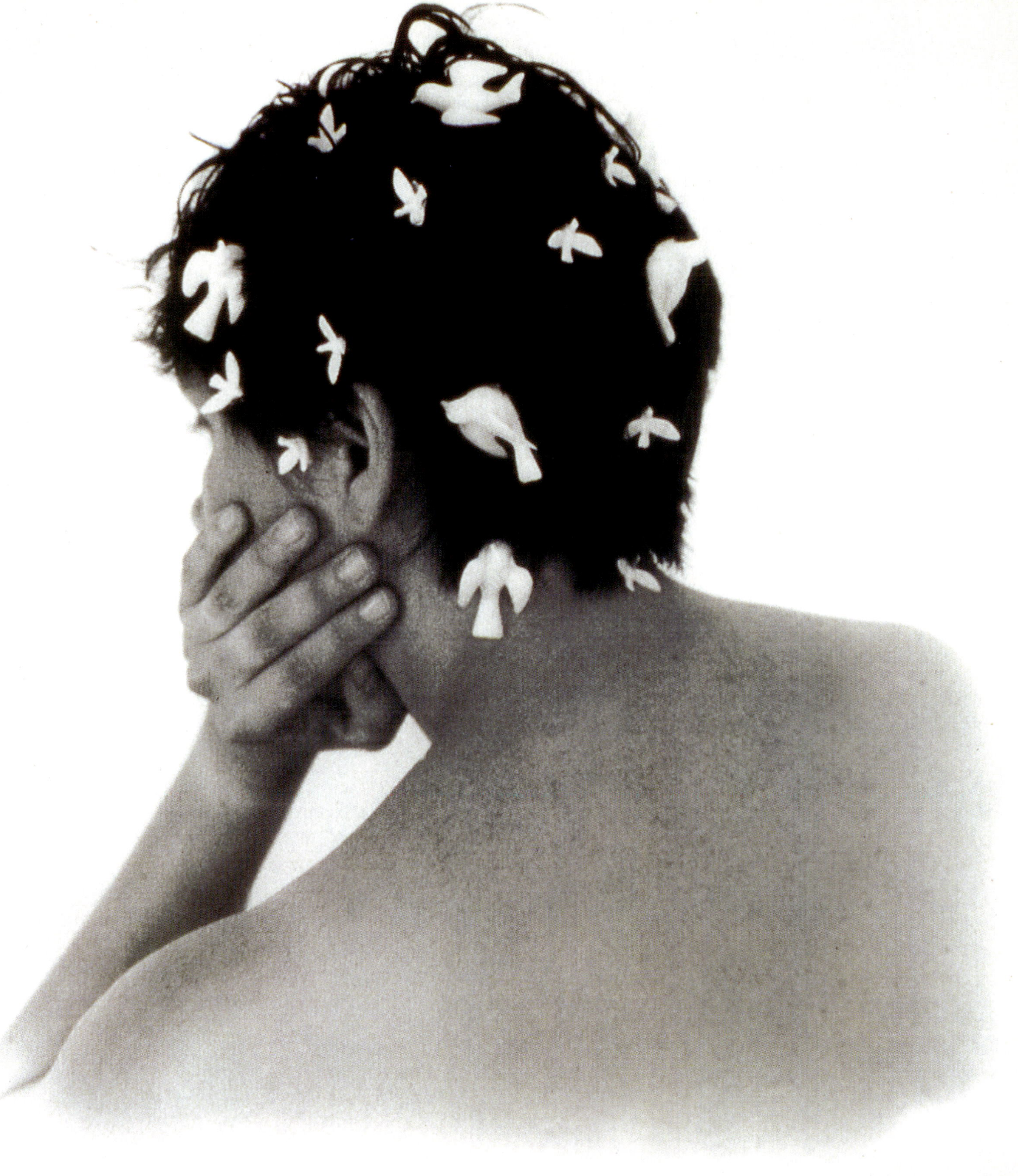

Below left *Todo lo tengo, todo me falta* (*All I Have, All I Need*), 1997. B&W photographic print, 150 x 122 cm (59 x 48 in). Private collection.
White symbolizes the god of purity and creativity, Obatala; he is also the god of the head where, in Yoruba belief, the soul resides.

Below right *Maleficio* (*Curse*), 1992. B&W photographic print, 150 x 122 cm (59 x 48 in). Private collection.

Right *Tiene la llave del destino (I Hold the Key of Destiny)*, 1992. B&W photographic print, 150 x 122 cm (59 x 48 in). Private collection.
'I hold the key of destiny', which will release all from the shackles that bind them.

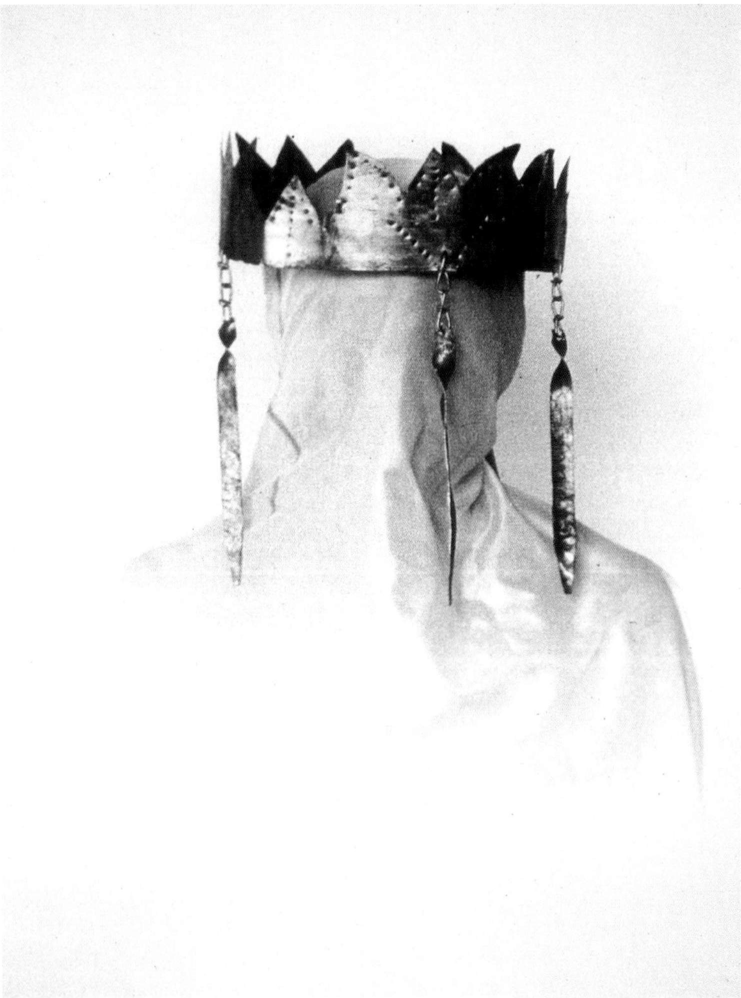

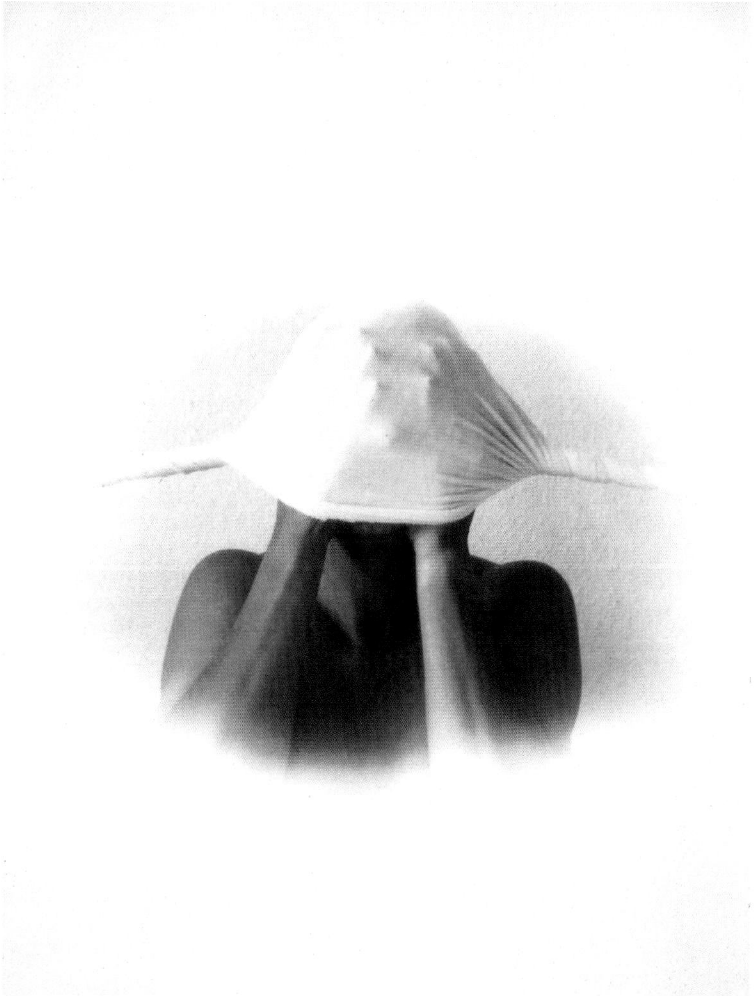

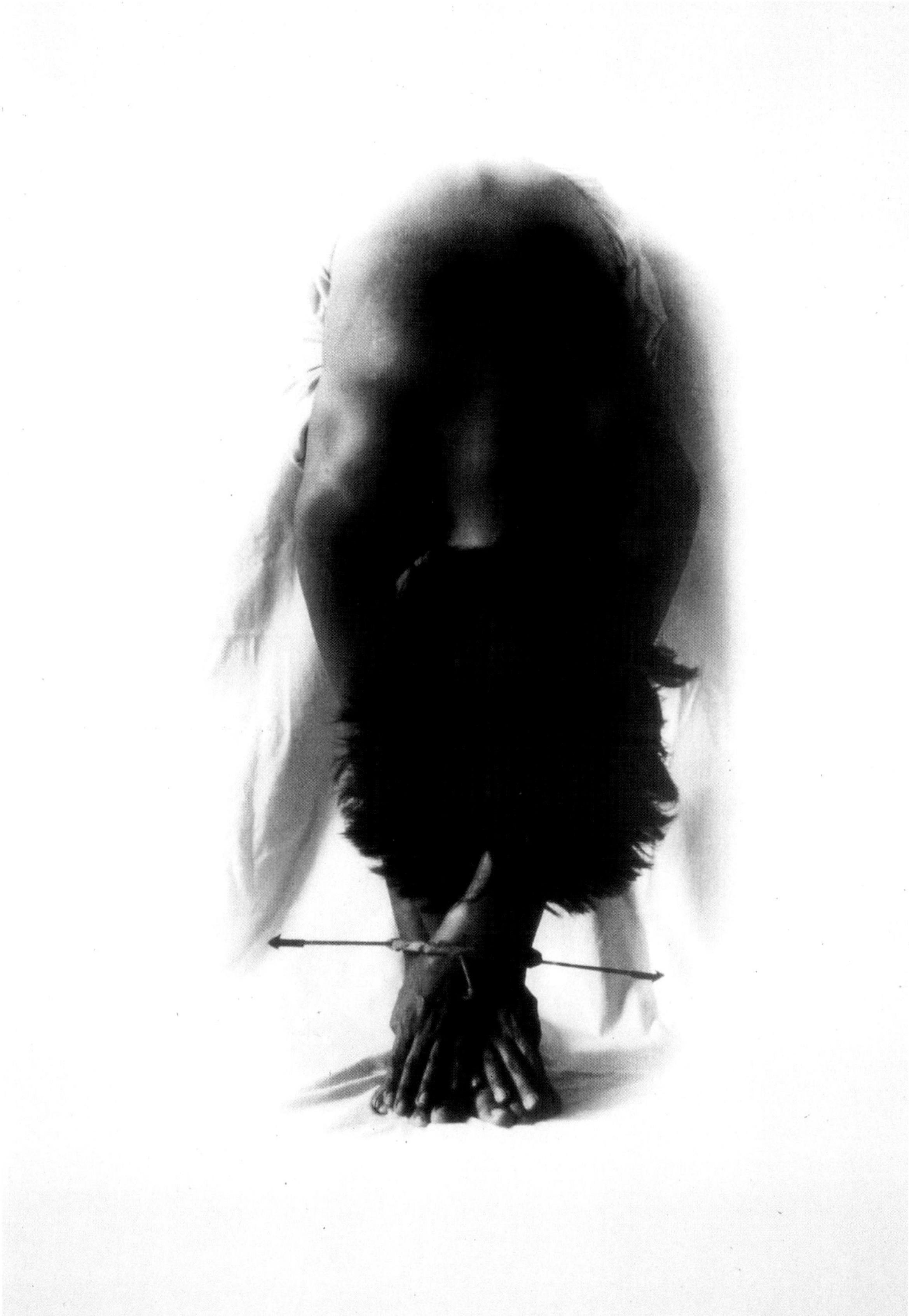

JOHANNES PHOKELA
SOUTH AFRICA

Below *Pantomime Mortal Quiz (after Jacob de Gheyns' Death Allegory)*, 2002. Oil on canvas, 198 x 168 cm (78 x 66 in). Collection De Castro Family Trust.
'Pantomime is an odd English dramatic tradition which I feel has similarities to an African sense of humour. There is a South African proverb that translates as "the worst death is laughter".' The red noses worn by the skulls appear regularly in Phokela's paintings and refer to, 'one incident where I bought a red nose and it fell off when I tried to fit it on to my nose. That's when I found out that the noses were not designed to be worn by someone with a flat nose like mine.'

Right *Tender, Loving, Care (after Adriaen van de Venne)*, 2006. Oil on canvas, 210 x 180 cm (82⅔ x 70⅘ in). gordonschachatcollection.
'The *TLC* [*Tender Loving Care*] triptych engages the notion of commodity fetishism from an art historical context, from the seventeenth century up to the present.' Van de Venne's *Allegory of Poverty* (c. 1630s) has the motto: 'They are feeble legs which must carry poverty.'

Growing up in Soweto, South Africa, where he was born in 1966, Johannes Phokela was fascinated by the Dutch Old Master prints owned by many people in the town, wondering why they were so popular. Most of the original paintings were created at a time when the Dutch were beginning to colonize South Africa, so Phokela uses the images as historical sounding boards to test and comment on the subsequent collision between Africa and Europe, with its ongoing consequences. He often superimposes a grid of lines on the paintings, which refers, amongst other things, to the golden mean in Western art, the perfect compositional balance between elements of a work of art as witnessed, for example, in the paintings of Johannes Vermeer. In the context of recent South African history, the grids reference divisions of another kind and draw the viewer's attention to parts of the painting that Phokela wishes to emphasize.

Johannes Phokela began his training as a painter at the Federated Union of Black Artists (FUBA) in Newtown, under the guidance of the renowned teacher Durant Sihlali. Subsequently, he moved to London, and studied at St Martin's School of Art and at the Royal College of Art, where he developed his exceptional skills in life drawing and painting, graduating with a Masters degree in painting in 1993. He is the winner of several prizes and honours, including the John Moore and the BP National Gallery Portrait Award.

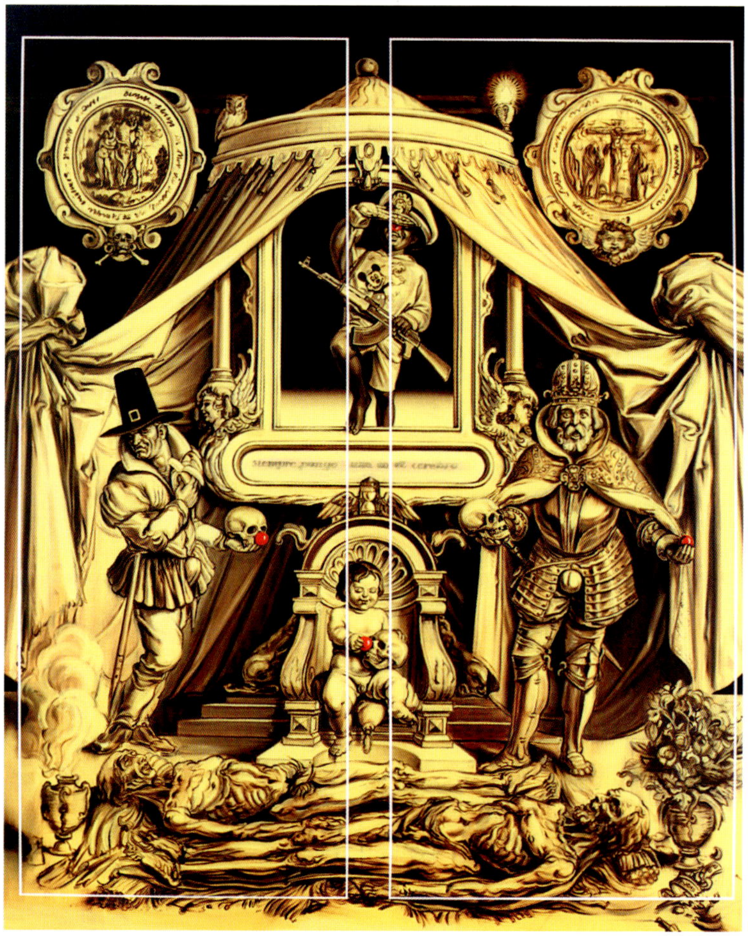

> 'Most of my work is a contemporary take on Dutch and Flemish Old Masters, where I take on what is perceived to be Europe's grandiose history of art as a medium to convey values and ideals represented within a global context of cultural elitism.'
> *Johannes Phokela*

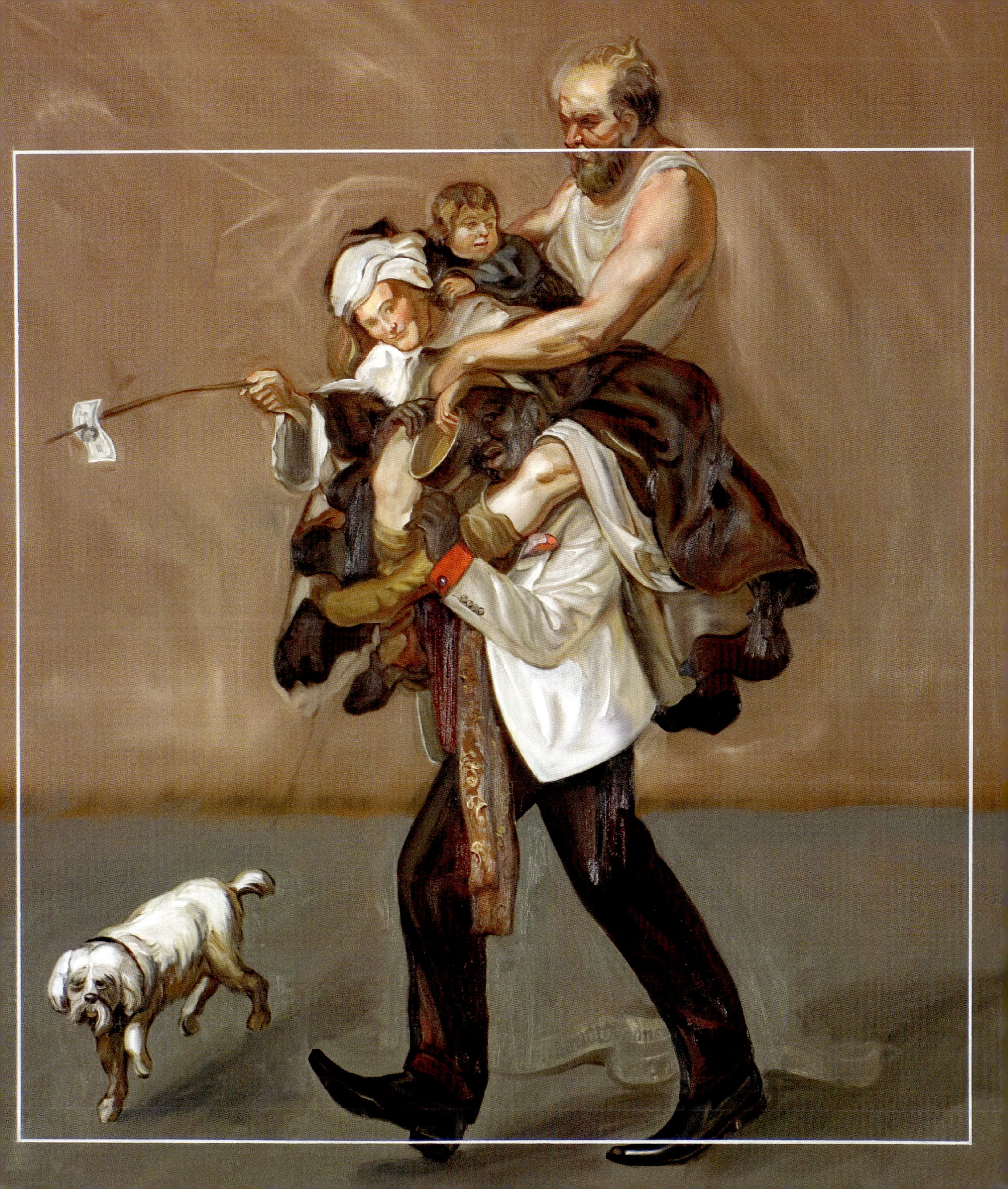

Below *Tender, Loving, Care (after Nicholaes Berchem)*, 2006. Oil on canvas, 210 x 180 cm (82⅔ x 70⅘ in).

Right *Tender, Loving, Care (after William Hogarth's* The Gate of Calais; O, the Roast Beef of Old England*)*, 2006. Oil on canvas, 210 x 180 cm (82⅔ x 70⅘ in). gordonschachatcollection.

'Through pastiche, the subject matter of *TLC* concerns the inevitability of inequality in trade value systems amongst individuals, then alluding to nations and to the extent of continental spheres.' Phokela has removed all the details from Berchem's *A Moor Presenting a Parrot to A Lady* (mid-1660s) except for the transaction.

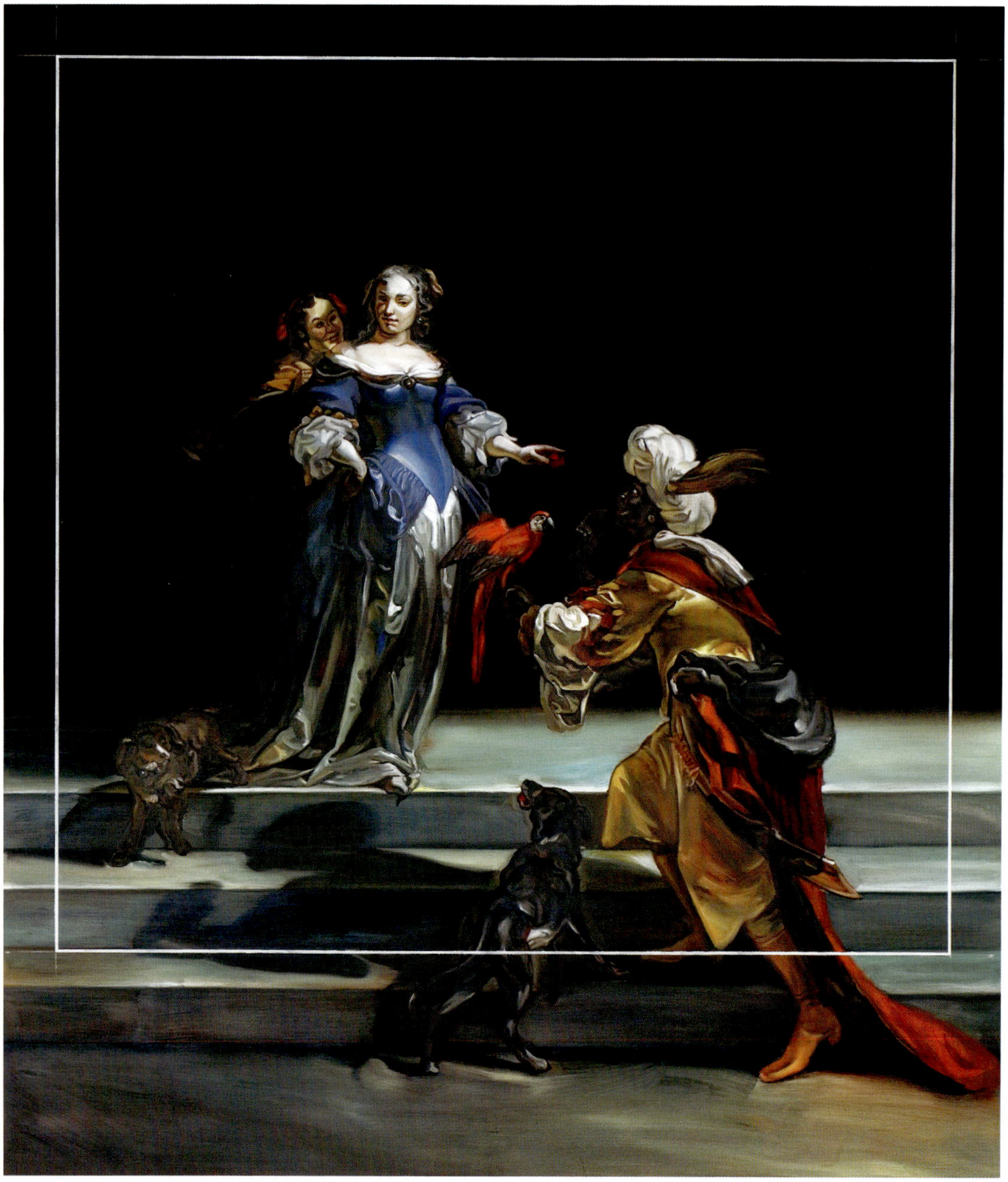

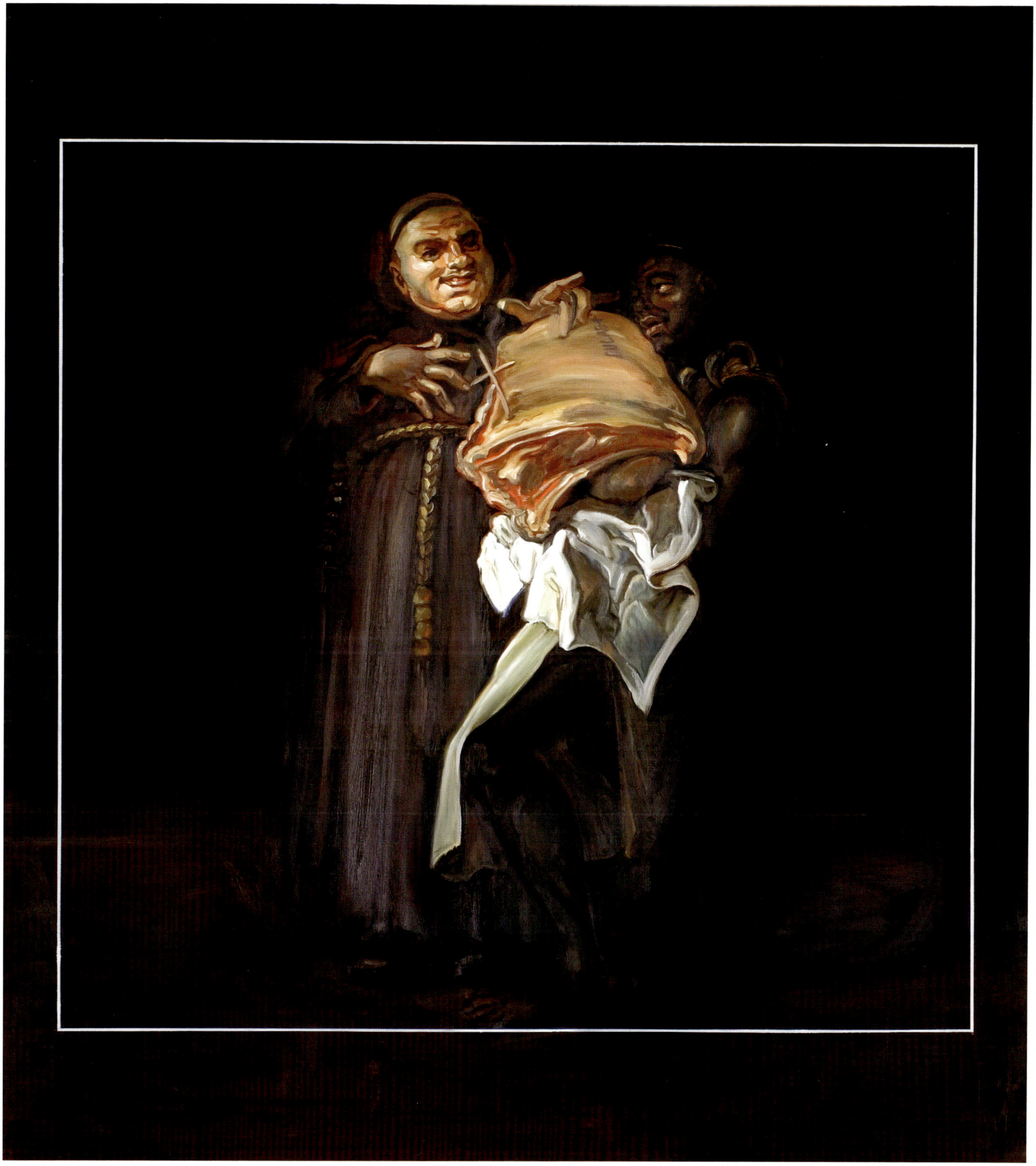

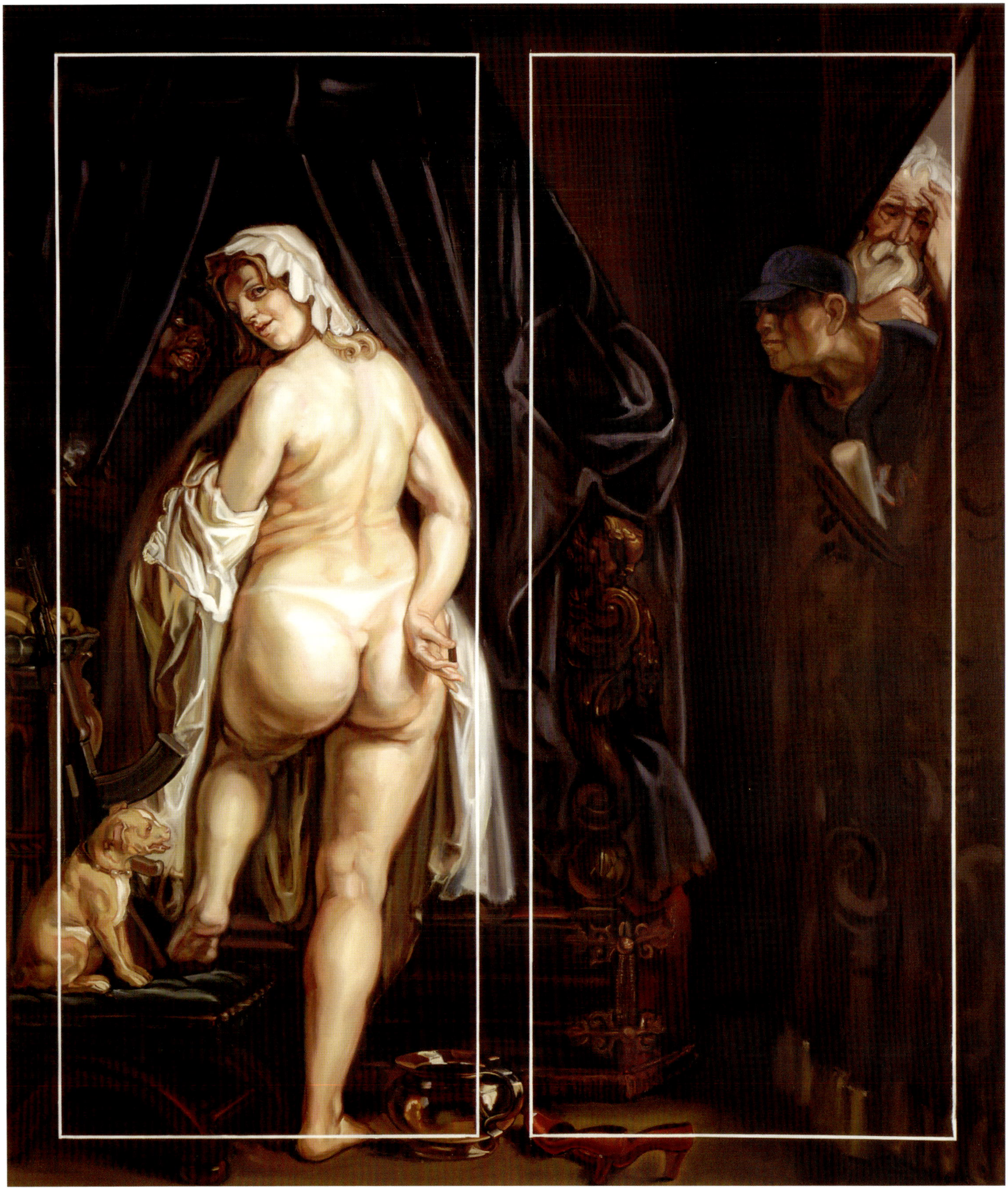

'Who said life drawing was only for Europeans? The European art market will always marginalize African art. The only way to fight that is not to make "African" art.'
Johannes Phokela

Left *Chocolat (after Jacob Jordaens's* King Candaules of Lydia Showing his Wife to Gyges, *1646)*, 2004. Oil on canvas, 198 x 168 cm (78 x 66 in). Johannesburg Art Gallery (JAG).
'Europeans wore much more clothing than Africans when they arrived, and today it is the opposite. Traditional South Africans are offended by semi-naked Europeans sunbathing in bikinis, as they perceive it as a violation of common decency and Christian morality. In some ways they have coveted each other, and yet the economic relationship between the two remains ambivalent.'

Below *Land of Cockaigne (after Pieter Bruegel the Elder's* The Land of Cockaigne, *1567)*, 1998. Oil on canvas, 122 x 152 cm (48 x 59⁴⁄₅ in). Private collection.
'Bruegel's *Land of Cockaigne* is based on a Utopian idea. My version introduces a sea nymph fountain into Bruegel's composition. I am responding to or commenting on an old allegorical tradition of the Renaissance. The fountain represents raw materials or mineral resources, and the figures below represent those who appropriate them for refinement and profit. There is often conflict in those countries where there is mineral wealth.'

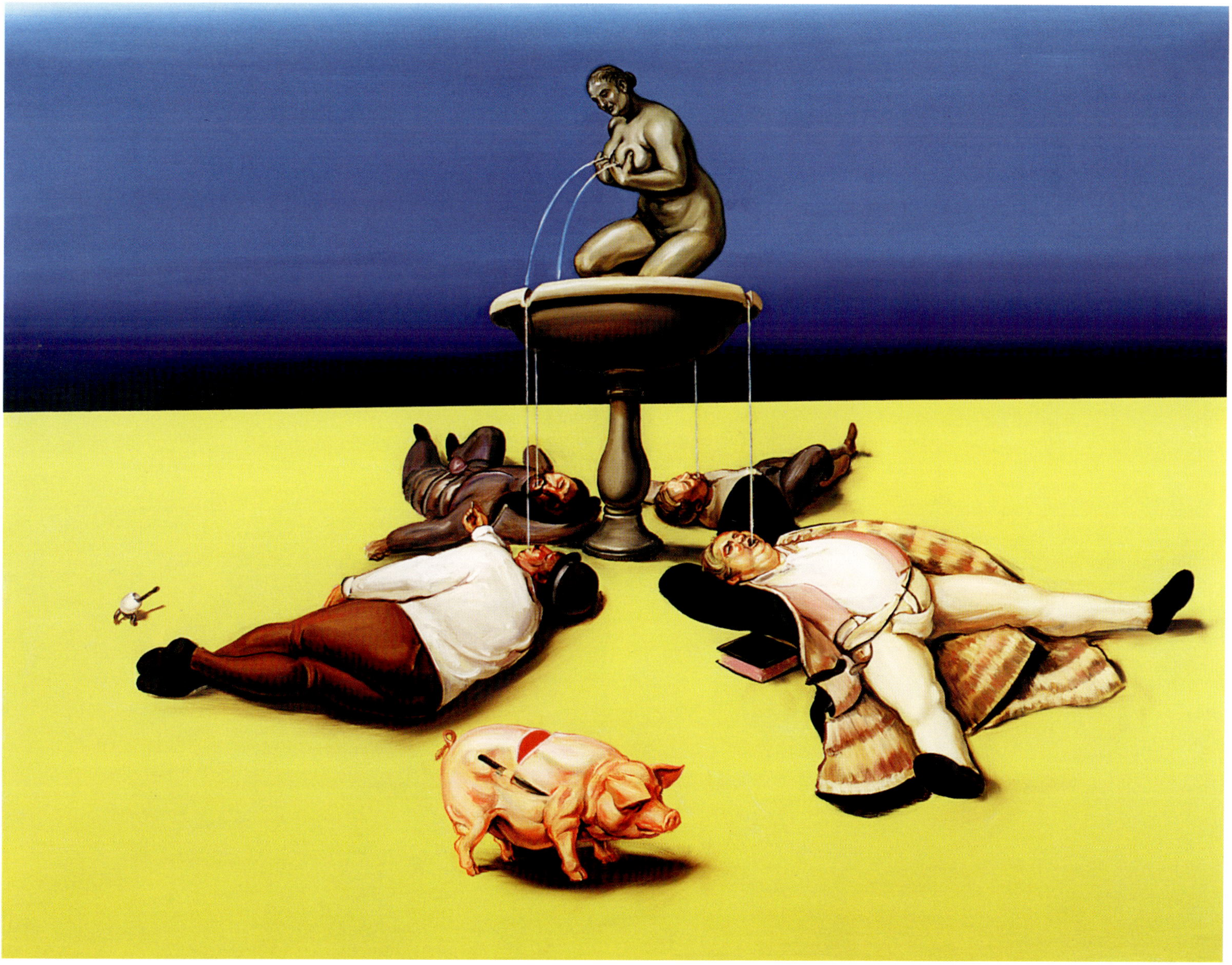

TRACEY ROSE
SOUTH AFRICA

Below *Mami*, 2001. Lambda print. 127 x 127 cm (50 x 50 in). Private collection.
Mami is one of many female characters who first appeared in Rose's video installation *Ciao Bella* at the Venice Biennale (2001). She is the archetypal establishment figure in tweed twinset, perhaps a headmistress standing proudly at the gates of her school. She can't stand mess, and when Bunny shoots a number of the other characters in the video, Mami efficiently wipes off the blood spattered on the screen.

Right *Bunny*, 2001. Lambda print, 127 x 127 cm (50 x 50 in). Private collection.
Bunny is in some ways the opposite of Mami – a male sexual fantasy, a 'playgirl' who wastes people for fun with her pump-action shotgun. Yet in some ways she, too, is an establishment figure, standing guard in front of barbed wire and a brick wall. The brick wall features graffiti of a black hand reaching up despairingly towards a white face – perhaps a banker or an industrialist with pince-nez glasses and a big moustache.

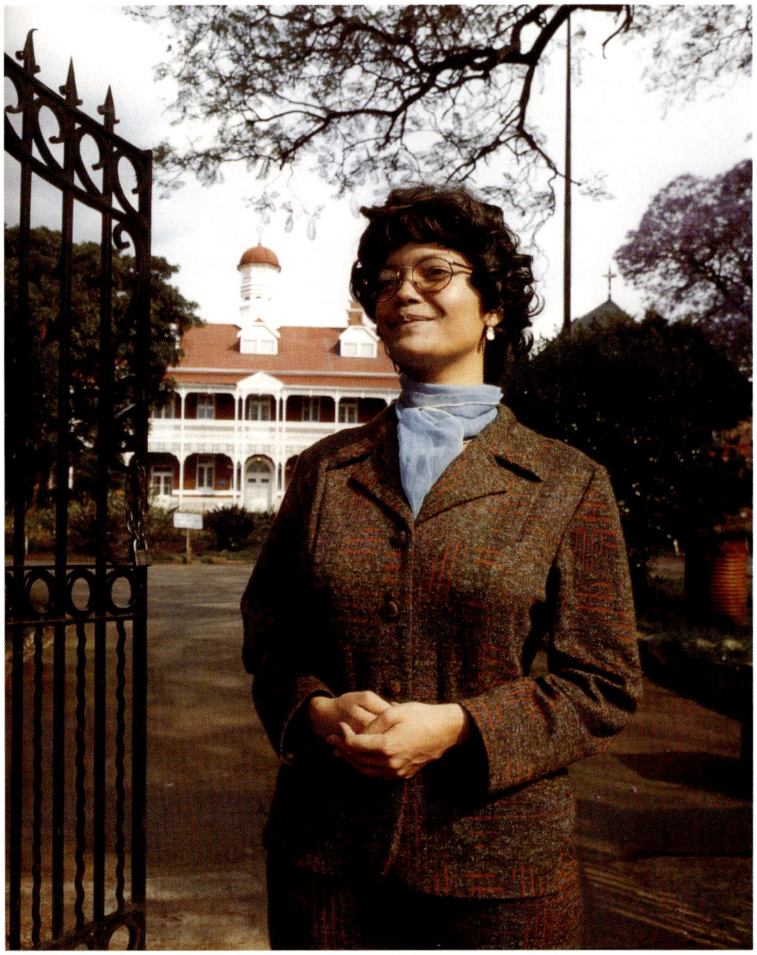

Tracey Rose was born in Durban, South Africa in 1974. She gained a BA in Fine Arts (Honors) at the University of the Witwatersrand, Johannesburg (1996), studied at the South African School of Motion Picture Medium and Live Performance (2004), and has recently completed a Masters degree in Fine Arts at Goldsmiths College, London (2007). She has shown her work at many prestigious venues worldwide, including the Venice Biennales of 2001 and 2007, and has completed residencies in India, the UK, South Africa, the USA and Austria.

Rose's work is painstakingly prepared; she may take years to develop a concept to a conclusion that meets her meticulous standards. She is a performance and video artist who has created an array of characters and persona to illustrate themes of race, gender, religion, politics and identity. These themes, together with her own Catholic upbringing and mixed racial heritage, including European and Khoisan ancestry, are bravely examined through the medium of her own voice, hair and body – both vulnerable and all-powerful. Sometimes characters from earlier projects reappear in later works in recognizable but slightly different guises, giving Rose's whole body of work a feeling of dynamism and exploration.

The subjects of Tracey Rose's work flow easily from the very distant past, in her celebration of the first hominid, the three-million-year-old 'Lucy' of Ethiopia, to the religious divisions of today and their terrible consequences. In her video *Waiting for God* (2005), created during her residency at the London School of Hygiene and Tropical Medicine, Rose suggests a healing and meditative solution as we look down with her from the Mount of Olives as the sun rises and sets over a church and a mosque in the city of Jerusalem below.

'Making work is a documentation of a journey – each stage, each process, each dilemma has to be worked through. At one time I felt pressured to do a lot of things at the same time, but now I want to take one step at a time. When you make an artwork you're not just doing something at that moment, you're contributing to an entire history of art-making.'
Tracey Rose

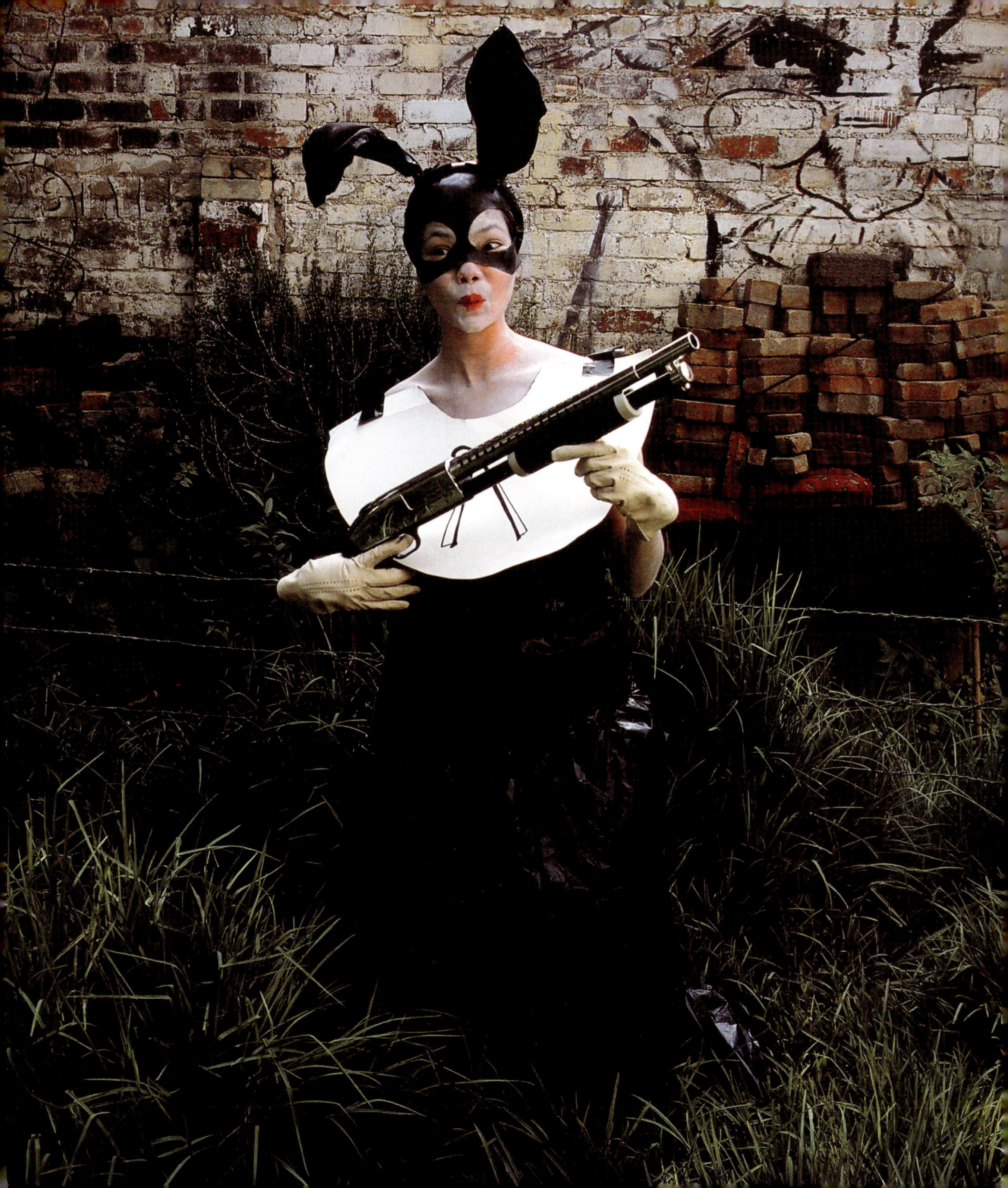

Below *Lucie's Fur: The Prelude*, 2004. Installation view of single channel DVD on rear projection, 60 x 125 cm (23½ x 48¾ in). Private collection.
This image is part of a series, the title of which refers to the 1974 discovery in Ethiopia of 'Lucy', the remains of a female hominid over three million years old, the discovery of which sparked a heated debate around evolution, gender and race. Rose's persona in this image references the *thokoloshi*, a South African evil spirit that, according to folklore, has a penis so long that it has to be slung over its shoulder.

Right *Lucie's Fur Version 1:1:1 – Adam and Yves, B.C.* 2003, 2004. Iris print, 82 x 82 cm (32¼ x 32¼ in). Private collection.
When the three-million-year-old remains of 'Lucy' were discovered, she was immediately dubbed the 'African Eve'. Rose stirs the pot of Judaeo-Christian mythology by picturing the primordial couple as a pair of gay lovers.

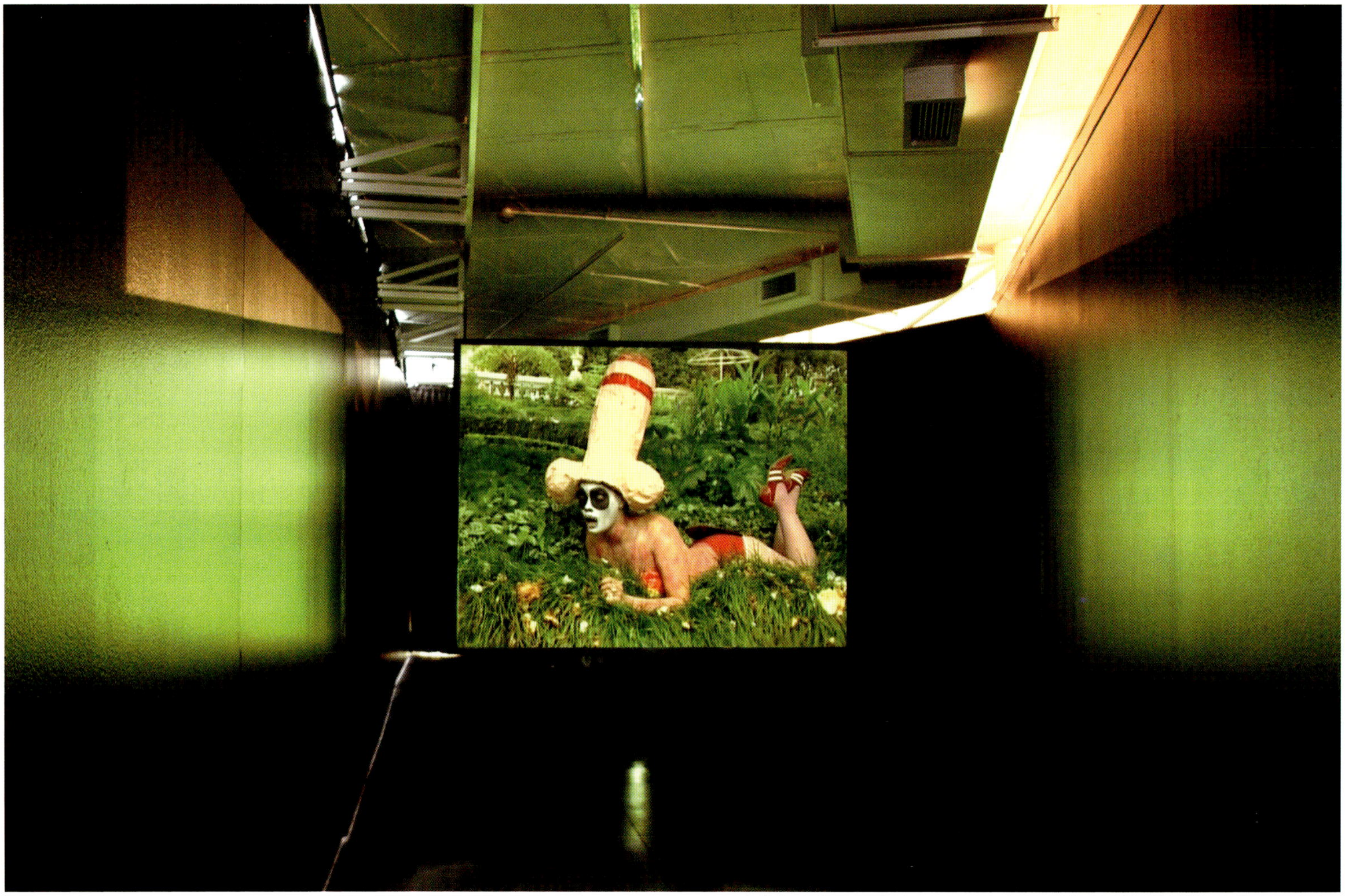

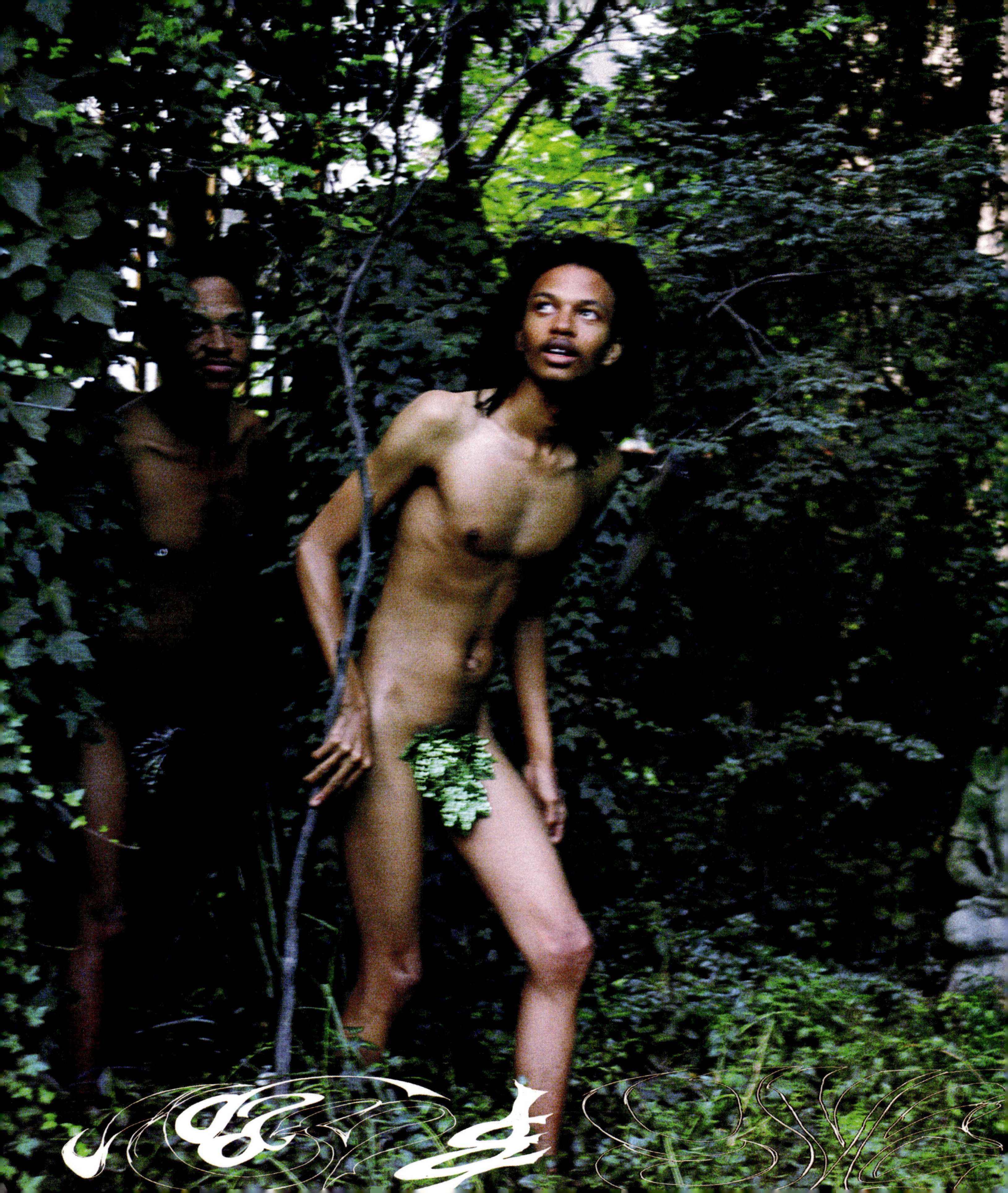

REINATA SADHIMBA
MOZAMBIQUE

Below Ceramic figures in Reinata Sadhimba's studio, Maputo, 2004.

Right *Shetani (An Unpredictable Spirit)*, 1995. Baked clay, height 34 cm (13²/₅ in). Private collection. This was the first piece made at the Triangle Arts Pamoja Workshop, Yorkshire Sculpture Park, 1995.

Reinata Sadhimba was born in 1945 in Nimu Village, Cabo Delgado Province, northern Mozambique. She received the traditional education of a Makonde woman, which includes learning the art of pottery. She married and began a family life, giving birth to eight children. Opposition to the Portuguese colonial administration had been growing in the early 1960s, and when the war of independence began she carried arms and ammunition for the soldiers of Frelimo for whom her husband fought. Her husband left her shortly after independence in 1975; six of her eight children had been killed in the war.

In deep despair, Reinata dreamed one night that she saw clay to one side and money to the other. At that point Reinata is said to have started to make her clay figures, though she would have been considered odd, as among the Makonde – and most peoples of sub-Saharan Africa – the making of figurative sculpture in any material is considered men's work. In the 1980s, some of her work was purchased by the Musée de l'Art Brut in Lausanne, which helped to bring her to international recognition. Today, her works are held in public and private collections all over the world; she lives and works in Maputo, Mozambique with her studio in the grounds of the Natural History Museum.

Reinata's work must be seen as an ongoing story or set of stories, each individual piece playing a part in that story. When asked about the primary motivation behind her work she replied, 'What life is like for myself as a Makonde person.' Her studio in Maputo is often overflowing with work and, viewing the serried ranks of ceramics that line the shelves and jostle for space on the floor, you get some idea of the many stories Reinata tells, which in the end combine into a single tale of epic proportions. In some ways it might be viewed as the oral history of the Makonde people in clay. Though she's getting used to it now, Reinata still gets quite upset if her visitors adopt the accepted Western approach to viewing works of art in a respectful, reverential silence. Silence to her is a sign of disapproval, so she is much happier talking with and embracing her visitors in a language that all people should understand.

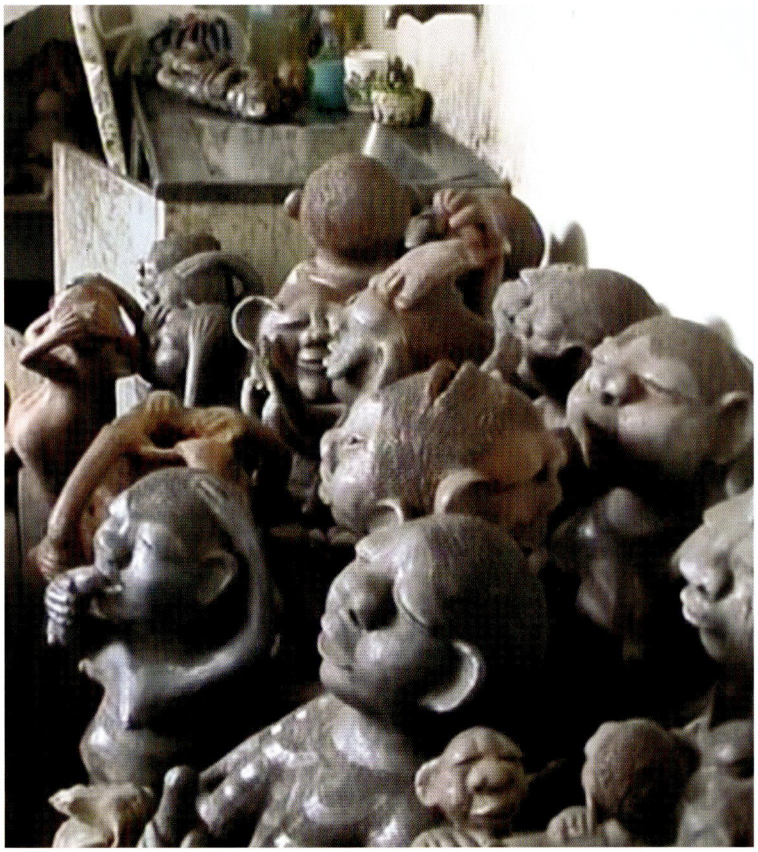

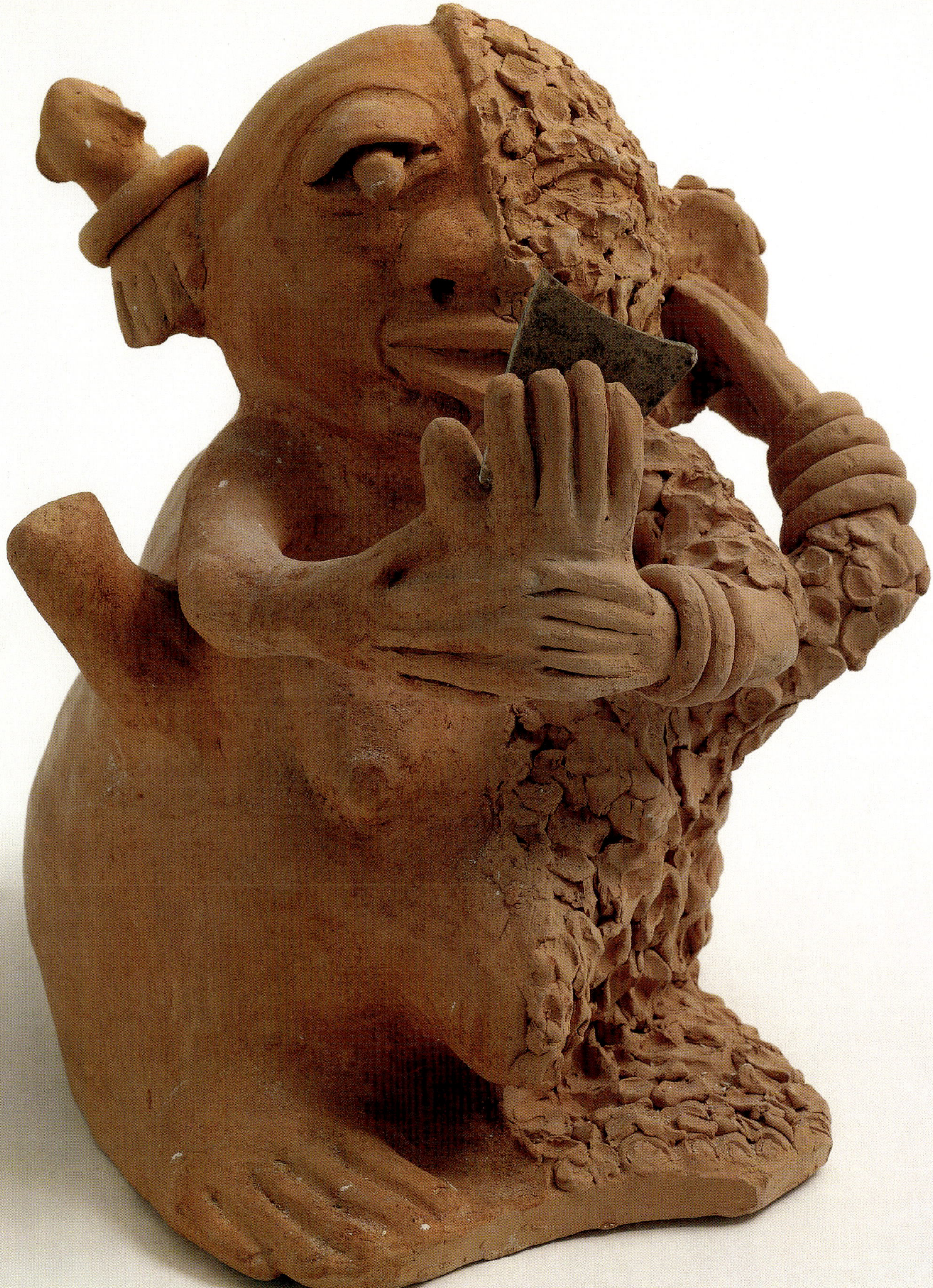

Below *Pregnant Woman Holding Her Stomach*, 1995. Baked clay, height 53 cm (20⅘ in). Private collection.

Right *Mother Giving Birth*, 1995. Baked clay, 14 x 35 cm (5½ x 13¾ in). Private collection.

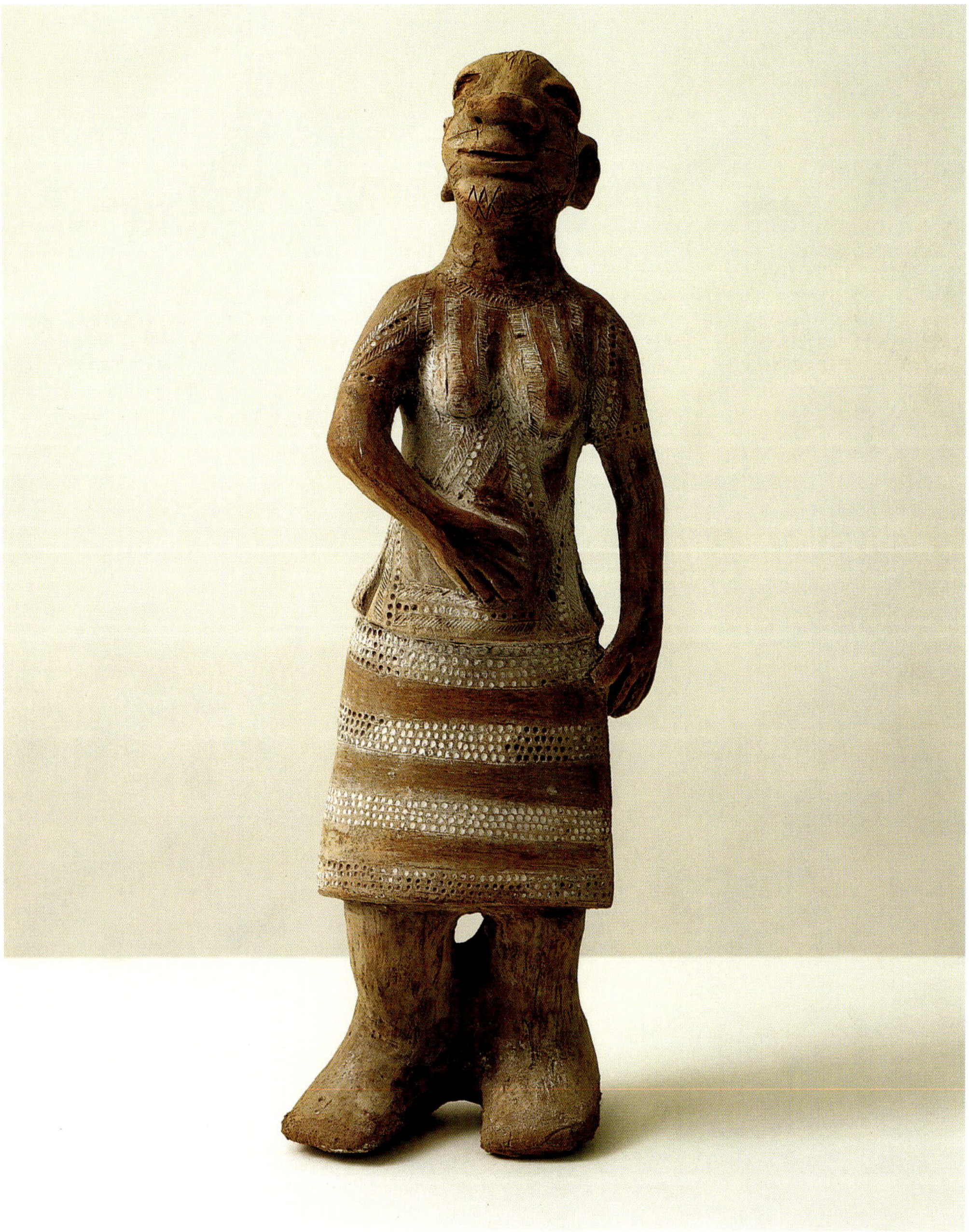

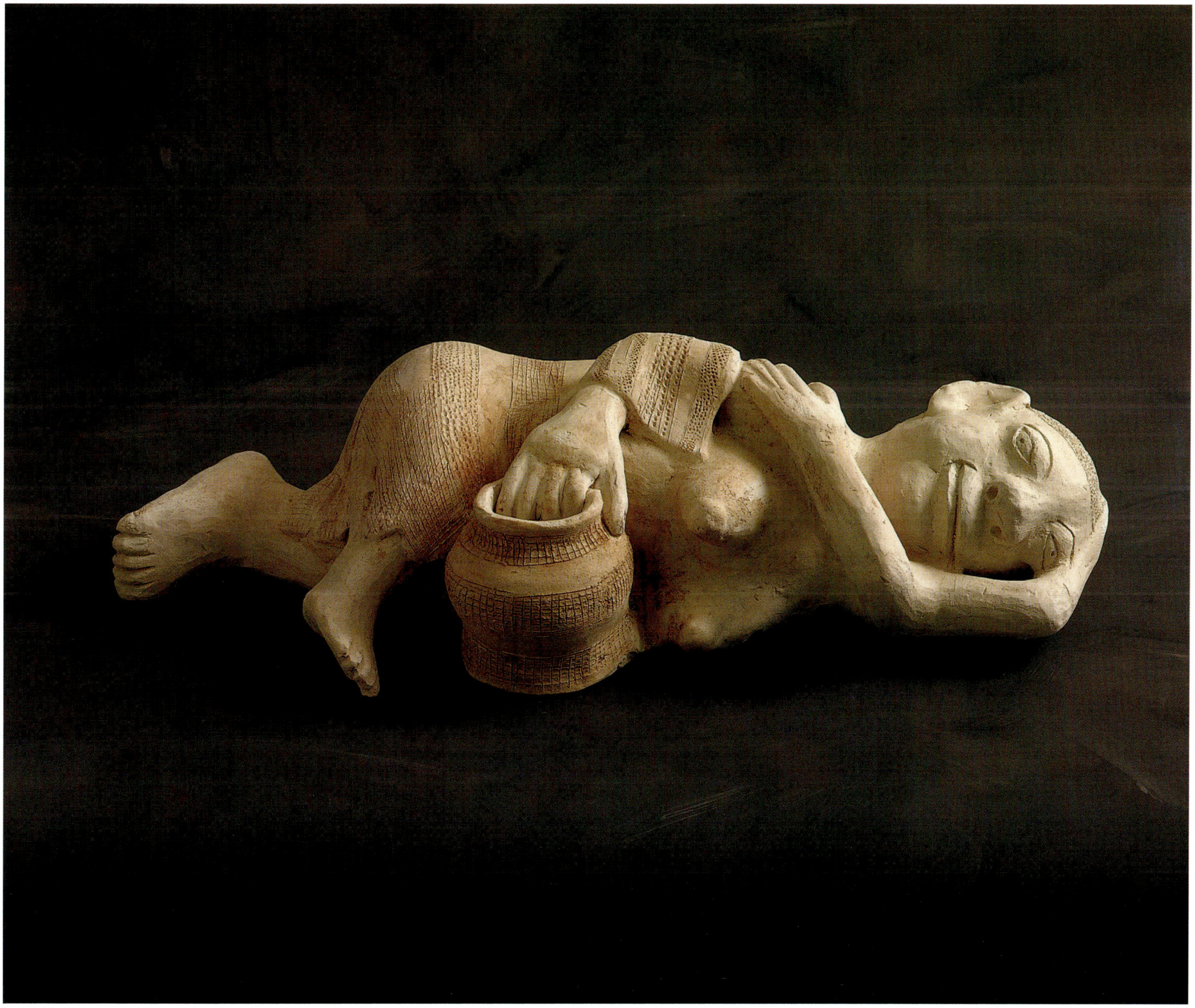

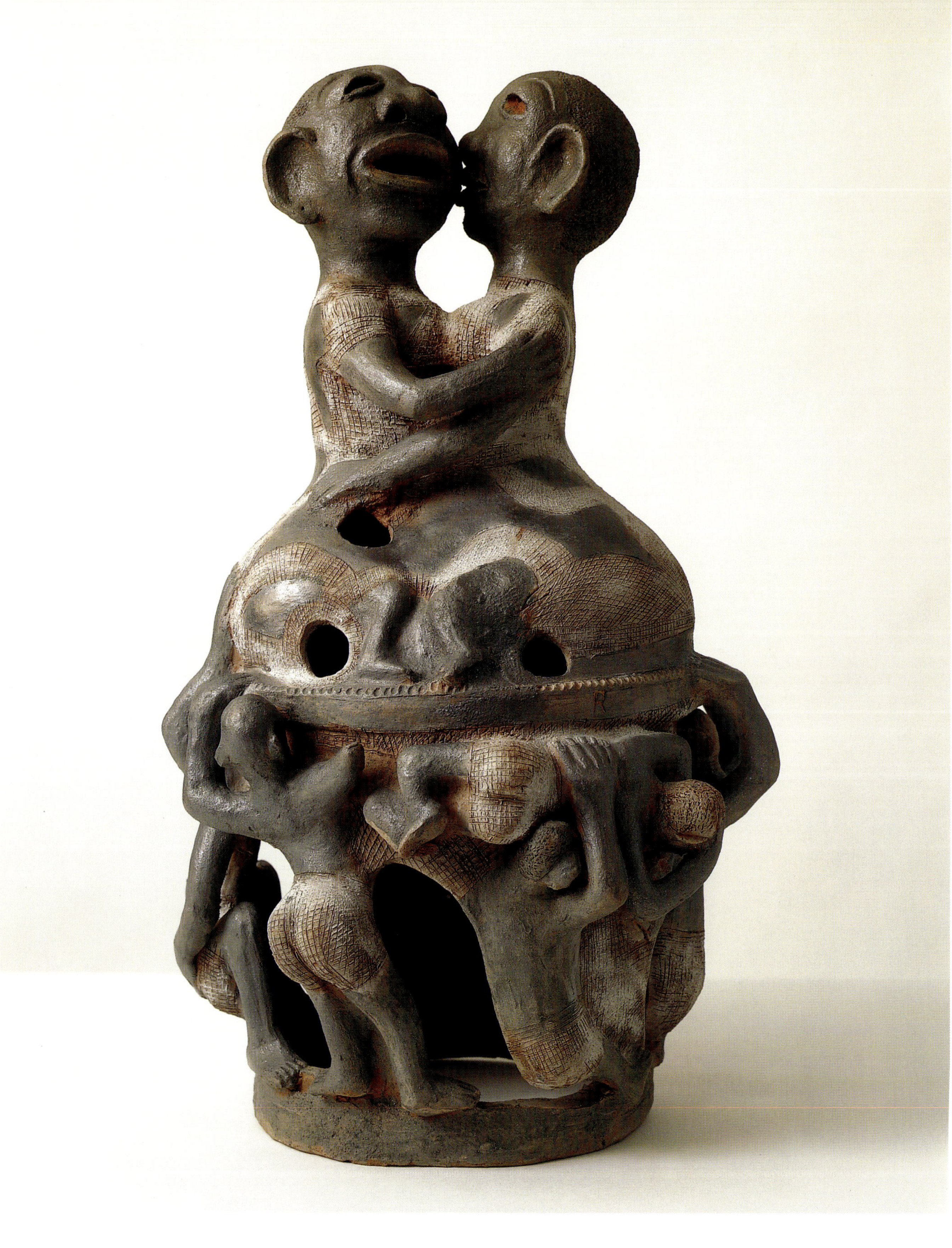

Left *Ceramic Pot Figures,* c. 1980s. Baked clay, height 64 cm (25 in). Private collection.

Below left *Woman Combing Her Hair* 1992. Baked Clay, height 46 cm (18 in). Private collection.

Below right *Robert* 1995. Baked clay, straw hat and sunglasses, height 68 cm (26¾ in). Private collection. Reinata made this piece at the Pamoja Workshop after Robert Loder, co-founder of the International Triangle Workshop Movement and of Africa '95. Reinata initially called the piece *Munu Juluku* (*The Money Man*), until she learned Robert's name.

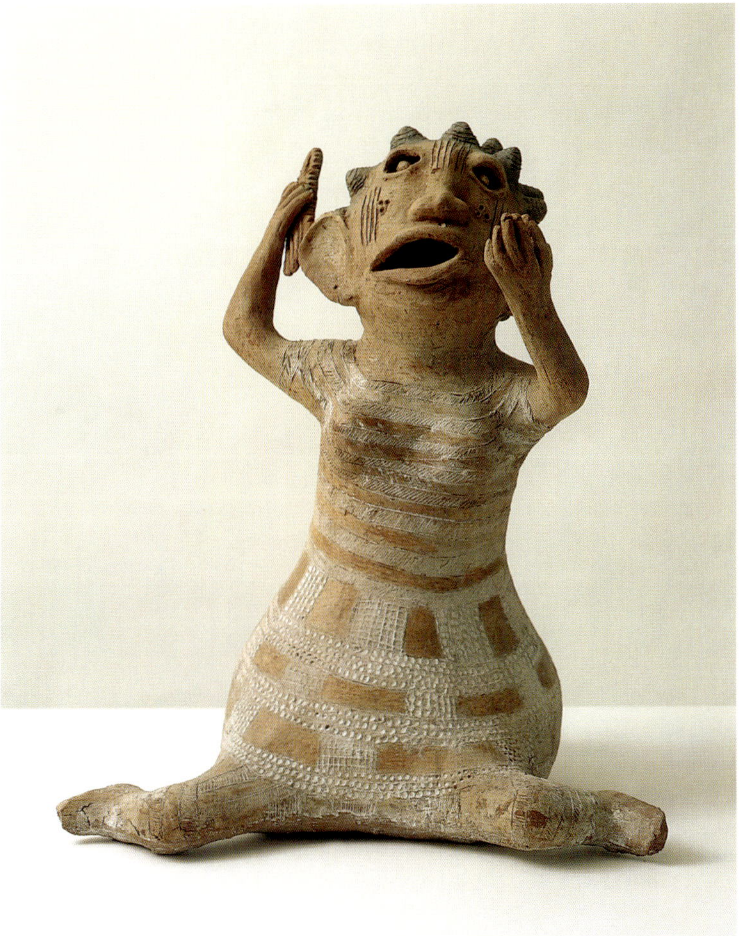

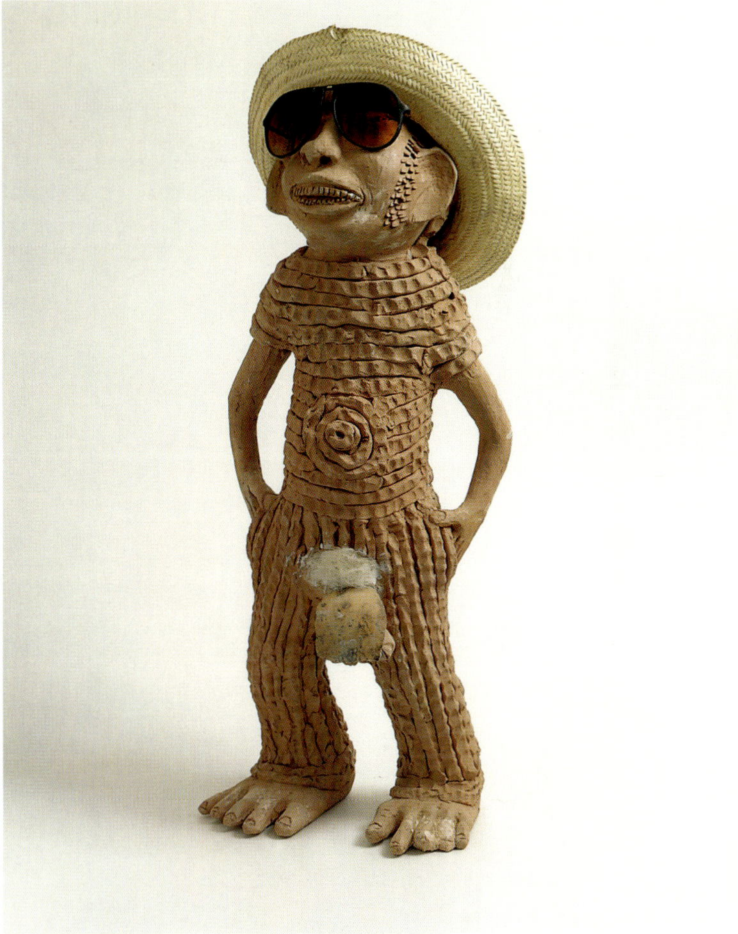

IBRAHIM EL SALAHI
SUDAN/UK

Below *Two Heads Tree*, 2001. Coloured inks on watercolour paper, approximately 35 x 26 cm (13¾ x 10¼ in). Oxford Exhibition Services, Uffington, UK.
'There is no painting without drawing, and there is no shape without line... In the end all images can be reduced to lines.'

Right From the *Tree* series, 2001 (detail). Coloured inks on watercolour paper, 35 x 26 cm (13¾ x 10¼ in). Collection of the artist.
In this work, El Salahi makes reference to the form of the *jubba* as well as to the human form, suggesting a Tree of Life in Sudan. The image can be viewed as an abstract assemblage of lines and colours or as a tree towering over a flat landscape at sunrise. The closely configured lines in the lower part of the picture suggest both the grain of the wood and the rising of life-sustaining moisture from the ground.

El Salahi was born in 1930 at Omdurman, Sudan. He was educated at the Gordon Memorial College and the Technical Institute, Khartoum, the Slade School, London and the Sudanese School for Administrative Science. His career-long involvement in cultural diplomacy, often related to pan-Africanism, includes solo or group exhibitions all over the world. El Salahi taught for many years at the College of Fine and Applied Art, Khartoum; in 1966, as Head of the Painting Department, he led the Sudanese delegation to the first Black Art Festival in Dakar, Senegal. He was jailed for six months in 1975 under the repressive Nimieri regime, and moved to the UK after his release.

The 'Khartoum School', under the leadership of El Salahi, began to be recognized in the 1960s as an emergent modernist movement with a distinctive means of expression known as *Sudanawiyya* – a synthesis of Western styles of art with other traditions, reflecting the remarkable ethnic, religious and cultural diversity of Sudan.

El Salahi is a Muslim and a member of a Sufi brotherhood. He often prays and washes before starting work. 'I always wash. I have to become clean outside, which leads to cleanliness within. And then I work.' Writing in 1998, the curator and academic Salah Hassan detected three distinct phases in El Salahi's work, the most recent of which consisted mainly of works in black and white. Since then El Salahi's work has changed yet again and is full of colour and light, drawing inspiration from the haraza tree that grows on the banks of the Nile:

> *There is a Sudanese saying about the haraza tree, which is often used to refer to someone who is difficult and obstinate. The idea behind the saying fascinates me, as it reminds me of some kind of inner nature in all of us humans; the resistance of the individual, the one who stands alone against all to say no when everyone else follows the crowd and says yes, be it socially, culturally, politically or otherwise.*

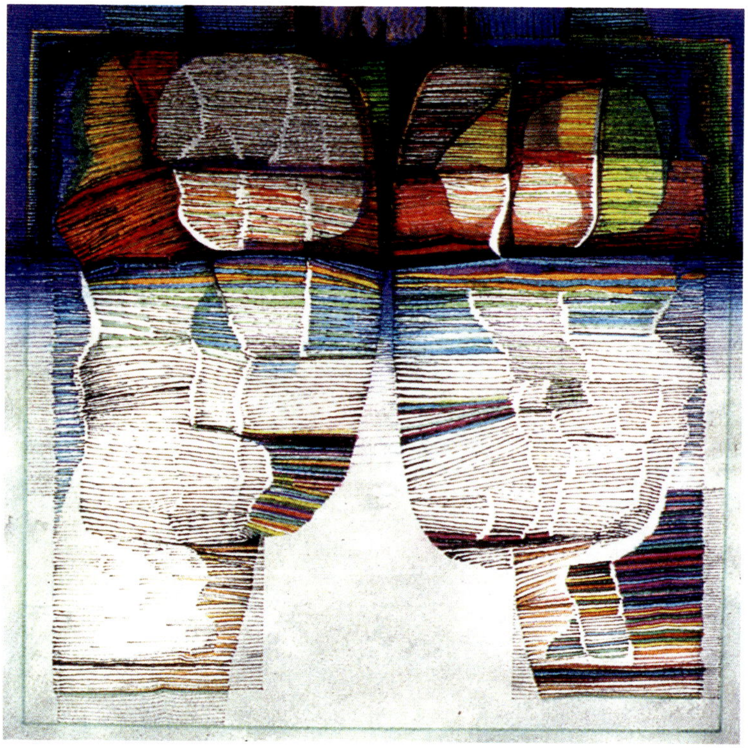

Below From the *Tree* series, 2001. Coloured inks on watercolour paper, approximately 35 x 26 cm (13¾ x 10¼ in). Private collection.
'Artists have to rest on solid ground as far as all elements and bases relating to their profession are concerned.'

Right *Jubba*, 2002. Coloured inks on board, 23 x 23 cm (9 x 9 in). Collection of the artist.
The patched tunic, *jubba*, was the distinctive dress of the followers of Muhammad Ahmad, the Mahdi ('rightly guided one'), who in 1885 overthrew the Turco–Egyptian government in Khartoum and established the Mahdist state. In this work, El Salahi uses the *jubba* as a metaphor for the remarkably diverse nature of Sudanese society, the patches symbolizing different cultures and beliefs in various parts of the country.

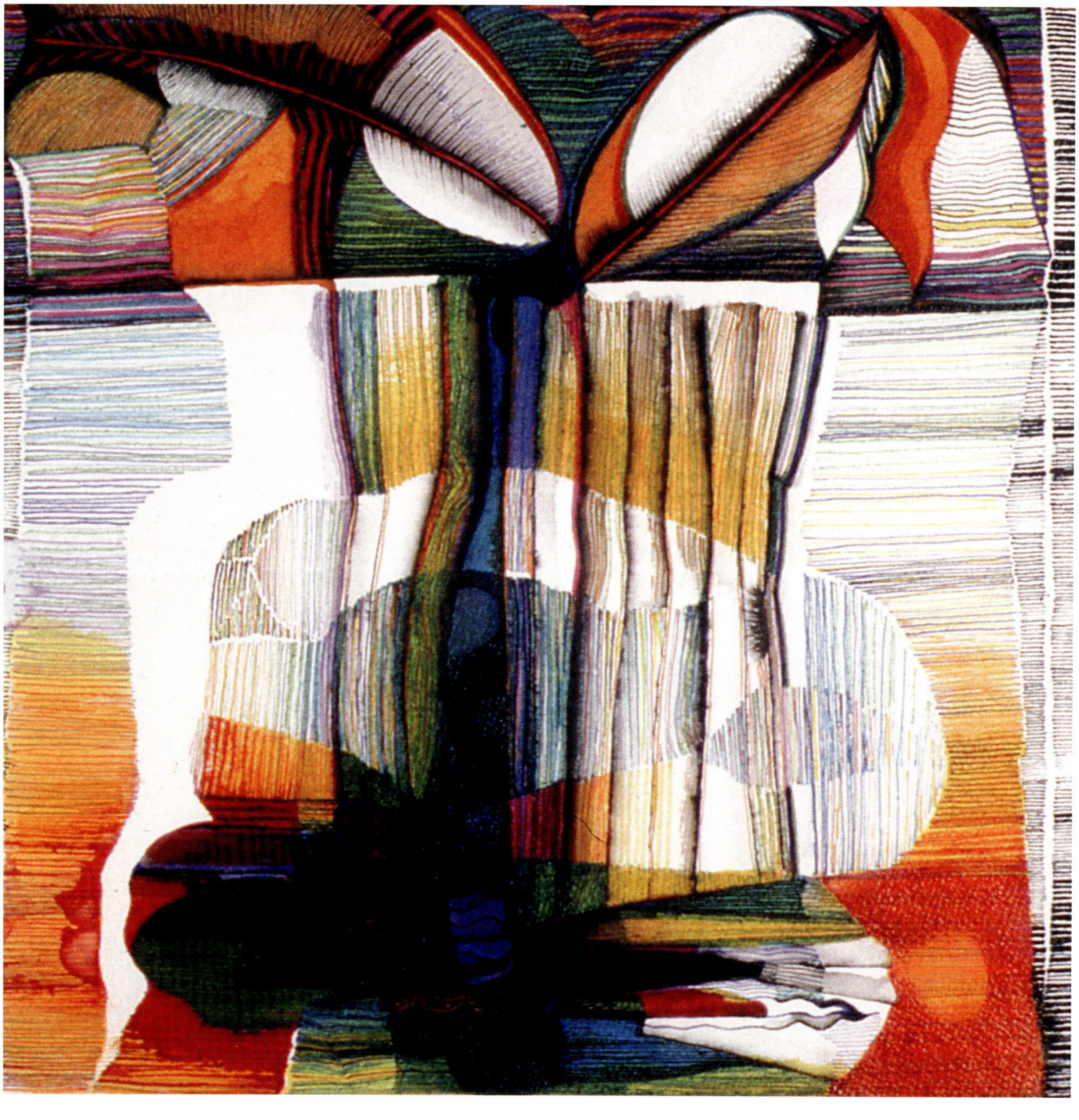

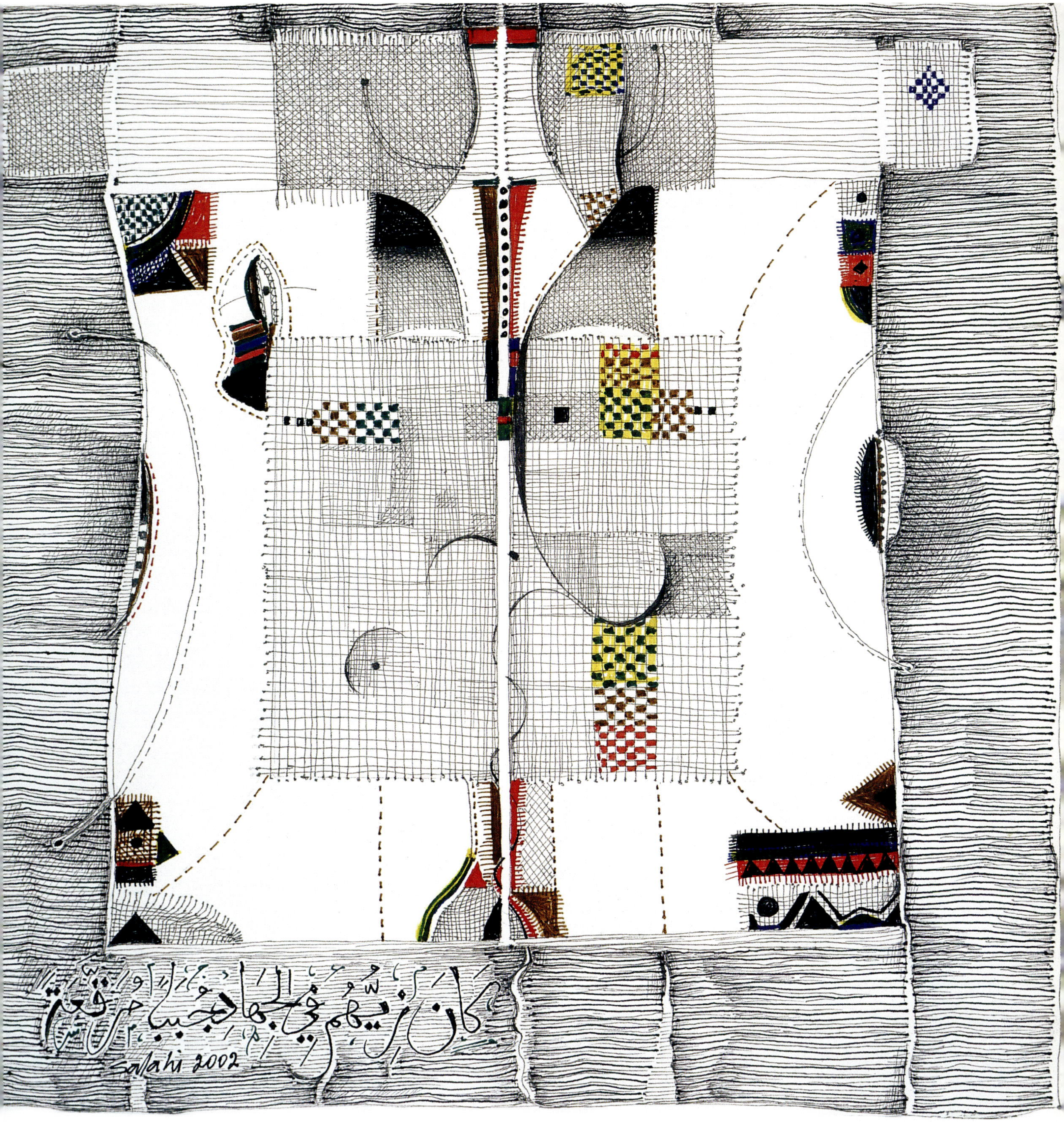
كان زيهم في الجهاد جبة مرقعة
Salahi 2002

Below left From the *Tree* series, 2001. Coloured inks on watercolour paper, approximately 35 x 26cm (13¾ x 10¼ in). Oxford Exhibition Services, Uffington, UK.

'Artists are observant people. They see everything so clearly and never miss a thing. They have worked in a flexible tradition of give and take throughout the ages but always bearing uppermost in mind that to preserve one's identity is the real order of the day.'

Below right From the *Tree* series, 2001. Coloured inks on watercolour paper, approximately 35 x 26cm (13¾ x 10¼ in). Oxford Exhibition Services, Uffington, UK.

Right From the *Tree* series, 2001. Coloured inks on watercolour paper, approximately 35 x 26cm (13¾ x 10¼ in). Oxford Exhibition Services, Uffington, UK.

'Many times I have said this to people – I realize the work comes through me. I am not the originator. It is originated by someone else – which is Allah, which is my God. And I have little bits. Sometimes the window opens and I can see things. I can follow them if I am clean; if I am not the window is closed and I don't see it...'

'Originality, human originality, does not mean creating something out of nothing, as such a claim is well beyond the capability of mankind. Originality, in my opinion, means to be able to create the new out of what is already there in existence. One simply makes a new addition, a sort of new idea, a fresh leaf atop that same old tree of creation.'
Ibrahim El Salahi

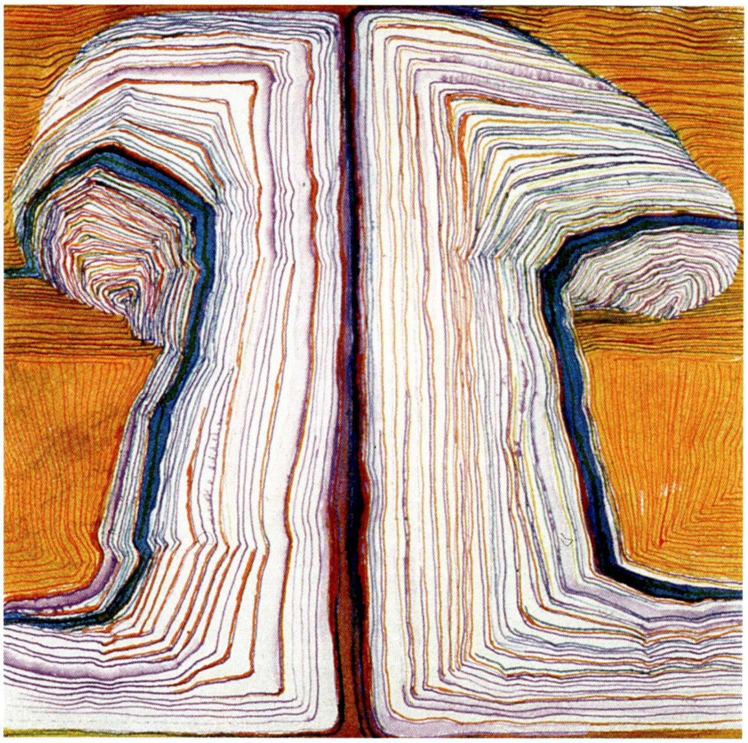

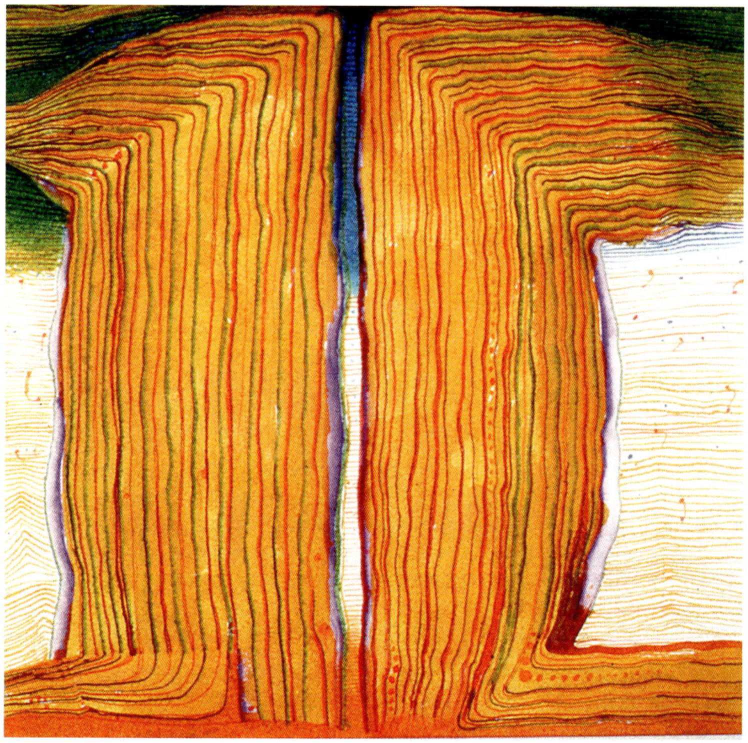

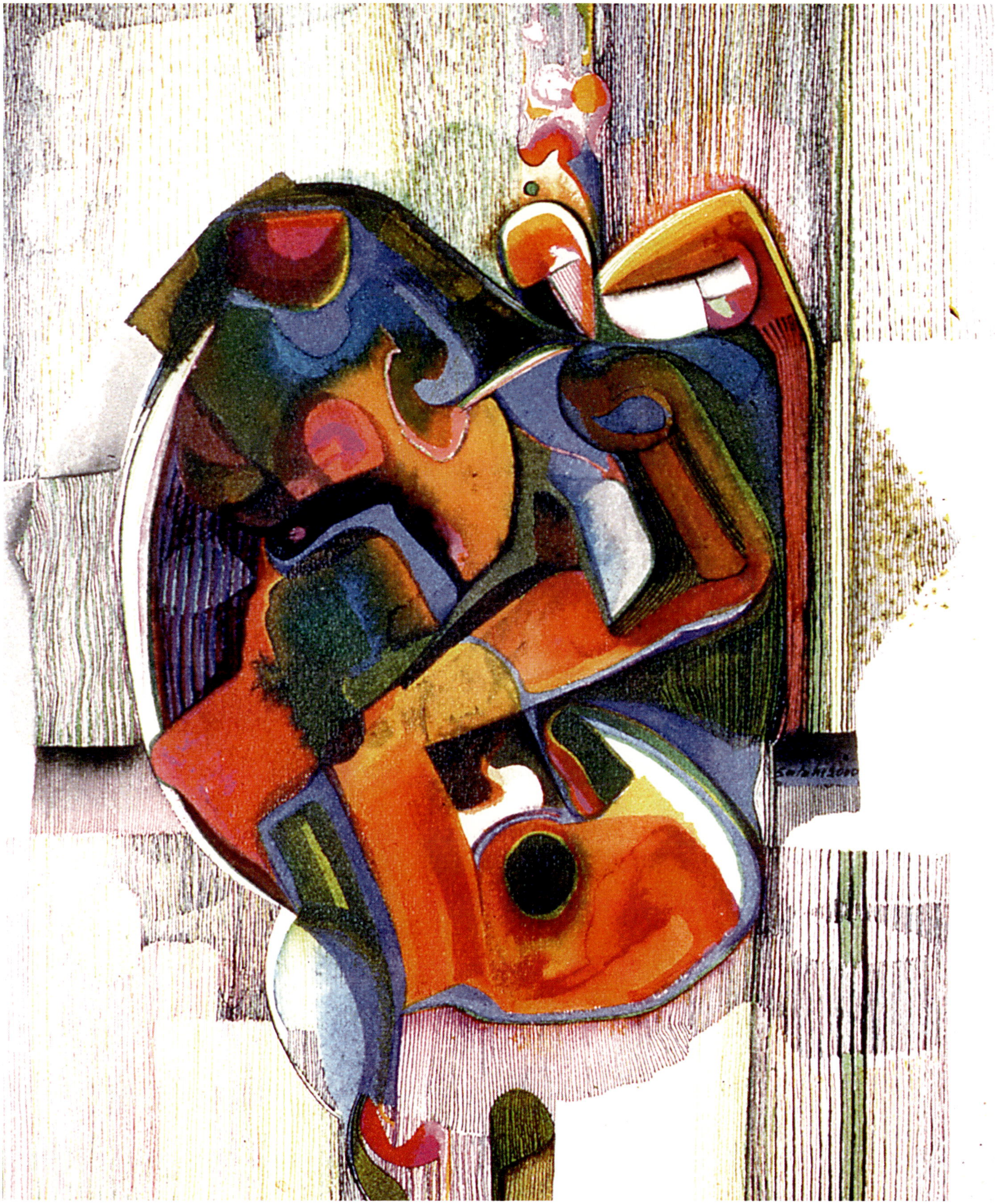

CHÉRI SAMBA
DEMOCRATIC REPUBLIC OF CONGO/FRANCE

Below *Collège de la Sagesse (College of Wisdom)*, 2004. Acrylic on canvas, 199.5 x 250 cm (78½ x 98⅖ in). CAAC–The Pigozzi Collection, Geneva.
'My painting is concerned with people's lives. I'm not interested in myths or beliefs. That's not my goal. I want to change our mentality that keeps us isolated from the world.'

Right *Little Kadogo*, 2004. Acrylic on canvas, 200 x 269 cm (78¾ x 106 in). CAAC–The Pigozzi Collection, Geneva.
Kadogo, the slang for a child soldier, comes from the KiSwahili word *kidogo* meaning 'a little'. Though the child has surrendered, the armed adult hand behind him will make sure he keeps on killing. Many thousands of child soldiers have died in wars throughout Africa; for those who survive, the experience leaves them deeply and irrevocably scarred.

Chéri Samba was born in 1956 in Kinto M'Vuila, Democratic Republic of Congo. He left school at sixteen to apprentice himself to the sign-painters on Kasa Vubu Avenue, Kinshasa.

He produced comic strips as well as billboards, and soon developed a distinctive style in his street paintings that incorporated text as well as images:

> *I had noticed that people in the street would walk by paintings, glance at them and keep going. I thought that if I added a bit of text, people would have to stop and take time to read it, to get more into the painting and to admire it. That's what I called 'the Samba Signature'. From then on I put text in all my paintings.*

Samba first came to the attention of a worldwide audience through inclusion in the exhibition 'Magiciens de la Terre' at the Pompidou Centre in Paris in 1989. His highly politicized and satirical subject matter, laced with sex and violence and often drawing attention to the impact of globalization on ordinary people's lives in Africa, was immediately appealing to a Western audience eager to have their preconceptions of Africa confirmed. Yet the pictures are painted for Africans, not for Westerners, and, despite their ribald humour and grotesquery, they have serious points to make:

> *There's poverty, stupidity, corruption, chaos, universal decadence... I like to think that artists can change people's mentality; I stimulate people's consciousness; artists should make people think.*

Chéri Samba has had numerous solo exhibitions worldwide, including at the Centre Culturel du Zoo, Kinshasa (2000), the Musée Royal de l'Afrique, Tervuren (2003), Fondation Cartier, Paris (2004) and the Tate Gallery, London (2007).

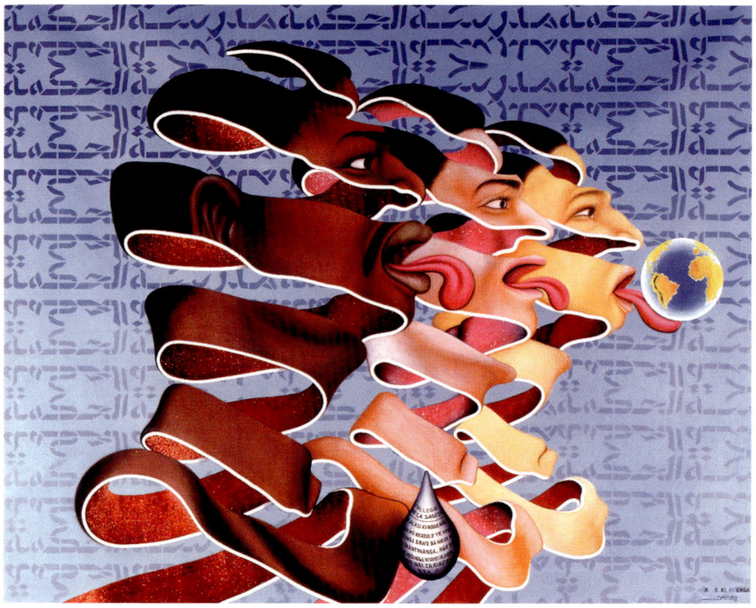

'The day I opened my studio, I hung a big painting outside in the street; it was about a war between two tribes and showed lots of naked people fighting. It quickly drew a crowd and by mid-morning there was a terrible traffic jam. The police arrested me for causing a disturbance and for disrespecting Congo's history.'
Chéri Samba

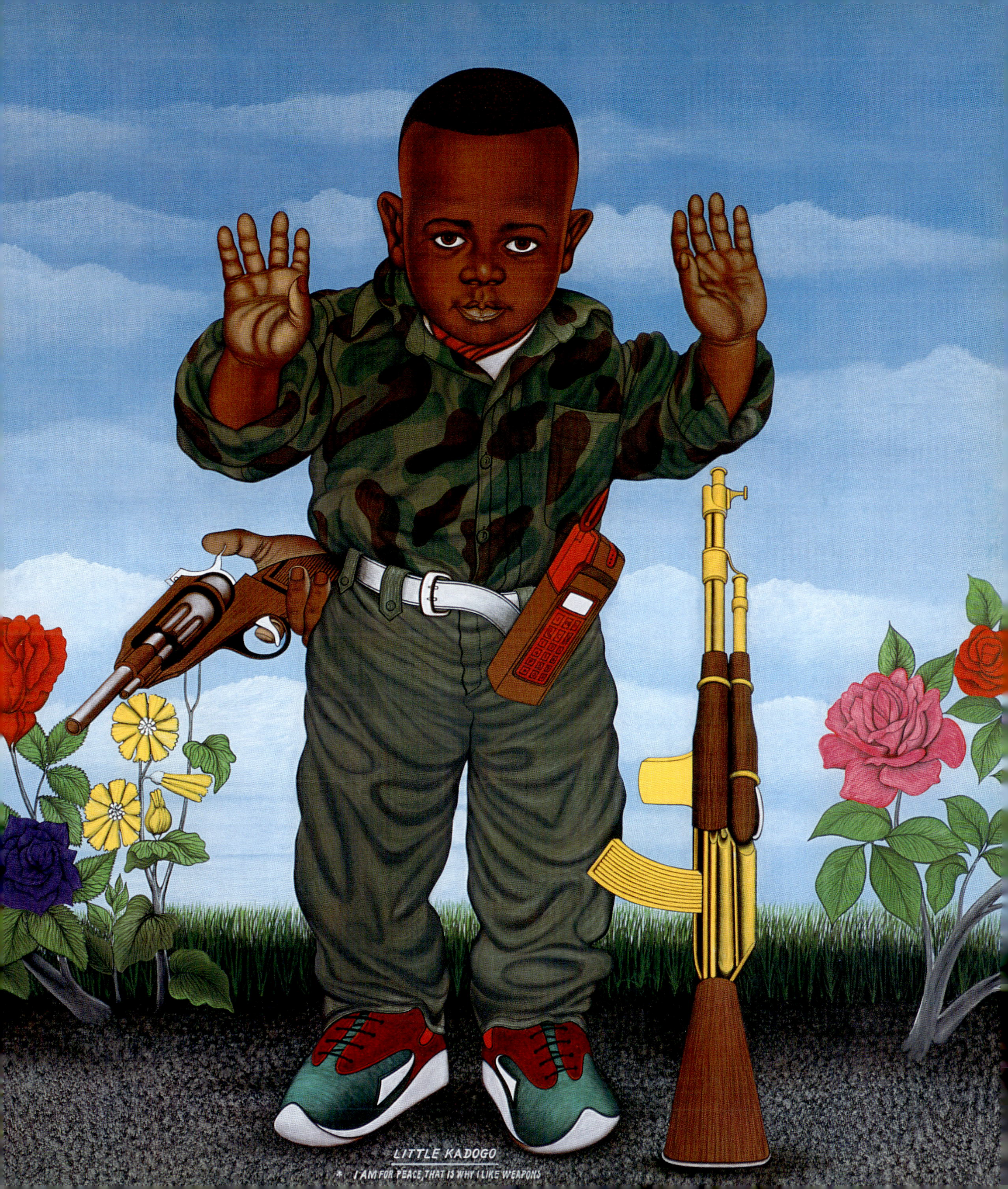
LITTLE KADOGO
* I AM FOR PEACE, THAT IS WHY I LIKE WEAPONS

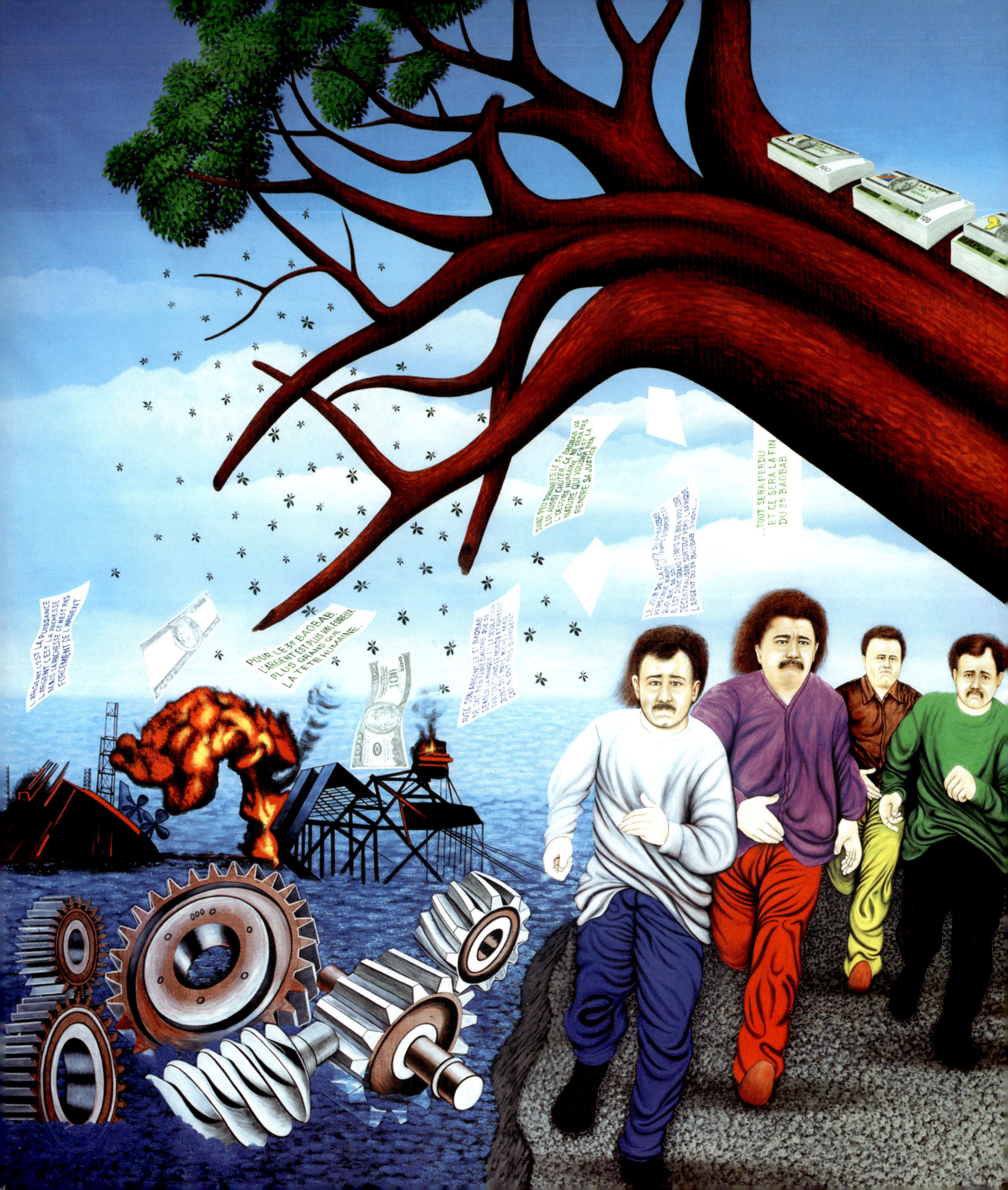
L'ARGENT C'EST LA PUISSANCE
L'ARGENT C'EST LA RICHESSE
MAIS LA RICHESSE CE N'EST PAS
FORCEMENT DE L'ARGENT.
POUR LE 3e BAOBAB,
L'ARGENT EST PLUS VALEUREUX
PLUS GRAND QUE
LA TETE HUMAINE.
AVEC SON ARGENT LE 3e BAOBAB
NE SAIT RIEN FAIRE D'AUTRE QUE DE
SEMER LA PANIQUE ET LA DESOLATION
PARTOUT DANS LE MONDE ET SURTOUT
DANS DES PAYS RICHES MAIS
QUI N'ONT PAS D'ARGENT
DANS PEU D'ANNEES LE 3e BAOBAB VA
LUI AUSSI CHUTER. CA NE SERA PAS
L'OEUVRE HUMAINE, C'EST LA
NATURE QUI VOUDRA BIEN
RENDRE SA JUSTICE
LE JOUR DE LA CHUTE DU 3e BAOBAB
PERSONNE N'AURA LE TEMPS D'EMPORTER
QUOI QUE SE SOIT.
IL EST DONC GRAND TEMPS DE BIEN VOULOIR
DECENTRALISER SURTOUT VERS L'AFRIQUE
L'ARGENT DU 3e BAOBAB. SINON...
...TOUT SERA PERDU
ET CE SERA LA FIN
DU 3e BAOBAB

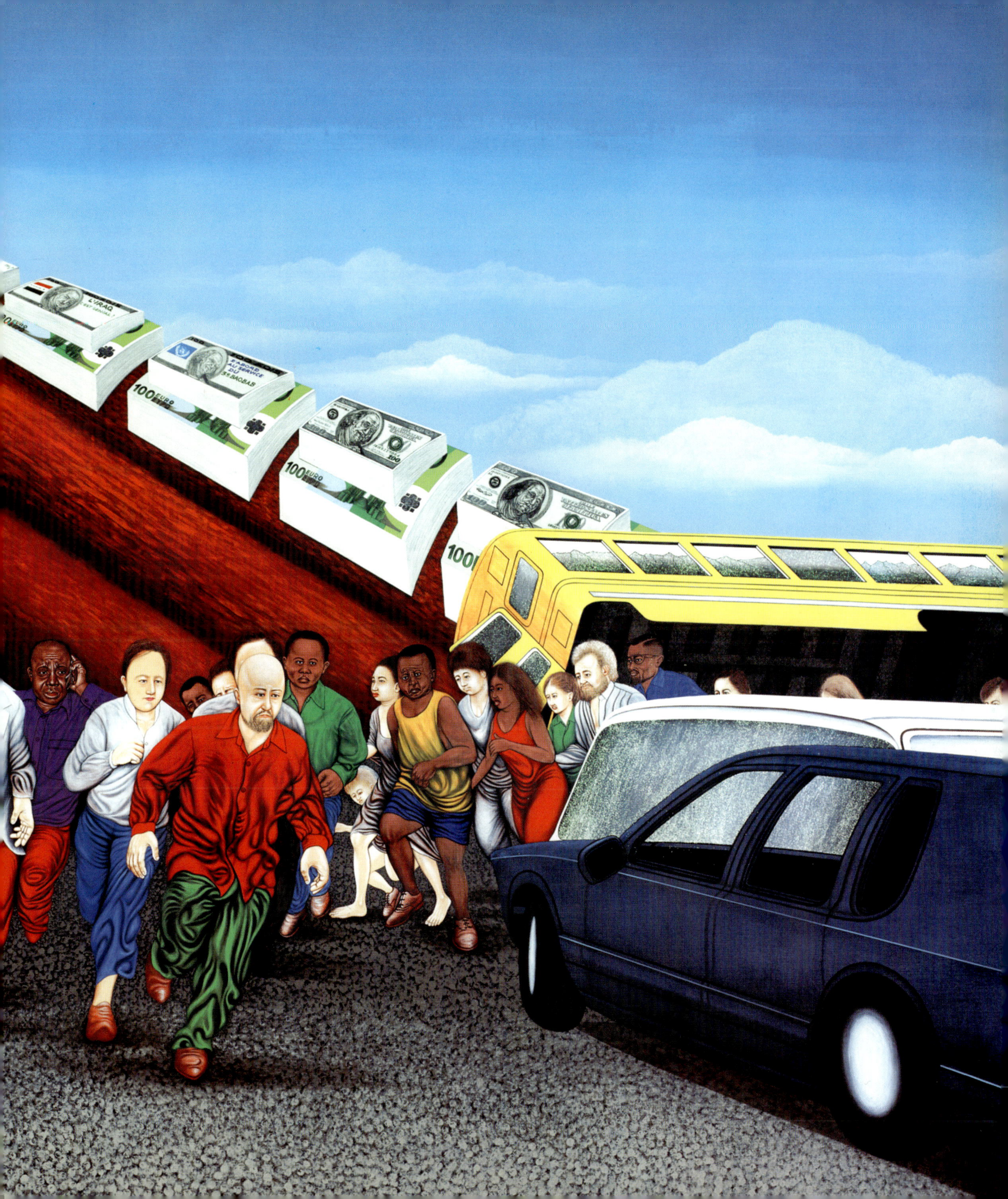
L'IRAQ
AU SERVICE
DU
BAOBAB
100 EURO
100 EURO
100 EURO

Previous spread *La Chute du 3e Baobab (The Fall of the 3rd Baobab)*, 2006. Acrylic and glitter on canvas, 300 x 496.6 cm (118 x 195½ in). CAAC–The Pigozzi Collection, Geneva.
The ancient baobab tree of Africa is a source of food, water and raw materials, and is the home of ancestral spirits. When greed, exploitation and contempt for the environment finally bring it down, the world will face disaster on an unimaginable scale.

Below *Quant il n'y avait plus rien d'autre que... l'Afrique restait une pensée (As there was nothing left... Africa remained a thought)*, 1997. Oil on canvas, 81 x 101 cm (31⅞ x 39¾ in). Private collection.
Picasso's ignorance of Africa is matched only by his debt to the continent.

Right *Le Monde Vomissant (The World Vomiting)*, 2004. Acrylic on canvas, 200 x 260 cm (78¾ x 102⅓ in). CAAC–The Pigozzi Collection, Geneva.

Where is the seriousness?
Where is democracy?
Should we just talk about
Majority or minority?

The United States of America
in the face of the World,
'they are the great Dictators'.

They provoke wars
everywhere and the entire
world vomits on them
because of the unjust war
in Iraq.

Chéri Samba, Sept. 2004
(Translated from the French)

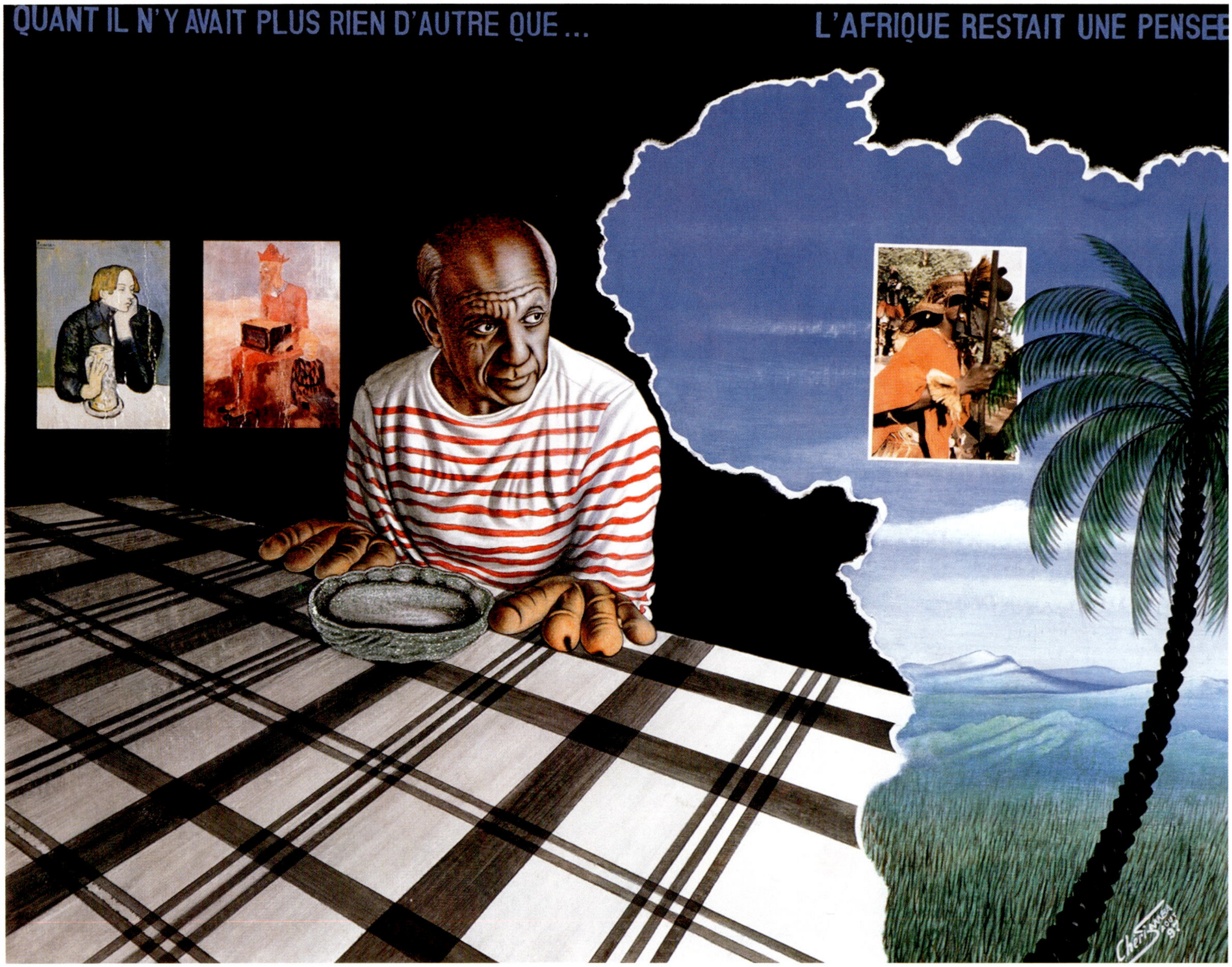

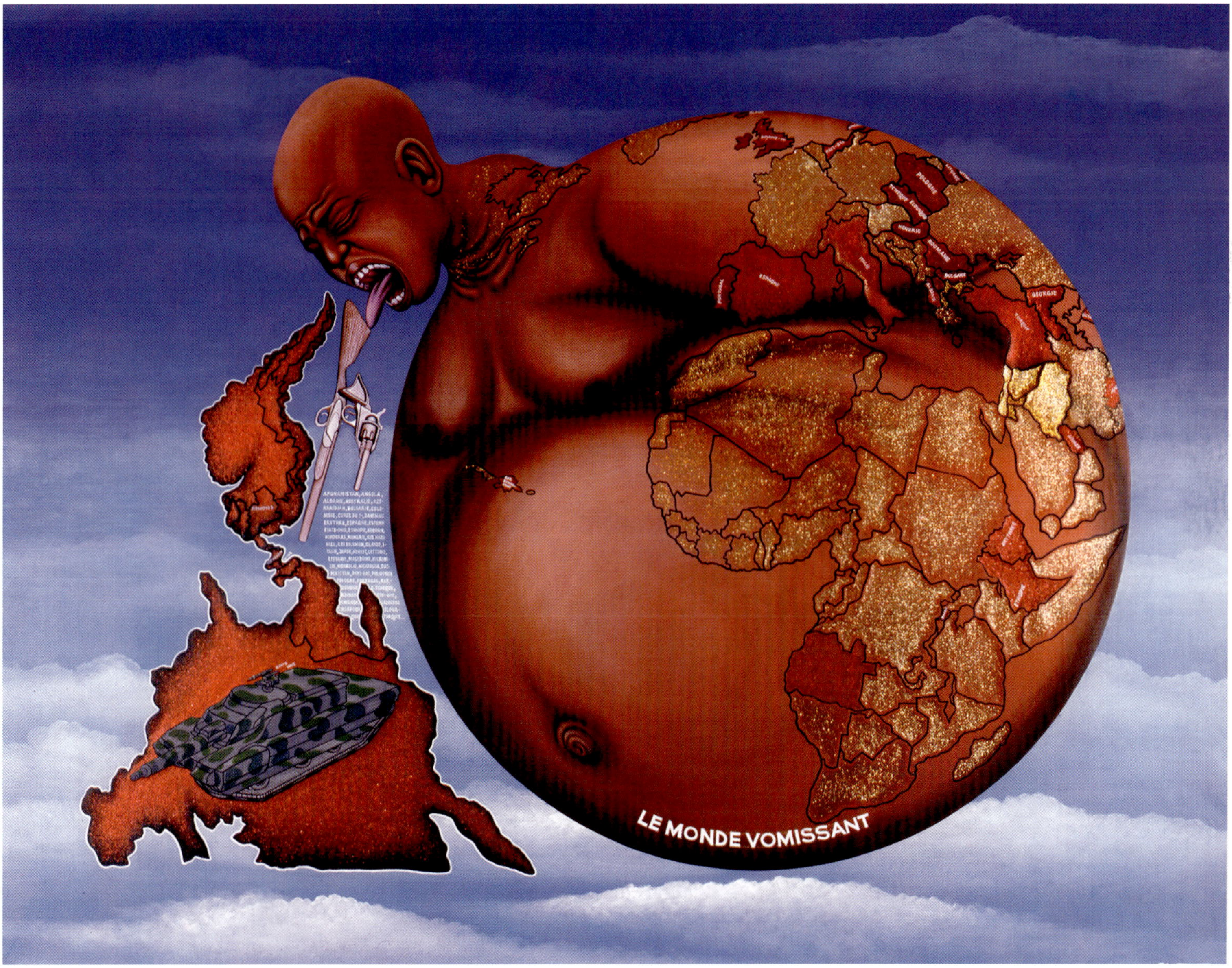
LE MONDE VOMISSANT

YINKA SHONIBARE, MBE
UK/NIGERIA

Below *Colonel Tarleton and Mrs Oswald Shooting*, 2007 (detail). Installation view of the exhibition 'Scratch the Surface', National Gallery, London.

Right *The Crowning (after Fragonard)*, 2007. Two mannequins, Dutch wax printed cotton textile, shoes, coir matting, artificial silk flowers, 160 x 280 x 210 cm (63 x 110 x 88 in). Collection of the artist.

'I was actually surprised when I came to England and found out that there was this notion that if you were black you were somehow disadvantaged – I thought that was hilarious. But then you either dwell on those issues or turn them to your advantage.'

Humour, parody and irony are essential elements in Yinka Shonibare, MBE's work, though the laughter that the artist encourages is also part of the technique he uses to emphasize the serious and deeply felt issues raised by his work. 'I realized that I didn't have to accept my designation as some sort of doomed "other". I could challenge my relationship to authority with humour and parody in mimicking and mirroring.' For Shonibare, 'culture' is an artificial construct, and the 'African' textiles that feature in one way or another in all his major pieces – and have become his artistic signature – are part of that construct. 'The fabrics are not really authentically African the way people think. They prove to have a crossbred cultural background quite of their own. And it's the fallacy of that signification that I like.'

Shonibare was born in London in 1962. At the age of three he moved to Lagos with his Nigerian parents. His decision to go to art school in London was brutally postponed by a rare illness that left him paralyzed down one side of his body. As soon as he was well enough, he continued his studies at the Byam Shaw School of Art (1984–89) and at Goldsmiths College (1989–91). He has held numerous solo exhibitions since 1994, and his work was included in the major touring exhibitions 'Sensation' (1997) and 'Africa Remix' (2004–7). He was a Turner Prize nominee in 2004 and was awarded the MBE in 2005. In 2007, Shonibare contributed to a number of exhibitions in London marking the bicentenary of the abolition of the Atlantic slave trade, including 'Uncomfortable Truths' at the Victoria and Albert Museum, and 'Scratch the Surface' at the National Gallery.

Much of Shonibare's work references the hedonistic lifestyle of eighteenth- and nineteenth-century European aristocracy, wealthy traders and industrialists, a lifestyle that was dependent first upon the slave trade and then upon the unseen labour of African and other peoples during the colonial period. Yet Shonibare also considers himself a hedonist:

> *I think that pleasure is king – as well as a very strong base for being subversive... I view pleasure as so important, and use it in my work as an intellectual basis for questioning a lot of things I believe in very deeply. I crave the trappings of wealth like anyone else, but politically I do question the means by which that is achieved.*

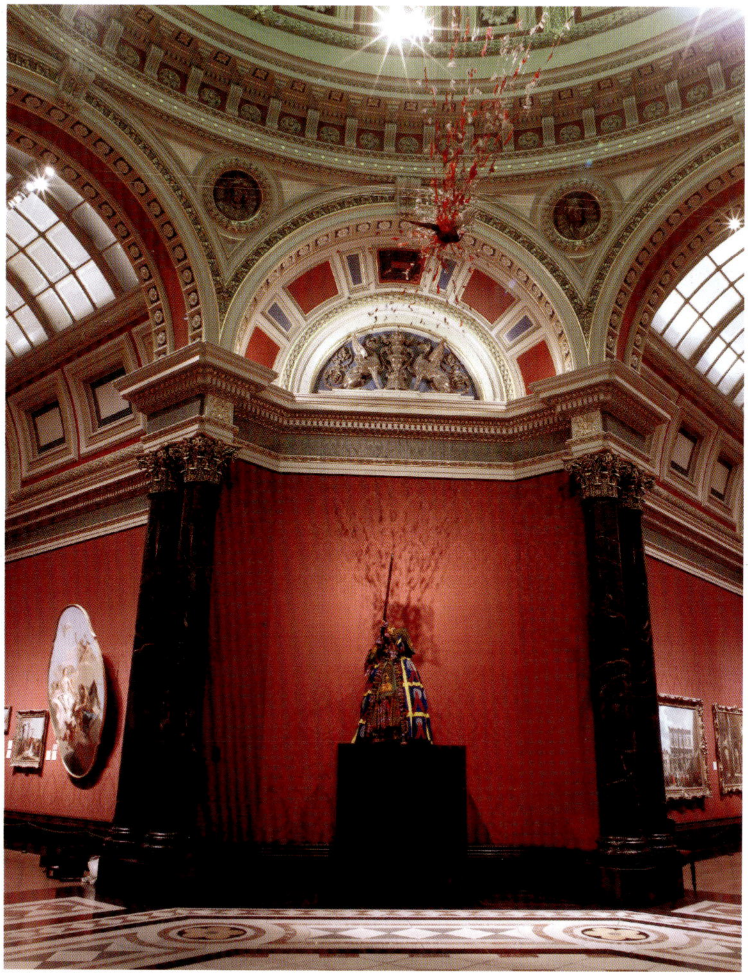

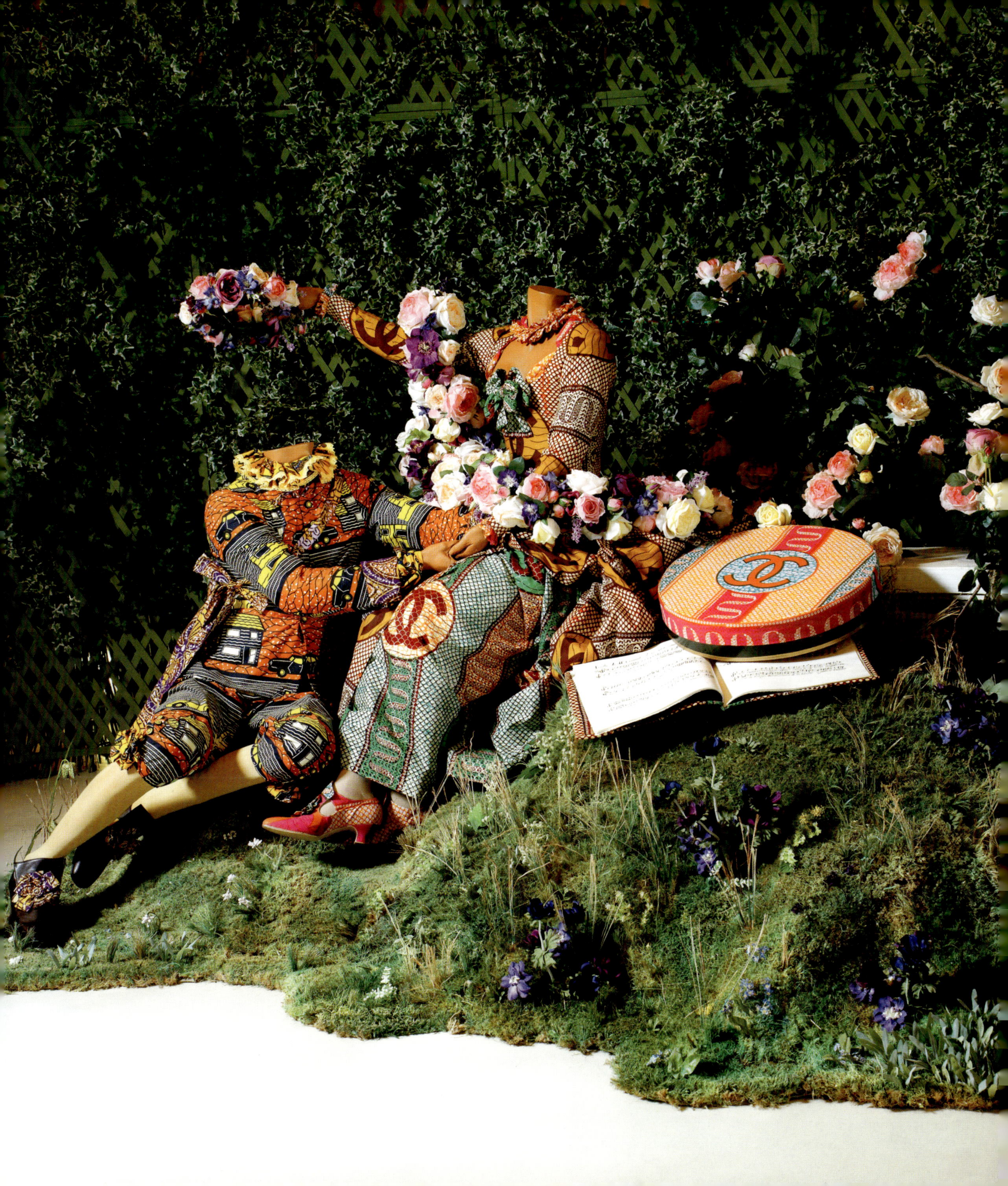

Below *Black Gold I*, 2006. Acrylic on canvas and 25 Dutch wax-printed cotton canvases, 330 x 673 cm (128¾ x 262½ in). Collection of the artist.

While painting at the Byam Shaw School of Art, Shonibare recalls, 'Then this tutor came to me and said, "You're African aren't you? Why don't you make work about traditional African art?" – meaning I should make neo-primitive art or something. I am a contemporary African. I did not understand what constitutes "traditional African art" and actually went to the British Museum to find out what he meant.'

Right *Dysfunctional Family*, 1999. Wax-printed cotton textile, polyester, wood, plastic, four figures, from left to right – Mother: 150 x 52 x 37 cm (59 x 20½ x 14½ in), Boy: 89 x 54 x 46 cm (35 x 21¼ x 18 in), Girl: 69 x 36 x 30 cm (27⅙ x 14⅕ x 11⅘ in), Father: 148 x 40 x 36 cm (58¼ x 15¾ x 14⅕ in). Walker Art Center, Minneapolis, Butler Family Fund, 2000.

'I am very interested in the politics of representation as opposed to the representation of politics.'

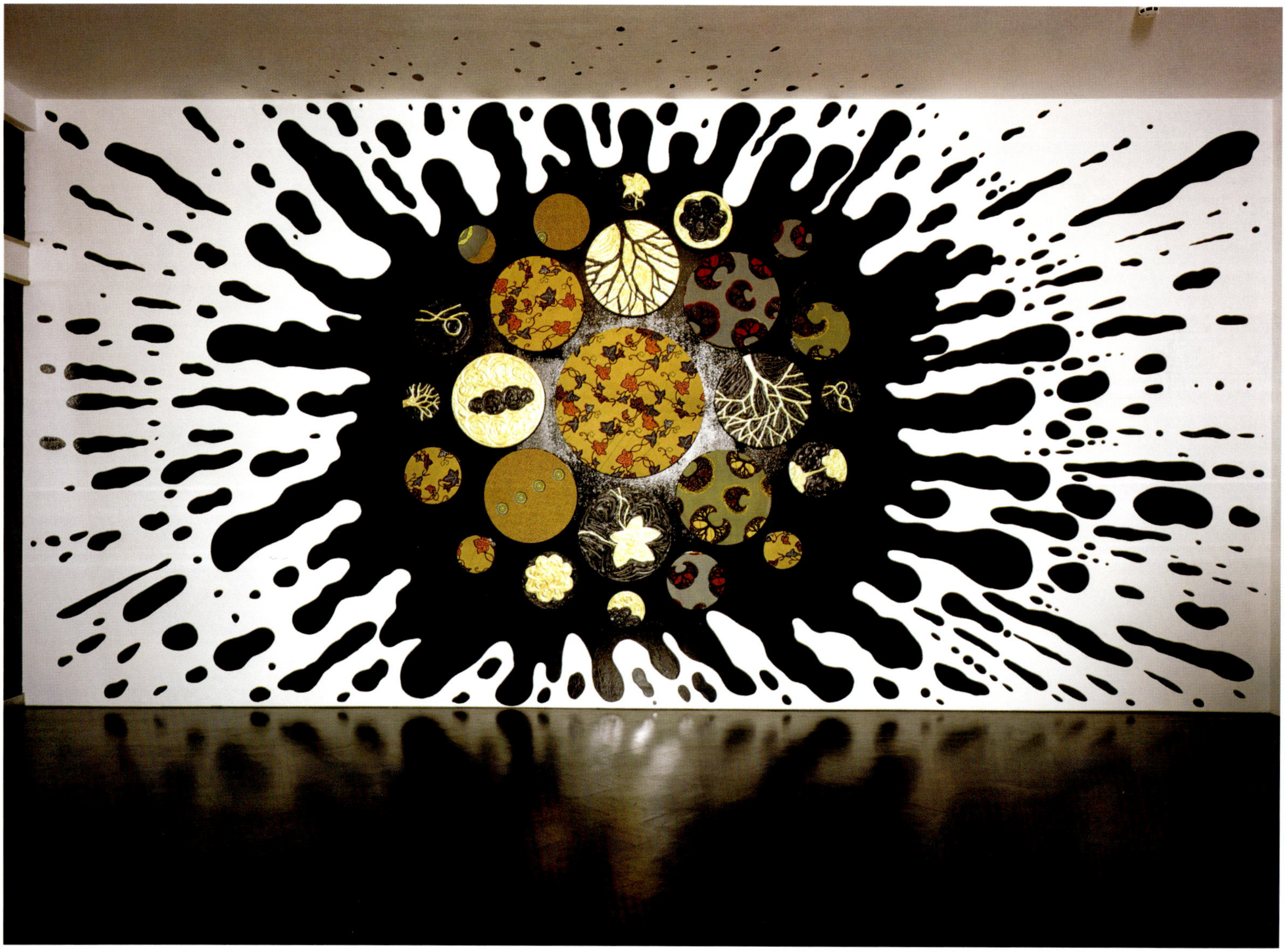

'Black people can laugh too. We are not serious all the time.'
Yinka Shonibare, MBE

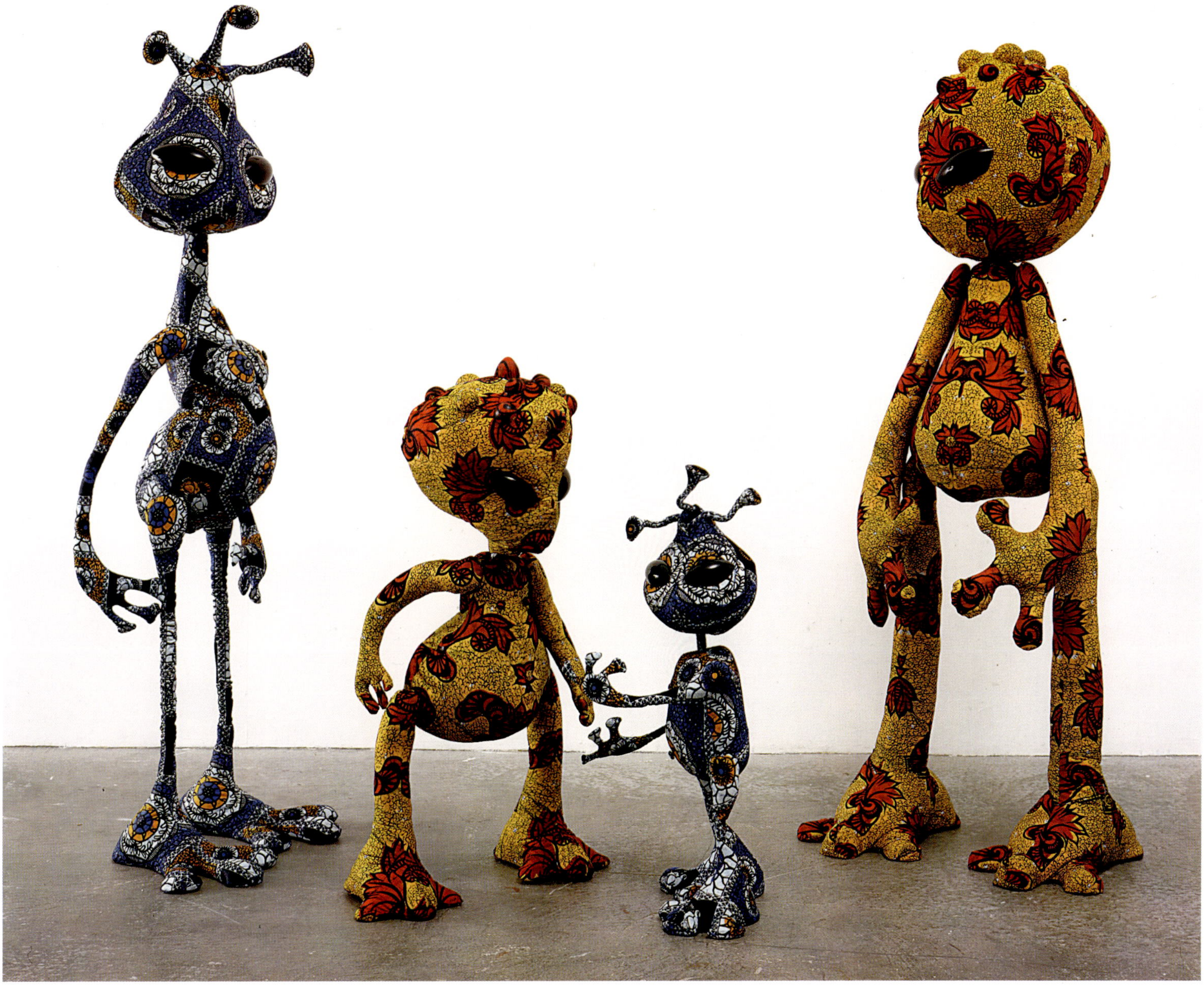

Below *Mr and Mrs Andrews Without Their Heads (after Gainsborough)*, 1998. Wax-print cotton costumes on armatures, dog mannequin, bench and gun, 254 x 570 x 165 cm (100 x 224²/₅ x 65 in). National Gallery of Canada, Ottawa.
None of Shonibare's mannequin figures have heads; heads, minds and faces are a distraction from the broader historical and political points he is trying to make. The only 'complete' figures with visible heads are his 'aliens' – those whom society considers abnormal.

Right *Diary of a Victorian Dandy: 17.00 hours*, 1998. C-type print, edition of 3, 183 x 228.6 cm (71½ x 89¾ in). Collection of the artist.
One of a set of five photographs that show the artist as dandy, progressing through a wonderfully decadent and narcissistic day; though set in Victorian times, the series nods to eighteenth-century humorous morality sequences such as Hogarth's *Rake's Progress*. Shonibare is fascinated by Oscar Wilde, 'a man of Irish origin who tried to move up in English society through his wit, style and writing. He was an outsider who parodied Englishness, in a way, and a gay man who thus challenged authority – though of course he paid for it in the end.'

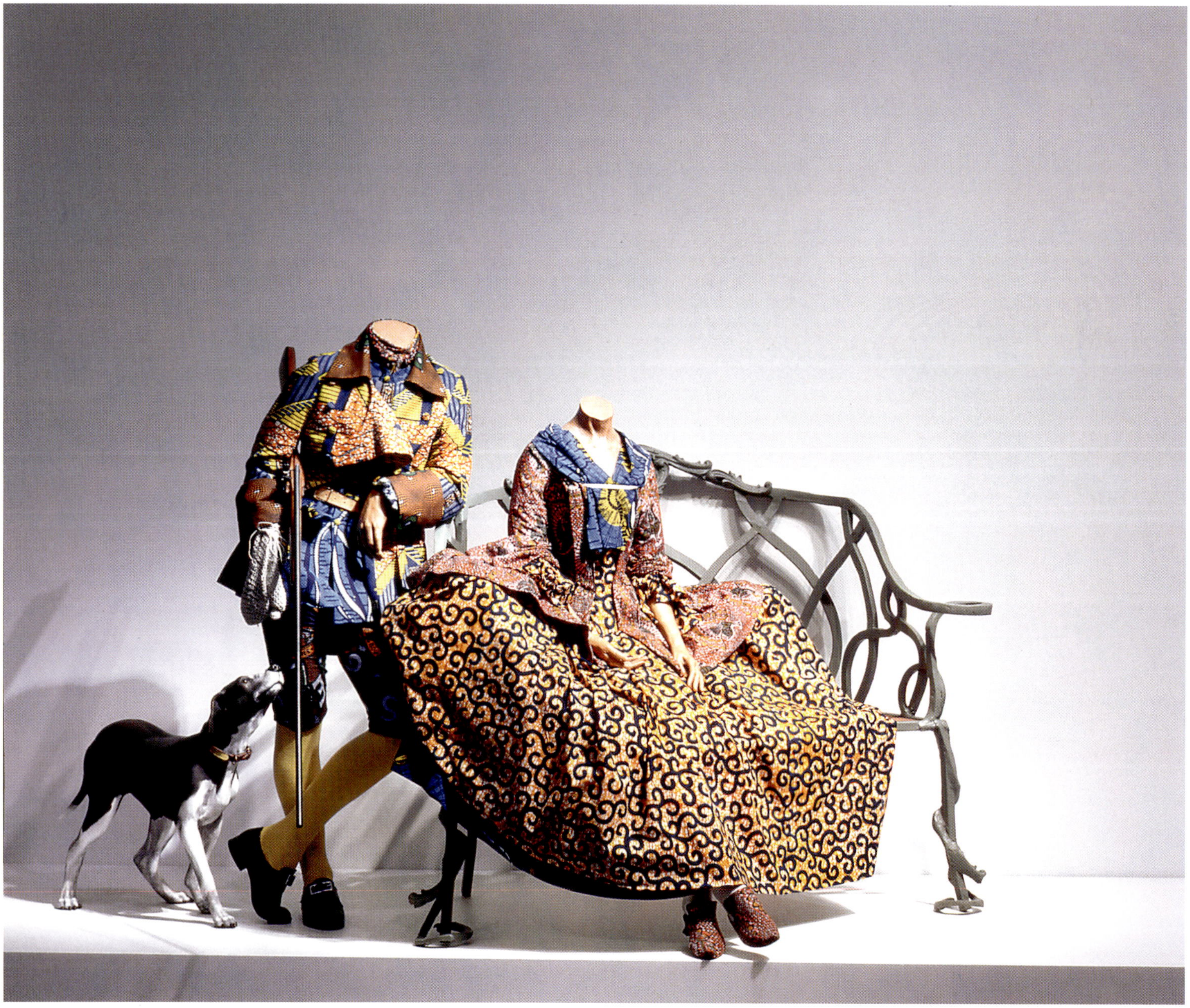

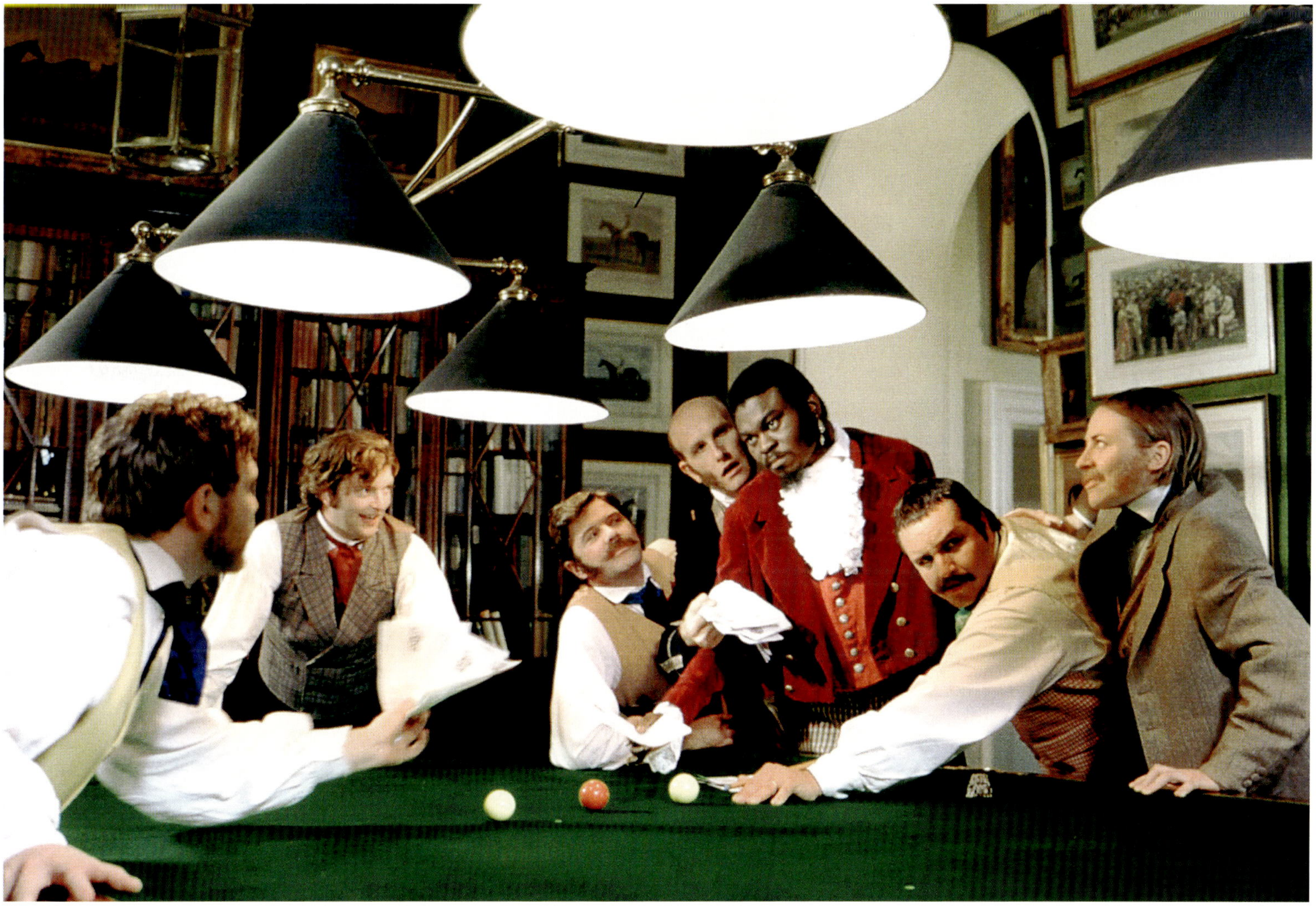

JULIEN SINZOGAN
REPUBLIC OF BENIN/ FRANCE

Below *Egun I*, 2007. Natural tint and oil on canvas, 130 x 90cm (51⅕ x 35⅖ in). Collection of the artist. An *egungun* dancer, swathed in rich cloth, honours the ancestors in the most complex of all Yoruba masquerades. Behind him are plaster reliefs that echo those on the walls of the palace of the ancient kingdom of Dahomey. The 'black sun' represents Yeku–meji in the Yoruba divinatory system *Ifa* and signifies remembrance of the dead by those still living.

Right *Dagbissou*, 2000 (detail). Acrylic on canvas, 100 x 75cm (39⅖ x 29½ in). Collection of the artist. Dagbissou or Daghesu is the goat-headed god of war in the pantheon of Fon gods, *vodun*. In his hand he carries a sabre (*gubasa*) and lightning springs from his mouth.

Sinzogan's work subtly expresses the way of life informed and inspired by the Yoruba divinatory and religious system known as *Ifa*. The Yoruba people of Nigeria and Benin in West Africa see life as taking a cyclical trajectory through which individuals experience the tangible world (*aye*), depart to the spirit world (*orun*) and are reborn. Sinzogan's works explore the journeys between these different but closely related worlds. The voyages between such realms lie at the heart of religious practice across much of the Atlantic world, a world for ever shaped by another voyage: the middle passage of the Atlantic slave trade.

Sinzogan's mixed-media and fine pen-and-ink works conjure the world of the spirits and their gods (*vodun* and *orisha*), the gods to whom millions of enslaved Africans would have prayed, departing through the 'Gates of No Return' in the slave ports of the West African coast. Yet Sinzogan does not portray these ports as sites of loss, but as triumphant arrival points for the homeward return of lost spirits about to be reborn. The galleons in his works are not the dark and evil slave ships of the Europeans, but are in the process of being transformed by their African cargoes into colourful and triumphant symbols of resistance.

Julien Sinzogan was born in 1957 in Porto-Novo, Republic of Benin. He studied architecture in Paris at the Ecole Spéciale des Travaux Public, and later ran a department of computer images before turning professionally to painting. He lives and works in France. Sinzogan has exhibited throughout Europe and Africa in group and solo shows, including 'Voyages' at the October Gallery, London (2007) and 'Uncomfortable Truths' at the Victoria and Albert Museum, London (2007).

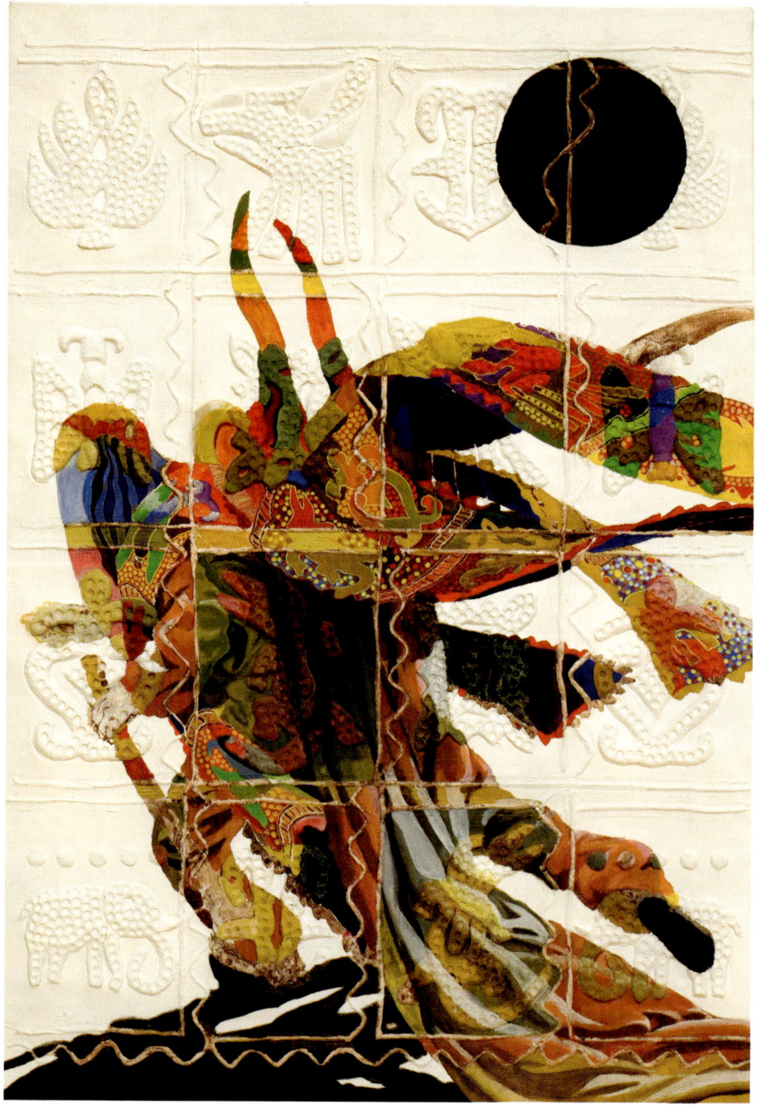

'There are voyages which should never have been... the middle passage, for example... there are spiritual voyages, such as a meeting with a *babalawo* [priest] well known for travelling between visible and invisible worlds... and there are imaginary voyages, through "Gates of Return" and "Gates of No-Return".'
Julien Sinzogan

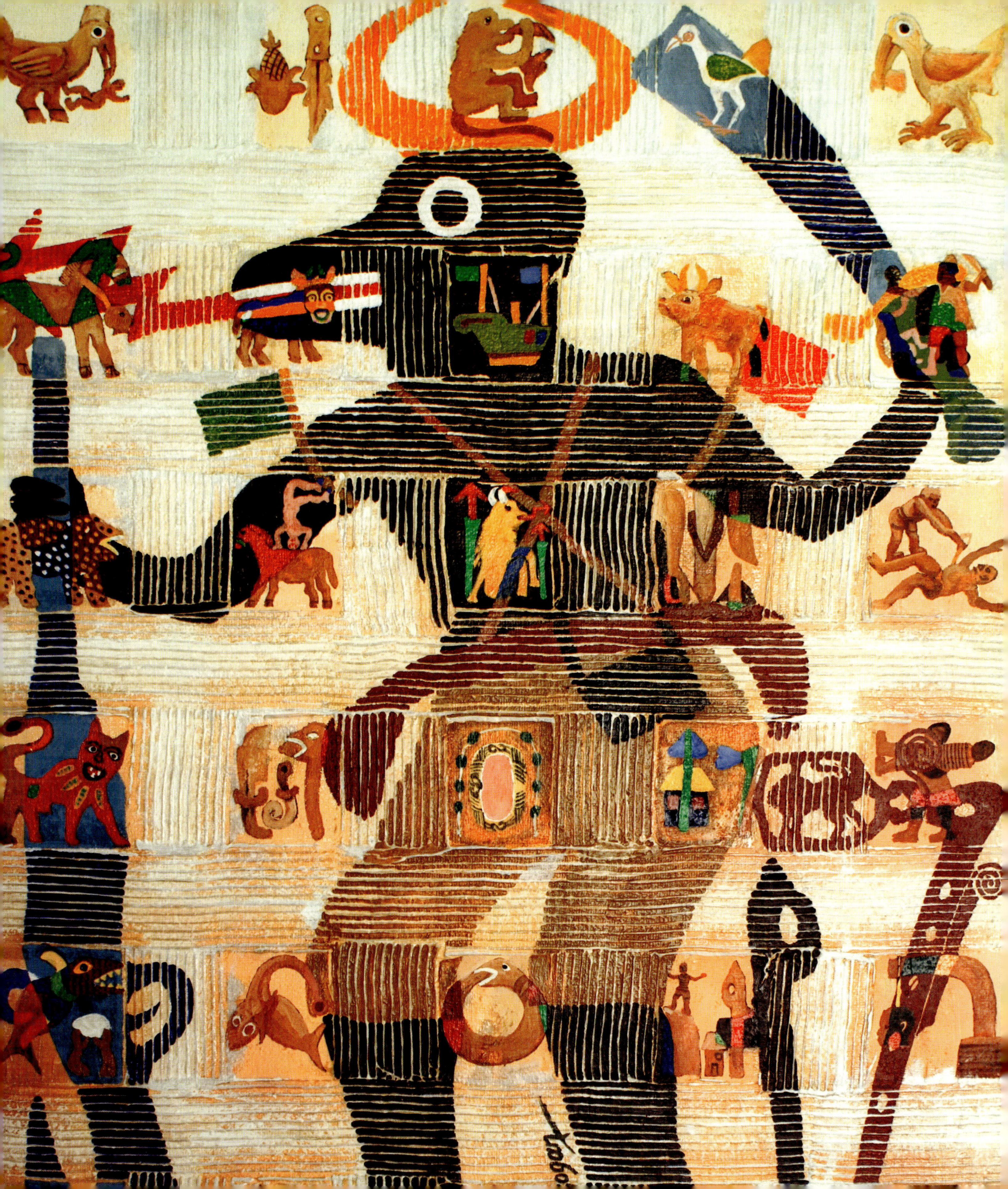

Below *Return of the Spirits*, 2000. Coloured inks on paper, 75 x 108 cm (29½ x 42½ in). Collection of the artist.
Returning spirits, in the forms of *egungun* masqueraders, have taken over a slave ship and are resurrecting those who have gone before.

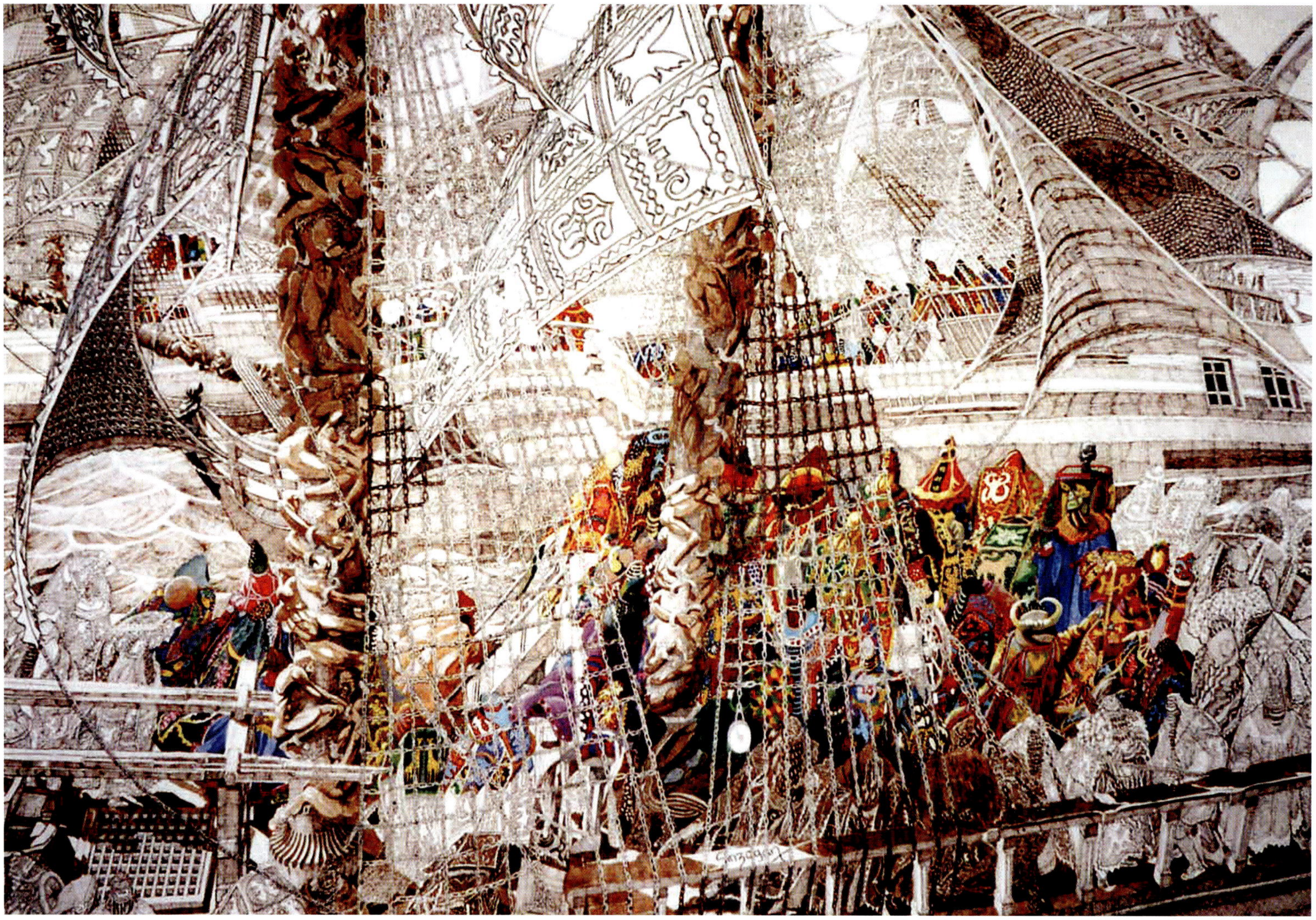

Below *Géléde Theatre,* 2000. Coloured inks on paper, 75 x 108 cm (29½ x 42½ in). Collection of the artist.
Gelede masquerades celebrate womankind, 'the mothers' without whom the Yoruba people would not exist.

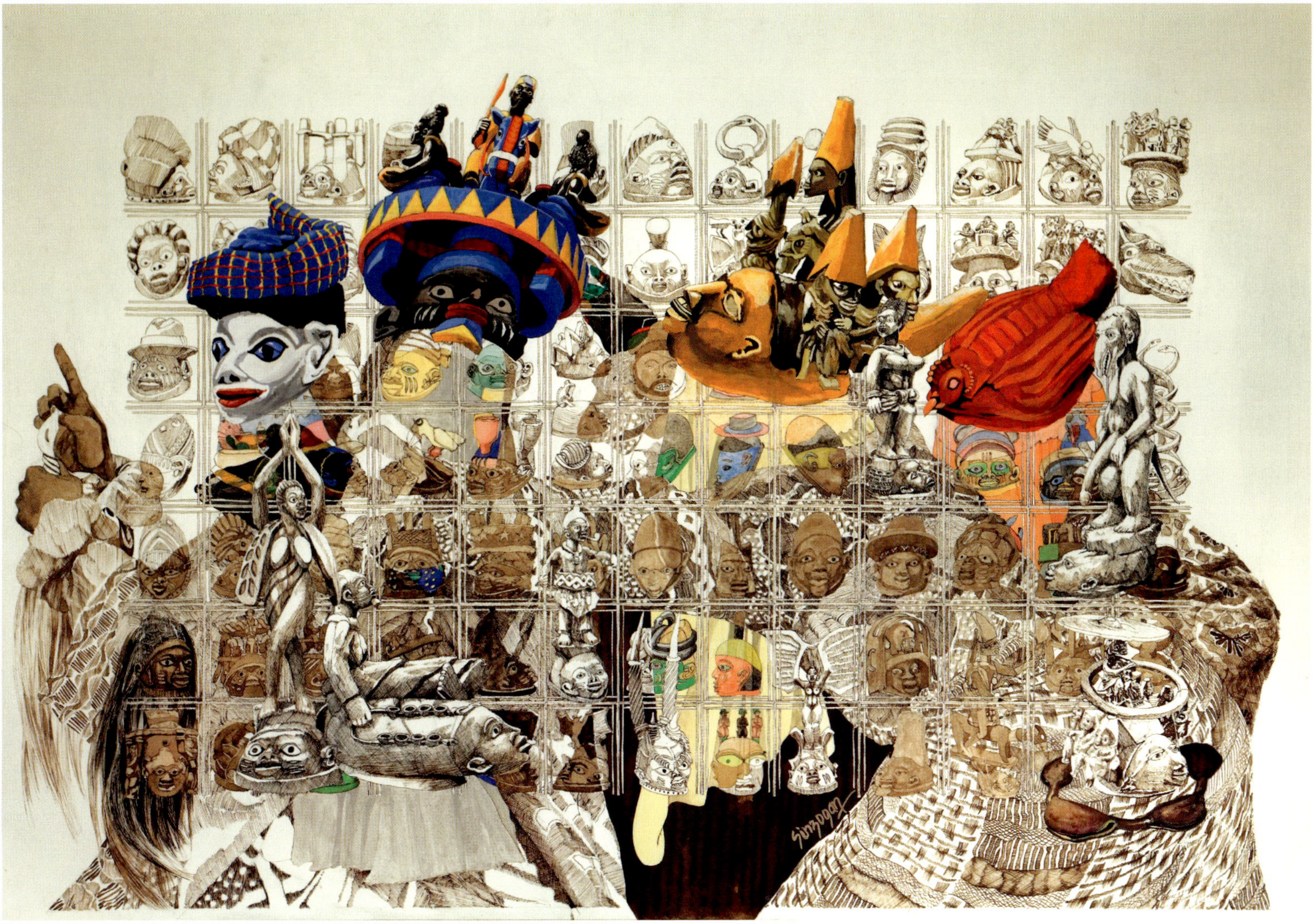

Below *The Gate of Return*, 2005. Coloured inks on paper, 150 x 206 cm (59 x 81 in). Olivier Doria d'Angri collection.
Sinzogan's spirit figures transform the 'Gates of no Return' in the slave forts along the West African coast into triumphal 'Gates of Return' through which the returning spirits are led by *Ifa* priests.

Right *Figurehead*, 1999. Mixed media collage on hardboard, 100 x 65 cm (39⅖ x 25⅗ in). Private collection.
In place of the European figurehead on the slave ship, the Yoruba spirit ship has an *Ifa* priest (*babalawo*) on its prow, carrying a huge diviner's staff in his hand.

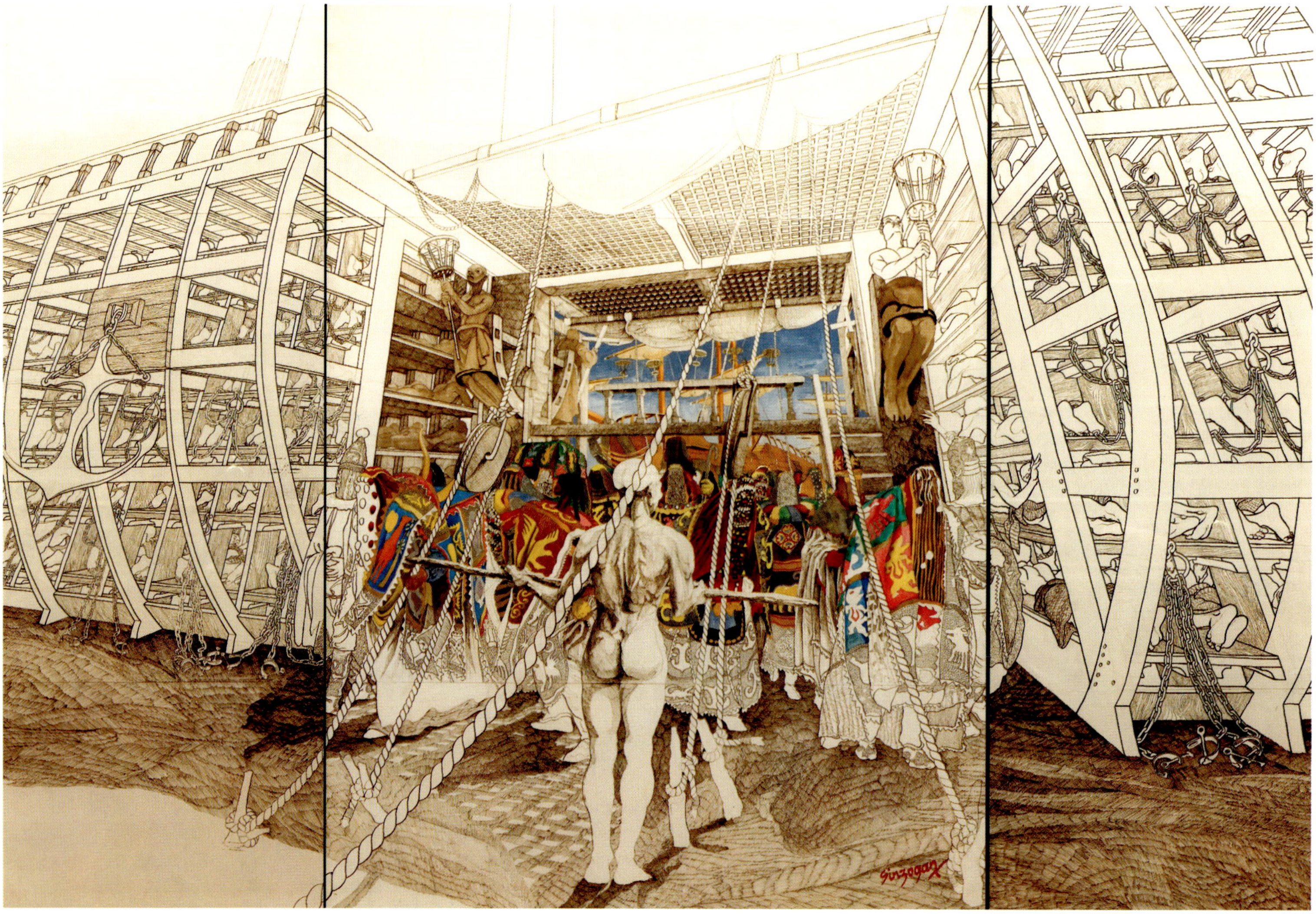

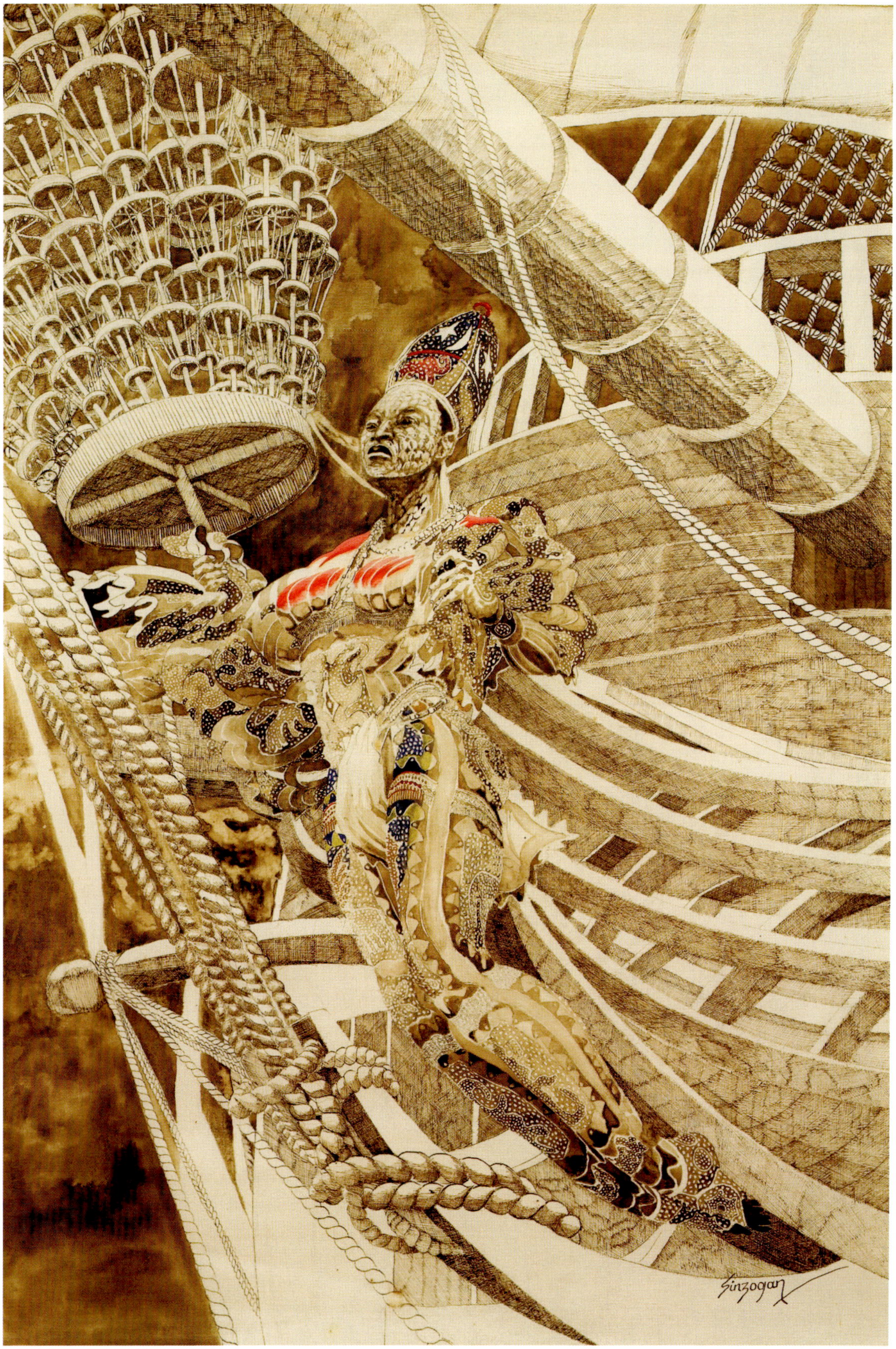
Sinzogan

KHALED BEN SLIMANE
TUNISIA

Below *Qinnina* (bottle) in the form of a Qu'ran board, 1988. Ceramic, 34 x 19 x 6cm (13⅖ x 7½ x 2⅓ in). British Museum, London. Slimane uses religious words and phrases that recur throughout his work, acting as a constant reminder of his deeply spiritual commitment. Here the normal function of the Qu'ran board is suggested by the written word '*Huwa*' ('He'; referring to God), while the work's hollow form suggests a mystical transformation into a receptacle for the word of God.

Right *Jadath* (*Gravestone*), 1992. Ceramic, 49 x 45 x 6cm (19⅖ x 17¾ x 2⅓ in). British Museum, London. 'From 1986 onwards, I created a number of horizontal and vertical stelae and tombstones... These two forms were used to symbolize the attitude of human beings to death. Some are frightened and lie down, while others accept its inevitability and remain standing.'

Producing ceramics is not just a question of technique, but first and foremost an art of living and a philosophy. Ceramics must express emotion and form a nexus for sharing and for the celebration of nature and man.

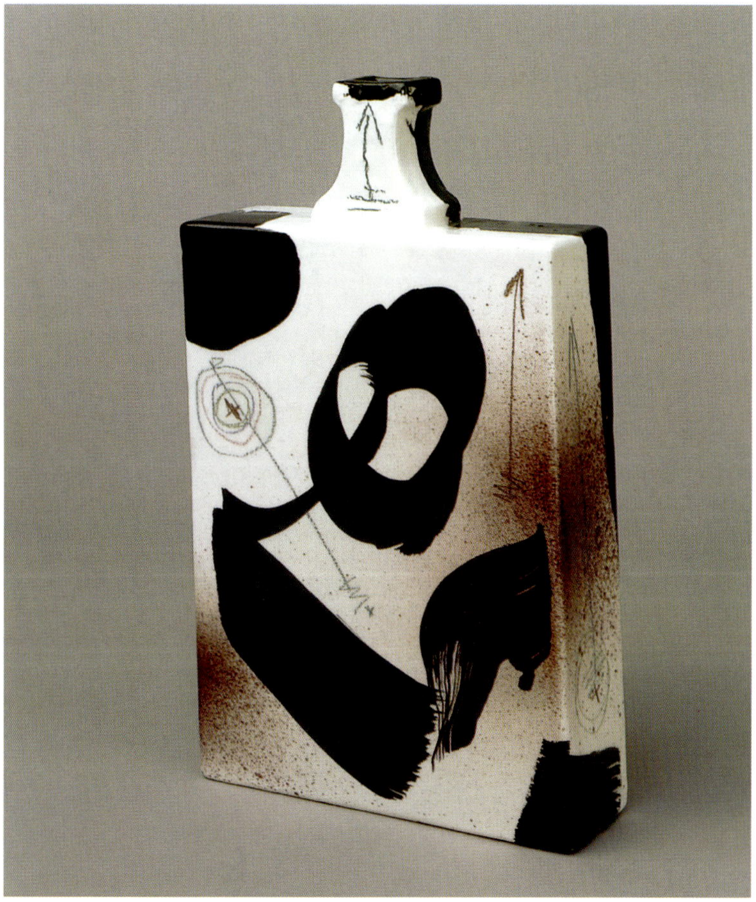

Khaled Ben Slimane was born in the town of Sousse, Tunisia, in 1951, though it was not until eight or nine years later that he feels he was 'really born' at Dar Oufa, near the little seaside village of Maamoura. 'I was watching the waves coming in and out. Like an obsession. I pretended to like fishing to be able to look at the ebb and flow of the water. An enthronement of sorts. I desperately needed to be alone... there was no bait at the end of the line.'

A deeply spiritual and entirely unpretentious man, Slimane has travelled far and wide in his quest for a deeper understanding of the relationship between man and the world – and the skills needed to express this philosophy. He trained in Tunis, Barcelona and on the island of Kyushu, Japan and travelled in Iran and India, though he found the true inspiration for his work in a trunk full of old property deeds in his grandfather's house in Maamoura. 'These deeds contained the history of the small seaside village, my birthplace, but the script particularly intrigued me, an enigmatic, undecipherable writing.'

Slimane is intensely aware of the past glories of Tunisian ceramics, which began to wane in the late nineteenth century, reaching their nadir in the 1950s. He passionately believes that it is his role to inject new life into these traditions, and that to do so a cultural dialogue and interaction with other countries, peoples and their traditions is essential. 'It is impossible to underestimate this dialogue between cultures.'

Khaled Ben Slimane's works are now to be found in the collections of more than thirty museums around the world, as well as in numerous private collections.

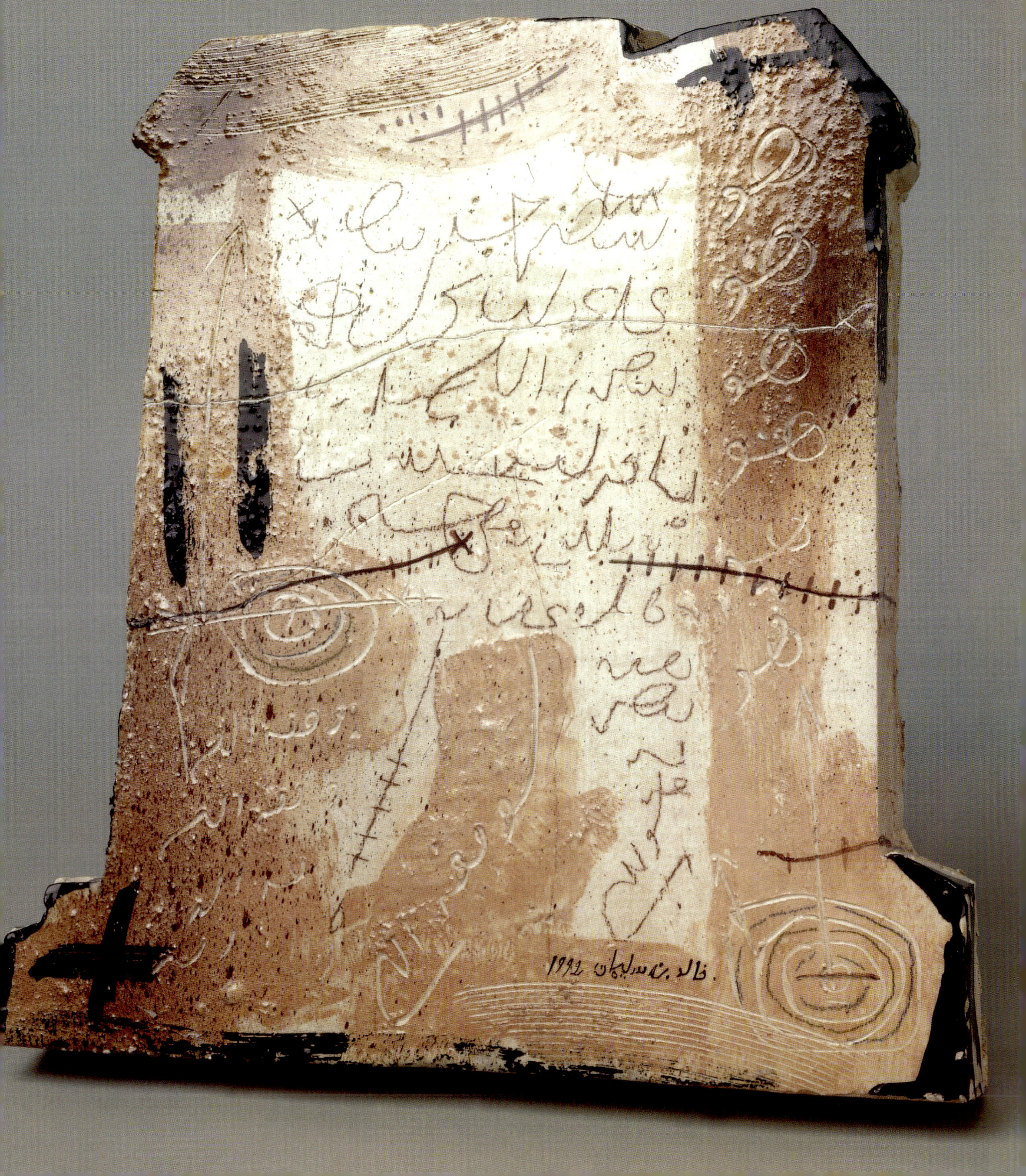
خالد بن سليمان 1992

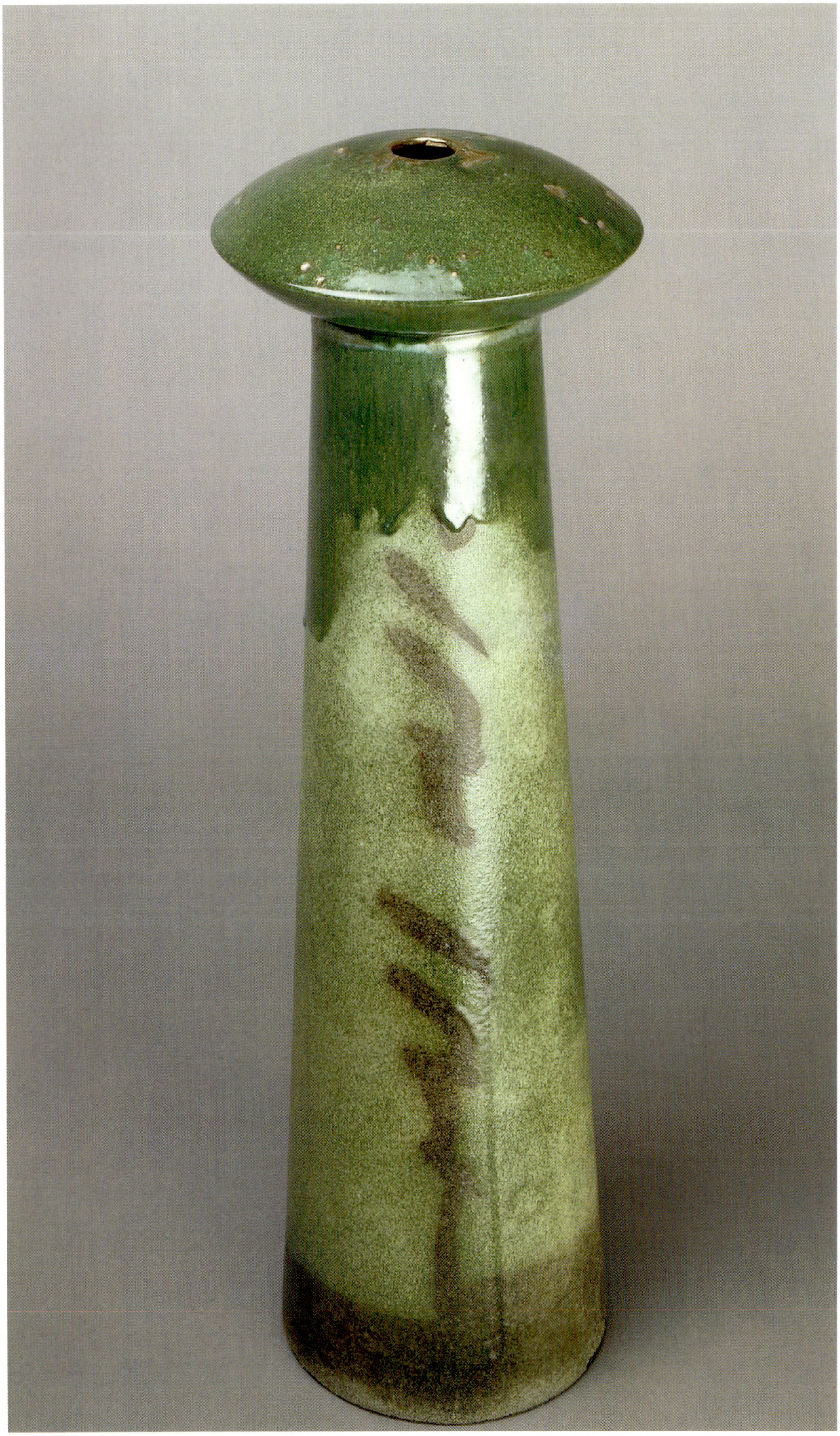

Left *Mazhariya* (*Invocation*), 1995. Ceramic, 57 x 20 cm (22⅖ x 8 in). British Museum, London.
The inscription on this vase reads: 'wafaqani Allah' ('God has brought me success'). Slimane fires his vessels twice. Following the first firing he applies the decoration, either by scratching or incising the slip-covered surface with signs, words and phrases, or by painting on coloured oxides with flat, wide brushes. He then applies a layer of clear glaze and fires for the second time.

Top right *Equilibrium*, 1994. Ceramic, 50 x 15 x 103 cm (19¾ x 6 x 40½ in). British Museum, London. 'A heritage frozen in time is a dead heritage, and in order to move it forward, it has to be open to other influences and welcome them with all their differences.' Slimane expresses the idea of the delicate balance of dialogue between peoples as a tightrope walk; the clay kiln temperature gauge perched on the end of the lower of the two projecting rods suggests, perhaps, the importance of constantly monitoring the progress of cultural interaction.

Bottom right *Misalla Ufqiya* (*Horizontal Funerary Stela*), 1989. Ceramic, 17 x 12 x 80 cm (6⅔ x 4¾ x 31½ in). British Museum, London. In the late 1980s and early 1990s, Slimane created a series of works inspired by forms of funerary architecture. During this period he visited many cemeteries, travelling from Mahdia in Tunisia to Oman. The form of this piece is inspired by Hafsid period (thirteenth–sixteenth century) prism stelae.

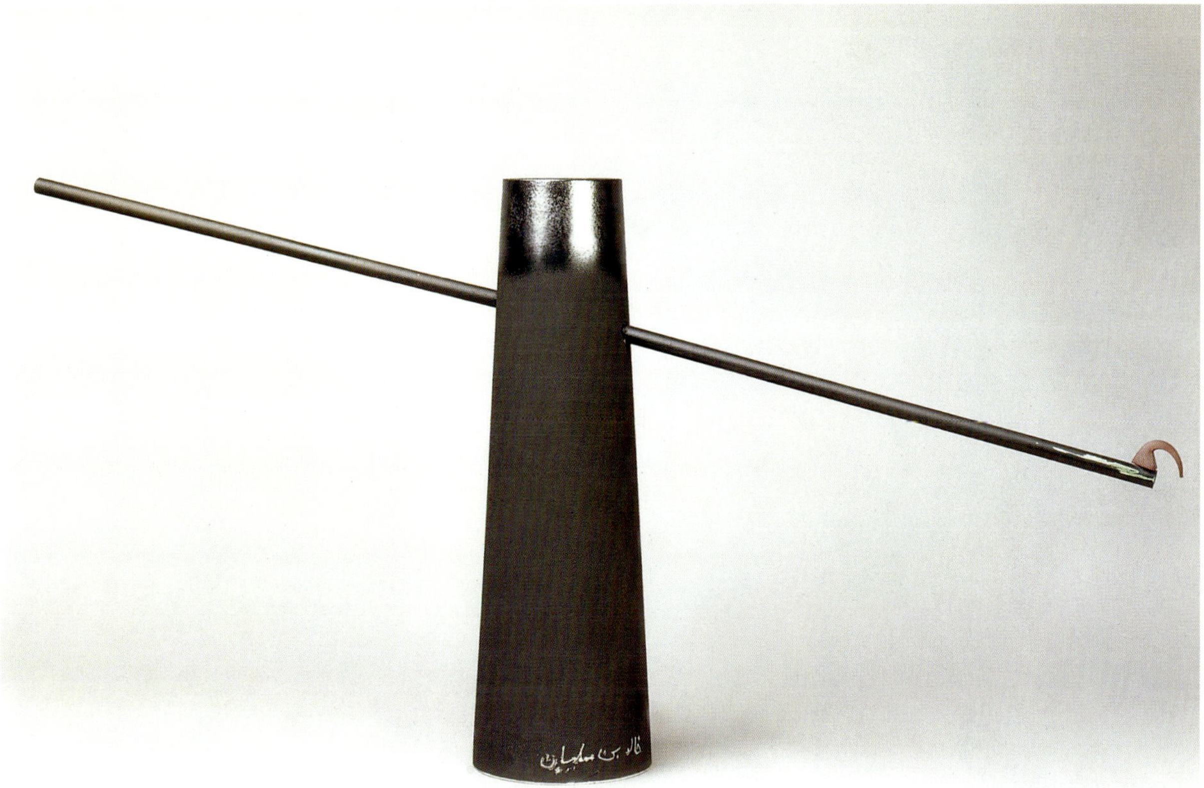

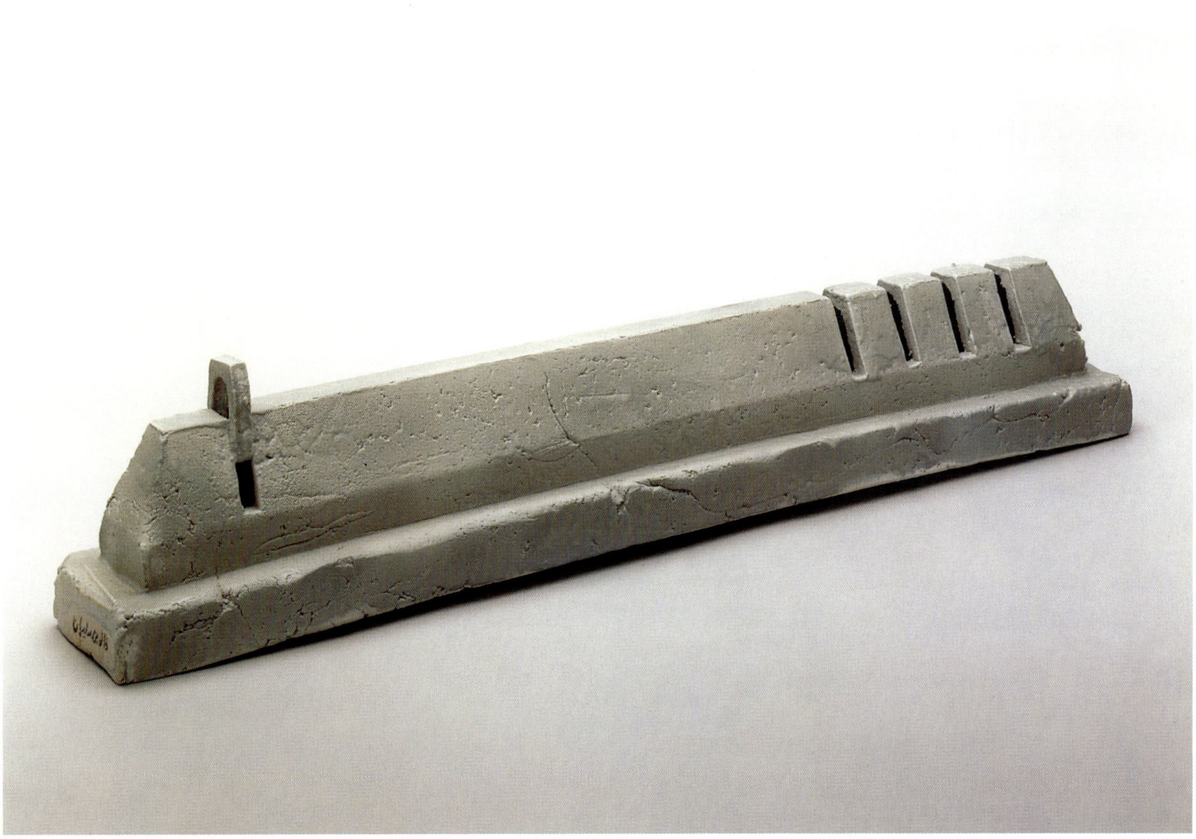

BARTHÉLÉMY TOGUO
CAMEROON/GERMANY/ FRANCE

Below *Nature Culture*, 2006. Photographic print of a performance, 130 x 130cm (51 x 51 in). Collection Bandjoun Station, Cameroon.

Right *Afrika Oil?*, 2006. Photographic print of a performance, 130 x 130 cm (51 x 51 in). Collection Bandjoun Station, Cameroon.
These images reflect Toguo's deep concern for the environment – deforestation, drought, the uncontrolled exploitation of oil and mineral resources – not just in Africa but around the world. They also reveal his humorous acceptance of how we are brainwashed by politicians and the headline writers – and what a source of inspiration they provide for his own art.

Barthélémy Toguo is a traveller, crossing boundaries of all sorts as his vision evolves. His travels are not just physical – though he has been to many places – but are also concerned with crossing the various borders, barriers and boundaries that human beings construct in their minds. He uses watercolour painting, photography, sculpture, installation, theatre and performance to try to explain to himself and to his audience the spectrum of human triumphs and tragedies he has encountered. His work is often concerned with ecological issues, not just in Africa but around the world, and he constantly campaigns on behalf of the exploited. 'What guides me is a constantly evolving aesthetic, but also a sense of ethics that makes a difference and structures my entire approach.'

Toguo sees the different elements in his work as an ongoing 'unfinished theatre', in which he is performer, audience and director. He is keenly aware that manipulation and exploitation take place in the art world as much as in any other field of human activity, and strives for a world 'in which art and ethics may cohabit'.

Barthélémy Toguo was born at M'Balmayo, Cameroon, in 1967. He studied at the École des Beaux-Arts d'Abidjan, Ivory Coast, the École d'Art de Grenoble, Switzerland and the Kunstakademie, Düsseldorf, Germany. He has had solo exhibitions in Africa, the USA and Europe, notably 'The Sick Opera' at the Palais de Tokyo, Paris (2004–5). He has also contributed work to numerous group shows, including the touring exhibition 'Africa Remix' (2004–7).

Toguo feels that his most important project to date is Bandjoun Station – an arts centre that he has built with his own resources in Cameroon. It is intended for artists from Cameroon, Africa and the international community, and includes space for studios, galleries, a library and a conference room.

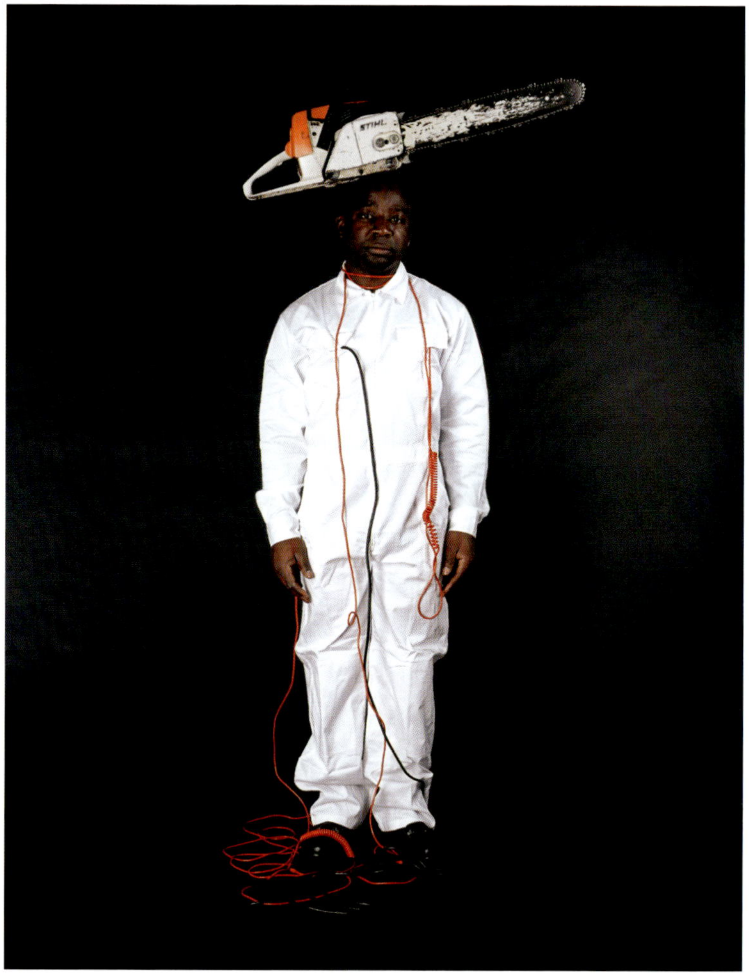

'Looking at our contemporary society I feel like being a stream of water, being the wind, being a migrating bird, being here and there and everywhere.'
Barthélémy Toguo

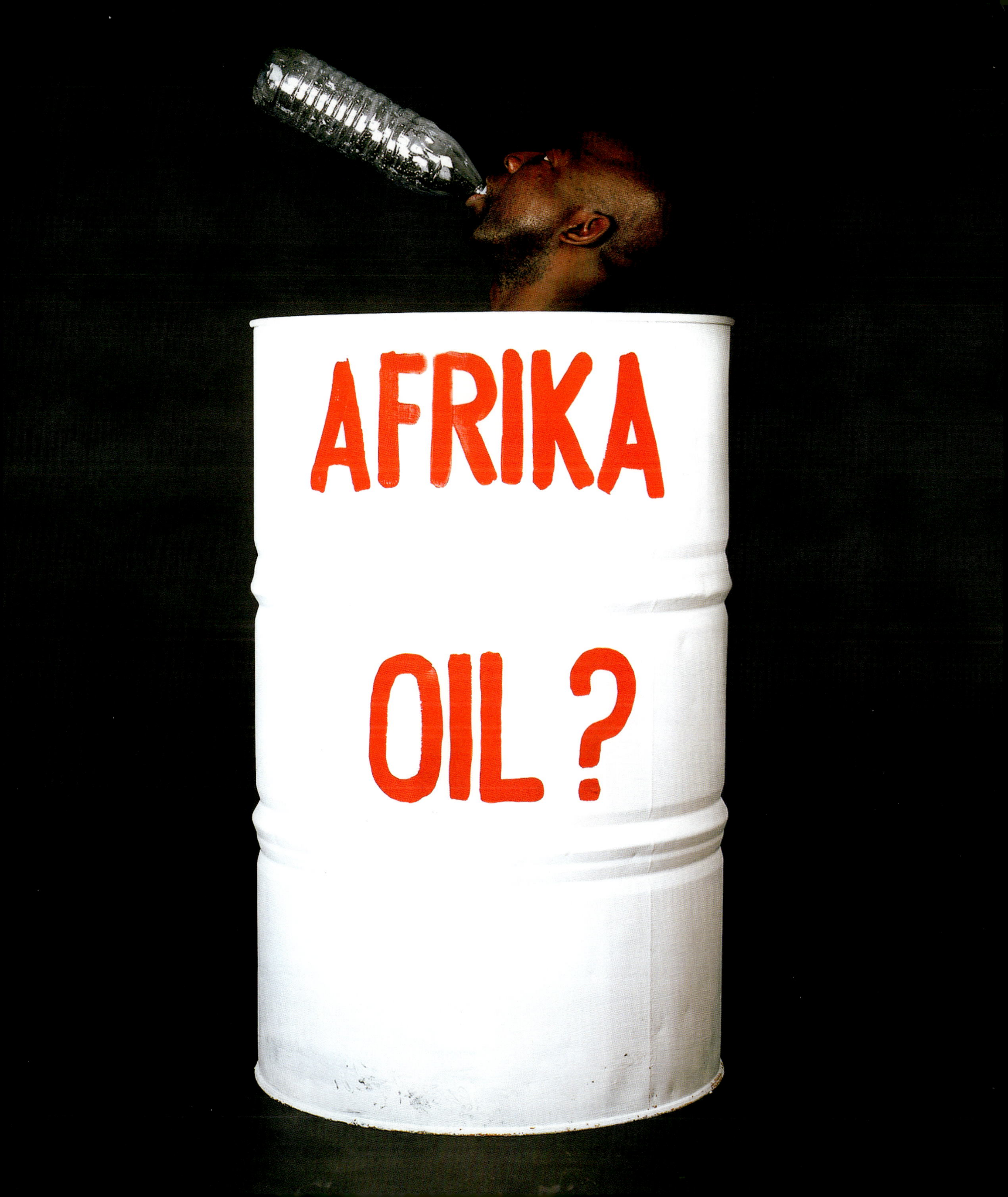
AFRIKA
OIL ?

‘I was born in Africa, I am Cameroonian and I see the corrupted political situation of the African continent which does not support access to true democracy.’
Barthélémy Toguo

Below *Unfinished Theatre*, 2000. Mixed media installation, 500 x 900 cm ($196\frac{4}{5}$ x $354\frac{1}{3}$ in). Musée contemporain de Lyon, France.
‘We are all in a permanent state of “transit”. It is a notion which is inherent in twentieth and twenty-first century man. Whether a man is white, black or yellow matters little; he is in any case a being who is potentially “exiled” … We leave one place for another… while bringing along with us… our culture, which runs up against the other. Of course this coming together can be either beautiful or difficult.’

Right *Stupid African President*, 2006. Photographic print of a performance, 150 x 150 cm (59 x 59 in). Collection Bandjoun Station, Cameroon.
‘I like to read the headlines of newspapers, comparing them to the current trends in politics. It is a compelling need to know what’s going on in the world. This overdose of information, of scoops, of scandals, of sensationalization of tabloid journalism, naturally inspires me a great deal. It is, however, necessary to have some perspective on what the media reports to be able to distinguish between actual news and tabloid journalism. But tabloid journalism is also a formidable source of inspiration.’
(Translated from the French)

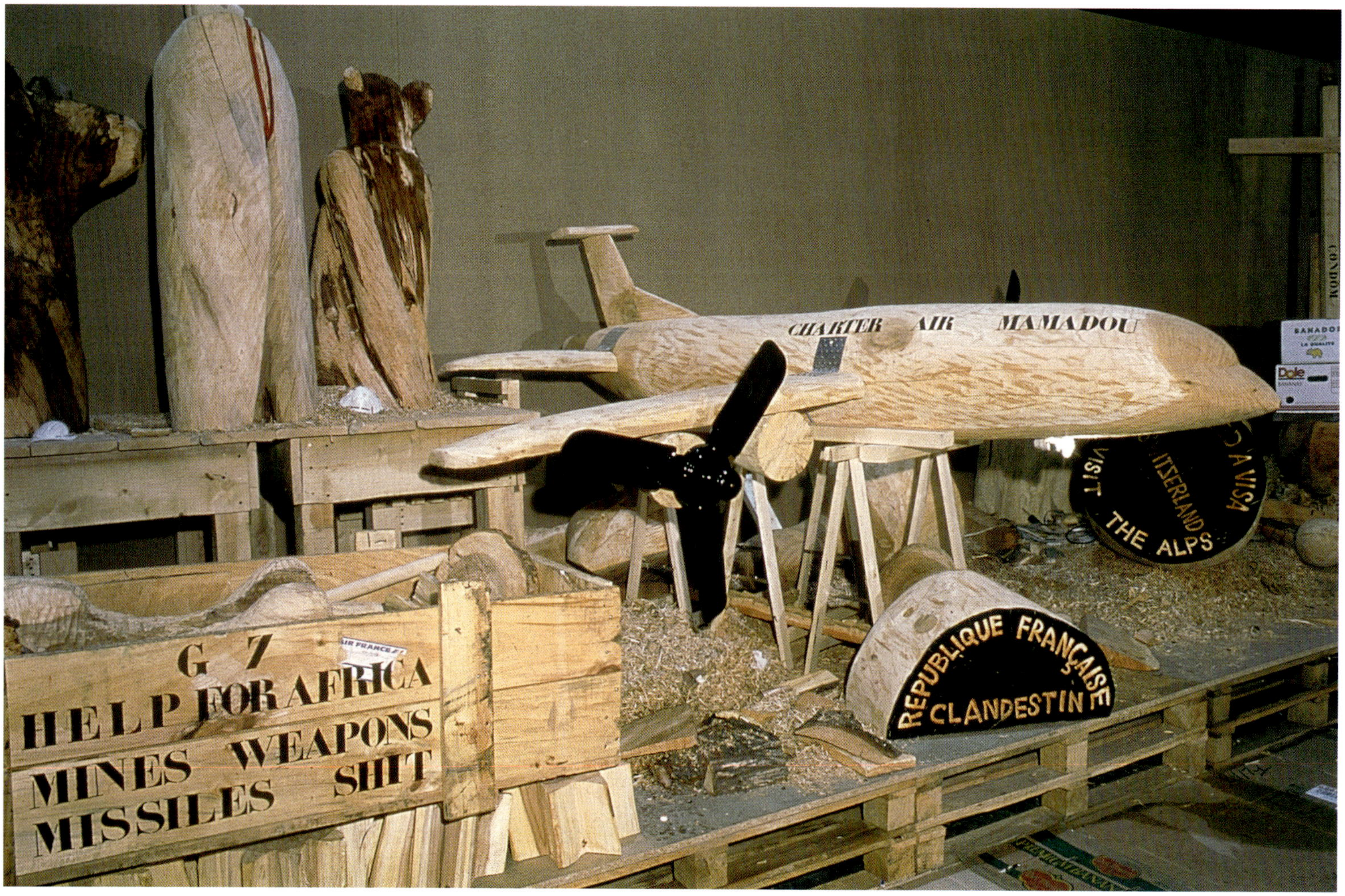

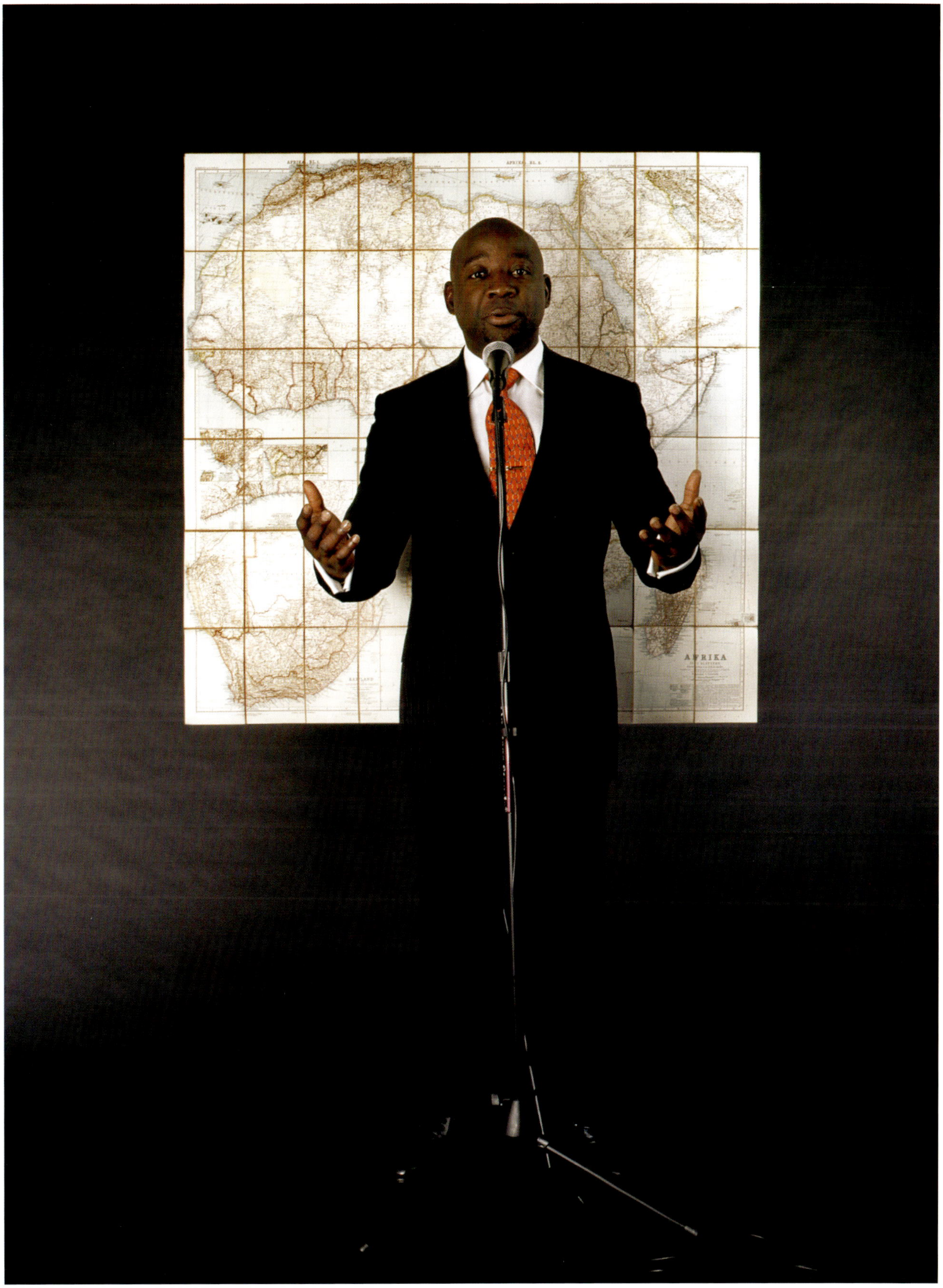

This spread *X, XII and XX,* from the *Purification* series, 2004. Watercolour on paper, each image: 110 x 110cm (43⅓ x 43⅓ in). Collection Bandjoun Station, Cameroon.
In this series of watercolours, Toguo portrays human beings, often bristling with nails, as well as animals and even plants excreting the toxins of life from every orifice in a kind of sensual orgy of 'purification'. These gruesome acts are balanced by the ethereal beauty of the paintings themselves, the various bodily fluids flowing together to form a kind of river of life.

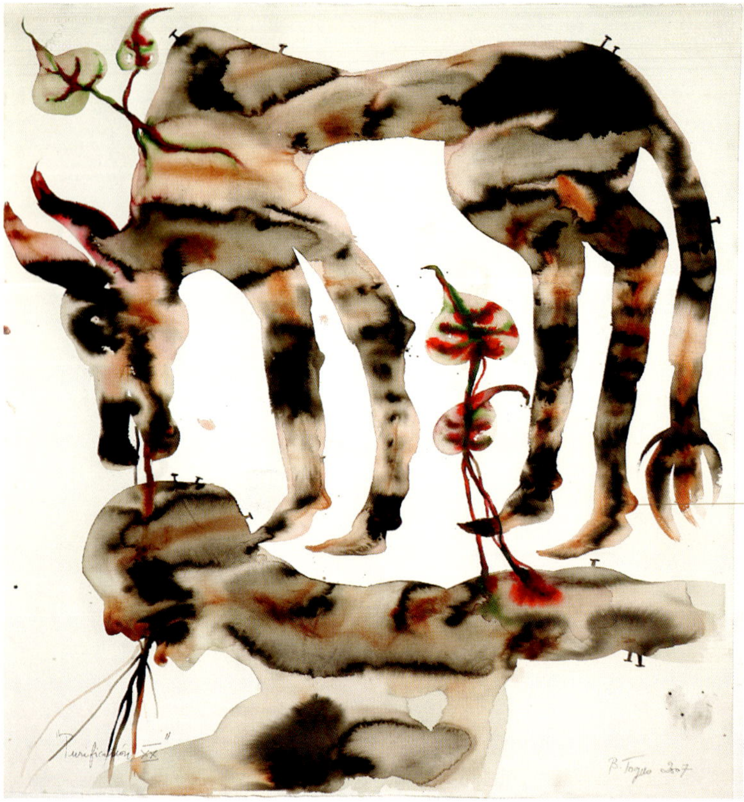

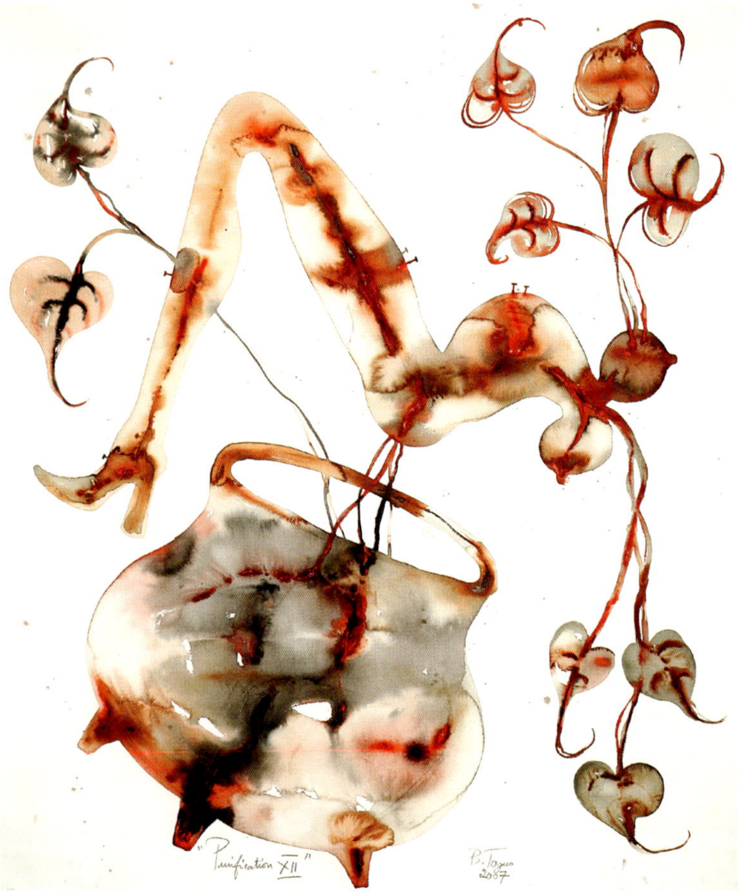

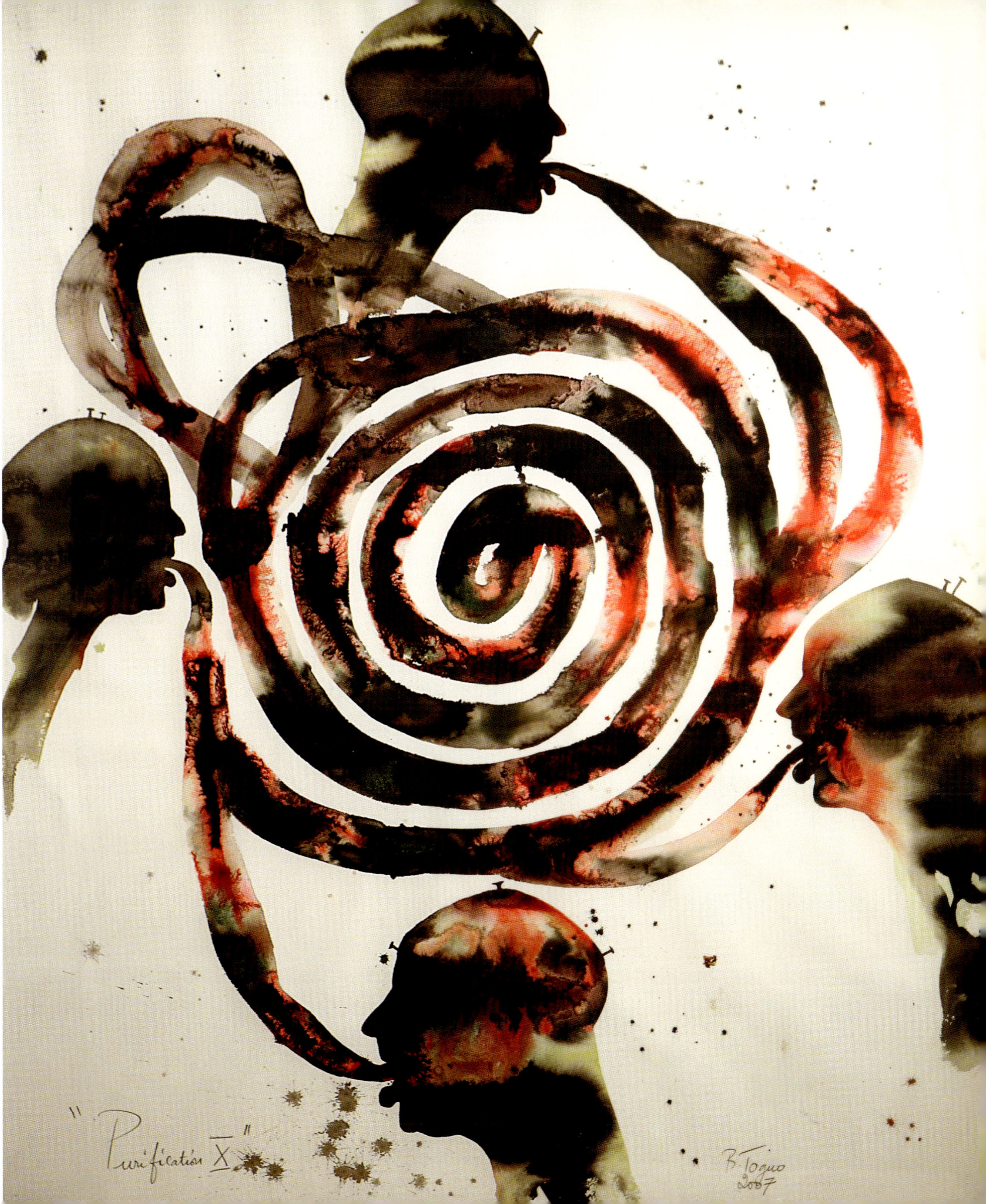
"Purification X"
B. Toguo
2007

SANE WADU
KENYA

Below Dress painted by Sane Wadu with texts including 'ABNORMALLY SANE', 2002.

Right *Joy Riders*, 1997. Acrylic on canvas, 87 x 114 cm (34¼ x 44⅘ in). Private collection.

In 1985, Sane Wadu Mbugua came into the Gallery Watatu in Nairobi, Kenya, carrying his paintings for sale. He wore a canvas suit on which various words and pictures were painted. Two years earlier Wadu had given up his steady job as a teacher to become an artist, an act that his bemused neighbours in his home village of Ngecha thought to be completely insane. However, against their expectations he immediately began to sell his paintings through the gallery. As a retort to his neighbours, Wadu adorned his suit with the slogan 'ABNORMALLY SANE' for all to see on his triumphant return to the village. From then on he became known as Sane Wadu. Wishing to share his success with his neighbours, despite their earlier mockery, Wadu set up a workshop in Ngecha with the backing of Ruth Schaffner, director of Gallery Watatu. The new group of artists who emerged from this workshop became known as the Ngecha Artists' Association.

Sane Wadu was born in 1954 in Nyathuna, Kenya. After high school he qualified as a teacher and wrote poetry and plays. For more than two decades however, he has been a professional painter, and now lives in Naivasha, Kenya with his wife and family. His early works took scenes of rural Kenya and wildlife as their subjects, but in the 1990s he began to address political and social issues. Wadu often includes a self-portrait amongst the large numbers of people on his canvases as a way of empathizing with their cares, concerns and suffering.

Sane Wadu has exhibited his work in solo and group shows in Africa, Europe and the USA. He also helped to organize the Triangle Arts Trust workshops at Wasanii on the shores of Lake Naivasha, and at the Kakuma and Dadaab refugee camps. Wadu's experiences at these workshops provided the subjects for a number of his most powerful paintings.

'As a painter your head can jump.'
Sane Wadu

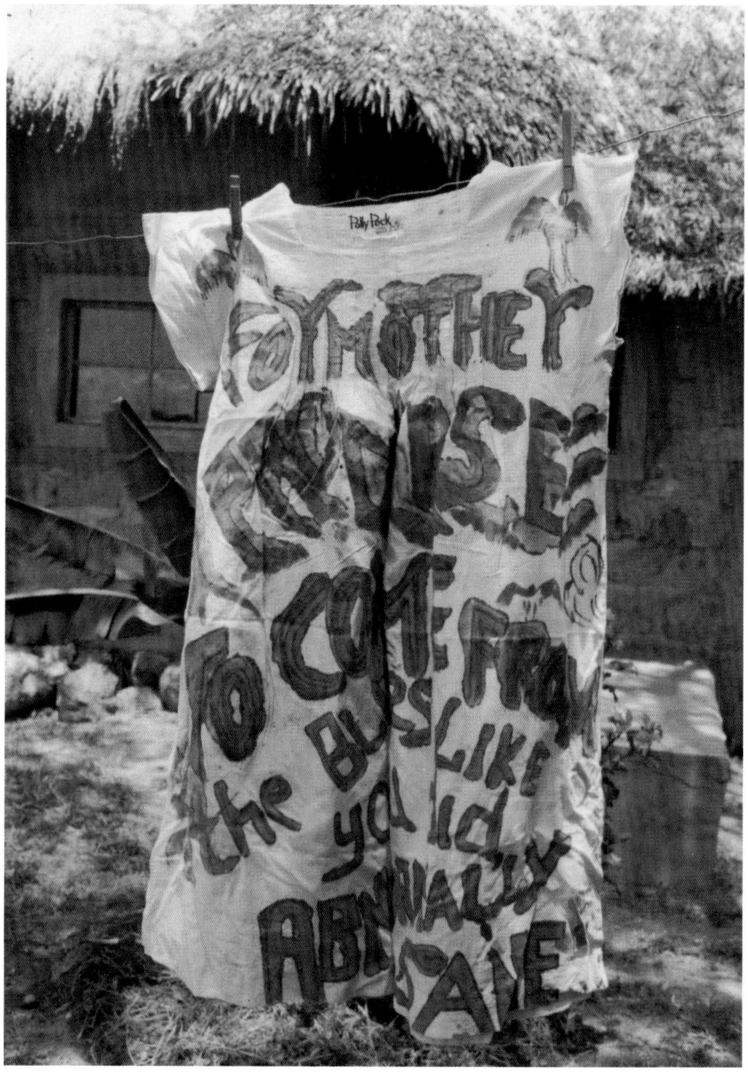

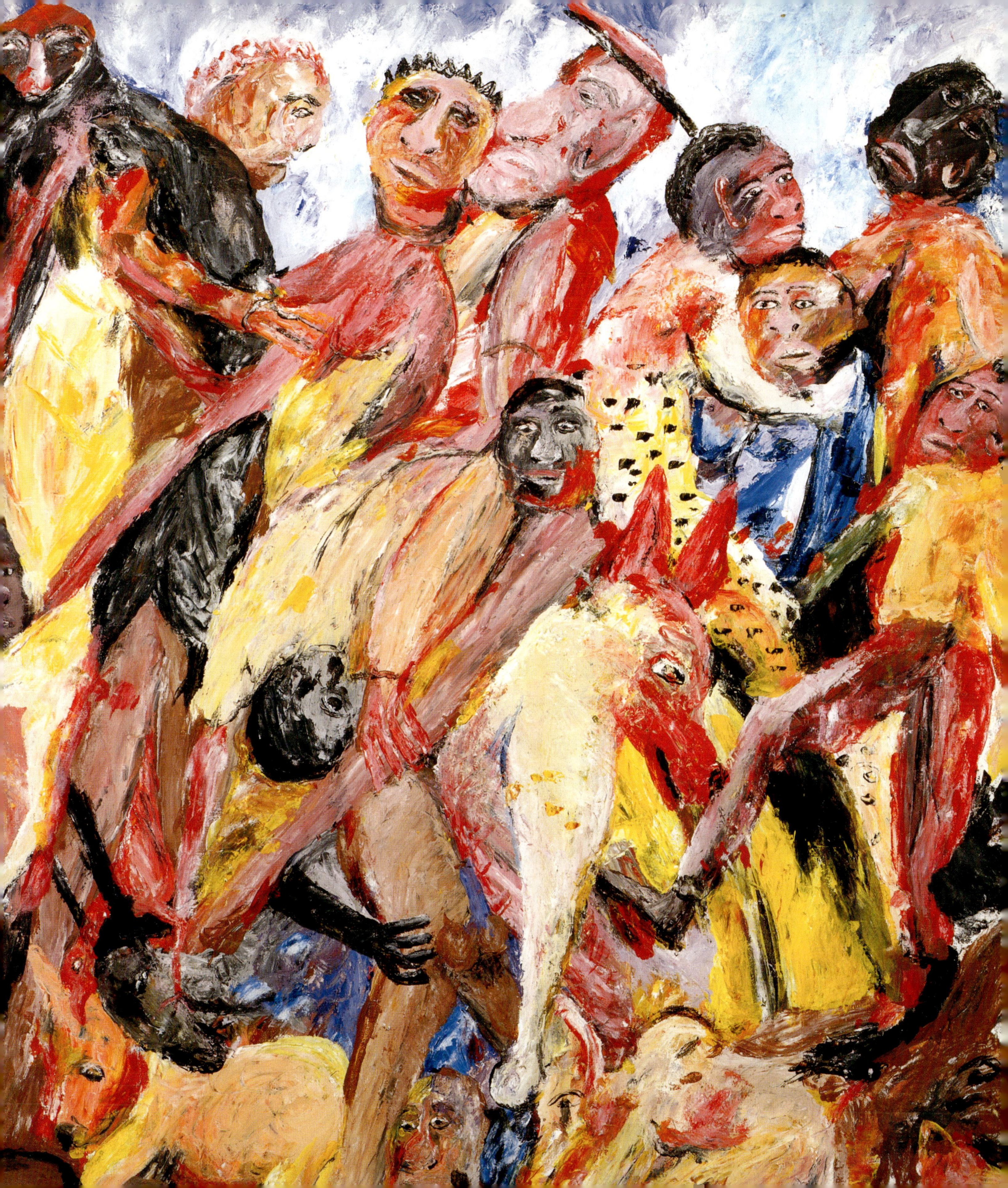

Below *Exodus*, 1998.
Acrylic on canvas, 120 x 173 cm (46½ x 67½ in).
Private collection.
Wadu assisted at a workshop organized by Kuona Trust in the Dadaab camp in northeastern Kenya, where many thousands of people, the majority from Somalia, come as refugees. It was an experience that inspired Wadu to paint this deeply moving portrayal of the suffering of displaced people, a scene repeated in many parts of Africa.

Right *Wasanii Workshop*, 1997. Acrylic on canvas, 113 x 123 cm (44 x 48 in).
Private collection.
Sane Wadu helped the Kuona Trust to organize the first Triangle Arts workshop at Wasanii on the shores of Lake Naivasha, Kenya, in 1997. The picture shows him, bare-chested and bearded, together with other artists at the workshop.

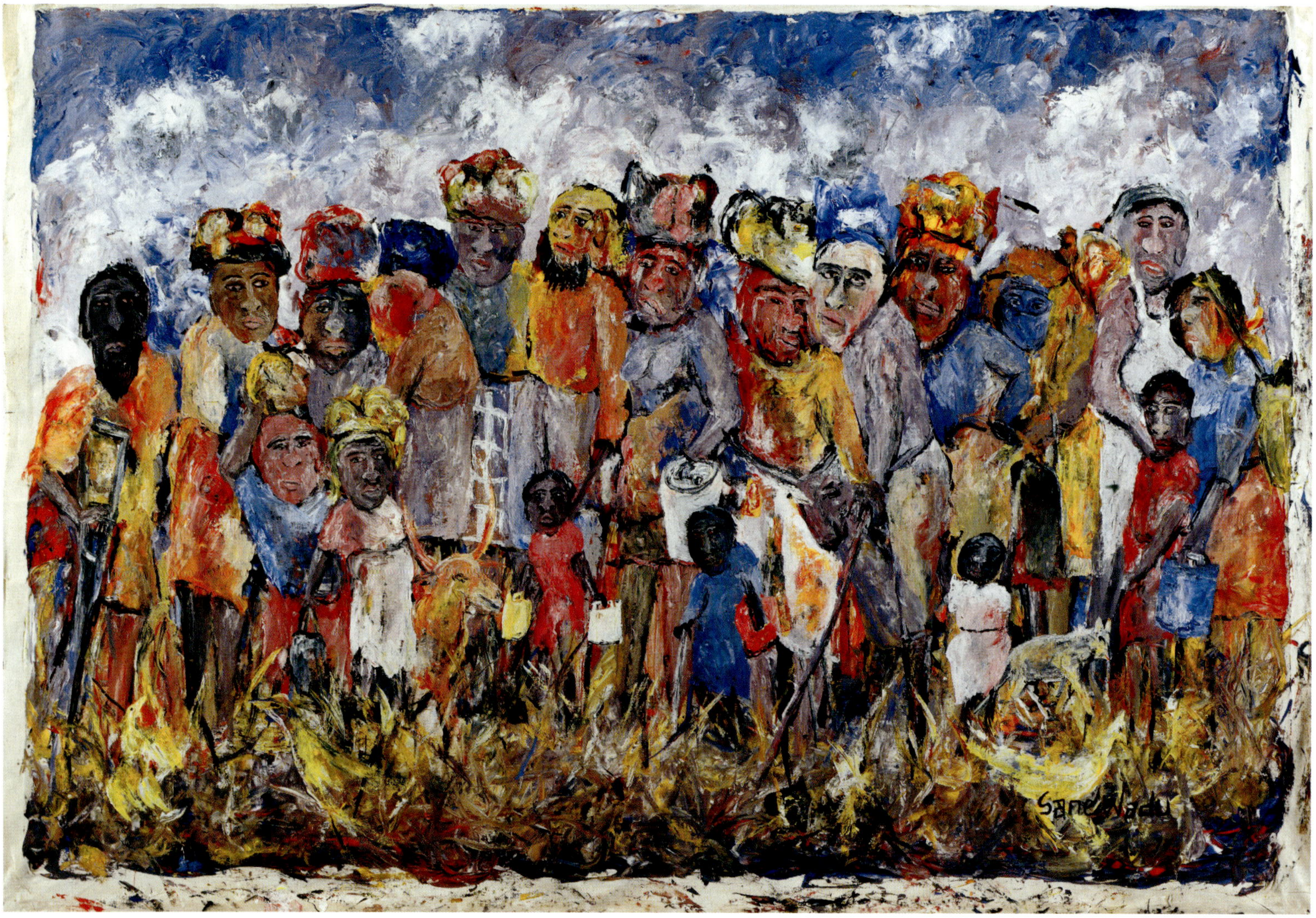

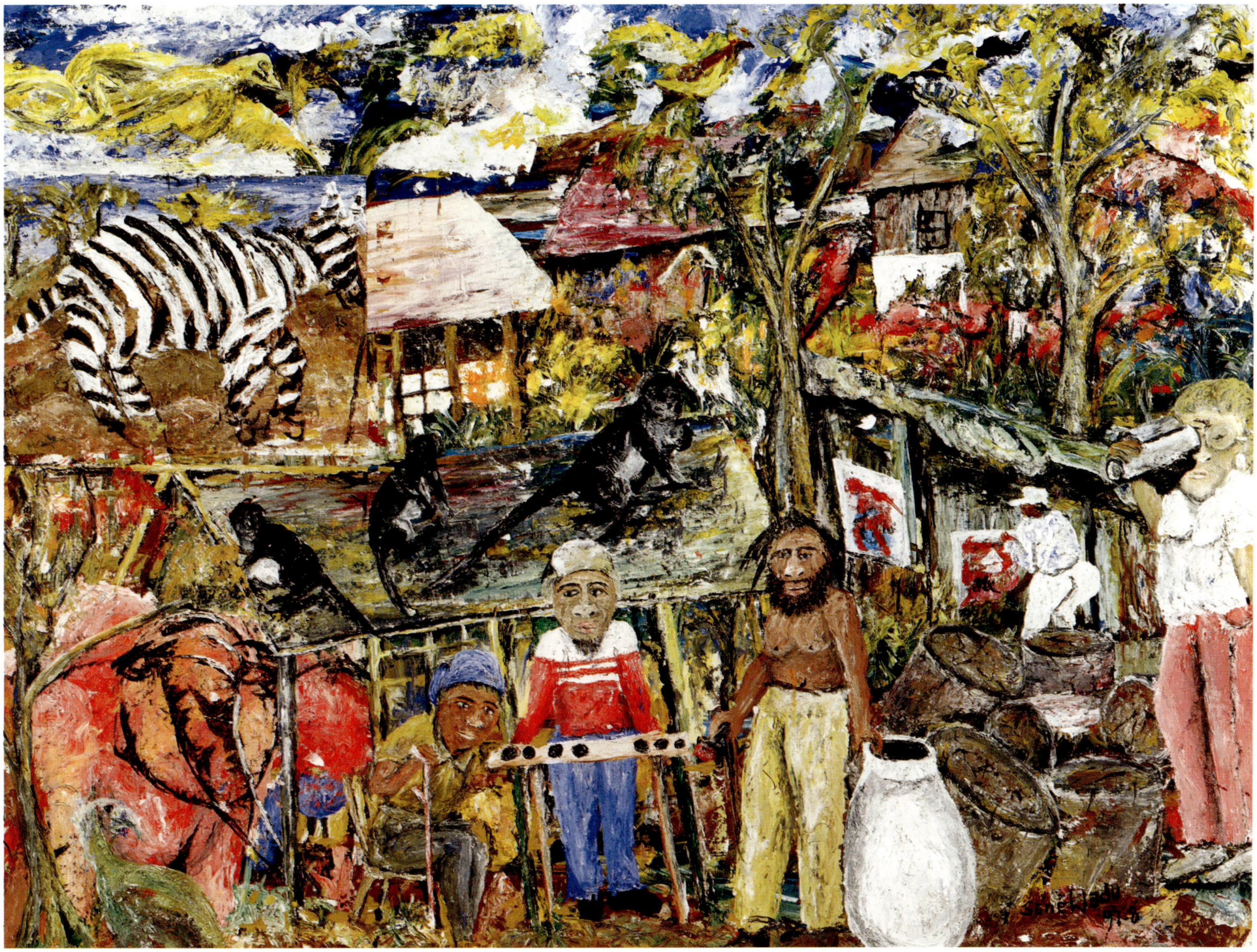

Below *Waiting*, 1991. Acrylic on canvas, 102 x 180cm (39¾ x 70 in). Private collection.
In this painting a group of prisoners await trial on the back of a lorry.

Right *Violence in Clash-torn Area*, 1996. Acrylic on canvas, 138 x 158cm (54⅓ x 62⅕ in). Private collection.

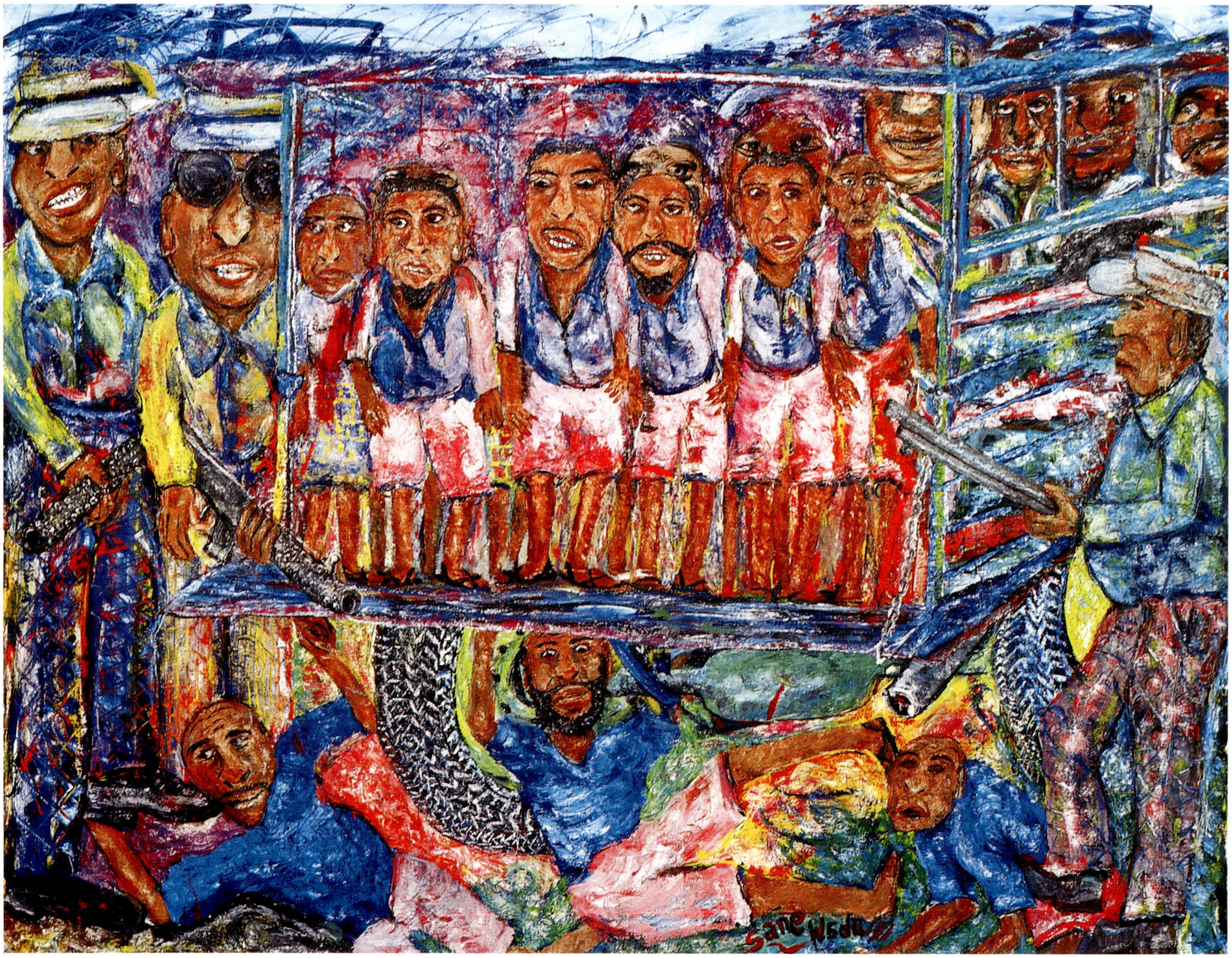

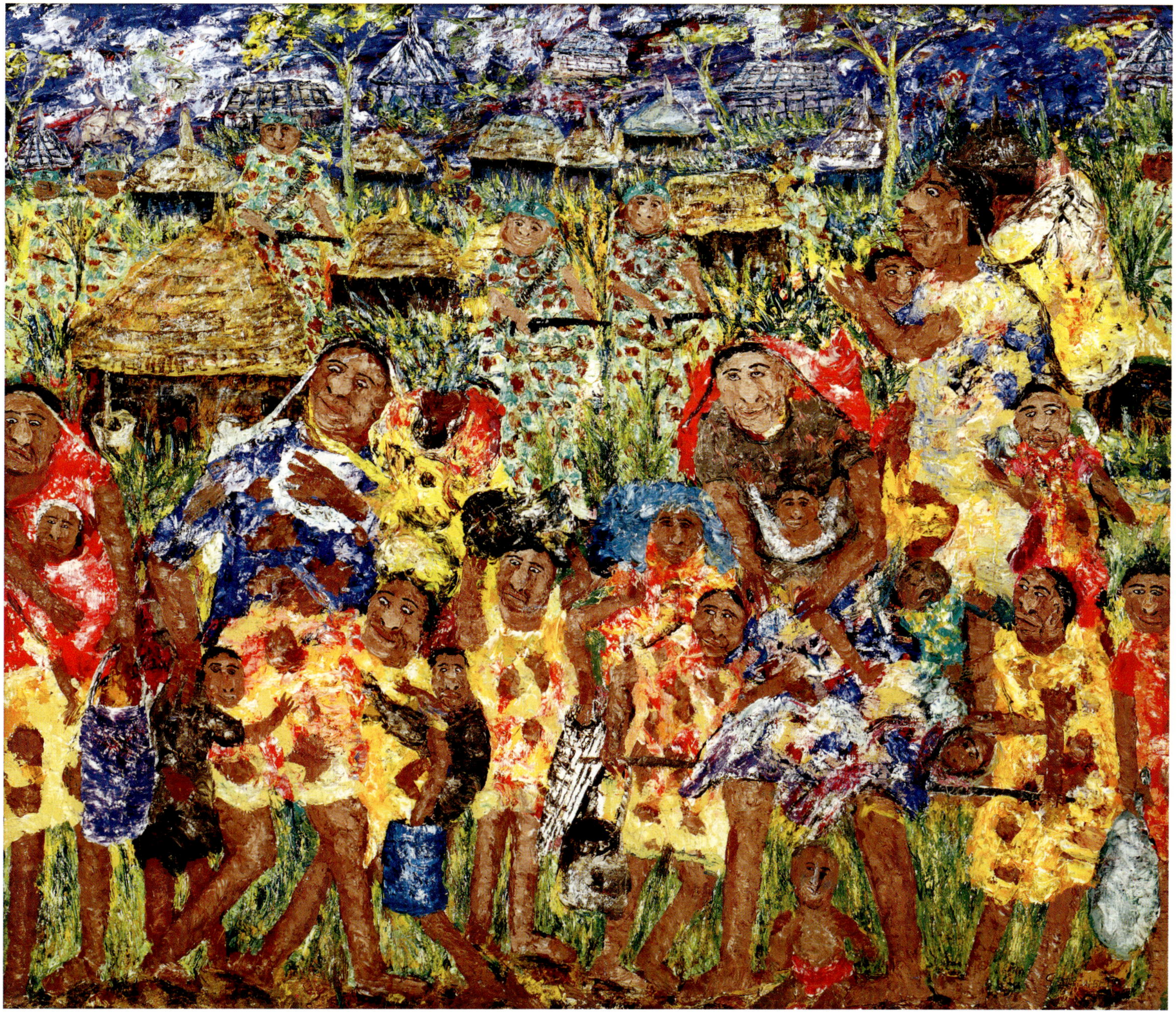

OUATTARA WATTS
IVORY COAST/USA

Ouattara was born in Abidjan, Ivory Coast in 1957. His father was a surgeon trained in Western biomedicine, but he was also a traditional healer. Elements of many religions were practised in the family home. At the age of seven, Ouattara attended a 'spirit school' in Abidjan. 'The spirit school permits you to understand the world. You are allowed a vision that is cosmic rather than a nationalistic or village-orientated one.' At sixteen, Ouattara left school to focus on his art, and at nineteen, he went to Paris to study at the École National des Beaux Arts (1980–84). In January 1988, he met Jean-Michel Basquiat in Paris who was greatly impressed with Ouattara's work and invited him to New York. Basquiat died in August 1988, but during those few short months the two artists' friendship had flourished and Ouattara's work began to reflect something of the synthesis of assimilated influences that characterized Basquiat's work. 'I needed to make a synthesis of everything I had learned in Africa and everything I was learning in the West. I had to assimilate it all.'

A string of solo exhibitions followed, including at the Marilyn Butler Gallery in Los Angeles (1989), the Gagosian Gallery, New York (1995) and the Mike Weiss Gallery, New York (2006). He also contributed to numerous group exhibitions, including the Venice Biennale in 1993.

Ouattara acknowledges the influence of modernism and technology in Africa as well as in the West. He also sees spirituality in both traditions, a spirituality that can help to harness technology for the benefit of humankind – and the important part that art can play in this healing process.

'When you talk about freedom, art is the liberator.'
Ouattara Watts

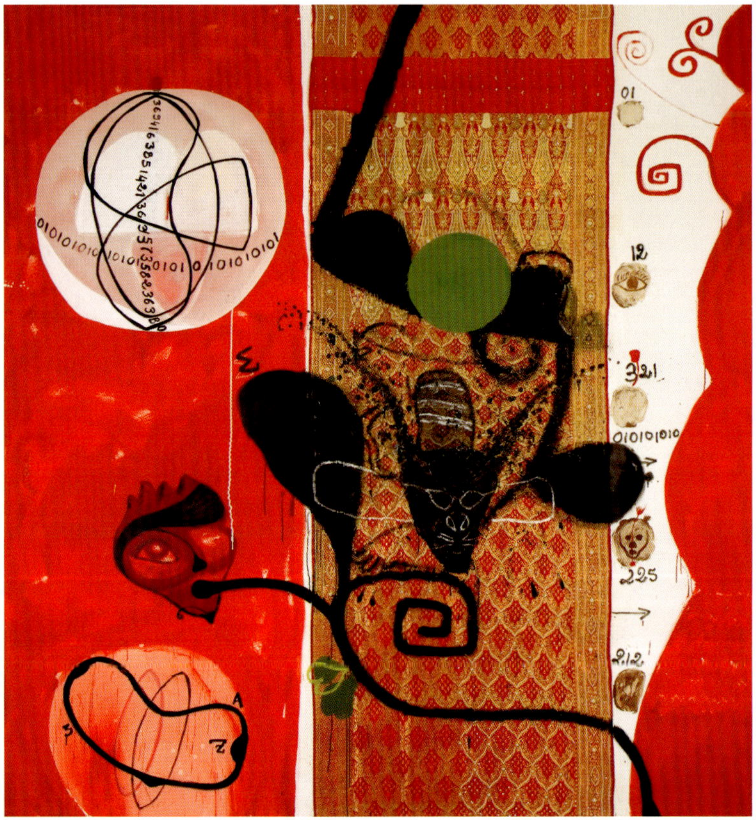

Below *Les Fleurs Du Mal I*, 2007. Mixed media on canvas, 308.6 x 278.1 cm (121½ x 109½ in). Mike Weiss Gallery, New York.

Right *So What*, 2007 (detail). Mixed media on canvas, 273 x 304.8 cm (107½ x 120 in). Mike Weiss Gallery, New York.

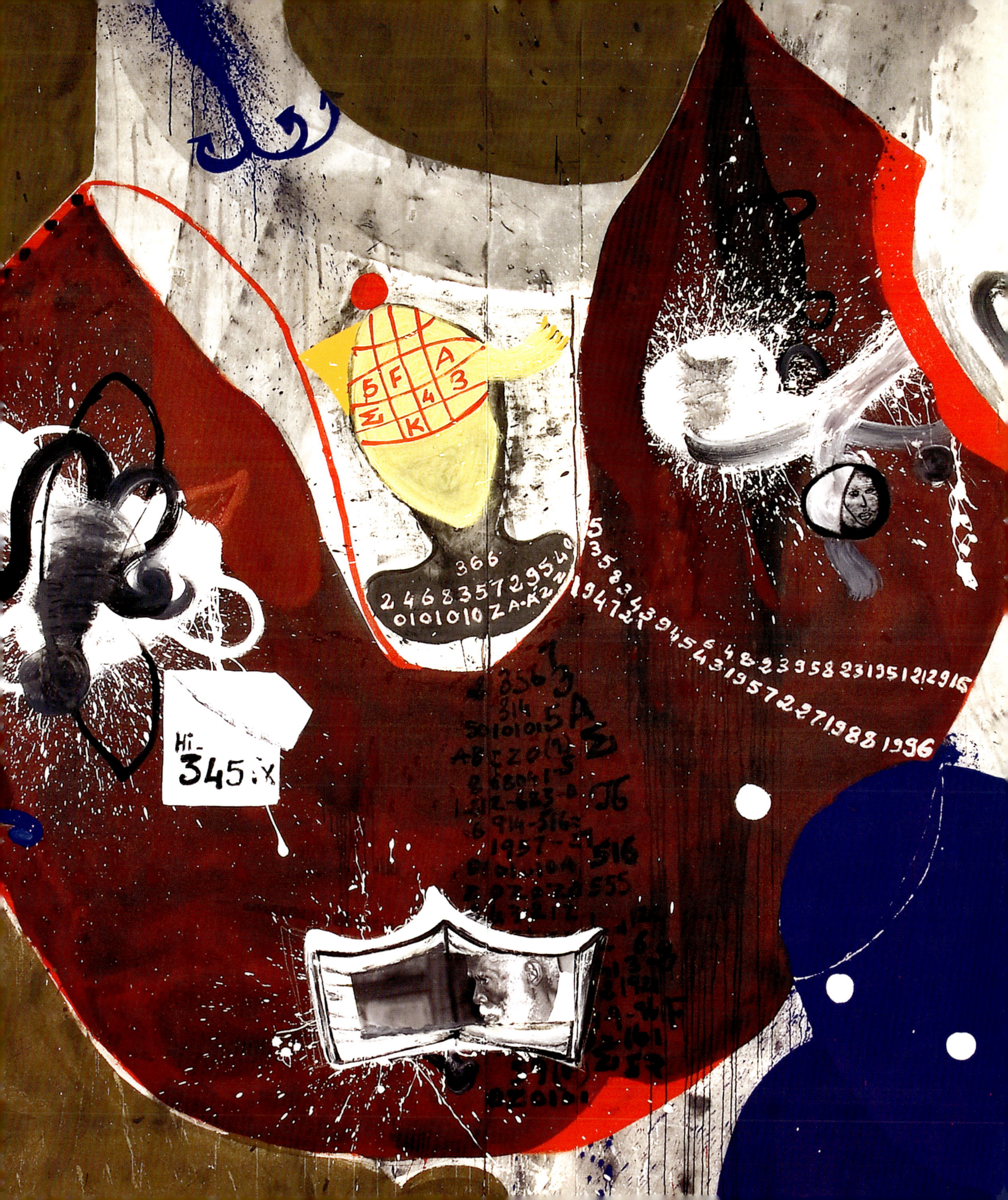
366
Hi-
1988 1996

'My vision is not based only on a country or a continent; it's beyond geography, or what is seen on a map. Even though I localize it to make it better understood, it is wider than that. It refers to the cosmos.'
Ouattara Watts

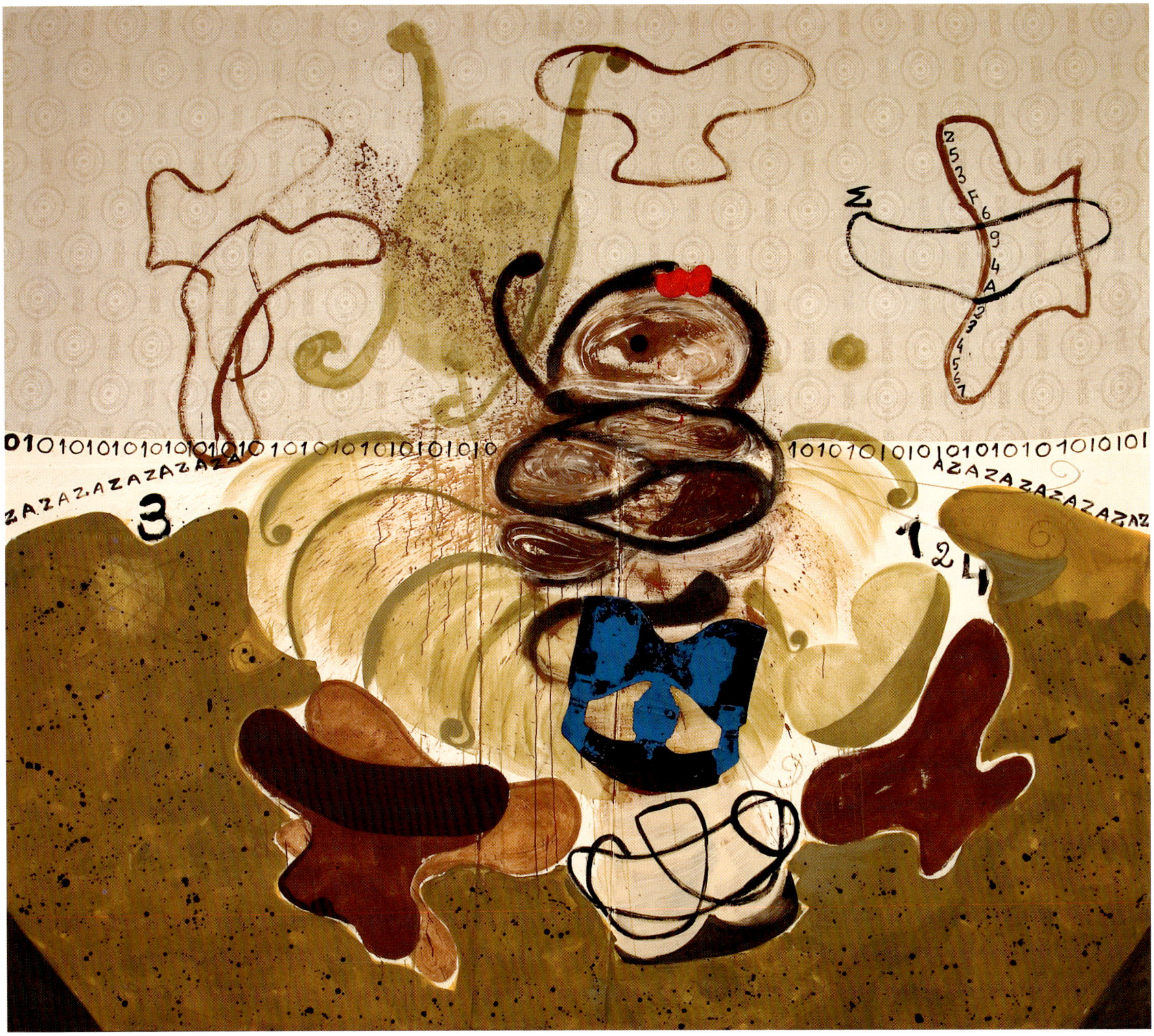

Left *Dream Support,* 2007. Mixed media on canvas, 278.1 x 308.6 cm (109½ x 121½ in). Mike Weiss Gallery, New York.
'Someone speaks about alchemy or magic, but this does not mean the transformation of lead into gold. Art is above all a transformation of our intellect and our psyche through the use of materials. I try to suggest through my paintings other rules and other visions.'

Below *Untitled,* 2007. Mixed media on canvas, 260.3 x 402.6 cm (102½ x 158½ in). Mike Weiss Gallery, New York.

Bottom *Sun Ra,* 2007. Mixed media on canvas, 209.5 x 299.7 cm (82½ x 118 in). Mike Weiss Gallery, New York.

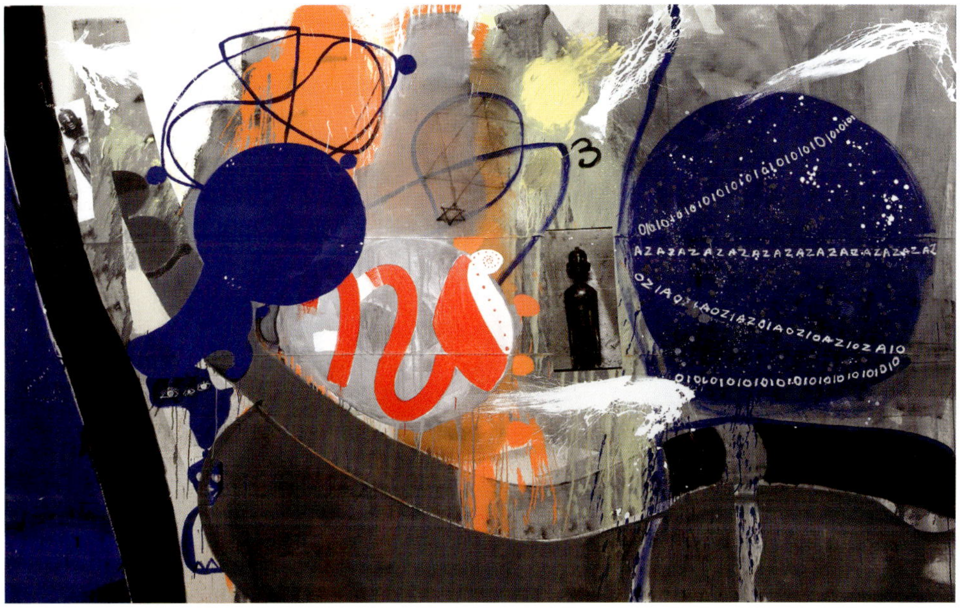

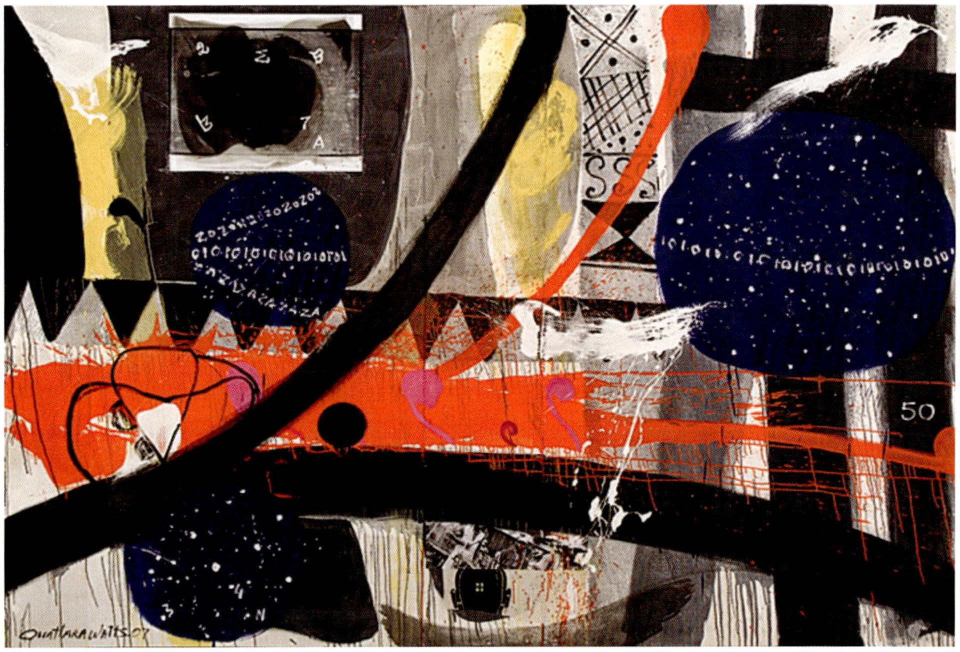

SANDILE ZULU
SOUTH AFRICA

This spread *Atomic Triptych – Birth of a New World*, 1996. Fire, water and earth on paper, each 103 x 78 cm (40 x 30½ in). Private collection.

'Fire and water, wind and soil allude to life, to creation and destruction, to colonization and decolonization, to revolution and liberation, to purgation and cleansing, to purification and renewal.' Zulu describes his working with fire as 'artomism', a force that, like nuclear energy, has the potential for creation or destruction on a massive scale.

Sandile Zulu is a poet and artist. He was born in 1960 in Ixopo, KwaZulu-Natal, and was educated at Rorke's Drift Art School (1982), at Technikon Natal, Durban (1983) and at the University of Witwatersrand, Johannesburg, graduating in 1993. Following his first solo exhibiton at the Rembrandt van Rijn gallery in Johannesburg (1995), Zulu has exhibited widely in South Africa, Europe and the USA. As part of the Africa '05 season, he had his first solo European show 'Fire This Time' at the October Gallery in London.

Zulu is passionately involved with examining ideas about time and the universe, both within and beyond the human body. The materials he uses – organic vegetal matter (roots, tubers, grasses) as well as barbed wire and synthetics – are at once the subject and the means towards his research and experimentation through the medium of fire. Zulu uses fire as his means of investigation, its light illuminating the way ahead like a miner's lamp, its heat transforming whatever lies on that path. The vegetal and metallic forms he uses – pumpkin seeds, beans, leaves, bundles of barbed wire – all leave their shadow of resistance to the fire of the blowtorch. Colin Richards of the University of Witwatersrand refers to the element of 'coolness' in Zulu's art – 'cool arson' he calls it, conjuring the image of a blacksmith heating the spearhead he works, then plunging it into water, hammering and polishing it again until it becomes razor-sharp, gleaming – and cold. Yet even in the metal's icy coldness burns the imprint of the refining fire that gave it form.

His work is highly structured and regimented, the forms often echoing those of Zulu *impis* and their shields and weaponry from a proud and ongoing history.

> *I regard my work as constructed structures. There is the sense of construction. It's a way, to me, of deconstructing the many social constructs. It's about attempting to emphasize the discourse in my work.*

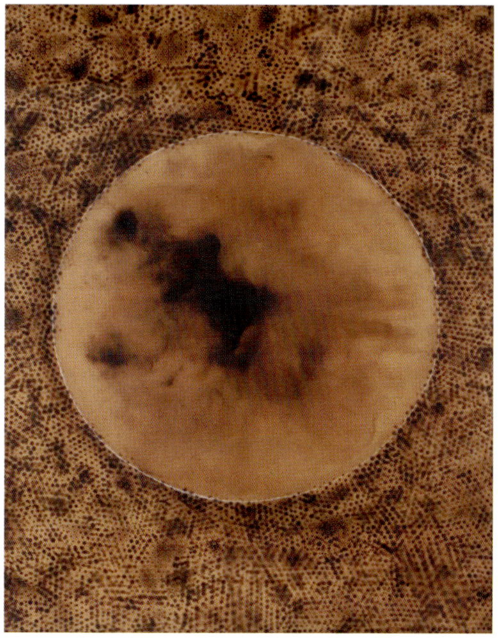

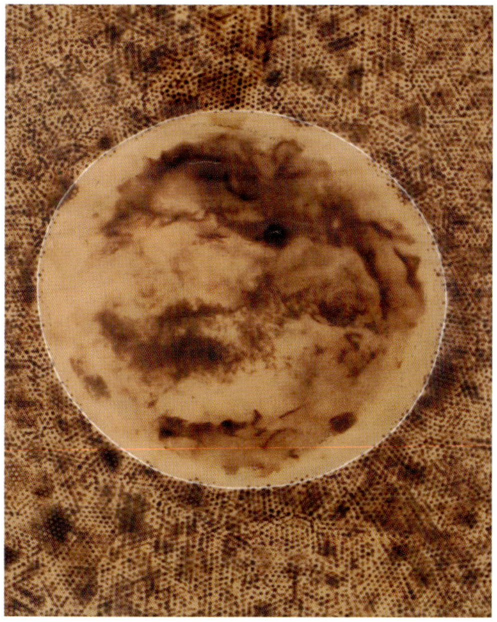

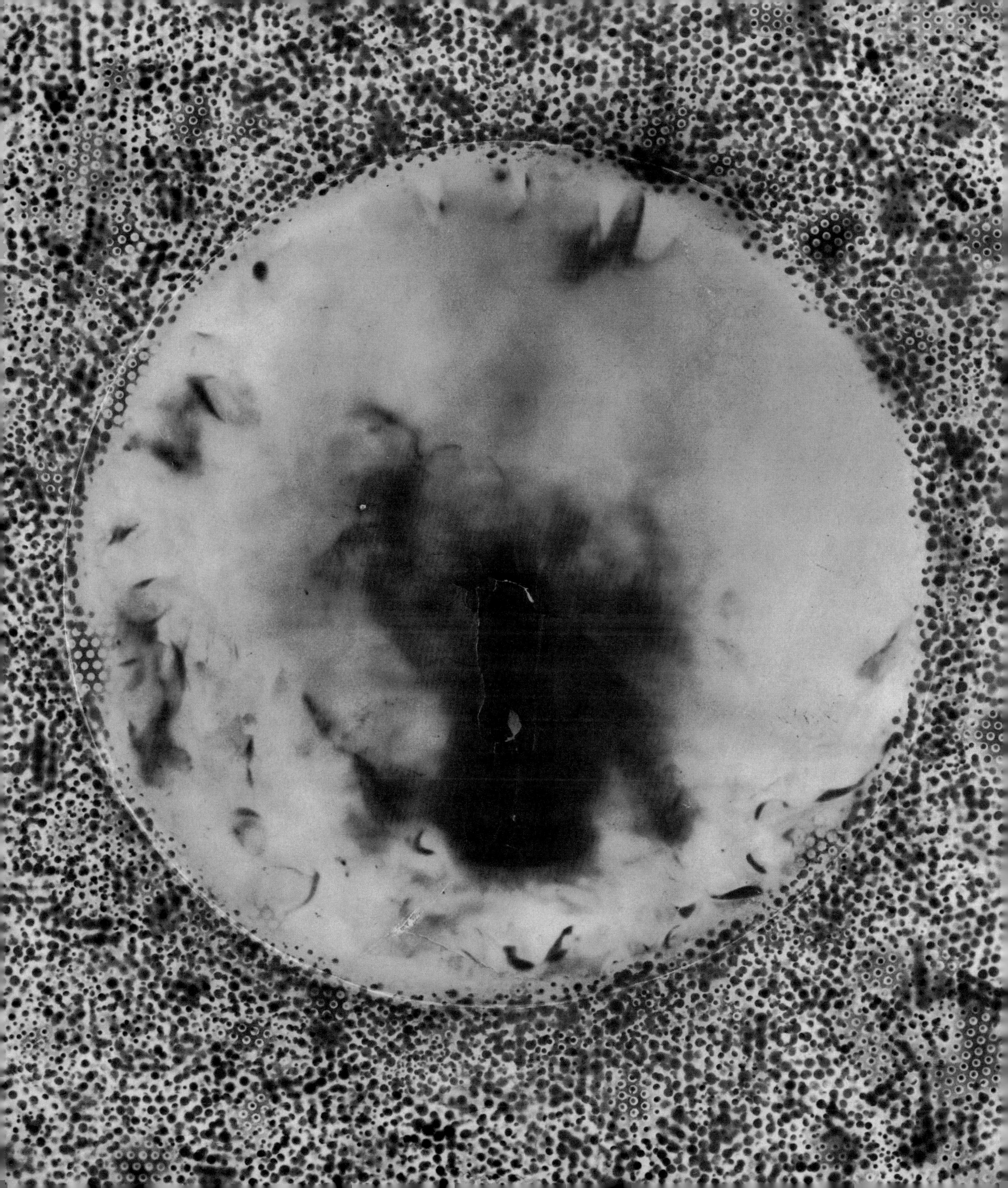

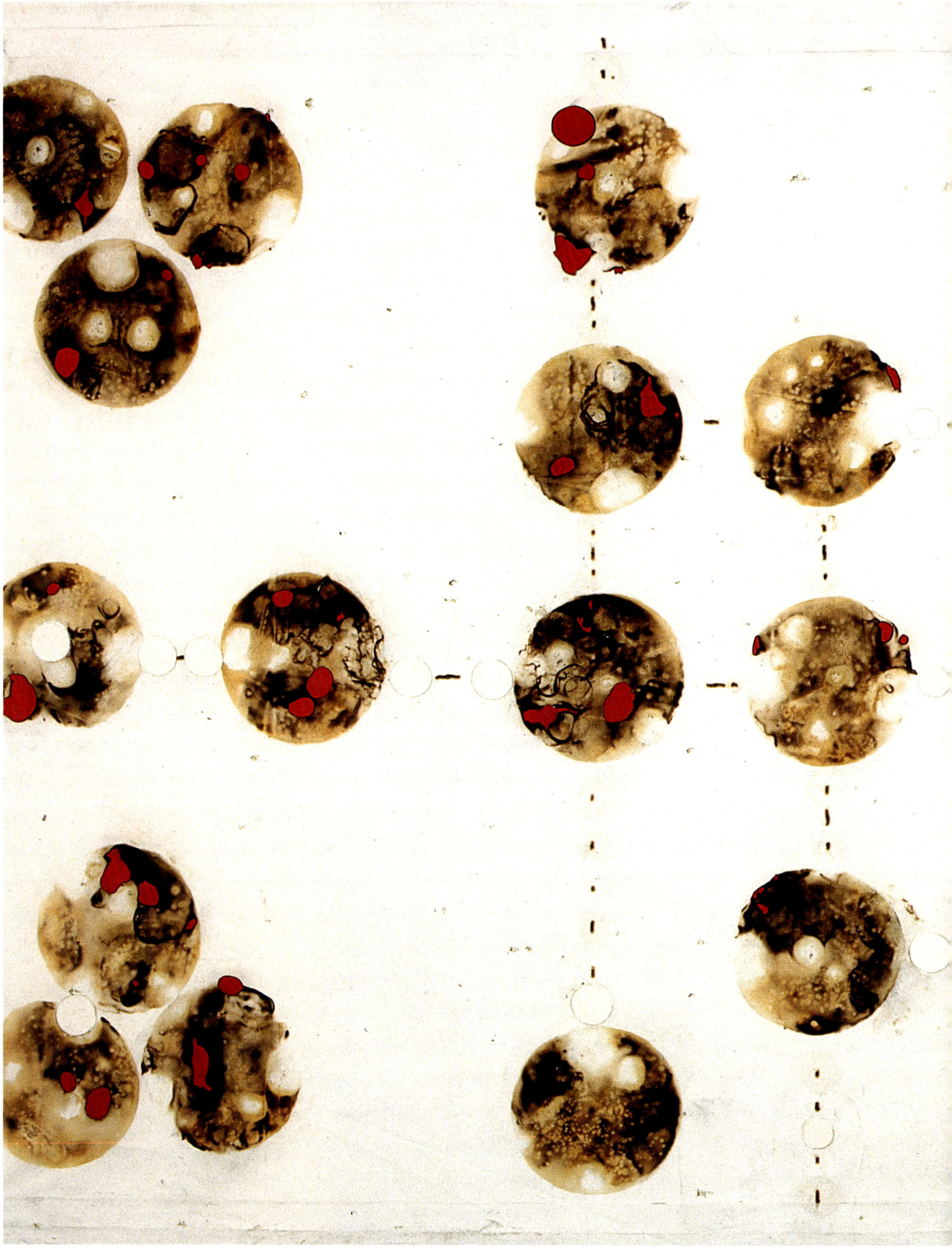

Right *Planetary Conception 5*, 2005. Fire, water and red cotton fabric on canvas, 149 x 298 cm (44½ x 116 in). Collection of the artist.

'...I draw upon scientific discourse, a discourse that encompasses the varied languages of astrology, physiology, psychology, histology and genealogy. At the same time, I am concerned with languages that describe the endless transformation of emotion, mind and spirit, and the integration of the internal and external spheres – languages that seek to describe the wholeness of the life force.'

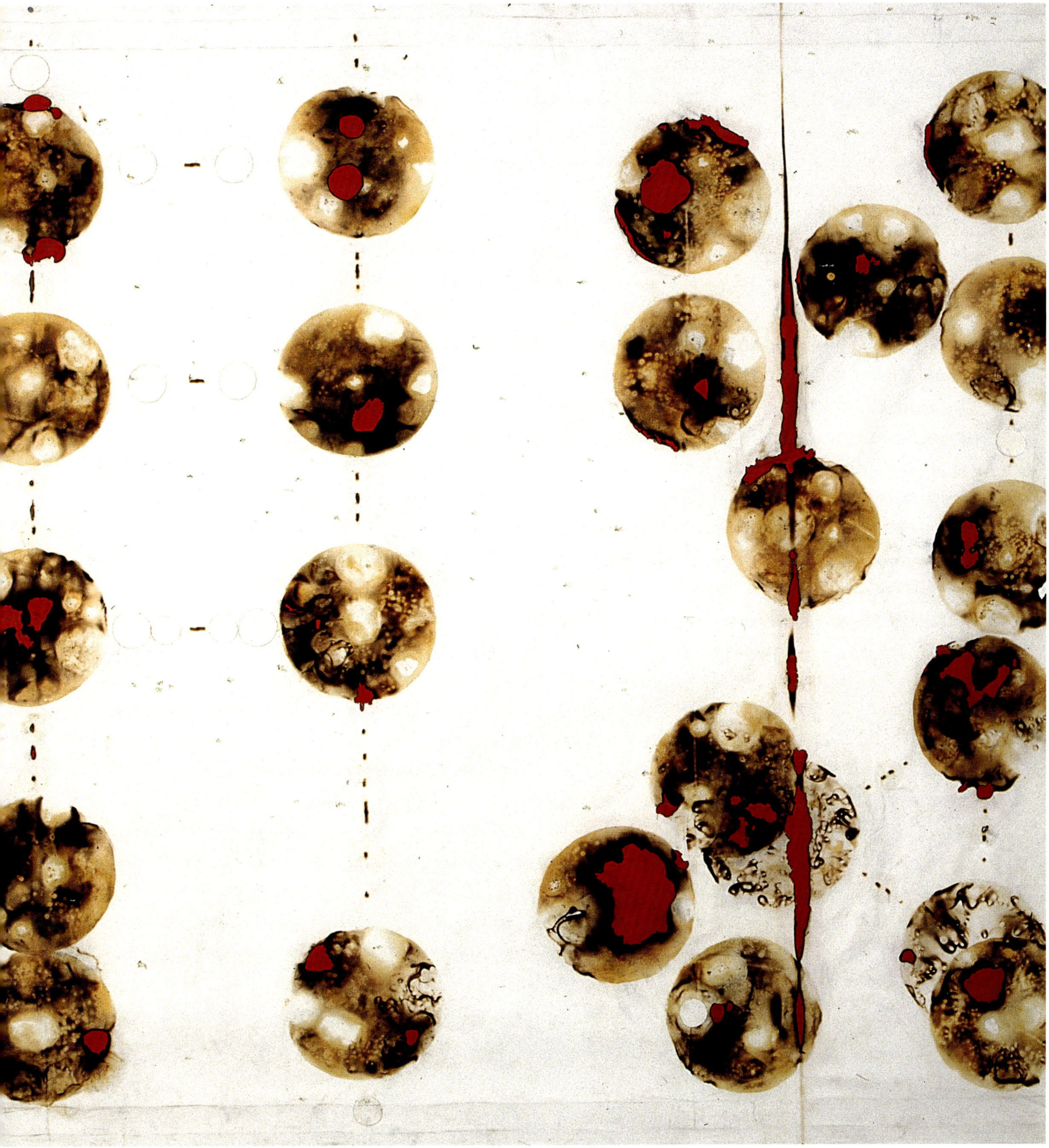

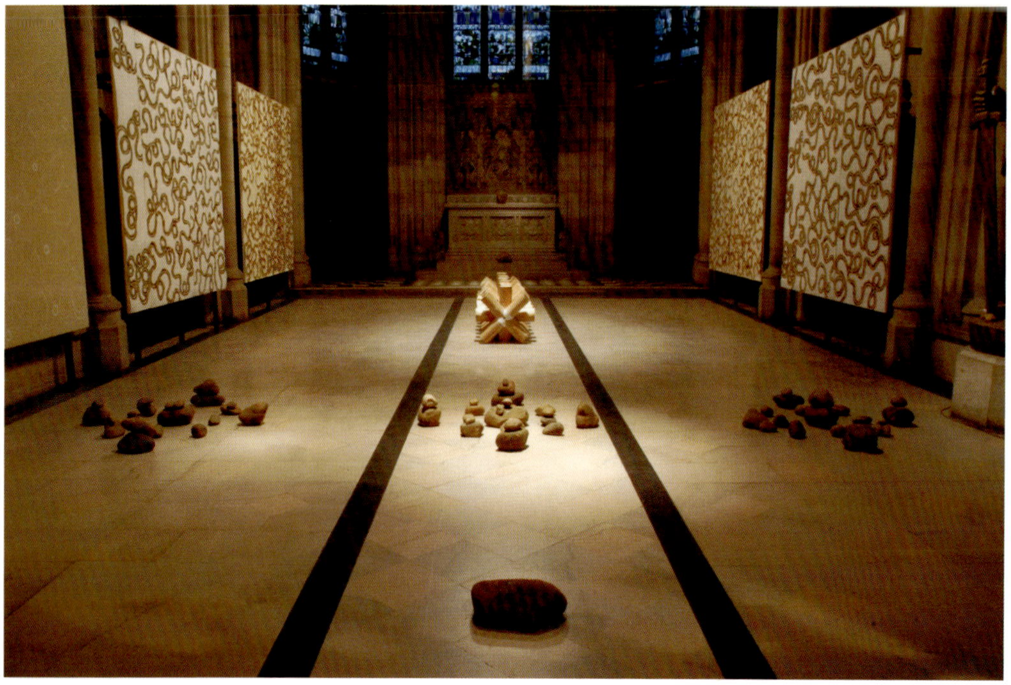

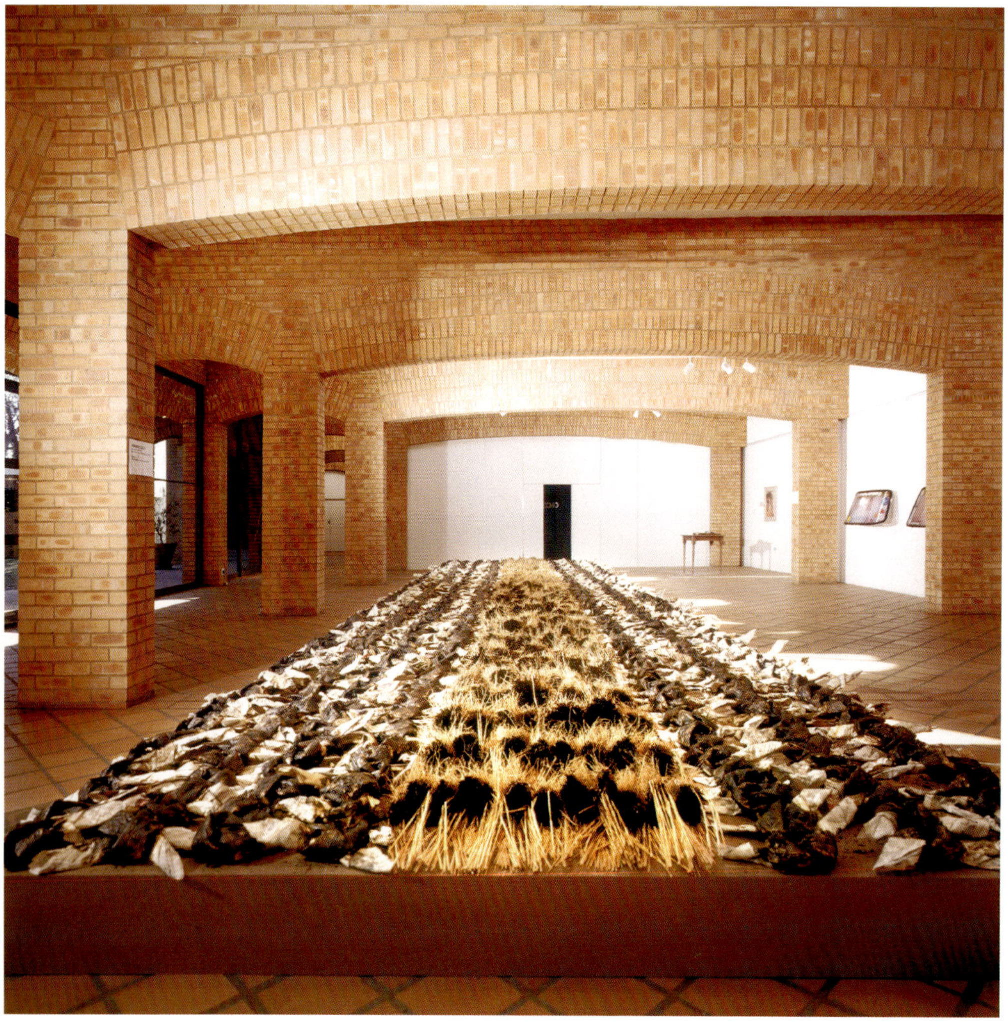

Top left *Lines of Origin (four paintings)*, 2004. *Spinal (sculpture)*, 2004. Fire, water, earth and fibreglass paper, each 243 x 243 cm (94½ x 94½ in). Wood, 230 x 58 x 54 cm (7½ x 22½ x 21 in). Installation at the Cathedral of St. John the Divine, New York.

Bottom left *Abduction of the Text – Main Theme Grassroots Frontline* 1998. Fire, water, earth, newsprint, grass and roots, 1200 x 300 x 30 cm (468 x 270 x 11½ in). Collection of the artist.
'The three main cultural influences on my work are the three values that you will find are held in humanist societies, and they are dignity, justice and freedom.' The burned bundles of newsprint refer not only to the suppression of information during the apartheid era, but also to the use of burning paper by protesters to mitigate the effects of tear gas used by the South African riot police.

Right *Camouflage 2*, 1998. Fire, water, earth, barbed wire, grass and canvas, 114 x 60 x 20 cm (102½ x 23½ x 7½ in). Collection of the artist.
'I do my work to enjoy what I'm doing and to make beautiful work even if it doesn't talk about beauty.' The title suggests a covering up or a disguising, but there's no mistaking the plumed shields and thrusting spears of proud history, as well as the divisive barbed wire of the apartheid era.

'Does it please you when before you still like death
I stand like ghosts of the dead and weep fire onto
your white face.'
Not Forever, *Sandile Zulu*

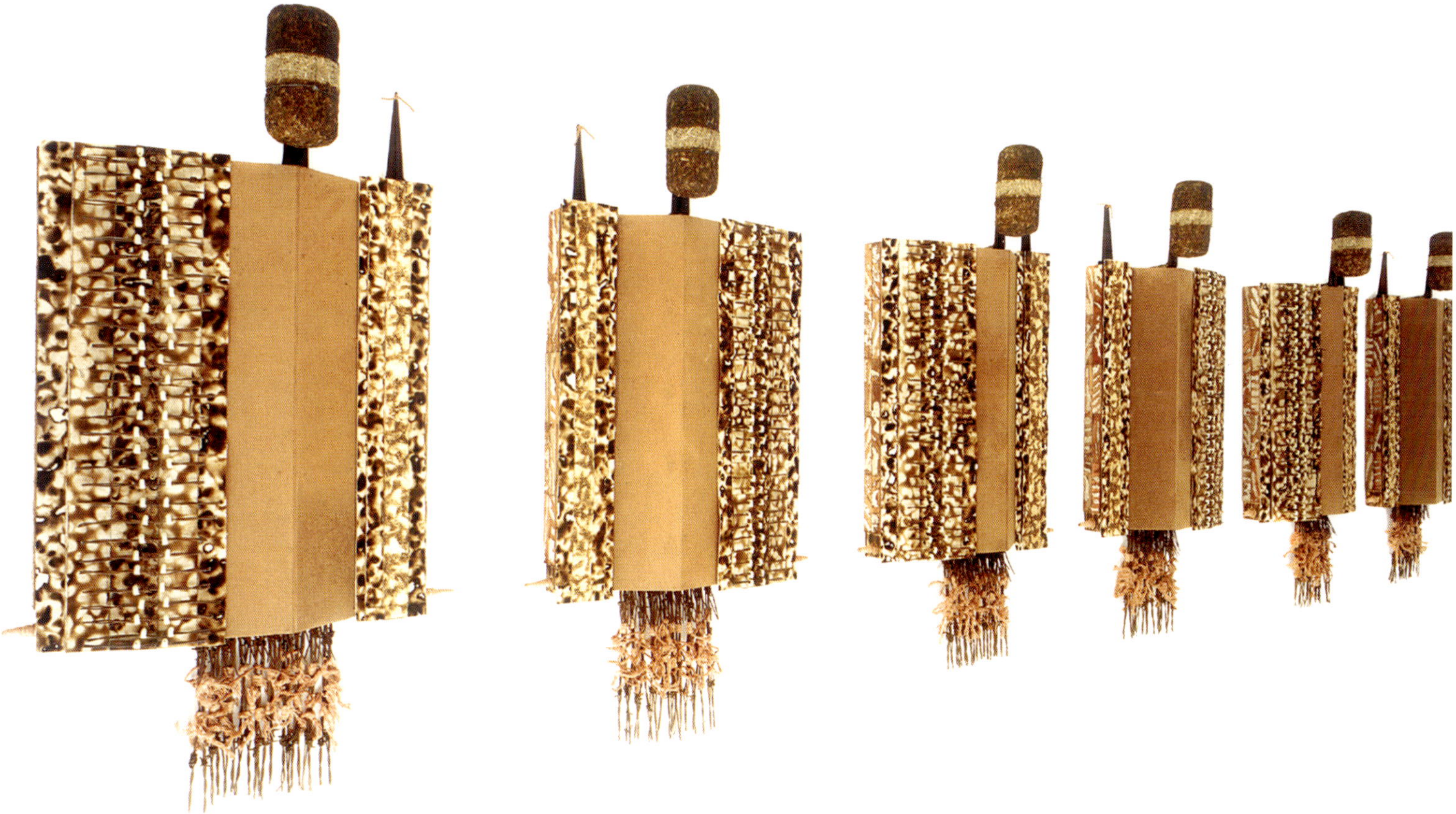

POSTSCRIPT NOEL WALLACE

Right *Black Man in White Space*, 2007. Colour Lambda print, 121.9 x 121.9 cm (48 x 48 in). © Chris Nash/Noel Wallace.

I want to end with an exhibition proposal by Noel Wallace that has nothing and everything to do with the other artists featured in this book. It is a proposal for an exhibition entitled 'CAPTURED: a Response to the Bicentenary of the Abolition of the Atlantic Slave Trade'. Noel was the English National Ballet's first black dancer. He subsequently danced for Bejart Ballet, choreographed at the South Bank Centre and collaborated with, among others, Brian Eno, the photographer Dennis Morris and David Fielding. He has been a resident artist at a number of arts institutions including the ICA, Metal, and the Greenwich Dance Agency in London.

> *Throughout this bicentennial year, most projects led by black people have been focused on the cathartic responses to slavery from people of the African diaspora. I am taking the opposite approach, by giving myself as a 'slave muse' to twenty white artists, moving the arena of expression regarding abolition to a new and more provocative territory.*
>
> *In this project, I surrender my artistic identity and independence to twenty world-renowned artists to create a pioneering exhibition, a contemporary memorial to the bicentenary of the abolition of the Atlantic slave trade... I want to use my body, my image as a muse in a way that will impact on contemporary culture, challenging our awareness and interpretation of history. Power, art, heritage and liberation are at the core of this idea, giving the collection of art works created as a result of this project a great historical significance.*
>
> *The combinations of artistic expression generated by this project will insure the objects and imagery created will have little chance of becoming cultural prisoners.*
>
> *I have chosen Caucasian artists for this project because I wanted to move outside the assumed familiar cultural-emotional experiences of black artists, creating a dynamic potential for debate. The only restriction on the artists in these collaborations will be that whatever work they produce must reflect 'slavery' or 'freedom' in some way. Questions about heritage, cultural stereotypes, sexuality, political belief and religion will be magnified as a result of this choice, heightening the creative risks and possibilities for this project. The works of the chosen artists, though well known, are currently experienced predominantly by white viewers – the subject matter of this project will attract a new audience to their work.*
>
> *I wanted the first artwork to be made on 25 March 2007, bicentennial day, and so it was – a photograph taken by photographer Chris Nash, entitled* Black Man in White Space. *I had some crack pipes made into a collar by George Tomlinson and took them to Chris; the rest, I hope, will make history.*
>
> *By offering myself as 'slave muse' to so many artists I want to use the paradigm of power as it shifts between artist and muse; it is my image as muse that brings the artists together; it is this transition from muse to facilitator that I want to use as a positive metaphor for freedom. Subsequently it will be the twenty works together which make the complete piece. Then the 'captured' will become the 'guardian', breaking new ground in the potential of portraiture. This coalition will produce compelling power paradoxes that will speak, through art, about slavery and freedom in a way that will go beyond the bicentenary.*

The first thing that struck me about Noel's proposal was its capacity to disturb, to force a rethink, to ask questions. One of the major achievements of the events marking the bicentenary of the abolition of the Atlantic slave trade has been to reveal new or hidden histories, to look again at received wisdom, accepted viewpoints, the real or imagined significance of individual people and events. I would hope that this book has achieved something similar through the remarkable vision of the artists represented in its pages.

The title 'CAPTURED' is ambiguous, suggesting both the process of the artist discovering the hidden depths of a subject, thus 'capturing' its essence, and the reverse, that this very essence is somehow imprisoned or enslaved. It could have been the title of this book. In the image of Wallace by the famous dance photographer Chris Nash entitled *Black Man in White Space*, Wallace stands on a white plinth like a work of classical sculpture, around his neck a yoke of crack-cocaine pipes. This is a profoundly disturbing image that conjures up the period in the European imagination when ideas of the 'other' were being formulated. This was a concept that represented the exact opposite of the neo-classical ideas of science and art that underpinned the period of the Enlightenment in Europe, a period roughly corresponding with the height of the Atlantic slave trade.

If the other artists whom Noel intends to recruit for his project provide an image that is as thought-provoking as that of Chris Nash, the resulting exhibition will be a very remarkable event. However, whether 'CAPTURED' comes to fruition or not, it is at the very least important to record the concept here, and to make that concept public knowledge as far as this book is able to do. This I am doing with the full agreement of Noel and Chris Nash. It is a concept that in many ways pushes the boundaries of our preconceptions of art and its subject matter, just as the artists in this book are doing. If together we manage to make a few cracks in the walls by which the world's understanding of Africa are bounded, we will have done our job.

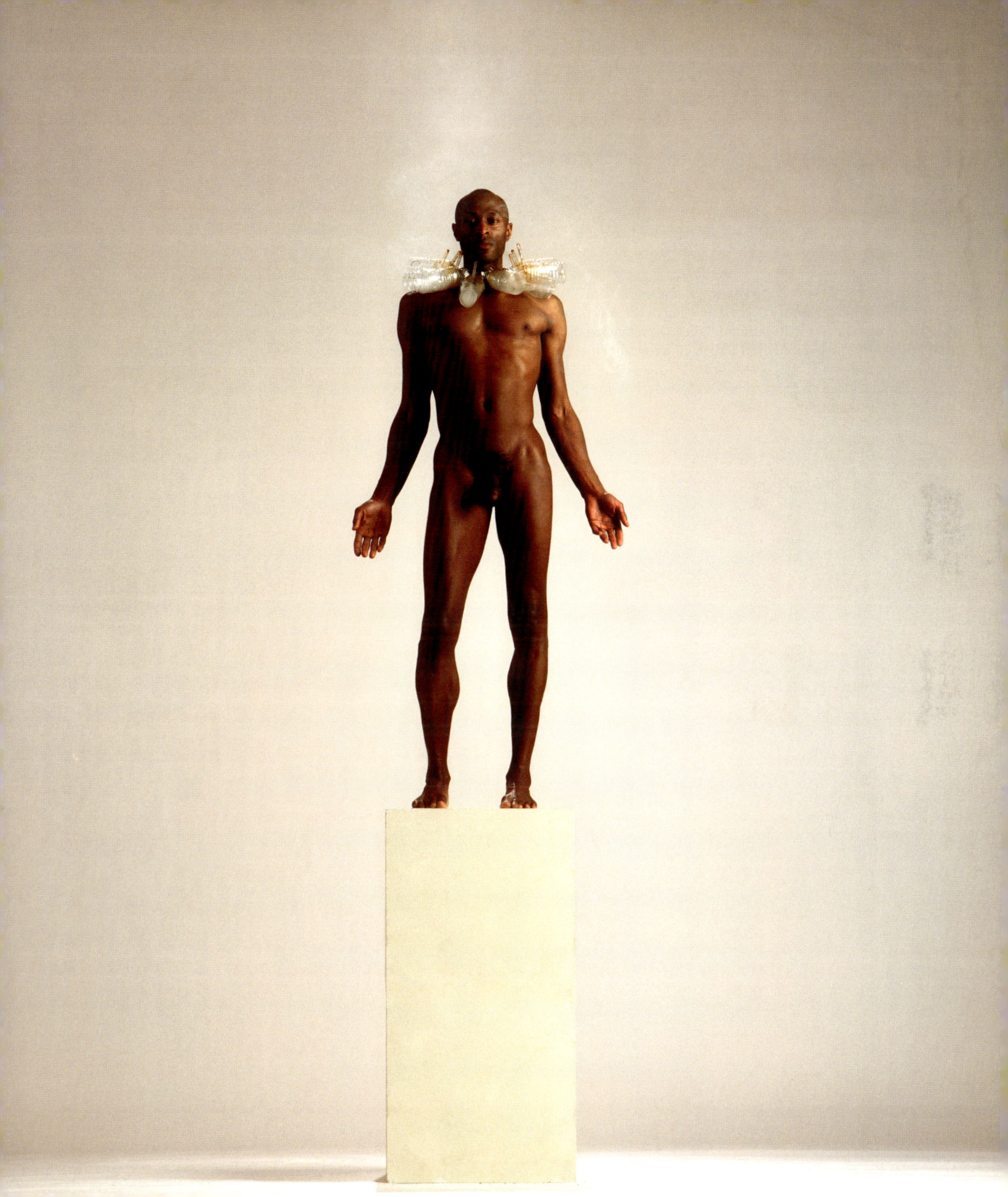

PICTURE CREDITS

Laurence King Publishing and the author wish to thank the institutions and individuals who have kindly provided photographic material. With the exception of those credits that appear with the image captions, all credit information is listed below. Numbers in bold refer to pages.

While every effort has been made to trace the present copyright holders, we apologize in advance for any unintentional omission or error, and will be pleased to insert the appropriate acknowledgment in any subsequent edition.

Cover: The following artists kindly allowed their art to be used in the creation of the cover design: El Anatsui, courtesy October Gallery, London; Chant Avedissian; Lara Baladi, © Lara Baladi, photography Robeya; Mario Benjamin, photography Marc Steed; Mohamed Omer Bushara, © Mohamed Omer Bushara, photography Roger Fawcett-Tang; Samuel Fosso, courtesy Jack Shainman Gallery, New York; Romuald Hazoumé, courtesy October Gallery, London; Abdoulaye Konaté; Atta Kwami, courtesy of Beardsmore Gallery, London, photography by Roger Fawcett-Tang; Nja Mahdaoui, © Nja Mahdaoui; Manuel Mendive, courtesy of the artist; Bruce Onobrakpeya, photography Bode Olaniran; Owusu-Ankomah, courtesy ARTCO Gallery Herzogenrath, Germany; Johannes Phokela, courtesy of MOMO Gallery, Johannesburg; Tree of Life, photography David Rose; Ibrahim El Salahi; Chéri Samba, Contemporary African Art Collection Limited/Corbis; Sane Wadu; Ouattara Watts, courtesy Mike Weiss Gallery, New York.

Endpapers: Owusu-Ankomah, *Rising*, 2006 (details). Acrylic on Canvas, 150 x 200 cm (59 x 79 in). Private Collection. Courtesy of October Gallery, London. Photography Roger Fawcett-Tang.

2 Mohamed Omer Bushara, *Untitled*, 2006 (detail), Collage, 20 x 20 cm (8 x 8 in) Private collection. Photography Roger Fawcett-Tang.

20–25 © Akinbode Akinbiyi. **27–29** © Jane Alexander, photography Mark Lewis. **30–31** © Jane Alexander, photography courtesy of the Tobu Museum, Tokyo. **32** © Jane Alexander, photography Luke Tan **35** Courtesy October Gallery, London; photography Jonathan Greet. **37–41** Courtesy October Gallery, London. **42–43** British Museum, London, AF1999,02.1 and AF1999,10.1. **48–49** © Lara Baladi; photography Robeya. **50–51** © Lara Baladi. **52–53** © Lara Baladi; produced by Sharjah Biennial. **58–59** Photography Marc Steed. **60** Photography David Damoison. **61** Photography Victor Petion. **62–65** Photography Roger Fawcett-Tang. **68–70** Photography Wim Botha/Michael Stevenson. **71** Photography Kathy Skead/Michael Stevenson. **72–79** © Mohamed Omer Bushara; photography Roger Fawcett-Tang. **84** Courtesy of the artist and La Petite Gallerie, Dar-Es-Salaam. **84–87** Roger Fawcett-Tang. **92–97** © Dilomprizulike. **98–101** © Sokari Douglas Camp / licensed by DACS 2007. **102–5** © Safaa Erruas. **106–11** Courtesy Jack Shainman Gallery, New York. **113–15** Courtesy Camden Arts Centre, London. **120**, **123–29** Courtesy October Gallery, London (*La Bouche du Roi* is now in British Museum, London, AF2006,20.1–405. **130** (below) Courtesy October Gallery, London; photography Romuald Hazoumé. **130** (right), **131** Courtesy October Gallery, London. **138** © Stadt Frankfurt am Main Museum der Weltkulturen. **139** Photography Roger Fawcett-Tang. **140–42** © Stadt Frankfurt am Main Museum der Weltkulturen. **144–49** Courtesy William Kentridge. **150** Photography David Rose. **151** British Museum, London, Af2002,01.1. **152–57** Photography David Rose (*Tree of Life*, *Monkey* and *Bird* now in British Museum, London, Af2005,01.1, Af2005,01.7, Af2005,01.2). **167** Courtesy Jean-Paul Blachère Collection. **168–69** Photography Roger Fawcett-Tang. **170** Courtesy October Gallery, London (now in British Museum, London, Af2004,02.15, purchased with support from the ArtFund). **171** Courtesy October Gallery, London; photography Laboratoire Sculpture Urbaine, Grenoble. **172–73** Courtesy October Gallery, London (now in British Museum, London, Af2004,02.16, Af2004,02.17, Af2004,02.19, Af2004,02.20; purchased with support from the ArtFund). **174–77** Courtesy Beardsmore Gallery, London; photography Roger Fawcett-Tang. **178–79** British Museum, London, Af1998,03.1. **180–81** © Nja Mahdaoui. **186–89** © Taslim Martin (*Secret Dovetail* now in British Museum, London, Af2006, 21.1). **190–91** Courtesy carlier/Gebauer and The Project. **192** Courtesy The Project; photography Erma Estwick. **193** Courtesy carlier/Gebauer; photography Erma Estwick. **194–97** Courtesy Manuel Mendive. **202–6** Courtesy Everard Read, Johannesburg. **207** Courtesy Zwelethu Mthethwa and Jack Shainman Gallery, New York. **208–13** © Hassan Musa. **214–17** © IngridMwangiRobertHutter. **218–20** Courtesy of Galleria Continua, San Gimignano. **222** AfriPics. **224–28** Photography Natasha Christopher. **230–33** Photography Roger Fawcett-Tang. **240–41** Courtesy Chris Ofili-Afroco and Victoria Miro Gallery, London; photography Stephen White. **242–43** Courtesy Chris Ofili-Afroco and Victoria Miro Gallery, London; photography Lyndon Douglas. **244** Courtesy Chris Ofili-Afroco and Victoria Miro Gallery, London; photography Stephen White. **245** Courtesy Chris Ofili-Afroco and Victoria Miro Gallery, London; photography Stephen White. **246–51** Photography Bode Olaniran. **252** Courtesy ARTCO Gallery Herzogenrath, Germany. **253–54** Courtesy October Gallery, London; photography Roger Fawcett-Tang. **255–57** Courtesy of ARTCO Gallery Herzogenrath, Germany. **258–59** Photography Roger Fawcett-Tang. **260** Courtesy Wolverhampton Art Gallery, Wolverhampton. **261** Photography Roger Fawcett-Tang. **262–65** Courtesy of Galleria Curti/Gambuzzi & co, Milan; Photography Foto Saporetti. **266–71** Courtesy MOMO Gallery, Johannesburg. **272–75** Courtesy Tracey Rose, The Project, New York and Linda Goodman Gallery, Johannesburg. **289** Contemporary African Art Collection Limited/Corbis. **292** Courtesy Alice Day Gallery, Brussels. **294** © Yinka Shonibare, MBE; courtesy the artist and Stephen Friedman Gallery, London; photography Stephen White. **295** © Yinka Shonibare, MBE; courtesy of the artist, Stephen Friedman Gallery, London and James Cohan Gallery, New York. **296** © Yinka Shonibare, MBE; courtesy the artist, Stephen Friedman Gallery, London and James Cohan Gallery, New York; photography Stephen White. **297** © Yinka Shonibare, MBE; courtesy the artist and Stephen Friedman Gallery, London. **298** © Yinka Shonibare, MBE; courtesy the artist and Stephen Friedman Gallery, London. **299** © Yinka Shonibare, MBE; courtesy the artist and Stephen Friedman Gallery, London. **300** Courtesy October Gallery, London; photography Jonathan Greet. **301** Photography Roger Fawcett-Tang. **302–3** Courtesy October Gallery, London. **304–5** Courtesy October Gallery, London; photography Jonathan Greet. **306–9** British Museum, London, Af1998,02.4, Af1998,02.2, Af1998,02.7, Af1998,02.6a–c, Af1998,02.9. **310–11** Courtesy Barthélémy Toguo; photography Teresa Correa. **312** Photography Barthélémy Toguo. **313** Courtesy Barthélémy Toguo; photography Teresa Correa. **314–15** Photography Colin Bourbon. **322–25** Courtesy Mike Weiss Gallery, New York. **326–27** Photography Roger Fawcett-Tang. **328–29** Courtesy October Gallery. **330** (bottom) Courtesy David Krut Publishing, photography John Hodgkiss. **331** Courtesy David Krut Publishing, photography Wayne Oosthuize.

NOTES

Quotations in the book are referenced below. Numbers in bold refer to pages in this book.

6 Hassan Musa in: Musa, Hassan, 'Comment expliquer "l'artafricanisme" a vos filles?' *Art*, no. 3, July-August 2005, p. 20. Yinka Shonibare, MBE in: Picton, John, 'Undressing Ethnicity', *African Arts*, Vol XXXIV, no.3, autumn 2001, p. 66. Owusu-Ankomah in: Melchers, Joachim ed., *FUTURE TRACK, Paintings 1990-2006*, Herzogenrath: ARTCO Gallery, 2006, p. 13. Kwame Anthony Appiah in: Phillips, Tom ed., *AFRICA: The Art of a Continent*, London: Royal Academy, pp. 23, 26. Olu Oguibe in: *Modern Painters*, June 2007, p. 87. Simon Njami in: *AFRICA REMIX*, London: Hayward Gallery, 2005, pp. 23, 13. **20–24** Personal communication with Akinbode Akinbiyi, 26 February 2007. **30–32** Nadine Gordimer, 'Censorship and its Aftermath', speech, 1990. J.M.Coetzee, Jerusalem Prize acceptance speech, 1987. **34–40** El Anatsui, in: *Journal of Contemporary African Art*, issue 1, 1994, p.37; *GAWU*, Llandudno: Oriel Mostyn Gallery, 2003, p. 24; *El Anatsui: a Man of the Earth*, Philadelphia: University of Pennsylvania African Studies Center, p. 2; Savage, Polly, 'Contexts, Textiles and Gin', *El Anatsui 2006*, New York and London: David Krut Publishing/October Gallery, 2006, p. 5; Mc Crickard, Kate, 'Telephone Interview', *El Anatsui 2006*, New York and London: David Krut Publishing/October Gallery, 2006, p. 4; *World Sculpture News*, vol. 4. no. 2, Spring 1998, p. 37. **42** Chant Avedissian in: Spring, Chris and Julie Hudson, 'North, Northeast Africa and the Sahara', in John Mack ed., *African Arts and Cultures*, London: British Museum Press, 2000, p. 81. **48** Lara Baladi in: Medlej, Joumana, article, *Daily Star*, Lebanon, December 2003; Karnouk, Liliane, *Contempoary Egyptian Art*, Cairo: American University in Cairo Press, 1995, p. 113. **54** Dominic Benhura in: *African Odyssey, 50 Years of Zimbabwean Stone Sculpture*, London: African Millennium Foundation, 2006, pp. 18, p. 30. **58** Mario Benjamin in: www.artfacts.net; *AFRONOVA*, Johannesburg: AFRONOVA, 2006, p.3; *Haitian Art: Food for the Spirit*, Pittsburgh: Galerie Macondo, 2006. **62–66** Willie Bester in: Loots, Andries 'Willie Bester', *ARTicle*, 20 February 2000, p. 2; Willie Bester, Los Angeles: Leslie Sacks Fine Art, 2007. 'Contemporary Art in South Africa', *ARTTHROB*, 1999; *A Journey through Resistance Art in South Africa*, Johannesburg: SARA, p. 1. **68** Wim Botha in: O'Toole, Sean, *ARTTHROB*, April 2003, p. 1. **72** Mohamed Omer Bushara in: statement as artist in residence at The Workshop Studio, Oxford 2007; *Mohamed Omer Bushara, Recent Works*, Anguilla: Savannah Gallery, 1993, p.15,17. **92–96** Dilomprizulike in: his 2007 powerpoint presentation 'Recent Creative Works of Dilomprizulike, the junkman from afrika'; Macaulay, Femi, 'Why artists must be far from the madding crowd-Junkman', *Daily Sun*, 26 April 2006. **98** Sokari Douglas Camp in: Aidin, Rose, 'Heavy Metal', *London Evening Standard*, 13 April 2000; www.sokari.co.uk. **102** Safaa Erruas in: Pappers, Daphne, 'Beyond the Exotic', *N.Paradoxa*, vol 19, 2007 pp. 54–61; www.wasla.net. **106–11** Samuel Fosso in: Taylor, Jessica, 'Here's looking at me', *The Guardian*, 27 June 2002; 'Art that gets to the heart of Africa', www.telegraph.co.uk, 22 January 2005. **116** Pompílio Hilário (Gemuce) in: artist's statement, *Deixar Andar/Letting things Go*, Maputo: MUVARTBiennale, 2005; *DAK'ART 2006, 7eme Biennale de l'art africain contemporain*, Dakar: Dak'Art, p.288. **120–23** Tapfuma Gutsa in: exhibition guide for 'Tapfuma Gutsa', October Gallery, London, 2 March–1 April 2006. Chikukwa, Raphael, 'Tapfuma Gutsa', *Contemporary Art*, no. 90, 2007; *GENESIS*, Emsdetten: Galerie MÜNSTERLAND, 1995, p. 35; exhibition guide for 'Uncomfortable Truths', Victoria and Albert Museum, London, 2007; Sanner, Pierre-Laurent, 'Tapfuma Gutsa', *REVUE NOIRE*, no. 28, 1998, p. 14. **124–31** Romuald Hazoumé in: Savage, Polly, *Romuald Hazoumé and the Art of Alchemy*, London: October Gallery, 2006. Marie-Cécile Zinsou in: *Romuald Hazoumé*, Cotonou: Fondation Zinsou, 2005, p. 9. **132–37** Jackson Hlungwani in: Hopkins, Pat, *Little Donkey – Jackson Hlungwani*, Randberg: Mukondeni Fine Arts Gallery, 2003.Robert Loder in: Picton, John and Jennifer Law eds, *Cross Currents—Contemporary Art Practice in South Africa*, Southport: Atkinson Gallery, 2000, p. 57. **138–43** Jak Katarikawe in: www.theartroom-sf.com/katarikawe.htm; www.africa-can.org/FILES/Webcompo/html/ken-index.html; Agthe, Johanna and Elsbeth Court, *Dreaming in Pictures*, Frankfurt: Museum der Weltkultuern, 2001, pp. 82, 128, 28, 90. **144–48** William Kentridge in: *Black Box/Chambre Noire*, Berlin: Deutsche Guggenheim, 2005, pp. 43–44, 99, 51; Tone, Lillian, 'William Kentridge: Stereoscope', at www.home.att.net/~artarchives/tonekentridge.htm. **150–56** Kester, Dos Santos, Nhatugueja and Maté in: the film 'Tree of Guns', BBC4/Christian Aid/Rooftop Productions, 2005. **158** David Koloane in: Williamson, Sue and Ashraf Jamal, *Art in South Africa*, Cape Town: David Philip, 1996, p. 56; Koloane, David, 'The Artist and His Community', in John Picton ed., *Image and Form*, London: SOAS, 1997, p.45. Robert Loder in: Loder, Robert, 'Image and Form in Africa', in John Picton ed., *Image and Form*, London: SOAS, 1997, p. 6. **164** Abdoulaye Konaté in: Turine, Roger Pierre , 'Portrait Konaté', in *Current and Contemporary Art of Africa*, Fondation Jean Paul Blachère, 2007. **174–77** Atta Kwami in: 'Statement of Work', curriculum vitae, 2006; www.web.onetel.net.uk/~herbertroese/africa5.htm. **178** Nja Mahdaoui in: Spring, Chris and Julie Hudson, 'North, Northeast Africa and the Sahara', in John Mack ed., *African Arts and Cultures*, London: British Museum Press, 2000, p. 77.

185 Malangatana Valente Ngwenya in: Pereira, Frederico, 'Speaking of Malangatana, Hearing Echoes of Matalana', in Júlio Navarro ed., *Malangatana*, Dar Es Salaam: Tanzania Publishing House, 2003, p. 19. **186–88** Taslim Martin in: artist's statement and interview in exhibition guide for 'Mixed Belongings', Crafts Council, London, 2005. **190–92** Julie Mehretu in: Plagens, Peter, 'Julie Mehretu', at www.msnbc.msn.com/id/6732507/site/newsweek; *Julie Mehretu*, Cleveland: Cleveland Museum of Art, 2004; Eleey, Peter, 'Julie Mehretu's "Perfect" Pictures"', *Afterfall*, no 14, Fall, 2006; interview with David Binkley and Kinsey Katchka, 'Ethiopian Passages: Dialogues in the Diaspora', March 28, 2003, at www.nmafa.si.edu/exhibits/passages/mehretu-conversation.html. **194** Manuel Mendive in: www.afrocubaweb.com/mendive/mendive2.htm; 'GRUPO ANTILLANO, a Black Consciousness Movement' in: Judith Bettelheim, *AFROCUBA:WORKS ON PAPER, 1962-2003*, San Francisco: San Francisco State University, 2005, p. 36. **198** Petrona Morrison in: www.panmedia.com.jm/archive/features/art96.htm. **202–6** Zwelethu Mthethwa in: Jamal, Ashraf, 'Zwelethu Mthethwa', in www.artthrob.co.za/99apr/artbio.htm; Mayne, Jayne, 'Zwelethu Mthethwa:Absolutely art', 21 Feb 2006, in www.lifestyle.africa.com/hislife/interview/911537.htm; *Zwelethu Mthethwa: Recent Paintings*, Johannesburg: Everard Read, 2006, p.3; www.chico.mweb.co.za/art/vita/artists/mthethwa.html. **208–12** Hassan Musa in: Musa, Hassan, 'Comment expliquer "l'artafricanisme" a vos filles?' *Art*, no. 3, July-August 2005, p.20; personal communication to Jean-Hubert Martin, 5 May 1999; artist's statement, curriculum vitae, 11 March 2005. **214–16** MwangiHutter in: www.acmi.net.au/2006/artists/acmi/mwangiandhutter.html; www.codezonline.com/2007/02/afrofuture.html; www.kenya.african colours.net/content/7589; www.ingridmwangi.de/mh/being_bamako_2007.html; www.ingridmwangi.de/mh/biography_exhibitions.html; www.ingridmwangi.de/mh/splayed_2004.html. **218–21** Moataz Nasr in: 'Echoes of Cairo in Monash Museum of Art', Monash Memo, 10 May 2006; Wabbeh, Ica, 'Moataz Nasr, Tamara Nouri & Juman

Nimri - Existential Introspection', *Jordan Times Weekender*, 14 September 2006. Simon Njami in: Njami, Simon, *Moataz Nasr or the Evidence of Things not Seen*, Amman: Darat al Funun, 2003. **224–28** Karel Nel and Emile Maurice in: Maurice, Emile ed., *Lost Light: Fugitive Images from Deep Space*, Standard Bank Gallery, 2007, pp. 8, 11, 13. **230** Robino Ntila in: Mkude, Daniel, Brian Cooksey, Lisbeth Levey eds, *Higher Education in Tanzania: a Case Study*, Oxford and Dar Es Salaam: James Currey and Mkuki na Nyota, 2003. **234–38** Magdalene Odundo in: Casely-Hayford, Augustus, *Magdalene Odundo*, Nairobi: British Council, 2005; Lucie-Smith, Edward *A Dialogue in Clay*, Prestbury: Artizana, 1999, p. 18; *Acknowledged Sources – Magdalene Odundo*, Bournemouth: Russell-Cotes Art Gallery and Museum, 2001, p.4. **240–44** Chris Ofili in: www.tate.org.uk/britain/turnerprize/history/ofili.htm; www.trianglearts.org; www.freeness.co.uk; *The Upper Room*, London: Victoria Miro Gallery, 2002. **246–50** Bruce Onobrakpeya in: Picton, John ed., 'Excerpts – Bruce Onobrakpeya' and 'Tracing the Lines of Art: Prints, Drawings and Sculpture from Nigeria and Southern Africa', in *Image and Form*, London: Brunei Gallery, 1997. **252–54** Owusu-Ankomah in: Melchers, Joachim ed., *FUTURE TRACK, Paintings 1990-2006*, Herzogenrath: ARTCO Gallery, 2006, pp. 13, 29, 41; artist's statement regarding work for the exhibition 'From Courage to Freedom', the October Gallery, London, 2007. **258–61** Eugene Palmer in: Archer-Straw, Petrine, *Conversations with Eugene Palmer*, Norwich: Norwich Gallery, 1993 pp. 10–13; artist's statement at www.thelondongroup.com/artists/palmer.html. **262–64** Marta María Pérez Bravo in conversation with Rosa Martinez, www.paolocurti.com/bravo/bravo.htm. **266–71** Johannes Phokela in: Dlamini, Ndaba, 'Phokela Exhibition Celebrates Mentor', 28 July 2006, www.joburg.org.za/2006/july/jul28_phokela.stm; Dilley, Ryan 'A New Look to African Art', 6 March 1999, www.news.bbc.co.uk/1/hi/entertainment/289022.stm; personal communication with the author, 2007; 'Johannes Phokela in conversation with Bruce Haines', INIVA archive, 2006, www.iniva.org/archive/resource/2253 **272** Tracey Rose in artist's statement for the conference 'In and Out of Africa', London, British Museum, 2005. **276** Reinata Sadhimba in: Bardhan, Rachel Lucy, 'It's rude to interrupt when someone is speaking" – africa95 and the Pamoja International Sculpture Workshop', PhD Thesis, SOAS, London, 2000, p. 313. **282–86** Ibrahim El Salahi in: *Salahi*, Khartoum: Dara Art Gallery, 2000; *The Oxford Show*, Oxford: Museum of Modern Art, 2003; Adams, Sarah, 'In My Garment There Is Nothing But God', *African Arts*, vol. XXXIX, no. 2, p. 27; Hassan, Salah, 'El Salahi', *Journal of Contemporary African Art*, Fall/Winter 1998, p.33. **288–92** Chéri Samba in: *artspace*, Amsterdam: Witzenhausen, 2007; Kwock-Silve, Sandra, 'Chéri Samba', *Parisvoice*, March 2004; www.aeroplastics.net/corpus_05/samba/samba_B.html. **294–98** Yinka Shonibare, MBE in: channel4.com – Turner Prize 2004; Holmes, Pernilla, 'The Empire's New Clothes', *ARTnews*, October 2002; artist's statement, 2001, collections.walkerart.org/item/text.html. **300** Julien Sinzogan in *Voyages – Crossing the Lake of Fire*, London: October Gallery, 2007. **306–9** Khaled Ben Slimane in: interview in exhibition guide for 'Mixed Belongings', Crafts Council, London, 2005; *Khaled Ben Slimane: Ceramics of Tunisia*, Tunis: SIMPACT, 2004, pp. 26, 33; Spring, Chris and Julie Hudson, 'North, Northeast Africa and the Sahara', in John Mack ed., *African Arts and Cultures*, London: British Museum Press, 2000, p.78. **310–12** Barthélémy Toguo in: statement at 2002 Montreal Biennale, www.ciac.ca/biennale2002/en/barth.htm; Longhi, Samantha, 'Barthelemy Toguo', www.paris-art.com; personal communication with the author, 16.March.2007; Stevenson, Michael, 'Barthélémy Toguo', 2006, www.michaelstevenson.com; 'Barthélémy Toguo – L'Art Comme Visa', in Christophe Domino and André Magnin, *L'art Africain Contemporain*, Paris: Scala, 2005, p. 104. **316** Sane Wadu in: Ernst-Luseno, Heidi, 'Sane Wadu', in *THELATHINI: 30 Faces of Contemporary art in Kenya*, Nairobi: Kuona Trust, 2003, p. 114. **322–25** Ouattara Watts in: *Fusion: West African artists at the Venice Biennale*, Munich: Prestel, 1992; Okwui Enwezor, *Ouattara Watts: Recent Works*, Rome: Warehouse Modern art, 2004. **326–31** Sandile Zulu in: Richards, Colin, *Sandile Zulu*, New York: David Krut Publishing, 2005; biography in exhibition guide for 'Mixed Belongings', Crafts Council, London, 2005; Richards, Colin, 'Sandile Zulu: Incendiary Devices', in Frank Herreman and Mark d'Amato eds, *Liberated Voices: Contemporary Art from South Africa*, Munich: Prestel, 1999, p. 153; Polly Savage, *Fire This Time: Sandile Zulu*, London: October Gallery, 2005.